A TRAVELLER IN ITALY

A TRAVELLER
IN ITALY

BY

H. V. MORTON

METHUEN

First published in Great Britain in 1964 by Methuen
This edition published in 2001 by Methuen Publishing Ltd
215 Vauxhall Bridge Rd, London SW1V 1EJ

Copyright © 1964 the Estate of H V Morton
The right of H V Morton to be identified
as the authors of this work has been asserted in accordance with the
Copyrights, Designs and Patents Act, 1988

Methuen Publishing Limited Reg. No. 3543167

A CIP catalogue record for this book is available from the British Library

ISBN 0 413 75430 8

Printed and bound in Great Britain by
Cox & Wyman Ltd, Reading

1 3 5 7 9 10 8 6 4 2

CONTENTS

ACKNOWLEDGEMENTS

The debt which every writer on Italy owes to those who have preceded him is indicated by the list of books at the end of this volume. I wish to thank the various managers of the *Ente Provinciale per il Turismo* in the regions and provinces through which I travelled and, in particular, Dr Francesco Borri of Parma and Dr A. M. Droandi of Arezzo. I should like also to thank Dr R. Guerrieri and Mr John Greenwood of the Italian State Information Office, London, as well as the authors and publishers of the following books from which I have quoted: Mr Harold Acton and Methuen & Co. Ltd for a passage from *The Last Medici*; Mr S. N. Behrman and Hamish Hamilton Ltd for a passage from *Duveen*; Mr L. Shirley-Price and Penguin Books Ltd for a passage from *The Little Flowers of S. Francis*; Mr Bernard Wall and Paul Elek Ltd for a passage from *Italian Life and Landscape*, Vol. 2.; and Allen & Unwin for passages from *Memories of a Renaissance Pope: The Commentaries of Pius II*. My thanks are also due to Signorina Laura Coletto and Signor Tullio Lanteri for their help.

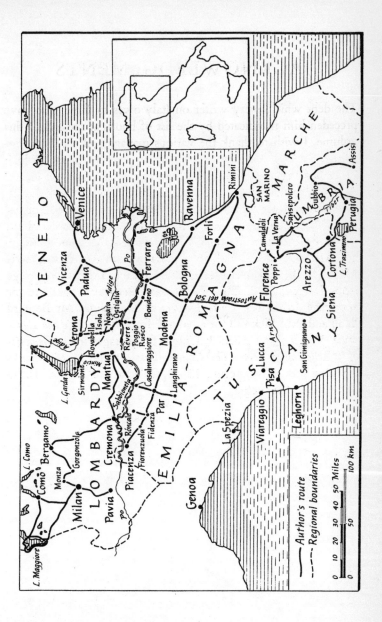

CHAPTER ONE

To Lombardy by Settebello – *Milan and its Cathedral – The Bones of S. Ambrose – The Conversion of S. Augustine – English Travellers in Milan – The Visconti – Chaucer and Milan – A Visit to* La Scala – *The Tomb of Verdi*

§ I

The hand-tended countryside slipped past in the sunlight. Castle looked across to castle, and village to village, from the summits of the terraced hills. Sometimes the train would sweep across a level crossing, and I would see in a flash a halted wagon drawn by immense white oxen which might have been harnessed by Virgil. Long may these beautiful creatures go swaying along the roads of Tuscany. Their horns are like the new moon and their eyes hold a measureless placidity. They are the oxen sacred to Jupiter, whitened, so the Roman poets said, by the waters of the Clitumnus.

The train in which I was travelling is the most elegant in Europe, probably, I should say, in the world. It has a name and a voice. The name, *Settebello* – the 'beautiful seven' – is that of an Italian card game in which the winning card is the Seven of Diamonds; and the accomplished voice of the train, speaking perfectly in English, French, and German, as well as in its native Italian, described to us the seven beautiful air-conditioned coaches which link Rome so pleasantly with Milan. The voice had the air of an Italian nobleman casually showing off the treasures of his palace to a guest. Listening to it, as it gently issued from concealed loud-speakers, and glancing round the cool drawing-room in which I sat, where all the luggage, and even the squalid parcels which one accumulates in Italy, were hidden behind panelling, I thought this was surely the most aristocratic form of movement since the coaches of the nobility rolled round Italy in the days of the Grand Tour. Indeed, I thought, had electric locomotives been invented during the Renaissance, this was just the kind of train that Ludovico Sforza and Beatrice d'Este would have owned, the restaurant car painted by Leonardo da Vinci.

My companions until Florence, where they left the train, were a jolly Canadian couple who told me they were paying their first visit to Europe. When I asked what had impressed them most in Rome, they replied the ghosts. I agreed, thinking that this was their way of describing the crowded events and characters of history; but no, they meant, literally, ghosts, spirits, phantoms. Their hotel in the middle of Rome had been haunted, and they had found the Colosseum as full of spirits as Cellini did when he spent a night there with a sorcerer. They did not actually complain of the spirits but mentioned them with amused tolerance, rather as good-natured travellers might refer to a lack of hot water or some other minor irritation. At the same time they gave the impression that they had stood no nonsense from them: they had kept the shades of Caesar and Borgia in their places. I can accept pale, nervous spiritualists who appear aware of the awful mysteries with which they are concerned, but jolly disciples of the occult who introduce a note of Rotarianism into their transactions with the other world are, to me, as frightening as a ghost itself. I waved to them at Florence and saw them vanish among porters and luggage (and goodness knows what else invisible to me), wondering which of the Medici they were about to buttonhole.

After Florence, I fell into conversation with a prosperous-looking business man. He smelt pleasantly of after-shave lotion and was a Latin version of the American tycoon. He had with him a limp document case and from it, first removing grey gloves, he drew forth letters and papers which he idly shuffled, and then turned to gaze wearily at the Tuscan landscape whose roads, vanishing in the distance, recalled alike processions of the Magi and the Eighth Army.

He told me that, as one of the directors of a Milanese company, it was his task to pay frequent visits to Rome to consult official bodies and government departments. This he disliked, partly because he detested the official mind and partly from a political conviction that the capital of Italy should be Milan, and that Parliament and Government Departments should be situated there. Rome, in his opinion, should be left to the Pope. From purely selfish reasons I was inclined to agree: it would be wonderful if the bureaucrats could be moved from the Renaissance palaces and Rome become less crowded and less noisy.

Meanwhile we descended from the hills of Tuscany into the plain of Northern Italy, that 'waveless plain of Lombardy' as it seemed to Shelley. The ox-cart and the peasant at work on his pocket-handkerchief of terraced soil had vanished; instead, I saw large, cultivated fields separated by windbreaks of poplars, a tree that is to Lombardy what the cypress is to Tuscany. When we rattled across the level crossings, similar poles however, barred the roads, and I saw tractors instead of ox-carts waiting for the train to pass. Presently we crossed the river Po, and I saw for the first time the great river that guides the Alpine rains into the Adriatic. It was a wide, dark river, flowing swiftly in places, sometimes lapping against long spits of sand; from Roman times onward it has been the backbone of an intricate system of water transport.

We sped with mellow flutings across the long-settled land, so crowded with life and so old, and as dusk was falling we exchanged the temperate climate of the *Settebello* for the warmth of a Milan evening.

§ 2

Rome, Milan, and Naples are the only three Italian cities which have a population of over a million, and at the time of my arrival in Milan it seemed to me that most of her inhabitants were packed into trains, trams, and buses, or crowded into the streets round the Cathedral. It was that hour in the evening when everyone is either rushing home or seeking some amusement. Milan has always been pictured to me as an Italian Manchester by friends who have attended the Fair. One glance showed me that this was not so.

One of my first impressions was that the Milanese walk twice as fast as the Romans, and, while walking, can tell a story or pass on a piece of scandal without stopping and blocking the pavement. The sound of the voices was different. The Milanese speak a more measured, less impetuous Italian; and I noticed everywhere a number of fair-haired women. Perhaps a Teutonic strain in the Milanese is responsible for those fair heads; if not, I recalled how noted Milan and Venice were during the Renaissance for hair-washes, bleaches and dyes. In one of her letters, Isabella d'Este wrote to her Milanese brother-in-law, Ludovico Sforza, asking how he managed to change the colour of his hair so quickly. And, writing of hair, surely the disappearance of the hat is one of the most curious social changes of our time. I can remember a more conventional age when a bare-headed person was stared at in the streets and laughed at by rude boys. Whether the hatlessness of the world, for all countries are now alike in their bare-headed crowds, is the successful work of the No Hat Brigade which operated before the First World War, or whether it is due to other and more complex forms of emancipation, I don't know, but hatlessness is now so general that the ancient trade of hatter will some day surely become extinct.

Though the Milanese may have given up his hat, he has a more visible choice of ties and shirts than in any other city I know. I soon gave up counting the numbers of small select shops in the streets leading to the cathedral, all aids to that Italian state of male well-being, *far figura*. You might translate it as cutting a dash, or, more accurately, as making a fine appearance. No Italian woman would think twice of a man who had no desire to do this, and you can see her helping to choose his ties and shirts, proud to minister to that male arrogance which shines in the faces of Italian portraits by the great masters, and even in the features of humble lute players and men-at-arms. Italy is a country where women allow men to believe themselves to be strong and master-ful, and it is part of the pretence perhaps that womens' shops should be hidden away; apart from the windows of the big stores, there is scarcely a hint in Milan that women need clothes at all.

It was a hot and humid night. Friends had told me that it is usually too hot or too cold in Milan, yet, they added, there is no place in the world where they would rather live. The crowds circulated in front of brilliantly lit shops in a piazza in the centre of which stands the largest cathedral in existence after S. Peter's in Rome. This trans-Alpine mastodon is a curiosity. It was begun in the late Middle Ages when Gothic architecture was in vogue and it was continued for centuries after it became unfashionable, but having been committed to such a vast construction, the builders were obliged to continue building it generation after generation in a spirit of conscious archaism. Naturally they overdid it. Whenever they were in doubt, a few saints were added to the building. Their numbers confounded even Baedeker, who says there are 'upwards' of two thousand statues in marble. Slender pinnacles rise everywhere, each one holding a saint. This pious encrustation culminates in a floodlit, golden Madonna – Milan's beloved Madonnina – who, when I first saw her, stood high against the dark sky gazing into the piazza far below, where Victor Emmanuel II rode a bronze charger.

A friend of mine, an Italian journalist, took me to the famous Galleria, which stands midway between the Cathedral and the Scala Opera House. It is probably the finest arcade in the world. It contains some of Milan's best shops, cafés, restaurants, travel offices, and even an *Albergo Diurno*, where the man whose *far figura* is at a low ebb can sit in a dressing-room and watch television while his suit is pressed. He can have his hair cut, his nails manicured, can buy a theatre ticket, (and a passage to New York if he has the money); and he can even hire an umbrella. My friend told me that these day hotels, which exist in most large Italian cities and are usually tucked away and better known to Italians than to foreigners, were originated by a man named Cleopatro Cobianchi.

We settled ourselves at a café table and enjoyed the most popular of Italian amusements – watching humanity. The Galleria seemed to me a modern version of the Roman forum. There is no traffic, people can shop there or just stroll about, gossip, and read the stock-market reports. All the characters of the ancient forum could be spotted: the lovers meeting at the appointed spot; the politician with the late edition of the *Corriere della Sera*; the woman of fashion; the rich man and his clients; even, who can doubt? – the adhesive bore! I never became tired of the Galleria, where human beings, removed from the noise and distractions of a street, walk as if on a stage where everyone is an actor and, at the same time, a spectator.

We dined in a restaurant at the back of the Galleria. Milan is in the heart of the rich butter region which stretches across the plain of Lombardy to the Adriatic, while Tuscany and southward belong to olive oil. Butter is, of course, a barbarian luxury, and even today if you ask for it in some of the small restaurants in Rome, particularly in the less sophisticated parts of Trastevere, they look at you as if you had asked for hair oil. Butter, said Pliny the Elder, is 'held as the most delicate food among barbarous nations, and one which distinguishes the wealthy from the multitude at large'.

We began our meal with a *Risotto Milanese*, in which the rice had been cooked in butter and chicken broth, and flavoured with saffron. It was sprinkled with Parmesan cheese and served with more butter. We had *Ossi Bucchi Milanese*, which I thought was delicious. The proprietor told us that the veal had been cooked with marrow in the bone, white wine and tomatoes, then sprinkled with parsley, and finally a touch of garlic was added, with a little grated lemon peel. He then produced a bunch of asparagus which, he said, had come that morning from Turin. It was served with melted butter and lemon juice. We drank an excellent red wine which came from Sondrino, about ninety miles north of Milan, in the Alpine highlands, a district watered by the Adda and known as the Valtellina.

As we drank our coffee, my friend said:

'Do you know that a Scottish village exists in the Alps, north of Lake Maggiore, in the Valle Cannobina? I have just sent a story about it to the United States. A friend and I went there by car a week or so ago. We started from Cannóbio and motored over a mountain track which led us to the lower slopes of Mount Zeda. There we found a picturesque cluster of tall houses with over-hanging storeys built together in narrow lanes. This was the village of Gurro. The first thing I noticed was that the moment

I took out my camera everybody vanished. It was impossible to photograph anyone, even with the help of the parish priest.

'The story is that when Francis I was defeated at Pavia in 1525, what was left of the royal bodyguard of Scottish archers fled north with the idea of finding their way back to France, perhaps even to Scotland! But they got no farther than Gurro. The snow came down and blocked the Simplon, and there they remained. In the spring they raided the mountain villages for brides and formed the community which exists today. The village and its people are different from anything else in the mountains: the houses are unusual, the villagers are mostly fair haired and the women wear a striped petticoat which looks like tartan. Everyone wears a peculiar form of shoe with a pom-pom on the toe, and an expert has detected eight hundred Scottish words in their dialect. I was amused to hear them say "Aye" instead of "Si", and "Nah" instead of "No". The priest showed me the parish registers. The name Macdonald has become Donaldi, Patrick has become Patritti, and Desmond is now Dresti. I was told that until about fifty years ago the men wore the kilt.'

We saw with surprise that it was after midnight.

§ 3

The next day my friend took me to the top of Milan's tallest and most admired skyscraper, a thin wedge of concrete that looked like the work of architecturally minded termites, and from the roof we looked into the dizzy depths of the streets below us, and outward to the green Plain of Lombardy. In the densely inhabited portions, which stretched for miles round the city, men were assembling motor cars, making transistor radios and, by no means the least interesting, arms and ammunition, a Milanese industry which extends back in time to the spears and breastplates of the Legions and the armour of mediaeval knights. Except in times of emergency and peril, I suppose the sound of hammered metal has been heard in Milan since the city was founded. How strange, as one looks down upon such a spread of human energy, to reflect that men may be making aeroplanes or television sets today upon the same ground where their forefathers of the Middle Ages mixed a little silver with the metal of their hawk bells.

> *Mei thinkes these Milan bels do sound too full*
> *And spoile the mounting of your hawke,*

wrote Thomas Heywood, though the opposite view was held by the sporting nun of St Albans, Juliana Berners, who liked the two-toned silver bells of Milan and thought them best of all, and the most expensive.

What is there, I wondered, about some places which consecrates them to human industry even in the face of what would seem impossible disasters? Milan suffered forty-four sieges; it was vanquished thirty-eight times, and was razed to the ground twice. Yet time after time the inhabitants rebuilt their walls, their homes and their workshops.

Beyond the miles of streets and factories we saw the green plain with its rich alluvial soil, intersected with irrigation channels and with windbreaks of acacia and poplar. The descendants of mulberry trees planted centuries ago are still feeding the silkworms, that ancient obsession of Lombardy, and fields of maize, wheat, barley, and rice stretched as far as I could see. To the north, looming in silhouette against the sky, I saw the Alps from whose passes the barbarians poured centuries ago to burgle the pleasant Roman world.

My companion was interested only in new suburbs and town planning, and after a time we began to bore each other since we were concerned with two different Milans – and both of them invisible! His Milan had not yet been born, and my Milan had vanished centuries ago.

As far as I know, the history of Mediolanum, or Roman Milan, has never been adequately written; and what a story it is. When the Emperors deserted Rome for military reasons about A.D. 300, they made Milan their capital, and for almost a century, while the imperial palaces stood deserted on the Palatine Hill in Rome, Milan was the most important city of the Roman west. Its provincial air vanished as architects built new and splendid buildings, as merchants flocked in from east and west, and as the luxury trades followed the court. The poet Ausonius, tutor to one of the princes, who lived in the 'Golden House', as the palace was called, has described the city as he saw it, glittering behind its walls with palaces and long marble colonnades surmounted with statues, where the citizens, as in Rome, could walk in shade during the summer and in shelter during the winter. He described a whole quarter of the city devoted to bathing, known as the Baths of Hercules, after the Emperor Maximianus. The coins which poured from the Imperial Mint were stamped with the letters MD or MED – Mediolanum. They often turn up at London coin auctions, the only visible relics, apart from a line of marble columns, of the vanished capital of the later Western Empire.

As I looked from a skyscraper upon the busy city, it was not possible to trace a Roman pattern in its streets, for no plan of the old city exists, but, I thought, in a similar crowded scene the last Emperors of the West had held court, and led their armies across the Alps to put down the barbarian raids. Milan was the scene in A.D. 313 of one of the most important events in the history of Western man. The victorious Emperor, Constantine the Great, issued from the 'Golden House' the famous Edict of Milan, which granted freedom of worship to Christians and emptied the prisons and the mines of Christ's limping champions. During the first Christian council that soon followed many of the attending bishops appeared on crutches, some maimed in the torture chamber and others scarred with the branding-iron. Such were the men who drew up the Nicene Creed. It is said that Constantine saluted one by kissing his empty eye-socket, surely one of the most extraordinary acts recorded of a Roman Emperor. If the story is true, possibly Constantine was not, as some scholars have believed, an entirely cynical convert.

One remembers, too, that Milan was the scene of the final battle between Christianity and paganism. Somewhere in the city, on a site now carrying maybe some massive erection of steel and concrete where the typewriters rattle, S. Ambrose, Bishop of Milan, wrote those famous letters to Rome which led to the expulsion of the golden Victory of Tarentum from the Senate House. Perhaps it was in the church which stood where the cathedral is now standing that S. Augustine was baptized by S. Ambrose. Somewhere else, where the domes and campanili of churches may be seen above the clustered roofs, S. Ambrose spoke the funeral orations over the bodies of four Emperors. Always, in Milan, one comes back to S. Ambrose. Even members of the local Communist Party like to refer to themselves as 'Ambrosiani', and you cannot read a newspaper printed in the diocese without coming across a reference to Milan as 'the Ambrosian City'. So much has happened since Ambrose was bishop of the city nearly seventeen centuries ago, so many sieges, burnings, and two complete obliterations, yet the corporate memory of Milan flies over the great gap of time to that Roman lawyer-churchman on every conceivable occasion. He is Milan's Romulus, Remus, and wolf all in one, and Milan's image of him is one of the oldest loyalties in Europe.

My friend came over and nudged me, feeling no doubt that I was not paying attention. He swept his arm across the horizon, indicating the site of new marshalling yards, new factories, new suburbs. He seemed to me like the spirit of Milan: that restless, acquisitive spirit which has led this great city through so many adventures to the busy present day. We returned to the lifts, and were transported silently to earth.

§ 4

During one of my early-morning walks I came unexpectedly upon the Ambrosian Basilica. Glancing through a gate across an austere paved atrium, I saw an old church which stands many centuries below the modern street level. It reminded me of early churches in Rome such as S. Clemente or S. Cecilia, both of which have retained similar paved courtyards. The basilica of S. Ambrose, with its air of Roman gravity, its silence and peace, and, above all, its antiquity, was a contrast to the lively morning bustle in the streets near by, where trams and buses were rumbling along, bearing to work the first wave of clerks and typists.

Crossing the atrium, I entered a dark Lombardic church, cold as an ice-box. As I stood shivering, I noticed a glimmer of light under the high altar. I walked towards it and, descending a flight of steps, entered a crypt where a number of old women dressed in black were waiting for early Mass to begin. They looked like a secret society or a gathering of primitive Christians. The verger hurried down with a bunch of keys. He unlocked the altar-piece in four places, and with four different keys, and this was then revealed as four painted steel panels which he cranked down into slots or grooves. As he did so, he revealed the object they had concealed and protected. As this came into view, the old women fell upon their knees and crossed themselves, for they were in the presence of one of the world's most awesome survivals.

All I could see at first was a sheet of plate-glass, but when the verger switched on the lights a gruesome and extraordinary sight sprang into view. Three clothed skeletons were lying side by side upon a bed, or bier, within a crystal shrine, the central skeleton resting upon a higher level than those on its right and left. This was my first sight of the bones of S. Ambrose, whose remains have been preserved in the basilica since his death in Mediolanum in A.D. 397. An antique mitre rested upon the saint's skull, upon the finger-bones were red episcopal gloves, upon the skeleton feet were golden slippers, and in the crook of the arm-bones lay a crozier. The skeletons on each side are those of the martyrs, S. Gervasius and S. Protasius, of whom little is known except that they were Roman soldiers said to have died for their faith long before the time even of S. Ambrose. Ambrose, who was a law unto himself, exhumed these martyrs and placed their bones in his basilica at a time when the Latin Church forbade the removal of saintly bones. This was, therefore, the first translation of relics into a Western Church, for the custom did not become general until after the desecration of the Catacombs many centuries later.

Immediately the Mass was over, the verger cranked up the steel shutters and no one could have imagined what lay on the other side. The bones of the great Roman bishop are rightly too sacred to be one of the sights of Milan, and I was interested, in the days that followed, to find out, when talking to visitors, how few who had been to the Basilica were aware that the relics of S. Ambrose are preserved there.

Naturally, one asks oneself what is the history of such an amazing relic? Are the bones authentic? How do we know that the skeleton is really that of S. Ambrose?

The saint died on the night of Good Friday in the year A.D. 397, On the following day his body lay in state in S. Maria Maggiore, the predecessor of Milan Cathedral. The next day, Easter Sunday, it was placed in a sarcophagus of porphyry and interred beneath the altar of his own Ambrosian Basilica, and, as he had requested, between the bones of S. Gervasius and S. Protasius. There it remained untouched for nearly four hundred and fifty years, throughout all the barbarian invasions. In A.D. 835 the Golden Altar, which still exists in the church above, was put into position, and while making the foundations for this the three burials were found below. The bones of S. Ambrose, together with those of the two saints, were placed in the porphyry sarcophagus, and this was reburied beneath the new altar. There they remained untouched for one thousand and twenty-nine years, which brings us to the year 1864.

When restorations were being made to the church in that year, the sarcophagus, flanked by two empty *loculi*, was found and was seen to contain the three skeletons. As soon as the lid was removed a careful drawing was made, which can be seen in the Archives of the Basilica; it is also reproduced in *Il Nostro Sommo Padre*, by E. Bernasconi, which can be found in any Milan bookshop. This was a difficult time for the Church in Italy, and it was not until after the establishment of the Italian State in 1870 that a scientific examination of the bones was made two years later. In 1873 Pius IX gave his authority to their authenticity, and during the examination an English visitor was present who described his impressions in a letter to Cardinal Newman. So far as I know, this letter has been printed only by Edward Hutton in *The Cities of Lombardy*.

The original is, so Mr Hutton tells me, in the Birmingham Oratory, and the writer's name was Newman's friend, St John.

'I was accidentally allowed to be present,' wrote Mr St John, 'at a private exposition of the relics of S. Ambrose and the SS. Gervasius and Protasius. I have seen complete every bone in S.

Ambrose' body. There were present a great many clergy, three *medici*, and Father Secchi, who was there, on account of his great knowledge of the Catacombs, to testify to the age etc., of the remains. . . . On a large table surrounded by ecclesiastics and medical men were three skeletons. The two were of immense size and very much alike, and bore the marks of a violent death; their age was determined to be about twenty-six years. When I entered the room Father Secchi was examining the marks of martyrdom on them. Their throats had been cut with great violence, and the neck vertebræ were injured on the inside. The *pomum Adami* had been broken, or was not there: I forget which. This bone was quite perfect in S. Ambrose; his body was wholly uninjured; the lower jaw (which was broken in one of the two martyrs) was wholly uninjured in him, beautifully formed, and every tooth, but one molar in the lower jaw, quite perfect and white and regular. His face had been long, thin, oval, with a high arched forehead. His bones were nearly white; those of the other two were very dark. His fingers long and very delicate; his bones were a marked contrast to those of the two martyrs.'

The writer does not mention a peculiarity of the skull of S. Ambrose which puzzled the doctors. The right upper eye tooth was deeply set in such a way as to suggest a slight facial deformity. It was left to Achille Ratti, afterwards Pope Pius XI, to point out in 1897, when Assistant Librarian and Prefect of the Ambrosian Library in Milan, that the right eye of S. Ambrose was slightly lower than the other. In support of this theory, he drew attention to the earliest portrait of the saint, the fifth century mosaic in the Ambrosian Basilica, in which this deformity is unmistakable, but until then it had been considered a defect due to the deficiency of the artist. The mosaic may therefore be a true portrait which reflects the recollections of those who knew the saint. He is seen wearing a tunic and dalmatic, a typical Roman of the fourth century, dark-eyed and dark-haired, with an oval face and a close-cut beard covering his cheeks and chin.

.   .   .   .   .

I returned to the basilica morning after morning, the only man among all the old women, until the priest, if he noticed me at all, must have thought me the most devout character in Milan. The skeleton of S. Ambrose fascinated me. I never tired of watching the sides of the altar-piece crank down to reveal what I consider one of the most impressive sights in Europe.

§ 5

S. Jerome said, in one of his letters, that when he was a schoolboy in Rome he sometimes went with other boys during the holidays to play in the Catacombs. The year was about A.D. 350, only thirty-seven years since the Edict of Milan and the toleration of Christianity, yet already the younger generation was taking freedom of worship for granted and playing hide-and-seek in those tunnels, among the tombs of saints and martyrs which their grand-fathers had approached on bended knee.

To a Christian over the age of forty, the times must have seemed incredible. Christianity was becoming fashionable. The Bishop of Rome lived in the imperial palace of the Lateran which Constantine had given to the Church. That Emperor had also built a basilica over the tomb of S. Peter and another above that of S. Paul. Everywhere in Rome pagan temples and churches stood open side by side, and a man had the right to attend a sacrifice to Jupiter Capitolinus or, if he wished, go to the new Basilica of S. Peter on the Mons Vaticanus and lower his handkerchief on a string to the grating above the tomb of the Apostle. Elderly Christians, who remembered the torture chambers, must have regarded their changed world with mixed feelings. It probably seemed to them that with toleration something noble had departed. Christianity had become popular, and rich women were to be seen relaxing upon silk cushions as they read costly versions of the Gospels. No one could have foreseen that in the next century Rome itself was to fall to the barbarian and many of the rich converts, becoming monks and nuns, would turn their palaces into convents.

In the meantime, however, Rome was still, in appearance, the rich and brilliant imperial capital, its streets bristling with statues and crowded with marble palaces, though the Emperors had deserted it and ruled, one from Milan, the other from Constantinople. Another Roman schoolboy at this time, said to have been born in the same year as Jerome, was Ambrose. He came of good family, and his mother, a widow, had brought him from the provinces to be educated in Rome with his brother and sister. They evidently moved in the highest Christian circles, for his sister Marcellina is said to have taken the veil at an early age from the hands of Pope Liberius himself, who reigned from A.D. 353-356. Ambrose, however, did not become a Christian and read law with the intention of entering government service. There is no record that he ever met Jerome, though they must surely have sat under the same roof at times: each of them was a law student and attended the law courts. It is interesting to think of those two boys, both to become two of the four Latin Fathers of the Church, as they walked about Rome with their law books in the first age of legalized Christianity. Ambrose was to become the mind behind the imperial decrees which eventually abolished paganism and closed the temples; Jerome was to live in Bethlehem and translate the Bible into Latin and, when an old man, to hear with horror, one day in the year A.D. 410, that the Goths had sacked Rome.

Those days were far off as the two boys passed through the Forum Romanum, noticing, as everyone did, the curl of smoke ascending from the small white temple where the Vestal Virgins fed the sacred flame. No one could have walked the streets of Rome for long without seeing a pagan sacrifice at one of the innumerable altars. Both boys may have seen the strange ceremony of the augurs feeding the sacred birds. Many a time, perhaps returning from a lecture, they must have heard the roar of thousands who were watching the games in the Colosseum, and it would not be fanciful to think that perhaps they sat on the marble seats of the Circus Maximus and watched the chariots come tearing round the course. Rome in A.D. 350 was, after all, still Rome.

Ambrose was officially a pagan, at any rate he had never

offered himself for baptism, when at the age of thirty he reached the top of his profession. Many ambitious men found promotion faster if they remained pagans, though only in name, and were thus linked to the vested interests of the State religion. Life was much simpler, especially in conservative circles, if a man were willing to cast a pinch of incense before a statue of Jupiter, or if he did not make a fuss should his steak have arrived in the kitchen from an altar. Yet for such little things a former generation had gone ham-strung to the mines.

There is no hint that Ambrose had any interest in the Church, or any leaning towards Christianity, when he was appointed consular magistrate, or governor, of the region of Emilia and Liguria, with headquarters in Milan. He was immensely important. When he appeared in public with his lictors it was the custom for all to uncover their heads; if he were encountered walking in the streets the crowds would make way for him; if he attended the circus, the theatre, or a public meeting, the audience would rise to its feet and remain standing until he was seated.

One of the trouble spots in his region was the Church in Milan, where riots often took place between the Orthodox and the Arians. The Arians had been giving trouble since the time of Constantine. Their heresy, which had been one of the chief items on the agenda of the Council of Nicaea, was the doctrine preached by Arius, Bishop of Alexandria, that, to put it simply, the Son of God was junior to God, and that God created Christ, who had not existed until that moment. The heresy was one which appealed to the barbarians, who remained Arians for centuries to come. The idea that a chief was more important than his son was one which they could understand more easily than the orthodox doctrine of the Trinity.

In the year A.D. 375 the authorities anticipated a riot between the Orthodox and the Arians during the election of a new bishop of Milan, and, with the idea that his official presence, accompanied by lictors and guards, might calm the situation, Ambrose decided to attend. The election was held in the cathedral, S. Maria Maggiore, the predecessor, as I have said, of the present building; and it was a noisy meeting. At the height of the tumult Ambrose was dismayed to hear the words, 'Let Ambrose be our bishop!' taking shape until it became a demand.

Election by acclamation was not exceptional at that time, and others like Ambrose, not even baptized, had been elected in that way to high positions in the Church. Ambrose protested that he did not wish to be made bishop and had never even been christened. He left Milan and went into hiding, but his admirers found him and brought him back in triumph. Eventually he capitulated, and ten days after his baptism he was consecrated bishop. So the State lost a distinguished governor and the Church gained its first statesman.

During the Ambrosian episcopate of twenty-two years the official end of paganism was effected, and the skeleton hand in the scarlet gauntlet, which you can see in the crypt of the Basilica, not only wrote the famous letters to Symmachus on superstition, but was the hand behind the various imperial decrees which finally closed the temples, disbanded the Vestal Virgins, and made worship of the old gods illegal. And, alas, during that victory the triumphant Christians began to persecute the pagans as in the old days they themselves had been persecuted.

Ambrose was friendly with Valentinian I, one of the greatest of the later emperors, and with his sons Gratian and Valentinian II, and with Theodosius the Great. Though Ambrose died at the comparatively early age of fifty-seven, the death rate of emperors during the Decline was such that he spoke the funeral oration on all four rulers. Valentinian I died the year after Ambrose had been elected. He had been campaigning against the tribes on the Danube and, being a man of fiery temper, was so enraged by the appearance of a group of sullen barbarian rebels that he had a stroke during an audience and died in an ante-room. It is tempting to believe that had this fine soldier lived – he was only fifty-four – the story of the declining Empire might have been different; for the lesson of history is that no harm comes to the strong. The new Emperor was Valentinian's sixteen-year-old son, Gratian, associated as co-ruler with his four-year-old stepbrother, Valentinian II. These imperial forays into barbarian country must have had a certain holiday aspect since the Empress

Justina, a beautiful Sicilian, was present with the infant Valentinian at the time of the Emperor's death. She left immediately with the child for Milan, where she acted as regent, and was fated to give Ambrose more trouble than anyone else in the course of his career.

Gratian, who now took command of the army, was one of those princes groomed for great things: he had been educated by Ausonius, and his spiritual father was Ambrose. He was intelligent, well-read, devout and clever, but his reign of eight years was a disaster. It sometimes happens, however, that a ruler who is himself a failure manages to hand the torch of success to someone else; and this Gratian did when he appointed Theodosius the Great as Emperor of the East, in place of his inept uncle, Valens, who had died in battle against the Goths. In a few years the handsome, clever young prince was himself dead. There are several accounts of his end, all different. In the eighth year of his reign, when he was twenty-four, a formidable general in Britain named Maximus, (pleasantly idealized by Kipling in *Puck of Pook's Hill*), revolted and, leading his armies across the Channel, defeated Gratian near Paris. The young Emperor fled with the idea of reaching Milan, but was caught near Lyons and slain. Another account says that he was decoyed to a banquet and killed; a third that he saw a covered litter approaching and, on being told that it contained his wife, hurried up and, parting the curtains, was stabbed by an assassin concealed within.

The death of his spiritual son was a blow to Ambrose, who now, on behalf of the young Valentinian II and his mother, Justina, twice crossed the Alps to Trèves to treat with Maximus. It was agreed that the usurper should be Emperor of Gaul, but that he should not cross the Alps. There were now three emperors: Maximus in Trèves, Valentinian II in Milan, and Theodosius in Constantinople. In four years time, however, Maximus disregarded his agreement, crossed the Alps and won Italy without fighting a battle. Justina, with Valentinian II, then twelve years of age, and three daughters, including a dazzling beauty named Galla, fled to Theodosius in the East to beg for help. It is said that she staged a pathetic scene for her first interview with Theodosius, presenting herself and her daughters in tears. The tableau was a success. Theodosius not only agreed to reconquer the West, but fell in love with Galla and married her. They had a daughter named Galla Placidia, whose tomb is one of the sights of Ravenna: she became Queen of the Goths, and later Empress of the West.

Theodosius defeated Maximus and restored Valentinian II to his throne in Milan. Justina was now dead and the young Emperor became friendly with S. Ambrose and relied upon him for spiritual advice as his stepbrother Gratian had done in former times. Four years after his restoration, Valentinian wrote to Ambrose from Vienna, asking him to go to that city and baptize him; but before the bishop could reach him, the young Emperor was found strangled in the palace. His death remained a mystery, though it was said that he had quarrelled with a barbarian general who had revenged himself by slaying his master. His body was taken to Milan for burial, and for the third time in seventeen years S. Ambrose spoke the funeral oration over the body of a Roman Emperor. Three years later he did so for the fourth time, for while on a visit to Milan Theodosius the Great died, worn out at forty-nine. Two years later S. Ambrose followed him to the grave.

I hope this bare framework of events will help anyone who stands in the crypt in Milan to place the great bishop in his period in history. As one thinks of those four emperors the clash of arms sounds from the frontiers, east and west, yet life went on as usual in the marble cities of the Empire: theologians engaged in furious argument, old men like Ausonius retired to their estates and wrote poems about country life, discontented young men like S. Augustine went about seeking jobs as lecturers in universities, and mobs attended the theatres and rioted, as they did once in Thessalonica because their favourite charioteer had been gaoled for immorality. Few people seem to have been aware that the pulse of civilization was beating more slowly, and indeed there are only one or two references in the whole mass of Ambrose's sermons, letters and addresses which show that he was conscious of the peril of barbarian invasion. Men still believed that Rome was eternal and that the Emperor and the army could hold the frontiers. Yet thirteen years after the death of S. Ambrose, the Goths sacked Rome. We who have seen a great Empire disintegrate in about the same time, and have experienced the revolution in thought which inspires such changes, are probably in a better position to understand this period than our more serene predecessors.

§ 6

The two best-known incidents in the life of S. Ambrose occurred during the anxious moments in Milan's history which followed the assassination of Gratian, and during the uneasy reign of the usurper Maximus in Gaul. These were the conflict between Ambrose and the Empress Justina, and the conversion and baptism of S. Augustine. It was in fact during the year of Gratian's murder, A.D. 383, that a young man of twenty-nine arrived in Milan with an illegitimate son called Adeodatus and a friend named Alypius. The young man wished to become a teacher of rhetoric and his name was Augustine. He was in the habit of sampling the rich variety of faiths available, pagan and Christian, orthodox and heretical, in the hope of finding something he could believe. He established himself with his child and his friend in a small rented house with a garden, and when he was not at work, presumably in the evenings, he would go out on his spiritual search, and in that way first heard S. Ambrose, but 'not with so good a frame of mind as I ought', as he confessed. Gradually he was drawn towards Ambrose, who was always surrounded by people and always accessible, yet Augustine at first hesitated to approach him, finding him either occupied with others or else reading to himself so intently that he did not care to interrupt him.

It was during this period that the conflict between the Empress Justina and Ambrose broke into open strife. While she had been married to Valentinian I, the Empress was able to conceal her Arianism, but as soon as she became a widow she placed herself at the head of the Arian party at court. This was a numerous and influential body, but under Ambrose all Arian places of worship had been either closed or had become orthodox, consequently these heretics had no church. The Empress asked for the use of two churches, one inside and the other outside the walls. This Ambrose refused. One day, while he was officiating in church, he was told that lictors from the palace were outside, fixing up the imperial draperies which indicated that the building had been taken over by the Treasury. Palace officials begged Ambrose to give way to the Empress and a body of troops surrounded the basilica, but these, hearing that the bishop intended to excommunicate them, crowded into the church and said they had come to pray and not to fight. For several days the church was surrounded by half-hearted troops, nevertheless Ambrose, fearing that the building might be seized during the night, organized all-night services. It was in order to relieve the tedium of these night watches that he taught the congregation to sing hymns composed by himself, the first time that hymns had been heard in a Western church.

Among those who sang was S. Augustine, who heard *Deus, Creator omnium* for the first time and copied down the words. Other hymns sung at this time are believed to have been *Eterne rerum Conditor, Veni redemptor gentium, O Lux beata Trinitas,* and *Jam surgit hora tertia.* It is sometimes claimed that others, including the *Te Deum,* were composed by S. Ambrose, but the five I have mentioned are considered to be authentic; and these, in the course of the fourth century, spread from Milan to every corner of Christendom.

In his *Confessions* S. Augustine gives many details of his four years stay in Milan. He was joined there by one of the most appealing female saints of the period, his loving mother, S. Monica. She fussed and worried over her son's spiritual search, and had only one desire, to see him baptized into the Church. One feels there were moments when S. Augustine must have found her solicitude rather overpowering. There is a vivid touch in his account of her arrival in Milan. She had come from a simple country parish where it was still the custom for earnest church workers to take baskets of food for the primitive *agape,* or love feast, to share with their poorer brethren after communion. She did not know that in large cities like Milan, and with the flocks of converts who were then entering the Church and were still pagans at heart, the custom had led to what we should call bottle parties, and was being sternly put down by the bishops. Accordingly, upon her arrival, S. Monica packed a basket of cheese-cakes, food and wine and went off to church. S. Augustine says that it was her habit to eat a little of 'these usual junkets' and give the rest away, and she carried about with her 'one small pot of wine well allayed with water, for her own sober palate, whence she might sip a mannerly draught'. This she also gave in 'small sups' to others, though the wine by that time, noted her son, was 'very lukewarm with carrying about.' However, when she arrived at the church door, the sexton looked sternly at her and told her she could not take drink into the building! S. Augustine, who thought his mother's dilemma amusing, was surprised that she, a determined and argumentative character, like many saints, should have given way without a protest because of her respect and reverence for S. Ambrose.

As I walked about Milan, I often wondered where the house with the garden had stood in which Augustine and Monica lived with the child Adeodatus and Alypius: what huge skyscraper, what block of flats, or what tramlines, now cover its site, and in what cellar below the modern level of the city is the spot, once a garden, where a man searching for God and haunted by Christ was eventually converted. One day, Augustine tells us, he went into the garden as far from the house as possible and flung himself down in an agony of spirit under a fig tree. Suddenly 'I heard a voice from some neighbour's house, as it had been of a boy or girl, I know not whether, in a singing tune saying, and often repeating: Take up and read, Take up and read'. He wondered whether it was a tune children sang when playing some game. Going indoors, he opened the Gospels and found his mind had changed: he believed at last. When he told S. Monica she leapt for joy.

Augustine, his son and Alypius, were baptized together at Easter by S. Ambrose in the year A.D. 387. Augustine was thirty-three years of age. Soon afterwards Ambrose was persuaded by the Empress Justina to cross the Alps on his second mission to Maximus, and at the same time Augustine and his little household decided to leave Milan and return to Tagaste in Numidia, which is now the town of Souk Ahras, on the borders of Algeria and

Tunisia. While they were waiting for a ship at Ostia, S. Monica caught a fever and died. Some days before, so wrote her son in one of the most tender passages in early Christian literature, she stood hand in hand with him at the window of the inn, looking down into a garden, and they began to talk of the Kingdom of Heaven and the eternal life of saints. A hush seems to fall over Augustine's narrative, and one feels that it must have been evening, with the sounds of the busy port silenced around them, as mother and son, like two swallows, took a spiritual flight together into the regions of faith. At the end she had a premonition of her death. God had granted her dearest wish, to see Augustine a Christian, and 'what then do I here any longer?' she asked. In a few days she caught a fever, and in a few more was dead. Before she died, she begged her son not to take her body back to Numidia but to bury it anywhere, 'because nowhere is far from God'.

Without a tear S. Augustine consigned her body to the earth, then swept by memories of the devoted mother, who never again would fuss over him and worry herself about him, was shaken to the heart. Like a true Roman, he went to the Baths in the hope that his grief might be eased, but found that 'the bitterness of my sorrow could not be sweat out of my heart'. Falling asleep, he awakened with the words passing through his mind which he and S. Monica had sung together in Milan when they were guarding the basilica from the Empress Justina – *Deus, Creator omnium*. So the great Augustine passed out of the history of Milan, where he had found God, with the words of Ambrose upon his lips.

S. Ambrose lived for ten years after the baptism of S. Augustine. During this time the fourth Emperor, whom he served, advised, and disciplined, was Theodosius the Great. Both men were great rulers and great fighters; and they were of much the same age. Perhaps the best-known story of Ambrose is that of the public penance he enforced upon the Emperor for a massacre at Thessalonica. The Bishop denied the church to Theodosius for eight months until he had humbly repented and promised to pass a law that no criminal should be executed for thirty days after his sentence.

Hardly had he spoken the funeral oration over the body of Theodosius than Ambrose's health began to fail and he soon followed the Emperor to the grave. He died on Good Friday, April 4, A.D. 397, and he was buried on Easter morning in the Ambrosian Basilica. It was noticed that among the enormous crowds who attended his funeral were many Jews and pagans.

Words inadequately express the sense of awe with which one stands beside the bones of the great Christian consul. His influence and authority in that fascinating period fifteen centuries ago, when society was half pagan and half Christian and Europe yet unborn, reminds one of a great pope of the Middle Ages. At seven o'clock in the morning I often think of the sexton cranking down the steel shutters and revealing the skeleton of the great Roman to a few old women in black.

§ 7

When in a strange city I have always been in the habit of roaming its streets in the early morning and watching it wake up. I like to be out before the dust-bins have been emptied and the blinds pulled up, to watch the street cleaners and caretakers arrive, and to see the first wave of the day's workers in buses and on bicycles.

Milan, like the City of London, has a cat population which vanishes before breakfast. Enormous tabbies investigate the overflowing dust-bins; embattled gingers emerge from arcades and side streets and blink contentedly at the new day. I saw one happily licking its paws outside a closed cinema which advertised a film from which the Milanesi were, no doubt, getting an odd idea of modern England – *La Saga dei Forsyte!*

The ancient Roman recipe for cleaning marble with damp sawdust is used in the Galleria just as it is at daybreak in S. Peter's in Rome. The returning traveller, indeed anyone who entered a friend's house in ancient Rome before the household was up, would have seen the slaves scattering sawdust on the marble floors and sweeping it up as men do today all over Italy, the unchanging routine of a land of marble floors.

The dust-bins of Milan are collected in a most gentlemanly way by automatic motor vans painted a hospital white. Two attendants – for the word 'dustman' conveys a different picture – wheel the bins to the van and attach a collar to them, whereupon the van vibrates with obscene but clinical pleasure as the refuse is sucked into it. They are like men leading round a hungry dragon. The interesting thing is that each van bears the words *Comune di Milano*. It has nothing to do with Russia, but takes the mind back to mediaeval Italy and the tug of war between Pope and Emperor, Guelph and Ghibbeline.

I found myself at the central station, where I watched the hurrying crowds of early workers pouring in from neighbouring towns and villages. I asked a passer-by to direct me to the garage upon whose girders the mob hung the bodies of Mussolini and Claretta Petacci in 1945. When I found the Piazzale Loreto, I was told that the garage had been reconstructed and all signs of that savage moment had been obliterated. Now that the end of the Dictator has become an historical event, it is seen to have been an outburst of mob fury that recalls the Italian Middle Ages: it was the same horrible end, with the savage humiliation of the corpse, meted out to Cola di Rienzo in Rome.

Walking on, I came to a circular fountain over which a cowled monk was leaning with an air of extraordinary intentness. I wondered what he was looking at in the water, then, as I approached, I saw that he was a life-sized bronze statue of S. Francis of Assisi, the most appealing I have ever seen. It was charming to watch some women, who kept a flower stall near by, go up and refresh their carnations in the water under the gentle and sympathetic scrutiny of the *Poverello*.

I shall always enjoy the memory of those early walks through a city which reminded me in some ways of the City of London. Like London, Milan is built on a vanished Roman city, and even more so than London the pattern of its streets is mediaeval, as you can see from the top of the cathedral or any high building; and, again like London, most of its treasures are hidden away so that the most casual of walks may become an exploration that some- times ends in a rewarding discovery. Hidden away in the city are many lovely Renaissance palaces, and a series of superb churches dating from the fourth century and restored and rebuilt at all periods from the eleventh to the sixteenth. A little corner of Milan that I thought charming was that part of the Corso di Porta Ticinese where a colonnade of sixteen Corinthian columns marches beside the tramlines, the only architectural relic left of Mediolanum, perhaps a fragment of the Baths of Hercules or one of the colonnades mentioned by Ausonius. It is a favourite resort of art students, and I often watched them invade the place with their easels and get down to work.

A few steps away from this dignified relic of Roman Milan, I saw the last visible proof that until the seventeenth century the city was an inland port, as Shakespeare knew, either from having been there or from having read books about Lombardy. This is a subterranean canal which emerges for a few hundred yards into the sunlight and vanishes again. There is even a small quay called the Darsena – the dock – and while I looked at this survival of a waterway known in the Middle Ages as the Ticinello, because it ran to the Ticino and on to Pavia, and in later times as the Naviglio Grande, a barge loaded with building material emerged from the darkness and disappeared again. How interest- ing it was to have seen the canal which once linked Milan with the Adriatic; and how odd to think that some scholars have criticized Shakespeare for making Prospero in *The Tempest* embark at the gates of Milan!

§ 8

In spite of its attractions, Milan has always been one of those cities visited on the way to somewhere else. To the churchmen of the Middle Ages, it was on the road to Rome; to the scholars of the Renaissance, it was on the road to Padua, Bologna, and Ferrara; to the young nobles of the seventeenth century who were finishing their education abroad, and to the amateur architects and the dilettanti of the eighteenth century, it was a stopping-place on the way to Venice, Florence, and Rome. And today it is still looked upon in much the same way by those who have come to see the sights of Italy: travellers are glad to spend a night there after having crossed the Alps, and when they have seen the Cathedral and the Scala Opera House they are off to the attractions of Venice or Florence.

Chaucer went to Milan on business, like so many before and after him, and he saw the city under the splendid rule of the Visconti. This family and its successor, the Sforza, monopolize the history of Milan through the Middle Ages to the Renaissance. Then came that event which cuts across Italian history, the European invasions which ended in the Spanish occupation of Milan, and then the Austrian occupation. According to the period, travellers saw either a French, a Spanish, or an Austrian army in control of Lombardy. Milan interested travellers as one of Europe's strong-points and everyone who passed through it wanted to see the great castle of the Sforza, which the Spaniards had fortified and filled with the best troops in Europe and the latest artillery. Montaigne, the best possible example of the happy traveller, always cheerful in spite of his gall-stones, saw Spanish Milan in 1581, and thought it like Paris, with its crowds of artisans and its varied merchandise. He walked round the Castle and noticed the cannon.

The first Englishman to describe the scene was that delightful Jacobean hiker, Tom Coryat, who was there in 1608, and whose *Crudities* is a sad omission from paperback classics. Coryat was a kind of unofficial jester in the Whitehall of James I, and is also an example of the world's willingness to take a man at his face value. No doubt it suited Tom, the son of a Somersetshire parson, who had scraped through Oxford without a degree, to be the funny man about Court; and it was in character when he announced that he was going to walk to Venice. Like the modern hiker, he accepted a lift whenever one was offered, and he travelled by way of Paris, Turin, and Milan. On his return home, he cere-moniously hung up his shoes in the church at Odcombe, near

Yeovil, and set about writing an account of his journey, which turned out to be the first modern travel book in English. Slightly earlier writers, such as Richard Guyleforde, Thomas Hoby, Robert Dallington, and even Fynes Moryson, had religious or political reasons for travel, but Coryat was the first Englishman to go abroad out of sheer curiosity to see the world and its people. He is clearly as much a character of the Renaissance as Lorenzo de' Medici. It is a pity that his fame as a clown followed him into authorship, which shows how dangerous a humorous reputation has always been in England. Even today many who have never read his *Crudities* imagine it to be a comic or an eccentric production and not, as it is, a learned and shrewdly observant book of travel.

Milton passed through Milan on his way home in 1639, almost a year after he had seen the leaves at Vallombrosa, considering it 'dishonourable to be enjoying myself at my ease in foreign lands while my countrymen were striking a blow for freedom'. Less heroic than Milton, John Evelyn, at the age of twenty-three, wished only to escape from the Civil War ('the ill-face of things at home'), and set out on his travels in Italy, arriving at Milan on his way back in 1646. While he was in Venice, he met the poet Edmund Waller, who had been banished from England for his part in a royalist plot, and they became travelling companions. They were joined by a Mr Abdy, and a Captain Wray, who was a convivial person described by Evelyn as a 'good drinking gentleman'. As they approached Milan there were nervous fears of the Spanish Inquisition and talk of throwing away some Protestant literature, but no trouble was experienced at the gate, and the Englishmen were allowed to pass on to their inn, the *Three Kings*.

Evelyn was an inquisitive and diligent sightseer in the modern manner. He had 'done' Rome as thoroughly as any American, with the aid of a 'sights-man', as a guide was called in those days, and he did not waste a moment in Milan. The 'sights' of 1646 were the same as those today: the cathedral, with the body of S. Charles Borromeo in the crypt; the Ambrosian Library; Leonardo da Vinci's *Last Supper*; and the Ambrosian Basilica, where Evelyn was told that the remains of the bishop, though not visible, were beneath the altar. While visiting the residence of the Spanish Governor and Constable of Castile, Evelyn happened to peep into a room, tempted by tapestries and pictures, and saw, to his consternation, that he had trespassed into a private place 'where the great man was under the barber's hands'. The Governor, noticing the intruder, sent a negro to ask questions, which Evelyn answered apologetically, but hearing the Governor say that he must be a spy, he took to his heels and managed to get out of the building and into the street. Most interesting of all, perhaps, is that Evelyn and his friends attended the matinée performance of an opera a good century and a half before *La Scala* was built. 'This afternoon,' he wrote, 'we were wholly taken up in seeing an opera represented by some Neapolitans, performed all in excellent music with rare scenes, in which there acted a celebrated beauty.'

There were just as many dispossessed persons, refugees, and spies wandering about the Continent in those days as today: Catholic exiles from Protestant countries, and Protestant refugees from Catholic countries, political refugees, agents and informers, and many exiled Scots, who were generally soldiers in the pay of some king or prince. One of these, a Scots colonel in the Spanish service, happened to hear Evelyn and his friends speaking English in the street and sent a servant to ask them to dinner. This alarmed them until they had made discreet inquiries about their host. They accepted, and found the colonel in 'a noble palace, richly furnished', with other guests, all soldiers, whom he had asked to meet them. After an excellent dinner with plenty of wine, the colonel gave Evelyn a Turkish saddle, on which he rode back to Paris and took to England. Then he led his guests to the stables and showed off his horses, and, against the advice of his groom, who saw that his master was 'a little spirited with wine', the colonel insisted on mounting an unbroken horse, which reared and crushed him against the wall. He was lifted from the saddle in great pain and carried speechless into the palace.

The next morning, when the Englishmen went to inquire after the colonel, they were appalled to see in front of the door lighted candles and the canopy which was carried over the Eucharist when it was taken to those *in extremis*. They went upstairs and found their host vomiting blood and able only to make signs to them. An Irish friar stood by the bedside confessing the dying man. The next morning they heard of his death, and also that the confession they had witnessed had been a piece of play-acting since the Scot was a Protestant and the friar his confidant. This was all that was necessary to send the nervous Englishmen on their way! Terrified that they might become involved with the Inquisition, they paid for their lodgings and hastily made for the Alps.

The last English writer to see a Spanish garrison in Milan was Thomas Addison, who was there in 1701, and until the close of the century those who came after him were to find the Austrians in possession, and so different were the two centuries that no one now worried about his Protestantism, neither did anyone think the garrison interesting or alarming. The young Boswell hurried to Milan in 1765 after his ludicrous attempt to become the lover of an elderly countess in Turin; he saw the builders at work on the cathedral, as they had been for centuries, and he climbed to the roof. Another member of the Johnsonian circle, Dr Burney, Fanny's attractive parent, spent nine days in Milan in 1770, during his musical tour of Europe. He had an introduction from Baretti to his brother, who lived in Milan, and he dined out a great deal and met many important people, including the Austrian Governor. He investigated the Ambrosian Chant and found that even the cathedral authorities were rather hazy about it. When he went to the opera, he sat in a box furnished with a fireplace and card-tables, and thought the orchestra too loud and with too much to do, and he noted that only the voices of the *baritoni* could fight against it. 'Not a lamp is to be seen in the whole city,' he wrote, 'every carriage must have a Flambeau, and every foot passenger a lanthorn. The lanthorn is very large and made of white paper. The carriages of the great are calculated for more than one servant behind, to stand one above the other.'

Dr Burney's description of Milan is the most interesting since that of Evelyn, but I think the best account of all is that of another Johnsonian, Mrs Thrale, who, when married to Piozzi, visited

Milan during the winter of 1785. Arriving on a dismal November day, she noted, as other travellers have done, how much the Italian temperament owes to sunlight: one wet day and despair closes in. It was not only wet during her visit, but also cold, and rain turned to snow, but even should four feet of snow fall in the night, she wrote, 'no one can see in the morning that even a flake has been there, so completely do the poor and the prisoners rid us of it all by throwing immense loads of it into a navigable canal that runs quite round the city'. Ladies took to church and the theatre fur-lined foot-warmers adorned with golden tassels, while poor women 'run about the streets with a little earthen pipkin on their arm, filled with fire'. She attended some formidable dinner parties. 'The common courses are eleven, and eleven small plates'. 'A footman's wages were a shilling a day, "like our common labourers", and they were paid every Saturday night.' Eight servants was a not unusual number, six of them men, and four of these in livery. 'When evening comes,' she wrote, 'it is the comicallest sight in the world to see them all go gravely home, and you may die in the night for want of help, though surrounded by showy attendants all day.' These flunkeys were great snobs. Coming out of church one day, Mrs Piozzi was attracted by a smart woman who was followed by two footmen. She asked her own attendant the name of the lady. '"*Non è dama*", replies the fellow, contemptuously smiling at my simplicity – *she is no lady*. I thought she might be somebody's kept mistress, and asked him whose. "*Dio mi liberi*," returns Peter in a kinder accent – for there *heart* came in and he would not injure her character – *God forbid: è moglie di un ricco banchiere* – she is a rich banker's wife. You may see, added he, that she is no lady if you look – the servants carry no velvet stool for her to kneel upon, and they have no coat armour in the lace to their liveries: *She a lady!* repeated he with infinite contempt.' Mrs Piozzi comments: 'I never in my whole life heard so much of birth and family as since I came to this town.' This was the result of two centuries of Spanish manners.

Between the visits of Dr Burney and Mrs Piozzi the flambeaux and the lanterns began to disappear, in fact while she was in Milan a man was arrested for breaking the new street lamps, 'lately set up with the intention of lighting the town in the manner of the streets at Paris', his reason, apparently, a desire to offend the Archduke, a sign perhaps of political agitation to come. Like Dr Burney, Mrs Piozzi admired the carriages on the Corso, but she gave a better description of them. 'The horses are long-tailed, heavy, and for the most part black with high rising foreheads, while the sinking of the back is artfully concealed by the harness of red Morocco leather richly ornamented, and white reins. To this magnificence much is added by large leopard, panther or tiger skins, beautifully striped or spotted by Nature's hand, and held fast on the horses by heavy shining tassels of gold, coloured lace, etc., wonderfully handsome; while the driver, clothed in a bright scarlet dress, adorned and trimmed with bear's skin, makes a noble figure on the box.' Napoleon selected Milan as the capital of his Cisalpine Republic, and it remained under French rule for seventeen years, from 1797 to 1814, a time when, of course, there were no English travellers. A glimpse of amorous French officers crowding into the red boxes of the Scala is given in the early pages of Stendhal's diaries; then came Waterloo and a return of the Austrians. This was the Milan seen by those early nineteenth century travellers in Italy, Samuel Rogers, Lady Morgan, Byron, and Shelley. Byron's impossible young Dr Polidori had a dispute with an Austrian officer in the Scala which ended in the Doctor's banishment from the city. From Milan, Byron, writing to Thomas Moore, excused the length of his letter because 'to be tiresome is the privilege of old age'. (He was not yet twenty-nine!)

This post-Napoleonic Milan was the city adored by Stendhal, who even enjoyed *une certaine odeur de fumier particulière à ses rues*. Behind the white tunics of the Austrian army, aristocratic conspirators in evening dress whispered their secrets over ices and sherbet in the plush boxes of *La Scala*; and in an appropriate atmosphere of opera the first revolutionaries exchanged their symbolic signs and countersigns, culled from the occupation of charcoal-burning. Byron became a *carbonaro*, and the Marchesa Origo, who examined the police records of many Italian towns while she was writing *The Last Attachment*, believed that he was more deeply involved than most of his biographers have imagined.

'Had he remained in Italy a few years longer,' she wrote, 'and met a *Sanfedista* bullet in the insurrection of 1831, he might have been the hero of the Italian war of Independence instead of that of Greece.'

§ 9

For centuries Milan cathedral has roused the wonder of visitors, even of those travellers who are familiar with the world's largest churches. It is one of the mightiest Gothic buildings ever erected, and among the most flamboyant. The multitude of saints with which it is encrusted ('more than the entire population of a German Duchy,' suggested the Princess Lieven), occupy countless pinnacles like mountaineers or steeplejacks. They bristle up everywhere, occupying dizzy positions on needles of stone, and one's first thought is that, like a bed of too exuberant lupins, they should be thinned; indeed it is amazing that this has not already occurred when one thinks how savagely the Alpine winds whip the Po Valley in the winter.

When, however, you have been in Milan for a short time, you would not abolish a pinnacle or prune a saint. By what magic such a mass of stone becomes friendly and companionable, indeed lovable, I cannot say, but it is a fact; and one soon understands why every native of Milan adores the Duomo. One gets into the habit of dropping into the cathedral as if it were the village church. Not only is it an ever-present haven, but it also offers an immediate transition from the noise and worries of a modern city to the calm and quiet of eternal values. It is like having a large cool forest in the middle of Milan into which one can retreat and take shelter from the sun and from one's fellow men.

For sheer size and mysterious gloom, it is unequalled, and I cannot recollect, even in Spain, that land of vast, dark churches, a more massive and tenebrous shrine. The nave columns and their height are fantastic, and on dull and sunless days one gropes one's way about like a dwarf lost in a wood, making for some distant gleam of candles as for a forester's hut. The twilight of some northern forest has been translated into stone and carried across the Alps. Shelley was fascinated by the building, inside and out, and he discovered 'one solitary spot' behind the high altar which he thought the most perfect of all places to read Dante. His eyesight must have been exceptional.

There is little except its colossal size to hold the attention for S. Charles Borromeo cleaned up the building in the seventeenth century and in doing so swept away several centuries of accumulated Milanese history. Many interesting relics must have vanished at that time. There still remains the gruesome statue of S. Bartholomew, which has been placed near the light from a side door so that you may miss no detail of the fact that he had been flayed, and is carrying his skin as a Scottish chieftain wears his plaid. A verger pointed to a cross suspended near the roof above the high altar and told me that it enshrines the bit of Constantine's horse, which was beaten out of a nail from the True Cross. He also said that the cross is lowered once a year, on May 3rd, when a machine invented by Leonardo da Vinci is still used to bring it safely to floor level. Unfortunately at that moment an important-looking cleric hissed at the verger and he hurried off, and I was never able to discover him again, neither could I find anyone to show me Leonardo's 'ladder'. Not a trace remains, of course, of the *Carroccio* of Milan, which was kept in the old church of S. Maria Maggiore; but it is interesting to think that this war chariot, which was eventually adopted by all the Italian communes, and was introduced into England at the Battle of the Standard in 1138, originated in Milan. It was the idea of Bishop Aribert, who about the time of the Norman Conquest roused the population of Milan against the Emperor, and gave them a rallying point in battle. Six white oxen in scarlet harness drew the *Carroccio*, priests said Mass at its altar, a crucifix was nailed to a tall mast, the battle standard flew from a yard-arm, and a bell gave signals to the army. The chariot was guarded by nine hundred picked horsemen and by three hundred young nobles, dramatically called the Company of Death, each of whom was pledged to die rather than let the *Carroccio* fall into the hands of the foe.

This was an Italian inspiration which evidently lost its efficacy across the Channel since, so far as I know, a battle-wagon was never employed in England except at that strange event at Northallerton in Yorkshire, in 1138, known as the Battle of the Standard. Perhaps Archbishop Thurston, who organized the English army against the Scots, had seen the Milan *Carroccio* during one of his visits to Rome; certainly he produced a faithful copy of it. The flag flew from a ship's mast mounted on a wagon on which priests stood with a pyx containing the Eucharist, while the wagon also displayed the banners of S. Peter of York, S. John of Beverley, and S. Wilfred of Ripon. Had the English lost the battle, one could understand why the *Carroccio* was not used again, but as they were victorious, it is strange that one never hears that it rumbled again on to an English battlefield.

The chief sight of the cathedral today is the tomb of S. Charles Borromeo, a member of the distinguished family whose present head is Prince Borromeo, the owner of the beautiful Isola Bella on Lake Maggiore. The remote ancestor of the family is said to have been a good roamer, or pilgrim – the *buon romeo* – which explains the family arms, a camel seated on a basket, a reference to the eastern wanderings and the patience of that virtuous wanderer. The saint was born in 1538, a few years after the Emperor Charles V had made Milan a dependency of the Spanish Crown, and his whole life was spent in Spanish Milan, and in the service of its people. His purity of mind, wrote Maria Bellonci, was 'so uncompromising that women were ashamed of their very existence in his presence'.

All day long visitors line up outside his tomb, waiting to be led down by a priest. The saint lies in a crystal sarcophagus given by that haunted monarch, Philip IV of Spain, whose plum-shaped face with its upturned moustaches Velazquez must have been able to paint in his sleep. I followed an expectant crowd into the darkness. The priest led us into an ornate crypt where a few lights shone upon silver and gilt decorations. As he pressed a button, the side of the shrine descended noiselessly, revealing the body of S. Charles Borromeo in full canonicals, lying in his illuminated crystal coffin. A gold mask lay upon his face and there were lace gloves on his hands. The Catholics knelt and crossed themselves; the Protestants cleared their throats and looked embarrassed. The

Milanese love their skeletons and enjoy – surely a legacy of Spain – the cold breath of the charnel house. I wondered what else a long Spanish occupation had bequeathed to Italy, besides formality of manners, saffron in the risotto, and an exaggerated passion for birth and rank. General Serbelloni was defeated in battle because he refused to open a letter on which some of his titles had been omitted! Above all, Spanish custom extinguished those lovely women of the Renaissance whose high spirits and intellect were so happily reflected as far off as England in Rosalind and Portia, and most of Shakespeare's heroines; and when we look again in Italy we see a guarded generation in black hooped dresses. The gaiety and the laughter have gone; instead, a century which seems to have been lived in sparkling sunlight is succeeded by one of dull, portentous skies.

This gigantic cathedral has an unusual history. It stands, as I have said, on the site formerly occupied by the ancient basilica of S. Maria Maggiore, probably the church which S. Ambrose defended from the Empress Justina and her Arians. If so, it was upon this spot that the first hymns were heard in the west, and here S. Augustine and S. Monica heard S. Ambrose preach and joined with him in the night-watch services. It is more than likely that S. Augustine was baptized in the old basilica.

The man who, in 1386, decided to demolish this building and erect the cathedral was one of the most notable characters of his time, Galeazzo Visconti III, the first Duke of Milan. His family had seized power in the early Middle Ages, and he was the richest, the most powerful and the most astute member of it. Like so many ambitious men, he dreamed of making himself King of Italy, and he was so confident of success that he had his crown and sceptre and his robes prepared for a coronation ceremony in the church, which he intended should be the cathedral church of a capital city. At that triumphant moment, to the relief of his enemies, he caught the plague and died in a few days. His chief object in committing Lombardy to such a giant structure was to make a votive offering to Heaven in the hope that, in return, he would have a son. The story is that a strange malady afflicted the women of Milan at the time, making it impossible for them to rear male infants. Galeazzo's three sons by Isabella of France had all died, leaving him without a male heir. The unusual words over the west door, *Mariae Nascenti*, dedicated the cathedral to the Mother of God, who brought the Saviour into the world. Though the first stones were laid in 1386, the church was still unfinished in the time of Napoleon; indeed one might say that it was not really finished until 1927, when the bronze doors were put in place.

 ·· The roof is unusual. I would never have believed that it could be so delightful to climb about the roof of a cathedral. In most cathedral cities this experience is not one to be recollected with any pleasure. There are usually narrow cat-walks and perilous little platforms, and you are perpetually being reminded to 'take care', and are only too willing to clutch the handrail: but the roof of Milan Cathedral was designed to be walked on, to be explored as if it were a large roof garden, as indeed it is. One treads solid blocks of stone and climbs from terrace to terrace, as it were, with stone rosettes and trefoil ornaments as one's flowers, while sainted pinnacles rise up like colossal foxgloves or snapdragons. Most travellers of the past thought it worth while to climb innumerable stone steps to the roof, but one may now ascend swiftly and painlessly in a lift. The view over Milan and the country beyond is superb, and one must not forget the hundred little glimpses of chimney-pot life all round one: a girl hanging out washing; waiters preparing tables for luncheon beneath the striped umbrellas of some costly-looking roof restaurants; workmen involved with recalcitrant water tanks and pipes, wearing that expression of savage exasperation which the trade of plumber seems to write upon the faces of its own; and, of course, the inevitable pigeons, on a lower level, blotting out tramcars and omnibuses beneath their wheeling flights, then settling in thousands upon the Piazza and covering the prancing figure of Victor Emmanuel.

 Near the little shed on the roof, where one can buy a cold drink or a film, stands a man with a telescope, ready to level it on the Alps. Every time I went up to the roof, they were invisible.

'Dear God,' said the man with the telescope the last time I was on the roof, 'if only you had come yesterday, or the day before, or last Friday, you could have seen Mont Blanc like an iced cake; and you would have seen the Great S. Bernard so clearly that you could have picked out the coaches coming down, while as for the Splügen – the Splügen! – you could have recognized the faces of friends!'

'Almost,' I said.

'Well, almost,' he replied.

§ 10

Returning to Milan one evening after a day in the country, I paused in delight before a scene which might have been in China or Japan. On each side of the road lay acres of shallow water which, seen against the late sunlight, had the appearance of sheets of silver. Every reed or plant growing round the lagoon was etched in deepest black. Moving in a line, and silhouetted against the water, were a number of bare-legged women, each of whom wore an enormous straw hat of the size and shape worn by coolies. Every now and again one would stoop and pull from the silver flood some tuft of grass or weed and place it in the wicker basket which each carried; as she did so drops of water fell like nuggets of gold. As if to make the scene more than ever like a wood-engraving by Hiroshige, the sun sank into a band of russet brown as a few birds, which in some mysterious way had evaded the *cacciatore*, flew up from the bushes.

I was told that the women were weeding one of the Lombardy rice-fields, which stretch for miles round Milan and many other parts of the Po Valley. That evening, as I enjoyed a superb saffron-flavoured dish of rice cooked in the Milanese way, I wondered how and when this alien seed had come to Italy. Its reception has been, to say the least, rapturous. It is so natural to assume that Marco Polo brought it from China, perhaps with noodles, which became *pasta,* that one is inclined to believe the question scarcely worth asking: but I did ask and found, rather surprisingly, that the story of rice and the Mediterranean has yet to be written. Marco

Polo apparently had nothing to do with its introduction, and its appearance in Italy was probably the work of the Arabs, perhaps in Sicily. In mediaeval Italy rice was handled not by the cook but by the doctor and the chemist, and a little evidently went a long way since it was not grown in any quantity, or for food, until Galeazzo Maria Sforza, the fifth Duke of Milan, introduced it to his duchy. The year before he died, 1475, he sent twelve sacks of rice to Ercole I to be grown at Ferrara.

Pasta was a more ancient food than rice. Boccaccio makes a picturesque reference to it in the *Decameron*: 'In a region called Bengodi where they tied the vines with sausages and where one can buy a goose for a farthing, and a gosling included, there is a mountain made of grated Parmesan cheese on which men worked all day making *pasta* and *ravioli*, cooking them in capon's sauce, and then rolling them down and who grabs most eats most . . .' Bengodi must surely have been somewhere in Lombardy or Emilia, the home of sausages and Parmesan cheese!

§ 11

Most people have heard of 'The Viper of Milan' and many may have read a novel with that title. Some may have seen a coat-of-arms which depicts a gigantic serpent standing on its tail, with a little man in its mouth, really a child which it is devouring. Such was the unpleasant badge of the Visconti, and the story is that a member of the family, while on a crusade, slew a Saracen who bore this device and adopted it himself. It suited the Visconti admirably, for they were serpentine enough and in the habit of devouring anything in their path.

They were the most able and crafty of the noble families who seized power in mediaeval Milan, and, having seized it, they held it for more than a century. There is little in the modern city to remind one of them except the cathedral, which, as I have said, they founded. When they died out in near lunacy and empty cradles, they managed to repeat and revive themselves in the Sforza who succeeded them, a genetic feat of some note. The last of the line, an illegitimate daughter, endowed the House of Sforza

with all the Visconti qualities, good and bad, and the second
family is like a reflection of the first, even to the Visconti family
name, Galeazzo Maria, which the Sforza perpetuated. This extraordinary name, which occurs nowhere else in Italy, was given to
the son of Matteo il Grande, it is said, because he was born on a
January night in 1277, *ad cantu galli*, as the cocks were crowing;
and the name Maria was given to all male Visconti after Galeazzo
III's prayer to the Virgin for an heir had been answered.

The Visconti are also associated with the Plantagenets. To me
nothing could be more fascinating than to think, as I wandered
about Milan, that Chaucer might once have been encountered
in its streets; that Lionel, Duke of Clarence, the tallest and
most handsome of Edward III's sons, was married here to Violante, the daughter of Galeazzo II, and that Bolingbroke, long
before he became Henry IV, visited the Court of Milan and
became friends with Galeazzo III. Henry even turned the head of
a young Visconti heiress, who failed to turn his or she might have
become Queen of England.

In what frame of mind, I wonder, did Plantagenet Englishmen
set out for Lombardy, as Lionel's wedding party did in 1368, a
cavalcade of five hundred noblemen and more than a thousand
horses. They were going to a land of wealthy men, and the richest
of these were the Visconti. It was also a land of self-made men,
rulers who were not gentlemen in the feudal sense and had no
king, but owed a shadowy allegiance to an absentee emperor.
Travellers would have prepared them for a strange land whose
nobles, such as they were, did not live in their castles, but within
the walls of cities like merchants, as indeed, many of them were.
It was clearly a land in which nothing would have surprised them.
Yet when they saw this strange new world for themselves, how
astonishing it must have been to find rulers who bought their
armies under contract and never went to war themselves, but sat,
like merchants, fighting battles at their desks and not from the
saddle like kings. Already the new world of the Renaissance was
visible, and the crafty prince was in command long before
Machiavelli had been heard of. The riches of Milan continued to
astonish feudal visitors for a century and more. The paved streets,

the stone palaces, the busy shops and factories impressed strangers much in the way that the United States surprised travellers from older countries at the turn of the century. Everything made in Milan was the best of its kind. They bred the best war-horses and they made the best armour; it was said that upon state occasions the armourers of Milan lined both sides of their street with mounted effigies encased in inlaid steel. Milanese silk was famous all over Europe, as it still is, so was its wool, grown in England and France, but spun and dyed in Milan, and so were the splendid war-horses reared in well watered pastures.

At the time of the Plantagenet-Visconti wedding, Milan possessed two vipers: Galeazzo II and his brother Bernabò, who shared the state equally. Two men could scarcely have been more unlike each other. Bernabò was a tough old warrior who was married to Beatrice della Scala of Verona, whose name is still on the lips of music lovers. He had a large family and, in spite of some thirty-six bastards, is said to have been dearly loved by his wife. He was an equally redoubtable dog-lover. He owned five thousand hounds which he boarded out on the unfortunate peasantry. Men with missing fingers or only one eye had probably been unkind to a hound, or had allowed it to become too thin or too fat to hunt. Bernabò's sense of humour was, like everything about him, robust. Once, disliking a letter sent to him by the Pope, he forced it down the throats of the messengers, two Benedictine abbots, and made them finish up with the seal and the silk cords. Chaucer must have been interested in him, for he it was with whom the poet had his business in Milan. The other brother, Galeazzo II, was a more subtle character and less paternal. He had only two children, Violante, and a son who became Galeazzo III and turned out to be the most powerful and sinister Visconti of them all. That, however, was ten years off in the future as the wedding party from England rode up to the gates of Milan in 1368.

They were greeted by the whole court, led by Galeazzo II himself, who wore a wreath of roses on his fair hair. The marriage took place before the doors of S. Maria Maggiore, and at the wedding feast even the meats were gilded. Every time the trumpets announced the arrival of another of the sixteen courses, the guests received gifts. Some were given suits of armour, or hounds wearing golden collars; some received bolts of silk and brocade, or hawks chained by links of gold to perches covered with velvet and gold lace. Petrarch is said to have been among the guests, a sign that the new world was on the way. Froissart was present, and how pleasant it is to think that maybe he sat next to Petrarch – the old world of romance and chivalry side by side with the new world of Platonic academies. The gift received by Froissart was a *cotehardie*, or tunic, of costly material that fitted him like a glove. Unfortunately the union between the Plantagenets and the Visconti was brief. Lionel, Duke of Clarence, died five months later, probably of hospitality in a warm climate. He was buried at Pavia and his remains were later taken to England and re-interred at Clare, in Suffolk.

Why Chaucer went to Milan some ten years later is unknown. The mission was a diplomatic one and was led by Sir Edward de Berkeley. As the business was with Bernabò Visconti, it has been conjectured that possibly it concerned the French wars, or perhaps a possible marriage between Bernabò's daughter Catherine and the eleven-year-old Richard II. The poet left London in May and came down into Lombardy, perhaps by the Simplon; but all we know about his travels is his expense account: he received a travelling allowance of 13s. 4d. a day. This was not Chaucer's first visit to Italy, for he had been to Genoa and Florence in 1372 and knew what to expect; even so, he probably contrasted the stone-built city of Milan with the unpaved London he had left. 'The gutters were new, the streets were paved with stone, and thieves were almost non-existent,' writes Marchette Chute in *Geoffrey Chaucer of England*. 'Each inn was responsible for checking its guests and notifying the official registrar of a new arrival, and the Visconti had a private postal system whose privileges they sometimes extended to individuals. Letters were stamped at the post office without being opened unless Bernabò had some reason to suspect their contents.'

Chaucer's quarters would have been in the old castle of the Visconti, on the site of the present castle, where Bernabò lived with his enormous legal and illegal brood. The English ambassadors would have discussed their business in the great hall, long since vanished, alas, which had been frescoed by Giotto. I can fancy Chaucer lying in a vast Italian bed in a tall stone room hung with tapestry, listening to the foreign noises of a Milan morning, and thinking of the little room over Aldgate where he kept his books, a room whose eastern windows looked across fields to Whitechapel. I can see him, too, in the library which Bernabò was collecting in the castle, and maybe the poet, like any tourist, would visit the house near S. Ambrogio where Petrarch had lived for some years. 'Italy was to Chaucer both what Europe is to a modern American, and what America is to a modern European,' wrote Dr Coulton. 'On the one hand, he found in Lombardy and Tuscany, even more than at Bruges, newer methods of trade and industry, and incomparably vaster business buildings, than even in his native London. On the other, he found in Italy what so delighted Ruskin at his first landing under Calais tower: here "the links are unbroken between the past and the present . . ."' If Chaucer ever met Petrarch and Boccaccio, it would have been during his earlier visit to Florence in 1372, for at the time of his later visit they were no longer alive, having died some five years before, within a year of each other.

How fascinating to imagine Chaucer walking the streets of Florence a good seventy years before the days of Lorenzo de' Medici and Botticelli. He must have spoken to elderly Florentines who had seen Giotto at work on the Campanile. 'Of all that makes the traveller's joy in modern Italy, the greater part was already there for Chaucer to see,' wrote Dr Coulton, 'with much more that he saw and that we never shall. . . . The pale ghosts of frescoes which we study so regretfully were then in their first freshness, with thousands more which have long since disappeared.' As he trod the streets of Boccaccio's Florence, he saw the very trees on the slopes of Fiesole under which the lovers of the *Decameron* had sat to tell their stories. Chaucer was then in his thirties and had not yet written a line of *The Canterbury Tales*. When he did so, he remembered Bernabò Visconti, and in *The Monk's Tale* mentioned his death, which occurred in 1385, seven years after the poet's visit to Milan. This is, says Mr Nevill

Coghill in the Penguin Classics edition of *The Canterbury Tales*, the most recent historical event mentioned in the poem. Chaucer's lines on Bernabò's death are (in Mr Coghill's version), as follows:

> *Great Bernabò Visconti of Milan,*
> *God of indulgence, scourge of Lombardy,*
> *Should I not tell of thee, unhappy man,*
> *That scaled the summit of felicity?*
> *Thy brother's son, so doubly bound to thee,*
> *Being thy nephew and thy son-in-law,*
> *Yet in his prison wrought thy misery*
> *And death, but how or why I never saw.*

This is a reference to the most crafty and dramatic episode in the history of mediaeval Milan, and many an Englishman had met the author of it. He was Gian Galeazzo, the only son of Galeazzo II, who was fifteen when his sister married Lionel of Clarence. The lad appeared at the wedding feast, gorgeously dressed, in command of a mounted company of youths who were clad in suits of steel made by the best armourers in Milan. Galeazzo was studious and shy. He gave the impression of being a gentle bookworm who was happier in his library than anywhere else. When his father died in 1378 and he became Galeazzo III at the age of twenty-five, his tough old uncle, Bernabò, with whom he shared the state, thought him a bit soft. For seven years Galeazzo was a model prince whose kindness and humanity made countless friends for him in Pavia, where he lived, while Bernabò, in Milan, became, with old age, more ill-tempered and tyrannous. One day Galeazzo decided to visit the shrine of the Virgin at Varese, and said he would like to embrace his dearly loved uncle on his way through Milan. Bernabò rode out to meet his nephew and smiled to note how timid the poor fellow was: he had brought with him for a short journey through Visconti territory a guard of four hundred men-at-arms. At a whispered word from Galeazzo, the guard closed in and Bernabò Visconti was led back to Milan a prisoner. The people and the garrison rose instantly, the palace was sacked, and members of Bernabò's large family were killed. Galeazzo was hailed as sole ruler. Seven months later old Bernabò died in prison and, of course, poison was suspected.

The viper of Milan ruled for seventeen years. Though he never saw a battlefield, his arms were victorious everywhere, and as he paced the corridors of his palace he plotted the end of friend or foe. He was successful in everything except parenthood. As I have said before, the cathedral of Milan is the colossal memorial to his longing for an heir. This was the Visconti, the greatest ruler of his time, who became friends with Bolingbroke years before he became Henry IV of England.

Henry, though a rather dull monarch, was an adventurous and much travelled prince. He was by nature something of a knight errant, and he loved to travel about England and the Continent, attending tournaments and jousts. In 1393, when he was twenty-six, he had completed two hunting seasons with the Teutonic Knights, the hunted being the unfortunate Lithuanians, who, incidentally, were Christians. This 'crusade' over, Henry Bolingbroke, whose title was then Earl of Derby, accompanied by his friends and servants, began his homeward journey by way of Vienna and Venice. The Doge received him in state and the Senate gave permission for him to hire a galley to take him to the Holy Land. When he was back in Venice again, he and his companions fitted themselves out with new silk and velvet gowns and set off for home. Henry travelled in state, preceded by two heralds who went ahead to select houses and stables and to fix heraldic shields on the lodgings.

When he arrived in Milan, he found that Galeazzo was glad to claim kinship through the ill-fated union between Lionel and Violante of thirty years earlier. Though Bolingbroke was in his twenties and Galeazzo was nearly fifty, they became friends; and once again the possibility of another marriage was discussed between an English prince and a Visconti. The girl was fifteen-year-old Lucia, who made matters difficult by saying that she had fallen in love with Bolingbroke and would marry no one else! One would like to know more of this apparently one-sided love affair, since Lucia, though she never married her hero, was fated to live and die in England. In fourteen years time, when

Bolingbroke was Henry IV, he remembered his 'excellent and virtuous kinswoman' and found an English husband for her, the handsome and gallant young Edmund Holland, Earl of Kent. The same ill fortune that attended the earlier Anglo-Visconti marriage widowed Lucia within a year, when her husband was killed in Brittany while besieging a castle. She did not, however, return to Milan. She continued to stay in England and outlived the King she had loved, and also his son, Henry V. She died in 1427, in the land she would never have seen had the Plantagenet prince not visited Milan.

When the time came for Bolingbroke to fight his trial by combat with Mowbray, which, as readers of Shakespeare will remember, was forbidden by Richard II, the armour he proposed to wear was bought in Milan; and so anxious was Galeazzo that his English friend should be well protected that he sent to England some of Milan's leading armourers to see that he was properly bolted and screwed down.

Of greater interest are Bolingbroke's intellectual pursuits. Should we not claim him as the first Englishman interested in the new learning rather than his son, the good Duke Humphrey, who is always given that honour? He was the first English king to collect books and seems to have handed on a love of learning to his sons. He was also a generous patron to scholars and writers. He doubled Chaucer's pension, he encouraged John Gower, and he invited the poetess Christine de Pisan to make her home at his Court. And I wonder whether he knew any Greek. At any rate it is likely that he met two important Greeks when he was in Milan: one was Peter Philargos, Archbishop of Milan, who had been a student at Oxford: in six years Bolingbroke would be Henry IV and Philargos would become Pope Alexander IV. The other distinguished Greek was the first teacher of classical Greek, Emanuel Chrysolaras, who may have been lecturing at Pavia when Henry was there; at any rate Chrysolaras came to London when Henry was King and visited cathedral libraries, looking for ancient manuscripts. Duke Humphrey clearly owed a great deal to his father.

Whenever I saw Milan Cathedral, I thought in passing of the vanity of human aspirations and the disappointments of parenthood, for Galeazzo III believed that his gift of the cathedral to the Virgin had been rapidly reciprocated. When the walls were only a few feet high his second wife, Caterina, who was also his cousin, produced a son and heir and, four years later, a second. In his joy and gratitude, Galeazzo decreed that his descendants should for ever bear the name Maria. It was merciful that he could not know that his dynasty would end with the answer to his prayers – Giovanni Maria and his brother, Filippo Maria.

The second duke, Giovanni Maria, was a young sadist who enjoyed the sight of criminals torn to pieces by wolf hounds. This curious passion for large and savage dogs seems to have been a Visconti peculiarity. One remembers Bernabò Visconti and his five thousand hounds. The story went that his grandson, not content with hunting animals, roamed the streets of Milan at night with his huntsman, Squarcia Giramo, and a savage pack which was unleashed on anyone found moving in the city. When the second Duke was twenty-four years of age, three Milanese nobles murdered him and flung his body into the cathedral, the church which had been founded by his father as a votive offering for an heir.

The third and last Visconti duke, Filippo Maria, was a different character, brilliant, intuitive, crafty, and a good judge of men. He employed the best generals and lived in dread of them. Not only did he restore order to his distracted realm, but he also piled up more treasure and once again made the name Visconti feared in Florence and Venice. Like his ancestors, he worked in secret, and his intelligence department was unrivalled. He himself was a miserable creature. He was so frightened of thunder that he had a sound-proof room made in the castle in which he would tremble during storms, while the same effect was being produced by his edicts on entire states and governments! He married a woman twice his age, but when she had served his political purpose he charged her with adultery and had her executed. In middle age he became fat and was so sensitive about his appearance that he would never have his portrait painted or be seen in public. He surrounded himself with astrologers and sorcerers, and his subjects, who caught an occasional glimpse of him slipping about at night, or came upon him furtively and silently sailing along the canals, felt there was something devilish about him. Reluctantly he married a second time, but as a dog howled dismally on the wedding night, (the Visconti hound again!), he would have nothing to do with his bride, but locked her away with women and spies. Oddly enough, Filippo Maria had a few devoted friends, and the affection, which he retained for years, of a talented mistress, Agnese del Maino, makes one wonder whether all the stories told about him are true. Surely no monster could have earned the devotion of a woman as good as Agnese del Maino is said to have been. They had an only daughter, the illegitimate Bianca Maria, who was good, charming and capable, and when young fell in love with her father's grizzled general, Francesco Sforza, and founded a family which, as I have said, turned out to be the Visconti all over again.

§ 12

The Scala Opera House occupies a site in the centre of Milan upon which, six hundred years ago, Regina della Scala, of the great Veronese family of the Scaligeri, erected a church in gratitude to God for having given her an heir. She was the wife of Bernabò Visconti. During the eighteenth century S. Maria della Scala became derelict and the site was sold cheaply to the *palchettisti*, or box-holders, of the old Ducal Theatre, who wished to build a new opera house. Mrs Piozzi, who went to the opera when the Scala was new, said that many families would never enter the building, shocked that a theatre should have been erected on what was once consecrated ground.

How curious it is that the name Scala should have been taken up by the film industry, which thus carries into modern life the name of the great family whose mediaeval tombs, surmounted by knights in armour, are one of the sights of Verona. Then the names that appeal to this industry are indeed strange – Colosseum, Plaza, Criterion, Tivoli, and oddly enough, Alhambra, and, still stranger, Curzon, while names such as Prado and Pitti, which have important associations with pictures, are not used.

One evening I bought myself a stall and went to the Scala. The opera was *La Bohême*. No one could believe that the building was a total wreck at the end of the last war, so perfectly has it now been restored. More remarkable still, and obvious even to someone who has never been there before, the atmosphere of two hundred years of first nights has in some miraculous way returned to take up its abode in the new building. The foyer with its glittering lights, the busts of famous composers, the chattering crowd, as animated as if *La Bohême* were being heard for the first time, and the grave attendants whose air, like that of the acolytes or priests of some pleasant and solemn cult, built up an atmosphere of expectancy which adult theatre-goers are not often fortunate enough to experience.

I was shown to my seat by a chamberlain in black who wore a gold chain round his neck – another relic of Spanish days? – and, as he bowed gravely, I felt that I had met Malvolio. I glanced round at the elegant semi-circle of red and gold boxes and was again struck by the Italian genius for reconstruction. Everything had been lovingly recreated: the crystal chandeliers, the cleverly adapted gas globes, the strange clock above the proscenium, which tells the time in Arabic numerals every five minutes (as if that mattered in the Scala, or, indeed, in Italy!), and I found it difficult to believe that the boxes were not those in which Byron had sat, in which Stendhal had enjoyed iced sherry water, and from which Samuel Rogers watched horses prance upon the stage during the ballet. Both Rogers and Lady Morgan noted that the Scala was lighted only from the stage, and Rogers commented, 'the Italians like to sit in the dark, some that they may go undrest, others perhaps from other motives.'

It was entertaining to watch the audience assemble – Italians who knew *La Bohême* by heart, visitors like myself, matrons who, when they returned to New York and Chicago, would stun any operatic discussion with a sentence beginning, 'When I heard So-and-so at the Scala . . .' Then the orchestra, invisible as all orchestras should be, began to make those furtive pipings and flutings which precede melody, and, at last, the conductor strode to his rostrum with the air of a colonel on parade. There was silence. Slowly, lights in the theatre began to dim and go out, until the huge arena was filled with a reflected rosiness, the only light coming from the red and gold boxes, an impressive and magical moment, and a traditional one.

I sat enchanted by *La Bohême*, which I felt I had never really heard before. The stage is so enormous that crowd scenes are essential unless the singers are to appear lonely; and I have never seen better. The scene outside the Café Momus in the Latin Quarter, with a nineteenth century crowd on the stage, including a company of infantry, was a tremendous spectacle which brought down the first curtain.

During the interval I met by chance an old friend who has written a great deal about music and musicians, and to him I confided my surprise that the Scala should specialize in spectacles which could not be done better by the Casino de Paris. He told me that it had always been so and advised me to look up the records of the opening night in 1778, when *Europa Riconosciuta* was produced, which I did. This must have been a wonderful evening. The curtain went up on a storm at sea, with flashes of lightning, trees on shore shook in the wind, ships were driven on rocks, then eventually the actors disembarked from a vessel; armed bands skirmished on the stage, aided by thirty-six horses; there were fights, fires, struggles with wild beasts, and Phaethon fell to earth struck by lightning.

I asked my friend how opera had originated and received the surprising reply that it really began with Galileo's father, who loved to sing or chant to the lute before an interested audience of Renaissance intellectuals in the Bardi mansion at Florence. These *dilettanti* were under the impression that they were reviving Greek tragedy rather than developing Italian opera.

Manners at the opera have changed in the last hundred and fifty years. They were once as hearty as those of the old London music halls. Lalande in his *Voyage en Italie* mentions the goings on at the old Ducal Opera House in Milan, which he visited before the Scala was built. Here opera lovers would arrive with their servants and their dinners, which were heated up in a restaurant on the premises. The boxes had sitting-rooms with fireplaces and card-tables – as noted by Dr Burney, Fanny's father, – and the Grand Duke's box even had a bedroom. Berlioz mentions in his *Mémoires* that he could not follow the opera because of the clatter of crockery. This, however, was nothing compared with the festivities usual at *La Cannobiana*, which opened in Milan in 1779, where patrons were served with steaming plates of minestrone and ate enormous veal steaks during the performance. Only during a popular *aria* was the rattle of knives and forks stilled; then a reverent silence was absolute. Mrs Piozzi mentions the curious sight at the Scala of a number of women in the audience dressed as men. 'There is however a degree of effrontery among the women that amazes me,' she wrote, 'and of which I had no idea, till a friend showed me one evening from my own box at the opera, fifty or a hundred low shopkeepers' wives, dispersed about the pit at the theatre, dressed in men's clothes, *per disimpegno*, as they call it; that they might be more at liberty forsooth to clap and hiss, and quarrel and jostle, etc. I felt shocked.'

In another interval I found that the Scala Museum was open. It is housed in a marble palace adjoining the theatre, and I thought it enchanting and nearly missed the rest of the opera as I went from room to exquisite room, looking at all kinds of related objects shown with perfect taste. There was a room full of Greek and Roman theatrical bronzes and terracottas; wrestlers, tumblers, coins showing circuses and amphitheatres; a whole room devoted to the *Commedia dell' Arte*; another contained Sicilian puppets, manuscripts of Donizetti, a cast of Chopin's delicate hand and another of Verdi's workmanlike one. To those like myself, for whom musicians have a mystery which writers and painters do not possess, the collection was fascinating and touching: indeed I enjoyed it so much that I returned the next morning. As I wandered round the rooms I heard the tinkling of a piano from the opera house and, passing along the narrow passage which connects the museum with the *loggie*, I came suddenly in sight of a rehearsal. The theatre was now empty and dark; the stage was stripped bare of illusion. A group of people in ordinary dress were gathered there. Some whispered in corners, some tried out little gestures and bits of 'business', while in the centre two formidable looking women in skirts and blouses were singing loudly as a few graceful young dancers undulated and pirouetted round them. A disillusioned man in a brown pinstripe suit played a piano, but whenever the singers reached a certain note the producer sprang out of the encircling darkness and stopped them, making them begin again. Nothing strips magic from the footlights more surely than a rehearsal, with its air of inexorable frustration, its atmosphere of impending failure and of striving towards some unattainable ideal. At least the writer and the painter are privileged to suffer in solitude.

I was told by a member of the management that the Scala produces sixteen different operas every season, and six are always selected from a list of thirty box-office certainties. Tradition demands that at least one work each by Rossini, Bellini, Donizetti, Verdi, and Puccini should be produced. The season begins in December and ends in June, and is followed by a short season in July at popular prices.

The orchestra numbers a hundred and seven, the chorus, a hundred, and the technical staff also numbers a hundred. Until the time of Toscanini the Scala was considered a singers' opera house, but since his time the conductor has been the absolute monarch. The theatre holds an audience of three thousand, and an average of five hundred thousand tickets are sold a year. I particularly like the by-law by which any deficit at the Scala is made up by the City's tax on cinema and other entertainments.

§ 13

Though Verdi died in a Milan hotel only about sixty years ago, I could not find his tomb in any of the churches, and sextons and priests, when asked where I could find his grave, sighed, blew out their lips, shrugged, spread out their arms in the national gesture of despair, and suggested that he must have been interred near Parma.

I happened to mention this to a publisher of books on music with whom I was lunching, who was shocked to think that some of his compatriots did not know where Italy's favourite musician is buried.

'It is fantastic!' he cried. 'If anybody but you had told me,' he added politely, 'I should have disbelieved him. Surely everybody in Milan must know that Verdi is not buried in a Church, but in the Piazza Buonarroti!'

After lunch he said, 'Let us go there.'

It was quite a long drive to the west of Milan, among broad avenues whose names are a curious historical medley: Via Elba; Via dei Gracchi; Via Vespri Siciliani; Via Giorgio Washington. Here, in the centre of the Piazza Buonarroti, we found a statue of Verdi escorted by an unusual group of allegorical figures, such as the Peace of Country Life, the Poetry of Patriotism, and the Tragedy of Hatred. My friend pointed to the gates of a building opposite. 'There,' he said, 'Verdi is buried.' We crossed over and entered the *Casa di Riposo per i Musicisti*.

In 1899, two years before he died, Verdi directed that after his death the royalties from his operas should be devoted to a home for a hundred poor musicians, men and women. The building in which the old men live is faced across a pleasant courtyard by that in which live the old women. A path goes on beyond the courtyard to a vault whose arches are covered with mosaics. We looked down from a marble balustrade upon the grave of Verdi, side by side with that of his second wife, Giuseppina Strepponi. A tablet on the wall commemorates the brief, ill-fated marriage of his youth with Margherita Barezzi. His epitaph, inscribed above the bronze tombs, is *Pianse ed amò per tutti* – he wept for, and loved, all.

The gate-keeper told us that there were sixty old men and forty old women living in the pleasant little flats. Unfortunately, he added, Verdi's copyrights were running out, and it would soon be necessary to find some other source of income.

It was the siesta hour, and none of the old musicians was visible or audible. We reflected that if an octogenarian existed among them it is possible that he, or she, when young, might have known the *maestro*. It is a pleasant thought that whenever a Verdi opera has been performed since the composer's death, it has helped to support musicians who possessed neither Verdi's genius, good fortune, nor, one might add, his remarkable business sense.

CHAPTER TWO

The Castle of the Sforza – Ludovico il Moro, and Beatrice d'Este –
Murder in the Cathedral – The Last Supper – Leonardo's Scientific
Inventions – Byron In The Ambrosiana – Lucrezia Borgia's Hair –
Pavia and its University – The Certosa and the story of a Tomb

§ I

The red brick castle of the Sforza stands in an immense square on whose edges the buses leave for such charming places as Bergamo. The building was falling to pieces when the city inherited it about a century ago, but, instead of pulling it down, as they might well have done as a symbol of ancient oppression, they restored it with such loving care that it is now difficult to believe that anything more exciting than a municipal council meeting ever occurred there. As I crossed the bridge to the main gate, I noticed gardeners mowing in the moat, and inside, where once clustered a swashbuckling military town full of Spanish culverins, I saw park-like lawns and flower-beds. Yet this was the castle described by seventeenth century travellers as one of the mighty strongholds of Europe.

High marble halls succeed one another, and the restorers have managed to obliterate the marks of French, Spanish, and Austrian occupation and to discover the castle as it was known to the Sforza. As I walked through these halls, which now house the city museum, I was escorted from one to another by voluble and well-informed attendants who bowed politely at the confines of their territory and handed me on to a compatriot. It would seem to be practically impossible for any literate Italian to spend his life in a museum without becoming an amateur historian or an art critic, and I could not help contrasting them with some English attendants I have known who were strong-minded enough to spend a lifetime resisting even the British Museum.

I gratified one of the attendants by telling him that Francesco Sforza was my favourite *condottiere*. As a reward, he took me to a window where we looked down over the square where one of the world's great masterpieces was shot to pieces by bored French archers. This was the clay model of the huge equestrian statue of Francesco Sforza which his son Ludovico Sforza commissioned Leonardo da Vinci to make in bronze, but because of the French invasion and the fall of Ludovico Sforza it was never completed. Who can doubt that it would have been the finest mounted statue ever designed?

The history of this work happened to be the guide's pet subject, and as we leaned out of the window above the square we recalled the low survival value of Leonardo's work. He told me that, anxious to outdo Verrocchio's statue of Colleoni in Venice and Donatello's Gattamelata at Padua, Leonardo at first wished to place Francesco upon the back of a charger prancing in battle, a feat which no sculptor had been able to achieve. There is a sketch of this horse in the Royal Collection at Windsor, but the problems of casting such a work were too great, and Leonardo's clay model, which was one of the sights of Milan, was the usual walking horse. He worked on this while he was painting the *Last Supper*, but after the French invasion the tons of metal assembled for the casting of the statue were sent by Ludovico Sforza to his brother-in-law at Ferrara to be made into cannon. I think I am right in saying that the world had to wait nearly a hundred years before the statue of a man on a prancing horse was seen, and it is still prancing, with Philip III of Spain in the saddle, among the flower-beds of the royal palace in Madrid.

'And when the French occupied this castle,' said the guide indignantly, 'the Gascon archers used the immortal horse of Leonardo as a target! What barbarians!'

'How would you like to have been a *condottiere*?' I asked.

'When I was a boy,' he replied, 'I should have said "yes", but not now. I have seen too much war.' He told me that he had been a prisoner of war in Pretoria.

To be a mercenary captain was, until the sixteenth century, the quickest road to fame and riches in Italy. Many of the *condottieri* were old soldiers, like the Englishman, Sir John Hawkwood, who at the end of the Anglo-French wars went on fighting Crécy and Poitiers on a reduced scale in the Po Valley; others were Italians, some of noble, others of humble, birth; all of them, like Pistol, saw the world as their oyster. They would train a band of troops and sign on for the duration of a war with any one of the city states, and, as the system was riddled with bribery, some could be persuaded to go over to the enemy at a critical moment. A reputation for comparative honesty was consequently valued, and this rare virtue was said to distinguish such commanders as Hawkwood, Colleoni, and Sforza. To us, who know how dangerous war can be, the charm of the system was its harmlessness. Never before, and certainly never since, had war been so safe. One has only to look at the statues of Colleoni and Gattamelata to see that the *condottieri* preserved all the pomp and plumes of war while at the same time they did their best to make it as safe as, say, steeple-chasing or Rugby football. The people who suffered most were the wretched peasantry outside the walled cities, who had their houses destroyed and their crops and livestock stolen.

The aim of the *condottieri* was to keep wars going as long as possible and to preserve the lives of their men, since the commander who was foolish enough to lose men in battle lost his capital and faced bankruptcy. The system lent itself to every kind of secret arrangement and bargain, and if ever soldiers could be described as a band of brothers, the phrase fits the *condottieri*. Their relationship to one another was not unlike that of the modern barrister: they could put up a noisy fight and be seen lunching together afterwards. This spirit was well expressed by two notorious enemies who in private life were devoted friends and had each made a will appointing the other the guardian of his family!

I explored the halls of the Castello Sforzesco with the thought that this building is probably the most spectacular monument in existence to the position in life attainable by a *condottiere*. Starting with nothing but his horse and his sword, and paternal advice, Francesco Sforza was able in middle age to make himself Duke of Milan and to found one of the great Italian dynasties. His father's advice, which was that of a tough old soldier, was: never make love to another man's wife, never beat a servant but, should you be forced to do so, get rid of him immediately, and never ride a horse with a hard mouth.

Such simple advice seems hardly adequate for the world of villainy, intrigue, and high politics in which the young Francesco found himself. It was the age of the great *condottieri*, when the mercenary commanders, as if aware that the end of their supremacy was approaching with the invasion of the bloodthirsty armies of France, kept Italy in a turmoil as they played off state against state and carved out principalities for themselves. It was, of course, a dangerous game and even the most adroit practitioners were liable to be caught out, like the mighty Francesco Bussone of Carmagnola who, responding to a polite invitation to visit his masters in Venice, was seen dead one morning, swinging by one leg between the columns in the Piazzetta of S. Mark, clothed in scarlet and with a gag in his mouth.

The prince with whom the young Sforza linked his destiny was the last of the Visconti, Filippo Maria, third Duke of Milan. I have mentioned some of his peculiarities: his fear of being seen: his habit of travelling at night along the silent canals: his fear of thunder as he cowered in a sound-proof room: his suspicion of everyone, which made it prudent to keep away from windows when having an audience with him. The most harmless individual who happened to lean on a window-sill, from which he could have signalled to someone standing below, stood a good chance of being knifed by the guard. His suspicion extended with good reason to his commanders. The shrewd paranoic knew that a moment would arrive in the careers of soldiers of fortune when they could no longer remain subjects. No wonder he felt himself to be a sitting target. He was the last of his line, his only child an illegitimate girl. Her name was Bianca. When she was in the nursery Filippo Maria had promised her in marriage to more than one powerful individual in the hope of attaching them to himself by bonds of interest. Among these hypothetical sons-in-law was Francesco Sforza. He was then thirty-one and Bianca Visconti was eight. It is said, and it is probably true, that when in her 'teens she fell romantically in love with her father's attractive and powerful general. Nine years later, when Bianca was seventeen and Francesco was forty, they were married, and by that time Francesco had fathered twenty-two bastards. During the Renaissance, however, no young wife who knew the facts of life was surprised to find herself surrounded by a crowd of stepchildren older than herself. The marriage turned out to be a success.

When Filippo Maria died in 1447, the Milanese pulled down the Visconti castle and proclaimed a republic which ran an uneasy course for three years. At last, surrounded by enemies, the citizens were glad to welcome Francesco Sforza and Bianca Visconti, (who were financially supported by Cosimo de' Medici), as their fourth duke and duchess. So the old *condottiere*, now a Duke, rode into Milan one day in the year 1450, followed by his troops, who were festooned with loaves of bread, for Milan, after a long siege, was starving.

After the extravagant rule of the Visconti it was probably pleasant to have rulers who had to spend carefully. At first Bianca had only four ladies-in-waiting, and on one occasion Francesco wrote to the Marquis of Mantua suggesting that he should not arrive in Milan on a Saturday because 'on that day the women will be washing their hair and the troops have their work to do'. Unlike the Visconti, who all cowered before their astrologers, Francesco openly scoffed at the soothsayer and declined to consult the stars when something had to be done; and to someone who wished to cast his horoscope he said that he had forgotten the day of his birth, but no doubt his secretary had a note of it somewhere. He was accessible, bluff and good-natured, and he was gifted with that memory for names and faces which is supposed to be the birthright of princes. He remembered not only the names of his old soldiers but those of their horses, a feat which was also attributed to Hernan Cortés.

The castle of Milan was a wreck. The citizens had tried to stamp out all memories of the Visconti. At the same time that Francesco Sforza was winning all hearts with his affability and his soldierly sense of humour and justice, he was also employing three thousand men on the rebuilding of the castle. It was a sign that another dynasty was on the way. He and Bianca never lived there, but in a little palace called the Corte d'Arego, which has unfortunately vanished. How delightful it must have been. It was decorated by such artists as Foppa and Moretti, and one court was frescoed with heroes of antiquity and another with portraits of Francesco's fellow *condottieri*, friends and enemies alike.

The young duchess and her elderly husband had a large family and he left to her the education of the children. She employed the celebrated but unpleasant scholar, Filelfo, who had been settled in Milan for years, and he filled the children with elegant Latin, the girls as well as the boys. It is on record that the Emperor Frederick III said that one of the most remarkable things he had heard in Italy was the speech of welcome made to him by Francesco's first-born, Galeazzo Maria Sforza, then aged eight. Scholars still have some difficulty in defining the beginning of the Renaissance, but we can be sure it was well under way when we read of those infant orators lisping their hexameters before Pope or Emperor. One might suspect a certain amount of yawning on such occasions, but it was not so: wonder and admiration were always aroused by the learned infants. Some high levels in priggishness were achieved in letters home, such as the letter in faultless Latin sent by one of the Sforza children to his mother, telling her that he had been out hawking and had killed seventy quail, two partridges, and a pheasant, ending with 'not that your Ladyship should think I am forgetting my work, which will bring me much more profit than hawking'. One can positively hear Filelfo breathing down his pupil's neck.

There is an endearing glimpse of one of these miniature scholars in the Wallace Collection in London, the well-known fresco attributed to Bramantino, and more recently to Foppa, 'Gian Galeazzo Sforza reading Cicero', a study that must have charmed and amused many. We see a little boy of perhaps six or seven in his schoolroom, seated on a hard bench of a design still used in village schools today, with an open window behind him and one little leg resting on a window-seat as he pensively reads; near by another book is open which may be a Latin dictionary. No more charming glimpse exists of that stormy period.

Though Francesco was content to allow his wife to bring up the family, he could not resist the paternal privilege of laying down certain rules of conduct for his eldest son, Galeazzo Maria, possibly remembering the advice given to him when he was young by his father. His *Suggerimenti di Buon Vivere* begins charmingly and disarmingly with: 'Galeazzo, you know that until now we have never been angry with you nor have we given you a single blow,' and goes on to lay down some rules of life: he must honour God and the Church; be respectful and obedient to his parents; be polite to all; be pleasant of speech to servants; he must never lose his temper about trifles; he must cultivate a sense of justice and mercy; he must not wish to possess everything he sees and must learn to do without anything he cannot get honestly; he must not be deceitful, or tell lies, or listen to slander, and – he must choose good horses.

The maxims which parents draw up for the good of their offspring often make sad reading in the light of future events, and they also endow the state of parenthood with a touching pathos and irony; but the *Suggerimenti*, if they fell on deaf ears, at least reveal the writer as a good, kind, and simple man with much about him, despite his power and grandeur as a self-made prince, of the shrewd peasant stock from which he sprang. Certainly none of his sons, living in a wealthier and more sophisticated world, could have written such an artless guide for the young. And such documents, the first of their kind during the Renaissance, reveal the arrival of a new age, and of ordinary men anxious to give expression to their hopes and longings and their fears.

Francesco's last great state occasion, a few years before his death, was his appearance at the Congress of Mantua in 1459, when Pius II attempted to rouse the rulers of Europe to go on crusade against the Turk. The deputation left in a Milanese fleet of forty-seven ships and, sailing down the Po and up the Mincio, arrived in splendour at Mantua. Pius wrote of the Milanese in his *Commentaries* that 'no one could be seen whose garments did not glitter with gold or shine with silver'; but the best gold of all was the advice given to the Pope by Francesco Sforza, that the projected crusade was out of date and impossible; other potentates expressed the same opinion, less pleasantly, by their absence.

Francesco's death was preceded by a severe attack of dropsy. He died suddenly in 1466, aged sixty-five. The distracted Bianca sent messengers to recall her eldest son, Galeazzo Maria, who was in France. He travelled home disguised as a merchant and approached the city garbed in mourning and riding a black horse. A deputation met him at the gates with the ducal emblems; he dressed in splendid garments and, upon a white horse, rode into the saddened city to take up his inheritance. He was the fifth Duke of Milan and he was twenty-two.

Those who wander listlessly through the great red castle of Milan, looking for an anchorage for their thoughts, may like to know that Galeazzo Maria was the first of his family to inhabit the rebuilt stronghold. They may also like to reflect, as I have already said, that the Sforza, as far as character and temperament go, were the Visconti over again. One of the mysteries of generation is that strong men often produce weak sons and clever men produce fools, and though the descendants of Francesco Sforza were neither weak nor foolish, their great sire had been unable to endow them with his good qualities. Their mother's blood had proved stronger, and instead of the solid qualities of the old *condottiere* one sees the craft and the guile of the earlier dynasty and also a touch of the Visconti *stravaganza*. The likeness was made even closer by the revival of the Visconti names – Galeazzo and Maria.

At the time of Galeazzo Maria's accession, his brother Ludovico – the most interesting member of the family – was only fifteen. There were three other brothers, two nonentities and the third, Ascanio, who became a worldly Renaissance cardinal. He had a house in the Piazza Navona, in Rome, where one of the narrow lanes that leads into the piazza from the south is still called Vicolo d'Ascanio. The amazed Romans used to turn out when they heard trumpets to see the cardinal return from hunting, with hounds, huntsmen, and game carts. In years to come he was to be the chief influence in the election of the Borgia Pope, Alexander VI, and it is therefore perhaps not surprising to know that he once paid a hundred ducats for a parrot that could say the Creed.

At the suggestion of Louis XI, Galeazzo Maria married the French king's sister-in-law, Bona of Savoy, a young woman of unusual beauty, according to the Milanese ambassador, who sent in the usual confidential report, adding with diplomatic caution that he had only had a front view of her. A more detailed description was that of Galeazzo's brother, Tristano, who was sent to France to marry Bona by proxy. 'First and foremost,' he wrote, 'she seems to me to have a beautiful figure, well suited to child-bearing, then a face neither long nor broad, beautiful eyes, though they might be darker, a good nose and mouth, a lovely neck, good teeth and hands; above all, she has the most gentle and winning manners.' He reported that after the ceremony he had, according to custom, ceremoniously touched the bride's thigh in bed with his leg. Bona of Savoy was one of a number of princesses at the time who might have been Queen of England had Edward IV not fallen in love with Elizabeth Woodville; indeed at one time she was betrothed to him.

When Bona reached Milan, she and Galeazzo Maria spent their honeymoon in a little house on an island in the park, while the builders and decorators worked away at the colossal castle. How big it was, and is, can be judged from the words of a contemporary writer who, wishing to localize an event, said it took place in a room 'at the head of the stairs up which one goes by horse'. It was indeed a fine roomy background for the reign of extravagance that now began. The coffers of Milan were brimming over once again, and one marvels at the vitality and resilience of this city which throughout history could be in distress at one moment and rolling in money the next.

It is not, of course, fair to contrast a man with his father, as if both breathed the same mental climate. Francesco's world had been the austere one of his friend, Cosimo de' Medici; Galeazzo Maria's world was that of Lorenzo the Magnificent. The wealth piled up by careful fathers was being spent by their sons.

Extravagance and amusement were in the air, and the Duke and Duchess of Milan were rich.

There is a portrait of Galeazzo Maria by Pollaiuolo in the Uffizi in Florence which shows what a strange man he was: elegant, lean, neurotic, with a great hooked nose of the kind called 'Roman', deep-set dark eyes and slender hands with long, nervous fingers. Of his father's robust heartiness and balance there is no trace. He was a Visconti risen from the dead. When his mother died unexpectedly it was whispered that he had poisoned her and, though this is almost certainly untrue, such a rumour tells its own story. Accompanied by his young wife, he flashed about the Duchy, clothed in the gaudy parti-coloured dress affected by the Sforza, one leg red, the other half white and half blue, a doublet of cloth of gold, long hair falling from his shoulders; and for the first time since the remote days of S. Ambrose we hear of someone in Milan who was devoted to music and singing. The Duke imported his singers from Flanders, which at that period was said to produce the best voices, and he took great pleasure in a large and costly orchestra and choir. An order has been preserved which allowed his musicians to be as drunk as they liked except on concert nights. He prided himself that his court was the most splendid in Europe and – another link with his Visconti ancestors – his hawks perched on velvet edged with silver and gold. He added splendidly to his libraries and even encouraged the printing press at a time when some book collectors would not look at a mechanically produced book. The first Greek book printed in Italy appeared in his time: it was the Grammar of Lascaris, produced in 1476.

His ten-year reign ended in his murder. It was one of the most foolish and pointless crimes in Milan's history, but it is interesting as a Renaissance crime based on classical example. Among the pupils of a Humanist named Cola Montana, a man who had a grievance against the Duke, were two bad characters and a young fanatic who fancied himself as another Brutus. Montana so worked upon the feelings of these three young men that they decided to re-enact the murder of Caesar.

It was Christmas-time in the year 1476 and the Duke, who had been absent from Milan, rode there for the celebrations, full of uneasy forebodings. The whole story reads like a chapter of Visconti history transposed into the Sforza period. On his way to Milan various omens alarmed the Duke: he saw a comet; a room caught fire; ravens flew across his path. His superstitious Visconti blood warned him to turn back. However, he went on and his fears, increasing, took on a macabre and dramatic form. He put his choir into mourning and ordered Lauds for the Dead to be sung every morning. Though this must have had a chilly effect on the festive season, Christmas passed off merrily, and Galeazzo Maria cheered up sufficiently to fly his hawks in the afternoon. On the following morning he was due to go in state to attend High Mass in the Church of S. Stephen. He rejected a breastplate because it made him look too fat and, instead, wore a red robe lined with ermine over the Sforza hose and a hat of the Sforza brown. An immense crowd had assembled in the bitterly cold morning to see him enter the church, and, as he did so, they heard the choir suddenly break into *Sic transit gloria mundi*. Here the murderers were waiting.

They had attended an early Mass to ask blessing for their enterprise and pardon from S. Stephen for shedding blood in his church. They carried daggers under robes of crimson satin. As the Duke advanced between the ambassadors of Ferrara and Mantua, one of the three men stepped out and knelt, as if to present a petition, playing the role of Tullius Cimber. The Duke paused, and the next moment three knives were buried in his body, and he fell dead almost at once. The murderers were quickly seized, hanged, drawn, and quartered, and small boys dragged what remained of them round the frosty streets of Milan.

The Milanese chronicler, Bernadino Corio, was present and saw the murder; even the confession of one of the murderers, most dramatically taken down in the present tense, has been preserved. Hard things have been said of Galeazzo Maria, but he was an intelligent and scholarly ruler, perhaps, like his maternal grandfather, a bit crazy, but with three obvious claims to be remembered. He had an illegitimate daughter, Catherine Sforza, who became one of the great Amazons of the Renaissance, and also one of the most beautiful women of her time. Her beauty preparations were famous, and it was her wish that her book of recipes, which has survived, should be generally known for the benefit of her sex. He also stimulated the silk industry by ordering five mulberry trees to be planted on every hundred poles of land; and, more important still, he is said to have introduced rice to Lombardy.

With the murder of Galeazzo Maria begins the last chapter in the history of the Sforza. Lurking in the shadows of the lecture-room where the wretched Montano had turned the brains of his pupils were three centuries of servitude for Italy. Of all the daggers that have flashed in Italy, none poisoned the future more surely than those which slew the fifth Duke of Milan. Only sixteen years remained and then the story of Italy is one of foreign invasion. It is hard to see how centuries of tragedy should have been poised on the points of three daggers; but this was so. 'Today the peace of Italy is dead,' exclaimed Sixtus IV when they brought him news of the murder. He was right.

The heir to the Duchy was Galeazzo Maria's seven-year-old son, Gian Galeazzo, the charming little boy in the Wallace Collection. His mother, Bona of Savoy, was appointed to be his regent: beautiful, gay, light-hearted, but, as Philip de Commines, who knew her put it, *une dame de petit sens*. She soon lost her head over a handsome carver in her household upon whom she heaped gifts and privileges. Her enemies enjoyed watching her ride out into Milan pillion with Tassino, which was the young man's name. No one was more interested than her brother-in-law, Ludovico Sforza il Moro, then a man of twenty-five, with the wicked uncle's historical possibilities. He was a man of great charm and ability, but history insists that he was a villain.

He was called il Moro – the Moor – not because he was of dark skin but because having been given the name Ludovico Maurus, he took, as a pun on his second name, the emblems of a Moor's head and a mulberry tree. He also engaged Moorish or African servants, which then became the fashion in Milan, as mulberry became popular as a colour for women's dresses. One of the best portraits of Ludovico is the altar-piece, said to be by Zenale, in the Brera, Milan, which reveals a more refined and sophisticated version of his great father, for the bluff humour of the old soldier has been replaced by a courtly grace, a calculated charm, indeed all that Italians mean by *amabilità*. The type is by no means extinct. One can see men not unlike il Moro stepping from chauffeur-driven cars outside expensive restaurants in Milan.

There is no evidence that he intended to supplant his young nephew in the early stages of the Tassino affair, but when the regent's favourite became more ducal than any duke and was supported by his mistress, he was told to go. This was rather an unusual occurrence in Italian history since a knife was the normal way of parting with such young men. Tassino evidently thought so too, since he took the hint and vanished, taking with him a fortune in jewels. Bona fled after him like a madwoman, but they never came together and she lived the rather shabby, tolerated life reserved for such women at the court of France. In this situation Ludovico il Moro took over the guardianship of his nephew. When the child was ten, he was dressed in white velvet and crowned in Milan Cathedral as sixth Duke. His loving uncle was beside him, a tower of strength; and the young man gave to Ludovico the affection he might have given to his dead father.

In northern Italy, after every great ruler's death, Fate would give a shake to the political kaleidoscope and the powers would regroup themselves into a different pattern. Old allies would find themselves to be enemies; old foes would become temporary friends; the balance of power which was created at this time was a delicate piece of mechanism and responded to fear like a seismograph to earth tremors. It was during the three years war, in the course of which Milan, Florence, and Naples together rescued Ferrara from the designs of Venice and the Papacy, that there arrived in Milan a strange man, a genius, whose letter of recommendation from Lorenzo de' Medici described him as an inventor of military machines, a designer of artillery, an erector of bridges, a maker of canals, an architect, a sculptor and, almost as an afterthought, a painter. This was Leonardo da Vinci, who was then thirty.

Ludovico had no need of Leonardo's military machines, for the war was ended, to be followed by twelve of the most brilliant and extravagant years in the history of Milan. One reason why I admire Ludovico Sforza is that Leonardo da Vinci, not the easiest person to get on with, found him a congenial employer and spent sixteen years in his service. Between painting immortal pictures, and working at the 'Colossus', as the mounted statue of Francesco Sforza became known, Leonardo designed machinery for masques, costumes for masquerades, and even for a Turkish bath. The popular conception of this most intellectual of the artists living a life of luxury, and in style and prosperity, is probably untrue. He was a vague, unbusiness-like genius, and one of those perfectionists who can never finish anything to his satisfaction. If the assumptions of some art critics are correct, a visit to his studio in Milan would have been interesting. Among the unfinished pictures on which he may have been working at odd moments, and when the spirit moved him, are the *Mona Lisa*, the *Virgin of the Rocks*, and the *Virgin and Child with Saint Anne*, all now in the Louvre. Though fortunes seem to have been squandered every day, his salary was often unpaid, and among his worst payers were the monks.

When the young Duke Gian Galeazzo was twenty he was married to Isabella d'Aragon, the daughter of Alfonso of Calabria, who detested Ludovico. The young Duke had grown up to be a weak, pleasure-loving nonentity well content to stay in the background as long as his loving uncle did the work. The marriage was a brilliant occasion, and even the cooks, someone noted, wore satin and silk. In the following year, 1491, Ludovico Sforza, the power behind the throne, decided at last to marry. His choice had fallen on the elder daughter of the Duke of Ferrara, Isabella d'Este, but as she was already betrothed to the heir of the Marquis of Mantua, Francesco Gonzaga, he was offered, and accepted, her younger sister, Beatrice d'Este, and one wonders, reading his history, if Italian history might have taken a different course had he married, instead of the gay and laughing Beatrice, her tough, iron-willed sister.

However, in freezing January weather in 1491 a fleet of battered ships, escorting the gilded state barge of Ferrara, put into the Ticino and docked at Pavia, full of young women who had erased the ravages of days of hunger and illness and now stood in their most splendid dresses, eagerly looking towards the cavaliers on the bank; and the most vivacious was the young bride herself, Beatrice d'Este, aged sixteen. How one would love to have seen that arrival, and the meeting of Beatrice d'Este with her forty-year-old husband. She was fated to die six years later, but in that brief period she became one of the best-known women of the Renaissance.

Her life with Ludovico repeated in a different age the felicity of Francesco Sforza's marriage with Bianca Visconti, and there was much the same age gap between them. They lived during the greatest prosperity and splendour that even Milan had known. The wealth of the Dukedom was fantastic. So apparently was taxation. The goldsmiths of Milan were famous and the armourers, as in the days of the Visconti, could put hundreds of lay figures in the streets clothed, horse and man, in the finest armour that could be bought. Building was going on everywhere. The white cathedral, more than ever a curious throw-back to the Gothic age, was rising slowly, but the Certosa of Pavia compensated for such an architectural anachronism. Great canals and hydraulic works were being undertaken. At the time one might have met Bramante building the dome of S. Maria delle Grazie, or have seen Leonardo da Vinci sketching faces in the market, or dreaming of building an aeroplane, or slipping off in the morning to the refectory of S. Maria delle Grazie to add a few brush strokes to the *Last Supper*. At the centre of all the activity, hurrying on the architects and the artists, inspecting the new irrigation schemes, rebuilding churches, adding to libraries, attracting scholars to the universities, was Ludovico il Moro, working with that frenzy which sometimes overtakes those for whom life has not reserved much time. The revenue of his small state is said to have been more than half the total revenue of France.

His affection for his young wife extended to members of her family, and he organized a weekly post between Milan and Mantua, so that she and her sister, Isabella, Marchioness of Mantua, might exchange news. The messenger carried, as well as Beatrice's letters, gifts of truffles and, in season, hares and venison, and he returned with letters from Isabella and gifts of trout from Lake Garda. Isabella regarded her sister as the rich member of the family and was sometimes unable to contrast without a tinge of envy the luxury in which she lived in Milan compared with the often empty treasury at Mantua. Beatrice enjoyed every moment of her good fortune.

'There is literally no end to the pleasures and amusements we have here,' wrote Ludovico to his sister-in-law. 'I could not tell you one thousandth part of the tricks and games in which the Duchess of Milan and my wife indulge. In the country they spend their time in riding races and galloping up behind their ladies at full speed, so as to make them fall off their horses. And now that we are back here in Milan, they are always inventing some new form of amusement. They started yesterday in the rain on foot, with five or six of their ladies, wearing cloths or towels over their heads, and walked through the streets of the city to buy provisions. But since it is not the custom of women to wear cloths on their heads here, some of the women in the street began to laugh at them and make rude remarks, upon which my wife fired up and replied in the same manner, so much so that they almost came to blows. In the end they came home all muddy and bedraggled, and were a fine sight!'

In his next letter to Isabella he says that, while staying at Pavia, Beatrice and Isabella d'Aragon went to the Certosa to spend the day, and he rode out in the evening to meet them. To his surprise he found them all dressed in Turkish costumes.

'These disguises were invented by my wife,' he explains, 'who had all the dresses made in one night! It seems that when they began to set to work about noon yesterday, the Duchess of Milan could not contain her amazement at seeing my wife sewing with as much vigour and energy as any old woman. And my wife told her that, whatever she did, whether it were jest or earnest, she liked to throw her whole heart into it and try to do it as well as possible.'

This remarkable young woman was sent when she was not yet twenty to represent her husband at the most crafty and cynical court in the world, the Signory of Venice. She travelled with her mother, the Duchess of Ferrara, and a company of over a thousand. The practical joker and tom-boy was then seen as a cool, self-possessed young woman who had no hesitation in addressing the Doge assembled in state with his Council, an ordeal which had made many an experienced ambassador weak at the knees. After seven days of gaieties and festivities, Beatrice and her mother attended the Great Council in the Doge's Palace, and Beatrice sent an account of the event to her husband.

'Here in the centre of the hall we found the Prince [the Doge] who had descended from his rooms to meet us,' she wrote, 'and accompanied us to the tribunal, where we sat in our usual order, and the Council began to vote by ballot for elections to two different offices. When this was over, my lady mother thanked the Prince for all the honours which have been paid us, and took her leave. When she had finished speaking, I did the same; then, following the instructions which you had given me in your letter I offered myself as a daughter to obey all the Doge's commands.'

Her earlier letters from Venice have a singularly modern ring to them. She described her sightseeing tours.

'We landed at the Rialto,' she wrote, 'and went on foot up those streets which are called the Merceria, where we saw the shops of spices and silks and other merchandise, all in fair order and excellent quality and in great quantity and variety of goods for sale. And of other crafts there was also a goodly display, so much so that we stopped constantly to look at now one thing, and now at another, and were quite sorry when we reached St Mark's. Here our trumpets sounded from a loggia in front of the church . . .'

Of another expedition, she wrote: 'And as we walked from shop to shop, everyone turned to look at the jewels which I wore in the velvet cap on my head, and on the vest embroidered with the towers of the Port of Genoa, and especially at the large diamond which I wore at my breast. And I heard people saying to one another – "That is the wife of Signor Ludovico. Look what fine jewels she wears! What splendid rubies and diamonds she has."' In another letter she tells Ludovico how she had teased the Bishop of Como, who, exhausted with sightseeing, had complained, as every tourist has done in Italy from that day to this, 'My legs are worn out!'

Alas, the laughter and the glitter of gold and diamonds were to be extinguished in six years. Beatrice had two sons, and it was now believed that Ludovico would put away the sickly young Duke and his family and usurp the Dukedom. So sure was Naples that this was in the air, so miserable was Isabella d'Aragon, that the southern kingdom was ready to go to war with Milan on behalf of the Duke and his Neapolitan wife. Feeling himself surrounded by enemies, Ludovico invited the French to come to Italy and assert their ancient claim to Naples.

Perhaps he did not really believe that they would come; perhaps he wished only to frighten Naples; perhaps he hoped to create some re-grouping of power from which he could profit. Who can say? The fact is that the French did come, led by a courtly but ugly little gnome, Charles VIII, and at that dangerous moment Gian Galeazzo, Duke of Milan, died. It was believed that his uncle Ludovico had poisoned him. Most historians still believe that he did so. Ludovico hurried to Milan and offered loyalty to the dead man's infant son, but the Council would not hear of it: Ludovico had been duke in all but name for years, and at a time when the state needed a firm hand, and not another regency, he was asked to become Duke. He and Beatrice d'Este became the seventh Duke and Duchess in 1494.

In the meantime, Italy, accustomed for centuries to mild *condottieri* warfare, was appalled by the ferocity of the French army. The very sight of it was startling. The vanguard consisted of eight thousand Swiss; gigantic archers from Scotland seemed to a contemporary observer to be beast-like men – *parevano uomini bestiali* – while at the head of the army 'marched' a monster of a man with a polished sword like a spit for roast pork, and then four big drums played with both hands, and accompanied by two pipes, making an infernal noise such as one heard at a fair. The cavalry was terrifying, astride chargers with clipped ears; the artillery was drawn, not by oxen, but by teams of horses, and the shining cannon moved as quickly as the infantry. Italians, who think so much of personal appearance, were shocked most of all by the master of all this, a little man in black velvet with a huge nose and mouth, and stick-like legs, who sat a magnificent war horse.

The French took Naples without a battle, and Ludovico,

turning his coat, formed a league of states against them, and the invaders had to fight their way out of Italy. There was only one real battle, which lasted fifteen minutes and is chiefly remarkable for the sudden transformation of the deformed little French king into a hero when, presumably inspired by his ancestors, he called upon the chivalry of France to die with him and led them into battle. The Italian commander, Francesco Gonzaga, husband of Isabella d'Este, captured the royal tent, in which was found the curious assortment of objects which a monarch at that date liked to have with him on the battlefield. There was a helmet and a sword said to have belonged to Charlemagne, a reliquary containing a thorn from the Crown of Thorns, a piece of the True Cross, one of the limbs of S. Denis, and a book full of pictures of the Italian ladies whose beauty had caught the royal eye.

The year after the French left Italy, (with full knowledge of her wealth and her weakness), Fate struck the first blow at Ludovico. Beatrice felt unwell and later that same night died in giving birth to a still-born child. She was only twenty-two. For days Ludovico would see no one; then it is recorded he was found lying clothed in sackcloth in a dark room hung with black velvet. He ordered that Beatrice should be buried before the high altar of S. Maria delle Grazie.

When the Ferrarese ambassador was admitted to see him, Ludovico confided that whenever he had prayed in his later years he had asked God to let him die first, but, as God had willed otherwise, he was now praying that, should it be possible for a living man to see the dead, he might be permitted to see and speak with Beatrice once again. Many of the historians who have written of this period have acknowledged the debt which this accomplished ruler of forty-six owed to the cool and capable brains of his young wife; and it has been said that had she been beside him in the storms that were gathering, he might not have lost everything, as he did.

In the following year Charles VIII of France, on his way to watch a tennis match, hit his head, small as he was, on a low archway, and a few hours later died of a cerebral haemorrhage, aged twenty-seven. His successor was the deadly enemy of Ludovico, the Duke of Orleans, who became Louis XII. His grandmother had been Valentina Visconti, daughter of Gian Galeazzo Visconti, and Louis, who regarded himself as the true heir to the Duchy, with a claim that went back beyond the Sforza, decided to invade Lombardy.

Ludovico found himself deserted, and was forced to fly. He staged a brief return but was betrayed to the French as he stood among the troops, disguised as a Swiss mercenary. Louis showed him no mercy. He was taken to France and imprisoned in various places, eventually at Loches. Those who have visited the *châteaux* of the Loire, and have gone a little way south of Tours, will have seen the grey towers and keep of Loches rising above the river Indre. Visitors are taken down to the dungeon in which the once splendid Ludovico il Moro spent the last years of his life. A mark on the stone indicates the only daylight that ever entered his cell. There are some frescoes and rude drawings on the wall which are said to be the last signs of one who made so many marks upon the age in which he lived. His captivity lasted for eight years, and he was fifty-seven at his death.

His two sons both succeeded to the Duchy, but as the puppets of foreign governments. When his second son, Francesco II, died in 1535, France had been expelled from Italy by the Emperor Charles V, (who was also King of Spain), and Spain was to be the dominant power in Milan for a hundred and seventy-eight years.

In the course of his tour through the Castle of Milan, the visitor will hear a confusing catalogue of names and dates, but I think the men and women I have mentioned are those whose triumphs and disasters should interest us most as we visit the scenes in which they lived.

There was one pathetic relic, which I came on by chance in the castle, exposed in a pitiless light. This was the last work of Michelangelo, the Rondanini Pietà, a fearful revelation of the cruel triumph of age. The sculptor was nearly ninety as he struggled to release those two figures from the stone, but the old hands would no longer obey the still questing brain. He 'hacked away the marble until nothing but a skeleton remained', says John Pope-Hennessy in his *Italian High Renaissance and Baroque Sculpture*: and while it is bad enough to see how the power and the glory had departed, it is worse to think that the old man knew it. Vasari tells how he visited Michelangelo in Rome a short while before his death, and how the sculptor saw his visitor's eyes straying towards the pathetic group on which he was engaged. It was night, and Michelangelo held a lantern. 'I am so old,' he said, 'that Death frequently drags at my mantle to take me, and one day my person will fall – like this!' And he dropped the lantern and plunged the studio in darkness so that Vasari should see no more.

§ 2

One day I happened to notice a crowd outside a church, and someone told me they were waiting to see Leonardo da Vinci's *Last Supper*. The ordeal of queuing up to see a picture which I knew to be the ghost of a picture, and one I had seen so often in reproduction, caused me to postpone a visit there. However, one morning I stopped a taxi and said to the driver, 'Il Cenacolo,' while he, casting away the butt of a cigarette, nodded with complete comprehension and drove off without a word into the traffic. I thought there can be few cities in the world in which you can give the title of a great picture as a topographical direction.

I arrived at the church of S. Maria delle Grazie, in whose adjoining refectory Leonardo painted his famous fresco, certainly one of the most ill-fated of the world's masterpieces. A crowd was still waiting and the turnstiles were clicking as I went almost reluctantly to experience what I felt would be a disappointment. I found myself in a gaunt hall in which the friars ate their meals when S. Maria delle Grazie was a Dominican monastery. The painting covers the end wall, so that it would have appeared to the friars that the life-sized figures supping at a table on a slightly higher level were a continuation of their own repasts. That, of course, was Leonardo's intention, and it must indeed have been a wonderful sight to have entered this hall when it was still in use, the friars seated on each side and the Prior facing the table occupied by Christ and His disciples. The crowd stood whispering, probably as surprised as I was, to see a much larger and less shadowy picture than I had expected.

I knew that Leonardo had painted this picture not in fresco but in oils on a wall so damp that even in early times the paint had begun to crack and peel, and in recent years was in such a desperate condition that the wall was heated in an attempt to keep it dry. The restorers touched up the picture century after century until there was probably little of the original left. Then what might well have caused complete destruction was a bomb in August, 1943, during an air raid on Milan, which demolished the roof of the refectory and one of the walls, but did not destroy the picture. A photograph of the chaotic scene after the bomb had fallen hangs in the refectory. When the last in the long line of restorers took down the sandbags they found Leonardo's masterpiece covered with a thick mould. In 1947 the *Last Supper* was restored by scientific experts supervised by a Government Commission; and, as one of the aims before the restorers was to remove the touching-up of former times and the preservation of every particle of Leonardo's pigments, it is probable that the picture is more like the original today than it has been for many a century.

I was astonished by it almost against my will. It cannot be reproduced. The postcards and even full-page illustrations in art books cannot convey more than the vaguest impression of this enormous work, which is approximately thirty feet long and fifteen feet wide. Though the colour has gone and the expressions on the faces are largely conjectural, one thing is as clear as ever: the steel-like framework or skeleton of a triumphant composition: two groups of agitated men in rhythmic movement, separated by the calm figure of Christ. I forgot that I was looking at the ruin of a picture and thought I might be seeing it in the early months of its creation when Leonardo was slowly, and bit by bit, building it up. What observation had gone into this work! How many supper-tables in Milan did Leonardo frequent to capture all those gestures and attitudes; how many men cutting a loaf of bread in an inn, or upsetting the salt, or whispering something to his neighbour, could have guessed that their actions were to be immortal?

Leonardo was forty-three and had worked in Milan for thirteen years when the Duke Ludovico commissioned the *Last Supper*. It was a part of his scheme for the aggrandizement of S. Maria delle Grazie as the Sforza mausoleum. At the same time he engaged Bramante to design the superb dome. Most critics think that Leonardo began his painting in 1495 and took two years to finish it. A young novice in the monastery often watched Leonardo at work: he was Matteo Bandello, the novelist, who sometimes saw the artist arrive early in the morning and mount the scaffolding.

'From sunrise to twilight,' he wrote, 'he did not put down his brush or think of eating or drinking but painted without interruption. Then perhaps two, three or four days would elapse without his touching the picture. But even so he would spend one or two hours there looking at the figures, reflecting and coming to a decision after turning the matter over in his mind. According to his humour, I have seen him go from the Corte Vecchia where he was sculpting the amazing horse, straight to the monastery at midday when the sun stood high in the sky. There he climbed the scaffolding, painted a few strokes and immediately went away again.'

There were naturally many stories about those two years. The best known is that the monks, seeing the faces of Christ and Judas unfinished for months on end, complained to the Duke that the artist was not really trying. Leonardo replied that every day, morning and night, for more than a year he had been going to the Borghetto to search the faces of the abandoned and the criminal for one suitable to be Judas. If necessary, he went on, he would use that of the Prior instead!

Years of thought went to the making of this picture, and it lives because it is life observed by eyes that missed nothing. 'When you are out for a walk,' Leonardo once wrote for the instruction of young artists, 'see to it that you watch and consider men's postures and actions as they talk, argue, laugh, or scuffle together: their own actions and those of their supporters and onlookers: and make a note of these with a few strokes in your little book which you must always carry with you.' From the age of thirty, ('an age when the average busy man ceases to take notes', comments Sir Kenneth Clark), Leonardo was never without his notebook, jotting down things he saw and things he imagined. For days he would follow people whose appearance interested him, and we know that he even wrote down their addresses. 'Giovanina, fantastic face, is at Saint Catherine's hospital', was one of his entries. The habits and methods of genius are always of interest, but there is no way of taking genius apart to see how it works. No notebook or technical achievement can explain that moment when Leonardo rejected as the theme of his picture the institution of the Eucharist but selected instead the terrible moment when Jesus said, 'But, behold, the hand of him that betrayeth me is with me on the table.'

A short street called the Via Zenale, almost opposite S. Maria delle Grazie, took me to the Via S. Vittore, where I found the Museum of Science and Technology. To me, this is one of the most fascinating museums in Milan. I saw a long gallery in which were displayed wheeled vehicles, machinery, a life-sized diver in suit and helmet, bombs, shells, cannon, and many strange objects whose purpose was not immediately apparent. These were the inventions, (which included the tank, the submarine, and the aeroplane), which occupied so much of Leonardo da Vinci's time and thought.

As I passed from one to another I thought that Leonardo would have been more interested in this gallery than in any of his paintings, for even to him these inventions remained diagrams and sketches in his notebooks, and here he could have seen them transformed into working models by Italian engineers and craftsmen.

One speaks of Leonardo's restless curiosity, but it takes on a new dimension when you stand before these extraordinary prophetic glimpses of a world still to come, a world in which men can travel under water and through the air. To the men of Leonardo's day this was sheer fantasy, and a contemporary, turning the pages of his notebooks and seeing his design for a submarine or a flying machine, would have put him down as mad. To us, who live in a world of specialization where it is not unusual to meet an ignoramus who can weigh a star, the general sweep of Leonardo's mind is uncanny. How his eyes would have sparkled could he have seen this hall where his dreams have become reality, and how well this hall helps us to understand how one of the world's greatest painters found painting a bore and a nuisance, something that kept him from serious things such as the flight of birds or the movement of fish. 'His mathematical experiments have absorbed his mind so entirely that he cannot bear the sight of a paintbrush', a correspondent once wrote to Isabella d'Este after a visit to Leonardo's studio, to explain why the artist would not paint a picture for her.

That morning the only other visitor to the museum was a man who, perhaps recognizing me as a fellow countryman, came up and wished to share his astonishment.

'If this fellow had known anything of steam, petrol, or electricity,' he said, 'men would have been rushing about in trains and motor cars four hundred years ago!'

I agreed that this was possible: the one thing Leonardo lacked was mechanical power.

'Just look at this!' said my companion, 'a perfectly good tank worked by man- or horse-power!'

Leonardo's 'armoured vehicle' was a mushroom-shaped tank large enough to hold several men. It ran on four wheels, moved by men or horses, it carried three cannon, and the sides were pierced by a line of loopholes that ventilated it and also served for musketeers. The commander stood on a stout wooden platform in the centre and could look out from a turret like that of a modern tank and direct the vehicle's movements and fire. Like most of Leonardo's inventions, this was never made: his idea had to wait for the petrol engine and the caterpillar tractor.

His paddle-steamer lacked nothing but a steam boiler: it was precisely the same type of craft that crossed the Channel within living memory and used to thrash its way noisily round the seaside towns of Kent. Leonardo, however, having no knowledge of steam power, had fitted it with a piece of massive clockwork like a child's toy. His diver's suit looked absolutely modern, as did a snorkel. There was a model of a double flying staircase of a kind now seen in modern flats; there were girder bridges, river locks, and multiple traffic lanes.

As we went round exchanging comment on these beautifully made models, I tried to 'place' my companion, but found him difficult. At first I thought he might be an art critic, though he exuded an air of wealth which does not always go with that calling; then I thought he might be a rich picture collector. This he certainly was not since, when we reached the end of the gallery, he turned to me with the astonishing remark, 'Who was this extraordinary fellow?'

I expressed surprise that he did not know he had been looking at the inventions of Leonardo da Vinci.

'I hadn't the slightest idea,' he replied. 'I saw the words Science and Technology outside and thought I might see something interesting.'

He paused and looked at me suspiciously, as if I were trying to mislead him. 'I thought Leonardo da Vinci was a painter!' His tone of voice, however, managed to suggest that da Vinci, the engineer-artist, had shot up in his estimation!

I thought it might be interesting to see the effect of the *Last Supper* on him, and as we walked to S. Maria delle Grazie he told me that he was a manufacturer of typewriters and adding machines and had come to Milan on his company's business.

'How interested Leonardo would have been to meet you and to hear of your machines,' I said. 'Oddly enough, a typewriter, which might well have been invented during the Renaissance, was one of the things he never contemplated.'

We entered the refectory and looked at Leonardo's masterpiece.

'There's nothing left of it,' he said. 'Too bad . . .'

We wondered, as we walked on, if Leonardo would have been willing to exchange his own glorious age, or so it seems to us, for our own age of invention, so filled with objects that would have delighted him – aeroplanes, railway trains, motor cars, electricity, the camera, the microscope, wireless, and, above all, atomic research and the conquest of space.

§ 3

Byron once expressed the contempt for Petrarch which a practical man sometimes feels for a theorist. 'I detest Petrarch so much,' he wrote, 'that I would not be the man even to have obtained his Laura, which the metaphysical, whining dotard never could.' And Don Juan, summing up his creator's views on matrimony, asked:

> *Think you, if Laura had been Petrarch's wife,*
> *He would have written sonnets all his life?*

Such being Byron's opinions, it must have been amusing to have seen his face when, on a visit to the Ambrosian Library, in 1816 the librarian pressed upon him the Library's greatest treasure – Petrarch's copy of Virgil! How natural to assume that the English poet would be interested! Byron, who could be blunt enough when bored, could say nothing since, having seen something that interested him more than the Virgil, he had no wish to offend the Librarian. This was a tress of Lucrezia Borgia's blonde hair.

I was reminded of this when, calling at the Ambrosiana and presenting a letter of introduction to the librarian, I was told rather than asked, 'Of course you would like to see Petrarch's copy of Virgil'. A man in a black smock went away to obtain this treasure.

The Library is housed in one of those old palaces which appears small from the street, yet inside is discovered to be enormous, indeed a positive labyrinth of inter-communicating rooms, marble staircases and galleries constructed round an inner court-yard. The reading-room is a small domed hall adorned with allegorical statues and furnished with tables and shaded lights. Six or seven elderly scholars sat there surrounded by folios and manuscripts, most of them sunk in a coma of creation and wearing that expression of despair so familiar to the wives of writers. A brighter feature was a young woman, maybe an American research scholar, who appeared to be racing through cursive script as if she were reading the *Ladies' Home Journal*.

The Virgil, when it came, was astonishing: a huge codex which I assumed to be a facsimile. When I realized that it was the original, I was reluctant to turn the pages, and the librarian, noticing this, courteously descended from his dais and we turned the pages together. I suppose this Virgil is priceless, and it must also be high among those books which, in booksellers' language, have an 'association interest', for on the fly-leaf Petrarch described in his own exquisite script his first sight of Laura and how, after an interval of twenty-one years, he heard of her death.

The adventures of such a book must be astonishing: the various hazards of ownership over six and a half centuries, the comparative haven of libraries, the peril of war and conquest, and the risk of fire. I asked the librarian to tell me what is known of its history. He told me that it had belonged at first to Petrarch's father, but was stolen in 1326, after the family had settled at Avignon. Twelve years later Petrarch found it again, or possibly the guilty thief returned it; at any rate, from that day in 1338 it never left the poet's possession. After Petrarch's death, the Virgil went with his other books to the Visconti library at Pavia, where it remained until the French conquest of 1499, when it passed through a number of hands until Cardinal Borromeo bought it for the Ambrosiana in the sixteenth century. Still its adventures were not over. Napoleon removed it to Paris, but it was returned to Milan in 1815.

No doubt in his joy at the recovery of the book in 1338, the poet wished to make it even more beautiful, and persuaded his friend, Simone Martini of Siena, who was then working at the papal court at Avignon, to illuminate it for him. The splendid decorations appear as fresh as when they were painted more than six centuries ago: but even more valuable is the famous inscription which Petrarch added. This is what he wrote:

'Laura, with all her illustrious virtues and long celebrated in my poems, first appeared to my eyes in my early manhood on the sixth day of April in the year of our Lord 1327, in the church of St Claire in Avignon, in the early morning. And in the same city at the same hour of Prime of the same day in the same

94

month of April, but in the year 1348, that light was withdrawn from our day, while I was by chance at Verona, ignorant – alas – of my fate. The sorrowful news reached me at Parma in a letter from my friend, Ludwig, on the morning of the 19th day of May in the same year. Her chaste and most beautiful body was laid in the church of the Franciscans on the very day of her death, at evening. Her soul, however, I am persuaded – as Seneca says of Africanus – has returned to heaven, which was its home. I have felt a kind of bitter-sweetness in writing this as a memorial of my sorrow, and have chosen this place as one that often meets the eye, so that I may reflect that no pleasures remain for me in this life, and that I may be warned by constantly looking at these words, and by the thought of the rapid flight of years, that it is high time to fly from the world. This, by God's grace, will be easy to me when I consider my past life's idle cares, the emptiness of its hopes, and its extraordinary issues.'

The problem of Laura – was she a real or an imaginary woman? – was of such interest in the sixteenth century that two enthusiastic Petrarchians opened a tomb in Avignon and claimed to have found her skeleton and a lead box containing a sonnet by Petrarch; but Cardinal Bembo, the great expert of the time, rejected the poem as a fake. Though she is still a mystery, most scholars believe that she was Laura de Noves, who married Hugh de Sade at Avignon in 1325, and that Petrarch, when he saw her with her fair hair falling to her shoulders, was transformed into a poet and, like any mediaeval knight or troubadour, chose her as his ideal lady.

Though Byron refused to show any interest in ideal love and despised sonnets, ('the most puling, petrifying, stupidly platonic compositions'), he nevertheless haunted the Ambrosiana to sigh with a sentimentality greater than Petrarch's over the letters of Lucrezia Borgia to Cardinal Bembo, and to gloat over a tress of her fair hair. 'I mean to get some of it if I can', he confessed in a letter to Augusta Leigh, and, when no one was looking, the inveterate collector of relics and love tokens abstracted 'one single hair'.

I asked if the hair and the correspondence could be seen and was told that after Byron's theft was known, it was decided to put the hair in a reliquary, which was done in 1828, and it is no longer to be seen, as Byron saw it, with the letters. These were, however, immediately produced for me, bound in sheepskin. There are nine of them, written in Latin and Italian in Lucrezia's own hand, and a song in Spanish, all addressed 'to my dearest M. Pietro Bembo': but, like so many women, Lucrezia omitted to date her letters, and Bembo did so in his own hand. Byron wished to believe that they were romantic and passionate epistles, but the probability is that they were not burning protestations of love at all, but the polished rhetorical compositions which ladies who carried the heavy burden of Renaissance learning were in the habit of writing to cultivated men friends. Indeed, had Byron only known it, Bembo and Lucrezia were probably as platonic as Laura and Petrarch!

I went upstairs to see Lucrezia Borgia's hair, which is now in the museum. There is a long outside gallery from which you look down into a dank courtyard where two statues stand among depressing shrubs; one was recognizable as Manzoni; the other, a gay young spark in trunk hose, turned out to be Shakespeare. Leading from this gallery is the museum where I saw Lucrezia's hair in a glass reliquary as if it were the hair of a saint: fine, fair hair, just a thin tress, the kind of keepsake which Byron knew so well. I remembered with what care Lucrezia tended this fair hair, and how often her wedding journey to Ferrara was interrupted so that she could wash her head. The reliquary is exquisite: the glass oval is surrounded with pearls from which hang two beautiful little pendants; on one is the Borgia bull in red; the other is an eagle, perhaps the white eagle of Este. Near by, with that irrelevance which makes some museums so fascinating, is a pair of chamois gloves worn by Napoleon at Waterloo.

In an adjoining room I saw the crystal box in which lies the famous *Codice Atlantico*, full of Leonardo da Vinci's prophetic and scientific drawings, sketches, and writings, together with the letter of introduction to Ludovico il Moro, in which the artist is described as an engineer.

Nothing, however, in the Ambrosiana delighted me more than

the celebrated profile of that enchanting young woman who was once known as 'Beatrice d'Este', by Leonardo da Vinci, and is now 'Portrait of a Young Lady', by Ambroglio da Predis. She has come down to us over four centuries bringing in her young face all that is sweet and innocent in girlhood, and though the experts do not appear to think so highly of the painting as they did, she seems to me the most charming and the most touching of all the female faces which have survived from the brilliant age in which she lived. Everyone must know her: the young profile, the auburn hair caught up at the back in a gossamer fillet edged with pearls, the net secured to her head by a jewelled ribbon from which hangs a pearl drop in the centre of her forehead. Her nose is slightly *retroussé*, her expression is solemn, but with just a hint that at any moment she might turn and smile, and beneath her chin, in the fashion of the time, are trained a few strands of her auburn hair. I once knew a young man who carried a coloured postcard of her safely through the First World War. She was his idea of perfect female beauty and, looking at the original, I thought to myself not a bad ideal for a young man to have had.

Of all the women whom she might have been, probably the most likely is Bianca, the illegitimate daughter of Ludovico il Morò, and Bernadina de' Corradis. She sparkled happily through the brilliant days of Beatrice's short reign and both Ludovico and Beatrice were plunged into sorrow when she died only a few months after her marriage to Galeazzo Sanseverino. What a kind and tender-hearted man Ludovico was: a letter in the Milan archives to his former mistress is a model of what such a difficult and civilized letter should be:

'Although we cannot speak of the sudden death of our darling child, Bianca, without the bitterest anguish,' he wrote, 'yet since you are her mother, we feel that it would be a grave failure of duty on our part if we did not inform you of this sad event with our own hand, this being unlike any loss that has befallen us. Yesterday morning at nine o'clock, having been apparently in perfect health up to this hour, she fell into a sudden fainting fit, and in spite of all the doctors could do for her, grew steadily worse, until at five o'clock this evening she ended her life on earth. The event has caused us the most unutterable grief, both for the loss of such a daughter and because the blow was so sudden and unexpected. We know that it will be a great shock to your heart, but we must bear with patience the trials that are sent us here, and bow to the unalterable laws of nature. We entreat you, therefore, to bear this loss with patience and courage, and assure you that you will be no less beloved by us in future, than if Bianca were yet alive.'

Ludovico also wrote to the Archbishop of Milan, asking that his daughter be buried exactly behind the high altar in S. Maria delle Grazie, 'as I do not wish Bianca to be buried in a place where I can see her grave'.

§ 4

The fen-like countryside south of Milan, with its irrigation channels and its rice-fields, wears a placid non-Italian charm. The silvery poplars trembling in the slightest wind lend to the landscape an air of Holland or France, and it is almost surprising to meet upon the roads those unmistakably Latin countenances, furrowed, brick-red, with big noses and dark eyes, which have not changed since they were painted as the Magi. Twenty miles south of Milan I came, on a calm summer's morning, to the ancient town of Pavia, the capital of one of Lombardy's nine provinces. There was a slight heat mist over it and the old town clustering on the banks of the Ticino, which is crossed by an unusual covered bridge, had the look of a Dutch landscape of the seventeenth century. But even as I thought so, the mist began to lift and with every second Pavia retreated from Holland and looked more Italian, or Lombardic, until the town stood revealed in all its shades of mustard-yellow and Siena-brown; and the cathedral, as if to signal the transformation, rang its urgent Catholic bells.

I was met by a friend who had been asked to lecture at the University and was staying in Pavia. He rushed me round from church to church, casting scraps of information at me, as to a hungry dog, until I refused to digest any more. This is a familiar moment to most strangers in Italy. The riches of the country, architecturally, historically, artistically, become at times intolerable, and one envies the specialist who is interested in only one period of history or in the work of one painter. Also there is so much to see and understand that a guide almost drives one mad: one must find one's own way in one's own time and make one's own selection.

We came to the Castle of Pavia, built by the Visconti and inherited by the Sforza, an immense structure with a grassy moat and terminal towers which bore a family resemblance to the Castle of Milan. This was the building in which the famous wedding feast took place, attended by Petrarch and Froissart, when Lionel, Duke of Clarence, was married to Violante Visconti. Later, it was the palace in which Ludovico Sforza and Beatrice d'Este spent some of their happiest hours.

Such a place, of course, had also plenty of room for tragedy. Here at the same time lived the pathetic Gian Galeazzo Sforza, sixth Duke of Milan, trusting and loving his uncle, drinking a little too much and finding himself unequal to life, to the sorrow of his angry, disillusioned wife. In this castle he died after a long, slow decline in health until he could not stand upright, which made many at the time say that he had been poisoned by his uncle. Yet Ludovico detested cruelty of any kind and, as far as one can possibly say, was not the type of man to kill anyone who trusted him. On the other hand, he did pass over his nephew's son and take the Dukedom.

I felt in Pavia, as I have felt so often in Spain, the awful oppressive weight of Time. I would not call it the most beautiful of Italian cities, but I had seen none which gave me a greater sense of age, of buried cities one above the other, extending back beyond the Romans to the Gauls. The roadway slopes downward, the incline representing the passing of centuries, to the west doors of the church of S. Pietro in Ciel d'Oro. Here my friend took me into the crypt and pointed out the tomb of S. Augustine. Such transitions from the fifteenth to the fifth century are usual in Italy. How S. Augustine, who had died during the siege of Hippo in North Africa in A.D. 430, should have been buried in Pavia seemed a little puzzling until a priest, who said that he was writing something about the wandering of the saintly bones, explained it to us.

'When Hippo fell to the Vandals in A.D. 430,' he said, 'the leading Christians were exiled to Sardinia. They were not allowed to take the relics of their beloved bishop with them, but they never ceased to hope that some day they might be translated. This did not happen for sixty years when they were taken to Cagliostro, in Sardinia. Two hundred years later, when the island was over-run by the Saracens, Liutprand, King of the Lombards, offered the infidels sixty thousand golden crowns for the bones of S. Augustine. This they were only too glad to accept, and they shipped the relics to Italy in A.D. 710 and the king had them interred here at Pavia, which was then his capital.'

That, briefly, was the story. The chest in which the relics were placed has been opened from time to time; men have gazed reverently upon the remains of the great Father of the Church and have chosen the right moment to steal a little bone for themselves. In 1787 a heel-bone was given to the Duke of Parma. I looked at the exquisite marble shrine crowded with little figures, beautifully carved and their eye-balls painted black, and wondered how much of Christianity's most popular convert it now contains.

My friend then rushed me to the University where I saw a series of dignified courtyards, Siena-brown in colour, each one with a balcony where one could lean and watch the march of neatly dressed undergraduates to and from lectures.

'Oxford might have been a bit like this in the fifteenth century,' said my friend. 'Small, quiet, no traffic and, of course, no bicycles!'

In one of the courtyards we came upon the statue of Alessandro Volta, the most distinguished of the University's professors, a stately eighteenth century figure whose name is invoked every time we buy an electric light bulb.

'Do you realize,' asked my companion, 'that the history of this university goes back to Roman times? Later, Charlemagne was one of its beneficiaries and Lanfranc, who became Archbishop of Canterbury, was a native of Pavia and read law here.'

We were greeted by a science don who took us into a museum where the glass bottles and metallic sandwiches are to be seen which helped Volta to produce the first volts. I have no idea whether electricians ever make pilgrimages to the shrines of their gods; if they do, this is obviously the place to go. This fantastic collection of glass retorts and bottles and zinc and metal tanks, of machines with brass knobs and mahogany handles whose purpose cannot be explained by anyone in less than half an hour, fills several rooms. The don explained the first voltaic pile and as he did so it occurred to me how civilized our ancestors were. The new source of power did not threaten the existence of mankind, or fall into the hands of crooks and bullies. No one, as far as I know, ever threatened to electrocute the world. The playful lecture-room spark of those early days, with which electricity proclaimed its presence, seems now, as we look back from the atomic age, to have been the star on the wand of a fairy godmother who watched over Volta's globes. Of all the great inventions, I thought, electricity seems almost alone in having roused no evil spirit.

We passed through an anatomical museum, hardly the best preparation for lunch, where among the objects which I strove hard not to see was a human head, the face a ghastly green in colour, the hair still horribly auburn, floating in a jar of oil. I was told it was the head of an anatomical professor who had died a century or so ago, bequeathing his body to his students.

I had been invited to lunch at the Ghislieri College, which was founded by Pope Pius V, whose name was Michele Ghislieri. He began life as a poor lad who knew how difficult it was to obtain a good education. The moment he was elected Pope, he founded a college at Pavia with the object of helping young men who were not well off. Facing the College is a spirited statue of Pius, a lean, white-bearded ascetic who had been Grand Inquisitor and took his hair shirt with him into the Vatican. He walked barefoot in public ceremonies and refused to exchange his white Dominican habit for the red robes of the Pope; since that time the Pope has always worn white. He was the Pope who helped to raise the fleet that triumphed over the Turks at Lepanto, and he also, incidentally, excommunicated Elizabeth Tudor.

The College is a stately marble palace designed in the style of the late sixteenth century. The rector showed me the best pictures,

(Lepanto, of course), and the tapestries: we then ascended a regal stairway and passed along a corridor from which the under- graduates' rooms led left and right, their doors bearing such messages as 'Wake me at ten'. An English scholar would perhaps think the rooms at Ghislieri rather magnificent and lacking in 'snugness', the usual English complaint about Italian palaces in the eighteenth century. But each one has running water, each is high and spacious, and in addition to a bed, has an inviting desk and a fine range of bookshelves, but no broken-down basket chairs and no evidence of hospitality. The rector told me that the most famous man of letters amongst the alumni was the playwright Goldoni, who, however, was 'sent down' in 1725 for composing a shocking satire on the daughters of Pavia's nobility.

The hundred residents of the Ghislieri dine together in a long white sixteenth century refectory. There is no high table. The undergraduates sit ten to a table down both sides of the room. Waiters who wear white cotton gloves carry round the menu to each table. I found myself seated next to the only English scholar at Pavia, a young man from Leeds and recently of Merton College, Oxford. He told me he had come to Pavia to write a thesis on what seemed to him an unusual aspect of Roman history, but what it was he did not tell me, and I did not ask. We ate an excellent lunch of gnocchi, followed by grilled sole, fruit, and cheese. There was red and white wine on the table. It was rather formal and dignified, and I thought the young Italians already looked like young doctors, lawyers, and engineers.

§ 5

The word Certosa in Italy, Chartreuse in France, and Charter- house in England, indicates a Carthusian monastery. About five miles from Pavia is one of the most famous of these, the Certosa of Pavia, which has inspired an architectural literature of its own. It is something of an experience in modern Europe to find oneself alone with a famous monument, yet on that bright forenoon I was the only visitor, and the silence was made more absolute because the Certosa is no longer inhabited.

I saw the extravagant building, framed in the archway of the entrance gate, lying some distance away at the end of a long wide road. It must be the most sumptuous and costly monastery ever built; both Visconti and Sforza lavished immense fortunes upon it, hoping to receive their dividends in heaven. And indeed should there be any spiritual merit in erecting a church-palace, (and after all the Visconti and Sforza could easily have spent the money on themselves), surely the heads of these families must have received a few words of celestial approval. It was surprising to see medallions of the twelve Caesars on the west front, side by side with the Apostles, and delightful to notice how pedantically the Renaissance had designed a toga for what is, after all, a Gothic framework. The fourteen side-chapels which line the aisles are each a marmoreal symposium, and the beauty and variety of the marbles in which masons have succeeded in recovering from the earth all the colours of the spectrum, are only less amazing than the skill of those who dovetailed them in such brilliant harmony.

But more interesting to me than any of this splendour was the tomb of Beatrice d'Este and Ludovico in the centre of the church. The history of this monument is curious. The tomb is empty and was originally erected before the high altar in S. Maria delle Grazie in Milan when Beatrice died. She was buried there, shortly before Ludovico's fortunes crashed and he ended his life in a French prison. For reasons I do not know, the Dominicans of S. Maria offered the tomb for sale and it was bought for practically nothing by the Carthusians of Pavia, who evidently had longer memories. They gave it the place of honour in their church, but in the move, apparently, the bones of gay, charming little Beatrice were lost.

Upon the tomb, lying in robes of state, are the life-sized effigies of Beatrice and Ludovico. The hunchback, Christoforo Solari of Milan, was commissioned by il Moro to make both figures, though he, Ludovico, was still alive. It was his wish that future ages should see his beloved Beatrice as she had been seen by her friends and servants, and the sculptor took great pains to make the figure a true portrait. I thought it one of the most touching tombs I have ever seen. There is a hint about these two figures, a young girl and a man much her senior, perhaps of tragedy or romance, which must cause some who do not know their history to gaze into their faces with interest and curiosity.

Though I knew that Beatrice died at the age of twenty-two, I hardly expected her to look so like a schoolgirl. She wears one of her most splendid gowns and, like so many celebrated women, she was tiny; and I noticed that her toes were slipped into pattens, or possibly they were Venetian *choppines*, whose soles were at least four inches thick. This was the young woman whose laughter and love of life had made Milan the gayest court in Europe, and who, at the same time, was able to advise a husband twenty years older than herself. Ludovico is portrayed lying at her side in the full splendour of his fortunes, his long hair falling upon the pillow, his ducal cap in his hands.

I have mentioned Beatrice's death, and I thought of it again as I stood beside her tomb effigy. Possibly, I thought, a first-year medical student today might have saved her life. The account of her sudden end is unusually detailed. She was advanced in pregnancy and in perfect health, but in low spirits. On the evening of January 2, 1497, probably in an attempt to amuse her, there was dancing in her rooms in the Castle of Milan, which was cut short when Beatrice suddenly said she felt ill. She gave birth to a still-born son, and died soon after. From his darkened room, the distracted Ludovico dictated letters to the courts of Italy.

'My wife was taken with sudden pains at eight o'clock last night,' he wrote. 'At eleven she gave birth to a dead son, and at half past twelve she gave back her spirit to God. This cruel and premature end has filled me with bitter and indescribable anguish, so much so that I would rather have died myself than lose the dearest and most precious thing I had in the world.' So he broke the news to Beatrice's father, Ercole I, Duke of Ferrara, and to his brother-in-law, Francesco Gonzaga, Marquis of Mantua.

He was in no condition to attend the funeral which, according to the custom of the time, was held at night. By the light of a thousand torches, the court, the ambassadors, and the leading citizens of Milan, wearing long cloaks of black, followed the hearse to S. Maria delle Grazie. Leonardo da Vinci was working on the *Last Supper* at this time and must have seen the funeral procession; possibly he even walked in it. The body of Beatrice was clothed in one of her richest gowns of gold brocade, and was carried to the high altar, where among the candles of unbleached wax and the purple draperies the Cardinal-Legate waited to receive it. No one saw Ludovico for a fortnight after the funeral. His rooms remained hung with black, and he took all his meals standing. Once a day he put on a long mourning cloak and hurried to his wife's grave.

Such sombre events are in sharp contrast to the gaiety and brilliance which the word Renaissance calls up. On the walls of innumerable art galleries, as in a looking-glass, we see only the happy moments of that age, and we look into the eyes of men and women who were clearly in love with living; possibly for that very reason death, when it surprised those gay and happy people, revealed that they had imbibed insufficient stoicism with the classics. Certainly, when sorrow struck a Renaissance palace, there was no attempt at a stiff upper lip. It was usual for the grief-stricken to hide themselves away, as Ludovico did, and for those admitted to their darkened rooms to emerge in floods of sympathetic tears.

When Guidobaldo I, Duke of Urbino, died at the age of thirty-five of what was called 'the gout', a secretary of Isabella d'Este was admitted to the room in which his widow, Elizabeth Gonzaga was mourning. He wrote:

'I found this illustrious Madonna surrounded by her women in a room hung with black, with the windows all closed, and only one candle on the floor. She was sitting on a mattress spread on the floor, with a black veil over her face and a black vest up to her throat, and it was so dark I could hardly see, and had to be led up to her like a blind man by my cloak. She took my hand and we both began to weep, and it was some time before her sobs and my own allowed me to speak . . . Today we spent more than three hours together, and I induced her to talk of other subjects, and even made her laugh, which no one had as yet succeeded in doing. I begged her to open the shutters, which no one had dared suggest, and I think that in two days time she will consent to do this. She still eats her food on the floor . . .' Who could recognize in that bleak figure the gay and brilliant Duchess mentioned in Castiglione's *Il Cortegiano*, who quoted and smiled her way through so many learned evenings at Urbino?

A prowling guide attached himself to me and we went off to see the cells of the monks, if you can call such delightful suites of rooms, built of marble by the best masters of the Renaissance, by that name. Each monk occupied a self-contained flat or maison-nette containing a bedroom and a study, beneath which was a woodshed and a workroom and a charming little garden. Each 'cell' was enclosed by a wall and a decorative arch whose door, fitted with a *rota*, or turntable, accepted the monk's vegetarian meals, cooked and delivered by lay brothers.

Three times in the twenty-four hours a bell would summon him to church for Mass, Vespers, and the Midnight Office, and after dark he would hurry across the cloisters holding a lantern. I remember a friend who had attended Matins and Lauds in a Carthusian monastery telling me that he had never witnessed any-thing more impressive than the cowled figures seen only by the glow of their lanterns. A rule of silence was observed and relaxed only during a weekly walk of two or three hours.

The Carthusian Order is remarkable among monastic orders in never having been reformed, ('Never reformed because never deformed', a Carthusian will tell you!), and the rules of a life modelled on that of the hermits of the Egyptian desert were laid down by S. Bruno in the mountains above Grenoble, about the time that William of Normandy was invading England. The Grande Chartreuse, as the mother house was called, stands in magnificent mountain scenery, though the monks were expelled from France at the end of the eighteenth century. Oddly enough the word Chartreuse, which in past centuries called up a vision of a life of severe privation, to most people now suggests convivial occasions. The distillation of the famous green and yellow liqueur is a recent event in Carthusian history and the great amount of money made by the monks was devoted by them to charitable and religious objects. Since their expulsion from the Grande Chartreuse, the liqueur has been made by a French company, but the monks opened a distillery at Tarragona, in Spain, and make what they naturally claim to be the original article. I remember a monk in Spain telling me that green Chartreuse is the strongest and the best, yellow the most popular, and white the least known.

I found an old gentleman in the gatehouse of the Certosa presiding over a museum and a plentiful supply of a liqueur called *Gra-Car*. He gave me his visiting card, on which I read 'Cavaliere Maddelina', and told me that he distils the liqueur according to an ancient monkish recipe and gathers the necessary herbs himself. I bought two bottles of *Gra-Car*, but unfortunately, such are the hazards of travel, left them unopened in a hotel wardrobe. I hope they were enjoyed.

§ 6

A great park called Mirabello stretches from the Certosa to the Castle at Pavia. It was one of the famous hunting grounds of the Dukes of Milan, and was stocked with deer and other animals. The biggest game run to earth there was Francis I, King of France, who was captured early on the morning of February 25, 1525, by the army of Charles V, King of Spain and Roman Emperor.

It is the endearing characteristic of kings to be, at the same time, foolish and brave, and those qualities were revealed when Francis I, after leading a charge straight across the field of fire of his own artillery, fought like a lion and was nearly killed, while the nobility of France fell around him. That was the battle of Pavia. Francis spent a year or so as a prisoner of war in Madrid; and the gates of Italy were opened wide to Spain.

CHAPTER THREE

The canals of ancient Lombardy – Lake Maggiore and Isola Bella –
A visit to Pliny's Villa on Lake Como – How Mussolini died – The
Iron Crown of Lombardy – Theodolinda's chickens and her oil bottles –
The town of Gorgonzola

§ 1

If anyone who had known Lombardy centuries ago could see it
today, nothing would surprise him more than the absence of
boats and sails. Until modern times the towns and cities of the
Po Valley were connected by an intricate system of waterways
which transformed the large towns into inland ports. Shakespeare
was aware that in his time one could go by ship from Milan to the
Adriatic, and from Verona by canal barge and river boat to Milan.
Throughout the Middle Ages the cargoes of Venice were delivered on the quaysides of Milan, Verona, Mantua, and Ferrara,
and barges unloaded stone for the building of Milan's cathedral on
the site in the centre of the city. There was even a time when
Milan ranked as a naval power and maintained a fleet of warships
that challenged the galleys of Venice.

The river and canal traffic gave a distinctive flavour to life in
Lombardy. The inns were full of boatmen who possessed the
inherited knowledge of those who for centuries had humoured a
dangerous river. Many early travel writers describe the silence and
ease of gliding through Lombardy by barge and boat. The
regularity and safety with which cargoes could be delivered had an
effect upon the civilization of the Renaissance: there were no
oceans to cross, no pirates to fear, no mountain passes, no bandits
or highwaymen; and the city states of the Po Valley were the first
to receive the spices, the embroideries, and the Greek manuscripts
from the East.

Scarcely a trace of this system of communications exists today.

It began to disintegrate with the political troubles of the sixteenth century, when, as ducal states declined or changed ownership, the canals became clogged and were filled in. The coming of the railway in the last century delivered the final blow. Sometimes you will see in a town the word *canale* on a street sign, instead of *via*, the only indication that it once formed part of the inland waterways.

The system went back to Roman times. In those far-off days a service of packet-boats called *cursoriae* plied between the various towns and accepted ordinary passengers as well as the mails and official messengers. In a delightful letter written about A.D. 450, Apollinaris Sidonius described how he had glided along in a *cursoria*, on a voyage from a place near Milan, to Ravenna, singing as he went. One of his songs was evidently suggested by the Lombardic landscape, its theme being the death of Phaethon, who, unable to manage the Sun God's horses, crashed fatally into the Eridanus (as the Po was then called); and at his death his weeping sisters were turned into poplar trees. It is pleasant to think of Sidonius associating the windbreaks with this old legend, singing away and ready to explain to anyone who did not know that the tears of the weeping sisters were turned by the sun into the sticky gum which oozes from the poplar buds.

The best time of all to have seen the canal and river traffic of Lombardy must have been during the Renaissance. A lovely sight which has vanished for ever from the world was one which often caused the peasant to forget his pruning-hook as he saw, approaching through the vineyards, to the sound of music, a carved and gilded barge. Every Renaissance potentate owned one of these vessels called, after the Dogal galley of Venice, a bucentaur. They were built entirely for show and entertainment, and were used to convey distinguished guests to the ducal capitals, to carry daughters to their weddings, and to add an extra touch of allegorical splendour to the courtly pageants. A Pope, or the Roman Emperor himself, was handed from duke to duke, and gilded barge to gilded barge, until eventually he arrived at his destination, where, drawn up upon the river bank, he would see the archers and men-at-arms of the ruler, and, as the musicians struck up, a water pageant would begin and the guest be greeted by mermaids and tritons. The best description of such an occasion was written by Pius II in his *Commentaries*. On his way to the Congress of Mantua in 1459, the Pope travelled overland from Rome to Bologna by way of Florence, but on leaving Bologna he took a barge on the river Reno and sailed up that river, and the Po, to Ferrara. The Duke of Ferrara, in his bucentaur, conveyed him up the Po to Revere, on the Mantuan border, where another bucentaur, that of the Marquess of Mantua, was waiting. Pius, writing in the Caesarian third person, described the meeting of the Ferrarese and the Mantuan fleets. 'The former was carrying Pius,' he wrote, 'the latter hoped to carry him. On both, trumpeters filled all the surrounding valley with an extraordinary din, and displayed a whole forest of banners tossing in the wind. The inhabitants, seated along the banks, implored the Pope's benediction and when he blessed them, they shouted '*Viva!*'

Having spent the night in the Gonzaga palace at Revere, which was then only half completed, the Pope embarked on the bucentaur of Mantua and continued up the Po to its junction with the Mincio. As they glided smoothly round the bends and loops, someone pointed out to Pius 'a hill held sacred by the Mantuans where they say the divine Virgil lived'. They spent the night on a Gonzaga estate so that the entry into Mantua might take place the following morning.

Upon his return to Rome, during bitter winter weather, the 'aged Pope' as he called himself, (he was fifty-five), left in the Mantuan bucentaur and sailed, or was rowed, down the chilly Mincio to the Po. 'Trumpets and pipes of all sorts of instruments made sweet music from the lofty sterns. There were impersonations of various gods and goddesses, giants and virtues on the dykes that prevent the river from overflowing.' When Pius reached Ferrara, he was in such a hurry that he declined an invitation to stay there and insisted on pressing forward in small boats across the shallow and freezing marshes to the Reno. When it became impossible to hack a way with axes through the ice, the Pope was warmly wrapped up and carried in a chair. The cardinals had to walk. Somehow they got to Bologna and, crossing the mountains by carriage and horseback, reached Florence and Siena.

It is surprising to know how many important voyages were made in winter. The Po must have been under better control than it is today. Women also set off on long journeys in the worst time of year. When Isabella d'Este left in her father's bucentaur for Mantua to marry Francesco Gonzaga in February, 1490, the storm encountered on the Po was so violent that upon arrival the court painter had been so sick that he fled back to Ferrara by land without even saying good-bye to his mistress! Isabella's sister, Beatrice d'Este, left Ferrara in December of the same year, also in the bucentaur, for Milan, where she was to marry Ludovico Sforza. The snow lay three feet high in the streets of Ferrara. The bride and her ladies-in-waiting endured five days of discomfort in a state barge which was designed only for ceremony and pageants, whose living quarters were minute, and in which there was, of course, no artificial heating. To make matters worse, the store ship with the food and the cooks was lost and there was nothing to eat for an entire day. As Beatrice, hungry and huddled in her furs, was drawn slowly across the white landscape she was heard to utter the wish of the sea-sick – 'I want to die!' So resilient is youth, however, and particularly perhaps bridal youth, that the moment the bucentaur approached Pavia, Beatrice and her ladies appeared on deck, their hair faultless, their make-up perfect, and their gowns a subject of conversation among the ladies of Milan for weeks.

If such hardships were experienced by the nobility, one can imagine what winter travel must have been like by ordinary public transport. The boats were often unpleasantly crowded, and Fynes Moryson recommended passengers to take with them rose leaves, lemons, oranges, cloves, and rosemary, to counteract the smells of the boat. However, everything depended on the season of the year, and it must have been delightful to leave the roads in spring and early summer and to glide smoothly and silently across the plain. Oddly enough, few travellers thought the charm of such a voyage worth writing about.

Cellini gives a picture of water travel from Ferrara to Venice in

1535, from which we learn that the boatmen touted for custom in the Ferrara inns, and a bargain could be struck beforehand so that a traveller might have the boat to himself. Having killed a man in Rome, Cellini had prudently retired in company with an old friend, the timid sculptor, Niccolò de Raffaello, known as Il Tribolo, because, says Vasari, he was always in trouble at school. When at Ferrara this ill-assorted couple became involved in a tavern brawl, in the course of which Cellini drew his sword and threatened to kill everyone. 'I rushed onward,' he wrote, 'brandishing my sword along the walls with fury, and shouting: "I will kill you all," but I took good care not to do them any harm.'

'After we had supped,' he writes, 'a bargeman appeared, and offered to take us to Venice. I asked if he would let us have the boat to ourselves: he was willing, and so we made our bargain. In the morning we rose early, and mounted our horses for the port, which is a few miles distant from Ferrara.' Here three men, who had been concerned in the tavern brawl the night before, were waiting, armed with lances. Swords were supposed to be carried bound up so that they could not be drawn. Cellini had bought a stout pike in Ferrara with which he instantly attacked the men while his terrified companion took refuge in the boat. Cellini followed, and the boat set off down the Po while the three men followed in a skiff and, coming up with them ten miles down the river, shouted, 'Go thy ways this time, Benvenuto; we shall meet in Venice!' Immediately he reached Venice, Cellini went to a brother of Cardinal Cornaro and asked permission to carry arms, but fortunately his enemies did not appear.

On the way back, also by water, Cellini exhibited, and described without shame, the violent side of his character. They spent the night at an inn at the end of the Chioggia canal, where travellers would transfer to a barge which was drawn by horses. The innkeeper annoyed Cellini by demanding payment overnight and there were angry words, which terrified Il Tribolo, who nudged his friend to be quiet. Cellini was forced to pay and was so furious with the landlord that he was unable to sleep. 'We had, I must admit,' he wrote, 'the most capital beds, new in every particular, and as clean as they could be. Nevertheless I did not get one wink of sleep, because I kept on thinking how I could revenge myself. At one time it came into my head to set fire to his house: at another to cut the throats of four fine horses which he had in the stable.' These revolting thoughts were not carried into action, and in the morning Cellini and Il Tribolo, and the other passengers, took their places in the boat; but when the horses had been harnessed to the cable, Cellini pretended that he had left a pair of slippers in the bedroom and ran back to get them. It seems that he wished to have a last-minute fight with the innkeeper, for he called to him and got an insulting reply from behind a bedroom door.

'There was a ragged stable-boy, half asleep, who cried out to me: "The master would not move to please the Pope, because he has got a wench in bed with him, who he has been wanting this long while." Then he asked me for a tip, and I gave him a few Venetian coppers, and told him to make the bargeman wait till I had found my slippers and returned. I went upstairs, took out a little knife as sharp as a razor, and cut the four beds that I found there into ribbons. I had the satisfaction of knowing I had done a damage of more than fifty crowns. Then I ran down to the boat with some pieces of the bed-covers in my pouch, and bade the bargee start at once without delay.' This was the man who designed the exquisite golden salt-cellar for Francis I, and whose statue of Perseus still stands in the main square of Florence!

The regular service between Venice and Padua, and between Ferrara and Bologna, remained in repair and resisted all political changes, and the extinction of the great families, until the end of the eighteenth century. Dr Burney, in the course of his musical tour in 1770, said that he was advised not to take the *barchio* which ran regularly from Padua along the Brenta to Venice, as the journey was tedious and the company usually bad. There was an old saying that the Brenta boat would sink if it did not contain a monk, a student, and a courtesan. Nevertheless, Burney had a look at the boats and thought them 'gay' and 'inviting'. On his return journey he decided to travel by water, starting in the *corriera* which carried the Venetian mail-bags, 'a kind of barge with a large covered cabin in the middle for passengers'. His fellow voyagers were a mixed lot. 'However,' he wrote, 'beds were spread on the floor, and we all pigged together – the Courier, one female, with several ordinary people, and we all slept and grumbled the greatest part of a terrible night of thunder, lightning and rain, and in as much noise, though less danger, as on board a ship in the most violent storm.'

The next morning they came to the Po and changed to a larger boat. 'The country grew a little better by degrees, and we supped on board not unpleasantly. We pigged as the night before.' Early the next day they arrived at Francolino, a few miles from Ferrara, where the passengers left their luggage on the boat and were driven in a coach and four to the city. Time was allowed for a meal, but instead of eating, Dr Burney rushed round as many churches as possible, and copied the inscription on Ariosto's tomb, before joining the coach again. This took the travellers ten miles to a place where they found their luggage stacked on the banks of a canal. They had to wait for three hours, ('in the hottest weather I ever felt'), for the boat to arrive, which then pressed itself along a canal so full of weeds that it could hardly pass. 'It resembles the Po dyke and several dykes of Marshland in Norfolk,' Dr Burney noted. When they reached Malalbergo they were obliged to change into a larger boat on a different canal, 'and in this we were all night only going twenty miles to Bologna. The banks of this canal were pleasant, and had it not been for the voracious gnats, it would have been an agreeable voyage, as the weather was fine'.

Burney's brief voyage illustrates how desperately slow canal and river travel was, and how frequently the passenger had to change boats. The weed-grown canal, still in use, suggests too that the marvellous waterways of earlier centuries were neglected and about to fall into decay.

Nevertheless, sixteen years later the Brenta boat was still going strong. Goethe, on his way to Venice in the autumn of 1786, enjoyed the voyage enormously, and said how delightful it was to float along admiring the noble palaces and gardens, and how pleasant, when the vessel was held up in a lock, to step ashore for a moment and eat fruit offered by those on the banks. He met two strange travellers on this boat, Germans from the Paderborn district, dressed like mediaeval pilgrims, even to floppy hats, long staves and cockle-shells. They confessed to Goethe that in the course of their wanderings they had been treated better by Protestants than by their fellow Catholics. What a scene this was: Goethe, who was described by a contemporary as 'the most oppressively handsome man I ever saw', seated on the little gangway that led to the deck, questioning the pilgrims and passing on the information to the steersman and a group of curious passengers. And the passengers disembarked at Venice with no idea that their fellow traveller was Goethe who, at the request of the pilgrims, had handed round 'some little consecrated tickets on which might be seen the representation of the three sainted kings'.

§ 2

The road from Milan to Lake Maggiore is an unhappy example of the unfortunate Italian habit, so old-fashioned in these days of radio and television, of advertising, every few yards, olive oil, sewing-machines, tyres, vermouth, typewriters, and other things it is not easy to care very much about when you are travelling at sixty miles an hour.

The road passes through a countryside which is fighting a rearguard action with industry. Factories straggle out into the fields, and one sees workers, who are taking a few minutes off from the making of plastics, exchanging comments and jokes with women who are hoeing a field of melons or tomatoes. As you near the lake, however, the last factory is left behind and the land takes on the well groomed, obedient look of earth which has been tended for centuries. The Italian farmer is a hard worker, and uses every inch of soil: he keeps animals whenever he can, and near his farmhouse stand those delicious-looking little haystacks, built round a central pole, that cut like cake and look as eatable as gingerbread. The countryside is crossed everywhere by irrigation canals and by windbreaks of poplar and acacia. Before the Romans came, the Gauls cultivated this beautiful black earth; and what more could any farmer want than flat, rich soil, plenty of water and sunlight? Every Milanese lawyer and merchant once had his smallholding not too far from the walls of mediaeval and Renaissance Milan, where he produced his own oil, cheese, wine, and milk. Travellers have described the evening trek of cows back to the safety of the walls of Milan, which explains why Stendhal, as late as the nineteenth century, mentioned the smell of manure, which he liked so much, in the streets. The concern of the town dweller with agriculture is said to have been one of several reasons why the barrier between classes, and between the nobility and the merchant, broke down as early as the Middle Ages, to the astonishment of the aristocratically-minded French in the fifteenth century.

The countryside is that of Manzoni's *I Promessi Sposi*, and I could never for a moment forget that great novel any more than I could forget *Don Quixote* in Spain. It is one of a small number of novels in which the spirit of a countryside appears to have taken possession of the writer. Perhaps the only reader who was allergic to it, or had the courage to admit it, was Longfellow, who said that it sent him to sleep. It is as long-winded in parts as any other novel written in 1827, but I have never found anything soporific about it. Verdi, a son of the Po Valley, knew the country described, and the people, and he confessed, after meeting Manzoni, 'I could have gone down on my knees to him.' But he did even better: after Manzoni's death, he composed his famous Requiem.

When crossing the gaunt plain of La Mancha, the traveller searches the faces of approaching Spaniards for some look of Don Quixote or Sancho Panza; so in the soft Milanese countryside he fancies that the young man cycling to the silk factory might be the honest Renzo; the old woman with the hoe in the melon patch could be none other than Agnese with her endless hoard of proverbial wisdom; and, as he passes through a small town, the priest, plump and anxious, who glances swiftly at him before hurrying on his way, must surely be the timid Don Abbondio.

To create characters who seem to contemporary readers to sum up the faults and virtues they have noticed in others is a gift granted to few writers, though it is impossible for anyone today, as he reads *I Promessi Sposi*, even in Italian, to have a true idea of its effect upon an Italian public which spoke Spanish, German, or French, and could read into the narrative all manner of veiled political allusions, and for whom the language in which the book was written came like a clean breath of their native countryside. What a tribute it is to this novel that people still read it with pleasure. Manzoni also cleverly indicated the peculiar political atmosphere of the Po Valley in the seventeenth century – the period of his tale – when no one lived far from the frontier of a neighbouring self-contained little state – such a boon to the evil-doer. All a wanted man had to do was to slip across the frontier of the next state, where he was safe as long as he lay low for a while. The question of extradition was conducted in a gentlemanly way by a letter from one ruler to another, but in an age of secretaries and filing systems there must have been every chance that a letter might be lost for years, should the request for some reason be a disagreeable one.

Millions of copies of *I Promessi Sposi* must have been printed in various languages since it made its first appearance. Writing to a friend, Manzoni's daughter, Juliet, said that six hundred copies had been sold in twenty days – '*c'est une vraie fureur,*' she added. Juliet's husband, the Marquis of Azeglio, remains in my memory for one of the few witty death-bed remarks I can recollect. After Juliet's death, he married a girl named Luisa Blondel. Husband and wife did not get on, however, and, though they had parted, she hurried to him when he was dying. 'Ah, Luisa,' he said with a smile, 'you always arrive just as I'm leaving.'

As I went on across a landscape as flat as Norfolk, I saw at last the outline of mountains and the glitter of blue water, though the distant Alps were not visible: but before I left the fields of tomatoes, maize, and melons, and the windbreaks which tell one that these fields are sometimes whipped by savage gales from the Alps, I remembered that Manzoni gave another, and lesser known gift than his novel, to Lombardy. He was a great gardener and is said to have introduced the acacia to this part of the world.

§ 3

All lakes are beautiful in summer, and Maggiore, enormous, blue, and windless, shared the tranquillity of air, water, and mountain which is found more perfectly here than anywhere else in Nature. The waves scarcely lapped the shore, the mountains were reflected in the water, and boats glided across the surface in the summer haze. I was sorry to find that the distant Alps were still invisible and wished that I might have seen them towering at the northern end, which is Switzerland. When I came to Stresa, the sight of the Borromean Islands, with Isola Bella in their midst like some triumphant Venetian galley, took my breath away. The shops facing the lake were crowded with tourists examining an assortment of little wooden chalets, musical boxes, and suchlike, which had been blown into Italy by some wind from Switzerland.

I had lunch in a large, Edwardian-looking hotel where an enormous dining-room was set for hundreds of guests, and where the waiters stood about with an air of disillusioned expectancy. The main dish was lake trout cooked over a charcoal fire. The fish had been caught in the lake that morning and were as good as trout which one has been lucky enough to eat beside a stream in Scotland. Suddenly the waiters became alert as a confused sound echoed through the hotel. The double doors were opened and into the room trooped about a hundred people whose appearance would have caused astonishment and amusement even fifty years ago. They had come in coaches from Interlaken and down through the Simplon Pass without, so far as I could judge, feeling any awe or wonder at their achievement. There were Germans, French, some varied Nordics, and a few English, dressed as if for the subjugation of some tropical island, though, instead of axes, they carried cameras. They had the appearance of being the sunburned survivors of some shipwreck, who, having been hastily fitted out with odds and ends from a children's outfitters, were now led in to the hotel by a kind and watchful official, a brisk young man in normal clothes, who counted them as they entered as if some, still suffering from shock, might have got lost.

I hope Mr James Laver is making notes of modern tourist

costume, surely one of the curiosities of our age. Why should the act of leaving home and crossing a frontier cause a massive matron to reveal her proportions in beach pyjamas; can it be that an urge to nudism is inspired by some romantic dream of Italy as the land of eternal sunlight and passion? It would be interesting to know what countries and which sports have contributed to the extra-ordinary collection of peaked caps, lumber jackets, espadrilles, coloured socks, sandals, and the richly decorated shirts worn by both sexes. How extraordinary it is to see a coachful of tourists today, boiled red as lobsters, and to reflect that early photographs exist which picture men in hard hats and tweed suits, and women in bustles, crossing ice-fields and glaciers, while members of the same hardy generation have been immortalized wearing city clothes in some of the hottest parts of the Middle East. Earlier travellers thought of sunlight as something to be avoided with the aid of dark clothes and sunshades, and it was valued only as an enhancement of the southern landscape. 'To explain the first voluntarily sunburned English female cheek would involve a profound socio-anthropological study,' wrote J. R. Hale in his introduction to the *Italian Journal of Samuel Rogers*. My own guess is that it all began in Germany after the First World War, when, in the craze for physical fitness, a generation starved by the Allied submarine blockade took to hiking and sun-bathing.

A pleasant little man dressed for football or hockey was placed at my table. He came from South Shields and did not know he had crossed the frontier into Italy. When I told him so, he said, 'Go on! Fancy that!' I managed to ask tactfully why he had come to Italy: he replied it was because his wife liked the pictures of Venice in the travel agent's brochures. After lunch I was surprised to hear a member of this party, an elderly woman, speaking faultless Italian to one of the waiters. She told me that she had lived in Florence for over twenty years, but had not been back since the war. She was like the Prioress in this hearty and mixed pilgrimage.

After lunch I walked to the next village, Baveno, where a num-ber of enchanting villas stand above the lake, surrounded by woodlands and terraced gardens, exquisite places in spring and summer, but terrible beyond words, I should say, in winter when storms lash down from the Alps and the lake is hidden by sheets of icy rain. Among the villas is the Castello Branco, which was known as the Villa Clara when Queen Victoria spent nearly a month there in 1874. The popular idea of the Queen in old age as a static widow seated at a little lace covered side-table is entirely erroneous: on the contrary, she was almost what was known in those days as a globe-trotter. The royal yacht frequently steamed off to take her to see relatives on the Continent, and in 1889 she appeared, most improbably, in Spain, the only reigning British monarch ever to have done so. Old people in Baveno remember the stories told by their parents of alfresco tea-drinking under the trees in the garden of the Villa Clara, so English and eccentric; and they still show the cedar and the cypress which Queen Victoria planted.

I bought a ticket for a trip to Isola Bella, and in company with a number of the pioneers from the hotel we exploded on our way to the fantastic floating vision which, as we drew nearer, resolved itself into a lordly palace and terraced Baroque gardens. The boatman told us that the island belonged to Prince Borromeo, who lived in Milan but often came to stay on the lake. We landed on a stone quay and, mounting narrow Capri-like streets, came to the gate of the palace, where we were welcomed as expertly as if we had arrived at Woburn Abbey. A major-domo who spoke several languages took us through a series of princely apartments decorated in egg-shell blue with white Baroque decorations. I looked down from a balcony overhanging the lake where perhaps fifty trout were swimming of a size one would be proud to catch; in another I saw a bust of S. Charles Borromeo, with his hooked nose, gazing towards two ancient chests bound in red velvet, full, I was told, of his vestments.

The garden was, to me, the great delight of Isola Bella. Every inch of its soil had been brought from the mainland by Count Vitaliano three hundred years ago. He must have been a man who delighted in difficulties. His work endures in a series of ten terraces planted with hibiscus, orange, lemon, camellia, magnolia, box, ilex, laurel, and cypress. Like the earlier gardens of the Renaissance, those of later times obeyed the same rules and were designed as an extension of the house and a place of shade and pleasantry where all mean and unhappy thoughts should be abandoned. I thought perhaps its most attractive feature was the sight of the lake and the surrounding mountains which are seen from every point of view, framed in the leaves of ancient trees and lying beneath the uplifted arms of time-worn statues.

Legend, which must have its romance, says that when the isle was barren rock it appealed to a Borromeo as the perfect place to conceal a young woman named Isabella from the eyes of a jealous wife. History, on the other hand, says that in 1630 Count Carlo Borromeo wished to cultivate the isle and call it 'Isola Isabella' in honour of his wife, but, dying before his plans could mature, his scheme was carried out by his son, Vitaliano. To me, infinitely more fantastic even than the pleasure dome itself is the thought that the first Briton to describe it was Bishop Burnet author of the *History of his Own Time*, who was there in 1684.

§ 4

A car ferry crosses Lake Maggiore to Laveno on the east bank, and I soon found myself in the charming town of Como.

By one of the pleasanter ironies of time, the Younger Pliny is to be seen seated in a niche on one side of the doors of Como Cathedral, while his uncle, the Elder Pliny, occupies one on the opposite side. What, one wonders, would they have said could they have seen themselves, much troubled by pigeons and often mistaken by the hasty visitor for saints, in such incongruous positions? Even local pride scarcely seemed to me to justify the elevation of two such charming pagans to two such niches, especially as the Younger Pliny's only recorded association with the Church was the torture of two deaconesses in an attempt to find an answer to Trajan's questions about Christianity.

Both uncle and nephew had villas on Lake Como, and the Italians, with their endearing respect for writers, a feeling which they share with the Irish and, of course, the Welsh, have never forgotten them. Even today the boatmen will point out the sites of the villas they occupied eighteen centuries ago, and the most humble fisherman knows that the Younger Pliny wrote a number of famous letters and that Pliny the Elder was asphyxiated during the eruption of Vesuvius while attempting to rescue people from Pompeii.

From where I was sitting, I could see, mirrored in the lake, a charming white temple in the public gardens. It is a temple to the memory of Volta and, like the museum at Pavia University, contains more souvenirs of his life.

It was pleasant to sit idly watching the boats come and go in this happy, tranquil scene, enlivened by the laughter of young people and the cries of the boatmen. I thought that some Italian landscapes have such a strong look of the classical world about them that one might almost believe one had been projected back in time. I have felt this strongly on Lake Albano, near Rome, where the villas that dot the hills for miles around might still be occupied by Horace and his friends; and I had the same impression at Como. The lake is narrower than Maggiore and enclosed by taller mountains; and, seen from a distance, the villas that stand upon the shore and rise everywhere upon the slopes and summits of the mountains repeated, I thought, the first century landscape. After many centuries civilization has again climbed back to much the same standard of culture and comfort. There are libraries round the lake as there used to be. Central heating and electric immersion heaters have replaced the hypocaust; and perhaps a Roman of imperial times would admit, could he see Como today, that life is as comfortable as it was. He might even find it preferable. I am sure that both the Plinys would have appreciated television and an Alfa Romeo.

§ 5

I was told how to find my way to Pliny's villa beside the Lake of Como, and found myself travelling along a steep mountain road on which there was no stopping or turning back. At last I came to a house beside the road, high above the lake, where a barefoot lad of about twelve years of age, an Italian Huckleberry Finn, was sitting on a wall wearing a pair of tattered khaki shorts and whittling a stick with a penknife. My question, 'Where is the Villa Pliniana?' was evidently one he was accustomed to, for with an eager expression he leapt from the wall and led the way down a steep path through a dense brake of hazel and bramble.

It was a hot day, and the young faun sped swiftly ahead over flint and stone, pausing from time to time and chewing the end of his stick as he waited for me to come up with him. I nearly always carry a bag of sweets in my pocket as an offering to such fauns, for nothing else so easily dissolves the barrier of age, but unhappily I had forgotten them; so we descended in silence, scornful on his part as I came slowly after him, thinking how far below was the lake and how narrow and twisting the path.

The Younger Pliny had several villas on Como and the one I was trying to find was the lakeside villa which possessed the spring whose rise and fall so interested and puzzled the owner. I had the feeling, as I followed the lad, that perhaps I was bound on a fool's errand and that there might be nothing at the end of this painful descent except a few stones in the wood or a bit of tessellated pavement. However, as we arrived at lake level, we heard a dog bark and came to a cottage and some hens. My first feeling of disappointment vanished when, looking beyond the cottage, I saw a Renaissance villa standing upon a stone terrace above the water. A woman came out of the cottage and told me that she was the caretaker of the villa, which at that moment was not occupied. She was a character straight out of *I Promessi Sposi*: a bold-eyed, big-bosomed, redoubtable female.

She told me that she felt sure that the marchesa, who lived in Turin, would not mind if I saw the villa, and together we walked towards the old house, with which I immediately fell in love. It was small for an Italian villa and was built about twenty feet above the lake, in two wings linked by an open courtyard in the centre of which a bronze statue of Neptune, with poised trident, rose above a circle of flowers. Columns supported a narrow, covered arcade and framed everywhere lovely vistas of blue water and green mountains.

At the back of the courtyard Pliny's spring wells out of the rock in a mossy cavern. It fills a pool about three feet deep and the overflow is carried to the lake by a hidden pipe beneath the courtyard. It was wonderful to see this spring still alive after all these centuries and just as Pliny knew it in the reign of Trajan. The woman told me that it rises for six hours and then falls for six hours, which is much as Pliny had said. I asked if she could find a glass or a cup for me, which she did, and, dipping this in the spring, I drank the icy water from the heart of the mountain. This is what Pliny wrote about the spring to his friend Licinius.

'I have brought you as a present out of the country, a query which well deserves the consideration of your extensive erudition. There is a spring which rises in a neighbouring mountain, and running among the rocks is received into a little banqueting hall, from whence, after being detained a short time, it falls into the Larian lake. The nature of this spring is extremely surprising; it ebbs and flows regularly three times a day. This increase and decrease is plainly visible, and very entertaining to observe. You sit down beside the fountain, and whilst you are taking a repast and drinking its water, which is extremely cool, you see it gradually rise and fall. If you place a ring or anything else at the bottom when it is dry, the stream reaches it by degrees till it is entirely covered, and then again gently retires from it; and this you may see it do three times successively. Shall we say that some secret current of air stops and opens the fountain-head as it advances or recedes from it, as we see in bottles, and other vessels of that nature, where there is not a free and open passage, tho' you turn their necks downward, yet the outward air obstructing the vent, they discharge their contents as it were by starts? Or may it not be accounted for upon the same principle as the flux and reflux of the sea? or as those rivers which discharge themselves into the sea, meeting with contrary winds and the swell of the ocean, are forced back in their channels; so may there not be something that checks this fountain, for a time, in its progress? Or is there rather a certain reservoir that contains these waters in the bowels of the earth, which while it is recruiting its discharges, the stream flows more slowly and in less quantity, but when it has collected its due measure, it runs again in its usual strength and fullness? Or, lastly, is there I know not what subterranean poise that throws up the water when the fountain is dry, and repels it when it is full? You who are so well qualified for this inquiry will examine the reasons of this wonderful appearance; and it will be sufficient for me if I have given you a clear description of it. Farewell.'

As I drank my cup of spring water, I noticed a trout-rod leaning against the side of the house near the balustrade. I walked over and saw fish in great numbers, some of them about two pounds in weight, nosing the water of the spring as it fell into the lake; and I remembered Pliny's remark that in his villa on Como he could fish from his bed as if he were in a boat. Under the spell of such continuity I felt that Pliny himself might appear, weary from Rome, tired of pleading before the Centumviri, a court which he considered noisy, vulgar, and fallen from its ancient austerity, and anxious only to forget the ceremonial toga and put on a country tunic and tell his troubles to Calpurnia. She was his second wife and much his junior; and she adored him. When he was pleading in Rome, she would send messengers to the courts from time to time to tell her how the case was proceeding; when Pliny gave a public reading of a manuscript at one of those dreary pre-publication functions so usual in ancient Rome – an ancient spectre of the publisher's cocktail party or the 'literary luncheon' – she would hide behind a curtain to enjoy the applause given to him; she even set his poems to music and sang them to a lyre.

One of the surprising things about rich Romans of the Augustan age was the multiplicity of their houses. There were many like Pliny who had villas all over the country, and though some of these may have been simple shooting-boxes or bungalows, others were enormous establishments, such as Pliny's villa at Tifernum Tiberiana, (now Città di Castello, north of Perugia), which had dining-rooms for winter and summer, elaborate baths, and a marble alcove under a vine trellis where Pliny and Calpurnia sometimes dined on hot days. They reclined round the basin of a fountain that never overflowed, and the dishes, shaped like ships and ducks, floated on the water.

The caretaker conducted me through the villa, which is occupied only in the summer. Furniture lay beneath sheets from which peeped Baroque gilt foliation; the wall lights and chandeliers were encased in paper bags, and in the centre of the marble floor in the drawing-room lay two motor boats covered with canvas.

The villa was built about 1570 by Giovanni d'Anguisciola, one of the men who put to death the son of Pope Paul III, Piero Luigi Farnese, Duke of Parma and Piacenza, a man whose misdeeds, by all accounts, make the life of Cesare Borgia appear comparatively blameless. The caretaker told me that Rossini composed *Tancred* in the villa, and, pointing to a small Buhl desk, said that Napoleon had signed the treaty of Campo Formio upon it; two facts which I have been unable to verify: but I did, months later, come across a reference to the villa by Shelley, who in April, 1818, tried to rent it. He said that the house, once a magnificent palace, was in ruins. 'The apartments are immensely large, but ill-furnished and antique. The terraces, which overlook the lake and conduct one under the shade of noble laurels, are most delightful.'

As I was leaving, the caretaker pointed to a door that evidently led down to cellars and spoke mysteriously of horrible orgies enacted there in Roman times. How this would have amused Pliny! She said there used to be a huge wheel which chopped up women and flung the pieces into the lake. This is a prevalent rustic idea of high life in other days that I have heard in widely separated places.

The young faun led me back through the hazel wood and we said good-bye on the road. The charm of Pliny's villa continued to haunt me and it will always do so. I know what my books would look like there, and where I would put my desk. It was one of those places, and they are few, where I knew I could be happy and content until the end of my days.

§ 6

As you travel along the north-eastern shore of Lake Como you come, after descending a steep hill, to a bridge and the surprisingly large piazza of a town called Dongo. It is a charming scene: the lake steamers call at the jetty in the tranquil bay, tourists gather on the promenade to admire the lake, houses climb the hills and the holiday villas descend to the water's edge. On a summer's day, while young girls are laughing in the sunlight and boys are putting up the sail of a yacht, it is hard to believe that anything tragic could have happened there. But in the piazza of Dongo, upon a wet April day in 1945, Mussolini was discovered hiding in a German lorry, on his way to the Swiss frontier, and was arrested by Italian partisans.

The last chapter in the downfall of that almost Renaissance politician is tragic beyond words, and time has now placed him and his death in historical perspective. I once shook hands with him, and twice was able to study him at close quarters on public occasions, and I thought him one of the most effective actors of the day; he was also one of several megalomaniacs whom I have known who felt a strong affinity with Napoleon. Even when, as Hitler's despised victim, he headed the futile Salo Republic centred on Lake Garda, he compared that squalid come-back to Napoleon's Hundred Days. I remember reading of his downfall with gratification and of his murder with disgust.

John Addington Symonds, who died when Mussolini was ten years of age, might have been writing of Lake Como, and reflecting upon the dictator's death, when he wrote: 'So extraordinary were the social conditions of Renaissance Italy, that almost at every turn, on her seaboard, in her cities, from her hilltops, and by her lakes, we are compelled to blend our admiration for the loveliest and purest works of art amid the choicest scenes of nature, with memories of execrable crimes and lawless characters.' Is it possible that social conditions had less to do with Renaissance crime than the Italian temperament? Certainly there is no event in Italian history that more closely resembles the death of Mussolini than the end of Cola di Rienzo in 1354, a dictator who was murdered in cold blood and his body dragged round Rome.

It is impossible to travel the western shores of Como, through the little villages where men still remember the events of April 28,

1945, without dwelling upon the death of Mussolini. Glancing back to the spring of that year, one has the feeling that Aeschylus or Sophocles had taken over the direction of the war. Two days after Mussolini was shot with Claretta Petacci, Hitler committed suicide with Eva Braun. One searches history for a parallel to such a drama. Both events have inspired several first-rate books, among them H. R. Trevor-Roper's *The Last Days of Hitler*, Roman Dombrowski's *Mussolini: Twilight and Fall*, and the more recent *Benito Mussolini* by Christopher Hibbert. I believe that these carefully documented books will outlive many of the military memoirs of the period, for both Hitler and Mussolini will continue to interest and provoke the curiosity of men; and such contemporary records of their deaths have a value that will increase with time. Hitler's end had a certain crazy grandeur, that of a Viking launched into Eternity in a ship of flame; but Mussolini's end was that of a Renaissance despot. Yet, oddly enough, he had the detachment to know, as he said, that history, judging between himself and Hitler, would award the palm to the one who had made the better end. He knew perfectly well that death was the penalty of defeat, yet he was too much of an opportunist to be capable of suicide: he always believed that something would turn up at the last moment. Also he feared death, and during his last days would quote the answer that Achilles gave to Odysseus in the *Odyssey*, that it was better to be a living serf than king of the dead.

The Americans were only fifty miles from Milan when Mussolini, a prey to panic and bereft of will, put off the problem of flight until April 25. Early in the day he had discussed his surrender with the Committee of National Liberation at a meeting which, with the help of Cardinal Schuster, took place in the episcopal palace in Milan. The Cardinal has described what happened. Mussolini, no longer the triumphant leader but a haggard, broken man, entered the room looking so ill that the Cardinal thought he should be given a drink to pull him together. 'I kept him company,' wrote the Cardinal, 'and I thought of St Benedict, who ordered the abbot to do the same when receiving a guest in his monastery'; then he added the biting, but delicious, thought, 'he himself must have done so when meeting Totila at Monte Cassino.'

Mussolini asked for an hour to consider the terms, but he never returned. Instead, under cover of a dark, rainy night, he fled with a few remaining henchmen along the road to Como, with the idea of getting over the Swiss frontier. He looked out beyond the blurred windscreen at the autostrada and said, 'Nobody can ever deny that I made this road. It will be here after I am gone.' The cars reached Como at nine o'clock in the evening; at midnight it was learnt that the Americans were by-passing Milan, and it was decided to push on to Menaggio, on the west side of the lake. Before he left, Mussolini rang up his wife, Rachele, who in the days of grandeur had never changed her peasant way of life, and told her that, as she had prophesied, he was now deserted. He asked her forgiveness for everything and wished her good-bye. Menaggio was reached at eight o'clock in the morning, on April 26, and Mussolini went to the Villa Castelli, the home of the local Fascist leader.

Some hours later a smartly dressed party arrived in a Hispano-Suiza, a young man, two women, and two children. The man was Marcello Petacci, the brother of Claretta Petacci, Mussolini's mistress, the two women were his wife and Claretta. They were all travelling with forged Spanish passports. When Claretta heard that Mussolini was there, she asked to see him, but he refused to see her. 'What has she come here for?' he asked. 'Is she so anxious to die as all that?' She created a scene and wept, and at length Mussolini consented. Shortly afterwards it was decided to make a dash for the Swiss frontier by the road that branches to the west at Menaggio, towards Lugano. Three cars set out. The first contained Fascists, the second Claretta and her relatives, the third, Mussolini. They had not been travelling for more than five miles when, at a place called Grandola, the first car was held up by partisans and there was an exchange of fire. Some of the Fascists were captured and the other two cars, hastily reversing, rushed back to Menaggio. Here Mussolini told Claretta that it was too dangerous for her to be seen with him, and they took cover in separate houses, she still maintaining her part as the sister of the

'Spanish ambassador'. They remained concealed, awaiting the arrival of a motorized German column that was in flight towards Austria and was due to arrive later. It arrived in the small hours. It consisted of thirty-eight lorries and about three hundred disheartened Germans.

The convoy moved off at 5 o'clock in the morning and did not meet any opposition until it was passing through a little village near Dongo, where it was halted by a partisan road block. This was at about half-past seven on the morning of the 27th. Mussolini asked the name of the village and the surprising reply was 'Musso'. 'There are times when names acquire a mysterious symbolic quality,' writes Roman Dombrowski. 'All through Hitler's life the name of Braun was associated with him in one way or another. He was born in Braunau, the Nazi movement was a "brownshirt" movement, his mistress was Eva Braun. Mussolini reached the climax of his attempt to escape at Musso, a small village of which quite possibly he had never heard before. And after his death he was buried in the cemetery of Musoco.'

The result of the hold-up was a long parley between the German commander and the partisans, during which Mussolini managed to climb unseen into one of the lorries and cover himself with a Luftwaffe greatcoat. Eventually, after hours of delay, it was agreed that the partisans should check up on the identity of all those in the convoy in the piazza of Dongo. The Fascists charged the German Commander with betraying them. They began firing at the partisans. Some were killed and others were rounded up, but Mussolini remained quietly in his lorry. The convoy drew up in Dongo. All the remaining Fascists were arrested. Some accounts say that Marcello Petacci gave himself away when interrogated by a partisan who could speak Spanish; at any rate he, his wife, and their children, together with Claretta, were detained. There are two accounts of the detection of Mussolini. One is that a partisan, having checked the identity papers of the Germans in the lorry, noticed a figure huddled in a dark corner, covered with a coat and with a helmet pulled down over his face. What seemed chiefly suspicious to the partisan was that this individual was wearing a pair of polished field boots. The Germans, when asked who the man was, merely shrugged and laughingly said it was a drunken comrade. The partisan stirred Mussolini with his foot and asked, 'You are an Italian, aren't you?' Mussolini could speak German well enough to have replied in that language, but, instead, he said in Italian, 'Yes, I am an Italian.' He was then lost. The other account of his discovery is that the check-up on the lorry had been completed, and Mussolini had not been detected, until a German jumped out on the road and winked to indicate that there was someone inside who had not been found.

Mussolini was recognized at once, and perhaps it might be said that the spell he had cast upon his country for twenty years still endured when, with a start of amazement, his captor addressed him as 'Excellency'. He was assured that no harm would come to him, to which he replied strangely, as if he were still the Duce receiving an address of welcome, 'I know the people of Dongo wish me well.' It was now three o'clock on the 27th. He was led to the mayor's office while a courier was sent in haste to the Committee of Liberation in Milan to announce the capture, and to ask for orders. Meanwhile, a fantastic scene was taking place in the mayor's office. Mussolini, in his grey-green Fascist uniform with the emblem of the lictor's rods, was patiently giving an account of his actions to the small town magnates, the mayor, the doctor and the veterinary surgeon.

As time wore on the partisans began to feel anxious for the safety of their prisoner. What if another German column came through and decided to rescue him? It was therefore decided to lodge him in the Customs House at Germasino, where Mussolini made a startling request, and one which must have been inspired by a gambler's conviction that a trump card had turned up and everything was going to be all right. He told his guards that the 'Spanish signorina' whom they had arrested at Dongo was Claretta Petacci, and that he would like to see her. In doing so, as things turned out, he had condemned her to death. While the partisan commander went to find Claretta, Mussolini dined with his guards, most of them young Communists, and again Italy's man of destiny explained his actions to these young men, after which

131

he retired exhausted to the little lock-up kept for those who try to smuggle things over the frontier.

When Claretta Petacci was given Mussolini's message, she pretended at first that she did not know him. When told that Mussolini had revealed her identity, her mood changed.

'You all hate me,' she cried. 'You think I went after him for his money and his power . . . Can you do something for me? I want you to lock me up in the same place with him. I want to share his fate. If you kill him, kill me too.' The partisan was astonished. This was not the Claretta Petacci of popular legend. He went away without a word.

At two o'clock in the morning Mussolini was roused and told to get dressed. It had been decided to lodge him with Claretta at Brunate, near Como. The two cars met at the Ponte di Albano, but as they drew near to Como they saw that the black-out had been lifted and they heard the sound of rifle shots. They concluded that the Americans had arrived, and changed their plans. Turning, they went to the village of Azzano, on the west side of Como, some fifteen miles south of Dongo, where one of the partisans had a farmer friend named Giacomo De Maria.

Although Dombrowski investigated the death of the Dictator within three years of its occurrence, he encountered so many contradictions and inconsistencies, even on the part of eye-witnesses, that he wrote, 'we are driven to query whether there is such a thing as objective historical truth, and to wonder how many lies and distortions lie concealed in the pages of history.' Ten years later, Christopher Hibbert, covering the same ground, but with even more authorities to consult, as his bibliography proves, adds many additional details, and it is interesting to compare these two admirable books. The dreary tragedy of that wet and windy night is vividly conveyed by Mr Hibbert, who tells how the fallen Dictator, a dripping blanket cast over his shoulders, and Claretta grasping his arm, was led up a rough track to a cottage on the side of the mountain. The farmer had often hidden anti-Fascists on the run, and it was perhaps not the first time he had been awakened at three-thirty in the morning by a signal, 'coaxing, penetrating, and repetitive – that farmers use to call their animals.' He admitted the two drenched and exhausted fugitives without question, and while he made them some ersatz coffee his wife went upstairs and turned her two sons out of a double bed into the loft and prepared the room for the strangers. Oddly enough, the farmer did not at first recognize Mussolini, who at once retired with Claretta to the room upstairs. As they undressed and got into bed the two sentries listened at the door and fancied they heard Mussolini say, 'I'm sure they won't kill me', then something like 'Can you forgive me?' and, later on, in reply to something Claretta had said, 'That doesn't matter any more.' The rain continued to fall.

While they slept their last sleep on earth their murderer, or 'executioner', was hurrying from Milan. His name was Walter Audisio, whose partisan pseudonym was 'Valerio'. Some of the Como partisans were opposed to the 'execution' of Mussolini, and demanded written assurance that the National Liberation Committee had commanded 'Valerio' to kill him. It is not certain that any such document was produced. Nevertheless 'Valerio' carried his point, and at half-past three on the afternoon of April 28 he arrived at the cottage near Azzano, accompanied by two companions.

Valerio had no shame in describing the 'execution' in the Communist newspaper *Unità* some days after. He wrote that when he entered the little bedroom Mussolini was standing near the bed, wearing a brown overcoat and the cap of the Republican National Guard without insignia.

'His boots were down at heel. He had a lost look in his eyes, which were protruding, and his lower lip was trembling – he was a terrified man. His first words were "What's the matter?" I had planned to carry out the execution not far from the house. To get him there, I had to resort to a stratagem. I said, "I have come to liberate you . . . hurry, we have little time to lose . . ." Mussolini pointed to Claretta Petacci . . . "She must go first," he said. She seemed unable to understand what was going on, and rushed about gathering up her personal belongings. Mussolini kept urging her to hurry. Losing patience, he eventually left the hut before her. Once in the open, Mussolini's face changed and, turning towards me, he said, "I offer you an Empire." We were still on the threshold. Instead of answering, I told Petacci to come on and join us.

'She drew level with Mussolini, followed by me, and they walked down a mule track which led towards the road where a car was parked. On the way, Mussolini looked at me only once, with a look as though he were grateful. At this point I whispered to him, "I have also liberated your son Vittorio." I wanted him to think we were taking him to Vittorio. Mussolini answered, "I thank you from the bottom of my heart." When we reached the car Mussolini seemed convinced that he was a free man. He motioned to Petacci to precede him into the car, but I told him, "You go first. You are better concealed, but with that Fascist cap it is a little risky." He took it off, and patting his bald head, said, "And this?" I told him, "Pull the peak low over your eyes."

'I stopped the car, motioning to Mussolini with my hand not to talk. In a low voice I told him, "I heard a noise. I am going to investigate." I jumped off the running board and walked to the end of the stone wall. "Get over in that corner," I said. Even though Mussolini obeyed promptly he no longer appeared to be convinced, but obediently stood with his back to the wall at the place I indicated. Petacci was on his right. There was silence. Suddenly I pronounced sentence against the war criminal. "By the order of the General Command of the Liberty Volunteer Corps I am entrusted with rendering justice to the Italian people." Mussolini was terror-stricken. Petacci threw her arms round his shoulders and screamed, "He must not die." I said, "Get back in your place if you don't want to die too." The woman jumped back to her place. From a distance of three paces I shot five bursts into Mussolini, who slumped to his knees with his head slightly bent. Then it was Petacci's turn.'

As she rushed to Mussolini's body, 'Valerio' shot her in the back. Why did he murder her? Her name was not included in the Committee's order, if such an order ever existed; and even this has never been proved. So a woman who had been execrated for years by the whole of Italy redeemed her life by the loyalty of her last hour.

How strange it is that there should have existed in Italy, even in the days of the Dictator's power, an old wives' tale that Mussolini would die, after a victory over France, at the hands of three soldiers. The prophecy was considered too absurd to mention, even after Italy's entry into the war, for hardly a shot had been fired by her in France. Nevertheless, a French delegation had capitulated to Italian headquarters and, technically, Italy had beaten France. Now, on this cloudy April afternoon, the three soldiers of the prophecy stood above the dead body of the Duce.

The barbaric scenes in Milan, when the bodies of Mussolini and Claretta were hung heads down from the girders of a garage in the Piazzale Loreto, have their parallel in the Italian Middle Ages. A South African journalist, Alan Forrest, who was serving with the Allied armies, recalls in his book, *Italian Interlude*, a fact I have seen mentioned nowhere else in accounts of that revolting display of savagery. 'Clara's dress hung down exposing her under-garments,' he writes, 'and the British commander of an armoured car which drove into the square, seeing this, climbed down from his car, mounted a pair of steps which stood near and pulled up the woman's skirt fastening it round her knees with his webbing belt. The crowd howled at him but he paid no attention. The armoured car drove nearer with machine guns swinging down to discourage any ambitious hooligans who might interfere.'

It is good that the act of a civilized man at such a moment should be remembered.

Como, blue and windless under the hills, the town of Dongo full of trippers, the village of Azzano lying in the summer heat, a little girl with a basket over her arm ascending the mule track to De Maria's cottage – is it possible that tragedy and murder had ever invaded this paradise? That is a question which those who attempt to reconcile landscape with history are always asking.

§ 7

One day I went to Monza to see the Iron Crown of Lombardy and the Treasure of Theodolinda. It is a little town about nine miles to the north of Milan, on the main road to Lecco, one of those industrial towns which one would usually pass through, as indeed many do. To most people it is known as the scene of international motor races; and the majority of its inhabitants are engaged in the making of felt hats and carpets.

When I arrived, the cathedral had just closed for the siesta and there was nothing to do but have lunch and wait for it to open. Delicious smells were invading the piazza from a restaurant near by, where I found the local business men enduring with admirable complacency the rigours of a fast day; for it was Friday. Their contentment was soon evident. An enormous mound of ravioli, stuffed with spinach and herbs instead of meat, and served with melted butter, was succeeded by a noble cold fish, the size of a fourteen-pound salmon, its flanks decorated with mayonnaise, which the proprietor himself wheeled round on a trolley. It was a sea bass from the Adriatic, known as *bronzino* in Lombardy and *spigola* on the west coast, and in the South of France as *loup de mer*. This was served cold with salad. After a slice of iced cake, the fasters retired to tables on the pavement to meditate under an awning while they drank coffee and contemplated the striped Saracen-like façade of the cathedral.

My own meditations concerned Theodolinda and Gregory the Great, in whose anxious and fearful reign she lived. Hers is a beautiful yet slightly ominous name: it might be that of a princess in a fairy tale. If I say it has never been used in England, I shall receive letters from a dozen Theodolindas, therefore I say that it has never been used to my knowledge, neither can I recollect ever having come across it in any English novel or biography. Oddly enough, Theophania was once used, so was Theophila, a name that would obviously run in families and crop up proudly like red hair or a particular kind of nose. Generally speaking, however, English people have never cared for these Greek names, and even Theodora, the loveliest of all, is not common, though in the reversed and less distinguished form of Dorothy it has been popular for centuries.

The Theodolinda with whom I was concerned was a Bavarian princess born somewhere about A.D. 570, whose flaxen beauty was so striking that reports of it crossed the Alps into the badly conducted shambles which was then Italy. Legend says that in an age when the Lombards were fighting the Exarch, besieging the Pope, and committing enormities which led Gregory the Great to believe that the end of the world was approaching, Authuri, the Lombard King, put on a disguise and went to Bavaria to see if the accounts of Theodolinda's beauty were true. A Lombard monk, who lived two hundred years later and knew all the stories of the royal house, says that as Theodolinda offered the stranger a goblet of wine, Authuri managed to entwine his fingers with hers and, as he bent to drink, moved her fingers caressingly over his face. The princess, not unpleasantly alarmed, confided her experience to her nurse, that immortal old confidante, as naughty and as ready for any intrigue in A.D. 580 as at all later periods, and the old woman advised that with silence and caution everything would come right; as it did.

Theodolinda became Queen of the Lombards, but in a year's time Authuri suddenly died. The Lombards then asked her to choose another husband, whom they promised to obey as king. It would be pleasant to relate that she hesitated from loyalty to her romantic lover, but nothing like that happened. She immediately chose the bravest and toughest of her young warriors, and proposed to him. His name was Agilulf, and she sought him out in his duchy of Turin. Legend relates that 'with a blushing smile' she made her motives clear and allowed him to kiss her on the lips. So Agilulf found himself King of the Lombards, with a beautiful wife and all the woes of Lombardy. Fortunately he was able to handle them both, and they reigned together for twenty years.

Theodolinda was one of several influential queens with whom Gregory the Great corresponded; another was Bertha, Queen of Kent, who at this period was assisting S. Augustine to convert her husband, Ethelbert. The Pope was grateful to Theodolinda for her calming influence on her aggressive husband, and he sometimes sent presents to her, one of which, it is said, was the Iron Crown of Lombardy.

The Iron Crown is kept under lock and key upon the altar, in a side chapel, but a perfect replica, which many a visitor mistakes for the real crown, is suspended on chains above the altar. When I told the sexton that I wished to see the genuine crown, he went off and returned with one of the canons, who turned out to be an authority on Lombardic history and the author of many articles on the Treasury. First, he took me into the apse and pointed out a massive stone sarcophagus which bears the words *Theodolindæ Langobardorum Reginæ*, and told me that there had always been a prejudice in the town against opening the Queen's tomb. However, in 1941 the war offered a sufficient diversion and the sarcophagus was secretly opened. Those who had hoped that Theodolinda would be found within, as she had been placed there at her death in A.D. 626, were disappointed. The tomb had been rifled at some remote time and all that was discovered were a few of the Queen's bones lying in the dust of ages.

The priest said he would show me the Iron Crown. He entered the sacristy and returned wearing a surplice and accompanied by the sexton, who carried a lighted taper. Two candles were lit upon the altar, the priest genuflected, then unlocked a steel safe from which he drew forward a plate-glass case that ran on rails. He switched on a light and I saw a Byzantine coronet, or diadem, of gold and enamel, richly decorated with floral patterns and set with large uncut jewels. As the canon turned a screw at the side of the case, he caused the Iron Crown to revolve slowly, so that one could examine every portion of it. It is made of six plates of gold held together by golden hinges; each plate is divided into panels and each panel contains three vertical gems. The enamel is glassy green in colour. The canon directed my attention to a thin ring of iron inside the crown, inset into the gold and secured with pins. This iron gives the diadem its title, for it is said to be one of the nails of the Cross which S. Helena brought from Jerusalem and gave to her son, Constantine the Great.

The story is that when Gregory the Great was Nuncio in Constantinople, one of the nails came, with other sacred relics, into his possession, and that he gave it to Theodolinda, who presumably had it beaten out and inset into the golden crown. Many believe this was the crown placed upon the head of Charlemagne in S. Peter's on Christmas Day, A.D. 800; and it is undoubtedly the crown used at many imperial coronations, including those of Barbarossa, Charles V at Bologna, and Napoleon at Milan, in 1805. On that occasion it was taken from Monza in a carriage in which the Master of Ceremonies of the Imperial Court sat holding it upon a velvet cushion, while a cavalry escort jingled along beside. Its arrival in Milan was announced by a salute of artillery. The more I examined the Iron Crown, the more puzzling I thought it. First of all, it is too small to cover the head of any adult man. It cannot be more than about six inches in diameter, perhaps a trifle less. When we read that emperors were crowned with it, they must have either held it above their heads, or else it must have rested there for a brief, symbolic moment. I did not care to suggest to the canon, who, for all I knew, may have believed implicitly in all the legends, that it looked to me like one of the votive Byzantine crowns which were often suspended above altars, but that is what I thought. The question, too, why Gregory the Great should have given such a superlative relic to a Lombard queen is a difficult one. Apparently this crossed the ecclesiastical mind three centuries ago, when on several occasions the Church suspended reverence for the Iron Crown. A process instituted before the Congregation of Relics in Rome lingered on for years and ended in leaving undecided the identity of the iron ring within the crown. Therefore those who wish to believe it to be Constantine's nail may do so, but the Church takes no responsibility for it. None of this, of course, can take away from the Iron Crown one bit of its unique character or its importance as a marvellous example of the goldsmith's art in that remote age. As the priest wheeled the crown back into its safe, he turned his head to me and remarked that forty-four emperors had been crowned with it, the last being Ferdinand of Austria in 1836.

We entered the Treasury. I saw a windowless, octagonal

building filled with display cases full of gold monstrances, chalices and silver reliquaries, crosses, statues, pyxes, and every type of ecclesiastical ornament. In a case by themselves were the presents sent by Gregory to Theodolinda thirteen hundred years ago: the crosses, crowns, and rings, many of which the good Pope must himself have handled as they were selected from the papal treasury. Theodolinda's fan and her comb are surprising survivals, so also is her large blue goblet, cut from a single piece of sapphire, the largest in the world, the canon said, which was believed to be proof against poison. She had poison on her mind, and perhaps with reason, for a near predecessor had died when forced to drink a draught which she had prepared for her husband.

The most delightful of the four surviving letters from Gregory to Theodolinda was written towards the close of his life, when his infirmities made it difficult for him to leave his bed. He wrote to congratulate the Queen and her husband upon the birth of a son, who had been baptized a Catholic. He sent the infant a cross containing a piece of the True Cross and also a reading from the Gospels in a Persian case. To Theodolinda's daughter he sent three rings, two of them set with jacinths and one with pearls. The canon pointed these out to me. The feeling of awe with which, some time before, I had first seen the body of S. Ambrose in Milan, returned to me as I examined these presents sent to two children thirteen hundred years ago by one of the best and most harassed of popes.

We then turned to examine another part of the Treasury, where Theodolinda's Hen and Chickens are to be seen. This is a circular platter of silver-gilt upon which are mounted a hen and seven chickens, about the size of bantams, in the act of pecking grains of corn. It is an enchanting piece of work in which the goldsmith has frozen a common farmyard scene, though neither hen nor chicks are the domestic breeds we know today: they are more like game birds, and the chickens are longer in the leg than their modern descendants. No one knows whether this charming work was merely decorative or had some symbolic significance. The canon suggested that it might be symbolic of Lombardy and its dukedoms.

Then I saw what, to me, will always remain the outstanding memory of the Treasure of Monza. Standing by themselves, and looking incredibly humble and shabby amid so much gold and silver, were a row of Roman phials two or three inches high, some of glass and some of pewter. Everyone who has studied the topography of early Christian Rome has heard of this unique collection of pilgrims' oil bottles, the only one to survive as a collection of all the millions that once existed. At some time about A.D. 590 an abbot named John was commissioned by Theodolinda to bring relics to her from Rome. In those days the only relics allowed by the Latin Church were oil from the lamps burning above the martyrs' tombs in the Catacombs, or cloths which had been in contact with the tombs. The removal of human remains from their original burial places was abhorrent to Rome and was only forced upon the Church at a late period, the eighth century, when barbarian raids on the cemeteries became so terrible that the Church, to rescue the bones of the martyrs from destruction, took them into the churches; and so began the epoch of translated relics. When the Abbot went to Rome, however, the Catacombs had not yet been violated, and Christian pilgrimage consisted of making a tour of them and collecting from each tomb some of the oil from the lamps that burned there. Whether the pilgrims were allowed to fill the little bottles themselves, or, what is perhaps more likely, whether they bought them, already labelled, at the entrance to the Catacombs, is not known.

There were originally more than seventy oil flasks at Monza, but now only forty-two remain, twenty-six of glass and sixteen of pewter. Several of them still bear the labels which were attached to them thirteen hundred years ago, and several still carry the string, but no label. A remarkable survival is a papyrus which gives a complete list of the seventy odd bottles, with the various places from which they were collected and the saints commemorated there. This is the famous *Index Oleorum*, which has inspired so much learned discussion. It ends with the words, 'The holy oil which in the time of our Lord, Pope Gregory, the unworthy sinner, John, brought from Rome to the Lady, Queen Theodolinda'. Scholars have argued that if the abbot had himself walked round the Catacombs collecting the oil, the list, if read in the right order, is of the greatest topographical interest, as showing the route taken by a sixth century pilgrim round Rome.

As I looked with amazement at these frail objects, marvelling at their safe arrival from the Rome of Gregory the Great to the equally dangerous world of today, I thought infinitely touching the little brown tags attached to them on which one could just make out a few words of Latin; and one bottle, I noticed, had cracked and the oil inside had crystallized and looked like brown sugar. I thought of the diligent John going round the tombs for Theodolinda in a Rome that, in spite of Goth and Vandal, was still imperial in outline. The golden tiles had not yet been stripped from the Pantheon; the Colosseum was intact; the Caesarian palaces on the Palatine Hill were more or less habitable; there were still statues of bronze and marble in the streets; and poets still read their works in the Forum of Trajan, where probably Gregory had seen the angelic Saxons; the Pope in the Lateran was writing to his bishops like a Caesar to his governors, calmly and courteously, with no hint of the despair which sometimes filled his heart. It was indeed a sad and battered Rome, not classical and not yet mediaeval, a Rome in transition, of which Gregory himself wrote, 'We live in the midst of a ruined world.'

I turned to the canon and told him what was passing in my mind; he smiled and remarked that when he unlocked the Treasury in the morning, he, too, had often fancied he could hear the distant clamour of S. Gregory's Rome. Passing to the survival of material objects and the often accidental, indeed, frequently flippant, circumstances which decided it, I said how strange it was to think that while the cathedral and the palace of Theodolinda had vanished, her fragile keepsakes and treasures should have outlived bronze and marble. He told me the reason. From the earliest times they had been concealed in either wood or marble, near or beneath the altars of the three churches that have stood on the site. Those who would have destroyed them in their search for gold, as Theodolinda's sarcophagus was violated, never discovered them; and so they remained hidden until 1881, when it was decided to place them in their present position.

On the way back to Milan, I thought how wonderful it was to have found all this in a town that makes felt hats and carpets, and holds motor races; and someone told me that the local Communists and anti-clericals would, if necessary, fight to the death in defence of the Iron Crown and the Treasury.

§ 8

I had always believed that the town of Gorgonzola was isolated somewhere in the Italian Alps. It was with surprise that I came to it one morning, about ten miles from Milan, along the road to Bergamo. I saw a small industrial town of the Lombardy plain. During my first steps along its main street I noticed that by no hint, suspicion, or fall-out was the famous product suggested; in fact I had to ask a policeman to be kind enough to point out a cheese factory.

Gorgonzola has been made in the town for so long that it has lost its original name, which was Argenza. In the old days – how long ago I am unable to say – herds of cows which had been pastured in the Lomellina, south of Milan, were driven north towards the mountains and milked at Gorgonzola. The villagers, finding themselves with a great quantity of milk on their hands, began to make cheese. Only cows which had been pastured on certain grasslands yielded the right milk for Argenza, or Gorgonzola. The cheeses were then taken to mature in cold caves in the mountains at Ballabio in Valtellina, near Bergamo, where some caves are still in use: but with refrigeration the cheese is made more easily and in greater quantities and with no loss of quality. Though the day was warm, two men wearing several sweaters and girt about with oilskin aprons conducted me through long sheds where thousands of cheeses were being salted. We then moved into icy sheds in which the temperature was five degrees above freezing; and here the cheeses were recognizable by nose and palate as Gorgonzola.

The process could not be simpler. A natural mould, which can be quickly induced by letting air into the curd with a copper wire, soon forms in the cheese, and the art then is to control its growth, which is a matter of keeping it in the correct temperature. These cheeses lay in their thousands, stacked to the ceiling on racks among which my guides moved with scoops, bringing back samples for me to taste. I had never before eaten so much Gorgonzola; certainly never at eleven o'clock in the morning, but it was impossible to refuse without hurting the feelings of the two enthusiasts.

When I say I do not care for Gorgonzola cheese, I must qualify this by adding that I mean Gorgonzola as sold and eaten in England. In Italy it is a different cheese: pale, creamy, delicious, and only thinly veined with blue. My two experts agreed with me. They said that no Italian would eat Gorgonzola in the advanced stage of ripeness demanded by the English epicure. An Italian Gorgonzola takes two months to mature; one for the English market takes three and a half months. I was led onward to a kind of transept of Gorgonzola, where cheeses at full strength were pronounced just right for London. They fully justified the celebrated *Punch* joke of the last century, repeated so often and, one thought, so painfully, by one's grandfather on festive occasions: 'Let loose the Gorgonzola!'

Nothing irritates the cheese-makers more than a Frenchman who compares Gorgonzola with Roquefort. The Italians will tell you, scarcely disguising a shudder, that Roquefort is made of ewes' milk and is matured with the aid of mouldy bread. They are willing to admit that it is quite a good cheese – for those who like it – but it cannot be compared with Gorgonzola – *Il Re de Formaggio!*

'And what would you call the Queen of Cheeses?' I asked.

'Ah,' said the cheese-maker, wiping his scoop on a length of butter-muslin, 'that is not easy to say. Perhaps Bel Paese, perhaps not! There is really no cheese fit to share the throne with Gorgonzola!'

CHAPTER FOUR

The Beauty of Bergamo – Colleoni's Chapel – A Renaissance Farm –
San Pellegrino – the Violin-Makers of Cremona – Mantua and the
Gonzaga – A Mysterious Scotsman – The Palace of Isabella d'Este –
An Admirer of Henry VIII – An Early Glimpse of Ireland – The
Ghost Town of Sabbioneta – Lake Garda and Sirmione

§1

When the summer heat really hits Milan and you wake up feeling more exhausted than when you went to bed, young people who possess cars and scooters think nothing of dashing off to dine at Bergamo. It is thirty miles away to the north, in the clear air of a mountain some twelve hundred feet above the plain. I went there one day and liked Bergamo so much that, the moment I could do so, I returned to stay.

At the foot of the mountain is Bergamo Bassa, a busy, thriving modern Lombardic town devoted to textiles; on the hilltop is its ancient parent, Bergamo Alta, encircled by massive walls and full of mediaeval palaces and churches. The upper town is reached by a funicular railway and if you are anxious, as I was, to sleep as high up as possible, the funicular makes a short additional journey to the summit of the mountain, which is called S. Vigilio. Here nothing is immediately visible but the saint's white chapel and his bell tower against the sky, also a café for the convenience of those who are waiting for the funicular, a general store, and a delightful little country hotel. There is, however, a quiet prosperous life on the summit which is not at once apparent. The road which winds up from Upper Bergamo, encircling the mountain several times in the process, leads to the villas and gardens of many retired Milanese business men, while little restaurants concealed in the shade of chestnut trees cater for those driven to the mountain by the heat of the plain.

145

The funicular to S. Vigilio groans and shudders its way through an opulent gorge. Vines grow on the terraces, and in the autumn a passenger could easily pick figs, loquats, pears and apples, as the cars make their almost perpendicular ascent. When I stepped into the cool air, which seemed to me to be coming straight from Alpine peaks, I said to myself: if I cannot have Pliny's villa on Como, this is where I should choose to live.

The hotel proved to be the kind of place I like. It was as if I had been incorporated in the warm embrace of a cheerful Italian family. Even the two waiters were full of willing kindness, while the family who owned the hotel lived on springs, ready to leap up and anticipate the wishes of their guests. My bedroom looked towards the foothills of the Alps. I could follow cars and carts for miles along the white threads that went northward through the valleys, and in the haze of mountains some forty miles away was the Bernina Pass. The terrace below my window was hidden by a pergola, and here the young people from Milan were fond of dining late at night. I would hear their engines boiling up the mountain road, or the exhausted panting of a gallant Vespa, then an unceasing bird-like flow of jokes and compliments, sometimes a song, until the moment came when, with a fusillade of backfires and much girlish laughter, they would wind their way down the mountain to the plain. Then silence until the new day dawned, with bird song and S. Vigilio's bell ringing for early Mass.

There is a sense of happiness and well-being which is dependent upon sunshine and a blue sky, and I shall often remember those enchanted mornings when, after the coffee and the crisp rolls, which came up in the first *funiculare*, I would walk in the little garden where the rosemary, bay leaves, and basil grew which flavoured so many of the meats and sauces; and looking down over the sweep of hills, valleys, and streams touched by the early sun, I would think how grateful I should be for such brief carefree moments. It was pleasant to walk a few paces to a seat below the chapel, where a walled terrace under chestnut trees afforded a marvellous view of Upper Bergamo, its roofs, towers, and walls, and beyond, stretching as far as one could see, the misty flat land in whose hazy reaches lay Cremona, Parma, Modena, and other cities of the plain.

The two Bergamos appear to be a perfect solution to the problem of development. Old Bergamo needed the mountain for protection, modern Bergamo needs the plain and the railway for its factories, so it has moved down to them, leaving the old city upon its hill free of traffic and crowds. In ancient times it must have been as impregnable as any town in Italy, and as remote, and one can understand how natural it was that its famous dialect continued to figure in Italian comedy. One remembers the 'merrie prancke' described by Castiglione, when a cowman of Bergamo was passed off on the ladies of a Renaissance court as the greatest courtier in Spain; and while the 'sillie fellow' sat speaking the incomprehensible jargon of Bergamo, the ladies outdid each other in respect and courtesy, while the courtiers split their sides with laughter. Harlequin is a Bergamasque peasant, and some believe that Bergamo was the home of the *Commedia dell' Arte*.

The most famous citizen was the *condottiere*, Bartolomeo Colleoni, remembered by every visitor to Venice. Long before he enlisted under the banner of S. Mark, his native town had become the most westward of the mainland possessions of Venice; consequently when the Serenissima wished to reward the general, it was able to offer him an estate in his own country.

§ 2

The road to the old city leads down between garden walls which drip cascades of bougainvillaea. At first sight the piazza seems too perfect to be entirely credible. In the centre of a square set with worn old brick, a fountain sends up a single jet into a marble basin. The basin is guarded by small, kindly lions seated upon their haunches and linked by a heavy iron chain looped from mouth to mouth. And what good, obedient lions they are; survivors, maybe, of a breed long since extinct which perhaps Marco Polo brought from China, where they must surely have been bred to match the Pekinese! Obviously no unworthy thought, much less a bloodthirsty one, ever entered their heads: they sit on trust, holding the chain as if it were an evening paper.

The piazza is surrounded by a rich harmony of architecture, with a few ordinary houses, some general shops, a café, and a restaurant, just to prove that this is not the result of a competition, but of long and dignified life. Had Shakespeare written *The Two Gentlemen of Bergamo*, this scene would have been an exquisite background for Act I –'Bergamo. A public place'. Facing each other across the square are twelfth and seventeenth century buildings. One is a lovely Palladian palace which receives the afternoon sun; it is built above an arcade and contains, so I was told, two hundred thousand books and several illuminated codices. Where but in Italy would a town of this size have a library of such quality, and where, save in Italy, would they have built a palace for it? Opposite the library is one of the oldest town halls in the world, the *Palazzo della Ragione,* a massive old fortress with Gothic windows also built above an arcade; and fitting into this scheme, as if perfectly placed there by some master hand, are an ancient bell tower – the *Torre del Comune* – and a flight of stone steps whose tiled roof is supported by romanesque columns.

The *Palazzo della Ragione* conceals one of the most beautiful sights in Lombardy. As you walk forward, you see beyond, framed in the arches which support the old building, a tiny piazza containing a glittering assembly of small and exquisite buildings: a church, the Colleoni Chapel, a cathedral, and a baptistry. Your eye goes instantly to the Saracenic-looking church porch built of horizontally-striped marble, supported by columns which rest upon the backs of stone lions. The porch in true Lombardic style is a stage on which are life-sized figures: a mounted knight in armour, lance in hand, flanked by two saints. The knight is S. Alexander, who lived in some remote Roman period and is the patron saint of Bergamo. He has the stiff alert appearance of those mechanical figures on horseback which ride out of mediaeval clocks. Above these figures is a smaller stage where the Virgin and Child stand with a saint on either hand. This mediaeval porch is the entrance to a church which was entirely re-designed in the baroque period. The contrast is surprising. In a side-chapel I came across the tomb of a great Bergamasque, the prolific composer Donizetti, who overworked himself into a mental home.

The gem of Bergamo is the building next to this church: the chapel built to the memory of Colleoni with money left by him for this purpose in his will. It was built at the beginning of the Renaissance, when architects erected the usual mediaeval church with a rose window and an open arcade, but, to be classically fashionable, covered it with medallions of ancient heroes strangely contrasted with scenes from holy writ. Anyone who has seen the Certosa of Pavia will recognize in this marvellous little chapel the master hand of Amadeo. It is almost as if one had cast a toga over a saint. Inside, the great soldier is seen, baton in hand, mounted upon a charger of gilded wood. He wears a cap of state and a quilted tunic with leg armour; his horse is stepping out with a gay, sprightly parade step. This work of a German wood carver, Sixtus Siry of Nuremberg, is extraordinarily dignified and impressive and one feels that this is exactly how Colleoni must have appeared to the Doge and Senators of Venice on many a fortunate day. I think no other soldier in history has been commemorated by two such statues as this one and the famous statue by Verrocchio in Venice.

In another part of the little chapel is Medea, Colleoni's favourite daughter, carved in white marble, who died seven years before her father. She was not a great beauty, and the fashion of plucking the hair high upon the forehead did not suit her. Nevertheless she lives again in the resurrective art of sculpture in a marble gown of figured brocade, her head upon a tasselled pillow. Her delicate, intelligent face, and her slender neck, remain one of the memories of Bergamo.

On the boundary of the lower town an old palace stands in a dank garden, and its upper floors have been modernized to house the famous collection of pictures known as the Carrara Academy. There are exquisite Bellinis and important Titians; and I saw Pisanello's marvellous profile of Leonello d'Este, one of the most attractive of the early Renaissance scholars, and also Botticelli's portrait of Giuliano, the young Medici who was murdered during High Mass in Florence. I came across the original of a portrait I have seen in many a book: a crafty-looking young fellow with a downward moustache and a chin tuft, whose long straight hair falls from a jaunty cap or beret. If it be true that he is Caesar Borgia, perhaps the tiny couple in the far distance, who have been caught in a cloudburst, symbolize his victims! I was struck by a curious little group painted by some unknown Lombard artist in the fifteenth century, which at first I took to be a group of Turks. On closer examination they proved to be fashionable men and women dressed in the Byzantine costumes which the Turks adopted when they captured Constantinople.

It was in Bergamo about seventy years ago that the oracle and Sherlock Holmes of art, Bernard Berenson, dedicated himself to connoisseurship. He was then a penniless young student, the son of Jewish emigrants to America, living in Italy on a travelling scholarship. Seventy years later he was a world-famous authority and a millionaire who left his estate in Florence, and his superb library, to Harvard University. It is interesting to think of him in Bergamo, eager to become an art connoisseur with 'no thought of reward', as he put it in *Sketch for a Self Portrait*. As he and a young fellow student sat at a café table, he said: 'We shall give ourselves up to learning, to distinguish between the authentic works of an Italian painter of the fifteenth or sixteenth century, and those commonly ascribed to him. Here at Bergamo, and in all the fragrant and romantic valleys that branch out northward, we must not stop till we are sure that every Lotto is a Lotto, every Cariani a Cariani, every Previtali a Previtali, every Santa Croce a Santa Croce; and that we know to whom of the several Santa Croces a picture is to be attributed. . . .'

It was a brave ambition of Berenson's to remove the false labels which dealers and owners have for centuries attached to pictures and to replace them with true ones. The poor young man who was ready to do this with 'no thought of reward' could not have imagined the existence of Lord Duveen, or of American million-aires who in days to come would be willing to pay heavily for a certificate of authenticity.

§ 3

When America was discovered, Italy treated the potato with suspicion, but eagerly accepted maize. The Italian word for it, *granturco*, proves that people of the time believed that it came from the East. (The French *blé de Turquie* shows the same belief.) In Lombardy especially, but generally throughout the Po Valley, a pudding made of maize-meal, called *polenta*, is to the Italian peasant what porridge used to be to the Highland crofter. You find it everywhere in the villages and on the farms; every family has a special polenta pot and a big wooden spoon, or a stick, to stir the meal. Having been boiled, *polenta* resembles a stiff brown porridge and can be eaten hot or cold. It can be served up again grilled, fried or baked with almost anything, though cheese and tomato sauce seem to be the most usual accompaniments. I had never tasted it until I went to the excellent little restaurant in the main piazza of Upper Bergamo and saw that polenta was on the menu – *polenta con gli uccellini*. It was brought to me hot and boiled with a roast quail on top. It is obviously one of those dishes to which one must become sentimentally attached in infancy. To me, *polenta* was stodgy and uninteresting. I was sorry, since I was aware that I had not appreciated something as genuinely Lombardic as a poplar! Yet in the way things happen, that disappointing meal remains a memorable one. My table was set on the pavement under the restaurant awning; a few feet away the fountain played, and the lions, with their mouths full of chain, looked like rewarded dogs; from the balconies women and children gazed down on the little piazza, and there was not a single car in sight, or a tourist. The sunlight fell upon a scene of great beauty and nobility; and I knew that I had only to take a few steps under the arches of the *Palazzo della Ragione* to see Colleoni riding his golden horse and Medea asleep upon her marble couch.

§ 4

Anyone who has been in Italy long enough to drink anything must have become familiar with San Pellegrino; some may even have wondered who the saint was and where the mineral water comes from. The town lies about fifteen miles from Bergamo, in the valley of the Brembo, which is one of the many exquisite valleys that run northward towards the Alps. A cheerful spa stands on the banks of the river and the hills are dotted with villas and hotels: there is even a Kursaal. It was built at the turn of the century when the popularity of spas induced in architects a positive frenzy of bad taste. In such places nude bronze beauties with fashionable wasp waists hold flambeaux at the foot of stairways to light the way to card-rooms, ballrooms, even to theatres. Everything was on a large and sumptuous scale. The world in those days was full of profitable ailments, and no one could foresee a day, as in England, when pump-rooms and assembly-rooms would be taken over by the health services, or, as on the Continent, pervaded by an air of suspended animation as if the spirit of the place, like the Sleeping Beauty, were waiting for the sound upon the gravel of a two-horse brougham and the awakening kiss of some liverish royalty.

San Pellegrino Terme is, however, a lively spa. I noted a ball-room, designed originally for duchesses, where the local boys and girls had been dancing amid bamboo tables. I was given a brochure prepared by the information bureau which depicts upon its cover, not the elderly invalids for whom such places were created, but a number of athletic young people setting out to climb mountains, to play golf and tennis, and to fish. Not a hint of old age and arthritis. No doubt that is the right approach, and one could indeed spend a happy and vigorous holiday on the banks of the Brembo and the green slopes of its hills. Pellegrino means, of course, 'pilgrim', but I could not discover who the pilgrim was who gave his name to this now famous little town.

'The story is,' said the local historian, 'that when the French under Charles VIII came to Italy, they were so well fed by the people here that, as a sign of their gratitude, they left on their departure the finger-bone of a saint called Pellegrino. But who he was, I cannot tell you. The relic was considered so precious that the town changed its name to his.'

The San Pellegrino water wells up out of the earth at a temperature of 80 degrees Fahrenheit. I was given a glass straight from the source, but was surprised to find that the characteristic sparkle was absent. I asked about this and was told that it is artificially injected in the form of a natural gas from S. Giovanni Valdarno, in Tuscany, incidentally the birthplace of Masaccio. I was taken over a model factory where the water is bottled. Hundreds of white-coated and rubber-gloved San Pellegrinas stood guard over maddeningly intelligent machines which washed bottles swiftly and angrily and revolved them to other machines which in jerky, exasperated movements, like a rebellious butler, filled them, slapped labels on them and sent them on their way to hotels and restaurants all over the world. In the packing-shed they were sending some cases to Somaliland and some to Caracas. I think, however, the most extraordinary thing I saw was a swimming-bath full of San Pellegrino water.

I drove back to Bergamo through the lovely valley, thinking that among the sights we shall never see again is that of a footman tucking rugs round elderly invalids in a Daimler, while hotel managers, doctors, and nurses beam happily from the steps of the Spa Hotel. The very word spa has now a period ring to it. It suggests that kindly age when the goddess Hypochrondria had many a costly and pleasant temple where a string orchestra sought to lull the uncertainties of digestion.

§ 5

When Colleoni in middle age was not leading the armies of Venice, he was enjoying the life of a country squire on his farm at Malpaga, near Bergamo, which is still in existence. The romantic organization of this estate has never been forgotten in Bergamo: almost anyone will tell you how the old soldier retired with a bodyguard of his comrades and lived in state, farming the land, but ready to arm and saddle at a moment's notice. Together with the Essex man, Sir John Hawkwood, Bartolomeo Colleoni was the most respected of the *condottieri*. He was sufficiently foxy to have survived in that tough age, but what distinguished him from his fellows was that while they piled up fortunes by treachery, he had a loyalty to his employers which, one is glad to say, turned out to be as profitable in the long run.

He was born in the year 1400 and lived to be seventy-six, so that his life spanned all that was finest in the Renaissance. J. A. Symonds noted that he was one of those Italians who owed his start in life to the murder of his father, which is another way of saying that, had he not been forced to shift for himself, he might not have joined a band of mercenaries as a private. Then again, as one looks at his statues, there seems no other profession but that of arms which he could possibly have adopted. He was trained by two of the most famous *condottieri* of the day, Braccio da Montane, and the rich and powerful commander of the Venetian armies, Count Bussone da Carmagnola. Most of the *condottieri* are merely shadowy soldiers marching and counter-marching, and changing sides, during the almost perpetual quarrels of the Italian states, but Colleoni, because of his desire for statues and memorials and his good fortune in having been commemorated by great artists, lives on as an individual. As a soldier, he was invariably on the winning side. He acquired a great deal of territory for Venice, and though he had his quarrels with the Republic, indeed he was once nearly assassinated by an angry Senate, he always went back to her and served her faithfully. When he was fifty-five Venice paid him a tribute which that crafty and suspicious state never paid to anyone else: he was made life-long commander of her armies. This rank he enjoyed for about twenty years, together with a monumental salary designed to make bribery pointless.

When he was dying, Venice sent a deputation to express the respect and gratitude of the Republic. The old soldier must have sent a chill down the spine of the assembled senators when he said: 'Never give another general the power you gave to me. I could have done you much harm.' So over the death bed of this loyal servant hovered the spectre of old bribes and treacheries. As he had no heir, Colleoni left his vast fortune to Venice. Thus he tried to repay her for her unusual faith in him.

. . . . .

I found Malpaga eight miles south of Bergamo in a network of side-roads not far from the river Serio. Expecting to see a ruin, I was faced by a Renaissance farm in working order, and still in the possession of a branch of the Colleoni family. Herds of glossy little satin-grey cows, of the *bruno Alpino* breed, were grazing on well watered meadows which have fed their predecessors for centuries. The farm buildings occupy an immense square like a Roman camp, in the centre of which stands the castle with its fishtail battlements rising above a dry moat. The old soldier designed it as if it would have to endure a siege, and when I saw the castle, it occurred to me that anyone born in 1400 still had one foot in the Middle Ages. Here was a distinguished man who had lived through the best years of the Renaissance, yet when he came to retire and build himself a place for his old age, he erected a mediaeval keep. While the farm bailiff went off for the keys, I looked with pleasure at the life which has continued to exist at Malpaga without a break for five centuries. The farm buildings are two storeys in height, and in the lower are the barns and storehouses, the granaries and stables and cow-byres, and above are the dwellings of the farm labourers.

Professor Gilbert Highet, in his *Poets in a Landscape*, describes a similar farm near Mantua, *La Virgiliana*, where he found eight or ten families living 'in a state of cheerful and sleazy confusion', a condition absent from Malpaga where life seems to be going on as it must have done in the time of Colleoni. I admired an ox-wagon which came swaying in under the central archway of the castrum, loaded with root crops, a sight that took the mind beyond the Renaissance to the classical world.

Colleoni's estate was probably modelled on the finest farms he had seen in the various ducal states during the course of his soldiering. The most famous was the Sforza farm at Vigevano, near Milan, which astonished the French who accompanied Louis XII into Italy. Here they saw for the first time agricultural experiments with crops and the scientific breeding of farm stock. Robert Gaugin was astonished by the care which was devoted to each department. 'The exact weight of everything, that is to say of the hay, milk, butter, and cheese, is carefully recorded,' he wrote.

Louis XII was particularly attracted to what were called the Milan cheeses, perhaps a type of Parmesan, notable for their size and weight. He took a great number back to France with him and built a special room at Blois where he kept them for years, preserved in oil.

The bailiff returned with the keys and we crossed the moat. The castle is in good repair and, apart from its interest as the home of the most attractive of the *condottieri*, is a rare example of the surroundings of a rich country magnate of the Renaissance. We know how they lived in camps, but here we see the rooms in which they administered their estates, the halls in which they feasted, and their kitchens. A picturesque courtyard, surrounded by colonnades, the inner curves of the arches decorated with frescoed grotesques, leads by way of several outside stairways to the upper storeys. Frescoes cover the walls, some religious, others illustrating a great event of Colleoni's retirement, the visit to him of King Christian I of Denmark on his return from a pilgrimage to Rome. As the walls prove, the guest was treated to a royal round of hunting parties and tournaments. The barrier between the Renaissance and the Middle Ages was extremely thin at times: on such occasions, dressed in armour and grasping long jousting lances, the lords of the Renaissance rode back easily into the twelfth century. I saw a mediaeval scene of this kind pictured on the walls of Malpaga as two knights with visors down crashed together on heraldically barded chargers, while the fair ladies, seated in tiers like a girls' school, occupied a pavilion on the shady side of the lists.

We climbed up and down stone stairways, sometimes arriving on an inner balcony with a good view down to the herring-bone brick of the courtyard; sometimes emerging in the sunlight of a pillared loggia high up under the roof of the castle, a vantage point from which the old soldier could review his agricultural command at a glance. Few tales of him survive, save that he lived in military pomp, surrounded by six hundred of his veterans, and that living with him were his two daughters, to whom he was devoted. Cassandra married the *erudito cavaliere*, Nicolà da Correggio, but Medea never married, and lies now, as I had seen her, like some marble Ophelia, in the lovely chapel at Bergamo. It is said that her death broke her father's heart. I was shown the now bare room in which Colleoni is believed to have died, perhaps the room in which the Venetian envoys stood round his bed and learnt with astonishment that he had left the bulk of his great fortune to its source.

I was taken round the farm buildings to admire the colts and the young oxen; I saw firewood stacked for the winter and the last of the hay, and heard much talk of wheat and maize. After some discussion over pig-sties, cow-byres, and in the washed-down cleanliness of dairies, I left with the pleasant feeling that there are some places where time, it seems, has stood still.

§ 6

I set off early on a summer morning to motor from Bergamo to Cremona through a level landscape where the small country towns were just awakening. The bells were ringing for early Mass, the shops were still closed, and the umbrellas and awnings were still folded in the market places. Upon the outskirts of a little town called Crema I came with surprise to a huge round church which looked as though someone had dropped the Pantheon in a village. Peeping inside, I saw that Mass had just ended. The priest was carrying the chalice from the altar, while a boy in a ragged suit was reaching up to snuff out the candles. The first few rows of seats were occupied by small boys about eight or ten years of age who were intoning an elaborate 'amen' in trebles while an old priest, wearing a long black overcoat, faced them and beat time rather angrily with a walking-stick. When he dismissed them, the children rushed in a body towards the door, making a terrible clatter, and I noticed that they were all wearing clogs, or sandals with wooden soles. It was one of those curious little scenes that somehow persist in the memory.

When I arrived in Cremona, which is a rosy-red town of old brick, terracotta decoration and mulberry-red roof tiles, I was impressed by the nobility of the piazza, and stood looking at the cathedral, the campanile, the baptistry, and the town hall as if I had never before seen this famous quartette: and I thought that each of these Italian cities, holding to its heart the ghost of ancient enmities, is a law unto itself and is still, no matter what the maps say, surrounded by spectral walls. One would have to be a Bergamasque or a Cremonese to know how deep this goes, but any stranger can sense the individuality, the local pride, and the local prejudice. Looking down the long avenue of time, one can discern a moment in the early Middle Ages when these towns vied with each other in the size and beauty of their cathedrals, the height of their towers, the dignity of their town halls, and, though they used the same formula, each city created something different. Such conformity, yet such lovely variety, in cities separated rarely by more than thirty miles, is as though a number of musicians had all composed variations on the same theme.

The cathedral is a gem. The marble columns of the porch carry it forward from the building and rest upon the backs of seated lions. Above, as if standing in Romanesque windows and gazing down into the square, are life-sized statues of the Virgin and Child, attended by the patron saint of Cremona, known locally by the strange name of S. Omobono and elsewhere as S. Homobonus. Above the tableau is a fine rose window of the thirteenth century, and on either side, running almost the entire length of the façade, is a graceful Romanesque arcade in two sections, one above the other.

These porch tableaux of Lombardy fascinate me. They go back to a time before the fresco described the sacred story to those who were unable to read. The church porch, of course, tells a simpler tale, nevertheless it is an important one and proclaims the best of news : that the local saint stands in attendance upon the Mother of God.

The inside of the cathedral scarcely fulfilled the Romanesque promise of the façade, so I returned to linger in the early sunshine and admire the piazza, and to watch, in an adjoining street, a colourful little market take shape under awnings of all colours. This market, in which one could buy fruit, vegetables, meat, poultry, and even old clothes sold by Jews, gives the last perfect mediaeval touch to the majestic piazza of Cremona. I walked out to S. Agostino, the church which Francesco Sforza built on the site of an earlier one to commemorate his marriage to Bianca Maria. This was, as I have said, an ideal marriage and also the foundation of the Sforza fortunes. I saw a picture in which they were kneeling face to face, looking rather more portly and middle-aged than I had expected; and the light was switched on by a little nun who, as I entered the church, was tenderly sponging the leaves of an aspidistra in the chancel.

When I returned to Cremona, I came upon the most remarkable of its features, a fine public garden and park in the centre of the town. There were lawns, a fountain, a bandstand, well-grown chestnut trees, polled acacias, beds of hydrangeas, and seats dotted about as if one were in England or France. Such a garden in the heart of an ancient Italian town is unusual. The Latin mind has always kept vegetation in its place, which is the country, and if trees or flowers do happen to invade a town, they are immediately imprisoned in stone. I asked the history of this park and eventually found someone who told me that an unpopular Dominican monastery, the headquarters of the Inquisition, was pulled down shortly after the Risorgimento and the site made into a municipal garden. While wandering about this unlikely greenery, I came upon a still more improbable sight, the tombstone of Antonio Stradivari, once in the Dominican church and now in the open air.

When you mention the name of Stradivari in this town the Cremonese eye lights up and you are directed to the *Scuola Internazionale di Luteria*, in a modern building not far from the cathedral. Here I was greeted by a powerful smell of varnish and wood, and by a man who thought I was a musician in search of a violin; for here instruments are made to the ancient formula. So far from being a musician, I was obliged to confess that I knew little about Stradivari save that, like Tompion and Graham, he was a genius who had carried his craft to its highest possible point. I begged them to tell me something about him, and discovered that the life of a man who had lived to be ninety-three could be briefly told. He was born in 1644 and married a widow older than himself. He had three children, and remarried the year after his first wife died and had five more children. He died in 1737. Little is known of his tastes and idiosyncrasies save that he was said to have been fond of money – he charged four pounds for a violin, quite a sum in those days – and he worked rapidly and contentedly, wearing a white leather apron and a white cap. One of Stradivari's few reputed remarks to a pupil was: 'You will never make a violin better than mine.' I was told that he had made one thousand, one hundred and sixteen violins, viols, and violoncellos, which, in a working life of about seventy years, is an average of sixteen a year. There is an old saying in Cremona, 'as rich as Stradivari', so that he was probably not only happy, but also careful. I asked how many of his violins still exist. They said about six hundred, and, of course, thousands of fakes. Many of his violins have perished, others may still lie hidden, and a great number of people are always looking for them. Also, I was told, everyone who owns a violin more than a hundred years old believes it to be a genuine Stradivari. The fakers of these instruments reproduce the printed label which the *maestro* attached to his works, yet they always manage to get something wrong. It is extraordinary how many mistakes can be made in reproducing a label as simple as this: 'Antonius Stradivarius Cremonenis. Faciebat anno. . . .', the date being in Arabic numerals. I asked what a genuine Stradivari is worth today. They said anything between £1,500 and £15,000, though an exceptionally fine one was sold in London some years ago for £24,000.

In the workshops upstairs I was introduced to the *maestro* who, girded with an apron, was overseeing the work of fourteen apprentices. The scene was much as I imagine any violin workshop to have been in the time of Stradivari: clumsy wooden tables; the walls hung with the templates of violins and parts of violins, with swanlike necks, with backs, fronts, and sides; racks filled with tools; various grained and differently coloured woods, wafer-thin but tough; and, of course, the pervading smell of hot varnish, glue, and sawdust. I was told that more than seventy pieces of different wood are dovetailed and glued together to make a violin.

Reflecting that I had not picked up a violin since I was a schoolboy, when my mother fondly believed me to show the makings of another Kreisler, I idly took one up and lifted it to my shoulder.

'Ah!' cried the *maestro* with Italian impetuosity, 'you are a musician!' and, advancing excitedly, he placed a bow in my hands and stood back waiting for the opening notes of some divine concerto.

I did not tell him that ages before he was born my music master practically went down on his knees and begged for me to be removed from his sight. So, fearing to give even a tentative scrape, yet perversely longing to hear again one of those fearful cat-like wailings which I used to draw from this instrument, I handed it back with a sigh. The *maestro* took it, closed his eyes, snuggled the instrument into his neck and, with a graceful sweep of the bow, played like an angel. Dissatisfied with the acoustics of the workshop, he went out into the passage and played there. The instruments produced in the *Scuola* are bought by musicians from many parts of the world, most of whom come to Cremona to try them out. They cost from twenty to a hundred and twenty pounds. It is still believed that Stradivari had a secret, either in his selection of the wood or in his varnish. I asked the *maestro*, who told me he had played many a Stradivari, in what lies their singular excellence.

'*Anima!*' he cried. 'In the soul, in the response, in the ease with which they render all that a violinist is able to express.'

'And do you believe in the secret of the varnish?'

'Yes, and also in the way Stradivari varnished.'

I was fascinated by the stories that have accumulated round the creations of this extraordinary genius. All the finest violins by Stradivari have pedigrees and also names, such as the *Viotti*, the *Vieuxtemps*, and the *Tuscan*, while some are called after their celebrated owners, Sarasate and Paganini. One Stradivari is believed to have a curse on it, but whether this instrument is still in existence no one could tell me. It was owned in the eighteenth century by Romeo Danni, a professional violinist, who bought it, unaware of its rather disconcerting habit of suddenly becoming silent after having played beautifully for an hour or so. When this occurred during one of Danni's concerts, he charged his rival Salvadossi with having perpetrated some trick on him, and challenged him to a duel. Danni was killed, and thus began a vendetta which ultimately cost twenty-two lives. The most extraordinary Stradivari story, however, concerns a mysterious individual named Luigi Terisio who lived in the first part of the nineteenth century. He was in the habit of travelling, disguised as a pedlar, all over Italy with a pack on his back full of new violins which he offered to exchange for old ones. The dealers in Paris were astonished when he arrived there with an incredible collection which included violins not only by Stradivari but also by the earlier Amati, by Guarneri, and Guadagnini and others. In the year 1854 one of these dealers, J. B. Vuillaume, learning that Terisio had died in Milan, hurried there in the hope of being able to buy whatever collection of instruments might remain. He was shown to the miserable room in which Terisio had died surrounded by more than two hundred violins, viols, and violoncellos by all the great masters. Vuillaume was speechless with astonishment. He was then taken to a small farm where Terisio had hidden away more violins, and, while he was examining this collection, he pulled open a drawer and gazed with amazement at a new Stradivari, the *Messiah*, an instrument which had never been played. This violin had been sold by a descendant of Stradivari to Count Cozio de Salabue, who had never used it, and in whose possession it had remained until Terisio found it. It is still in mint condition just as it left the workshop in Cremona, and was presented to the Ashmolean Museum at Oxford by Arthur and Alfred Hill, the foremost authorities on Stradivari.

Having listened to these stories, I recollected that I had a Stradivari story of my own, which I told them. Some years ago, when I was staying in Madrid, a friend rang me up one night and asked, 'Would you like to hear four Stradivari violins being played at the same time?' In a few minutes he called at my hotel, and, as we drove off to the royal Palace, my friend explained that after Alfonso XIII had left Spain in 1931, a chest was opened in the Chapel Royal in which a number of fiddles, which were sometimes played during services, were seen jumbled together in the dust. On examination, four of the instruments were found to be by Stradivari and were rescued from their squalor. They were restored, and are now occasionally used during concerts given by a select little musical society of which my friend was a member. We drove into the desolate courtyard and made for a distant archway whose lamp spilt a faint light upon a stairway. We ascended and tiptoed in conspiratorial silence along dark corridors until we came to a door, which was opened by a palace servant. In a drawing-room lit by sparkling chandeliers perhaps a hundred persons sat facing a little dais on which a string orchestra was seated. The pianist led the way, and the time came when the four violinists drew their bows across the four precious instruments. It was a great moment. In no capital of Europe could one have seen a more courtly audience: such dark, discreet eyes, such silvery hair, such neat imperials, and such a gathering of elderly duchesses, with bosoms generous or meagre, upon which jewels burned and glittered. In those sudden silences which occur in music, as if the composer were determined to discover a whisperer, there would be no sound but the faint tap of a monocle meeting a shirt-front. All about us lay the dead and silent palace. One thought of the throne-room of all the Spains lying dark, the chandeliers in bags; and there we sat, listening to music from the magic boxes of Stradivari, like some fragment of a pleasantly privileged society which, for some inscrutable reason, had been lost by enchantment in the palace and was happily unaware of the ugly world without. After the concert I was allowed to carry a Stradivari to the strong-room next door, and I helped to lock up all four of them for the night.

I said good-bye to my friends of the *Scuola*, thinking how odd it was that Dr Burney, while on his musical tour of Europe only thirty-three years after Stradivari's death, never even mentioned him, nor did he even visit Cremona. A traveller who did visit Cremona, however, thirty-six years before Stradivari was born, was dear old Tom Coryat. He wrote: 'I did eat fried Frogges in this citie, which is a dish much used in many cities of Italy: they were so curiously dressed, that they did exceedingly delight my palat, the head and the forepart being cut off.'

§ 7

As I drove on to Mantua, which is only about forty miles east of Cremona, I reflected that such famous towns, so close together, cannot be seen elsewhere in the world. One comes to them every thirty or forty miles, each one a place with a noble pedigree and a distinguished history. Once they were a day's journey apart, but now they are only an hour's drive from each other. Milan and Pavia are twenty miles apart; Pavia and Piacenza are thirty miles apart, and Cremona and Parma only twenty-five; thirty miles separate Parma from Modena, and only twenty-five miles lie between Modena and Bologna: and so one could go on across the map of this great plain. Many of the cities still preserve impressive stretches of their fortifications, and all are still surrounded by spiritual walls: a sense of separateness, the last relic of that civic pride which makes the history of northern Italy remind one at every point of the Greek states in the fourth century before Christ. Local dialect is still spoken everywhere, but that is something which a traveller like myself can sense rather than know. One would have to be in intimate contact with the peasants of Lombardy to understand how important this is, and to what extent bi-lingualism fosters that secret identity which goes back to an earlier world. When Stuart Hood was an escaped prisoner in Lombardy and Emilia during the last war, he wrote, in the account of his experiences with the Italian Underground, that: 'From village to village and from valley to valley the dialect changed, but basically it kept its nasals and its modified "u". "*Fueg*", they said and meant *fuoco*: fire. *Vin*, they said with a long "i" and a nasal: wine. Trousers were *braghe* – breeks. I remembered that this was once Cisalpine Gaul.'

When I walked out into Mantua that night, a full moon was transforming the city into the backcloth of an opera. The moonlight, accentuating the shadows, made each colonnade a scene for drama, and every street corner had the appearance of a romantic trysting-place. Towers and domes, rising from immense shadows, shone in a green wash of light, and most striking of all was the rambling palace of the Gonzaga, the open beaks of its merlature touched by moonlight as it stood upon the edge of a lake, crouched in profound darkness. One looked at the rows of windows and imagined behind them the empty palace with its silent marble staircases and its deserted audience chambers, the moonlight falling in angles and bars across the floor; and I looked up half expecting to see a white face watching the moonlit square.

Unfortunately the orchestra which this scene demanded was absent; instead, as if Satan were running his pitchfork across the railings of hell, young men mounted upon red motor-cycles raced each other through the streets, and every colonnade multiplied and echoed the hideousness of their passing. Sometimes I could hear them a long way off and so prepare myself to meet the approaching explosions, but often they would arrive suddenly, in full pandemonium, sending their deafening racket into every nook and crevice of the ancient town.

While I was seated in a café, loathing the motorists and admiring the moonlight, a sad little Italian, whose melancholy face looked as though it had witnessed every conceivable disaster, came to my table and said he could tell I was an American. When we had straightened that out, he explained that he had been an interpreter with the American army. I invited him to my table and ordered an *espresso* for him. He was a pleasant little man and knew a great deal about the history of Mantua.

He told me that there is still a Count Castiglione, who lives in the Castiglione Palace in Mantua and who possesses the manuscript of his ancestor's work, *Il Cortegiano*. The book, he said, was kept in a velvet-lined box in a bank, and he had seen it, beautifully written in Renaissance script.

Passing to more mundane things, he said how rich and prosperous life was outside Italy. If only he could get to America, even at his age. He told me that his salary ran out on the fifteenth of every month and he was always on the look-out for temporary jobs to keep him going until the next pay packet arrived. Quite bluntly he conveyed that he would not be too proud to accept a few lire for showing me round Mantua. I hinted that I should much like to see the manuscript of *The Courtier*, but he thought that would be difficult as the Count was not in Mantua at that moment. Changing the subject hastily, he asked if I knew of a distinguished Englishman named Signor Giacomo Critonio who had died in Mantua. I said it was not a common English name, but he insisted that I must have heard of the man and offered to take me to the church and show me his tomb. It was already fairly late, but I thought it would be interesting to wander round Mantua, and so we were soon strolling through silent back streets which, with the coming of darkness, appeared to have retreated beyond the Renaissance to the Middle Ages. We came at length to the church of S. Simone which was, as I had expected, closed and locked for the night. This did not worry my acquaintance, however, and, asking me to wait for a moment, he vanished into the darkness.

We were in a shabby little back street where the lamplight fell upon ancient shuttered houses and upon an arcade whose shadows were impenetrable. I felt that in some preposterous way I had been cast for a minor part in a Shakespearean comedy. Some absurd character like Gobbo, I reflected, might open one of the shuttered windows with a 'God bless your worship'. Almost as if in answer to my mood, the little Italian appeared under a lamp at a near-by turning and motioned dramatically for me to follow him. We crossed a stretch of waste land and came to the backyard of a house where an old woman was standing with a bunch of keys. She opened a heavy old gate and we entered an icy darkness fragrant with incense. We had come into the church by a back door. My friend led the way, grasping a lighted taper, which he held above an inscription let into the wall. I read:

To the Memory of
James Crichton of Eliock and Cluny
From the splendour of his talents and the universal
range of his accomplishments known to history as
the Admirable Crichton.
He expired in early manhood already renowned
For scholarly and courtly attainments,
for ideals of knighthood and honour
combined with wide erudition and skill in arms,
and eloquence and powers of reason.
Born at Eliock, Dumfriesshire,
Scotland, 19 August 1560
Died at Mantua 3 July 1582.
His remains were buried in this church.

'You see,' he said, holding the taper an inch from the name, 'Giacomo Critonio.'

'Yes,' I replied, 'I have heard of him. How did he die?'

'In a duel,' he replied, 'about a woman.'

I do not know if this is the true explanation. I do know, however, that a young Scotsman named James Crichton arrived in Italy in the late sixteenth century and dazzled everyone by his gift of tongues, his ability to turn out Latin odes at a moment's notice, and his skill in debate. He had everything, it seemed, but money. He caused a sensation in Venice, it was said, by vanquishing the local dons in public argument, and from Venice he arrived at the court of Guglielmo Gonzaga, third Duke of Mantua. Crichton made an instant conquest of the Duke, who was a clever, sour little man who had inherited the Gonzaga curse, a spinal defect which made him almost a hunchback. He detested his son and heir, Vincenzo, who was a gay and handsome young man with a straight back, and only slightly younger than Crichton. While the Duke persecuted his son for his extravagance and his gallantries, he made Crichton one of his councillors and enjoyed long discussions with him on learned subjects.

On the night of July 3, 1582, Crichton left the palace, accompanied by a servant, for a walk through the deserted streets. It was a night of the full moon. As the two men entered a narrow lane they saw two cloaked figures approaching who, as they passed, jostled Crichton so insultingly that he drew a dagger and plunged it into the back of the man nearest to him. His friend drew a sword and ran Crichton through the body. As he fell, the Scotsman recognized the prince, Vincenzo. He staggered to an apothecary, in whose house he died. Crichton's servant, who could have described what happened, disappeared and was never heard of again. Whether Crichton's death was an accident or a planned assassination due to jealousy, who can say? It will probably never be known. The Duke threatened to have his son tried for murder, but the affair blew over. About twenty years afterwards, when Vincenzo was Duke of Mantua, he wrote a letter to a friend in which he mentioned the Admirable Crichton's death. 'It was a case of pure misadventure,' he wrote, 'and if I had been dealing with anyone but a "barbarian" so much harm would not have followed.'

As we walked back through the same lanes and arcades, lit by the same green wash of moonlight, my acquaintance pointed out to me the Palazzo Sordello, the thirteenth century palace which the Castiglione family still inhabit. We found the café open and sat down at a table.

'It must be a fine thing,' said the Italian, 'to live in an affluent society.'

But I was conscious that something even finer had happened to Mantua. The motor-cyclists had gone to bed.

§ 8

The market women were already sheltering beneath their awnings and busily selling their cabbages and aubergines when I walked to the Reggia to see the palace of the Gonzaga. The enormous building was not yet open and a strange-looking group of visitors lingered near, dressed in eccentric wayfaring costumes. There was a bearded man in flannel trousers and sandals, wearing a beach shirt decorated with prismatic fish; there was a middle-aged woman who might have dismayed even Rubens; and there was a bland little man in yellow shorts with the chubby knees of a Mantegna cherub, who wore a Tyrolean hat and had three cameras slung about him. He was accompanied by a doting wife and two schoolgirl daughters. He spoke to me in German, then in fluent English. He told me he was making a photographic record of every Italian town mentioned by Shakespeare.

'Oh yes,' I said. 'Didn't Romeo come to Mantua after Tybalt's murder to buy some poison here?'

'Yes, yes, of course!' cried the little man delightedly, 'and do not forget *Love's Labour's Lost*. Here lived the poet Mantuano, the "good old Mantuan".'

He had come from Milan, which he said is mentioned by Shakespeare twenty-five times, and he was on his way to Padua (twenty-two references) and then on to Venice, which is mentioned more frequently than any other Italian city: it has fifty-two references. What a world it is, how amusing and how unexpected! Every time the little German made a statement, his wife supported him admiringly with nods and smiles, while the two girls gazed at their father with the eyes of young calves.

While we were talking, a coach drew up in the piazza and from its high windows about fifty faces gazed without much enthusiasm at the graceful sweep of mediaeval colonnade and merlatured battlement. A guide with a microphone said in French, 'Ladies and gentleman, we have here the famous palace of the Dukes of Mantua. The part of the building that you see dates from the fourteenth century. Here lived Isabella d'Este, the most famous of the marchionesses of Mantua.' The faces continued to look out while a few travellers lowered windows and aimed their cameras at the Reggia before the coach slipped into gear and disappeared on its way to Venice. At this point the enormous palace of the Gonzaga opened its gates and we all trooped into the cool darkness. The guide gazed sadly over us in search of an attractive female and settled upon the two little German girls. He led us to an inscription on a wall on which we read: 'Upon this spot was decapitated on February 7, 1391, Agnese Visconti, wife of Francesco Gonzaga, Captain of the People. She was twenty-three years old.' Someone asked why this had happened to her. The guide said that a handsome young man named Vincenzo da Scandiano was strangled at the same time in the dungeons. Everyone nodded broadmindedly, but I remembered that this intrigue has never been proved. There is a good chance that the poor girl was innocent, and that her jealous husband was the victim of one of Gian Galeazzo Visconti's Iago-like plots.

We entered the confusing building, which might be called a history in stone of the Gonzaga captaincy, marquisate, and, eventually, dukedom. Its complexity would defy anyone but a determined architect, and it seemed to be of three periods, the late mediaeval, the Renaissance, and the seventeenth century. We were told that there are five hundred rooms in it, as well as fifteen court-yards. We trooped up the grand staircase into enormous empty halls and came to the *Sala dei Duchi*, where we saw portraits of the Gonzaga, beginning with Luigi in 1328 and ending with the last duke in 1708, nearly four centuries of them: four captains of the people, four marquesses, and eleven dukes. I reflected that the Gonzaga of Mantua and the Montefeltri of Urbino were the most attractive and comprehensible of the princely families, perhaps because they had a respect for learning and a love of art, and certainly because their secretaries kept their archives so perfectly that we, who are able to read their secret thoughts, know their joys and sorrows, and their fears, as well or even better than their contemporaries can have done. The Gonzaga were a military family. One marquess drew most of his income as commander of the Milanese armies, another was Captain-General of Venice, and a third commanded the forces of Florence. The spinal deformity to which I have already referred is believed to have been introduced into the family by Paola Malatesta da Rimini, who married the first Marquess Gianfrancesco, about 1414. The disease did not show itself until she was in her thirties, but it appeared in her descend-ants at intervals through the long family history. Two of her sons, Gianlucido and Alessandro, were cut off from normal life and sought comfort in the classics. It was said that Gianlucido knew the whole of Virgil by heart. One of Paola's grand-daughters, Susanna, grew up into a hunchback. This poor girl had been betrothed in infancy to Galeazzo Maria Sforza before her deformity had been noticed, and had the ignominy of seeing her name struck out of the marriage contract and that of her sister, Dorotea, substituted. Then it was whispered that she also was deformed and the Sforza demanded a medical examination, which her father, Ludovico Gonzaga, indignantly refused to permit: he also resigned his position as commander of the Milanese armies. The eldest sons seem to have escaped the family curse until 1538 when Guglielmo, who befriended the Admirable Crichton, was born a hunchback; by that time, however, the family had passed its zenith and was on its way out through extravagance, reluctant bridegrooms, and empty cradles. One enters these halls aware that riches and galleries full of Mantegnas, Titians, and Bellinis cannot compensate for a defective spinal column; and while the guide was extolling the military triumphs of the family and was bidding us to remember various battlefields, I visualized the Gonzaga, not upon their war-horses, but bending apprehensively above the ducal cradles.

We were led through a number of great halls, most of them battered by time and military occupation and all of varied periods. This dodging about in time was a bit disconcerting, but was to be expected in a building that had housed a wealthy family through the fashions of nearly four centuries. We saw the halls where the Gonzaga received in state under the cold gaze of classical busts in niches and embrasures, and under ceilings where cupids played and whispered among the signs of the Zodiac; we walked the length of a great gallery looking over a tilt-yard at whose windows the ladies of the court would watch their sweethearts and husbands crashing together on horseback as if it were 1324 and not 1524. I noted with interest that Giulio Romano, who had built the gallery, had introduced the twisted or barley-sugar column there a good century before Bernini's canopy in S. Peter's.

Then we came to what I shall always remember as the sheerest fantasy – the Apartments of the Dwarfs.

In the heart of the palace, built to scale for inhabitants about three feet high, is a suite of rooms, or rather a miniature house, with midget staircases and even a tiny chapel in which I had to bend double. As I explored the rooms, I thought it a curious mark of affection which would not have surprised me in some old and eccentric palace in Spain, but here in Mantua surely the strangest possession for a family who had cause to dread deformity. Like all noble families in past centuries, the Gonzaga loved their dwarfs, whose names and escapades are merrily scattered through the ducal archives. Isabella d'Este, when Marchioness of Mantua, aged twenty-two and temporarily miserable during her husband's absence on some warlike occasion, wrote to her father at Ferrara to ask him to send Fritello to her. He was the Este dwarf who never failed to convulse the family with his tricks. He danced, sang and turned somersaults, and greatly cheered the Estensi during their dark moments. Her own favourite dwarf, Mattello, came to the rescue of the lonely marchioness (we learn in a later letter) and made her laugh with his imitation of a drunken man, and also, upon another occasion when, having been announced as the venerable Padre Bernadino Mattello, he entered her room dressed as a tiny Franciscan. Two years later she sent Mattello to Ferrara to minister to her brother, Alfonso, who was disconsolate after the death of his wife, Lucrezia Borgia. Evidently the cure worked, for Alfonso wrote to say that he considered Mattello more valuable than the gift of a fine castle. When Mattello died and was laid in his little grave, the usual Latin epitaphs were written, and the poet Pistoia wrote that 'if Mattello is in Paradise he is making all the saints and angels laugh'.

Another popular Mantuan dwarf was Nanino who, like Mattello, was fond of putting on an ecclesiastical act. When the melancholy Maximilian, Duke of Milan, visited his aunt, Isabella, Nanino alone was able to make the young man smile. One of Nanino's side-splitting feats was a hunting burlesque in the course of which he had a wrestling match with a goat. It is indeed odd to think of the grave and arrogant lords and ladies painted by Titian moving sadly and disconsolately against their tapestries and their gilt cupids until, sending in despair to the dwarfs' quarters, they received from them the healing gift of laughter. Throughout the Renaissance there was a brisk interchange of dwarfs and buffoons between related houses, notably Mantua and Ferrara, and one can imagine how the pampered, jealous little favourites eyed each other with suspicion on these occasions, and how they sulked at the appearance of a rival from a neighbouring court. The management of the dwarfs must have called for that blend of firmness and flattery now expended upon temperamental film stars. It is perhaps understandable that dwarfdom has not featured much in poetry, though it attracted the attention of painters, notably Velazquez. I do, however, recollect one charming little English poem by Waller on the marriage of Richard Gibson and Anne Shepherd, both three feet ten inches in height, the court-dwarfs of Charles I and Henrietta Maria. Charles gave the bride away, and this is what Waller wrote:

Design or chance make others wive
But nature did this match contrive:
Eve might as well have Adam fled
As she denied her little bed
To him, for whom Heaven seemed to frame
And measure out this little dame.

On we went, getting now a little footsore, and came to what were to me the most fascinating rooms in the whole palace: all that is left of the famous *Paradiso* of Isabella d'Este. These are three little jewel-box rooms leading one to the other, scarred by time and military occupation and denuded by thieves and art dealers; yet they still have about them something of the happiness of the days when their owner sat surrounded by her treasures, playing the lute or singing, or perhaps unwrapping the latest Aldine classic printed on vellum specially selected for her, page by page, by Aldo Manuzio himself. Isabella was sixteen when she left her father's court at Ferrara to marry the young Francesco Gonzaga, the third Marquess of Mantua, and a great deal of one's interest in her concerns this lifelong search for a retreat or haven filled with the pictures, the books, the musical instruments, and the jewels and bronzes that she loved; a place where she could retire in a congenial projection of her own personality to forget the woes of life; and she experienced many. Even in her twenties Isabella was a fully fledged art critic and connoisseur, and so she remained all her life, becoming perhaps more exacting and more acquisitive as the years went on; and this passion for beautifying her surroundings was as strong when she was seventeen as it was forty-eight years later when she died.

The intricately carved ceilings of the *Paradiso* have defied destruction. They still shine with gold-leaf and glow with colour, and upon them I traced the mottoes and symbols which Isabella loved and on whose composition she spent so much time. I saw the Roman numbers XXVII (*vinte le sette*) by which she intended to say, so I believe, that she had vanquished all her enemies; I saw the three letters U.T.S., the monogram Ys, the open pack of playing-cards, and the bunch of twigs bound with a ribbon, less easy to explain. One of the most beautiful marble doorways I have ever seen, with sculptured medallions by Christoforo Romano, led into a perfect little room with a gold coffered ceiling where I picked out more of Isabella's symbols and designs, and also her famous motto, *Nec spe, nec metu* – 'Neither with hope nor fear'. So this was the *Paradiso*, its possessions now scattered all over the world. It was not, of course, Isabella's first haven, but her last. Her original *studiolo*, made when she was a young bride, was not in the palace, but in the ancient castle which adjoins it. When later her rooms became crowded, she asked her son Francesco to allow her to migrate to the ground floor of the palace, where she designed her charming *Grotta*. This was the retreat for whose walls Mantegna, Perugino, and Costa painted the involved allegorical pictures now to be seen in the Louvre.

Two thousand of Isabella's letters have been found in the Mantuan Archives alone; we know her in all her moods, loving, angry, haughty, sad, and in youth, in middle age, and old age. While she was sitting for some of the world's greatest painters, she was unaware that she herself was leaving to posterity a more revealing portrait in her correspondence. Leonardo da Vinci's red chalk drawing of her in the Louvre shows a rather full-blown young woman of twenty-five, not particularly good-looking, but pleasant and capable, wearing a flimsy low-cut gown. Vienna possesses two portraits by Titian, one of Isabella aged fifty-five and the other his copy of a portrait by Francia when she was a young girl. 'I doubt if we were ever as beautiful as this,' she wrote when she saw Titian's copy. This canvas shows a beautiful girl dressed in the height of fashion, jewelled and brocaded, a fur thrown over one shoulder, her fairish hair crowned by an elaborate jewelled construction which one hesitates to call a hat. One has only to look at the decisive line of her mouth to know that this haughty young dame had always had her own way and would continue to do so. This was clearly the Isabella who bulldozed her path through the studios of the Renaissance, getting what she wanted; this was the Isabella who laughed and danced with the French in her dead sister's palace in Milan; who threatened the wretched painter Luca Liombeni 'If our *studiolo* is not finished on our return we intend to put you into the dungeon of the Castello. And this, we assure you, is no jest on our part.' This was also the Isabella who stretched out no helping hand to the impoverished and dying Mantegna, but, instead, tried to bargain with him for his most treasured possession, a bust of Faustina. That, however, was only one side of Isabella, and it may be that Leonardo caught the real Isabella in his gentle profile in the Louvre. This is the submissive Isabella who could write to her lord: 'Of course if Your Highness thinks differently, I will set out tomorrow, even if I have to travel alone and in my chemise.'

So far from setting out in her chemise, Isabella, when summoned to Milan to her sister's wedding, began to assemble new dresses, furs, and jewels. She wrote to the Gonzaga agent in Venice, asking him to search all the shops for eighty of the finest sables. 'Try to find one with the head of the animal,' she wrote, 'to make a muff which I can carry in my hand . . . You must also buy eight yards of the best crimson satin which you can find in Venice to line the said *sbernia*, and for God's sake use all your accustomed diligence.' There, at the age of seventeen, sounded from Mantua the authentic voice which Gonzaga agents everywhere, artists, sculptors, architects, printers, antique dealers, goldsmiths, and dressmakers, were to hear for the next half century.

Like most wealthy people in an age of pomp, Isabella was extravagant, and she spent her money on rare objects which could be pawned in hard times. There was nothing furtive or discreditable about pawning in past ages: kings and princes practised it shamelessly. The Crown of Thorns was pawned in Venice and, when unredeemed, was bought by Louis XI, who built the Sainte Chapelle as a shrine for it. Life in Mantua alternated between moments when Francesco sent agents to Spain to buy costly Arab stallions while Isabella bought jewels, furs, brocades, and pictures, and both travelled about with hundreds of courtiers, sailing up the waterways in their gold bucentaur, the minstrels playing; and times when Isabella sent her jewels to the money-lenders in Venice and a cold chill of economic depression settled like one of the marsh fogs over the Reggia. Typical of the kind of letters which passed between husband and wife were those of 1495, when Isabella was in Mantua and Francesco was in Milan, anxious to make a brave show at the installation of Ludovico Sforza as Duke. He wrote to Isabella asking her to lend him her finest jewels, and she sent him all she had, for 'I would not only give my treasure, but my blood, for your honour and that of your house'. She ended by reminding him gently that a number of her jewels were already in pawn in Venice. A year or so later she sounds rather irritated when Francesco asks her to raise money on her jewels to buy a cardinal's hat for his brother. 'I have only four jewels left in the house – the large balass ruby which you gave me when my first child was born, my favourite diamond, and the last ones which you gave me. If I pledge these I shall be left entirely without jewels and shall be obliged to wear black, because to appear in coloured silks and brocades without jewels would be ridiculous.' Fortunately the cardinal's hat was not at that moment forthcoming and Isabella was allowed to keep her jewels.

Such periods of relative penury were relieved by sunny periods of sudden affluence like that after the dubious victory of Fornovo, when the Venetian Signory increased the salary of their commander-in-chief by two thousand ducats, and even gave Isabella a pension of a thousand ducats, a timely windfall for her. She immediately wrote to her Venetian agent asking him to settle her debts and spend what was left on fine pieces of *tabì*. What a queer word this is, applied now only to cats. In Isabella's time it was watered silk made originally in the Attabiya quarter of Baghdad, named after Attab, a contemporary of the Prophet. The word, as *taby* and *tabby*, has come to settle down and purr contentedly beside the fire by way of Elizabeth Tudor's silver and white tabby gown, Pepys's new waistcoat, and Fanny Burney's lilac dress.

Isabella had six children, three boys and three girls, and as the girls arrived first, she characteristically refused to allow them to use the ducal cradle which had been prepared for a son and heir. One fancies that the little girls had a rather lean time until, at the age of twenty-six, Isabella felt herself fulfilled and justified by the birth of her adored Federigo. It was during her first year of mother-hood, in 1493, that an interesting letter arrived in Mantua from a faithful servant who had been sent by Francesco to buy horses in Spain. 'A Savona sailor named Columbus,' he wrote from Cadiz, 'has landed here, bringing 30,000 ducats in gold, as well as pepper and other spices, and parrots as big as falcons and as red as pheasants. They found trees bearing fine wool, and others which produce wax and linen fibres, and men like Tartars, tall and active, with long hair falling over their shoulders. They eat human flesh, and fatten men as we do capons, and are called cannibals . . . It is certain that these sailors have brought back a great quantity of gold, sandal-wood and spices, and what I myself have seen – sixty parrots of variegated colours, eight of them as big as falcons – as well as twelve Indians, who have been sent to the King. And in that land they found great forests in which the trees grow so thickly you could hardly see the sky, and if some men had not climbed to the top of the trees they would never have got out again, and many other things of which I have not time to tell.'

Isabella's fame as a collector and patron of the arts has obscured the part she played in the history of her time. She saw her husband's state, and those of her father and kinsmen, shaken in the storm after the French invasion; twice she welcomed as exiles her brother and sister-in-law, and her daughter and son-in-law when they were driven from Urbino by the schemes of the Borgia and, later, of Clement VII. When on a visit to Rome in 1527, she heard the guns of the Castel S. Angelo booming during the sack of Rome and barricading herself in the Palazzo Colonna, she gave shelter to hundreds of terrified people. During those frightful days, as the cries of murdered men and women reached her from the streets, there reposed in a room in the palace the cardinal's hat which she had gone to Rome to procure for her younger son, Ercole, so that in the worst moments, when her dwarf Morgentino clung to her skirts in terror, and the mob of drunken Spaniards, Swiss, and Germans was reeling down the streets draped in copes and chasubles, she, though the world seemed about to end, had at last collected the red hat she had wanted for years! She was then fifty-three and her husband, Francesco, had been dead for eight years. Their early married life had been ideal; later the demands of his profession in an age of invasion, political misfortunes, bad health, and a mistress or two, made him irritable and morose. I think he was an appealing character, as some will possibly agree who have studied his sad face in the great picture by Mantegna, *Our Lady of Victories*, in the Louvre. He was small, swarthy, and ugly; how ugly one can tell from Mantegna's bronze at Mantua, which has something Caliban-like about it, for he had obviously escaped the Gonzaga hunchback only by a miracle. At the battle of Fornovo three horses were killed under him and he continued to fight on foot until his sword broke. Nevertheless Francesco was completely obscured by his gifted wife. To be married to such a famous collector and critic could not have been easy, but never did he interfere with her pursuits or rebuke her for extravagance. She gave him the stability he lacked, but she could not give him health. For some years before he died, Francesco sank into a state of melancholy fretfulness, and even his famous stud seems to have had no further attraction for him. As a young man his passion was horse-breeding and racing. When he was not leading the armies of one state or another, he was attending the races and often bringing home the *palio*, and the Mantuan stud became the most famous in Europe. Henry VIII once told a friend of Isabella's that he always rode a Mantuan horse on state occasions. Thus the visitor to Henry's London might have seen Gonzaga horses being groomed in the Royal Mews – now Trafalgar Square.

On an April evening, in the year 1519, Isabella and her family gathered round Francesco's bedside. He told her that he had always placed his whole trust and confidence in her. Later that night he died, aged fifty-three. In a few days his nineteen-year-old son, Federigo, clad in white from head to foot, received the sceptre upon the steps of the cathedral, and was hailed as the fifth Marquess of Mantua. Isabella had twenty years more of life. She had known sorrow when her young sister, Beatrice, died; she had been hurt when her husband had strayed from her; but she had never been humiliated until her favourite son took as his mistress a beautiful young woman named Isabella Boschetti, who sought every opportunity to make trouble between mother and son.

Never can the *Paradiso* have been more precious than in those bitter days when she saw a spiteful young woman in the place she had graced for thirty years; but maybe she is not really to be pitied, for she must have known that trouble has a way of straightening itself out if you continue to collect books and to read them. The Sack of Rome was the end of an age. When the Emperor Charles V came to bring peace to Italy, the sun shone again as the Gonzaga accepted the hand of friendship which the master of Europe held out to them. They could not have foreseen that Italy was merely exchanging the tyranny of France for that of Spain, but Isabella enjoyed a moment of great pride. In a ceremony at Mantua, upon the steps of the cathedral where her son had recently been proclaimed Marquess, the Emperor Charles created him first Duke of Mantua.

Growing stout and approaching the sixties, Isabella was still young in mind. Her letters are as vivid and as interested in life as they were when she was twenty. Titian was now her favourite painter and she was as impatient to see a finished picture as she had been twenty and thirty years before, when the painters had been Mantegna and the dilatory Perugino. 'And since we desire to have the picture immediately, we send a courier to Venice forthwith, in order that he may bring it back with him.' She had not altered! She died at the age of sixty-five, still full of interest in the world and filled with concern and affection for those around her.

One looks in vain for the tomb of this woman, the most attractive and the best known of the Renaissance. She was buried beside her husband in the Capella dei Signori in the Church of S. Francesco in Mantua. She lay there for two and a half centuries until the French revolutionary armies captured Mantua after a long siege, and the greatest tomb-robbers of modern history, whose path across Europe is marked by shattered coffins, broke in, in search of gold and jewels, and scattered the bones of the Gonzaga to the wind.

§ 9

The guide pointed out a roof garden where box hedges ran among tangled flower-beds, and told us that it was the graveyard of Isabella's pet dogs and birds. I remembered the various accounts I had read in her letters of sad little funerals attended by the Court and of bereavements commemorated by odes and elegies by the best Latin scholars of the day. Someone who knew her mentioned that her arrival was always announced by the barking of her little dogs.

We trooped across a courtyard and entered the ancient castle of S. George, which stands picturesquely upon the lagoons at a point where miles of stagnant water and close-packed beds of reeds stretch into the distance. The lagoon is crossed by a long bridge, which is really the main road to Nogara, and is to be seen in the background of Mantegna's *Death of the Virgin* in the Prado, in Madrid. The building itself is a huge, uncompromising square keep with massive terminal towers, and was built by the same mediaeval castle builder who erected the Este castle in Ferrara, so that when Isabella d'Este married Francesco, she exchanged one castle for another exactly like it.

The treasure of the castle is one of the most distinguished rooms in Italy, the *Camera degli Sposi*, the bridal chamber. Every inch of the walls and the groined ceiling are covered with frescoes by Mantegna. Above the door, held by a flight of cupids with the wings of butterflies, is a beautifully lettered inscription which says that the artist painted the room in the year 1474 – incidentally the year that Isabella d'Este was born at Ferrara. Above the mantelpiece, and as if standing upon it without any loss of dignity, is a life-sized group of men and women. We see Ludovico, the second Marquess, then aged sixty, with his placid and intelligent German wife, Barbara of Brandenburg, surrounded by their family and courtiers. They are richly dressed in cloth of gold, stiff brocades, and satins, and all the men are clean-shaven and wear red hats, either the Byzantine fez or brimless caps. They are assembled to greet one whose identity has started a number of attractive hares. Whoever he is, he briskly approaches a flight of steps where dashing young men, wearing short pleated tunics and coloured hose, wait to greet him and escort him to the Marquess.

Ludovico sits in an arm-chair upholstered in the Italian style, and is wearing a long gown edged with ermine and a wide linen collar not unlike those worn by the Puritans in England much later in history. Beneath his chair reposes in a rush basket a large old dog of Renaissance breed, obviously a privileged favourite. The Marquess half turns, holding a letter in his hand, and whispers an aside to a courtier who, cap in hand, bends forward to hear his master with the expressionless face of the perfect confidential secretary.

There are various theories about this scene. One suggestion is that the stranger is an ambassador arriving from the Duke of Würtemberg to ask for the hand of Barbara Gonzaga, then a girl of about seventeen. Another is that the picture represents the reconciliation between Ludovico and his eldest son, Federigo, after the young man's absence in Naples. This theory, which has had some doubt cast upon it, is interesting as an example of the involved intrigues which occur so often in Italian life. The story is that when a marriage embassy arrived at Mantua to arrange a match between Margaret of Bavaria and Federigo, the young prince was appalled by the appearance and manners of the Bavarians, and, to make matters worse, he heard that Margaret was short, fat, and unable to speak a word of Italian. He took to his heels and fled with six companions to Naples. On the way the party was robbed and arrived penniless. As Federigo was in hiding and travelling under another name, he could appeal to no one. He took lodgings in a poor part of the city, and when he fell ill his six companions became porters and casual labourers in order to support their prince. He was eventually discovered and persuaded to return home by means of an inquiry about 'seven men of Lombardy' which his mother, Barbara of Brandenberg, sent round to all the courts of Italy. It only remains to be said that Federigo did, after all, marry Margaret of Bavaria, who turned out to be a pleasant little blonde. I cannot, however, believe that any family should have thought it desirable to perpetuate the story of a reluctant bridegroom on the walls of its bridal chamber.

The other scene is not so controversial. It represents the arrival from Rome, in 1472, of Francesco, the first Gonzaga to achieve a red hat. The proud Marquess Ludovico has ridden out to greet his son, wearing hunting dress, and the old dog of the former picture is still in attendance. Other members of the family stand round the two chief figures beneath a beautiful tree; in the background a tantalizing road winds in and out and up to a shining classical city which may be Rome. There are three generations of Marquesees of Mantua in this picture; Ludovico, his son Federigo, and his grandson Francesco, who, though only six years old, is already, with his mop of hair and his protruding forehead, the appealing figure who kneels in armour in *Our Lady of Victories*. Experts have recognized other characters in this group, including a self-portrait of the artist. There are more frescoes, including one of the famous Mantuan war horses and some staghounds.

I went to see the massive summer palace of the Gonzaga called by the strange name, the Palazzo del Te, but whether from the T-shape of the avenues which lead up to it, or from the many *tigli* – linden trees – which grow there, I am unable to say. To me, the most attractive of the frescoes, which cover every inch of walls and ceilings, are six life-sized horses, two chestnuts, three greys, and a black, and the two favourites stand on each side of the fireplace with blue plumes in their head-collars. It was interesting to see this memory of the famous Gonzaga stud, and to notice that the animals had been painted in profile with the sole object of showing off their points. A difficult room to live with, and one worthy of Newmarket or the Curragh.

§ 10

Among Isabella's most lively correspondents was Francesco Chiericati, who, as papal nuncio, paid a visit to England from 1515 to 1517. The Mantuan archives contain a number of letters in which the writer describes the Court of Whitehall in the days when Henry VIII was twenty-four years of age. Those whose sad experience it is to have gained an impression of an historical period from the cinema must think of Tudor days as a time when bawdy monarchs sat down to dinner wearing velvet, satin, and ermine, and tore meat to pieces like starving savages. It is delightful to read the impressions of a cultured humanist, familiar with the highest society of the Renaissance, who found England to be not the barbaric land he had been led to expect but a country of wealth and culture, and the Court distinguished for its elegance, its love of scholarship and the graces of life. Chiericati could not sufficiently praise Henry for his statesmanship, his personal appearance, his geniality in private conversation, and his interest in learning and the arts. During a Sunday which he spent in the King's company, Henry told him that he was proud of the Mantuan horses in the royal mews. On another occasion a week's festivities were held to welcome an embassy from the Emperor Charles V, led by Count Jacques of Luxembourg. The nuncio was present at a reception where the King appeared wearing a royal robe of cloth of gold cut in the Hungarian style, while the English nobles, who wore the finest gold chains and collars the writer had ever seen, were clothed in gold brocade. In the days that followed, banquets were given to the ambassadors by the King, by Cardinal Wolsey, and by the Lord Mayor of London. One day Henry invited the ambassadors and the nuncio to dine with him privately in the Queen's apartments.

'This, I am told, is a very unusual thing,' wrote Chiericati to Isabella. 'The King himself sang and played all kinds of instruments with rare talent, and then danced, and made the Count dance, and gave him a fine horse with rich trappings, and a vest of gold brocade, worth seven hundred ducats.' The climax of the week's festivities was a tournament held in a tilt-yard described by Chiericati as 'a piazza three times as large as that of S. Pietro of Mantua, surrounded by walls, with tiers of seats occupied by thousands of spectators, with two great pavilions of cloth of gold on either side'. Henry appeared on horseback from one pavilion, wearing over his armour a surcoat of white damask, embroidered with Tudor roses in rubies and diamonds. Forty knights on white chargers followed him. Their bridles and harness were of silver. At the same moment, from the opposite pavilion rode out 'the Duke of Suforche' (Suffolk), at the head of a similar troop of knights, 'and when he met the King in single fight, we seemed to see Hector and Achilles'. After this encounter the King, removing his armour, appeared in blue velvet embroidered with golden bells, and attended by twenty-four pages in the same livery, 'rode before the Queen on a very tall white horse, prancing and leaping as it went, and when he had tired out one horse, he went back to his tent and mounted another'.

The banquet that followed in the Palace surprised Chiericati by its splendour and lavishness. Every variety of fish, meat, poultry, and game was served, and all the dishes were borne in front of the King by figures of elephants, panthers, tigers, and other animals. What delighted the nuncio were the jellies made in the shape of castles, churches, and animals. 'To sum up,' he adds, 'most illustrious Madama, here in England we find all the wealth and delights in the world. Those who call the English barbarians are themselves barbarians! Here we see magnificent costumes, rare virtues and the finest courtesy. And, best of all, here we have this invincible King, who is endowed with so many excellent virtues that he seems to me to surpass all others who wear a crown in these times. Blessed and happy is the country which is ruled by so worthy and excellent a prince! I would rather live under his mild and gentle sway than enjoy the greatest freedom under any other form of government!'

Chiericati was not the only Italian to think highly of Henry VIII. At about the same period two Venetian ambassadors, Piero Pasqualigo and Sebastiano Giustiniani, went gathering May-dew at Greenwich with Henry and Katherine of Aragon; the King, mounted on a bay Frieslander, was dressed entirely in green velvet. Pasqualigo said that he fancied himself looking at Mars. Henry spoke to the Italians and asked if Francis I, King of France, whom he had not yet met, was as tall as he was. The Italians said they were much the same height. Henry asked, 'Is he as stout?' The Italians replied no. Henry then asked, 'What sort of legs has he?' They said, 'Spare.' Whereupon the King 'opened the front of his doublet, and placing his hand on his thigh, said, "Look here! and I have also a good calf to my leg".' Pasqualigo concluded: 'His Majesty is the handsomest potentate I ever set eyes on.'

Ambassadors and nuncios, of course, move only in exalted society, and we rarely hear from them about ordinary folk. There was, however, an Italian in London when Chiericati was there who could have said quite a lot about them. He was Torrigiano, who was just finishing the bronze effigies of Henry VII and Elizabeth of York in Westminster Abbey. The sculptor had lived in London for some years (it is said, on Old London Bridge), and he must have known a good cross-section of English life from the King down to the humblest of Londoners, and he called the English 'bears'. He was, however, a quarrelsome, blustering fellow who perhaps did not bring out the best in his neighbours. As a young man he broke Michelangelo's nose during a studio row in Florence, and when he returned to that city to recruit artists to work in England, his accounts of his fights and brawls were evidently so hair-raising that even Benvenuto Cellini, himself no mean filibuster, declined to be enlisted. Nevertheless Chiericati was to leave the international aristocracy of the English Court and to plunge into the reality of Ireland; and these are, I think, the most interesting of all his letters.

He and his suite wished to make their devotions at S. Patrick's Purgatory, then, as now, a popular place of pilgrimage. They travelled north to 'Chiustra' (Chester), and after a day and a night at sea reached 'Dublino'. As they began to cross Ireland to Lough Derg, in Donegal, their adventures began, and the brilliant Renaissance Court they had left behind in London must have seemed like a glimpse of another world, as indeed it was. The Irish, wrote Chiericati, are 'clever and cunning, and very warlike, and are always quarrelling among themselves ... The men wear cloth shirts dipped in saffron from head to foot, shoes without stockings, and a grey cloak and felt hat, and are always closely shaven, excepting on the chin. The women are very white and beautiful, but dirty ... In the northern highlands the people, I hear, are still more savage; they go naked, live in caverns and eat raw meat'.

Modern Irishmen and women, in fulfilment of a vow or penance, still go on pilgrimage to Lough Derg, as I saw myself the last time I was in Donegal, in 1958. A queue of people who had come from all parts of the country was waiting for the boat to take them to the little rock of S. Patrick's Purgatory in the centre of the lake. On the way over they remove their shoes and stockings and remain barefoot for their three days on the island. Some fast for three days or eat only a little oat cake and drink weak tea. They spend the three days in prayer and in a barefoot circuit of the various shrines. Every pilgrim concludes his visit with a long period of prayer in S. Patrick's cave. This is a milder version of the routine followed by Chiericati and his friends in 1517, when pilgrims spent ten days on the island, ending with, an incarceration of twenty-four hours in the cave where extraordinary and terrifying things were to be seen. After sounding a horn and waving a white cloth on the end of a pole, the Italians managed to attract the attention of the three canons who inhabited the rock. A boat was sent over for them. On arrival, they found a little oratory, a well, and the cave in which S. Patrick is said to have slept. Chiericati did not go inside, 'fearing to see terrible things'. Two of his companions, however, entered the cave with five other pilgrims. 'I think my penance was worse than theirs,' he commented, 'as I had to wait their return almost ten days! And during that time I consumed the greater part of the victuals we had brought with us. On the day of your arrival you make your will, if you have anything to leave! Then you confess and fast on bread and water for nine days and visit the three cabins every hour, saying any number of prayers. And you have to stand in the lake, some up to the knees, others half-way up their bodies, and some up to their necks! At the end of nine days you hear mass, communicate, and are blessed and signed with holy water, and go with the cross before you to the gate of S. Patrick's well. Then you go inside and the door is closed and not opened until the next day, as you have to stay there twenty-four hours. . . . Of those who entered the cave when I was present, two saw such fearful things that one went out of his mind, and when he was questioned declared that he had been beaten violently, but by whom he did not know. Another had seen beautiful women, who invited him to eat with them, and offered him fruit and food of all sorts, and these were almost vanquished. The others saw and felt nothing but great cold, hunger and weakness, and came out half dead the next day.'

The Italians then left Lough Derg gladly enough, and returned to Dublin by way of Downpatrick where, writes Chiericati, 'I could not walk about the streets without being pursued by people, who came running out of their houses to kiss my clothes when they heard that I was the Pope's nuncio, so I was forced to stay at home. Such is the annoyance which arises from over-much religion!'

The richness of the libraries in the old duchies of Italy are unbelievable. Where else in the world would a town of forty thousand inhabitants possess a municipal library of two hundred and fifty thousand volumes, including more than a thousand and two hundred incunabula, also rare editions of the sixteenth century, a collection of early Virgils, books printed by Bodoni, including the famous *Homer* of Napoleon, and over a thousand codices, most of them on vellum and many richly illuminated. The Austrian Government of the nineteenth century must have been a good deal more honest than most to have allowed such a collection to pass intact into the possession of the Mantuan municipality. The German historian, Gregorovius, author of the great *History of the City of Rome in the Middle Ages,* found undreamt of treasures at Mantua, though he had been told by his friend, Ranke, the historian of the Papacy, that nothing new was to be discovered anywhere after the Sack of Rome. Gregorovius left Munich one bitter day in December, 1871, in eighteen degrees of frost. He sat chilled in a railway carriage, his feet on hot water tins, and, during the long journey across the Alps, his left hand became numb. When he arrived at Mantua the sky was blue, but the temperature was below freezing and the lakes and marshes were covered with ice. His sufferings were rewarded when he began to work in the archives and found letter after letter, including many from Caesar Borgia, from Castiglione, when he was Clement VII's nuncio in Madrid, and from others who were present at the Sack of Rome in 1527. 'Have never suffered from cold as I did at Mantua,' Gregorovius wrote in his diary. 'I hardly expected to leave the place alive, and it was only the joy over my discoveries in the archives that sustained my vitality.'

§ 11

The end of the Gonzaga has an unusual interest for English people since the family, when in the last stages of decline, sold its famous collection of pictures to Charles I of England. I was discussing this with an Italian friend, who asked if I had ever heard of 'the greatest scandal of the sixteenth century', which, in his opinion, was the beginning of the end of the House of Gonzaga. This is the almost unbelievable story.

The gay young Vincenzo, heir to Guglielmo, third Duke of Mantua (the same young man who killed the Admirable Crichton), was married in the year 1581 to fourteen-year-old Margharita Farnese of Parma. A wedding of the utmost magnificence was followed some days later by a rumour that a panel of doctors had certified that the bride could not become a wife without a surgical operation which they were unable to perform. The girl, who was deeply in love with her handsome young prince, was sent weeping back to Parma. Then followed two years of medico-ecclesiastical conferences which must be unique in the history even of the Vatican. Finally the Pope, one reads with some surprise, appointed the unworldly Cardinal Carlo Borromeo to be the arbiter, and he, after consulting the physicians, decided that Margharita should enter a convent. So in October, 1583, at the age of sixteen, Margharita Farnese, under the name of Sister Maura Lucenia, vanished from history, but not from life, since she lived to be nearly eighty in a world from which every person associated with her tragedy had long since departed. Her disappearance cleared the way, so far as canon law was concerned, for another marriage.

It was now proposed that Vincenzo should marry Leonora de' Medici, daughter of Francesco, Grand Duke of Tuscany, but a situation then arose which might have been devised by Congreve or Wycherley. During the nullification of Vincenzo's marriage the whole of Italy had, of course, discussed the matter and had taken sides, and many believed that the break-up of the marriage was due not to any defect in the bride but to the impotency of the prince. The Medici pretended to believe this. The Grand Duchess, who before her marriage had been the notorious Bianca Cappello and had several old scores to work off against the Duke of Mantua, insisted that before any marriage contract was drawn up Vincenzo should be asked to provide proof of his virility. If her intention was to humiliate and insult the Gonzaga, her plan failed, for both the old Duke, Guglielmo, and Vincenzo at once eagerly agreed to co-operate in the preposterous arrangement. The plan was that Vincenzo should spend a night with some young woman chosen by the Medici. The Pope indignantly objected to a mortal sin as a preliminary to a sacrament, but this had no effect on anyone concerned.

Alfonso d'Este, a close friend, offered to find a girl for the test. Living in Ferrara at that time were the widow and daughters of that neglected genius Pirro Ligorio, one of the most accomplished architects and archaeologists of the time of Pius IV. He had designed the water-gardens at Tivoli and the exquisite Villa Pia in the Vatican gardens, but he could never keep any money, and when in his sixties was glad to take the post of court antiquary to Duke Alfonso II at Ferrara. After his death his wife and family lived in poverty, and Alfonso, knowing how welcome money would be to them, approached the widow and told her of the dowry offered by the Duke of Tuscany to a suitable collaborator. However, the widow and her daughters preferred their poverty to a part in such a shameful plan. Eventually Alfonso discovered in some religious institution in Ferrara a modest and devout maiden who was willing to be dressed up and taken to a country house with four matrons and guards; there she waited with her rosary. Vincenzo arrived at Ferrara, but it was carnival time and he plunged into a whirl of dances and masquerades and showed no inclination to go through with his test. He quarrelled with those acting for the Medici, and at last left without seeing the girl, who was discreetly returned to the religious institution. The scene then moved to Venice. The Medici, exasperated by the inefficiency which had until then ruined their scheme, searched the orphanages of Florence and produced their own candidate, a good-looking young woman of twenty, named Giulia, an illegitimate daughter of good family. A new touch of the preposterous was the decision that Giulia, accompanied by the Chancellor of the Grand Duchy, should travel in disguise to Venice; and though the Chancellor was recognized in all the inns along the route, he told an elaborate story to the effect that he was taking the daughter of an old friend, a German captain, to meet her father. How the innkeepers must have laughed as the Chancellor, dressed as a private citizen, departed upon this peculiar journey! Having arrived in Venice, Giulia was installed in a palazzo belonging to the Grand Duke of Tuscany, near the Grand Canal, and while matrons looked after her and saw that she was fashionably dressed and her hair done in the latest style, the girl's first air of innocence began to change to one of expectancy.

Shortly before the 'bridegroom' was due to appear, the Medici agent who lived in the palazzo died, probably of excitement. His body was carried into the nearest church and the house set to rights. When the young prince appeared he was in a jolly, careless mood, having dined too well. Laughingly he retired for the night, while the Chancellor stood guard on the other side of the bedroom door. But after three hours the prince burst from the room doubled up with colic and was taken to his own lodgings; and it was discovered, to the sniggers of the Florentines and the dismay of the Mantuans, that the problem was still in doubt. Vincenzo returned at a later date and was so successful that the marriage contract was signed, and later in the year, 1584, he was married, amid the usual rejoicings and glittering scenes of splendour, to Leonora de' Medici. It is a strange commentary on the morals and thought of the time that though the bride was perfectly aware of the events, she evidently thought no less of her husband and fell deeply in love with his handsome face and figure and his attractive ways. They had sons and daughters, and Vincenzo, as anybody who knew him might have predicted, continued to manifest his virility in various directions until the end of his life. So ended, to our way of thinking, a shameful and, one would have thought, entirely unnecessary episode.

Time with its usual irony was to see that the name which Giulia was to bear would, in centuries to come, be better known than the mighty names of those whom her humble life had crossed. Shortly after the 'Congress of Venice', as the episode was called, she was given an ample dowry and married to a musician at the Court of Tuscany named Giulio Caccini. His passion was song-writing, and he was experimenting with his friend, Jacopo Peri, in a new form of music and declamation which developed into opera. There are doubtless students of music today who are more familiar with his name in this connection, and as the compiler of a collection of songs which he called *Le nuove musiche*, than they are with the names of Medici and Gonzaga.

The Gonzaga decline set in with the three sons of Vincenzo and Leonora, who succeeded each other as Dukes of Mantua, and with whom the Mantuan dynasty came to an end. First came Francesco, who succeeded in 1613, a young man of twenty-seven with an infant son, but within ten months of his accession both died of smallpox. The next male heir was Cardinal Ferdinand, who, hearing of his brother's death, posted to Mantua and took over the Government. He renounced his Cardinal's hat, and is remembered today only by numismatists for his splendid large gold coin, which fetches about £600 in auctions when it comes up, and is known as the 'eight doppia piece'. He struck the coin to celebrate his accession, and it shows him in biretta and ducal chain, looking much older than his twenty-six years. He was succeeded by his brother, Vincenzo II, and just as the lives of the early Gonzaga each made its contribution to the fame and grandeur of the family, so those of the last two undermined its fall.

Both were married to women whom they repudiated. Ferdinand married a young girl of fifteen named Camilla, and Vincenzo married a widow many years his senior and already the mother of seven sons. Ferdinand locked away his young wife and destroyed proof of the marriage in order to make what he considered a profitable political union with Catherine de' Medici, sister of Cosimo II. In doing so, he disinherited a fine young boy, his son by Camilla, who possibly might have saved the fortunes of the Gonzaga. His marriage with Catherine turned out to be both miserable and childless. Ferdinand sank down entangled in the self-made nets of his deceit and dishonesty, while his Duchess lived in jealous fear of her cast-off rival and her son. This grim situation ended only when Ferdinand died, an old man at thirty-nine. Vincenzo II followed Ferdinand and reigned for only a year, twelve gruesome months which might have been a continuation of his brother's life. Instead of a miserable young woman, the background to his woes was an enraged old one, for his Duchess, furious at having at one time been publicly defamed and charged with sorcery, gave him little consolation. He attempted to forget the chaos of his affairs, and his mounting debts, by planning extravagant masquerades, and in hiring comedians, and in that strange obsession of the Gonzaga, dwarfs. How macabre, considering the physical deformity which haunted the family, was the infatuation of the last Mantuan duke for a female dwarf named Crestina.

Vincenzo was the duke who sold a great part of the famous Mantuan art collection to Charles I of England. The intermediary was the first of the gentlemanly art dealers, a skilful person named Daniel Nys, who bought pictures by Mantegna, Titian, Correggio, Raphael, Michelangelo, Andrea del Sarto, Tintoretto, and various other works, for £10,500. Even this sum Charles I found difficult to raise in 1627, for he was as pressed for money as the Duke of Mantua. However, it was somehow found, and the masterpieces joined the marvellous collection in Whitehall Palace made by the only royal virtuoso in English history. The collection included all the pictures inherited by the Crown from the Plantagenet and the Tudor kings. What a national treasure this collection would have been had the Puritans, after burning all superstitious images and representations of saints and the Blessed Virgin, not sold it by public auction and so dispersed it throughout the world.

For nearly thirty years the eyes of France and Spain had been fixed with greedy interest upon the empty cradles of Mantua. International rivalry and family feuds were both concerned with the delightful possibility that the rich dukedom with its valuable art treasures would soon be vacant. The Gonzaga had intermarried with many of the royal and noble families of Europe, all of whom were interested in the problem of the Mantuan succession, and their ambassadors and spies created a fog of intrigue in the Mantuan palace. Spain and Austria, jealous of France, backed one candidate; France supported a cadet member of the house, the Prince of Nevers and Rethel. While the conspirators plotted, the sickly Duke drifted through the last months of his life, eagerly sending for Oriental pearls, which he bought by the pound to crush in his potions, playing with his dwarfs, and devising new comedies and consulting his astrologers, as if, poor man, there could be a single star left in his favour. As he lay on his death-bed, a young girl was hurried out of a convent in the middle of the night and married to Carlo, Prince of Nevers. She was Maria Gonzaga, Vincenzo's niece and the daughter of the brother who had died of smallpox fifteen years previously. So the French branch of the family assumed the Dukedom as the last Duke of the Mantuan line expired, aged thirty, of a complication of diseases called dropsy and 'cancrena'. With the victory of the French candidate, the Spanish and Austrian armies prepared to move, and the end of the Mantuan dukes brought with it the sack of Mantua, a savage event whose marks can still be seen upon the walls of its great palace.

§ 12

About four miles from Mantua upon the western edge of the lagoons I came to a church that has been accumulating a strange collection of ex-votos for many centuries. It is the Sanctuary of the Madonna delle Grazie. She is celebrated for her compassionate interest in the misfortunes of humanity and for her willingness to extend a helping hand from time to time. The church is in itself a votive offering, having been built by Francesco Gonzaga in 1399 in gratitude to Our Lady for having saved Mantua from the plague. It was enlarged in slightly later times and has now become one of the most popular pilgrimage shrines of Northern Italy. As soon as I stepped inside, I glanced with surprise at a scene which bore a strong resemblance to Madame Tussaud's. A dignified Renaissance building without an aisle had been swamped by exotic decoration and by the construction of two tiers of opera-like boxes on both sides of the church, each box occupied by a life-sized waxwork figure. The effigies were clothed in the dusty garments of centuries ago. There were men and women whose agonized or devout expressions and attitudes saved them from the appearance of attending a theatre. The priest, who took my remarks in good part, told me that in the sixteenth century, when the church was occupied by the Franciscans, a certain Brother Francesco d'Aquanegra, who had a talent for making waxwork figures, was given a free hand to represent some of the distinguished recipients of the divine compassion.

Fortunately the friar's zeal stopped short at the mortuary chapels where, among various Gonzaga, I found the tomb of that celebrated Renaissance writer, diplomat and gentleman, Baldassare Castiglione. He belongs to that select company whose immortality rests upon one book and, though I knew he had died in Spain, I had no idea he was buried in Italy.

The priest offered to show me some votive offerings which are unique. He led the way into a corridor which was hung with some fascinating catastrophes in oil and water colour, but he hurried me on. They were nothing compared with what he was about to show me! So, with a hasty glance at the terrible accidents and near death-bed scenes, neatly framed and bearing the letters P.G.R. (*Pro Gratia Recepta* or perhaps *Per Grazia Ricevuta*), we entered an old and abandoned Franciscan monastery in whose gaunt halls the priest had contrived a spartan little flat. Opening the door of a long gallery, he waved his hand towards seventeen suits of armour.

He told me that until about twenty years ago, seventeen wax figures clothed in armour had been one of the chief features of the church. The armour had belonged to members of the House of Gonzaga, who had given them, *Pro Gratia Recepta*, on their safe return from battle. At the same time there was another story that the armour, together with the dummies inside, was the work of the industrious Brother d'Aquanegra. So matters rested until 1929, when an Englishman visited Mantua and proved the suits to be genuine and of great interest. The priest hurried away and returned with two reprints from *Archaeologia*. The visiting Englishman was Sir James Mann, then Master of the Armouries of the Tower of London and Keeper of the Wallace Collection. I smiled to think how little escapes the expert.

Shortly before his recent death, I asked Sir James to tell me how he had come to hear of the armour. He said that when he was in Florence in 1926, the Baron de Cosson showed him a photograph of the church and its wax figures and mentioned a legend which said that some of the armour had come from the battlefield of Marignano, in 1515. Three years later Sir James went to Mantua and, though the local people told him that the armour was made of *papier-mâché*, managed to borrow a ladder in the village and satisfied himself that it was not. In 1930 he read a paper to the Society of Antiquaries, based on the notes he had made from the top of the ladder, and this eventually came to the notice of the Bishop of Mantua. He became interested and had one of the suits taken out and scraped. Beneath layers of paint various armourer's marks were discovered, and in 1937, at the invitation of the Bishop, Sir James went to Mantua and supervised the dismounting of the seventeen armoured knights. The appearance of the ragged regiment was fantastic as they were lined up against a wall, still wearing wooden plumes in their helmets and grasping swords, each figure thick with the filth of centuries. A fire was made in the yard of the monastery and the armour was boiled in a huge cauldron. This, said Sir James, is the proper way to remove stiff coatings of old paint, for it avoids all risk of the scratching and erosion which have ruined armour in many collections when over-cleaned with acid. The armour is the largest collection of mortuary or ex-voto armour in existence, the gifts of Gonzaga who had returned safely from battle. One of the breastplates, which had a large dent in it, was accompanied by an inscription which stated that the owner had been struck by a cannon-ball, but that his life had been preserved by the Madonna delle Grazie.

I never realized until I read Sir James Mann's account of the armour that a breastplate has as high a survival value as a pair of legs has a low one. The breastplate is a decorative object and can be hung on any wall, but a pair of legs demands a life-sized figure, and consequently they become separated from the rest of the armour and are lost. The survival of six sets of leg armour of the fifteenth century is therefore something to make the expert's eye glisten. It is, I think, a pity that the armour, having led such a public existence for about five centuries, should now be hidden away in a back room of the monastery. The right place for it is a hall in the Reggia, where the Gonzaga originally clanked about in it, no doubt admiring their well-turned steel calves before kissing their wives and riding to war.

§ 13

The guide books call Sabbioneta a 'ghost city', or a 'Renaissance Pompeii' and, having been there, I cannot imagine how it managed to escape the attention of the English romantics: it has everything they liked: a touch of the macabre and the right amount of sin and aristocratic melancholy. Shelley, Byron, and Browning would all have found inspiration there, and, earlier still, Walpole might have discerned in its deserted streets, and the story of its unhappy duke, the perfect sequel to *The Castle of Otranto*.

I left Mantua early one morning and travelling across a placid landscape came after twenty miles or so to a walled town standing among fields of sugar-beet, maize, vines, and mulberries. A stone bridge spanned a dry moat and led to a fine classical gate on which I read the name 'Vespasiano Dux', and the date 1579. Except for one small section, which might be measured in yards, the circuit of the walls is complete. And they are unusual walls. The town of Sabbioneta lies within an enormous star-shaped fortress of the late sixteenth century, the five points of its bastions thrusting mighty stone wedges into the vineyards. During the ten minutes or so that I stayed there no cart, wagon, or car passed in or out of the splendid gateway. Neither could I hear the noises of a town beyond the wall. I crossed the bridge and entered the most impressive exercise in architecture I have ever seen. The ideal of the Renaissance, as rectangular in its lay-out as New York, lay there in fine streets, colonnades, palaces, squares, and churches; and there was hardly a soul to be seen. I looked round at the palaces which surround the chief piazza, and saw only a woman draping some bedding on an aristocratic balcony, and a cat asleep under an arcade. The silence of this miniature city was profound, and I thought how strange it was in these days to be the only visitor in an Italian town. I mounted the steps of the ducal palace, now the town hall, but found the building locked. While I waited for someone to appear, I sat contentedly on the ducal terrace and recalled all I knew of this place and its builder.

His name was Vespasiano Gonzaga, a member of the younger branch of the family. He was born in 1531, and when fifteen years of age was sent to be educated in Madrid at the Court of the King of Spain. Years later, when a commander in the Spanish army, he fell in love with and married Diana di Cordona, with whom he returned to Italy. In those days Sabbioneta consisted of an ancient castle rising above a stagnant moat with a few cottages clustering round it. As he surveyed this gloomy scene, Vespasiano resolved to build the ideal city, a place where artists and writers could live in close collaboration with the perfect patron. Italian princes had been building and rebuilding for a hundred years, but no one had ever tackled a completely new city. He drew up his first plans, but was then called away to take command of Spanish troops in various parts of Europe. Upon his return he discovered that his wife had been unfaithful and, like a true Italian, he murdered her and her lover. The popular belief, though unsupported by anything more than his temperament, is that he locked the unhappy woman in a room with the corpse of her lover and appeared daily holding a glass of poisoned wine, saying only one word, *bevi* – 'drink'. At the end of three days it is said Diana seized the cup and drained it. It is, however, a fact that, when describing her death to a relative, Vespasiano remarked, 'God called my wife suddenly to Himself before she could utter a word.'

He went off to Spain to forget his tragedy and there he met and married Doña Aña de Aragon, a connection of Philip II. They had a daughter, and then a son, for whose birthday celebrations they returned to Sabbioneta, then rising in all its Vitruvian splendour behind the scaffolding. The classical obsession seems to have been more violent for having struck so late in history, since, as part of the celebrations, jesters dressed as pagan priests led garlanded oxen crowned with ivy and myrtle into the main square. Here the animals were 'sacrificed', and the population enjoyed a gigantic feast. In three years time tragedy struck again. Vespasiano's second wife became a hopeless melancholic and went away to live in solitude, refusing to see her husband or her two young children, and in a year or so she died. Once again he returned to Spain, where Philip II appointed him Viceroy of Navarre, then of Valencia. Here his passion for building took a military turn and inspired the fortifications of Cartagena and the massive bastions, similar to those at Sabbioneta, which still surround Pamplona.

At the age of forty-seven Vespasiano retired to Sabbioneta to live. The town was then almost complete and the peasants from the surrounding countryside had been rounded up and forced to live there, which annoyed them exceedingly, for they had no interest in architraves and pilasters, and, it might be said, had already had enough of the ancient world in their habits and fairy-tales. With the Virgilian ox-carts rumbling in at the gates every evening, the architect's dream seemed now to be a reality. Then tragedy struck for the third time. Vespasiano's son and heir, Luigi, was now fifteen. One day, while out riding, father and son met, and Vespasiano rebuked the lad for failing to greet him with respect. Luigi became rude and his father aimed a kick which, catching the boy in the groin, developed into an injury from which he died. Vespasiano continued to forget his mounting sorrows in architecture, and more buildings were added to his town. He married a third time and fate, as far as one knows, held its hand. Philip II thought so highly of Vespasiano that he awarded him the 'Golden Fleece'. His last years were spent on ladders and scaffolding, with architects, painters, printers, and the designers of his coinage. At the age of sixty he endured a trepanning operation and one day, sitting up in bed, remarked, 'I am cured'; and fell back dead.

While I was thinking about Vespasiano, an old man emerged from one of the side streets and passed below me on the pavement. In answer to my appeal, he mounted the steps and began to bang on the door of the town hall with his closed fist. Eventually there was a shuffle on the other side as of the approach of a venerable elephant, and the door was opened an inch by an old man wearing carpet slippers. As he peered at us, first in bewilderment and then with pleasure, he had the air of some aged servitor who had long given up hope that his lord would ever return. We entered and, ascending a worn marble staircase, came to a depressing scene. Vespasiano's splendid palace with its gilded ceilings has been split up by thin partitions and doors of fumed oak into offices for the municipality. Medallions depicting the lords of Sabbioneta and their wives gaze down upon notices about electricity and the payment of rates. In one of the main halls stand four superb life-sized statues in wood, still partly coloured and gilded, of the Sabbonieta dukes in armour upon their war-horses. They ride forward proudly, baton in hand, as if the chatter of the Olivettis were the applause of their people. Once there were twenty of these horsemen, and the four survivors are, Ludovico II, the Gonzaga of the *Camera degli Sposi* frescoes, and his son, Gian-francesco, the founder of the Sabbioneta branch; Luigi, who is remembered for having helped Clement VII to escape in disguise during the Sack of Rome, and Vespasiano, the builder of Sab-bioneta. I thought the four horsemen magnificent, seated upon chargers which must have been sired by those ridden by Colleoni in Venice and Gattamelata in Padua. These splendid Gonzaga stallions, prancing proudly forward with uplifted forelegs, are among the less known treasures of Lombardy. I was told by an official in the secretariat that they are said to have been carved by a Venetian sculptor in the style of Lorenzo Bregno. Glancing out of a window of the palace into the ducal garden, I saw the melon-shaped bowl of a dead fountain rising from a tangle of weeds and bushes. An old man was sitting in the sun; a woman was putting out washing; a dog was scratching in the dust. This is all that is left of the enclosed garden where Hamlet-like Vespasiano once cultivated his genius for melancholy.

I was asked if I would like to see Scamozzi's theatre, one of the most interesting sights in Sabbonieta. Led by the old man, I explored the streets of the town. Clever little vistas had been contrived so that the eye should not be wearied, and I could imagine Vespasiano saying to his architects, 'perhaps a church at the end of this street'. The theatre, named like its parent at Vicenza, the *Teatro Olimpico*, is at the corner of the Via Vespasiano Gonzaga and the Via del Teatro, which leads back into the main square. We found the keys and entered a scene of some confusion. Builders were reconstructing the stage and the proscenium, and that part of the building was piled with bricks, sand, cement, and scaffolds: but the glorious little auditorium is more or less intact; and it is a gem. Above what one might call the orchestra stalls, which could seat about a hundred on five semi-circular tiers of what are now hard wooden benches, rises a screen of twelve Corinthian columns supporting an entablature upon which are mounted twelve gods and goddesses. The columns follow the curve of the auditorium and are linked by a balustrade, and the wall behind is covered with a number of charming frescoes. We see Roman emperors in classical niches, and above them is a terrace where stand courtiers, wearing what we should call Elizabethan or Jacobean costume. The audience, which I noticed includes an intent and critical dog, has been watching the stage with courtly smiles for some three and a half centuries.

This beautiful little theatre is a contrast to the famous Palladian theatre at Vicenza, where the interest is entirely on the stage with its astonishing perspectives. Here the interest is in the auditorium, and I wondered whether a private ducal theatre of this period is to be seen anywhere else in such fine condition. I felt close to the mysterious inhabitants of this make-believe audience and fancied them in their brocades, pearls, and starched ruffs, accompanying their Duke to the little playhouse to laugh and chatter beneath the Corinthian columns, pretending that they did not know each other as well as the members of a small garrison town always do. The old man knew nothing of the history of the building, though he did remember having seen a play there many years ago before the stage collapsed. I was able to find out little about the theatre save that it was the last of Vespasiano's contributions to his town. As soon as Scamozzi had finished the *Teatro Olimpico* at Vicenza, after the death of Palladio, which took place while the building was still incomplete, he went to Sabbioneta at the request of the Duke and began the theatre in 1588, finishing it two years later.

My guide took me to the other ducal palace, a sight which deepens the air of fantasy, the Palazzo del Giardino, still within the fortifications and only a few minutes walk from the main piazza. Here Vespasiano housed his collection of Greek and Roman antiquities in a long gallery with a beautifully built red-brick exterior supported on arches. The wall still holds, as indeed most of the walls in Sabbioneta do, the iron brackets or funnels for torches. The palace inside has been a good deal knocked about, but the ceilings are magnificent, and the frescoes and panels form several hundred square yards of allegory. Here Daphne, with her nightdress blowing round her neck, is turning into a tree, there Icarus is making his disastrous landing, and not far away Phaethon, having parted company with his steeds, is obeying the force of gravity. There is a charming little *saletta* devoted to the Æneid: we see the Laocoön, the Trojan Horse, the flight of Anchises, and various other episodes. And there is not a sound in the whole palace, save the banging of a door or the fluttering of a bird which has found its way in through a broken window pane. This sophisticated building was erected in 1584, a time when, in England, Elizabeth had been on the throne for twenty-six years, when Mary Stuart was still alive, when the Armada was four years away, and when Shakespeare, aged twenty, had not been heard of. A building of this elegance and style was not to be seen in England for another fifty years, when Inigo Jones built the banqueting hall of Whitehall Palace. The English countryside saw nothing like it until the eighteenth century, in the age of Burlington and Kent.

We came at length to the Church of the Incoronata and to what is the finest thing to be seen in Sabbioneta, the tomb of its founder. Vespasiano's remains rest in a sarcophagus of veined marble beneath a classical niche. His right hand is outstretched in what is perhaps intended to be a gesture of command, but no general ever commanded with an expression of such sorrow and compassion. It is the same expression of habitual melancholy seen on the face of the mounted statue in the ducal palace. His sorrowful face turns the gesture into one of commiseration, as if reprieving some poor sinner. No one, facing this unhappy, benevolent image, could believe Vespasiano to be other than a victim of fate.

Here is a town founded on its owner's melancholy. 'My only amusement,' he once said to a friend, 'is to raise new walls and to give life to material work in contrast to my empty soul.' And what is there so familiar in that gloomy pose, the weary line of the head with its crisp curls: of course, Byron. It is extraordinary that the poet should never, so far as I know, have found this other nobleman whose brooding air of melancholy was so like his conception of himself.

I said farewell to the old man and returned to Mantua in the twilight. I awakened in the night and found myself thinking of Sabbioneta and its strange founder. I imagined him riding forward so proudly and so pathetically in the darkness of the old palace; and I thought of him seated in the church, making in the darkness that sad gesture of forbearance.

§ 14

The Virgilian landscape stretched northward to Garda in the profound hush of a Sunday morning. There was not a sign of those who had dug, irrigated, and pruned this landscape into shape, had polled the willows and made the dykes and planted the windbreaks: and, as in Lincolnshire and Suffolk, I heard church bells ringing across the flat country long before I came to town or village.

Virgil mentions the 'marriage' of vine and elm, and one might well wonder what he meant had one not seen this unlikely union in the Mantuan countryside. Having lived in a wine-producing country and having owned a vineyard, I found the system peculiar, yet practical and obviously archaic. It is to plant at regular intervals dwarf elms and other trees which will not take too much out of the soil, and allow the vines to climb them in such a way that the runners can be festooned from tree to tree. This gives the land an air of gaiety as if garlanded pages were advancing at some festival or tournament. In summer the draped vines lend the land a characteristic and unusual appearance, and it is strange that this system of Roman viticulture should have survived all the changes and invasions of Lombardy, suggesting maybe that the Roman farmer remained on his land and continued to prune and festoon his vines as his ancestors had done in the days of Virgil. Apart from the fact that many of the farmers are now Communists, perhaps Virgil would recognize them and their methods as survivals of the Augustan age.

As I approached the little town of Rovabella, which is surrounded by peach and pear orchards, a traffic policeman stopped me, but his bows and smiles immediately set at rest any anxiety I might have felt. He pointed to a notice in English, French, and German, which called upon all foreign travellers to stop and accept, during Rovabella's peach week, a basket of peaches with the compliments of the town. The main street was *en fête*; girls were running about to a number of halted cars with baskets of peaches, and one pretty young woman came to me and, in the most charming way, handed me a basket of fruit. When she realized that I was English, she asked me to stay and, going over to a fruit stall which had been erected at the cross-roads, returned with a little girl of about ten, who told me her name was Hazel and that she came from Leytonstone. She was the child of an English soldier and an Italian mother, and she was spending a holiday with her grandparents. That Hazel should have met someone who knew Leytonstone, and had even been there, struck these jolly Rovabellans as delightful, with the result that I was introduced to Hazel's grandmother, who introduced me to the chief of police, who introduced me to the *sindaco*, or mayor, who invited me to have a drink in the town hall.

Round a table littered with glasses stood the fruit growers and the peasant farmers of the district, toasting each other in vermouth and in Campari Soda. They were the modern equivalent of those Roman shepherds, agriculturists, and bee-keepers who passed hesitantly but relentlessly across one's youthful horizon. They were wearing the dark suits worn at weddings, funerals, and high mass on saints' days; country and town are side by side in the Po Valley and there is little, save perhaps an extra touch of sunburn, to distinguish the farmer from the townsman. I thought how different they were from a similar gathering of vine and olive men in out of the way places in Spain, such as Martos or Jaen, where upon occasions such as this one might fancy oneself back in the Middle Ages.

I spoke to some farmers who were exchanging reminiscences of the past winter and its rigours like veterans at a regimental reunion. One of them turned to me and explained that those who came to Italy in the summer (presumably people like myself) had no idea what the Italians had to endure in the winter. I listened sympathetically to their stories of every kind of climatic disaster: floods, snow, egg-sized hailstones, sudden frosts just when the peach blossom was setting, and, as for the vines, they talked like doctors who had managed to bring a patient back from the brink of death. Then we spoke of blight, pests, and sprays. It crossed my mind that this was a picture of the Mantuan scene very different from that of the *Georgics*; indeed the Virgilian vines appear to have been free from Phylloxera and from Guignardia Bidwellii, which turns the grapes into little black nuts, and from a hundred other woes of today. It is difficult to imagine Tityrus with a sulphur spray. One receives an impression from the *Georgics* that Nature in those days was in an unrecognizably benevolent mood; that cows and bees were eager to increase the milk and honey yields, and that agricultural life was really a long, happy holiday in the country. It was fascinating to listen to the stories of the descendants of Tityrus who were waging an endless war against mildew, fungus, and insects.

The mayor led the way to a packing-shed in which a number of haughty-looking dark-eyed girls with their mothers, old and wrinkled at forty, and their grandmothers, were busily grading and packing the fruit, which was then placed in chilled railway vans and consigned to Germany. I bade my host good-bye and was soon on my way to Sirmione.

The Mincio, which I hoped to see, was hidden among side roads and well groomed vineyards, and it was not until I came to Valeggio that I saw it as Milton did, 'smooth-sliding' and ice-green. I crossed the river by a fine old bridge and came to a delightful and welcome scene. A number of dining-tables, the cloths secured from the wind by stones from the bed of the Mincio, were set out beside a river wall and in the shade of lime trees. The boundaries of the little restaurant were prettily limited by tubs of hibiscus, oleanders, and hydrangeas. In the background stood an experienced old building in which one would guess many a plot had been conceived centuries ago, and many a strange guest received after dark. On this bright Sunday, however, the Locanda Mincio, as the inn is called, was loud with feminine chatter and argument, and from its open door shot from time to time young women in black dresses and aprons bearing steaming dishes, as if expelled from a stormy session of some female parliament. Beneath the lime trees sat the usual pleasant Italian Sunday morning crowd, neatly and decently dressed, the children in their Sunday clothes, the girls in pretty frocks, the boys in sailor suits. A prestige Pekinese caused amusement as it pranced about putting larger dogs to flight. Now and again the popping of a Vespa or Lambretta would announce the arrival of a young man and his pillion maiden; and I thought of the freedom this invention has bestowed upon the lives of young Italians, and how they ride these machines at the gallop as if they were horses.

I ordered grilled trout. While it was being cooked, I sat in the shade and looked beyond into the white glare of heat across the Mincio to the hilly vineyards opposite, where now and again a neat electric train would slide incongruously, and as smoothly as the river, on its way to Mantua. To my amazement, for the noon sun was brilliant and the water clear as glass, a fisherman appeared upon the opposite bank and began to cast, and, again to my astonishment, no sooner had he cast than he hooked and landed what looked remarkably like a half-pound trout. He did this six or seven times in as many minutes like someone fishing in a shoal of mackerel. The waitress told me the fish were *cavazzini* and were easily caught with bread.

Continuing my journey, I passed through idyllic country, the Mincio again invisible in woodland on my left, until I came to the southern end of Lake Garda, where I saw the river leaving the lake on its meandering journey to Mantua and the Po. It was here, near the town of Peschiera, that one of the most dramatic and important meetings in history is said to have taken place. In A.D. 452 Attila and his Huns, having wiped out the city of Aquileia (many of whose inhabitants fled to the lagoons and founded Venice), were camped on the Mincio, contemplating the sack of Rome. The cowardly panic of forty-two years previously, when Alaric and the Goths had sacked the city, was repeated, and Leo I was persuaded to head an embassy to the barbarian. The King of the Huns was an arrogant, bullying savage and, in appearance, small, broad-shouldered, with a flat Mongol nose and a thin wispy beard. It is said that he trod the earth proudly and haughtily as if he owned it. What Leo said to him will never be known and that the 'Scourge of God' should have turned away from Rome is one of the mysteries of history. We may assume that Leo reminded him of the fate of Alaric, who, only a few weeks after his sack of Rome in 410, unexpectedly and mysteriously died.

I had always imagined the site of the famous interview to have been a sombre blend of forest and mountain, but it is a peaceful scene of great beauty. The pale, clear river, rushing out of the southern extremity of the lake, carves its way through hills and vineyards. Near by lies Garda, calm and blue as I saw it on this windless summer afternoon, with the mountains around it rising to the mighty summits of the Austrian Alps. In such a sylvan paradise it was not particularly easy to imagine the wiry little Huns watering their shaggy ponies, or to think of the stately figure of S. Leo and his white-robed Roman emissaries approaching the tent of the barbarian.

Sirmione is a thin strip of land that protrudes into Lake Garda under the dead eyes of a superb castle built by the Veronese Scaligeri in the Middle Ages. In summer the slender peninsula receives whatever winds may blow and enjoys the coolness of water on each side of it; in winter there must be days when it is almost unhabitable. As I saw it on a hot Sunday afternoon, the hotels and bathing-beaches were crowded and young women in bikinis, and wearing large straw hats, lay or strolled upon the beaches and in the shady pinewoods near the shore, lending to the place the air of one of those allegorical paintings so prized during the Renaissance.

This summer calm was no doubt the lake as Catullus preferred it, and as Tennyson saw it, rippling with 'Lydian laughter', its banks 'olive silvery' in the sunlight. The villa of Catullus is a huge, incoherent mass of Roman masonry, of broken-down arches and roofless halls, in a fine situation overlooking the lake, but it is unlikely to have been what it claims to be. It is not old enough. The tradition, however, which associates the poet with this part of the lake is sound, and it must have been somewhere near at hand that he retired with the yacht which he had bought in Asia Minor, and in which he made a Byronic voyage home through the isles of Greece. The old caretaker of the villa of Catullus was indignant when I suggested that the ruins might be those of a large Roman hydropathic hotel: to him, and to everyone at Sirmione for centuries, it has been the villa of Catullus and to suggest anything else is heresy.

A boatman waved to me and I descended from the ruins to the rocks at the water's edge. He thrust forward a brown hand and helped me aboard. I sat in the welcome shade of a striped umbrella as he started up the little outboard motor, and we chugged across the lake while he told me stories which I suppose have circulated for centuries: that a sunken city is to be seen beneath the water and that Garda never gives up its dead. I made some remarks about the calmness of the water. He shrugged and said that I should see Garda during a winter's gale when a bitter wind is being funnelled through the gorges.

'*Fluctibus et fremitu . . .*' I said.

He looked a bit puzzled, but, with the willingness of the Italian to agree, he said '*Sì, sì,*' and rolled a cigarette in brown fingers.

CHAPTER FIVE

*The Via Emilia – Parma and Marie Louise – Parmesan and Parma
Ham – The Etruscan Liver of Piacenza – Where Verdi was Born –
A Visit to the Composer's Country House – The Este Archives at
Modena – Mary of Modena – Bologna – The Law Schools of the
Middle Ages – Undergraduates of the Renaissance – Women Professors –
The Stuarts in Bologna*

§ 1

A few miles south of Sabbioneta, at a town called Casal-
maggiore, the river Po sweeps round in a broad curve
with sand-bars in its brown waters. As I crossed the
bridge to the south bank, I said good-bye to beautiful Lombardy
and wondered what I should find in the region of Emilia which
lay ahead.

In shape, this region is a long, narrow wedge between Lombardy
and Venetia on the north, and Tuscany on the south, and it takes
its name from the consular road built nearly two hundred years
before Christ by M. Aemilius Lepidus, which runs for a hundred
and fifty miles from Rimini, on the Adriatic, to the Po at Piacenza.
This Roman road is still the backbone of the region; there is
hardly a bend in it, and it stretches on mile after mile like some
modern speedway. With the exception of Ravenna and Ferrara,
all the provincial towns are to be found along the Via Emilia.
Bologna, the first university town of Europe and the gastronomic
capital of Italy, is also the capital of the region. There are seven
other provinces: Ferrara, Forli, Modena, Parma, Piacenza, Ravenna, and Reggio Emilia. Three of these, Ravenna, Forli, and
Imola, form a sub-region known as the Romagna, one of the
most interesting place names in Italy. It perpetuates the Romans
of the Byzantine Exarchate.

Emilia is part plain and part hill-country: the plain is the southern valley of the Po and the hills are the northerly heights and spurs of the Apennines. Like most parts of northern Italy, Emilia can be bitterly cold in winter and ferociously hot in summer. The farmers are accustomed to fighting heat and floods, and I was soon to learn that they are a tough, bronzed race who can switch into dialect and baffle even an Italian from other regions.

The story of Emilia is a confused one: it is that of a group of rival mediaeval Communes which changed into duchies, some of which have survived into modern times and others which became incorporated in the States of the Church. I looked forward to seeing Ferrara, where the Estensi ruled for centuries, and, above all, Ravenna, where the last Western emperor abdicated, and Modena, which gave a queen to England, and Parma, famous for hams and violets. As I went on, I thought what a pretty word Emilia is, and how long it is since I have heard of a girl called Emilia or Emily. It was Boccaccio who popularized 'Emilia' and Chaucer who altered it to 'Emily' or 'Emelye', but the name seems to have been out of fashion since the last century, or perhaps I have just had bad luck.

I arrived in Parma as it was growing dark. I had an impression of crowded streets, lots of Lambrettas and buzz bicycles, of noble towers lifted against the last of the sunset, and a hotel facing a river embankment. While I was contemplating my bedroom, and a minute green bathroom designed for a dwarf, the telephone rang and the concierge, in whose voice I detected a note of reverence, said that Dr Borri was in the lounge. I did not then know that Dr Borri is, to all intents and purposes, Parma. By profession a banker, by inclination and opportunity a connoisseur and a gourmet, he is one of those already much employed people who nevertheless find time to be the president of innumerable societies and to be aware of everything that happens in the town. Multiply him by ten or twenty thousand and you begin to understand the intense municipal rivalries of mediaeval Italy.

I saw a small man filled with vitality and enthusiasm, of indeterminate middle age, yet young as all enthusiasts are. Having exhausted various minor topics of conversation, he looked at his watch and suggested that we might dine together. We took our seats in a chauffeur-driven car which left Parma and sped along the autostrada. To be whirled off, during one's first moments in a town one has never seen, is disconcerting: everything seems dream-like and there are no landmarks.

Dr Borri, politely brushing aside my reminiscences of Lombardy, briskly brought me face to face with the beauties and characteristics of the region which he is convinced is the finest in Italy – his own. And I thought how difficult it is for anyone to understand Italy unless he is sensitive to these regional and even provincial differences, which are more sharply defined and more numerous in the north than elsewhere. Stendhal was well aware of them and said they took the form, in his opinion, of unabated loathing of one town for another and of the mistrust of one individual for the next; and, writing a good half century before the political unity of the country, he thought the most powerful influence upon Italy was a legacy of hatred lingering on from the Middle Ages. It would be interesting to know what he would have said could he have seen the mellowing of this fierce emotion into the determined local patriotism expressed by Dr Borri.

Glancing from the window, I saw that we were approaching a hillside scattered with lights, and the road led upward into the most northerly foothills of the Ligurian Apennines. Passing through the lively looking spa of Salsomaggiore, noting the rococo Thermæ, we drove through a garden and drew up at what was evidently a country club. A saxophone, lowing softly as a bereaved cow, was playing the insinuating melodies of yesterday, while a few couples in the rigid embrace of the 'thirties moved almost imperceptibly across a darkened floor.

We began dinner with Parma ham, of which there are many grades. The local epicure would not eat with much pleasure the Parma ham one buys in Soho, though it has always seemed delicious to me, neither would he view without suspicion the ham so popular in Rome in the summer and eaten with figs or melon. The only ham which satisfies his palate, I was told, must be grown

and fed round Langhirano – *capitale del prosciutto* – upon the hills
that rise above the river Parma; and, having been cured, it should
be selected by an expert and slices, thin as pink tissue paper, cut
from the centre and served with pats of butter but no bread. Such
a ham was produced for us on a trolley, to prove, once again, the
enormous difference between the good and the best. A special
Parmesan dish of *cappelletti* followed, and was served again with
butter. With this we drank the dry, sparkling Lambrusco, one of
the most distinguished wines of the province. Amid a great con-
flagration, peaches were then served in brandy and kirsch, and
with ice-cream.

Dr Borri asked what reaction the word 'Parma' roused in my
mind. I said violets, ham, cheese, Correggio, Stendhal, and
Napoleon's second wife. I recollected that when I was a young
man the cry 'Parma vi'lets, lidy, pennyabunch!' was heard every
day at the Eros Fountain in Piccadilly from a group of flower
'girls' (some were grandmothers) who, in their knitted shawls and
straw hats, were, in their own London way, a sight as picturesque
and charming as the flower sellers at the foot of the Spanish Steps.
But officials drove them off before the last war, and made way,
upon the steps of the fountain, for the dreariest-looking crowd to
be seen in Europe. My host was particularly pleased that I should
have remembered Marie Louise. He said that the making of scent
from Parma violets was a cottage industry in her time – 1815 – and
she it was who made it a commercial business. The Parma violet,
however, is not to be found there now, and visitors who expect to see fields of violets are disappointed, though many of the
more costly scents sold by Roman *couturiers* are distilled in
Parma. Another thing which visitors ask to see is the Chartreuse,
or Charterhouse, of Stendhal's novel, which, of course, never
existed.

From Renaissance times, Parma has a comparatively simple
history. Paul III, an outstanding example of the bracing effect of
S. Peter's Chair upon an apparently expiring invalid, annexed it
to the States of the Church, together with Piacenza, which he
formed into a duchy for his cruel and detested son, Pierluigi
Farnese. Titian's well-known portrait of the white-bearded old

Pope, frail, bent almost double, listening to the oily remarks of one of his equally disliked grandsons, is a revealing glimpse. It was painted a few years before Luigi was murdered in Piacenza, and the young man who is bending forward, a plausible, untrustworthy-looking fellow, is Pierluigi's son. This celebrated family, which rose to fame with the lover of Alexander VI, the *bellissima*, Julia Farnese, upon whose naked limbs in S. Peter's Bernini was ordered to fit a metal chemise (which is still there, but is detachable), held Parma until 1731. The duchy then passed to Spain and Austria and, after Waterloo, to Marie Louise.

As we drove back, we discussed enough history for me to realize that in Parma it is tactless to express anything except boundless admiration for Marie Louise. They still love her and remember a hundred kindly acts. Perhaps no other town in Italy would number among deeds to be remembered for ever the fact that their beloved duchess refused to sell a famous Correggio to Louis XVIII for a million francs.

In the morning when I looked out of my window I saw with some surprise that the embankment, which I had vaguely noticed when I arrived, confined no river. In a bed of stones and summer nettles an ancient figure, which might have been that of Time himself, was scything grass.

Parma remains in my memory as a town full of pleasant, cheerful people; and I think not only of the well-to-do, but also of those engaged in ordinary jobs, such as shopkeeping, the salting of hams, the keeping of pigs, the milking of cows, the making of cheese, not forgetting policemen, sextons, waiters, and the guardians in art galleries. Great crowds of suspicious tourists have not muddied here the crystal fount of Italian kindness and courtesy.

The town has a bustling activity which I found stimulating, and in the evening, when every café table was occupied in the Piazza Garibaldi, I rarely heard a word of English spoken, or, what is stranger in Italy these days, of German. The fine cathedral and the superlative Baptistry are not the centre of the town, and they retreat after dark to a mysterious mediaeval silence and darkness which I liked. Indeed, the back streets of Parma, which are so bustling and active by day, descend with the coming of darkness into an earlier world, and become scenes for cloaks, daggers, and *miching mallecho*. The transformation is extraordinary. Pausing one night, thinking how sinister they were, I realized that I was standing outside a little bookshop, scarcely recognizable in the lamplight and shadows, where during the day I bought my newspapers.

The mediaeval cathedral has lost its porch statues, giving it a forlorn air as of a stage temporarily empty. Upon the inside of the dome Correggio painted his famous Assumption, the Ascent of the Virgin into Heaven, and I looked up into what might be some enormous space capsule of the future whose passengers, released from the laws of gravity, still managed to behave gracefully. Not all of his contemporaries admired it, indeed one of them compared the audacious foreshortening to a 'hash of frogs'. It was Titian, however, who remarked, 'Reverse the cupola, and fill it with gold, and that will not be its money's worth.'

Vasari gives the impression that Correggio was unappreciated and underpaid. He also suffered from something more serious which he could do nothing about: an early death. Like Raphael ('his cousin in art descent', says Berenson), he died in the full promise of his life: he was forty, and Raphael was three years younger. Vasari tells a curious story of Correggio's death. He says that he carried a heavy bag of money home to his native village of Correggio (his real name was Antonio Allegri), the payment for a picture made, in order to annoy him, in copper coins. The fatigue of this induced a brief illness which developed into pleurisy, from which he died. Even as the crow flies, this village is some twenty-five miles from Parma, and it is inconceivable that anyone would have carried a bag of copper coins all that way when presumably he could have changed it for more portable denominations. Yet how strange a story to be invented.

In one of the aisles I came to the tomb of the most elegant printer of the eighteenth century, and read above it, in English, the following unexpected tribute:

In Enduring Recognition
Giambattista
Bodoni.
The Printers of the United States
of America.
MCMLVI.

Bodoni's press at Parma printed two English books which were enormously celebrated in their day, but are now read only by the curious; Thomson's *Seasons* and Horace Walpole's romance magnificently entitled *The Castle of Otranto*. The printing of Thomson's poem is understandable, for it was the kind of book which appeared in many fine editions, but I could not imagine why Walpole's novel, which some claim to have been the ancestor of the 'thriller', should have achieved such typographical glory. And the story is this. Among unusual Londoners in 1790 was a man named James Edwards, who made a fortune from selling rare books long before there was an American market. He was constantly crossing to the Continent to inspect libraries and to make purchases, and upon one of those occasions, meeting Bodoni in Parma, it occurred to him that Walpole's story, then a best-seller, would be a pleasant book to have as a well-printed quarto. Walpole approved and Edwards footed the bill for an edition of three hundred copies and five printed on vellum. The book had already gone into six English editions, and the sixth, printed by Dodsley, is known as the small paper edition to distinguish it from the sixth edition, Parma, 1791, printed by Bodoni. When Walpole saw the first copy, he found so many errors that publication was delayed while Bodoni prepared cancels; even then Walpole's comment was that the book was 'not fit to be sold' in England.

Perhaps noting my interest in the Baptistry, an old man who was seated outside the cathedral told me that he had been christened there seventy-five years ago, and he clearly believed that this had conferred some particular virtue upon him. By general consent Parma's Baptistry is the finest in the north, though I prefer the smaller one at Bergamo. Like all these octagonal towers, it stands by itself a few paces from the cathedral, and it was built when Richard the Lionheart was King in England and when Robin Hood was still alive. It is constructed of red Verona marble, and the features which distinguish the tower from other baptistries are the four pillared galleries, one above the other, on its eight sides, and a magnificent Romanesque doorway, fine enough for any cathedral.

Of the famous trio to be met with all over Italy – cathedral, campanile, and baptistry – the only one that now fulfils no useful purpose is the baptistry. It is generally locked, and the old man who has the key is often not to be found. If you do manage to get inside, you will see a gaunt mediaeval bath which has not been regularly used since total immersion went out of fashion : but of all the relics of the Middle Ages in Italy, none is more interesting.

Though the literature on baptism is formidable and the number of clergymen who have written about fonts is astonishing, as far as I know there is no book on these structures which perpetuated during the Middle Ages the baptismal practice of the early Church. When I first saw one, I was interested; when I had seen two or three, I was astonished, and after that I began to think of these baptistries as in their own way as strange and unique as the round towers of Ireland. Everywhere except, apparently, in Italy, the separate baptistry ceased to be built in the ninth century, when it became incorporated with the church, or disappeared altogether, while the font was removed into the church. During the great rebuilding boom in the Middle Ages in Italy, however, no such thing happened; the baptistry remained the detached octagonal building of the fourth century. This, of course, would seem to imply mass baptism, total immersion, and the holding of baptism at stated times, generally at Easter, Pentecost, or Epiphany, when the Bishop himself would officiate. In the cathedral at Parma there is a fresco of the Giotto period which depicts one of these mass baptisms in progress, and a peculiar scene it is. Eight naked people are crouched in one of the octagonal fonts, while the bishop stands sprinkling water on them. The fresco was paid for by the bakers of Parma in the early Middle Ages and depicts incidents in the lives of S. Fabian and S. Sebastian.

Why are these buildings so high? What purpose did the

galleries serve outside and inside? Is it possible that people gathered to watch the mass baptisms?

The interior of Parma's Baptistry was the finest I had seen. The building is full of interesting Romanesque carvings which depict husbandmen sowing, reaping, and riding out in spring-time; and there is a beautiful little series in which various figures symbolize the different months of the year. I liked January. It was the figure of a peasant with two heads seated by a fire. I thought this a delightful way to convey the idea that he was thinking back-ward to winter and forward to spring.

§ 2

They say that Parmesan cheese has been made along the Via Emilia for two thousand years. Like nearly everything eatable or drinkable in Italy, it tastes better in its native land than elsewhere. In Italy, should you still feel hungry after a meal, you can gnaw a nugget of Parmesan with enjoyment. Elizabeth David, whose *Italian Food* is a classic, explains that the fame of Parmesan in the kitchen is due to the almost unique quality that, during the process of cooking, it does not become like elastic. It is made all over the region of Emilia and (one whispers) also in Lombardy. Naturally, Parma believes that there is just a little something about its cheese that makes it superior to that produced in the neighbouring towns.

When I visited a cheese factory outside Parma, I was intro-duced to a man who was standing with a wooden paddle, stirring warm milk in a copper vat. He told me that the best Parmesan is made from the milk of cows fed on fresh pastures, and not on hay, and that the best production season is from April 1 to November 11 (S. Martin's Day); and it may be appropriate that S. Martin, who is the patron saint of repentant drunkards, should have such in-fluence over milk. The milk is skimmed, and the cream goes to the butter factory. When the curd has separated, the whey goes to the pigs, and so helps to make Parma ham.

The curd is put into large circular wooden forms, where it drains and dries for six months. It is then exposed to sunlight and can be turned out of the mould. The outside of the cheese is now painted with a black preservative which seals it from the air. There is nothing to do now but to allow it to mature for at least two years. Experts go round knocking at the cheeses with hammers, and can tell from the reverberations if all is well inside.

The ideal Parmesan is not the familiar and costly hard rock familiar to English kitchens, but a pale gold, close-textured cheese covered everywhere with innumerable pinpoint holes.

I drove up into the foothills of the Apennines, south of Parma, and came to the small town of Langhirano, beautifully situated in gentle hills beside a river. On the way I noticed a number of sheds whose shutters were arranged at such angles that the interior could be ventilated in a variety of ways, according to the direction of the wind and sun. These were the sheds where the famous hams are cured.

The manager of the curing factory, who was expecting me, led the way into a drawing-room in which his wife was seated with a small boy of about five, who needed only a pair of wings to be one of Raphael's cherubs. A few days previously, I was told, when walking across an open trap-door, he had vanished into a curing shed thirty feet below. They rushed in to pick up his body, to find him without a scratch. As they told me of this, his mother hugged him fiercely, while his father handed me a glass of wine, saying: 'It was a miracle. Madonna was with him that day.' The wine was Malvasia, a white wine made by the priest of Langhirano from grapes grown on the hill not far away.

When we entered the factory, the manager tugged at the mighty door of a giant refrigerator. Inside were four men like Arctic explorers, padded with clothing and wearing overcoats with fur collars, engaged in rubbing salt from Salsomaggiore into hams. There was frost on their eyebrows. They looked at us with their wintry faces and smiled and nodded agreeably before we shut them up again. Though the curing of Parma ham is a tricky business, it looks as though anyone could do it. Salt is rubbed into the hams and they are then left to mature for a year, and sometimes two, in the correct temperature. The mortality rate is high, which explains why Parma ham is expensive, even in Italy.

I went on to Torrechiara, a tiny hamlet under a hill upon which stands a castle which from a distance looks like an Aztec temple. The *Trattoria al Castello* gave me a huge plate of the finest ham, some homemade bread as sweet as the bread in Spain, and some cream cheese. The rough red wine was excellent, and when I asked where it came from, they pointed to the hills outside. The inn was full of countrymen in working clothes, drinking their watered wine sparingly and demolishing mounds of spaghetti. I have always found it wise in places like the *trattoria* to explain what I had been doing and what I was proposing to do. It makes for easiness all round.

Driving up to the castle of Torrechiara, I found to my disappointment that the postern gate was locked. I was turning away when a young girl came running with the keys from a near-by cottage, and we entered a castle which put Colleoni's stronghold at Malpaga completely in the shade.

This superb building with its palatial rooms, each one frescoed with Pompeii-like grotesques or with scenes, overlooks a grand sweep of rolling hills folded against each other to the horizon, and cultivated in long gold, green and olive-brown strips, each one separated from the next by a line of vines festooned from poplar to elm or mulberry. Some of the finest rooms opened on to covered porticoes – wonderful places to breakfast on a summer morning – where you could gaze at the hills and the roads threading their way and losing themselves in the valleys. The enormous Renaissance fireplaces spoke of the winter chill, but now, with the summer sun slanting in through the tall windows and gilding the frescoed walls, I refused to think of anything but the joy of living in such perfect surroundings, of wandering from room to room and looking down on the Virgilian countryside. I asked the girl why the men in the *trattoria* had referred to the castle as the 'castle of Bianca Pellegrini', and for answer she took me into a hall and pointed to the walls. Painted in fresco was the story of a beautiful young woman who was seen travelling from castle to castle and at last triumphantly finding her young man, while Cupid stood joyfully upon a pedestal. The girl told me that when the Rossi family were lords of Parma long years ago the owner of the castle, Pier Maria Rossi, went on a visit to the court of the Visconti in Milan. Here a young woman of the Pellegrini family, Bianca, the wife of a man called Melchiore d'Arluno, fell desperately in love with him. Though women in love are more curious even than usual, she knew no more about him when he departed than that he owned a castle near Parma. Deciding that life meant nothing without him, she dressed herself as a pilgrim and went to Parma, passing from castle to castle until she came to Torrechiara. The frescoes tell of this happy discovery and of their life together under her touching and optimistic motto, *Nunc et Semper*.

'And what happened?' I asked. 'Had they a family?'

'After many years,' answered the girl, 'he returned to his wife.'

'But what happened to Bianca?'

The girl gave me a slow smile and lifted her shoulders slightly, in which I seemed to detect a feminine insight into the inconstancy of man, and also a peasant resignation to the ups and downs of life.

§ 3

I have many varied and happy memories of Parma. There was the shop full of Parma violets – beautifully made of plastic.

There was the Benedictine monk who showed me the sixteenth century library of his monastery, with a fresco of Lepanto painted only a year after the battle, and maps with names written in the Parmesan dialect. He thought it amusing that S. Paul should be S. Pollo.

There was the spectacular apothecary's shop which was opened in 1201 and was Parma's only pharmacy until the eighteenth century. It is now a museum whose walnut shelves hold delightful blue and white jars bearing inscriptions such as *Bicarbonato di Sodio*. Never again will the world see a beautiful chemist's shop, a calm, dignified library of drugs.

There was the Palladian Theatre which was built in 1618, two years after Shakespeare's death, in the vast armoury of the Palazzo della Pilotta, and could hold an audience of five thousand. It was badly damaged by bombs during the last war and I saw carpenters at work restoring it. The entire classical proscenium had disintegrated, and several of the gods and goddesses were lying in corners like air-raid casualties. I was surprised to see that one apparently marble deity was made of plaster of Paris over a core of straw. I was told that this theatre was the first to have a revolving stage.

Then, of course, there was the memory of Marie Louise. It was a little trying to go round the art gallery with one of her most devout admirers, one who thought of her not only as a regal cornucopia whence flowed a stream of orphanages, bridges, roads, and maternity homes, but also as a perfect human being. I could not suggest that she was a lethargic woman with little mind of her own, who would have made herself content with any forceful male who happened to be on the spot. There were two revealing portraits of her in the gallery. One is a fine statue by Canova, made when she was Empress and showing her in classical robes as a daughter of the Caesars, which is how Napoleon imagined her, and the other is a portrait which shows her as she really was when Duchess of Parma, with her sleepy eyes, the Habsburg under-lip, and the expression of a sheep.

'How beautiful she was,' said my acquaintance. 'How queenly!'

I thought that had Napoleon won the Battle of Waterloo and re-established himself, he would inevitably have seen her true character When he was living in loneliness and defeat on Elba and writing pitiful letters, begging her to go to him – how little he knew her – she was having an affair with the one-eyed Count von Neipperg, who became her chancellor in Parma and governed her duchy well. All the praise lavished on Marie Louise by Parma should really go to von Neipperg. His tomb in the church of the Madonna of the Steccata in Parma shows a handsome hussar wearing a patch over an eye which was injured by a sabre cut when he was a young officer in the Austrian army. He was a fine example of the reformed rake. Beginning his association with Marie Louise as a cynical seducer, he ended as an exemplary prime minister and, dying at the age of fifty-four, a poor man, left only a cardboard box in which stars of all the most valued orders of chivalry were jumbled together.

Looking at Marie Louise's placid, empty face, one realizes how desperate was her need of a father figure. When Napoleon was dying on St Helena and ordering that his heart should be sent to her, the Duchess was about to present her lover with a second child.

I was carried unresisting to the stately palace at Colorno, some ten miles out, where Marie Louise held her court in summer. Here I saw a long, low, three-storey building about the size of Buckingham Palace, which stands in a stretch of neglected grassland. In a moment of absent-mindedness, Stendhal called it 'the Versailles of the Princess of Parma'; but then he saw it when it was alive. I saw it now in death and worse, for it is a lunatic asylum. In the country these old palaces have no hope of survival; in a town they do stand a chance of becoming at least the town hall. The uncurtained windows gaze hopelessly across the weed-grown drive along which no state landaus will ever come again. I thought the palace was architecturally attractive and it reminded me of some of the better Georgian country houses of England. It seemed scarcely credible that less than a century ago curtains hung on every window, the stables were full of horses and coaches, maids were running up and down stairs with cans of hot water and cups of chocolate, secretaries were planning dinner-parties, the fountains were gushing plumes of water; and that somewhere in the tall rooms, where the lunatics now sit idly, the Duchess of Parma's head was bent above her embroidery.

A near-by building is devoted to relics of Marie Louise: her diaries, her embroidery, and those little sketches and water colours which Napoleon, in the flush of his infatuation, thought so brilliant.

§ 4

During the course of a delicious lunch at Parma, a number of learned men were discussing fortune-telling and divination in general. One of them, I think it was Dr Borri, remarked that the astrologer was as important to an ancient ruler as a scientist is to the modern state. Someone made a joke about the Roman College of Augurs, to be rebuked by the curator of the museum, who said dryly that, to him, the feeding of sacred birds appeared no more ridiculous than other beliefs which Man has wrapped in dignity and mystery.

'Have you been to Piacenza yet, to see the *fegato*?' I was asked. As anyone who has ever handled an Italian menu knows, *fegato* is liver, and in that gastronomical atmosphere it took me a few moments to realize that the liver referred to was the famous Etruscan liver of bronze.

I thought it would be interesting to see this unique object, and so one bright morning I sped along the road to Piacenza, a town which is about thirty-five miles to the west of Parma, on the Via Emilia. The straight Roman road traverses a landscape as flat as Holland, and Piacenza is its western terminus and the point where it reaches the Po.

When I arrived, all thought of the bronze liver was driven from my mind by the beauty of the town. In the main square the morning sunlight was falling upon a battlemented palace built of rose-red brick. In front of it, outlined against a series of arches, and green as coins which have been buried for centuries, were two splendid bronze horsemen, Farnese dukes, riding forward upon prancing stallions into that vigorous breeze which blew round the Baroque world. The effect was magnificent, and I thought that neither Lombardy nor Emilia could show anything finer. The horseman on the left was Alessandro Farnese, who was practically a Spaniard and can hardly have known Piacenza at all. His whole life was spent warring in the Netherlands as one of Philip II's officers, and it was he who assembled the landing barges in the Low Countries for the invasion of England during the Armada. He fought at Lepanto, and when his uncle, the poor, ill-treated Don John of Austria, died miserably in a Flemish pigeon-loft, he was chief mourner as the funeral procession paraded between the regiments to Namur Cathedral. I think his own end was not without pathos. He bore the scars of a life spent in the service of a cold-blooded monarch, but he carried on, ill and wounded, until he died at Arras. His reward was a magnificent funeral in Brussels, but his body was taken home to Piacenza for burial.

I thought the situation of this town delightful, with the Po flowing to the north in a wide and majestic loop; and, as I went round the churches, it occurred to me that the people of Piacenza believe in the old saying that seeing is believing, for never have I encountered the bones of so many saints in glass coffins. S. Justina's bones are tied with red ribbon in the crypt of the cathedral; S. Antonianus, in the church of that name, is to be seen in an illuminated coffin under the high altar, neatly packed into a Roman cinerary urn; and the remains of S. Rita are visible in the church of S. Maria di Campagna. In the narrow streets some of the old palaces exposed barred and shuttered windows to the passer-by, looking unspeakably grim, as if an astrologer left over from the Renaissance were still at work there, or maybe even a stray alchemist with his retorts and a stuffed crocodile. I saw the palace from whose windows the murdered body of the detested Pierluigi Farnese was flung into the street.

Eventually I found the *fegato di Piacenza*, which was much smaller than I had expected. It is a highly polished bronze model of a sheep's liver, and is covered with those mysterious Etruscan inscriptions which look as if a blind man were trying to write Greek with a blunt nail. I do not know whether the bronze liver was a model to teach aspiring augurs what to look for in a real one, or whether it was an *ex-voto* commemorating some unusually informative liver. I do know that I was impressed by this proof of the technical complexity of augury.

Reading the life of S. Columbanus, at home in an easy chair, it may seem that a visit to Bobbio, the remote fastness in the Apennines given to him by Theodolinda and Aigiluf, would be an expedition of some magnitude: but it is nothing of the kind. A second-class road rambles for about thirty miles from Piacenza to the ancient retreat in the mountains. There is even an hotel. The small modern abbey church has a crypt in which stands a carved sarcophagus containing, it is believed, the remains of the Irishman.

Like all Celtic saints, he was kind but quarrelsome, and, again like Celtic saints, he anticipated by many centuries the intimacy which existed between S. Francis and the animal kingdom. It was said that birds would fly down to him to be petted, and that squirrels would snuggle into his cowl. The same love for animals was shown by many Irish saints, including, of course, the beloved Columcille, whose memory in Ireland today is as precious as that of S. Patrick. When Columcille felt death to be approaching, he went to say good-bye to an old horse which, as it rubbed its head against him, he blessed.

Columbanus was no longer young when he came to Bobbio. Having founded a great number of monasteries in his wanderings across Europe, he eventually came up against that terrifying woman, Brunhild, who, in order to retain power in her own hands, had become a procuress for her grandson, King Theodoric, and in the course of her activities had built up for him an extensive harem. The anger expressed by S. Columbanus made it prudent for him to cross the Alps, and anyone who has seen Monza and the Treasure of Theodolinda will like to think of that good queen and her husband befriending the saint in his latter years and giving him one of their loneliest mountains.

The treasures of Bobbio have enriched the libraries of Italy, for Columbanus, like other Irishmen of that age, was a classical scholar and could even read Greek and Hebrew. Among the most remarkable finds at Bobbio was the only known manuscript of Cicero's *De Republica*, which remained filed away in the Vatican Library for centuries until one day the great librarian, Cardinal Mai, recognized it for what it is.

§ 5

On a side road to the north of the Via Emilia, half-way between Piacenza and Parma, is the little village of Le Róncole, where Verdi was born. I decided to go there on my return to Parma, and, while I was on the way, I began to think about artists and money. I imagine that Verdi must have made more money, and have saved more, than any other musician in history; and he enjoyed doing so. The cherished illusion that a genius is above such mundane thoughts is not always borne out by facts. Many great artists have had a sense of money. Leonardo da Vinci once wrote to the Duke of Milan to complain that his salary had not been paid for two years. 'Gladly as I would undertake immortal works and show posterity that I have lived,' he wrote, 'I am obliged to earn my living.' That is the problem that has always faced genius; it is an unhappy fact that no butcher or grocer refrains from sending in his bill because his customer is an artist.

Leonardo, like a number of Renaissance artists and architects, was able to save money and to own property. When he was in his fifties he had six hundred gold florins to his account in the savings-bank at Florence, and when he died, as court painter to Francis I, in the comfortable surroundings of the Castle of Cloux, near Amboise, he had four hundred ducats at Florence, vineyards near Milan, and money in France, which he left to friends and servants, and to charity. Raphael was also comparatively well off when he died at the age of thirty-seven. He had bought a palace for three thousand, six hundred ducats, he received a salary of three hundred ducats a year as supervisor of the rebuilding of S. Peter's, and one thousand, two hundred scudi for each of the frescoes of the stanze. The fortune left at his death was said to have been sixteen thousand gold ducats, of which six hundred was invested in property. Another genius who managed to save money was Michelangelo. When he died at the age of eighty-three, the untidy rooms in which he had lived in bachelor squalor were found to contain a walnut chest with eight thousand, one hundred and ninety gold ducats in it, while about two hundred scudi were discovered tied up in handkerchiefs, or hastily thrust away in jars and pots. Cellini was able to take care of himself in a materialistic world and so was Shakespeare.

Verdi's earnings, however, make the finances of other artists appear trivial. He left about £282,000, which in the year of his death, 1901, was worth by modern standards more than half a million. He once wrote of London, 'Oh, if only I could stay here a couple of years and take away with me a sack full of blessed money!' At the zenith of his career, when the Khedive commissioned him to write an opera for the opening of the Suez Canal, he was in a position to demand an advance of £30,000 before a note of *Aïda* had been written. This may shock romantic people who like to believe that an artist should be indifferent to his own welfare and that of those dependent upon him, but it will please others who admire a genius who can take care of himself in a tough world.

I came to a network of quiet country roads where the sky was reflected in irrigation canals and where poplars shimmered as if their branches were loaded with silver coins. It was a crowded, agricultural country where every inch of soil was cultivated, and you could not walk ten yards without meeting someone. The little hamlets were as crowded together as in an English countryside, and had the same air of long-established resignation. When I arrived at Le Róncole, I saw a bronze bust in the front garden of a cottage, the bust of a bearded man who wore a winged collar and a neatly tied bronze bow-tie. This, of course, was Verdi, and behind was the little cottage with a long, low-pitched roof in which he was born. His expression was stern. From the garden he fiercely regards his admirers with a look once familiar to indifferent tenors at *La Scala*. There is nothing soulful about him: he might be a soldier of the Risorgimento, a politician or patriot like Cavour or Mazzini, or even a distinguished engineer.

When he was born, the stone cottage was the local wine shop and general store. Now it is a national monument. The caretaker removed her apron and led the way up the wooden staircase to the room under the bare rafters where Italy's most beloved composer was born. She then took me to the village church of S. Michael and, pointing up to a gilded Baroque organ loft, said that the organ is the same one which Verdi played at the age of eleven. From Le Róncole, Verdi went to Milan to learn music. There he encountered poverty and sorrow. He married and had two children. Four years later the two infants died and were followed to the grave by the mother, a situation which Francis Toye, in his life of Verdi, calls 'quite operatic in its exaggeration'. Also operatic is the fact that Verdi was at work on a comic opera at the time. The woman in Verdi's life was not his short-lived wife, but a singer named Giuseppina Strepponi, who knew the musical world inside out and had been acquainted with the composer from his days of struggle. No musician has been more fortunate in his life's companion. She was a woman of extraordinary sense and balance and, for a retired prima donna, of singular lack of vanity. When Verdi's operas became famous she never demanded to return to the limelight, but was content to housekeep and look after her husband. 'After all, everybody can't write *Aïda*,' she once said to a friend. 'Somebody is needed to pack and unpack trunks and make out the laundry lists.' Verdi and this sensible woman lived together for twelve years, then suddenly married. It was an ideal partnership. She dearly loved her irascible, rather fierce and hard-worked husband. She once wrote to him: 'That which makes the world raise its hat to you is something to which I never, or almost never, give a thought. I swear to you, and you will not find it difficult to believe me, that I often feel a sort of surprise that you know about music . . . The magic qualities in you that fascinate me, that I adore, are your character, your heart, your indulgence towards the errors of others while being, at the same time, so hard on yourself.'

Three miles from Le Róncole is the estate of Sant' Agata which Verdi bought in 1848, when the royalties were coming in from his earlier operas. Here he was to become the local squire, to live with his Giuseppina, to write *Rigoletto*, *Il Trovatore*, *La Traviata*, *Aïda*, and *Otello*; and here, too, forty-nine years later, after a long and happy life together, Giuseppina was to die and leave him a sad, silent, and bereft old man.

The house is surrounded by a high wall and is inhabited by Verdi's descendants. He and Giuseppina were childless, and his estate went to his niece, Maria Verdi Carrara. I was shown round by her great-grand-daughter. The house is rather English to look at, or it may be that the garden, laid out in the English style popular in the 1840's, with winding paths, shrubberies, rockeries, a lake, a belt of woodland, give it the look of a rambling early Victorian vicarage in Norfolk. There is something almost sinister about the house, standing surrounded by dark overgrown shrubberies and by colossal magnolias planted by Verdi for Giuseppina a hundred and twenty years ago, and now as tall as Burnham's beeches. It is obvious that the early Victorian garden, in which nothing had been changed or modernized since Verdi laid it out so long ago, has been kept alive by family piety. That much I could see at a glance. I was shown the seat where Verdi liked to sit. I was told that he would rise early in the morning and go round the estate inspecting the vines and the corn. He put down his occupation as 'farmer' on his identity card.

'He would walk round the garden every night,' said my guide, 'and if he found any implement out of place he would fine the careless gardener and put the money away and give it at the end of the year to a paralysed man. The result of this was that everything was very tidy. His old gardener died in 1956, well over ninety years of age.'

'What kind of a man was Verdi?'

'He was serious and pensive, but very *simpatico* and, though he frightened people by his manner, which could be gruff and harsh, he was tender-hearted and kind. But he didn't like anybody to suspect this.' We followed a little path which led to the grave of a Maltese terrier. I read the inscription, '*Alla Memoria di un vero amico.*'

'He was devoted to his dogs,' remarked his descendant. 'But now you must see the house.'

The garden should, I suppose, have prepared me for the even more remarkable survival of a country house of about 1850 or 1900, in which nothing appears to have been changed since Verdi's death half a century ago. The same family piety that has preserved the garden has forbidden the removal or destruction of anything that was there in the lifetime of the composer. It is a lived-in museum. I stood fascinated by the heavy plush curtains and mahogany furniture, and the oil paintings in their gilt frames, occupying the same places on the walls which they did when Verdi acquired them.

Verdi died, as I have mentioned earlier, in a Milan hotel, and so deep was the national sorrow engendered by the event that every article in his bedroom at the time of his death was sent to Sant' Agata and arranged just as it was on that January day in 1901, when the old man, while dressing, bent down to find a lost collar stud and was discovered some time later unable to move or speak. Verdi's own bedroom, likewise preserved, is rather more interesting. It contains a grand piano, a writing-desk, a print of Shakespeare, a gun and cartridges – he was a good shot – and the white kid gloves which he wore when he conducted his Requiem Mass for Manzoni. On top of a wardrobe is his leather silk hat-box with a 'Grand Hotel, Milan' label on it.

I was told that he never sat at the piano to compose, but wrote down the music as it came into his head. Nevertheless there are four pianos in the house, and I was told that, when Verdi wished one of them to be tuned, he would send it to Paris.

The room in which Giuseppina died is also kept as it was at the time of her death in 1897. In another room I was shown her favourite green Amazon parrot, Lorita, stuffed, and gazing round quizzically under an oval glass dome. This is the bird whose raucous screams so irritated Verdi that he once conspired to poison it. A friend of his went into town and returned with the poison to find that Verdi had changed his mind. 'Never mention the matter again,' he whispered. 'Just tell me how much I owe you for the poison and – forget it!'

Perhaps for associative reasons which go back to youth, Aïda is the opera I prefer to anything else that Verdi wrote, and I had always trustfully believed the story, first told to me in Egypt years ago, that the composer wandered up and down the Nile listening to the Arab tunes which he introduced so skilfully into the exquisite opening to Act III, as the priestesses of Isis dance in the moonlight above the tomb of the lovers. But I learnt at Sant' Agata that this was not so. Verdi, who detested the sea, never went to Egypt, and wrote every note of Aïda in his villa. It is strange to look round the rather stuffy, over-upholstered surroundings of a nineteenth century landowner, and to think of those melodies coming out of the air, as it might be, into the mind of the bearded man; and beyond the windows the magnolias were only half-grown and the shrubberies were still reasonably restrained.

Verdi achieved fame not only because he wrote melodious operas, but also for a political reason which has now been forgotten: he was a master of the musical *double entendre*. It was

Stendhal who, writing of the Italy of Verdi's day, said that music was the form in which Italians, tossed about politically between the French and the Austrians, remained victorious; music was the only form of political expression possible for them. As the forces grew which led to the Risorgimento and the political unification of Italy, patriots found in most of Verdi's operas stirring calls to be up and doing, and scenes bordering on riot became so frequent that attending a Verdi first night was a regular Austrian police routine. The political undertow must indeed have been powerful. A Florentine audience, attending the first performance of *Macbeth*, lost all control when hearing the aria containing the words:

> *La patria tradita*
> *Piangendo c'invita;*
> *Fratelli, gli oppressi*
> *Corriamo a salvar.*

The police had to be called to the theatre; and in the same way, in Venice, the chorus in *Ernani*, which begins *Si ridesti il Leon di Castiglia* (Rise up, Lion of Castile), was tumultuously interpreted by the audience as a reference to the Lion of S. Mark. During a performance in Rome of *Ernani*, an Italian gendarme in full dress uniform created a remarkable diversion. T. R. Ybarra, in his book on Verdi, says that he 'put one leg over the balustrade of the balcony in which he was seated, and lustily bellowing "Glory and honour to Pius IX", threw his ornate headgear into the pit, sent after it his coat and vest, and then hurled his unsheathed sword in the general direction of the stage, where it stuck in the woodwork behind the footlights to the dissatisfaction and considerable peril of adjacent singers and musicians. Next, teetering on the balustrade, he started to remove the remainder of his apparel and had almost succeeded in doing so when he was collared by a charging squad of other gendarmes and hounded from the theatre.' It is, however, a little difficult to know how much of this was political and how much, shall one say, musical intoxication. However, Verdi became the cryptic voice of the political underground, and it was natural that eventually, during the Risorgimento, the words 'Viva

Verdi' should have been one of the passwords. The letters of his name stood inevitably for 'Vittorio Emanuele Re d'Italia'.

As I was walking to the garden gate, a man passed whistling on the other side of the wall. I smiled. The tune was *La donna è mobile* from *Rigoletto*.

'You know the story?' asked my guide.

'No, except that it must be one of the most popular arias ever written.'

'It is, and Verdi knew that it would be. The opera was produced at Venice, and Verdi was well aware that if *La donna è mobile* were sung at rehearsals the whole of Venice would be whistling it before the opening night. The tenor was sworn never even to hum it and was not allowed to sing it until the final rehearsal, when the whole cast burst into applause. So the secret was kept. And Verdi was right. The next day every gondolier was singing it, and has been doing so ever since!'

§ 6

Modena is about thirty miles to the east of Parma, along the Via Emilia. Here Mary of Modena was born, the noble and unlucky consort of James II of England, who conveyed her dark eyes and hair to her son, the 'Blackbird' of Jacobite romance, James Francis Edward Stuart, the Old Chevalier.

Ferrari and Maserati racing cars are made at Modena, though you would never guess this: the old city appears untouched by industry, indeed when I arrived a cattle sale was under way and it was almost impossible, until a policeman came to my rescue, to find a way through narrow streets filled with carts and farmers with their cows and pigs, especially pigs. It was interesting to see these men in their Sunday best, like farmers everywhere, locked in the throes of deadly financial duels as they sat in the little wine shops sparingly sipping the local red wine. Yet there was something courtly about them. That drunkenness is a disgrace is one of the finest traits of the Latin character, in Italy as in Spain.

I had given a lift in my car to a friend from Parma, who had an appointment in Modena. When at last I found a parking-place near the cathedral, he said, 'I've just got time to show you the strangest thing in Modena.'

'What is it?'

'The most famous bucket in Italy.'

Beside the lovely cathedral stands a red brick campanile which bears some resemblance to the Giralda Tower in Seville, and was hailed as such by the Sephardic exiles, and to this we went. We had mounted a few steps in the Tower when my friend looked up in surprise.

'It isn't here!' he said. 'What can have happened?'

We found a caretaker who told us that the *secchia rapita* – which I suppose you could translate as the 'ravished bucket' – had been recently stolen by the students of Bologna University and had only just been recaptured by the students of Modena. It had not yet been suspended from its usual place in the tower, but if we would come with him, he could show it to us. He unlocked a room and handed us a venerable wooden pail bound with hoops of metal. I was told that it had been captured from the Bolognese by the Modenese during a battle in 1325, and for more than six hundred years it has been going home to Bologna and then returning to the campanile of Modena.

'We Italians are like that!' laughed my friend. 'If you go to Perugia, you will see the chains of Siena hanging on the walls of the Palazzo del Municipio.'

Arranging to meet for lunch, he sauntered off, only an hour late for his appointment. I went into the cathedral, where, by a slight stretch of the imagination, I might have been standing in one of the Norman cathedrals of England. The large, uncluttered church, with its massive round arches, its powerful pillars and triforium, had been built in what to us in England were Norman times, from bricks and tiles from the ruins of a Roman Modena, a town called Mutina. The altar was lifted high above the nave as if on a stage; beneath was a vaulted crypt where lie the bones of S. Geminianus, a contemporary of S. Ambrose, and a famous healer who once went to Constantinople to drive a little Greek devil out of a princess.

The charming town with its narrow streets and its picturesque colonnades was once traversed by canals, now filled in, but names like Corso Canal Grande perpetuate their memory. There was once a canal in front of a tremendous display of seventeenth century Baroque, the Ducal Palace built when the Este family, driven out of their ancient capital, Ferrara, migrated to Modena. It is the building in which Mary of Modena was born and in which, after bitter tears, this girl, scarcely fifteen years of age, was married by proxy to a widower of forty.

Not far away is one of the most admirably arranged picture galleries in Italy. I spent an enjoyable hour there, looking at the wonderful collection of pictures of the schools of Ferrara, Parma, and Modena. One of its chief treasures is not an Italian picture, but the beautiful portrait by Velazquez of Francis I, Duke of Modena, painted in Madrid in 1638. It shows him to the waist, in armour, a cloak over his shoulder, wearing the Golden Fleece; and he was so pleased with the portrait that he gave the painter a gold chain which Velazquez wore ever afterwards on state occasions. Eleven years later Velazquez, who was travelling in Italy with his devoted mulatto slave, Juan Pareja, snapping up Titians and Tintorettos for Philip IV, arrived in Modena. The Duke showed him great honour and led the painter to his own work, then occupying a place of importance in the palace.

A speciality of Modena cooking is *zamponi*, pigs' trotters stuffed with pork: and here I should say that nothing less like the spaghetti and tomato sauce conception of Italian cooking can be imagined than the food of this rich, buttery region of Emilia. The person who dislikes pasta, and is yet anxious to eat well, could chew his way along the Roman road from Piacenza, through Parma, Reggio, and Modena, to that culmination of gastronomy, Bologna, 'the Fat', without once tasting spaghetti. Those who consider the Italian cuisine to be limited would be astonished by the variety of the ham and pork dishes, never heard of outside Emilia, which depend for their excellence, like all Italian food, on the freshness and the quality of their ingredients and the care taken in their preparation.

After lunch I met Dr Ciavarella, the Librarian of the Biblioteca Estense, with whom I spent an afternoon among the records of the Este family. The extent of these archives – thirty-five kilometres of documents, I was told – is awesome. The treasures of the library, such as the Borso Bible, illustrated by Crivelli and probably the most lavishly decorated book in the world, are exposed in glass cases in a lower hall, but I was even more interested in the inter-communicating halls above where the Este records, from the Middle Ages to the eighteenth century, are piled to the ceiling. Thousands of these documents have been printed, but others have never been read since they were filed away centuries ago. It seemed to me that there can have been no waste-paper baskets in a Renaissance court: everything was kept. The precision with which letters were copied in days before typewriters and copying machines, and with which they were filed in days before 'systems', fills one with astonishment. No wonder an Italian secretary was considered a treasure in a Tudor court. The *secretarius* (one who is trusted with a secret) has a noble and romantic history: all the ducal secretaries were a reflection of that expert and learned department of state, the Papal Chancery.

How the dead years stir in one's mind in a place such as this, and with what reverence and curiosity one turns the brown membranes and the faded parchments, seeing in imagination the writer in some distant court, the messenger galloping across Italy or Europe, his arrival at the gate of a palace, then the crisp sound of an opened parchment against a background of tapestries and candlelight. And the brown words live still, although those who penned them, often so exquisitely, have long since gone. I was shown a document to which Charlemagne, who never managed to master the alphabet, had added a kind of schoolboy cross; another to which Matilda of Tuscany, on March 1, 1107, had written her name on each side of the arms of a cross – 'Matilda, by the Grace of God', then added modestly, 'If so she is.' I sat at a table, and there were laid before me letters written by Elizabeth of York, wife of Henry VII, to Ercole I, Duke of Ferrara; from Henry VIII to Alfonso I; from Thomas Cromwell to Ercole II; from the Borgia Pope, Alexander VI, to his beloved daughter,

Lucrezia Borgia, who had just become Duchess of Ferrara, and letters from Lucrezia to her brother, Caesar.

'And this might interest you,' they said, and placed in my hands a letter from Mary, Queen of Scots, written on August 26, 1579, to Cardinal Luigi d'Este.

Then I was handed an important-looking document to which was attached a wax seal the size of a plate. It was the marriage contract, signed and sealed by Charles II, between Mary of Modena and James, Duke of York. James, who gave his name to New York, and Beatrice Maria – as they call her in Modena – who cried and screamed for two whole days and nights before she left to marry the heir to the throne of England, and could only be pacified when her mother agreed to go with her. She was tall, slim, dark, good-looking, and only fifteen, and her middle-aged husband had suffered obviously from smallpox and stammered. She confessed in later life that her feelings, when she first saw him at Dover, could be expressed only by tears. Yet, so strange are human relationships, she soon became devoted to him, indeed the only trouble in the whole of their married life was the agony she suffered for a time through one of those mistresses who, as Charles II once said, were so unattractive that they must have been given to his brother as a penance by his confessor.

When this marriage contract was signed, everyone anticipated a dazzling future for the young bride: immediately the marriage by proxy was over she took precedence over members of her own family, even her mother, and was addressed as 'Your Royal Highness'. No one could have foreseen that tragic December night of wind and rain, only fifteen years away, when the Queen of England, with her infant son in her arms, was ferried across the Thames at dead of night on her flight to France. So began the life-long exile of James II and Mary of Modena, an exile dignified by their unswerving faith and made beautiful by their love. During her thirty years of exile, Mary never visited Modena, but the archives contain all the letters she wrote to members of her family. When James died, the woman who as a girl had been almost forcibly led weeping to him, wrote: 'My heart and soul are sad even unto death . . . I feel more and more the privation and separation from him who was dearer to me than my own life, and who alone rendered life sweet and supportable. I miss him every day more and more in a thousand ways.' James was one of England's least popular kings, but the woman who knew him best thought of him as a saint. And she was not an easy woman to please.

§ 7

I have said once, and must repeat it, that in no other part of the world are so many wonderful places so close together, and nowhere, even in the northern regions of Italy, are towns more accessible than upon the straight stretches of the Via Emilia. Within half an hour of having left Modena, signs of Bologna began to appear. Tuscany thrusts an impressive wedge of foothills into Emilia at this point, and Florence is only about fifty miles away over the mountains to the south. These foothills kept me company, coming closer as I drew near to Bologna, when a tall, detached peak became prominent, with a church on the summit which I was soon to know as the sanctuary of the Madonna di S. Luca. The capital of Emilia, one of the oldest cities in Italy, lies in the shadow of this peak.

I found my way through the busy streets to a secluded hotel where my usual fate overtook me. I was given a choice of several rooms and selected one that overlooked a narrow lane or passage. As I stood on the balcony I was enchanted, as always, by the fascinating microcosm of Italian life below. The lane was lined with small shops and houses. A girl with glossy hair was airing bedding on a flat roof, and upon an adjacent building several labourers wearing paper caps peeped through the rush mats which concealed their activities and shouted compliments to her, which she acknowledged with a petulant, but not displeased, lift of the shoulder. A woman was calling 'Gina!' from one of the houses (why is there always a missing child called Gina in an Italian town?), while a man with a cart came along uttering a word which resolved itself into '*ghiaccio!*' Such human sounds do not disturb me, but hardly had I decided on the room than the lane erupted with delivery vans, motor-cycles, and Vespas, making a din hideous enough but almost physically painful when magnified by the walls of the narrow passage. I had evidently made my choice during some temporary hold-up in Bologna's traffic.

Thinking how sorely at times Italy can try her lovers, I was surprised to hear the fearful racket majestically obliterated by a roll of thunder. The sun vanished and in a few moments a storm of rain descended upon Bologna. When summer rain falls in Latin countries it is as if the population has been betrayed. There is a dismayed rush for shelter; the streets empty; the waiters fall over each other to whip tablecloths, chairs and tables into safety; cars skid; drains become clogged; the electric light fails; the telephone refuses to work; and a few brave figures, head down before the storm, cross the flooded road with something about them which, were it not so ludicrous, would be a tragic reminder of those who fled before the red-hot dust of Vesuvius.

As the rain had set in for the afternoon, I went out to look at Bologna. I saw the largest city east of Milan, whose population just manages to exceed that of Venice. If the Roman Empire upon its death-bed gave to Venice the gift of commerce and ship-building, she gave to Bologna the tablets of the Law, and it was as the greatest law school in Europe that her University was famed from the earliest times.

I enjoyed the storm and smelt with pleasure the clean and sweetened air. I liked the sound of the gurgling down-pipes and enjoyed the sudden reversion to mediaeval practice as choked gutters discharged their contents directly on the pavements. The rain, perhaps by temporarily abolishing the car and giving to the few figures who braved the storm hoods or cloaks, seemed to return Bologna most appropriately to the thirteenth century and gave me the feeling, as I looked up at battlemented and merlatured buildings through the falling veil of grey, that I was a scholar or a pilgrim seeking lodgings in this apparently deserted city.

In spite of the Renaissance, Bologna, like many another Italian city, manages to look essentially and massively mediaeval, and she also wears the air of a provincial capital. The first travel writers of the seventeenth century said that she was famous for lutes, sausages, and 'little dogges for Ladyes', creatures so small, said Lascelles, 'that the ladies carrying them in their muffs have place enough for their hands too'; while a French traveller noted that 'the ladies here are reported very handsome, but have all flat noses like their dogs, but extreme good eyes'. The Bologna 'dogges' were evidently a breed of pug that had the nose flattened during puppyhood and were thought sufficiently curious to be bought by travellers and taken home with them from Italy. The Bologna sausage is still as famous as ever it was (our word 'Poloney' is said to be a corruption of 'Bologna'), and the city is proud of its reputation as the acknowledged headquarters of gastronomy.

Grim and mournful in the rain were those two strange and preposterous towers beautifully named Asinelli and Garisenda (obviously star-crossed lovers from Provence), which Bologna cherishes in the centre of the city. They were the first mediaeval towers of any size that I had seen in Italy and it would not be surprising to be told that they are haunted by the ghosts of astrologers. At a kiosk near by, I bought a postcard which pictured a reconstruction of Bologna in the time of Dante when such towers sprouted all over the town like a bed of asparagus. The history books tell you that they were built by the mediaeval nobles in opposition to the trade guilds, and grew taller and taller as no one could afford to let his neighbour's tower overlook his own.

The feature of Bologna that delighted me was the colonnades. I had seen colonnades in Modena and Mantua, and other places, but here one can walk for miles beneath them. There are long colonnaded streets intersected by other colonnades and so on throughout the city. I have been told that these originated in the desire to make extra room for University students, and the carrying forward of the houses on columns provided the necessary addition. As there are a number of conflicting explanations for everything in Italy and no one can tell you which is the correct one, I prefer my own theory: that colonnades are a survival, or revival, of Roman architecture. When I saw them for the first time – some of the columns painted Pompeian red – I felt that here was an amazing reconstruction of an ancient town. The whole population appeared to have sheltered beneath these colonnades to watch the rain descend as if in Augustan Rome.

A wet day was scarcely the perfect moment to admire the pride of Bologna, the Neptune Fountain, which John of Bologna designed in the hope that it might win the competition for the fountain in Florence. A Hercules of a Neptune, a sea god who has been given every opportunity to flex his muscles on land, stands above a collection of cherubs and mermaids mounted on sea monsters, while water spouts from every direction, even from the breasts of the mermaids. It is a singular and compelling work of the late Renaissance but the sound of the water from its many spouts, which refreshes the hot Bolognese summer, was now inaudible as the more powerful fountain of the skies continued to descend. Within a few steps I came upon men dry shod in a subway that was being constructed. They had just unearthed, surprisingly near the modern road level, a portion of the Via Emilia.

§ 8

Those who wish to see the University of Bologna are taken to a number of fine buildings in various parts of the town, where the eleven Faculties are situated; and here they will admire modern lecture-rooms, laboratories, libraries, and everything necessary for the creation of lawyers, doctors, dentists, chemists, engineers, and even a few classical scholars and philosophers. However, remembering the antiquity of Bologna University, and that it claims to have received Roman Law directly from the ancient world and to be the mother of all univerisites, it was disappointing to find no building as old or as beautiful as the average Oxford college. This may seem strange in a city that has preserved so many of its antiquities, but there is, of course, a reason for it and a curious one. The inquirer discovers that this venerable university, which will celebrate its nine hundredth anniversary in June, 1988, had no settled, permanent quarters until the year 1565. In order to explain this it is necessary to go back to the year one thousand, or thereabouts, when the revived study of Roman Law at Bologna seemed to many of the best brains of the time as though a long-dead lighthouse had been discovered and was once again casting its guiding beams upon dark waters. From many countries elderly and mostly wealthy men went to Bologna to study law. Some were priors and bishops, some were noblemen, some were ambitious careerists with their eyes on high offices of state, like Thomas à Becket, who studied here in the twelfth century. Such exceptional students created an unusual organization. The students hired the professors; they laid down the rates of payment and drew up conditions which their lecturers swore to obey, creating a master–servant relationship made possible by the age and status of those who were attending the schools. Later on, when Paris, Oxford, and Cambridge were founded, the relationship between teachers and taught was the more normal one of master and apprentice.

The peculiar constitution of the ancient law schools was carried over to the University, and throughout the Middle Ages the students of Bologna continued to be technically the masters, while the dons were their servants. Each body of students, and they were organized in national groups, elected a student to be its rector; and it was only in comparatively modern times that this dignity was transferred from the scholars to the professors. Until 1565 there were no university buildings. The professors continued, as in the earliest times, to lecture in their own homes or in hired rooms, or, if the attendance justified it, they wandered out like Greek philosophers into the gardens and public squares.

When Bologna came under Papal rule, it was decided to gather the scattered schools under one roof and to build a fine palace for them, which still exists in the centre of the city. I had passed this beautiful building with its noble arcades and its splendid courtyard many a time without knowing that it was the famous Archigymnasium. Unfortunately its present function as the municipal library has disguised its original purpose, but you can study what must be a joy to anyone interested in heraldry, a museum of some seven thousand armorial bearings covering the vaulting of the arcades, grouped above the architraves of doors and upon ceilings and walls, the blazons of all the rectors from 1563 until such signs of social distinction were abolished in 1797 in the revolutionary fervour of Napoleon's Cisalpine Republic. The pleasant custom of allowing the departing graduate to leave his coat-of-arms behind him has covered walls, passages, and archways with countless blazons, and I was shown the name which Bologna believes to be that of the first American to study in Europe – Pasquale Perez of Lima, who took his degree in 1608.

I was introduced to a young man who was writing an account of early English students at Bologna, though he confessed that it was chiefly a list of names and dates: but what an interesting one it was. Thomas à Becket is counted among the most distinguished of the early English scholars. He read law there at some time between 1143 and 1148 and he is said to have taken back to England with him the Italian lawyer, Vacarius, who gave the first lecture on Roman Law at Oxford. After Becket's martyrdom there must have been an English 'nation' at Bologna, since the records state that English students were expected to serve the altar of S. Thomas in the church of S. Salvatore. It is possible to read between the lines here and there and to discover that Norman and Plantagenet scholars suffered from those twin trials of university life down the ages, lack of money and the non-arrival of allowances. There are records of Englishmen who pawned their law books; a Master David of London got into debt in 1168, while others fell unwisely in love, and some were slain in brawls. An early Anglo-Scottish quarrel was that of 'Hugh Anglus', who accused 'Simon Scotus' of threats and robbery. An early English doctor who studied at Bologna was Nicholas of Farnham, who became physician to Henry III and Eleanor of Provence.

A professor told me of many a strange custom observed by the University in the Middle Ages, the oddest, I thought, being the presentation of the snow. This took place on the first heavy snow-fall of the year, when the Rectors of the various nations, attended by their beadles, carried a lordly platter containing a snowball to the chief city dignitaries, each of whom rewarded them with money. The sum collected was spent in feasting in the evening. This pleasant custom was abolished at some time in the fifteenth century.

I was curious to know something of the famous women

professors of Bologna who achieved academic distinction in the early Middle Ages. The story of one professor, who was so beautiful that she had to lecture from behind a screen in order not to distract her class, is one that you will be told in every Italian university, but it happens to be more or less true in Bologna. The lady was Novella Calderini, who lived in the early fourteenth century. She and her sister, Bettina, evidently inherited from their father, the distinguished jurist, Giovanni d'Andrea Calderini, a genius for legal studies which showed even when they were children. It is said that when the doctor was absent from Bologna on diplomatic missions, one of his daughters would take his place in the lecture-room. Novella was so beautiful that, in order to keep the students' minds on jurisprudence, she ascended her rostrum wearing a thick veil. This must be the origin of the story of the screen. She married a legal don, Giovanni Oldrendi da Legnano, whose chair she also took when he was obliged to be absent on state business. Urban V offered to make her husband a cardinal if she would retire to a nunnery, but the couple refused to give up their life together. Novella died in 1366, after a long and happy married life.

But she was not the first woman professor at Bologna. This was Bitisia Gozzadini, born in 1209, who won *la laurea* in both Civil and Canon Law. The last famous woman lecturer was Laura Bassi, born in 1711, who, like all her predecessors, seems to have been something of an infant prodigy, and astounded her elders when a child by her fluent Latin and her grasp of meta-physics. When she was twenty-one she was persuaded to give a typically mediaeval exhibition of her talents in public, the sort of academic brains trust that had been popular in Bologna for centuries. It is reported that she emerged triumphantly from the ordeal, having been quizzed and examined by five learned professors, and in a few weeks was accorded *la laurea* in Philosophy and a Chair in the University. Her real interest was the then fashionable one of electrical experiment, and before Galvani (whose graceful statue stands outside the Archigymnasium) had observed the twitching of the frogs' legs, or Volta had invented his electrical piles, Laura Bassi was inventing machines to produce charges of electricity. When Dr Burney visited Bologna in 1770, he presented a letter of introduction to her and found her 'between fifty and sixty; but though learned and a genius, not at all masculine or assuming'. She showed him some of her machines and made a few sparks for him, and told him a rather interesting story. When Dr Franklin had discovered the connection between electricity and lightning and had published his paper on conductors, she said that she had iron rods fixed on the roof of the Institute, but so great was the alarm of the populace that she had to take them down, in spite of a reassuring letter of approval from Pope Benedict XIV.

I was told of another woman, a contemporary of Laura Bassi's, who made a great name for herself in Bologna. She was Anna, the wife of a melancholy sculptor of anatomy named Giovanni Mazolini. Beautiful models of the human body in wood and wax were necessary after Bologna came under Papal rule since the Church rarely permitted the dissection of human bodies, and I do not know whether Giovanni's depression was caused by the thought that a box-wood liver or a wax kidney were of less use to science than the executed criminals used so freely in non-papal Padua. However, in an attempt to cheer him up, Anna took up the study of anatomy so that she could work beside him and she became so expert that her models were admired as much as his; also the inspiration which descended so freely upon the learned women of Bologna caused her to become a famous lecturer on anatomy.

The records of the University are extraordinarily full and vivid and contain many accounts of student life during the Middle Ages. The average student lived in one of fourteen residential colleges organized as 'nations' (the Spanish College still exists), though many boarded out with private citizens, and wealthy students, arriving with a train of servants and their own furniture, hired houses. Before the invention of printing only the rich scholar could hope to own his books, and these were evidently of formidable size and weight, for some contracts between student and householder provide for the services of a porter to carry the books to and from lodging to lecture hall. It seems that every opportunity was seized for a feast or a procession, and the students of a 'nation' often turned out in strength to welcome the son of a distinguished countryman. There were, of course, disputes between town and University, but these did not often end in casualties. Petrarch, who studied law at Bologna from 1323 to 1326, seems to have been a model undergraduate, diligent at work and fond, in his spare time, of wandering round the countryside with other undergraduates. He has described how he would return sometimes in the dark after the gates had been locked. One has always imagined that in 1323 every city was surrounded by impregnable walls, and it is surprising to be told by Petrarch that if the gates were shut he and his friends knew of places where the wall ended in 'brittle paling half rotten by age' where 'each of us could make entry where it suited his convenience'.

The final examination for a doctorate ended with a spectacular viva in the cathedral to which the candidate, wearing his best clothes, was conducted by his friends in a procession led by the beadles, the Archdeacon, and the professors. The candidates had to be at least twenty years of age and to have studied civil law for eight years (six years for Canon Law or five years for a degree in medicine). Two doctors, who had previously examined the candidate in private, acted as his sponsors and walked with him in the procession. Having arrived at the cathedral, the candidate delivered a thesis, after which he was questioned by the professors and by fellow students; if he emerged successfully, he was given the insignia of the *laurea* – book, ring, and biretta – and was then conducted to his 'chair'. This was often an imposing ceremony attended by pipers and trumpeters and by a great crowd of students of all nationalities. Nothing delighted Bologna more than a princely undergraduate, and when the son of one of the ruling houses took up residence, the town and the University really let themselves go. An occasion of this kind was the arrival, during the winter term of 1522, of the seventeen-year-old Ercole Gonzaga, in later life the distinguished and faultless cardinal, the second, and favourite, son of Isabella d'Este. His letter to his mother announcing his safe arrival, and his description of what one might euphemistically call his 'rooms', give a good idea of the state an aristocratic young undergraduate was expected to keep up. He wrote:

> 'Most excellent and illustrious Lady and dearest Mother,
>
> On my arrival yesterday, a great cavalcade rode out to meet me about eight miles from Bologna. First came my cousin, Pirro Gonzaga, with sixty other scholars, mostly of Mantuan birth, on horseback. These dismounted, and Pirro and I embraced each other tenderly. A little further we met a troop of Bolognese gentlemen, who all rejoiced at my coming: and yet further on came dear Maestro Pietro himself [Pietro Pomponazzi, the philosopher], with a number of learned doctors, who had ridden some way out of the town to meet me. So I entered Bologna about four o'clock with a train of two hundred horsemen, and the streets and gateways were crowded with men, and women stood at all the windows, crying out "Gonzaga!" When I reached my house I saw that its owner, Aliprando, had decorated the doorway with festoons of evergreens and shields bearing the arms of our house, of the Pope, and of the people and Governor of Bologna. After taking leave of these gentlemen, I got off my horse and visited my rooms, which pleased me immensely. First of all you enter a beautiful little *salotto*, hung with tapestries which I had sent on as well as several pictures in frames, which look very well, and containing a bed hung with crimson damask embroidered with various devices. From this room you enter a smaller one, also hung with tapestry, and containing two couches, one draped with cloth of gold, the other covered with linen. Within, there is a third room, with a couch hung with crimson velvet and cloth of gold, which I will use as a study. Certainly these lodgings are most excellent, and all my servants are quite satisfied, and indeed the house is as good and comfortable as possible. Last night my cousin Pirro and some of our Mantuan scholars supped with me. I kiss your hands reverently.'

The picture of a young Renaissance prince studying on a couch hung with crimson velvet and cloth of gold is happily tempered by hints (in the Mantuan archives), of rags and celebrations, and at least one tragic moment when a Mantuan student quarrelled with one from Modena and killed him. At Christmas-time there was a week's vacation and the University was given over to fun and feasting. The Mantuan students hung laurel wreaths over their prince's doorway and primed the college beadle to recite mock heroic verses in his honour, which was the cause of much merriment. When Christmas was over, Ercole attended an anatomy lecture at which a number of sculptors and painters were present, and saw the dissection of the body of a man who had been hanged for theft. Of course Ercole ran short of money, and there exists in the archives a pathetic letter to his mother from his tutor telling her that her poor son was down to his last penny! One hopes this did not reach Isabella during one of those not infrequent moments in her own affairs when her jewels had been pawned in Venice.

§ 9

Nothing is more worthy of admiration in Italy than the preservation of municipal archives, and every time one sees these mighty collections one wonders what may still be hidden away there awaiting discovery. Bologna's archives contain a number of little-known records of the Stuarts. It is strange that no Bologna guide-book so much as mentions the unhappy princes whose shabby court, with its impoverished loyalists and its spies, was in and out of Bologna for years; indeed no other city in Italy save Rome is so full of Jacobite memories. These associations began one evening in May, 1719, when there appeared at the Hotel Pellegrino, in the Via Ugo Bassi, a tired young girl of sixteen with four Irish officers. Her only luggage was a petticoat lined with ermine, three chemises, a few handkerchiefs, and a bag of brown cloth which contained the Crown Jewels of England. She was Clementina Sobieski, grand-daughter of the hero King of Poland. The Crown Jewels had been sent to her by James Stuart as a betrothal present, and the four Irish officers had just rescued her from prison in Innsbruck, where she was being held by the Emperor (an ally of George I), who thought that if he could prevent the marriage he would be assisting the Protestant succession. However, the four gallant Irish Jacobites broke into the castle on a snowy night and rescued the princess, leaving a servant girl dressed in her clothes, and after a terrible journey across the Alps made for the safety of the Pope's city of Bologna.

In the next few days Clementina's incognita wore so thinly at the hotel that it was thought prudent to move her to an uncomfortable private house, where she waited the arrival from Rome of James Murray, who was to marry her by proxy. There is a charming painting on vellum in the Bologna archives which shows the marriage. The commonplace little room has been decorated with a number of heraldic shields and contains nothing but a few chairs, a chest, two mirrors, and what looks like a divan bed. The princess, wearing a light-coloured dress with a train, a mob-cap, and a string of pearls, stands with a bridesmaid (the wife of one of her rescuers), and two men in long, brindled wigs, who wear swords slanting through the tails of their velvet coats, evidently two of the Irishmen. Facing her is a priest and two more courtly figures in long wigs, wearing velvet coats with swords, one of them James Murray. So began poor Clementina's frustrated life as would-be Queen of England. Romance has been kind to her, and after her death there was a movement for her beatification, but the truth is that she became a tiresome and neurotic woman and must have been a severe trial to live with. She had beautiful blonde hair which hung almost to her ankles, and this northern colouring she handed on to her son, Prince Charles Edward – 'Bonnie Prince Charlie'.

Charles's daughter, Charlotte, Duchess of Albany, whose mother was Clementina Walkinshaw, whom the prince had met in Scotland during the '45, died in Bologna, though the church in which she was buried was pulled down many years ago and even her tombstone has been lost. Few tears have been shed for her, though she was worthier than many of her relations. After having been slighted and neglected by her father for over thirty years, she instantly went to him in his sorrowful old age and introduced a note of calm and dignity into his disordered life. She survived him less than two years. Suffering from cancer, which was attributed to a fall from her horse, she went to Bologna to consult the surgeons, but died before she could be operated on.

A Jacobite, if any still exist, could spend a profitable hour in the Bologna archives and in wandering round the city looking out the palaces in which the Stuarts lived. There are several of them, though in the puzzling way of Italian palaces many have changed their names with their tenants. One, however, the Casa Belloni, carries a tablet on the staircase wall which states that James Francis Stuart once held his court there.

The archives also preserve in manuscript form the extraordinary story of the descendants of Queen Elizabeth's favourite, Robert Dudley, Earl of Leicester, who settled in Florence and Bologna. His son, Robert Dudley the second, in despair of being able to establish his legitimacy, decided to leave England. There may indeed have been other reasons, for, with the same casual attitude to marriage that distinguished his father, he left a wife and family and departed with a lovely young woman, Elizabeth Southwell, who accompanied him dressed as a page. They settled in Florence and eventually had a family of thirteen. Like so many men of his time, Dudley knew a great deal about seafaring, ships, and engineering, and he was also an amateur chemist and alchemist. As a dignitary at the court of Cosimo II, Duke of Tuscany, he drained the Pisa marshes, designed ships and compounded patent medicines, and became so well known and distinguished that the Emperor made him Earl of Warwick and Duke of Northumberland in the Holy Roman Empire. He also managed to obtain a dispensation to marry Elizabeth Southwell.

Their success was marred by the conduct of their eldest son, Cosimo, who turned out to be a rascal. As the second 'Duca di Northumbria', he married a French girl of good family and among their children was a sensationally beautiful girl named Cristina. After a scandalous youth she was married to the Marchese Paleotti of Bologna, and upon his death she turned the family palace into what might politely be called a matrimonial agency, which became popular with all the rich young men of the time. As she grew older, her ambition was to make a good marriage for her favourite daughter, Diana, a girl of seventeen, by all accounts a second edition of herself. And she succeeded, after various ruses which were the delight of Bologna, in capturing no less a bridegroom that Marc' Antonio Colonna.

The return to England of two members of this family was not the least fantastic episode in its history. This happened when a second daughter, Adelaide, without her mother's assistance, married the forty-five-year-old Charles Talbot, twelfth Earl of Shrewsbury, and so left the Italian scene for the land of her ancestors. Thus in the first decade of the eighteenth century a descendant of Elizabeth's Leicester attended the Court of Queen Anne and, later, achieved social success at the Court of George I. This was not lost on a scapegrace brother, Ferdinando, who had murdered, raped, and embezzled, and turned up in England to sponge on Lord and Lady Shrewsbury. Unfortunately for him, he flew into a rage one day in 1718 and killed his servant. He was brought to trial and condemned to be hanged at Tyburn. He was allowed to drive there in his own coach and was hanged with a silk rope entwined with threads of gold. 'Vain man!' commented the *Newgate Calendar*. 'Of what avail were his titles in the presence of the Almighty?'

The conduct and importunity of Ferdinando are said to have killed the Earl of Shrewsbury, and in far-away Bologna, Cristina di Northumbria, hearing of her son's death on the gallows, is said to have fainted. But by that time she had entered the familiar refuge of so many great courtesans, and was entirely given over to good works and to devotion. Anyone who wishes to read this story in detail will find it in *Vita Barocca*, by Corrado Ricci, who explored the Bologna archives with successful zest.

§ 10

As I have said, the Italian restaurant, notably in England, with its spaghetti drenched with tomato sauce and its flaccid Veal Milanese, has probably done more to frighten people from Italian cooking than anything else, and I would recommend, as a corrective, a tour through the region of Emilia. I have already indicated that in this opulent, buttery, and cheesey land every town vies with its neighbour in the richness of its local dishes, and all agree that the highest standards of gastronomy are achieved in Bologna, the Fat. It is unusual in Italy to find any town that will admit the superiority of another, but this the towns of Emilia do when they refer to the pork, the sausages, the creamy sauces, and the white truffles of Bologna. Rossini, who gave his name to many operas and one *tournedos*, and was as fond of food as he was of music, settled at Bologna because of its cuisine, and they will proudly point out the house in which the *maestro* digested so many rich meals.

I had heard so much of Bologna's food that I half expected to find a town of Falstaffs and was almost surprised to discover the people to be of moderate proportions. My own experiences were memorable. The first time I had luncheon at the Papagallo, I was comatose for the rest of the day, but the recollection of chickens' breasts cooked in butter and served with thin slices of white truffles, or, even richer, layers of turkey and ham oozing with butter, cheese, truffles, and mushrooms, and of the Lambrusco, the dry, sparkling Emilian red wine that seems made by Nature for Bolognese cooking, is one that will, I am sure, return poignantly if I am ever put on a diet. The great speciality of Bologna is a large sausage called Mortadella, which has been made for untold centuries and may even have been made by the Romans on the old Via Emilia. It is made of pork, but no doubt because I am not a great lover of sausages and salami, I could not understand its fame, or the affection with which it is spoken of all over the region.

When I was dining alone one evening I saw a sight which, more than a thousand recipes, explains why Bologna is so proud of its nickname, '*la Grassa*'. Seated near me were two women gastronomes dining together and unconscious of all save the food upon their plates. I have no idea what the bird-watching equivalent of such a rare sight may be – perhaps a couple of red-billed hoopoes – but I admit that these two women fascinated me, and I watched them out of the corner of my eye with the eagerness of a curious ornithologist. As every man knows, women left to themselves will live on buns, biscuits, and fruit salad, and there seemed to me something phenomenal about these two, who accepted the homage of proprietor, head waiter, and wine steward as a right, as if they were queens accepting the expected flattery of courtiers. Who were they, I wondered. Were they women who had abandoned themselves to the authorship of a cookery book; were they the wives or sweethearts of men who admired immense Rubenesque women, for that was obviously the shape of things to come? At the moment, however, both were young, and, though well covered, could not be called fat except perhaps by a dress designer. There must surely have been female epicures though no names spring readily to mind, and the fact that one has to invent an explanation for two such women proves how rare they must be. I would like to have seen the last stages of their banquet, but they drew it out so lovingly that I had to leave while they were still pondering, menu in hand, with the proprietor. I shall carry with me for a long time the memory of their happy faces and their shining noses.

§ II

The group of seven or eight churches called S. Stefano is a mediaeval attempt to create in Bologna a full-size replica of the Holy Sepulchre in Jerusalem. It is rather puzzling unless you know this. Anyone familiar with the Church of the Holy Sepulchre, however, will see that everything in S. Stefano falls into its proper place and, what is more interesting, reflects not the shabby present-day church, but the building as it was known to the Crusaders. The tomb of Christ in Jerusalem is covered today by an ugly structure, the work of a nineteenth century Greek architect, and the shrine which stands isolated in the rotunda at Bologna may be a copy of the Holy Sepulchre as seen by the mediaeval pilgrim. I thought S. Stefano one of the most fascinating churches I had seen in Italy, and one that was pervaded by an air of such remote antiquity that I was not surprised to come across a notice drawing attention to a column, or a stone, which had formed part of a temple of Isis which once stood on the site. The beautiful little cloister which leads to the rotunda dates from about the time of the Norman Conquest, and in the centre is a stone bowl on a more recent base which is called a font, but it is really a Byzantine receptacle for alms of a kind still to be seen sometimes on sacred sites in the Holy Land.

A dominating physical feature of Bologna is the steep hill, about a thousand feet high, which rises above the town and is called Monte della Guardia. I was told that it derives its name from the sentries who in former times were stationed there to keep an eye on Modena. There is a large pilgrimage church on the summit where yet another of S. Luke's miraculous Virgins has presided benevolently over Bologna since the Middle Ages. The church is connected with the town by an architectural *tour-de-force* in which Bologna's love of covered ways achieves an impressive climax. This is a colonnade two miles long, roofed with beautiful red tiles, and it strides boldly upward, reminding one of some great feat of Roman construction like Hadrian's Wall. It is also rather a touching colonnade. It was built by private citizens, guilds, and villages over a period of some sixty years; and those who contributed to a few yards of it are commemorated by little tablets fixed to the walls. It was built so that pilgrims might reach the sanctuary in all weathers, and also that the Virgin di S. Luca might descend under cover at Ascension-tide to visit the cathedral of Bologna.

Nowadays, though the colonnade is still used by pilgrimages, it is possible to take a tramcar to the foot of the mountain and then a cableway to the summit. Here is an astonishing view, one I thought finer than any I had seen since I looked north at Bergamo to the Alps and, in the other direction, over the Po Valley. Looking west, I saw the Via Emilia running straight as a spear to Modena and Parma, and the foothills of the Apennines stretching on into Tuscany and the south. Dim smudges of smoke in the north indicated the towns of Lombardy, and to the east the land melted away into a heat mist in which lay Ravenna and the Adriatic Sea.

Above the high altar of the church is the famous picture of the Madonna which, the story goes, was brought from Constantinople by a hermit in the Middle Ages. It is, presumably, a Byzantine ikon, though it is covered everywhere with silver and only the dark oval of the face is visible. There were several pilgrims kneeling before the altar, holding candles. A young priest came out and held out a replica of the ikon, which they kissed. I noticed that the priest was modern and hygienic. He wiped away each kiss with a face-towel before he offered the ikon to the next pilgrim.

CHAPTER SIX

Rimini – The Temple of Malatesta – A Man who was sent to Hell – Crossing the Rubicon – Ravenna and its revival – The Tomb of Galla Placidia – The Mosaics – The Fall of Rome – Ferrara and the Estensi – England's First Greek Scholars – Renaissance Space Travel – Where Lucrezia Borgia was buried

§ 1

Though I am not more compassionate or forgiving than most people, I sometimes feel sympathy for the really wicked people of history. I wonder whether they were as bad as their biographers have made them out to be, and there is no way of finding out. 'Men of past ages are merely problems which we endeavour to solve,' wrote Gregorovius, which is a kindly variation of Voltaire's 'History is, after all, nothing but a parcel of tricks that we play upon the dead.' And in a generous mood I approached the city associated with a man who, I suppose, most people would say is high up among the ten worst people who have ever lived – Sigismondo Malatesta of Rimini. He aroused the violent hatred of Pius II, otherwise a kindly and tolerant man, and few reputations, I suppose, could be expected to survive the ordeal of being publicly consigned to hell and burnt in effigy as Pius II consigned and burned the lord of Rimini.

When I arrived there – Rimini is seventy miles to the east of Bologna – I wanted to look at the Adriatic and so drove down to the beach. Instead of the gentle view which I had expected, with perhaps an odd sail or two, I saw twelve miles of sun-bathers lying on the sand or sprawled in canvas chairs. Most of the northern countries of Europe had contributed to this revelation though, listening to the voices, I should have said that Germany was responsible for much the greatest number of bodies. Once so remote, Rimini is now on the main road of the sun-bather; I witnessed a meeting between two English friends in a hotel lobby, one of whom had breakfasted that morning in London.

It does not take long to discover that Rimini, like the man whose name is associated with it, has a dual nature. There is the sun-bathing Rimini of the miles of striped umbrellas and huge summer hotels; and a couple of miles inland you find the quiet old Rimini of the past, still bearing signs of the air raids of the last war, the Rimini where the Via Emilia meets the Via Flaminia, where the noble Arch of Augustus stands near a Roman bridge which is still in use, and where they hold a crowded mediaeval market in the shadow of an ancient castle. There is a charming little temple, or shrine, in the middle of the road, full of flowers when I was there, which marks the place where the mule of S. Anthony of Padua knelt as the Sacrament went past. The greatest sight in Rimini, however, is the most unusual Christian church ever built, the Tempio Malatestiano, which Sigismondo erected in honour of S. Francis, but really to glorify and eventually to enshrine the remains of the woman he loved, and to whom he never even pretended to be faithful, Isotta degli Atti. It is indeed a temple to Isotta. His initials and hers, intertwined, are to be seen all over the church, and there is scarcely a Christian emblem anywhere.

Alberti's beautiful entrance, a Roman arch, prepared me for the exquisite classical interior. I entered a building of rare marbles with a number of side-chapels all richly decorated with carving and sculpture. The interlaced initials 'S.I.' are everywhere, and marble elephants are to be seen by the dozen. They support pilasters and sarcophagi, while decorations which, at a first glance, appear to be waving ribbons are really, on closer inspection, the trunks of elephants. This animal was the heraldic badge of the Malatesti, a strange one since no member of that warlike family had ever fought in Africa, or, so far as one knows, had anything to do with these creatures. Perhaps they adopted the emblem because bones supposed to be those of Hannibal's elephants were in distant times discovered in Malatesti territory, at the Furlo Pass near Fossambrone. The animals, beautifully carved in black marble, add much to the strangeness and the mystery of this building. Two support an urn in which, so a priest told me, the remains of Isotta still repose, and above her tomb two more wave their trunks. The elephants are, however, absent from the tomb of Sigismondo.

The celebrated picture by Piero della Francesca, of Sigismondo kneeling before his patron saint, is to be seen in the church, where, as usual, Malatesta is pictured in profile. It is a powerful, good-looking face and I doubt whether anyone unaware of his reputation would consider him 'sinister' or 'snake-like', which are the usual descriptions of him. He remains the great psychological mystery of the Renaissance. What is one to make of him? He was the most grasping and treacherous of the *condottieri* – itself no mean feat. His first wife was said to have been poisoned by him, his second wife was found one morning with a napkin tied tightly round her throat, and he is said to have debauched his daughters. At the same time he maintained a court full of artists, poets, and scholars, and his respect for learning was such that he allowed himself to be dictated to by a band of dreary pedants, whose tombs, under arched recesses, can be seen on the outside of the church. One of these is still believed to hold the ashes of the Byzantine scholar Gemisthus Plethon, which Sigismondo brought back from Mistra when he captured Sparta from the Turks: it was typical of him that he should have preferred to enshrine a Greek scholar rather than a Christian saint. Naturally his life-long love for Isotta, the inspiration of his poems and his glorious temple, has often been described, yet surely she is equally puzzling. Can one really believe that she was the one good influence in his life? Or was she an ambitious woman who overlooked his sins and his other mistresses and eventually married him and inherited his estate? Every time one tries to believe that Sigismondo was not as bad as he was painted, one comes up against the vilification of Pius II, who knew him and detested him. 'The poison of all Italy,' the Pope called him, and 'of all men who have ever lived, or ever will live, he was the worst scoundrel, the disgrace of Italy and the infamy of our times'. The Pope said:

'He had a thorough knowledge of history and no slight acquaintance with philosophy. Whatever he attempted he seemed born for, but the evil part of his character had the upper hand. He was such a slave to avarice that he was ready not only to plunder but to steal. His lust was so unbridled that he violated his daughters and his sons-in-law. He outdid all barbarians in cruelty. His bloody hand inflicted terrible punishments on innocent and guilty alike. He oppressed the poor, plundered the rich, spared neither widows nor orphans. No one felt safe under his rule. Wealth or a beautiful wife or handsome children were enough to cause a man to be accused of crime. He hated priests and despised religion. He had no belief in another world and thought the soul died with the body. Nevertheless he built at Rimini a splendid church dedicated to S. Francis, though he filled it so full of pagan works of art that it seemed less a Christian sanctuary than a temple of devil-worshippers. In it he erected for his mistress a tomb of magnificent marble and exquisite workmanship with an inscription in the pagan style as follows, "Sacred to the deified Isotta".'

In 1461 the Pope's detestation of Sigismondo forged a new weapon in the papal ordinance which, so far as I know, had never been fired before and has never been discharged since: the Pope publicly condemned Sigismondo to hell, and, in a curious reversal of the process of canonization, ordered a cardinal to investigate the case and report. 'No mortal heretofore has descended into Hell with the ceremony of canonization,' said Pius. 'Sigismondo shall be the first to be deemed worthy of such honour. By an edict of the Pope, he shall be enrolled in the company of Hell as comrade of the devils and the damned.' In the following year Sigismondo was excommunicated and a life-like effigy of him was burnt in front of S. Peter's in the presence of a large crowd. From the mouth of the dummy protruded an inscription which read, 'Sigismondo Malatesta, son of Pandolfo, king of traitors, hated of God and man, condemned to the flames by the vote of the holy senate.'

Though Sigismondo was amused by these events, a series of shattering defeats soon made it politic for him to make peace with the Church, and Pius, with an admirable display of Christian charity and forgiveness, lifted the excommunication and accepted Sigismondo's repentance. It was, however, scarcely even a formal admission of guilt for after the death of Pius, Sigismondo, offended by the new Pope, Paul II, set off for Rome with the intention of plunging a dagger into the pontiff during an audience.

The Pope, having been warned, it is said even the cardinals wore swords under their robes! Sigismondo eventually declined in fortune and health, and in a few years time died at the age of fifty-one, leaving Isotta in control of his affairs. He was a character impossible to whitewash, yet one looks at the lovely church which sprang from such a strange brain, mystified by the dualism of his nature.

A few miles north of Rimini, on the coast road to Ravenna, I came to a trickle of summer water that was flowing under a bridge. Its name was the Rubicon. It was once the boundary between Cisalpine Gaul and Rome, and any general who crossed it with his army, without the permission of the Senate, was committing rebellion. Caesar crossed it because his spies had told him that his enemies in the capital were plotting his downfall, and he knew that he had to march on Rome or perish. It was the greatest gamble of his life and, as he ordered his legions to advance, it is said he remarked, like a true gambler, *Alea jacta est* – 'the die is cast'; and ever since men have been casting their various dies and crossing their Rubicons. When a Roman army forded a river into enemy country, it was usual for a sacrifice to be offered to the river god, but, instead of slaying animals, Caesar dedicated a herd of horses to the Rubicon and set them free to roam the valley without a herdsman. Among the signs and portents that foretold his assassination was the behaviour of these horses, which were said to have been seen standing dolefully in their pastures, refusing to eat, and weeping bitterly.

It is curious how often famous rivers fail to live up to their associations: the Tiber is not much to look at, and the Jordan is hardly wider than the Rubicon. In winter, of course, the Rubicon, like all torrents, would be formidable, and Caesar forded it on January 10, in the year 48 B.C., which, as the unreformed calendar was about seven weeks ahead of the sun, would really have been during the November floods. As I stood looking at this stream, to me one of the most thought-provoking sights in Italy, cars, motor-cycles, scooters, coaches, and caravans continued to rush past; and during the few moments I was there several hundred people must have crossed the Rubicon without being aware of it.

§ 2

I went on to Ravenna thinking how strange it is that the Roman Empire should have been born there and have died in the same little country town. It had the whole known world to die in, yet it returned to that obscure place in the marshes. Caesar was in Ravenna when he marched on Rome and so set in motion forces which created Imperial Rome, and five centuries later it was to Ravenna that the last shadowy Emperors fled from Milan, with their Greek hair-cuts and their encrusted dalmatics, to seek safety from the barbarians. The town proved to be a good shelter which helped to prolong imperial history in the West for another seventy years.

The countryside has the uneasy appearance of having been deserted by the sea. The indomitable Italian farmer has tilled it and irrigated it, but still it has the look of land that remembers the movements of the tides, and I fancied that many a vine root goes down to coil itself round an anchor. Long before Venice had been heard of, Ravenna was a city surrounded by marshes, whose streets were canals and whose inhabitants went everywhere by boat and barge; and the Romans wrote about it much as we now write about its successor. It was notable in early times as a city that drank rain-water, as Venice used to do until recently, and in whose bracing air gladiators flourished. The last public engagement of Caesar before he crossed the Rubicon was to inspect a gladiatorial school and to watch a show put on for his approval.

When I arrived, I was prepared to see the 'dear dead town' of Byron's day. Instead, I joined a stream of traffic that crawled slowly through narrow streets designed for two horsemen riding abreast, until a traffic policeman waved me into a crowded little piazza, where café tables invaded the pavement. Everything I had read about Ravenna led me to expect a sleepy place of crumbling walls and tottering palaces where grass would be sprouting in the streets; but I saw instead a thriving market town filled with vitality and cheerful prosperity. The streets were packed with the tenant farmers of the district, who had come in from the country to do their week-end shopping; and I noticed a number of swarthy characters who bore a striking resemblance to Mussolini, evidently a local type, since the Dictator's birthplace, near Predappio, is not far away.

I was given a front room in an hotel overlooking a narrow road and a shop called 'Old England'. Here at last, I thought, I have found a quiet corner where the sleepy old Ravenna which I have read about still persists. Hardly had I thought this than the narrow streets roared with the noise of approaching motor coaches, which, by some miracle of driving, drew up before 'Old England' and discharged their passengers, then reversed into side turnings and waited. The hotel was immediately filled with feminine chatter, for most of the travellers were women. They filled every part of the building and overwhelmed the dining-room. Two of them, both English, sat at my table and asked if there was anything to see in Ravenna. It seemed a nice, clean little place, they thought. Venice had smelt; and it was such a pity that so many cabbage leaves were floating in the Grand Canal. Was Florence clean? They looked at their watches. They would be in Florence for tea. Would there be tea? I liked them both, and envied their ability to be conveyed pneumatically across Italy without a care, hearing no voices from the vasty deep, feeling no ghostly fingers: two nice, sensible women, unhampered by the past.

After lunch I faced the unpleasant trial of having my hair cut. The hateful ministrations of the barber vary in unpleasantness from country to country, but, I think, reach exasperation point in Italy, where his shop is a club and his looking-glasses reflect the faces of those who are in love with their appearance. I did think, however, that, if anywhere, I might in Ravenna find some quiet little place where I could have a hair-cut without fuss and bother, and quickly escape. Pushing aside a bead curtain, I found myself, alas, in the usual haunt of masculine vanity and self-approval. Old and young were being shaved and shorn as if in Martial's Rome. All snipping stopped when a young man entered with an illustrated paper and passed round a photograph of Venus Genetrix in the guise of Italy's most popular film actress. The comments were not flippant or coarse; indeed the connoisseurs might have been admiring a beautiful urn. Still, to them, the most satisfactory objects in sight were without any question their own reflections.

When my turn came, I remarked to the barber that Ravenna was far from the quiet, dead town I had expected, and he told me that the discovery of methane gas since the last war had brought a new and entirely unexpected prosperity. Ravenna, he said with pride, was now an industrial town and possesses more television sets than any other town of its size in Italy.

Instead of visiting the tombs of Galla Placidia and Dante, as I had expected to do that afternoon, I spent it in searching for what everyone calls E.N.I., which means Ente Nazionale Idrocarburi. It is five miles from the town, on the seven-mile-long canal which connects Ravenna with the Adriatic. Here I saw a huge modern plant with giant retorts and cooling towers, which covers about three hundred acres of ground. A wall encloses it and round the wall were hundreds of cars and more motor-scooters and bicycles than I have ever seen gathered in one place, all parked under concrete shelters round the main gates. Lacking an introduction, I could not enter the monster, but stood looking at it in amazement, wondering how such a place could have been created in ten years. Here obviously was the answer to Ravenna's air of energy and prosperity. Byron must have ridden over the site of E.N.I. when there was nothing but pine trees and silence. I thought it one of the most unexpected sights in Italy: the reawakening of Ravenna after thirteen centuries of slumber. I went on along the canal and came to the Adriatic at Port Corsini, which has recently been enlarged to take the tankers which come to E.N.I. from the Middle East and Russia.

Towards sunset I managed to find a vacant table in the delightful café that sprawls into the main piazza, and there I was joined by an acquaintance who lives in Ravenna. He told me that E.N.I. is already producing thousands of tons of fertilizers and synthetic rubber and, of course, petrol.

'Who owns it?' I asked.

'The State,' he replied.

To me the State and Ravenna suggested a few inept and short-lived emperors and a line of Exarchs; now it means Vespas and Lambrettas, television sets, bicycles and Fiats, and the reawakening of the aged streets to unexpected vitality. So far, industrialization has done nothing to change the noble and romantic appearance of Ravenna. Indeed, as we sat there in the evening, while the fishtail battlements of the old palaces cut the pale sky, music came from some open window, and there seemed to be magic in the air. We remained until it became chilly, then walked back to the hotel. We sat in the little bar with a German professor who had come from Munich to see the mosaics.

§ 3

I enjoyed a walk as the bells were ringing for early Mass and market women were arriving with their vegetables and fish. Here was the rustic Ravenna seen by former travellers, and the scene was one which Byron must have observed often, if he rose early enough to see it, in the days when he was making love to his plump little Countess Guiccioli.

I think that the street markets of Italy are worth perpetuating before the modern world sweeps them away. They are all different, yet are drawn to the same pattern, just as their backgrounds are a variation on that stately theme: the cathedral, the baptistry, the campanile, and the town hall. I wish some photographer as talented as Georgina Masson would devote a book to them. Eggs, poultry, and vegetables have never been sold in a nobler setting. It would be fascinating to compare the faces and market stalls of Mantua, Cremona, and Bologna with those of Ravenna, Rimini, and Padua. What glimpses of eternal types are to be seen in those morning hours as the sun descends from the red roof tiles and warms the streets: faces which Giotto painted glance up from baskets of plum-shaped tomatoes, and one looks into face after face, recognizing a Piero della Francesca here and a Bellini there, while a tilt of the head or an attitude carries the mind to a quayside by Carpaccio. I remember often vainly searching the faces in

Rome for a likely Caesar, but one would not have far to go in Ravenna. One might even buy a dozen new laid-eggs from the Mother of the Gracchi. The moment I saw the country people of the Romagna, I felt that I was in a different tribal area, a province full of forceful and expressive individuals who resembled their ancestors more closely than usual, even in Italy.

The tide of history has ebbed away from Ravenna, as the Adriatic has done, leaving behind some half-dozen shabby-looking red-brick churches, just as the sea deposits a microcosm of the departed ocean in a rock pool. The accidents of survival are surely among the strangest of phenomena. We all know of the glass of water which emerged intact from an air raid, and the churches of Ravenna, having resisted some of the worst blasts of history, wear something of the same air of miraculous survival. The palaces and other secular buildings, their contemporaries, whose occupants founded the churches, have utterly vanished; and one can only reflect that such unusual saints as Ursicinus, Nazarius, Celsus, Vitalis, and Apollinaris, to whom the churches are dedicated, have proved efficient guardians.

Nowhere else in the world are there such relics of the fifth and sixth centuries, and, unlike many Italian cities, Ravenna is easy to understand. The visitor is not required to leap mentally from century to century: everything he is shown is the result of events which occurred during what in Italy is a brief space of time, a mere century and a half – from A.D. 400 to A.D. 550. I set off to see these churches, impressed by the knowledge that I was about to enter buildings which had been erected and decorated a century and more before S. Augustine set off to convert the Saxons: and the storm which drove the last emperors into Ravenna, and elevated the town to the dignity of an imperial residence, was the same which summoned the Roman legions from Britain and terminated four centuries of Roman rule. It is curious to think that the crisis in Ravenna set up a chain reaction that was felt as far away as York and Chester.

The tomb of Galla Placidia is a small brick building which stands upon a stretch of rough grass. The contrast is startling as you leave the rough exterior and pass inside, to find yourself in a small building completely covered, floor, walls, and roof, with decorations designed about the year A.D. 446. One expects mosaics of this period to be fragmentary, but here is a complete chapel covered with them. My first impression was of blue, a luminous, rich dark blue, that covered ceilings, the dome, and the curves of arches. The blue was scattered everywhere with golden stars and rosettes, and the light, in which the mosaics seemed to change colour and shimmer, was like the filtered light of some palace under the sea as it glowed rather than shone through windows of biscuit-thin sheets of alabaster. The only time I truly felt I had passed into another age and century was many years ago, when I stood in the tomb of Tut-ankh-Amen at Luxor before the treasures had been removed. Something of this same awareness of the strangeness of the past came to me again in the Tomb of Galla Placidia.

The mosaics on the heavenly blue walls paint a number of pictures. The most interesting is that of Christ as a beardless young Roman, wearing a gold toga with blue *clavi*, and sandals, as he sits amid a rocky landscape and leans upon a tall Byzantine cross of gold. Around him graze symbolic white sheep, members of the same flock which stand in similar enamelled meadows in a few of the early churches of Rome. The Apostles, dressed as Roman senators, stand round the walls, S. Peter, so the learned say, grasping for the first time in art the keys of heaven.

A strange mosaic shows a fire crackling under an enormous grille. On one side stands an object which looks like a modern refrigerator whose open doors reveal on its shelves the four Gospels. It is a Roman book cupboard. On the other side, a saint in a toga, with a cross tilted across one shoulder, comes hurrying, almost running, to the fire, holding a massive codex bound in leather and open in the middle. Everyone is told that this is S. Lawrence tripping towards the gridiron, though to me he looks more like an outraged Orthodox saint about to commit an Arian volume to the flames.

Three sarcophagi stand under the star-spangled blue arches: the largest is said to be that of Galla Placidia, another is that of her husband, Constantius III, who reigned only from February to September in the year 421, and the third is that of their son,

Valentinian III, who was murdered in 455. Galla Placidia's sarcophagus seemed to me to make nonsense of the picturesque story, which even distinguished historians continue to repeat, that when the Empress died in 450, she was buried in her jewelled imperial robes, seated upon a throne of cypress wood. Her body is said to have been visible through a hole in the sarcophagus until 1577, when some children, in order to see the mummy better, thrust a torch inside and reduced the contents of the tomb to ashes. The story has always seemed to me unlikely, and a glance at the sarcophagus clearly proves it to be a fabrication, since it was too small to contain a body seated on a throne. I counted no fewer than twenty holes, or attempted holes, bored in the marble by treasure hunters of all periods.

A group of tourists entered with their guide, who reeled off names and dates and ended by telling them the story of the seated Empress in the stone coffin. 'Who was Galla Placidia?' asked an American matron. 'She was a Roman empress, madam,' replied the guide, then, hastily, with a glance at his wristwatch, 'We now go to see San Vitale!' And out they sped.

Galla Placidia was indeed a Roman empress. Her father was Theodosius the Great and she was half-sister to the Emperor Honorius, who succeeded to the shaky western half of the Roman Empire when eleven years of age. Theodosius seems to have handed on nothing of his vigour to Honorius, but quite a lot to Placidia. She was captured by Alaric when he and his Goths sacked Rome in 410, and she was wandering with the barbarian army in the south when Alaric died suddenly. She was present when he was secretly buried in the bed of the river Busento, whose waters were turned aside while his grave was dug and then returned to their channel. She married Alaric's successor, Ataulf, and reigned with him over the Goths, to the amazement and scandal of the Roman world. After a few years, which seem to have been happy, her husband was slain and she was exchanged for a few thousand wagon-loads of corn, and so returned to her imperial relatives. She was still in her twenties. Legend says that she unwillingly married a Roman general who was in love with her, and to him she bore a son who, at the age of six, became

Emperor of the West, as Valentinian III. As his regent and the power behind the throne, Galla Placidia was the most powerful influence in the tottering western world for the next twenty years. Of the churches and palaces she built, only her tomb remains, but once having seen the starry dome beneath which she elected to lie, the memory of her seems to haunt Ravenna. She was the most interesting woman of the Decline, and the first of the many women who played a spectacular part in the history of the Byzantine age. Her daughter Honoria resembled her, but in an extreme way. Whether Placidia was in the habit of picturing her life with the Goths as the happiest days of her life we cannot know, but her daughter had no hesitation, when frustrated in her love affairs, in offering herself in marriage to the revolting savage, Attila, King of the Huns. In order to claim her, and a part of the Western Empire as her dowry, Attila set loose his hordes on Italy, and it was during this time that Aquileia was ravaged and its inhabitants fled to the lagoons. How strange that when Honoria sent her ring to Attila, one of the results of that impulsive act was – Venice!

As I walked past S. Vitale the tourists were coming out, and I heard the American matron say to a friend, 'That was a very, very lovely relationship.' Whose could it have been, I wondered? Surely not Justinian and Theodora; perhaps Placidia and Ataulf; possibly Dante and Beatrice; maybe even Byron and Teresa!

§ 4

Some may think that illustrated books have made them familiar with the Ravenna mosaics. No illustrations, however, are able to convey the spirit of those curiously stylized and rigid decorations, least of all can they reproduce the glow or glitter, almost as if the little glass and stone cubes were fitted with their own illumination. This, I think, can be explained by the skilful way the cubes are cut so that they reflect light at various angles; and it may also explain why the colours seem to change at different times of the day.

It was still a Roman-looking world, this Ravenna on the eve of the imperial collapse. The saints are all beautifully dressed in white togas like Roman senators; Christ is the young, clean-shaven Christ of the Catacombs; and, as in the Catacombs, the Crucifixion was not considered a fit subject for art. I saw a remarkable mosaic of the Baptism on the ceiling of the Arian Baptistry. S. John, clothed in skins, is already the hermit saint of mediaeval art, but our Lord is a beardless youth, waist-deep in the Jordan, while – an extraordinary pagan touch – the old river god, Jordan himself, has emerged to take part in the ceremony, a typical Roman deity with curly beard and long white hair from which rise two red crab's claws. This mosaic fascinated me: S. John carried my mind into the future and Giotto; our Lord reminded me of the Catacombs; and the Jordan took me still farther back to Olympus.

Just as surprising, I thought, was the figure of Christ in the hall of the Archiepiscopal Chapel, a mosaic, I was told, that dates from the year 500. Our Lord is seen as a Roman officer in armour. He is young and beardless, and He wears the customary bronze breast-plate and a kilt of gilded leather, with a military cloak. He holds an open book which bears the words in Latin, 'I am the way, the truth and the life', and His feet, in Roman army sandals, rest, one upon the head of a lion and the other upon that of a snake. This struck me as the most singular portrait of Christ I had ever seen, and possibly also the earliest surviving representation of the Church Militant. I thought how perplexing it must have been for the fifth century church-goer to encounter this early Roman version of the Saviour side by side with the very different bearded Christ of the Byzantine Church which soon established itself in art, and has remained the accepted conception ever since.

Extraordinarily impressive are the long processions of saints, male on one side, female on the other, which decorate the nave of S. Apollinare Nuovo, each one holding his, or her, crown of martyrdom, and each passing down an avenue of date palms, a curiously African indication that the scene is set in heaven. They seem to smile with their lips, but their eyes remain dark and inscrutable.

Dr O. M. Dalton noticed that some of them have a strange habit of walking on their toes. There are fashions in walking as in every-thing else, and maybe fifth century clerics did trip along on tiptoe.

I noticed something which struck me as even more peculiar. It is to be seen in S. Apollinare as well as in most of the other churches in Ravenna. It is the way people who are wearing togas, which leave the left side of the body draped, hold objects in their left hands. It would be natural to us, indeed we constantly see this action on the stage, to fling back the toga in order to leave the left hand bare to hold something. But the Romans, or at any rate the saintly Romans of Ravenna, did not always do this: they held the object while their left hands were still covered with the cloth. Some of the saints in S. Apollinare hold their crowns of martrydom with both hands covered by their togas; the Christ in the Archiepiscopal Palace is holding the book with an invisible left hand draped in the fold of a military cloak; S. Peter in the Arian Baptistry is holding his keys in a draped hand; in the same way S. Luke holds his Gospel on the walls of S. Vitale. Perhaps some day I shall meet an expert on Roman costume who will be able to tell me if this was a general custom in polite society, or whether it was an ecclesiastical fashion of the time.

When I received an English periodical which contained an article on the fall of the Roman Empire, I happened to show it to a German professor who was staying in the hotel. He cried, ' I also have!' and produced a German periodical with an article on the same subject. Surely this is the longest post-mortem in history, and every year produces new witnesses, yet we seem as far off as ever from a verdict. The argument contains all the elements of eternity, as if it were some Russian diplomatic diversion. I was interested to read that the writer of the article in my magazine, Professor J. J. Saunders of New Zealand, asked: 'Is not the real mystery not the fall of empires but how men's outlook and belief change so radically that one generation finds the mental attitude of its predecessor wholly unintelligible?' One is always glad to see one's own opinion backed by a learned writer, and I read on: 'I do not believe that Rome was bound to fall or that the miseries of the Dark Ages were necessary for the rebuilding of civilization in Europe.'

Nevertheless, the western part of the Empire did terminate in Ravenna one day in 475, when a young boy in his 'teens, named pathetically Augustulus Romulus, was forced to abdicate by a Gothic overlord. No eye-witness has left an account of that fateful moment. We know nothing except that the boy was allowed to retire with a pension to a villa in the south, because his years were tender and he was good-looking. The lad had no right at all to be Emperor, and had been put forward by his ambitious father who, odd to relate, had been Attila's Latin secretary. One wonders what happened to this last of the Caesars. Did he grow up to manhood? It is unlikely that he was ever important enough to have been assassinated.

The fifty years of Gothic rule that followed have left one notable memorial in Ravenna, the tomb of Theodoric. It is a mile or so outside the town and is approached by a gravel path bordered by grass. The heavy stone rotunda, having settled into the soggy marshland, lies in a hollow. There is nothing to be seen inside, but the guide will ask you to admire the roof, which is hewn out of one colossal block of stone, and while you do so, he will tell the local story that Theodoric was so afraid of thunder that he built a sound-proof retreat in order to hide from the storm. It is said that in comparatively modern times workmen found remains which were said to be those of the Goth, together with a golden corselet, a sword, and a jewelled helmet.

Like Alaric and Ataulf, Theodoric was one of the cultivated barbarians. It is true that he seized power by inviting his fellow Goth, Odoacer, to dinner and killing him with his own hand (making the unpleasant remark that he appeared to have no bones), but apart from that, and one savage outburst in old age, Theodoric ruled wisely and is known as a civilized Goth who tidied up Rome after its years of misfortune. He even revived the ancient post of 'keeper of the statues', and his brickworks provided material for the repair of the city, each brick being stamped with his name. The archaeologist Lanciani wrote, 'I have never made or witnessed an excavation on the site of any of the great buildings of Rome without discovering one or more of Theodoric's bricks.' Yet the ruler who loved to reproduce his name so often was unable to write it himself: when it was necessary for him to sign a document, we are told he used a golden stencil.

After Theodoric's death, the Emperor Justinian began his campaign to reclaim those portions of Italy and Africa which had been overrun by the barbarians. After years of struggle the great soldier Belisarius defeated the Goths, whereupon Ravenna began a new chapter in its history, and for nearly two hundred years became the seat of an Exarch, or Viceroy, who ruled on behalf of the Byzantine Emperors. Of this period there is one superb monument in Ravenna, possibly the finest in the city, the church of S. Vitale. It seems that as soon as Justinian possessed Ravenna, he hastened to associate himself and his consort Theodora with the consecration of this church, which was probably built and decorated by his own architects. The consecration took place in the year 547, and everyone who has opened a book on the history of art will remember the beautiful mosaics in this church, which show Justinian and Theodora in their state robes, accompanied by their soldiers and courtiers. No finer imperial portraits of the period have survived.

The first time I entered this church, I was impressed by its air of ornate splendour, by a kind of solemn gaiety, an attempt to interpret the golden halls of heaven in terms of earthly grandeur. The light falls through thin sheets of marble and alabaster and, wherever I looked, I saw coloured marbles and glowing mosaics. It was as if I had entered one of those halls in the imperial palace of the Byzantine emperors which one has read about, whose floors were of silver-gilt and whose doors were of silver, ivory, and enamel.

I returned to the neighbouring tomb of Galla Placidia to stand in an atmosphere which is separated from S. Vitale by only a hundred yards, but by a hundred years of time. How curious it was to look round and to see nothing that did not turn the mind to Rome and the early Church, then to walk back to the Byzantine jewel-box, to find all one's thoughts flying east to Byzantium.

The mosaics of Justinian and Theodora are upon the walls of the apse. The Emperor is seen on the left wall of the apse, standing crowned in an imperial robe of purple, while he holds a golden bowl which he is about to present to the new church. On each side are courtiers wearing white dalmatics, priests in their vestments, and soldiers of the imperial bodyguard. The procession has not yet entered the church, or the Emperor would have removed his crown. On the wall facing this mosaic is the even more decorative one of Theodora and her ladies. The Empress wears her crown and a cascade of enormous pearls. The lower part of her purple mantle is embroidered with the three figures of the Magi in Persian dress, copied from the mosaic in S. Apollinare Nuovo. While the Empress carries a chalice, probably containing a gift of gold, a chamberlain holds back the curtain which leads presumably into the church. On Theodora's left stand a group of her ladies-in-waiting, dressed in the richest products of the Byzantine looms, yet in a manner not to outshine her imperial highness. I wondered if the prim-looking lady who stands next to the Empress, wearing a white drapery over a purple robe, might not be the unpleasant Antonina, wife of Belisarius, a woman whose origins and history were as notorious as those of Theodora herself.

If these are true portraits, as they are believed to be, Justinian and Theodora are portrayed as quite young people, whereas when S. Vitale was consecrated, Justinian was sixty-four years old, and Theodora must have been middle-aged and in the last year of her life.

Charlemagne was so impressed by the beauty of this church when he stood there two and a half centuries later, that he tried to reproduce it in Germany in the octagon of the cathedral of Aix-la-Chapelle, but the effect is earth-bound and heavy.

When I was leaving S. Vitale, I noticed a curious thing. A pool of water had gathered in the church which at first I thought to be rain-water, until it occurred to me that it was seeping up through the foundations. It is the last sign that Ravenna had once been a town of canals and boats, the last sign that the marsh is still there – the reason no doubt why the summer grass is so green in Ravenna – the same marsh that had protected the last emperors fifteen centuries ago.

. . . . .

About three miles from Ravenna, more or less in the direction of the departed sea, a gaunt old church rises above the flat land. It is S. Apollinare in Classe, the last relic of the thriving naval port of Classis which Augustus established as the permanent station of the Adriatic Fleet. Everything has gone – dockyards, harbours, houses, – leaving the basilica as a signpost to mark the spot. Its circular campanile, not unlike one of the round towers of Ireland, stands beside the church, and is said by some to have been built on the site of the lighthouse of Classis. In the church porch is a memorial in English, which is unique among the inscriptions of Ravenna. It reads:

> To the memory of Wladimir Peniakoff (Popski)
> Lieut.-Col., D.S.O., M.C., British Army (1896-1951)
> by whose efforts this church basilica was saved
> during the battle for the Liberation of Ravenna
> (18–19 Nov. 1944). The Municipality gave him
> honorary citizenship. This memorial was placed
> here by the wish of his widow and his friends
> with the consent and gratitude of the people of
> Ravenna. 15 May 1952.

In the final pages of his book, *Private Army*, which describes the exploits of a band of young British soldiers behind the enemy lines during the last war, Peniakoff mentioned this incident. Hearing that the campanile was to be shelled as a suspected German artillery observation post, and having heard vaguely of the beauty of the mosaics, he sent out a patrol to investigate. 'I proved the rumour to be unfounded,' he wrote, 'and saved the church'. He described this 'as an act of virtue, the first in a long career of destruction.'

Beyond the church stretches the famous pinewood, the *pineta* of Ravenna, which Dante loved, where Boccaccio placed his best ghost story, and where Byron liked to ride in the evening. Though not as dense as it was in Byron's time, it still stretches for miles and, especially in the evening, the huge dark umbrella pines are mysterious and eerie, and through their trunks one can catch a glimpse of the distant Adriatic. Byron sometimes rode there with his pretty young countess, Teresa Guiccioli, but she was not a good horsewoman, 'for she can't guide her horse and he runs after mine', he wrote, 'and tries to bite him, and then she begins screaming in a high hat and sky-blue riding habit, making a most absurd figure, and embarrassing me and both our grooms, who have the devil's own work to keep her from tumbling, or having her clothes torn off by the trees and thickets of the pine forest'. Shelley and Byron rode there and practised pistol shooting, for both were good shots, and sometimes Byron would dismount and aim at pumpkins, and at other times he would throw up silver coins; on these occasions he was followed by a crowd of little boys.

In Byron's day the Arcadian industries of Ravenna were wine, silk-worms, and *pinoli*, those oily little pine-kernels which have been a feature of Italian kitchens since classical times. Travellers of the last century have described how the local youths could be seen in the pine trees shaking down the loaded cones, from which the kernels were extracted while the husks were saved and burnt in braziers during the winter.

I suppose, in the hearts of its people, the most precious possession of Ravenna is the tomb of Dante. He spent the last three years of his life there and died of marsh fever. To have befriended the great poet in his last years is Ravenna's pride, and this is not lessened by the knowledge that a repentant Florence would dearly like to atone for having exiled him by welcoming him to a superb tomb.

Nevertheless, his bones still rest, so I am assured by one who claims to have seen them, in the sarcophagus within the stately little classical shrine erected two hundred years ago: but the battle for them continued for centuries, and Ravenna always managed to foil the most determined efforts of Florence. A dangerous moment occurred in 1519 when, with a Medici pope in power, the Florentines sent envoys armed with a papal injunction to demand the remains. The sarcophagus was opened and – found to be empty! Someone had been warned, but, in hiding the bones from Florence, Ravenna managed to lose them. They remained lost for three hundred and fifty years. They were not seen again until 1865, when workmen, making some repairs to a chapel near by, discovered a wooden box containing a complete skeleton and an inscription which said that these were the bones of Dante. Medical experts held a post-mortem and declared this to be so. They lay in state for three days while thousands of people filed past them.

Once again, during the last war, the bones were removed to a place of safety and afterwards returned to the sarcophagus.

§ 5

I drove from Ravenna to Ferrara, a distance of forty-six miles, along a flat, featureless road intersected by drainage dykes and canals, and traversed by meandering railway branch lines. Ferrara is to the north-west, and the main road crosses the plain that has been deposited during the centuries by the flood waters of the Po and the Adige. On the east stretches an almost unknown region inhabited by small farmers and fisherman, and on the south the coastline is an indented continuation of the Venetian lagoons.

In this lonely world of sandbars and islands, of creeks and estuaries where wild fowl breed, the fisherman, noiselessly passing in his canoe, might be a Neolithic man as he prods the mud for shellfish or draws his dripping nets from the lagoon. Only a few miles to the north a sophisticated society might be celebrating a film festival, while here, among inland lakes and along a rush-fringed, fretted coastline, the modern world is forgotten and life continues in a solitude where a poet might encounter the ghost of a Greek galley moving over the salty grass in the mists of morning. The plain is the graveyard of many a remote mistress of the Adriatic whose life was spent before Venice was thought of; even Ravenna was a late-comer to this region. Towns are not frequent, roads are few, and there is nothing to attract the ordinary traveller to a part of the world where there are so many adjacent and famous attractions.

One of the notable places in this delta is Comacchio, a shabby but fascinating little Venice, whose canals are choked in the autumn with eels fighting to begin their long journey to the Sargasso Sea.

At that moment the entire population wrestles so successfully with the invaders that the dried eels of Comacchio are known all over Italy. Locally they are cooked, sliced, and roasted between bay leaves, or served, like Kebab, on a skewer, well basted with oil and fat and smelling of rosemary. Farther north is the little town of Adria, which gave its name to the Adriatic Sea. There are places in the marsh like Pomposa, whose Benedictine monks were driven away by malaria in the ninth century. A few enthusiasts still find their way there to look at the mosaics and to remember Guido of Arezzo, a monk who devised the musical scale.

On the road to Ferrara I passed through the town of Argenta, which the Germans flooded in the winter of 1944 in an attempt to hold up the advance of the Eighth Army. I was again reminded of the war when I arrived at Ferrara. I had expected to see a city that was noted during the Renaissance for its fine palaces and parallel streets, and I saw instead a town full of new blocks of flats and factories built upon bombed sites. The international ugliness of these concrete boxes is nowhere more striking than in a town of Renaissance buildings. However, the hotel was new, pleasant, and air-conditioned, and fortunately bombs had not demolished the cathedral or the castle.

The old castle of Ferrara rises gloomily above its moat in the centre of the town and is approached by a serviceable drawbridge. It is undoubtedly a grim castle and as soon as I crossed the draw-bridge and encountered the custodian, I knew that I was going to hear a lot about dungeons.

In one of the gaunt, enormous halls an old looking-glass is set at a queer angle on the wall and the visitor is asked to look into it. Framed in it, he sees a certain window on the opposite side of a courtyard. 'It was while glancing into a mirror,' says the guide with enjoyment, 'that Niccolò III, Marquis of Ferrara, saw in that window across the way his lovely young wife, Parasina Malatesta, in the arms of his son, Ugo.'

The Italian guide loves to relate dramatic stories, often with a shrug of the shoulders and sometimes, as at Ferrara, with a jingle of keys and an invitation to descend and see the dungeons where Parasina and her stepson were entombed and eventually executed. There is, however, an even worse dungeon drama than this. It was the life imprisonment of Giulio and Ferrante d'Este for plotting against their brother, Alfonso I, the reigning Duke, in 1505. A few years previously Alfonso had married Lucrezia Borgia, who had brought with her from Rome a cousin of formidable attractions named Angela Borgia. This young woman turned the heads of the Estensi princes, including that of Cardinal Ippolito I, that unpriestly character whose preferment had been rapid even by Renaissance standards. He received the tonsure at the age of six; at eight he was an Apostolic Pronotary; at eleven he was Archbishop of Strigonia, in Hungary; at fourteen he acquired a cardinal's hat! One day, when he was paying court to Angela Borgia, she unwisely, and, of course, jokingly, remarked that his whole person was not worth the eyes of his brother, Giulio. The next day Giulio was attacked by a band of bravos while riding in the country, and it was said that the Cardinal looked on as the ruffians blinded him. He was led bleeding into Ferrara, screaming for justice against Ippolito, and the doctors managed to save the sight of one eye. His demand for justice was disregarded by Alfonso, who merely sent the Cardinal into banishment, which was scarcely even a technical punishment. Giulio then conspired with another brother, Ferrante, to kill Alfonso and place Ferrante on the throne. When the plot was discovered, Ferrante fell at his brother's feet and begged forgiveness. Alfonso, who was a powerful man with a violent temper, struck him across the face with his staff, smashing one of his eyes. Thus two Estensi had now blinded two of their brothers. Not content with this, Alfonso decreed that both Ferrante and Giulio must die. An elaborate execution scene was staged in the cortile of the castle, but at the last moment the Duke commuted their sentences to life imprisonment.

I wandered through the huge, gaunt halls and ante-rooms of the castle, wondering how the Estensi could have held dances and masques there, and have organized the elaborate banquets and merry-making of the time, knowing that beneath their feet the two half-blinded princes sat in silence and disgrace, year after year. Did anyone ever dare to smuggle down to them a roasted peacock? And how much did they know of what was going on above them? I was shown two appalling little cells below the water level of the moat, which I was told are those in which the brothers were imprisoned, but I cannot believe this. No one could have lived as long as they did in such places, for both Ferrante and Giulio enjoyed – if that is the correct word – the prisoner's revenge, which is to outlive his judge. They had been incarcerated a mere twenty-eight years when their brother Alfonso died and was succeeded by his son, Ercole II, a man of twenty-six. One might have thought that he would have set free his two middle-aged uncles – Ferrante was then fifty-seven and Giulio younger by a year – but he did not do so. During this reign Ferrante died in prison, aged sixty-three, but the once bright-eyed Giulio continued to live on. He was still alive when Ercole II died and was, in his turn, succeeded by his son, Alfonso II, who was also twenty-six years of age on his accession. He was, however, more compassionate than his father. He remembered the old man in the dungeons – his great-grandfather's illegitimate son – and upon the night of his coronation he gave orders for the prison doors to be opened. Giulio was then eighty-one. He was in the best of health and spirits. Ferrara saw with awe the return to life of this aged one-eyed prince, who wore the fashions of a past age and asked eagerly after men and women who had been dead for years. His last memory had been of Lucrezia Borgia and her bright hair, and she had been dead for forty years. He was followed about everywhere by cheering crowds. He was a huge man and he rode the largest horse he could find. He went round Ferrara trying to recognize the scenes of his youth, and it is related that even nuns living in the strictest seclusion welcomed him to their cloisters and let him embrace them, while he received their chaste kisses in return. Alas, so much freedom proved fatal. Worn out with delightful plans for the future, Giulio died suddenly and unexpectedly on the eve of a visit to Rome, some eighteen months after his release.

The Estensi were a fascinating family and perhaps it is a little

unfair to have stressed their two big scandals, for they were not
unusually violent. They were the first of the great town lords,
and as early as 1208 were invited to take over Ferrara by the
Commune itself, which had become tired of fighting its own
battles. The family took their name from the old Roman town of
Ateste, corrupted into Este, where they had their castle, a few
miles from Padua.

Even in an age of lax morality the House of Este was notorious
for its bastards, and Pius II reflected that, when he visited Ferrara
in 1459, not one of the seven princes who received him had been
born in wedlock. The greatest voluptuary was Niccolò III who,
says Ugo Caleffini in his rhymed history of the family, had eight
hundred mistresses, adding flatteringly that he would probably
have achieved a thousand had death not interrupted his activities.
Pius II, who detested Niccolò as 'a fat man, jolly, given up to lust',
said that he kept whole troops of concubines and was indiscrimin-
ate in his attentions. It is surprising to learn, therefore, that he
acknowledged only about twenty to thirty illegitimate children.
It was typical of Fate's usual jests that this notorious Lothario,
himself never faithful, yet demanding absolute fidelity in others,
should have been seen, as the chroniclers record, pacing the halls of
his castle in agony, and gnawing his sceptre with his teeth, the
night he had condemned to death his wife Parisina and his son
Ugo. No difference was ever made in the courts of Italy between
the legitimate and illegitimate offspring of a ruler; the children
were brought up together, shared the same nurseries and the same
teachers, and sometimes the legal heirs had to stand down while
an illegitimate brother succeeded by the will of their father.
Seniority was often of more importance than legitimacy. This
was so usual at Ferrara that it was exceptional for the reigning
sovereign to have been born in wedlock until the death of Duke
Borso in 1471. Niccolò's love-making was largely responsible for
this, and during his time the old castle must have resembled a
crèche. He was often short of money and his immense brood were
brought up in Bohemian lavishness varied by periods of excessive
penury, sleeping, it is recorded, on beds of straw, but covered with
quilts of gold brocade. The boys were kept short of money and

when at the university were forbidden to waste their allowances by inviting friends to dinner. Niccolò himself always appeared in magnificent clothes, and on state occasions the Court of Ferrara, by ransacking closets, wardrobes, and strong-rooms, could produce enough tapestries, plate, and cloth-of-gold to dazzle the most critical eye.

Niccolò III was one of those Renaissance characters who had one foot in the Middle Ages. As a young man he had made a pilgrimage to the Holy Land in company with some noble companions, coasting down the Adriatic in a Venetian galley, putting in at Corfu, listening to the singing of monks, and supping with the Venetian governor in his orange garden, all of which was delightfully described by a member of the party. When they reached Jerusalem in the year 1413, Niccolò knighted his companions after Mass at the Holy Sepulchre, then they ascended to the Chapel on Calvary, where he strapped on their golden spurs. Oddly enough, Niccolò himself had never obtained golden spurs and now he would permit only his left foot to be spurred, declaring that he would receive the other spur at the shrine of S. James in Galicia. A few years later we find this mediaeval character transformed into a Renaissance prince and patron and one of the first north Italian rulers to be interested in Greek. It was Niccolò who persuaded the first great collector of Greek manuscripts, Giovanni Aurispa, to come to Ferrara; he also revived the ancient University and attracted to his city the celebrated Paduan physician, Michele Savonarola, the grandfather of Girolamo; and when his son, Leonello, needed a tutor, Niccolò sought out one of the first Italians who had studied Greek in Constantinople, Guarino da Verona, and made him so happy at Ferrara that he spent the rest of his life there. It is strange that a ruler's sexual excesses should blind posterity to other aspects of his character and achievements – Henry VIII and Charles II are good examples – and it is a pity that this fascinating figure of the early Renaissance is chiefly remembered for having fathered a great number of bastards.

Two of these, Leonello and Borso, succeeded him, to be followed by that rare phenomenon, a legitimate son, Ercole I, the father of Beatrice and Isabella d'Este, and generally considered to be the hero of Ferrara. There is a fine portrait of him in Modena by Dosso Dossi, looking remarkably like some old Highland chieftain, due maybe to the bonnet or beret he is wearing, and also perhaps to his canny expression. In the National Gallery in London there is a profile portrait by Oriolo of Niccolò's immediate successor, Leonello d'Este, and an even better one by Pisanello, also a profile, but looking in the other direction, in the gallery at Bergamo. He is a lean young man with a mop of auburn hair, a long, intelligent, almost bridgeless nose, and, like many other sons of immoderate fathers, he was a model of sobriety and morality. Fate reserved nine happy years for him to reign, a paragon of all the virtues and one of the first of the scholar-princes. One sees him strolling, beautifully dressed, through his Platonic grove, followed by his amateur philosophers, and when he died at the age of forty-three, he was succeeded by Borso, a jolly, illiterate, and much-loved ruler who, like a true aristocrat, put literature in its place without entirely dislodging it. It was during his reign that the first English students of Greek found their way to Ferrara to attend the lectures of the then aged Guarino of Verona. This merry duke, say the chroniclers, was always smiling, and some of his smiles have adhered to the walls of the Palazzo di Schifanoia, where I saw them.

Ferrara is a wonderful place for those who care to moralize and reflect on the caprice of survival. The Schifanoia is the only one to survive of the great number of beautiful palaces which the Estensi built in and near Ferrara. Even the famous Belfiore has vanished, with its splendid gardens and the woods in which Benvenuto Cellini, when working at a silver jug for Cardinal Ippolito, shot peacocks that had become wild and taken to the trees. Schifanoia means literally 'carefree', the Italian equivalent of *Sans Souci*, and until recently it has been a tobacco factory. It is therefore, fortunate that the smiles of Duke Borso may still be discerned beneath the cracks, the dust, the retouching, and all the other accidents of time. We see a suave, smooth-faced man riding here and there on a beautiful charger, accompanied by an elegant and arrogant staff of courtiers, all of whom I noticed were wearing the red Byzantine fez. Around them peasants are working at the tasks of the year, sowing, and pruning the vines, while Borso, smiling eternally, rides out to the hunt, or on one of those splendid missions which he loved, when, surrounded by five hundred noblemen, and escorted by trumpeters and pipers, and accompanied by huntsmen and hounds and by Indians in charge of hunting leopards, he would take the road to Rome. One of the best-preserved frescoes shows the Duke with his favourite jester, Scocola, a deformed little man with a bull neck, who is evidently pleading with his smiling employer. Scocola was in perpetual need of money and is probably trying to wheedle some out of the Duke.

Alas, the charming fancies of the Court painters fade to nothing before the painful realities of history, for this prolific family terminated with an empty cradle. One may imagine the ghosts of the past gazing in bewilderment upon Alfonso II, the unfortunate last Duke of Ferrara. Three times he married and three times the hopes of the Court must have been lifted, until the moment arrived when no one even thought of the empty cradle. Alfonso II was like a man bewitched, for he lived under a threat. If he could not produce an heir, the Dukedom, a papal fief, would revert to the Holy See; and neither he nor his diplomats could do anything to deflect the Vatican from its ancient obsession to obtain Ferrara. The heir to the expiring Dukedom was Caesar, the grandson of Alfonso I and a beautiful woman, Laura Dianti, whom, it is said, he married on his death-bed. But the Vatican refused to admit the validity of this marriage and so caused a Dukedom, which so often in the past had gone to an illegitimate son, to be forfeit in the absence of a legal heir.

The end of the House of Este in Ferrara was accompanied by none of the usual sordid scenes of lunacy or impoverishment. The Dukedom expired like a liner that strikes an iceberg and goes down with all its lights on and the band playing. No sooner was Alfonso dead than the Papacy moved in and appointed a cardinal legate; and so began several centuries of maladministration and neglect. The land returned to swamps and the miserable inhabitants soon looked back on their ducal history as to a golden age. The family migrated with its archives to Modena, where it continued in the descendants of Alfonso and Laura Diante. They became Dukes of Modena, and that is why the traveller today comes upon the Este library and archives not in Ferrara, where they might be expected, but in Modena, where I had seen them. In 1658, just fifty-one years after the extinction of the direct line, a daughter was born to the reigning Duke of Modena, Alfonso IV, and his wife, Laura Martinozzi-Mazarini, and she was christened Maria-Beatrice d'Este. She became the Mary of Modena of English history, the consort of James II.

§ 6

The lawyer to whom I had been given an introduction turned out to be a pleasant young man in his twenties, who had recently taken his degree at Bologna. He was tall, thin, and dark, and had the air, like so many young Italians, of having stepped out of the background of an old master, a minor courtier maybe, or an arquebusier, or possibly a lute player. I liked him at once, recognizing in him the painful symtoms of deflation, so wounding to the tender self-esteem of youth. It often happens to young lawyers that, having passed their examinations, they find themselves, instead of delivering brilliant arguments in court, seated on shabby chairs in a back office licking stamps, which they consider they could have done just as well without a degree. My young friend was sometimes sent out to try and collect debts and we spent some time together, prowling the back streets and having long conversations with disarming individuals in tenement flats.

One morning we explored Ferrara's Gothic cathedral, whose exterior, with the Virgin enthroned above the west door, is one of the most impressive and decorative I had seen, but I thought the interior was disappointing. We climbed several staircases to the cathedral museum, and were rewarded by Cosimo Tura's two masterpieces, S. George rescuing a composed princess from the dragon, and an exquisite Annunciation, which was framed within a sumptuous Renaissance triumphal archway.

We wandered on, collecting rents or promises, and came to the house which the poet Ariosto built with the earnings of *Orlando Furioso*. It is flush with the street and bears the famous Latin inscription in which the poet says it is small, but suitable for him, and bought with his own money. 'It is home,' he concludes. I thought the inscription touching, remembering that the poet once said he would rather eat a turnip at home than a banquet at court. He detested courts with the hatred of a sixteenth century noble-man who was obliged to earn his living. He also disliked patronage, and one can sympathize with him, for he lived for fourteen years at the beck and call of the unpleasant Cardinal Ippolito I. Like the owners of stately homes in England, the tenants of this house are accustomed to find strangers wandering round and they go about their business as though the intruders were invisible. We looked at the small walled garden at the back where Ariosto applied the same methods to gardening that he did to authorship. He was one of those writers, detested by publishers, who rewrite their books in proof, and as a gardener he was just as restless, even digging up seeds to see if any were germinating. My young friend took me to the University, which was preparing to move into modern quarters from the beautiful old palace which it has inhabited for centuries. The porter was sitting in his lodge, against a sixteenth century fresco of Paradise. He glanced up and, recognizing the young lawyer, waved us on to a marble stairway flanked all the way up by busts of the Caesars, and I noticed that wherever these were to be reached by a pencil, they had been given mous-taches. I paused, surprised by a transformed Julius Caesar. Clothed in a suit and bowler hat, and carrying a rolled umbrella, he would have been admitted without question to any military club in London. Nero's fat and petulant face was much improved by an imperial, though he continued to look unreliable and might well have been a professional politician or a tricky financier. Some undergraduate had given Vespasian a walrus moustache which brought out all the sergeant-major in that tough old soldier and transformed him into a Roman 'Old Bill'.

At the end of a long hall in the library we saw the marble tomb of Ariosto, which one of Napoleon's generals had brought there from a derelict church during the French occupation of 1801. It completely filled one end of the hall and did not look at all out of place. In a cabinet near by, lying upon a piece of faded velvet, I was shown one of the poet's knuckle-bones, and was told that during the exhumation a professor of anatomy pocketed it while no one was looking and, remorsefully confessing the theft in his will, left the bone to the library. It was with interest that I took in my hands the original manuscript of *Orlando Furioso*, one of the most heavily corrected scripts I have ever seen. Ariosto knew that he would alter or eliminate whatever he had written and therefore used only the right-hand side of the paper, leaving the other side for corrections. He spent years altering his poem, all in a clear, confident Italic hand. The first edition was printed in Ferrara in 1532. There was an English translation by Sir John Harrington as early as 1591, and there is an amusing story about this. Harrington's parents were imprisoned in the Tower with Princess Elizabeth, who, when she became Queen, rewarded their loyalty by becoming godmother to their son John. He went from Eton to Cambridge, where he studied law, but he never practised; he then learnt Italian and became known at Court as a witty and naughty young man. In order to amuse Elizabeth's maids-of-honour, he translated the twenty-eighth book of *Orlando Furioso* – the story of Gioconda – which fell eventually into the Queen's hands. She scolded him for corrupting the morals of her ladies by translating the most improper portion of the poem, and as punishment banished him to the country until he had translated the whole work. So we owe the first English version of Ariosto to Queen Elizabeth I. (Harrington had another claim to fame: he invented the water-closet.)

The library possesses a collection of more than fifty early translations of *Orlando Furioso*, many of them illustrated with the woodcut portrait of Ariosto said to have been taken from a portrait by Titian, but the melancholic with untidy beard and hair is not at all my idea of the sprightly author of such a satirical, and, in parts, extremely funny idealization of mediaeval chivalry. Every English century except our own has been interested in the *Furioso*. Spenser modelled his *Faerie Queene* upon it; Wordsworth took the poem on his Alpine walking tour in 1790, just as Macaulay took it on the ship to India in 1834; Keats learnt Italian from it, struggling valiantly from stanza to stanza; Southey read it when he was a child; Scott, of course, loved it; Byron knew it in the original. Perhaps our own age, more occupied than any other with lunary madness, might take to it again, if only for the wonderful Canto Thirty-four, which describes Astolfo's flight to the moon, accompanied by S. John. They fly off in the chariot of Elijah, drawn by four steeds harnessed abreast, redder than fire, and in a short time make a successful landing. As they explore the desolate landscape, they come across all that Man has lost and wasted upon earth: unhappy marriages, sighs, tears, and vain hopes. They see heaps of twigs covered with birdlime, which are all that remain of the allurements of the world's lovers; they come upon a peculiar deposit which turns out to be the fame of great men, which had disintegrated with time. In the valley of lost things they see an enormous collection of vials filled with the lost wits of Mankind.

I was shown the uncomfortable wooden chair on which the poet is said to have sat as he worked at his poem, also his inkpot, an elaborate Renaissance work with a cupid on the lid, the gift of Alfonso I.

After this it was almost an anti-climax to come to the unhappy Tasso, whose *Gerusalemme Liberata* in manuscript was placed in my hands. He also, I saw, was a notable corrector. Every gondolier in Venice, I was told, once knew this poem by heart and they could be heard, on quiet nights, singing verses to one another along the canals; first a verse, then a pause, then from far off would come the next verse. It was the fashion among the romantics of Byron's time to believe Tasso to have been a much wronged man, imprisoned by a harsh prince because of his love for a noble lady. In reality he seems to have suffered from a persecution mania so appalling that he had to be locked up for his own good. There is no evidence that his prison was the dark cell in which Byron spent a ruminative hour and from whose door Shelley (who thought it 'a very decent dungeon'), cut a precious splinter of wood.

There are, unfortunately, no memories in the University of the small group of Englishmen, the first Greek scholars who came to Ferrara, during the reigns of Henry IV and Edward IV, to attend the lectures of Guarino da Verona. In those days the University, like that of Bologna, was a peripatetic institution and lectures were held in any convenient room or hall. The Englishmen were William Grey, who was in Ferrara in 1445, and became Bishop of Ely and left a hundred and fifty of his manuscripts to the library of Balliol College, Oxford; Robert Flemming, who was there in 1450, the nephew of the founder of Lincoln College, Oxford; John Free, a poor scholar and fellow of Balliol, who had a miserable time pawning his few possessions while he waited for his allowance to arrive; John Gunthorpe, who became Dean of Wells and the builder of the ancient deanery; and John Tiptoft, Earl of Worcester, who went to Ferrara about 1460 and ten years later was captured during the rebellion against Edward IV, and ended his life on the scaffold. Grey and Flemming must have seen and known the admirable Leonello d'Este, and may even have joined in the philosophical disputes among the box hedges and cypress avenues; the others studied in Ferrara during the reign of the smiling Borso. Thus contemporary English eyes saw that splendour-loving Duke ride out with hawks and hounds as modern English eyes can now trace out his dim shadow on the peeling walls of the Schifanoia Palace.

§ 7

When we left the University, I asked the young lawyer if he would take me to the Convent of Corpus Domini in which Lucrezia Borgia was buried. He said it was only a few hundred yards away, and we plunged into some of the shabbiest streets in the town. I asked if he believed Lucrezia Borgia to have been guilty of the enormities heaped upon her, but his humming and hawing and lack of decision, or of any desire either to prosecute or defend her, suggested to me that although he might turn out to be a good judge, he would probably never be much of an advocate. My own feelings about Lucrezia are clearly cut: I am definitely on the side of the defence. No one who knew her ever said a word against her: her detractors were the enemies of her father and brother. In moments of anger the Latin mind reverts instantly to certain basic themes, of which incest, prostitution, and libidinousness are the most popular, and the insults which two infuriated Italians will shout at each other today are practically the same as those which Suetonius directed against the Caesars, and which in later ages were directed against the Borgias.

As we went on, we found that the convent was securely hidden in the back streets, but at length we arrived at ancient looked doors upon which we hammered for a long time in vain. The difficulty of entering the Convent of Corpus Domini is apparently well known in Ferrara. The nuns live in strict seclusion and until recent times no one could enter without a letter from the Cardinal Archbishop. This may have led Gregorovius, in his life of Lucrezia Borgia, to say that her tomb was lost.

As we continued to knock, an angry old woman wearing an apron over a black dress appeared at the end of the street and began to shout at us. Finding that we were not officials, she became a pleasant and kindly old woman and led us by devious alleys and courtyards into the convent by a back way, and into the church, which even on this warm day held the chill of the grave. Here she asked us to wait. We were soon joined by two hooded figures. They were nuns who, to preserve their clausura, had pulled down their hoods to their mouths. All one could see of them were the veined hands of old women, but they were able to see us through the material which covered their faces. Led by the two ghosts, we passed from the church into the nuns' choir where, let into the pavement in front of the altar, we saw several tombs of ordinary grey stone. We spelt out the names of Lucrezia Borgia and her husband Alfonso I, son of Ercole I. Near by was the grave of Alfonso's mother, the elegant Eleanora of Aragon, at whose wedding feast, when she passed through Rome in 1473, the Seneschal changed his dress four times, while waiters in silk served roast boar, peacocks, and fish covered with silver, while sugar castles full of meat were stormed by the crowd. The ghosts nodded their heads. Yes; that was the grave of Eleanora, wife of Ercole I.

They silently pointed their fingers and, kneeling down, we made out the names of Alfonso II, the last of the Estensi, and his first wife. Nearby was Lucrezia's grave.

It was a strange scene: the sunlight penetrating the choir in dusty shafts; the two inscrutable figures like the Fates; my young lawyer, longing to escape to more congenial surroundings, and myself fascinated to be at the graveside of Lucrezia Borgia. She was not a great beauty, but, as a spy wrote to Ercole I, Duke of Ferrara, whose heir was to be her third husband, 'she has a sufficient share of good looks, and her pleasing expression and graceful manners make her seem more beautiful than she really is. In short, her qualities are such that I am sure there is nothing to fear from her, but rather everything to hope for'. At the same time Isabella d'Este had sent a spy to Rome to find out what her future sister-in-law was really like. He found her on a Sunday evening, seated with ten maids of honour. They soon began to dance. Lucrezia, he says, wore black velvet fringed with gold, and upon her cascade of golden hair rested a Juliet cap of green silk secured with a ruby clasp. These confidential reports prove the anxiety of the proud House of Este when the Pope's daughter, already twice married at twenty-two, had been forced upon them by the ambitions of Alexander VI and his son, Caesar. They must have been relieved to be told that Lucrezia was not the debauched character of Roman slander, but the charming and graceful young woman whose rather empty and pathetic little face, framed in its cloud of tresses, looks at us from Pinturicchio's frescoes in the Borgia apartments of the Vatican.

All her detractors were those with good reason to hate her father and her brother. Love had had nothing to do with her marriages: they were all inspired by Alexander's politics, and when better alliances offered, one husband was forced to sign an admission of impotence and was divorced; the other was strangled before Lucrezia's eyes at the order of her brother. She wept easily and, like many tearful women, soon washed away her troubles and emerged dry-eyed and smiling and ready for the next blow. Had there been any truth in the scandals about her, one would look for some mention of them by John Burchard, the papal Master of Ceremonies, who confided to his diary the many occasions on which he was shocked by the Borgias. He has described the Pope's frequent fainting fits, his liturgical incompetence and carelessness – Burchard once found a consecrated wafer on the altar steps where the Pope had dropped it – and he did not mince words in his horrifying description of Alexander's death and burial. That uncompromising observer, who knew Lucrezia well, did not write one word against her. From the moment she left Rome for Ferrara in 1502, at the age of twenty-two, until her death at the age of thirty-nine, no breath of scandal touched her again. Her adoring father watched her as she set off, mounted upon a white jennet and wearing a riding-habit of red silk and ermine and a jaunty hat trimmed with feathers. Two hundred men and women on horseback accompanied her: a hundred and fifty mules carried her trousseau, and among her wedding presents was a beautiful sedan chair of French make which could hold two people seated side by side. Musicians and Spanish clowns helped to relieve the tedium of the journey. Lucrezia's cavalcade slowly passed into northern Italy by way of Castelnuovo, Civita Castellana, Narni, Foligno, Urbino, then beside the Adriatic at Pesaro and on to Rimini and the Via Emilia to Bologna, thence, by canal and river boat, to Ferrara. The journey, which is just under three hundred miles, took them a month. 'The illustrious Donna Lucrezia is of a delicate constitution,' wrote one of the company, 'and, like her ladies, is unaccustomed to the saddle.' The cavalcade was sometimes held up for a day or more for Lucrezia to wash her head. This *lavarsi il capo* was evidently an elaborate business which took a whole day, during which Lucrezia was not visible. Then with the celebrated golden tresses gleaming, she would continue her journey. At Imola she attributed a headache to the fact that she had been unable to wash her head for eight days.

She rode into Ferrara, the central figure of the grandest pageant the city had ever known. Drums, trumpets, archers of the ducal bodyguard in the white and red livery of the House of Este, a fife band, the nobility of Ferrara, and the ambassadors of France, Rome, Venice, Florence, Siena, and Lucca, the bishops of Adria,

Comacchio and Cervia, court officials, pages, and maids of honour. Beneath a canopy carried by doctors of the University, was the bride herself, in glittering brocade, her golden hair streaming over her shoulders, a jewelled cap upon her head and round her throat a necklace of rubies and emeralds which had once belonged to Eleanora of Aragon. Isabella d'Este noticed her dead mother's jewels with a pang of anger and sorrow. Alfonso, the bridegroom, a big, tough soldier whose obsession was artillery and the casting of cannon, rode a bay horse and was dressed in a suit of grey velvet covered with scales of beaten gold, 'worth at least six thousand ducats', as his sister wrote to her husband, with the pawnbroker's eye to finery usual during the Renaissance. At first Alfonso had declined to contemplate marriage with Lucrezia Borgia, but fear of the Pope, and the fantastic dowry and tax exemption offered with the bride, brought him to heel. Nevertheless he was so anxious about the woman he had heard so much about, but had never seen, that he rode out in disguise to intercept the wedding procession, and having spent two hours with Lucrezia, went away delighted with her. It was one of history's pleasanter moments, for the marriage turned out to be a happy one.

Some historians have wondered whether Lucrezia's friendship with Cardinal Bembo were innocent, and whether her admiration for Federigo Gonzaga, the husband of her sister-in-law, was more than the platonic exercise fashionable at the time. The mistrust which Lucrezia continues to inspire has caused one investigator to wonder whether, as Isabella's feline suspicions were only thinly veiled, Lucrezia avenged herself by making love to the Marquess of Mantua. If this were so, it is curious that in seventeen years time, when Lucrezia died in the arms of her husband, among the first to whom the distracted Alfonso wrote, announcing her death, was the Marquess. 'I cannot write this without tears,' he wrote, 'knowing myself to be deprived of such a dear and sweet companion. For such her exemplary conduct, and the tender love which existed between us, made me to her.' Alfonso was brokenhearted. He fainted at her funeral. Her death at the age of thirty-nine followed the birth of a stillborn child, and she knew that she could not live. Upon the brink of the grave, she wrote the following letter to the Pope, Leo X:

'MOST HOLY FATHER AND HONOURED MASTER: With all respect I kiss your Holiness's feet and commend myself in all humility to your holy mercy. Having suffered for more than two months, early on the morning of the 14th of the present, as it pleased God, I gave birth to a daughter, and hoped then to find relief from my sufferings, but I did not, and shall be compelled to pay my debt to nature. So great is the favour which our merciful Creator has shown me, that I approach the end of my life with pleasure, knowing that in a few hours, after receiving for the last time all the holy sacraments of the Church, I shall be released. Having arrived at this moment, I desire as a Christian, although I am a sinner, to ask your Holiness, in your mercy, to give me all possible spiritual consolation and your Holiness's blessing for my soul. Therefore I offer myself to you in all humility and commend my husband and my children, all of whom are your servants, to your Holiness's mercy.

In Ferrara, June 22, 1519, at the fourteenth hour.

Your Holiness's humble servant,
Lucrezia d'Este.'

After her death it was said that she had worn a hair shirt, though it may have been the cord of the Third Order of S. Francis. She bore four children, and the eldest succeeded his father and became Ercole II, another son, Ippolito, became a cardinal and is known as Ippolito II to distinguish him from his unpleasant namesake and uncle.

Some of this ran through my mind as I stood beside the humble grave in Corpus Domini. I would like to have asked if any memory of Lucrezia survives in the community, or if her benefactions are remembered, or her retreat to the convent in times of sorrow, but the hooded figures scarcely encouraged conversation. As I was going out, I asked one of the sisters to place a small gift in the alms box, and I was conscious of eager bony fingers, and I thought I saw behind the veiling a face like a skull.

As we walked away, I asked my friend if the nuns were very poor.

'They are said to be starving,' he replied. 'You see, nobody cares. We have a lot of Communists in this town.'

CHAPTER SEVEN

Verona, a City of Red Marble – The Roman Amphitheatre – The Tomb of Juliet – Vicenza – The Palladian Theatre – Padua and its University – The Anatomy Theatre – English Medical Students – S. Anthony of Padua – The Road to Venice

§ 1

At the bridge over the Po at Portelagoscuro I left Emilia and, crossing to the northern bank, entered the region of the Veneto. The road lay temptingly ahead to Padua and Venice, but, with the feeling that I must be one of the few travellers who has deliberately chosen the other way, I went instead by devious roads westward to Verona. As in Lombardy, where the Simplon and the S. Gotthard lead down to the Italian Lakes and Milan, so in the Veneto the famous Brenner Pass leads to Lake Garda and Verona; and it is impossible to say which is the more enchanting gateway to Italy.

A man mounted on a ladder was pasting a poster upon a wall in Verona to advertise a film, *Arsenico e Vecchi Merletti*. I watched him with some interest, not because a venerable entertainment was about to visit an even more venerable city, but because he was obliterating a wall of pink marble. The act seemed to me characteristic of Verona, where marble is everywhere, even in the gutters. The most amazing display is, of course, the famous Roman amphitheatre with seating for twenty-two thousand, and all of it, even to the cheapest seats in the back row of the gallery, in solid marble.

You first begin to notice this pink marble, which some writers have called 'peach-blossom', as far off as Cremona, where an occasional column or a lion is made of it; but it bears no

293

resemblance to the glassy substance in restaurants and banks: it is a pinkish and unshining material which looks more like time-worn nougat than peach-blossom. Nevertheless it is marble, that mineral second only to gold in ministering to man's sense of the magnificent; and this may be the reason why some of Verona's squares resemble the halls of a gigantic unroofed palace.

Arriving in the early afternoon, I saw the city flushed with warm light; I saw the Adige flowing swiftly beneath the bridges, enfolding, in its reminiscent Venetian curve, squares, towers, and palaces; I saw the red *campanili* of many churches and, praise God, a main street closed to wheeled traffic. Think of it: a street from which the motor is banished; a street with no sounds but the delightful chatter of the Veronese, the echo of their feet upon the marble pavement, and the music of an aria floating pleasantly from a shop that sells gramophone records. In my first flush of pleasure I felt like echoing John Evelyn when he saw Verona three hundred years ago, 'here of all places I have seen in Italy would I fix a residence'.

I walked to the amphitheatre, which the Veronese call the arena, and was admitted to the great oval of marble, from which I looked down upon the best-preserved Roman circus in existence. On the far curve men were at work upon a stage built out over the lower tiers, erecting plywood trees and pavilions of lath and canvas, the scenery for a performance of a Verdi opera. I thought the men almost as notable a sight as the building in which they were at work. They were the latest in a line of impresarios, managers, and scene shifters going back in time to the Flavian age nineteen centuries ago. Men like them had laboured in the same building to prepare it for gladiators and wild beasts. (Surely it was Pliny, in one of his letters, who mentions that games were cancelled at Verona because the leopards did not arrive in time from Africa?) Men were still at work there in the Middle Ages preparing the amphitheatre for tournaments and bull-fights. It is the great-grandfather of all circuses, theatres, and concert halls: the oldest place of entertainment still in use in the world. When Dr Burney strolled into it a hundred and ninety years ago, just as I had done, he found the *Commedia dell' Arte* making such a din that for a moment he thought the wild beasts might have returned! So he sat on a marble seat and saw for the first time 'in true Italian purity' Harlequin, Columbine, and Pantaloon, 'all speaking the jargon or country dialect of different parts of Italy'. It must have been fascinating to have seen Harlequin, the descendant of the ancient Roman *sannio* (or 'zany'), against such an authentic background.

In tranquillity and safety I walked along the peaceful Via Mazzini to one of the most spectacular squares in Italy – the Piazza delle Erbe. It is an oblong piazza, its shape a reflection of the forum of Roman Verona, surrounded now by ochre-coloured houses whose balconies drip ferns and flowers and whose walls retain the shadow of old frescoes. The far end of the square is closed by a grand Baroque palace and a marble column upon which stands the winged lion of S. Mark. The centre of the square is a mass of coloured umbrellas and, taken together, these form a huge canvas awning down the entire length of the square; and here you can buy anything from a bale of cotton chintz to a canary. I have rarely seen a more lively mediaeval fair, and, dodging from umbrella to umbrella, each one shading its own little stall, I saw a wonderful selection of those traders who over the years have retained the right to sell the yellowest lemonade, the most chromatic sweets, vegetables, clothes, all of the cheapest kind, amid the marble glories of this city.

In the centre of the encampment sounds the lovely splash of water, where, rising from the umbrellas, and mounted above ancient basins of marble, stands a Roman statue which was found headless in the Middle Ages. Fitted now with a female head and also a spiked crown, it is reverenced throughout the province as 'Our Lady of Verona'.

But the most significant object in the square is the Lion of S. Mark; the sign, from here westward to Bergamo, that a city had accepted, as the phrase went, 'the protection of Messer San Marco'. This happened to Verona in 1405 when, the ruling Scaliger family having expired, the city, rather than expose itself to the turmoil of Italian politics, accepted annexation by Venice, and so began three hundred years of tranquillity and affluence. Whatever the sins of

Venice, among her virtues were the kindness, the mildness, the justice and the prosperity which descended upon cities with the arrival of the Evangelist's Lion. The Venetian connection explains much that strikes the visitor in his first impressionable hours. It tells him that the resemblance to Venice goes deeper than the Grand Canal-like curve of the Adige, and is rather an air of imperial splendour conferred upon the city in the days of Venetian power. I felt at times that I was looking at Venice, not as she is today, when her argosies are composed mostly of amateur photographers, but as she was; and sometimes when I saw the Veronese chatting together in the marble streets, or grouped under one of the many porticoes, I thought I detected the crafty air one associates with magnificoes, though they were, I am sure, discussing only that eternal Italian problem: what to do with the proceeds of a lottery not yet won. To me, Messer San Marco was the answer to the question: why is Verona so different from the cities of Lombardy and Emilia? Here for the first time I saw a city, the result not of local feeling and tradition, but of that cosmopolitanism which was the soul of the great maritime Republic. Already I seemed to smell the Adriatic and to fancy the fleets of the Serenissima homing from the Spice Islands while the bells rang. An archway leads from the Piazza delle Erbe to a scene of even greater splendour and beauty, the Piazza dei Signori. Not even in Rome, certainly not in Venice, are two such superb creations separated only by an arch. I explored no farther. I had seen enough for one afternoon. I had recognized one of the most noble cities in Italy.

You can set your watch by that moment in Verona, as the sun is setting, when the evening suddenly flowers with hundreds of young women in their best cotton frocks. This delightful survival of seventeenth century society, to be witnessed nowadays only in Spain and Italy, is the *passeggiata*. It takes place in the traffic-less Via Mazzini where one can watch it with pleasure and safety, admiring the neat heads, the well-shod feet, the pretty uncreased frocks. Dr Burney noted that 'the ladies here wear black silk hats, cocked like those of the men in England. The females in general wear black silk hoods'.

I was told that the moment a girl leaves work she runs home, tidies her hair, perhaps changes her stockings and shoes, and takes down from its special holder in her wardrobe her special *passeggiata* dress, which must be without a crease. It is never sat upon. In the act of sitting the dress is swiftly pulled up and the wearer sits upon her petticoat. Having dressed, the girl then meets her dearest female friend (of the moment), or perhaps several of them, at the corner of a street, and they begin together that slow perambulation up and down the Via Mazzini. It is like the preliminary mating habit of some species of pretty brown bird. It is amusing to notice the change that occurs in a spirited girl who has attracted a *fidanzato*, and now, having left the ranks of her own sex, has joined those who are engaged; for this parade is grimly serious. While with her own sex the girl appeared bold and capable of bearing all the burdens of life, now, beside a male, she conveys an impression of coyness and helplessness and, no matter how small and puny her admirer, suggests in her manner a charming deference to his masculinity. But this is nothing compared with the extraordinary change which occurs in him. Once a member of a wild-looking bachelor gang sprawled sneeringly outside a café, or charging pointlessly about on a Vespa, and as good an example as you will find in modern times of a young bravo, he is now transformed into a mild, obedient, but at the same time, haughty swain. The companions of his former days, still sitting cynically outside the café, may whisper together as he passes with his girl, and in the glance he returns may be detected the apprehension of one who has crossed his Rubicon.

§ 2

The people I met in Verona were brimming over with the Italian desire to charm, and I felt that their kindness and affability were, in a sense, a reflection of the beautiful city in which they had the good fortune to live. Of all the cities I had seen so far in Italy, Verona gave me the greatest pleasure. It was elegant, dignified, and beautiful. It was neither too large nor too small. Its colour was a joy: the pink brick of the mediaeval buildings with their fish-tail battlements, the dull reddish marble, the siena walls of the old palaces, the balconied houses with their scarlet geraniums, the blue loop of the river, all combined together to form a collaboration of the centuries which appealed as much to the eye as to the imagination.

Every morning I walked beneath the arch, reminiscent of the Bridge of Sighs, from the crowded Piazza delle Erbe into the lordly Piazza dei Signori. Here Dante brooded upon his pedestal, for Verona loves to remember that the court of the Scaligeri is said to have been the first refuge in his exile. A few paces away stood one of the loveliest buildings of the Renaissance, a little palace called La Loggia, built by some unknown genius in the late fifteenth century, someone with an affectionate feeling for the classical world not unlike that of Pirro Ligorio, whose summer house in the Vatican Gardens always seems to me one of the gayest, happiest buildings of that age.

A few paces from this square, and you come to a narrow street, and the most striking sight in Verona. At first the lane appears to be filled with Gothic tombs. Several shrines of white stone, encrusted with saints and pinnacles and topped with funeral effigies of knights in armour, almost fill the roadway. When you see them for the first time it is as though you had surprised some great funeral of the Middle Ages at a moment when the procession had halted in a side-street to set the hatchments straight, to pull down the black velvet and see the candles lit before it continued to the cathedral square. These are the tombs of the Scaligeri, the mediaeval lords of Verona.

They are too tall and elaborate to be enclosed within a building and stand in the street with the sunlight on them, surrounded by an iron grille of loose mesh so strong that it has weathered the storms of more than five hundred years, yet so light that you can take it in your hand and shake it like a coat of mail. Each link of the iron grille is in the form of a little five-runged ladder (*scala*), a reference to the story that the first Scaliger either made or sold ladders.

There are five tombs, three of them with mounted knights on

top. These lords of Verona lived during the Plantagenet period in England, a time when the later Capetians and the first Valois reigned in France, and while the imperial line in Germany changed from Hohenstaufen to Habsburg. In Italy, they were the contemporaries of the first Visconti, the remote Matteo, Galeazzo, and Azzo, but the other great seigniorial families had not yet asserted themselves. The Scaligeri carved out an empire in Verona and set that pattern of cruelty and luxury which was to become familiar in later times.

The greatest and most popular of them was Francesco, or Cangrande, the 'Great Dog', who seems to have been the first of his family to wear a helmet in the shape of a dog's head. He is to be seen on top of his tomb, riding his war-horse, which is covered from head to hoofs in a flowing housing. Cangrande is in armour, his dog-headed helmet thrown back upon his shoulder-blades. He grasps a sword, and his clean-shaven face wears a smile that can be seen from pavement level. This perpetuates the memory of his famous merriment – his *allegria* – that endeared him so much to the Veronese. I said to the little man, who unlocked the gate in the iron grille for me, that it was unusual to see a man laughing on his tomb. He looked at me solemnly and answered, 'We say in Verona that Cangrande was never afraid of anything.'

The contrast between the gay rider as he was seen in life and the lower stages of his monument is a strange one. Here Cangrande is seen carved in marble, lying in death, his sword between his folded hands; beneath is a beautiful sarcophagus resting upon the backs of two mastiffs.

Near the gate is the tomb of Mastino II, the nephew of Cangrande and the father of Beatrice della Scala, who married Bernabò Visconti and gave her name to La Scala in Milan. Her flock of ten daughters spread the Scaliger-Visconti blood through Europe. One became the Queen of Cyprus, another became the Duchess Leopold of Austria, while three married into the Wittelsbach dynasty.

Mastino was an odd and suspicious character who allowed his nerves to get the better of him. Once, while riding with a bishop, he suddenly drew his sword and killed the unfortunate prelate, his excuse being that he believed the bishop was plotting against him with Venice. His remorse was life-long. He is said never again to have been seen without a veil covering his face (perhaps a picturesque mediaeval way of saying that he grew a beard), and his tomb effigy is the only one with the visor closed. His son, Cansignorio, whose tomb is near by, was one of those rare characters who have gone down to history as a ruler who reduced taxes and sold corn in bad times at less than cost price. A peculiar event occurred in this churchyard after his death. It was discovered that he had made a fortune by farming out church benefices, and in other ways not above reproach, and it was felt that in doing so he must have committed grievous sins which had not been specifically absolved on his death-bed. It was therefore decided to give him posthumous absolution. Mass was said amid the tombs, then ladders were brought so that the Bishops of Verona and Vicenza might ascend and sprinkle holy water on the sarcophagus as they gave absolution to the dead man.

The Scaligeri were not, on the whole, an attractive family. They were fabulously rich, generous to those whom they liked, but full of distressing neuroses, with an emphasis on fratricide. Their attitude to the Muses was one of aristocratic indifference, yet, oddly enough, Cangrande's claim to fame is that Dante dedicated the *Paradiso* to him and is said to have sent him cantos of the poem from time to time as he wrote them. This picture of the war-lord as a literary critic and a patron may not be the true one, indeed it is said that Dante, when a guest at Verona, was sometimes an object of practical jokes. There is a story that buffoons and actors, resenting Dante's air of superiority, once sent a small boy to creep under the table and pile up at Dante's feet the bones which the diners had thrown down. When the table was removed, Cangrande, pretending to be astonished, said that he had no idea that Dante was so fond of meat, to which the poet is said to have replied, 'My lord, you would not have seen so many bones had I been a dog.'

However, if these stories are true, the poet cannot have been happy in such company. For years a literary battle, recently revived, has waged round the authenticity of Dante's *Epistle* to Cangrande in which he extols 'the illustrious renown of your

Magnificence', and mentions the splendour he had witnessed at the Scaliger court and the bounty he had received there.

It is curious to contrast the rough dining-room scene of the above story with the fact that certain Alpine villages were exempted from taxes as long as they kept the Scaliger ice-houses filled. Maybe the guests, having tossed their bones on the floor, were treated to refrigerated game or sophisticated iced drinks.

§ 3

The patron saint of Verona, S. Zeno, was a fisherman who may be seen in the church named after him, holding a rod with a fine silver fish on the end of it. When he was painted as a bishop, a fish was always attached to his crozier. His church was built when Richard, Cœur de Lion, was with the Crusades, and if you descend into the archaic crypt you will see the saint's bones in a crystal casket. The doors of the church are decorated with bronze panels in high relief, some of the figures standing out two and three inches from the background. While I was looking at these primitive scriptural scenes, a small car drove up from which two young men descended. While one ran up the steps of the church holding a canvas bag, the other walked to the end of the road and appeared to be keeping watch. The man with the bag swiftly produced from it a lump of modelling clay, or some similar substance, which he began to press upon the bronze panels. Having taken two or three impressions, he ran back to the car, where his companion joined him, and they drove away. The operation did not take more than three or four minutes. I wondered whether they were art students, souvenir hunters, or antique dealers, and resolved that if ever I saw a convincing bronze panel of the expulsion from Eden in an antique shop, I would pass by on the other side!

The impressive old baptistry of the cathedral solved a problem which I think first occurred to me in Parma, when I saw the font there, in size almost a small swimming-bath. During mass baptism, did the officiating cleric get into the font with the faithful or did he stand outside? This font in Verona answers the question: there is a priest's hole, or cavity, in the centre of which the bishop could stand dry-shod; and this, I suppose, must have been the custom everywhere.

To an English eye, I think the Giusti Garden in Verona is perhaps more attractive than the strictly formal Italian garden. It is backed by a steep hillside planted with beautiful trees. Enormous cypresses of immense antiquity cast their shade; trim box hedges enclose bright beds of cannas and geraniums; there are statues in exactly the right positions; there are tubs of clipped lemon trees, and fountains, while marble seats invite you to sit and think what a perfect background it is for *Twelfth Night*. The garden has been open for centuries. Tom Coryat became lost in a maze there in the reign of James I and had to be rescued; Goethe (who never even mentions the Scaliger tombs), enjoyed the Giusti Garden and caused a mild sensation by walking round Verona holding a spray of cypress with the cones attached, which he had got there, and a sprig of flowering caper.

The elegant little Roman theatre, all marble, of course, was not visible in his day. It was discovered in the last century beneath the buildings which once stood there. How Goethe would have loved that graceful semi-circle of marble seats now revealed in such good shape that plays are sometimes given there.

I was again reminded of Goethe when in one of the streets near the arena I heard the wireless-set of some short-wave listener booming out the signature tune of the British Broadcasting Corporation. 'The ballad of Marlbrook is heard in every street,' wrote Goethe in 1784.

I remembered once more the Italian genius for reconstruction, evident in the rebuilt opera house in Milan and, in Verona, by the rebuilding of the red-brick bridge which was blown up by the Germans in the last war as they retreated to the Brenner Pass. Who could believe, seeing this bridge now, with its romantic fish-tail battlements, that it is not the original built by Cangrande II in the fourteenth century? It leads to his castle, which is red-brick and crenellated like the bridge, indeed the two are one architectural group, the bridge a fortified passage across the river. Now the castle is a museum and art gallery, but the finest picture is the view from the windows to the blue sweep of the Adige and the bridge below. In the hall where one now admires many a famous picture, Count Ciano and his fellow rebels against Mussolini were sentenced to death in 1944. An adjoining room contains some gruesome photographs of Cangrande as he was revealed to those who opened his sarcophagus in 1921, also some pieces of the beautiful brocade in which the lord of Verona was buried six centuries ago.

§ 4

Verona pretends that Romeo and Juliet were historical characters. You will be told that they lived about the year 1303 during the reign of Cangrande's elder brother, Bartolomeo della Scala, and that Juliet was buried in the graveyard of the now disused Franciscan monastery, just outside the southern stretch of the town wall.

The story of the two lovers is an old and popular one, and in some versions the scene is not set in Verona. The first writer to tell the story as we know it was Luigi da Porto in his *Giulietta e Romeo* (and to this day Italians gallantly mention Juliet first), a version which was copied by others, and these, in translation, are believed to have been Shakespeare's sources. Such facts, however, mean little to the thousands from all countries who go to Verona to see, not the amphitheatre or the tombs of the Scaligeri, but the tomb of Juliet. Some may consider this deplorable, others may think it pathetic, while an Englishman may feel some pride as he sees Shakespeare guiding so many coaches from Hamburg, Oslo, Copenhagen, Vienna, and goodness knows where else, into Verona, full of those who have never heard of da Porto or Bandello and know the story of Romeo and Juliet only from Shakespeare's play.

Verona is a town of balconies, as da Porto, who lived near by at Vicenza, knew well; and once he had decided to localize the story in Verona it was an obvious local touch, which Shakespeare, in his turn, used so brilliantly. One balcony in Verona, in a picturesque mediaeval house in the Via Cappello, is pointed out to pilgrims as Juliet's, and a graceful but unhistorical inscription has been attached to the building. 'This was the house', it reads, 'of the Capulets, whence sprang Juliet, for whom so many gentle hearts have wept, and poets have sung.' Those two charming last lines, even more charming in the original – *per cui tanto piansero i cuori gentili e i poeti cantarono* – give one the eye of faith and send one off in an agreeably sentimental mood to Juliet's tomb.

A short walk from the Portoni della Brà brings one to an abandoned monastery whose custodian smilingly takes the gate money and waves one on into a delightful little cloister with a pretty, dove-haunted garden in the centre. A few steps descend to a vaulted room occupied by what appears to be an unusually large pink marble sarcophagus. Unsympathetic authorities, however, say it was once a horse-trough. As I came silently down the steps, I surprised a couple of young people standing on each side of it and, hand in hand across it, were bending forward to kiss each other. I heard afterwards that this is a common custom with lovers, who go there to wish and, as the young woman who told me this put it, 'if their hearts are pure, their wishes come true'. I thought the rendezvous a charming one. The vault was filled with a shell-pink light reflected from the cloister above, giving to the sarcophagus a delicate poetic look like pink alabaster at the bottom of the sea. It is almost impossible to look at it and fail to recall the lines,

> *For here lies Juliet, and her beauty makes*
> *This vault a feasting presence full of light.*

The zeal with which English visitors chipped off fragments of the 'tomb' in 1814 is mentioned by Samuel Rogers, and, of course, Byron added some to his sentimental museum. An unusually large piece must have gone to make the pair of bracelets which Marie Louise was wearing when Chateaubriand dined with her at Parma. All this pales, however, before the almost unbelievable fact, which I discovered by accident, that the Juliet cult is so popular today that she has a secretary to answer her fan mail!

While walking in the cloister, I noticed a small glass window inset in the wall, framed with a marble moulding and fitted with a slip for letters. Idly glancing inside, I saw a pile of notes scribbled hastily on scraps of paper, leaves torn from notebooks, old bills, and so forth, like the notes which children scribble to Father Christmas. Several of these had not been folded and two were decipherable. They were both in Italian and both began, 'Cara Giulietta'. One read, 'We are two young lovers travelling after our marriage. Help us, Juliet, so that our love may become greater every day'. The other read: 'My love is far from here. Let him come and see me very soon, and let us someday always be together'.

I was astonished. I wondered if the clergy of Verona knew that the old Franciscan monastery had become a shrine of Aphrodite! One of the attendants told me that the box in the wall holds only the letters written to Juliet on the spot; the greater part of her correspondence arrives by post from many countries and in many languages, and is indeed so formidable that the Municipality employs a secretary to handle it. The secretary was, I gathered, 'an elderly retired gentleman', a manifestation, I suppose, of old Friar Laurence.

'Are the letters from men or women?' I asked.

'Some are from men, but many more from women,' I was told.

On the way out I stood aside before an eager advancing crowd of travellers of varied nationality who had descended from two motor-coaches. I heard myself hailed and found myself shaking hands with the little German from Mantua, still slung about with cameras, and in the background his wife and the two adoring daughters. The Shakespearean associations of Verona were almost too much for him: he was breathless with excitement.

'Please,' he said, thrusting a camera into my hands, 'be so kind as to take my photograph here.'

Seizing the arm of a fellow passenger, he led him to the notice-board under the cypress trees which reads *Tomba di Giulietta*. There, arm in arm and at attention, I photographed them.

'You are so kind,' said the German. 'Do you know what I shall call that picture? Then I will tell you. The two gentlemen of Verona!'

With a merry laugh, he slung the camera round his neck and skipped heavily along the path to Juliet's tomb.

§ 5

The road from Verona to Vicenza lies through a lush country-side planted with beet, maize, and vines, and protected from Alpine blasts by windbreaks of acacia. The foothills undulate northward to the great mountains which lie around the Brenner, and I am told that on clear days you can see them in violet silhouette against the sky.

I had with me in the car a lively Italian acquaintance from Verona, a merchant of marble, who had some business in the hilly town of Montecchio Maggiore, which is just off the main road. To Signor X marble was more than a geological fact or a commercial product: it was a theory of life. To him, history was a simple matter of stonemason or carpenter. Stone represented civilization; wood, barbarism. He would argue that the Teutonic tribes, which invaded Italy in the Dark Ages, were forest men (the stranger is still a *forestiero*), who were scared by the magic world of marble that, to their amazement, had fallen to them, so scared in fact that they preferred to live in open country like the beasts. This enabled the Latin spirit to survive within the stone walls of the cities, and to reassert itself during the Middle Ages in stone cathedral and palazzo, and to develop into the full marble splendour of the Renaissance. He would quote Poggio and Tasso to prove how shocked were Italian travellers of the Renaissance by the ungainly wooden buildings of Paris and London, the abodes obviously of unarchitectural barbarians. The most scabrous tumbledown stone slum was, in his opinion, more suitable to the dignity of Man than any building of wood.

As we travelled through the fresh morning, we talked about marble and the decline in civilization implied, according to his theory, in the slump that has existed in the industry since 1929. By this time I was well instructed: I knew that the finest greys come from the provinces of Cuneo, Navara, and Gorizia; the best green from the Valle d'Aosta; a superb black from Bergamo and the famous 'pink' from Verona; and still the most prized marble today, as in classical times, is the chaste Carrara taken from the quarries of the Apuan Alps. He mentioned with satisfaction a profitable consignment which he had sent, of all places, to Saudi Arabia, maybe a cheering indication that though civilization appears to be losing ground here, it is perhaps gaining it elsewhere.

When I had dropped him at Montecchio, I went on to look at the ruins of two castles which face each other upon neighbouring hills. Legend claims them as castles of Montagu and Capulet, but I should think they were probably strongholds of the Scaligeri. Having ascended the hill, I entered the ruined courtyard of a castle to find two Canadian girls washing nylon garments in a canvas bucket. The castle is now a 'camping', with water and electric light laid on. A group of young hikers were setting off for Venice, laden like pack mules; cyclists were preparing to leave, drawn probably to the same inevitable magnet; there was a sumptuous trailer caravan in which a large German family existed amidst chromium gadgets as if living inside a Leica camera; and, as I took in this scene, a series of minor explosions announced the arrival of an Italian couple mounted upon that hero of the Italian highway, an overloaded Vespa. The Canadian girls thought it a wonderful 'camping' but confessed that the complexities of the simple life were relieved by the bar and restaurant of the near-by *Taverna di Giulietta*.

Never perhaps since the Middle Ages has travel been so casual, neither have so many travellers wandered afar apparently with so few means, moving happily from place to place, counting their pence, undismayed by the prospect of sleeping on bare boards or under the stars. I am not one of those who would willingly be twenty again, but if I were obliged to experience the joys of youth once more, I can think of no pleasanter way of seeing Italy for the first time than in the frugal company of this self-reliant generation.

Passing through Montecchio Maggiore again, there was Signor X waving to me from a café. He had concluded his business and said he would come with me to Vicenza. So off we went down the hill to the main road, where the looped vines strode across the country like garlanded pages, while the growing maize re-sembled the lances of advancing cavalry. Someone had told me that a few years ago Signor X had gone to London to see a firm of architects about marble for a bank or a skyscraper and had since become an authority on England. I referred to this as we went along and, rather to my surprise, found that he had discovered in England certain sturdy, old-fashioned virtues which some of us are unable to discern nowadays.

'I always tell those who come to me for advice when going to England,' he said, 'that if they think and behave in the opposite way from that to which they are accustomed in Italy, they cannot make a mistake!'

He thought the English eccentric and disciplined beyond belief. 'In the final deluge,' he remarked, 'all the English will die together, but here in Italy a few individualistic heads will pop up in the flood.'

Late one night, he told me, he went to Buckingham Palace to see if the sentries were still marching up and down.

'And they were,' he declared, 'with no one to see them but God. That could not happen in Italy.'

I reminded him of the two silent figures bowed in grief on each side of the Unknown Soldier's tomb in Rome.

'There is no comparison!' he cried. 'To you, they may seem silent figures. But *I* know they are speaking out of the sides of their mouths, and *I* know what they are saying. They are criticizing Vittorio Emanuele for having a monument; and the Unknown Soldier for having a tomb . . . That is the Italian way . . .'

I reminded him of the sentry of Pompeii.

'He must have been a Briton,' he said.

Arriving at Vicenza, we saw the morning sunlight falling upon a majestic scene which, probably more than any other in Italy, was reflected in the appearance of eighteenth century England. Upon every hand rose the tawny palaces built by the man who gave the much praised and much abused term Palladian to the English language. Born in 1518, he began life as a stonemason and was named Andrea di Pietro. In those happy days the gentry of a city could form a society called an academy and devote their lives to the most intoxicating of amateur occupations, building. One of the leaders of Vicenza's Academy was Count Trissino, who spotted the genius of the young stonemason and sent him to study architecture in Rome. He returned to Vicenza, the last great architect of the Renaissance, fired by an ambition to revive the austerities of Augustan architecture as expounded by Vitruvius; and during his triumphant career his patron persuaded him to change his name to Palladio.

Fourteen Palladian palaces were destroyed by bombs during the last war, but still the city can boast survivors in every street. How fortunate was Palladio to have found so many clients anxious and financially able to give him a free hand.

'Ah, but what a tragedy!' exclaimed Signor X, as we passed from palace to palace. 'So much classical splendour but no marble! It is all brick and stucco. Just imagine it in marble! How one's heart bleeds for poor Palladio!'

I reminded him that the buildings which Palladio would have liked to have built in stone were to rise, not in Italy, but in far-off London, and amid the woods and meadows of English counties. The library of Worcester College, Oxford, has a copy of Palladio's book on architecture which Inigo Jones carried everywhere with him during his second tour of Italy, and one hopes that the cure for indigestion which the owner memorized on one of the end-papers helped to make the tour more pleasant. He took back to England, two hundred years after it had run its majestic course in Italy, Architecture as opposed to Building; and every time one passes down Whitehall, there, awaiting one's admiration, is that Italian *palazzo*, blackened with more than three centuries of London grime, once the Banqueting Hall of Whitehall Palace, in which Inigo Jones expressed what he had learnt in Vicenza and other places in Italy. It was the first truly Renaissance building in England, and to those who saw it in 1622, when it was new – only six years after Shakespeare's death – it must have looked as strange as some of the experiments with glass and concrete do today.

Richard Boyle, third Earl of Burlington, was about twenty when he arrived in Vicenza a century later with those reels of waxed thread knotted together into foot lengths which serious-minded travellers of the time were advised to take to Italy with them. It was Burlington's boast that he had measured every building erected by Palladio. Returning home, and with the help of another timely genius, William Kent, the architectural earl began to translate his studies into stone. Old Burlington House in Piccadilly was given a Palladian face-lift modelled on the Palazzo Chiericati, now the Museum of Vicenza, but his most famous translation is the villa at Chiswick, based on the Villa Almerico. The Chiswick villa, which was in a state of collapse after the last war, has since been beautifully repaired and restored.

Why, of all the architecture to be sketched and measured in Italy, did the architecture of Palladio attract the English so much? Maybe the reserve of the Vitruvian resurrection appealed to the national character, as it then was, or possibly such restraint seemed more suitable to England than more pompous styles; or perhaps it was simply because Palladio had solved the problem of adapting classical splendour to the comparatively small country house. The Palladian villa still stands ('suitable for school or institution') in the English countryside, a monument under our pale skies to an enthusiasm we shall, alas, never see again.

We wandered through the bright and pleasant town and came to rest at a café table in the shadow of Palladio's masterpiece, the huge Gothic town hall to which he gave a classical façade. Two friends of Signor X came over to our table in a state of some excitement and described what I thought was a fantastic theft. During the night, it appeared, a thief had made off with a Lion's Mouth! These were the letter-boxes of the Venetian Republic, into which any informer might slip a denunciation for the attention of the secret service. They were called Lions' Mouths because the top portion of the box was a bronze lion's head and the letter was slipped into the open mouth.

We hurried off to the scene of the crime, which proved to be just round the corner, and found a small crowd of officials and police gathered round a gash in the wall. The thief had sawn through the metal clamps that secured the lion's head to the stone and had made off with it. Perhaps an American tourist, someone began. No, no, was the reply, what tourist would have had the good taste to steal such a bronze?

Signor X thought he could find another *Bocca di Leone* in position, but we looked in vain.

'What a shocking system it was,' I said, 'an invitation for citizens to spy on each other.'

'Yes,' he replied, 'but the Venetians were experts in sifting the letters. The man working off a grudge did not stand much of a chance. The real evil was the inspired denunciation slipped into the box to incriminate someone the Government wished to eliminate.'

The great sight of Vicenza is the *Teatro Olimpico* which Palladio was building at the time of his death. The first performance was given in 1584, and the stage looks much as it did then. The action takes place before a permanent architectural scene, which is a massive classical gateway through whose three arches one looks along three apparently long streets. The perspective is so brilliantly contrived that I went on to the stage to convince myself that these streets are really only a few yards in depth. I was told that, when a play is performed there, should it be necessary to give a semblance of life to the background, small children dressed as adults have to be used since the appearance of a full-grown man would instantly destroy the illusion. I noticed a great number of small glass oil-lamps at the back of the stage. When lighted, the effect of a Roman street at night, or in moonlight, must be enchanting.

Of the many Palladian villas around Vicenza, the Villa Almerico, or the Rotonda, is the best known and the most popular, but I prefer the Villa Valmarana, known as the Villa of the Dwarfs. One sees the Rotonda standing among its stone pines with a smile of recognition, for it is the parent of so many English houses. There were once four copies of it; now there remain the Burlington Villa at Chiswick, Mereworth Castle and Footscray, both in Kent.

The dwarfs of the Villa dei Nani are garden statues mounted upon the boundary wall so that they may be seen by all who pass along the road. No doubt generations of peasants are responsible for the tale I was told: that once a rich lord had a loved and only daughter who was a dwarf, and to keep the knowledge of her deformity from her she was never allowed to see anyone of normal height. One day, however, a handsome prince rode by and, so the story ends, the poor child committed suicide.

I liked this villa with its charming frescoes by Tiepolo and his son. The stables, though congested with wheelbarrows, hencoops, and suchlike objects, and with a number of pheasant chicks, struck me as a delightful and unusual glimpse of the Renaissance. The horse-troughs were of Verona marble, the hay-racks of wrought iron, and each stall was separated by a partition ending in a column crowned with a statue. The stables of the huge Villa Pisani at Stra are of almost identical design and are illustrated in Georgina Masson's beautiful *Italian Villas and Palaces*.

Vicenza and Padua are less than twenty miles apart and I saw little on the road save one Palladian villa. I approached Padua wondering if Shakespeare had ever been in Italy. Some believe that in the Italianate Tudor age he could easily have gained all the intimate detail he required over a bumper of sack in any London inn, but others think he must have known the country. Professor Ernesto Grillo believed that the poet had a working knowledge of Italian; Professor A. Lytton Sells thinks it not impossible that when the London theatres were closed by the plague in 1592–4, Shakespeare may have taken ship to Venice and have visited Padua, Vicenza, and Verona. 'He loved, in imagination, to dwell in Venetia more than in any other part of Italy,' he writes, 'and seven of his plays, if not more, are situated in or related to this region.'

§ 6

The hotel in Padua was large, dignified, and old-fashioned. Lifts of solid mahogany rose slowly to enormous bedrooms, and from my window I looked down upon – 'Padua: a Public Place.' Immediately below was a bus-stop with its ever-changing clientèle, and beyond stood an elegant Greek temple which, as I was soon to learn, specializes in *zabaione* and is celebrated in Italian history as the all-night Caffé Pedrocchi once frequented by the patriots of the Risorgimento.

How sweetly the name of Padua sounds in English ears. Shakespeare's Shrew was Katerina Moroni, renowned in Padua for her scolding tongue, and the action of the play takes place there. It was as a Paduan lawyer and 'his' clerk that Portia and Nerissa hurried to Venice to confound and defeat poor Shylock. One remembers too how closely the city was linked to Elizabethan England by generations of medical students who went off to 'fair Padua, nursery of the arts' to obtain the most reputable degree in Europe.

It is crowded, confusing, and delightful, and claims to be the oldest city in Italy. Its walls and bastions can be traced for long stretches while a stream or canal, one hardly knows which to call it, meanders pleasantly all over the map so that one is always crossing a bridge as if one were already in Venice. The crowded streets in the centre of the town are mediaeval in plan, but with an underlying rectangularity which reminds one that a Roman city was there first, and one in which it is said Livy was born. More famous now, however, is S. Anthony of Padua, whose tomb is here, a saint who, as an old man remarked to me, is the fastest worker in heaven if approached in the right spirit.

One of the first things I noticed was the technique of the conducted tour as the coaches came roaring into Padua to stop near the Scrovegni Chapel. While the passengers entered the chapel, the drivers reversed their coaches and were ready to rush off somewhere else when the travellers emerged. Not a minute is wasted. How wonderful to be carried swiftly from place to place with nothing to do but to lie back upon soft cushions! Only great lords and millionaires were once able to travel in such comfort.

Near by is a sad Augustinian church, sad because the famous Mantegna frescoes no longer exist. One night during the last war a young man somewhere in the sky above Padua released a bomb at the precise moment when the law of gravity was fated to bring it down upon the apse of the church and destroy Mantegna's work. In that unhappy moment Italy suffered the most serious art loss of the Second World War, but in some miraculous way, the adjacent Scrovegni Chapel, which would have been an even more disastrous loss, came through unharmed.

The chapel was built in 1305 by the son of a money-lender named Rinaldo degli Scrovegni, a man whom Dante had condemned to Hell to sit for ever with other usurers on burning sand. In the year 1305 Edward I was reigning in England; the Popes had not yet fled to Avignon; sixty years were to pass before Chaucer was born . . . so one struggled to place it in time. Nothing is known of the founder save that he was rich and that he employed the most revolutionary artist of the time to decorate the chapel, the ugly and lovable little genius known as Giotto.

Every inch of the building is covered in fresco; the vaulted ceiling is a blue heaven studded with gold stars, and the walls are an elaborate scheme designed to frame more than thirty of the best-known pictures ever painted: scenes from the life of Christ and the Blessed Virgin, and though these are illustrated in every book on art, even the best reproductions give a poor idea of the originals. In the chapel one also sees them not as detached pictures, but as a series and in their right order in the scheme of decoration. The colour is astonishing, even though it must have been touched up from time to time. The Sistine Chapel gives one the same impression of being enfolded in colour, mainly blue. It is not easy for anyone living today, with centuries of books behind him, to imagine the effect of Giotto's frescoes on spectators who could not read. This simple New Testament picture book did something more than tell a story; it told it in a new way. Some may even have thought it rather shocking to take Christ and Our Lady from the encrusted Byzantine heaven and place them in the ordinary workaday world. It must have been as startling as watching the first cinema.

Giotto was a peasant from that valley near Florence which produced the Medici, and his contemporaries, like true Italians, were fascinated by his ugliness. It is said that his friend Dante stayed with him in Padua and sometimes sat in the chapel watching him swiftly transferring his pictures to the wet plaster, reflecting how odd it was that a man who could create such beauty should have created six children, each one as ugly as himself.

With darkness, large areas of Padua return to the sixteenth century. Many an Englishman now abed at home in England in his parish church, beneath a Tudor effigy, would recognize the colonnaded streets where he lodged in his youth. The English and the Scots were always sufficiently numerous at the University to form a *langue*, or language group, known as a 'nation', and they seem to have been a high-spirited crowd. They were near enough to Venice to go there on public holidays and to cheer the arrival of a new English ambassador, and often, after drinking his health, to have brawls in the Piazza of S. Mark and end up in the police station. In Padua itself national rivalries would sometimes blaze up, or disputes would end in tragedy. One morning the son of Sir Julius Caesar, Chancellor of the Exchequer under James I, was found dead in the street after a quarrel with a fencer's usher.

Sometimes the valour of medical students was challenged by the presence in the town of soldiers. This explosive situation was noted by John Evelyn, who put in a winter's study at Padua in 1645. 'I returned to Padua,' he wrote, 'when that town was so infested with soldiers that many houses were broken open in the night, some murders committed, and the nuns next our lodging disturbed, so that we were forced to be on our guard with pistols and other firearms to defend our doors; and indeed the students themselves take a barbarous liberty in the evenings when they go to their strumpets, to stop all that pass by the house where any of their companions in folly are with them. This custom they call *chi vali*, so as the streets are very dangerous, when the evenings grow dark; nor is it easy to reform this intolerable usage, where there are so many strangers of several nations.'

§ 7

I found the old University in the centre of Padua only a few steps from my hotel. The building is now the administrative offices of the modern University, whose faculties are scattered about the city. I saw an impressive late Renaissance court-yard from which marble steps led into rooms whose walls are covered with the names and coats-of-arms of students of all nations. While I was waiting in the Great Hall, where degrees are still sometimes conferred, I glanced at the inscriptions and noticed the names of Robert Suvale ('Anglus'); Robert Bannerman ('Scoto Aberdonensis'); Thomas Shoct ('Anglus'); William Stokeham; Peter Balle; Thomas Sorus; John Finch, and James Murray.

A professor who kindly took me round the University told me that the earliest record of an English student is that of Hugh of Evesham, who became doctor to Pope Martin IV and was made a cardinal in 1281. Famous names like those of Robert Fleming (1447), founder of Lincoln College, Oxford, John Tiptoft (1460), the learned and notorious Earl of Worcester, John Free, the scholar, and Thomas Linacre, are on the walls and in the registers of the University.

We came to a hall known as the *Sala dei Quaranta,* from the forty distinguished scholars whose life-sized portraits decorate the walls. An object of great interest is the ancient desk at which Galileo taught for eighteen years. It is made of rough oak planks and is more like a pulpit than a desk, and was perhaps inherited by Galileo from some mediaeval predecessor. One sees this type of desk in early pictures of professors teaching their pupils, though Galileo's is a very battered example.

His career was not only a triumphant one, until he came into conflict with the Church, but it was also well paid, said the pro-fessor. Sometimes two thousand people clamoured to attend his lectures, among them many distinguished scholars who had come from all parts of Europe to hear him. While he was at Padua he made his first telescope, which magnified only three times, but he continued to experiment with lenses and at length was able to make instruments which magnified thirty-two times. With the help of such modest aids, he saw for the first time the moons of Jupiter and picked out the stars of the Milky Way.

When I turned to examine the portraits on the wall, I saw a number of English scholars among the famous 'Forty'. First was Thomas Linacre, who had the awesome task of being Henry VIII's doctor, and the more pleasant one of teaching Princess Mary her Latin. There, as large as life, stood Francis Walsingham, the head of Elizabeth's secret service; William Harvey; and, odd in such company, John Ruthven of the Gowrie Conspiracy. Most surprising of all, however, was the portrait of 'Oliver Goldsmith, Irlandese', whose academic career was, I had always believed, something of a mystery. However, Padua firmly claims him as her own. (I looked into this later in the University archives, and suspect a case of mistaken identity. On December 13, 1755, a Doctorate of Philosophy and Medicine was conferred upon '*Domini Guglielmo Oliver filii domini Gulielmi, Angli*', an unsatisfactory description of Goldsmith!)

We entered a room that was ready for a viva voce. A lonely seat was placed facing an inquisitorial array of arm-chairs. Also within sight of the candidate was a glass case containing eight human skulls.

'They are the skulls of professors who left their bodies for dissection', explained my guide.

To face dead professors as well as the living struck me as the worst kind of academic joke. We descended some stairs and came to a door at which the professor paused.

'You will now see,' he said, 'the oldest anatomy theatre in the world. It was built in 1594 for Fabrizio d'Acquapendente with whom your own great William Harvey studied, and in whose house he lodged.'

We passed into a macabre fragment of the sixteenth century. A circular lecture-hall, or theatre, rose about us, made of some light-coloured wood like pine, and capable of holding about two hundred students in six galleries, one above the other. There were no seats. The students would stand leaning on the balustrades, gazing down into the central circle in which was the dissection-table. An oblong about seven by four feet had been removed, and through the opening I looked into the vaults or cellars. I asked the reason for this. 'The mediaeval prejudice against the dissection of a human body lasted well into the Renaissance,' said the professor, 'and it was sometimes advisable, even in Padua, the least theological of all universities, to be able quickly to conceal the evidence of a post-mortem. At a sign from the anatomist, the table could be sunk into the cellar by way of this opening and all evidence concealed. Also, the bodies which were dissected were usually those of executed criminals, which were cut down from the gallows at night and hurried, by way of the cellars, into the anatomy theatre. That was why so many lectures were delivered by candle-light. Sometimes two men holding torches stood at each end of the table and directed the light here and there at the bidding of the professor.'

He told me that among the reasons why the medical school at Padua was so famous was that under the rule of Venice anatomical lectures and dissections were held more frequently than anywhere else in Europe. In Paris, for instance, at that period, the sixteenth century, only two bodies were allowed to be dissected annually, and such 'anatomies' cannot have been of much help to students. The lecturer, seated upon a high throne, would point with a white wand while a barber-surgeon dismembered the corpse of a felon. In Padua, on the other hand, the science of anatomy developed under the direction of the first of the great anatomists, Vesalius, who was able to persuade the local magistrates not to condemn criminals to be drawn and quartered. Students were able not only to attend the lectures and demonstrations of the great anatomists but also to buy accurate 'tables' of veins and arteries like those, now in the British Museum, which Evelyn took home with him from Padua and presented to the Royal Society.

No student became a more devoted surgeon than William Harvey, whose first thoughts on the circulation of the blood are believed to have occurred while he was leaning over this cock-pit in Padua. It is said that when his wife's parrot died he had the bird on the operating-table in a moment and proved that it had been masquerading as a male all its life! Another of his unusual 'anatomies' was held when James I asked him to give an opinion on a suspected witch. The old woman lived alone on the edge of Newmarket Heath, and did not admit her supernatural powers until Harvey confided to her that he was a wizard. Encouraged, the old dame promised to show him her familiar. Making clucking sounds, and placing a saucer of milk on the floor, she pointed to a toad that hopped out from beneath an oak chest. Harvey sent her away to bring a jug of ale and while she was absent, like a good pupil of Fabrizio, he had the toad dissected in a moment and found it 'in no wayes different from other toades'. Naturally, the old woman was annoyed to find that her familiar had been dissected, but she did not know that the operation had probably saved her from the stake.

'William Harvey lodged with Fabrizio d'Acquapendente,' said the professor, 'and it seems probable that the starting point of his thoughts on circulation may have been his master's discovery that the valves of the veins opened towards the heart.'

As I climbed about the galleries, I tried to imagine the faces of the students lit only by the torchlight from the gruesome pit into which they were gazing, a scene even more dramatic than that imagined by Rembrandt. There were no anaesthetics or microscopes when the students left Shakespeare's England to study here, and their knowledge of germs and infection was less than that of any ten-year-old today, yet when they returned with their saws and their probes, they were the most scientific and up-to-date practitioners of the time.

§ 8

In the early morning before the motorist is up a merciful silence broods over the city. Sunlight falls upon quiet squares and deserted colonnades, and the only signs of life are a few figures hurrying to early Mass. Like most of the cities of northern Italy, Padua is a perfect place to explore before breakfast, and it has all the features you expect: statues of Petrarch and Mazzini; a Via Dante; a Via Manzoni; a Piazza Garibaldi; and, rather more original, a Via Falloppio, a tribute to the anatomist; and the Via del Santo, which leads to the basilica of S. Anthony of Padua, one of the great pilgrimage churches of Italy. They tell you in Padua that it is the city of:

The Saint without a name
The Meadow without grass
The Coffee-house without doors.

These cryptic references are to S. Anthony, who is never given his name in Padua but is always 'Il Santo'; the Meadow without grass is the immense architectural square, the Prato della Valle ('Prato' meaning meadow), which is so much like a seventeenth century engraving that you expect a company of grenadiers to march across with a fife band and a negro cymbalist; and the doorless coffee-house is the Caffè Pedrocchi which once remained open all night. Perhaps one might add to Padua's cryptograms 'the Cat on horseback', being Donatello's mounted statue of Erasmo da Narni, the great Venetian commander known to everyone as Gattamelata.

The first portion of any Italian town to awaken is that part of it which is obviously linked to the Middle Ages by a continuous string of onions, the Piazza delle Erbe. In Padua there is also a Piazza dei Frutti, and both stand in the shadow of a vast town hall that looms over the busy scene like an old galleon above a quayside. It was amusing to watch the stall-holders arriving on buzz-bicycles, on motorized tricycles, in small vans, and even on motor-scooters fitted with home-made trailers, every vehicle loaded with lettuces, cabbages, aubergines, melons, tomatoes, and everything else which the finest market gardeners on earth can charm from the warm Italian soil.

In no time stalls were set out and canvas shades erected, and the market was ready for its first customers. At the same time the butchers, the bakers, and the fishmongers were opening shops under the Palazzo della Ragione, grouped together by trades, and I thought if Dante and Giotto could pass by, they would not see many changes.

I found the vast hall above the market occupied by a splendid horse of wood, left over maybe from some Renaissance triumph, and by two statues of the Egyptian cat goddess, the gift of Padua's giant son, Giovanni Belzoni. I fell under his spell in early life, and have often wondered why his exciting adventures among the tombs and Pyramids of Egypt, at a time long before anyone could read Ancient Egyptian hieroglyphs, have never been reprinted. He was an attractive, good-natured giant, six feet six inches in height, who delighted audiences at S. Bartholomew's Fair and Astley's Amphitheatre in London during the reign of George III when, dressed as Hercules, in a panther skin, he performed prodigious feats of strength. He attracted an equally large Amazon, who became Mrs Belzoni, and together the two giants went off to Egypt to sell hydraulic pumps to pashas. It was appropriate that the Paduan Hercules, who had studied engineering in Italy, should have been chosen to lift the colossal granite bust of Rameses II for transport to the British Museum; a feat which led him to explore tombs and temples up and down the Nile. He was the first man to excavate the temple of Abu Simbel, now a victim of 'vandalisme utilitaire', and he was the first European to penetrate to the mummy chamber of the Great Pyramid. Though Belzoni was no scholar, he was one of the greatest of the Near Eastern travellers, and his Narrative, with the large volume of highly-coloured tomb paintings drawn and tinted by himself, is the most fascinating early work of the kind in English. They still recall in Padua that when he returned in middle age, a famous traveller, bearing two cat goddesses as a gift to his native town, a gold medal was struck in his honour. Five years later the charming giant died on his way to Timbuktu.

I went to the Botanical Gardens, where you can sit in the shade of many a tree planted in the sixteenth century. In the centre one can trace the circular shape of the old Physic Garden, opened in 1545, where Tom Coryat tasted pistachio nuts and thought them 'farre more excellent than Apricocks', and where John Evelyn gathered those simples which are still preserved in the Library of Christ Church, Oxford. This claims to be the first scientific botanical garden in Europe.

It might be fanciful to say that England has impressed itself upon Padua, though true that one cannot walk its streets for long without recalling an English name. A highly improbable, yet possible, King of England died of fever while he was a political exile there: he was Edward Courtenay, Earl of Devonshire, whom many wished to see upon the throne with Elizabeth Tudor. Had he not died two years before she became Queen, who knows what new course history might have taken? Coryat saw his tomb in Padua, but I looked for it in vain on one of those typical Italian days when no one can tell you where anything is to be found.

A sad death in Padua was that of the art collector, Thomas Howard, Earl of Arundel, who had been driven abroad like many cavaliers, and settled miserably at Padua and, for him, in penury. Evelyn saw him on his death-bed. 'I took my leave of him in his bed,' he wrote, 'where I left that great and excellent man in tears on some private discourse of crosses that had befallen his illustrious family, particularly the undutifulness of his grandson Philip's turning Dominican Friar (since Cardinal of Norfolk), and the misery of his country now embroiled in civil war.'

Another Englishman who died in Padua was Lady Mary Wortley Montagu's eccentric son, Edward. It must be unusual for a mother to detest her son as much as she disliked Edward – possibly she saw him as a travesty of herself – and I suppose there can be no doubt that he was out of his mind. He was travelling to England dressed as a Turk when one night in Padua a fish-bone stuck in his throat and killed him, and, in spite of the fact that he was said to have become a Moslem, the kindly Augustinians buried him in the cloister of the Eremitani.

Pilgrims have been praying at the tomb of S. Anthony of Padua for seven centuries. Like his friend, S. Francis of Assisi, S. Anthony was one of the most gentle and sweet-natured of saints, a mighty preacher, a great consoler, the patron saint of travellers and of lost property. (How well these go together!) Like S. Christopher, he is depicted holding the Christ Child in his arms because once, during his devotions, he was seen holding the infant Jesus as he prayed.

His church is unexpected and exotic. The exterior, with its cluster of ribbed domes and its minaret-like towers, wears the unlikely air of a mosque; and this reminds one that S. Anthony – a Spaniard born in Lisbon – was on his way to the Moslem East when his ship was wrecked on the coast of Italy. Readers of the *Little Flowers* will remember that S. Anthony preached to the fishes, beginning his discourse in the true Franciscan manner with 'My brothers, the fish . . .' As he spoke, the fish 'raised their heads from the water and remained attentive, completely still, tame and orderly', and when told to praise their Creator, who had preserved them alone of all creatures during the Flood, 'began to open their mouths and bow their heads, and with such other signs of reverence as their nature permitted they gave thanks to God.'

I found the tomb of Il Santo in a side-chapel behind the altar. A crowd of people passed continuously in front of it, making a low whispering sound as they touched the marble with their fingers or rubbed their handkerchiefs along it in a touching desire to take some influence of it home with them. When Coryat was there he saw 'a certaine Demoniciall person' who had been brought to Il Santo in the hope that the 'devill' would be expelled, but unfortunately the exorcism did not work and, as Coryat relates, 'I left the fellow in as badde a case as I found him.'

I am told that were a referendum to be held in Italy on the two most popular saints, the result would be a tie between S. Francis of Assisi and S. Anthony of Padua. A good story is told by Bernard Wall of the cult of S. Anthony in his *Italian Life and Landscape*.

'A gnarled peasant woman was dying and the priest was anxious to have her consider the solemn moment when her soul would appear before God. "But I don't believe in God," said the cunning old woman. The priest was taken aback. Then he thought for a bit and said, "But everybody believes in something. It isn't possible to believe in nothing. Don't you believe in the Madonna and San Giuseppe? Don't you believe in the Church?" "No," said the old woman. "That's all rubbish and priests' stuff, *roba di preti*." The priest strove desperately for a straw in this shipwreck. "But think," he adjured her, "you, who are dying, what is going to happen to your soul if you believe in nothing?" The woman thought hard. Then her face lit up and she said, "But of course. *Credo in Sant' Antonio*." '

Outside the church the great *condottiere* Gattamelata, cast in bronze by Donatello, rides forward upon his war-horse. He wears twelve-inch-long spurs and has the air of a benevolent Caesar. It is impressive to reflect that he was the first great bronze rider to be cast since the days of ancient Rome, and the forerunner of that numerous cavalcade of emperors, kings, princes, dukes, and generals which has now pranced into all the best squares in the world.

Donatello and his works so delighted Padua that an attempt was made to persuade him to settle there, but the artist said no, he must get back to his native Florence or he would forget all he had ever learnt: in Padua, he said, everything he did was praised; in Florence he was always being blamed! But my favourite story is that in his old age the Medici, who were devoted to him, gave him a farm, and off went Donatello in high spirits to take possession. In the following year he begged the Medici to take back their gift since he would rather die of hunger than worry.

§ 9

A few miles to the south-west of Padua a miniature Switzerland rises with an air of enchantment against the sky – real hermit and dragon country. Those contorted volcanic heights, the Euganean Hills, seem much higher than they really are because of their sudden dramatic eruption from the level plain.

At the foot of the hills I came to the spa of Abano, where the Caesars took their gout. It is still celebrated, and its modern visitors, wrapped in their bath-towels, seem to be acting the parts of the arthritic proconsuls who limped about there long ago. The invalids are well looked after in attractive hotels where they can lie in radio-active mud and feel the rheumatism being soaked out of them. In a public park I saw a pleasant statue of Hygieia, standing above a bed of red flowers, and a rocky pool of steaming blue water straight from the mysterious furnaces which in some remote age shot the Euganean Hills into the air. I could not bear my hand in it.

I had been reading Iris Origo's book, *The Last Attachment*, which describes Byron's love affair with Countess Teresa Guiccioli, a liaison which was still more or less intact at the time of

Byron's death in Greece. At least, no one can say that had the poet lived they might not have come together, possibly even have married. However, in the first romantic flush of a new affair, Byron, whose contempt for Petrarch's platonic love had been vigorously expressed, allowed the young woman to take him on a romantic pilgrimage to the poet's house in the Euganean Hills. Here they both signed the visitors' book. I wondered whether this book still exists, and thought it might be interesting to go to Arqua in the hope of seeing the page signed by them.

No sooner had I left the main road than I found myself in winding lanes and cart tracks that ran here and there into the hills; and I was aware that I had left modern Italy behind on the main road. One sometimes comes across little areas like the Euganean Hills which have either defied the road-maker or else, for some other reason, have been left with their primeval footpaths and are less accessible than many genuinely remote parts of the world. More than once I had to pull into the side to let farm carts drawn by white oxen go past, and, turning a corner in a lane that might have been near Selborne, in Hampshire, I saw two sturdy girls ascending the hill with wooden yokes upon their shoulders from which hung pails of water. They resembled two milkmaids who had run away to Italy from *The Cries of London*. Villages were perched upon the volcanic slopes among vines, which love this type of soil, and the whole district seemed to be living in a past age.

Arqua is a small village with a church on one level, a wine shop on another and, highest of all, the house that Petrarch built. He went to live there in 1369, when he was sixty-five and in poor health, thinking it would be good to get away from the turmoil of Padua into the peace of the country, where he could read his books and write when he felt like it – the writer's dream in all ages. He was a warm-hearted man who was dependent upon friends, and these had died off, leaving him sad and lonely. His last great friend was Boccaccio to whom he wrote from his haven at Arqua, describing his quiet life and saying that he hoped death would call for him while he was either reading or writing. His wish came true. On the morning of his seventieth birthday he was found seated dead at his desk, the pages of the book he had been reading open before him.

The view from the house is of hills and vines and far distances. The building is small, solid, and stone-built, with a good-sized entrance-room whose ceiling is painted and divided into carved panels. Above the door an embalmed cat is seated, still with feline dignity, in a glass case, with a long explanation in Latin which says how devoted Petrarch was to the animal, which the writer calls Laura the second! There are some bad frescoes which the old dame, who shows visitors over the house, told me date from the poet's time; she showed me his chair, his attractive ink-pot, and the room in which he was found dead. These relics struck me as pathetic, and not as close to Petrarch as the little garden with its pomegranate trees where he must have walked and sat so often, looking down to the plain and thinking about the past.

When I asked about the visitors' book, the caretaker took me into the front room and pointed it out in a glass case among a number of odds and ends. But nothing would induce her to unlock the case, so that I was unable to see Byron's name side by side with that of Teresa.

I walked down to the church, thinking of the scene described by Iris Origo. It was in 1819, and the lovers, in the early stage of their affair, were on their way to Padua and Venice, behaving, so they imagined, with discretion. Teresa was travelling in her husband's coach-and-six with a maid and a manservant; Byron was following in his huge travelling carriage, modelled on that of Napoleon, which was large enough to take his bed, a small library, and a large amount of silver, china, and linen. The road, difficult enough today, was then so bad that the postillions refused to go on to the end, so the lovers completed their pilgrimage on foot. Maddening as Teresa's habit of reciting poetry on appropriate occasions must have been, Byron was then in that stage of infatuation when he probably enjoyed listening to the verses of Petrarch which his lover murmured as they approached the poet's house.

They found it half ruined, and the ground floor littered with domestic utensils and jars of wheat, but the mummified cat was there in its case. 'Of this Byron characteristically remarked,' writes

Iris Origo, 'that the hearts of animals were often better than ours – and that this animal's affection may well have put Laura's coldness to shame.' They walked down the road to the church and saw outside it a marble sarcophagus raised on four short marble columns, the tomb of Petrarch. Children brought them grapes and peaches, and Byron, who normally disliked to see a woman eating, noted that this was the first time he had seen Teresa doing so, and the sight was 'the fulfilment of one of his dreams.' The descendants of those children now offered me little bunches of flowers, and I was able to reward them with bags of sweets.

Petrarch and Laura . . . Byron and Teresa . . . sacred and profane love, if you like, but surely an interesting visit; and how foolish of those who look after this house to keep the visitors' book open at the wrong page. Of all those who have found their way to Petrarch's house, Byron and his 'last attachment' were the only two whose love affair is as celebrated in literature as that of Petrarch, though, as Byron would have been the first to admit, on possibly a less exalted, but more satisfactory, level.

Joining the main road I was soon in the town of Este, which the family owned before they were established at Ferrara. What, from a distance, appeared to be an immense mediaeval castle, is nothing more than its outer wall. A warlike exterior was never more deceptive. The wall encloses the town garden, where men-at-arms once assembled and war-horses were saddled; it is now planted with beds of salvia, petunias, and dahlias, and children play in the shade of gigantic magnolias and cypresses.

The villa, *I Cappuccini,* which Byron rented for two years and lent to Shelley, is still there, and it was in the summer-house at the end of the garden that Shelley wrote *Lines on the Euganean Hills* and began *Prometheus Unbound.* A tablet in the piazza states that Rome was proclaimed the capital of a united Italy in that small town.

§ 10

I set off in the morning for Venice.

The twenty-seven miles of autostrada were like a race track: coaches, motor-cars, caravans, motor-cyclists and cyclists were speeding along towards the Queen of the Adriatic; and I realized what a peaceful triangle is formed by Verona, Vicenza, and Padua at the heart of the typhoon.

I smiled to think that all this dashing about began when a Baptist missionary and teetotaller named Thomas Cook took converts on an excursion from Leicester to a temperance meeting at Loughborough in 1841. It was a fateful journey. As the travellers walked steadily to their railway coaches at the end of the day, already, in the eye of Time, the man from Cook's was standing on all the main stations of the world, a tactful compromise between a guide and the family adviser. It was a brave decision to extend the conducted tour from Ramsgate to the Continent in 1860, a period when travel, though no longer aristocratic, was still a preserve of the moneyed classes; and the dismay of some who saw the Continent invaded by governesses, clerks, members of working men's clubs, and 'young persons' of both sexes, was expressed by Charles Lever, the novelist, then British Consul at Spezia.

'The cities of Italy,' he wrote, 'were deluged with these creatures. I have just met three flocks, and anything so uncouth I never saw before, the men, mostly elderly, dreary, sad-looking; the women, somewhat younger, travel-tossed and crumpled, but intensely lively, wide-awake and facetious.' With typically Irish malice, Lever spread the story among influential Italians that the Cook's tourists were criminals who had been rejected by penal settlements and were being craftily dumped in Italy by the British Government. We who live in an age which knows that no lie, if repeated often enough, can be too preposterous to be believed, can understand that Mr Cook had to go to the Foreign Office and ask for help.

Now one sees upon the road to Venice how that distant cargo of abstainers has developed into a universal business, a share of which every nation strives to capture. No modern state is rich enough to be indifferent to the foreign currency produced by the tourists, and most Governments employ professional sirens to lure the traveller to their shores with posters and leaflets portraying countries, not as they are, but as the tourist hopes they will be. The posters show an ideal world where the sun always shines, where men are bursting with health and all the girls are in bathing costumes, while quaint, delightful characters, beaming smiles of welcome, are clothed in the regional costumes of the last century.

These appeals are among the few bright promises of our dark age, and it is touching to think that the tourists, having met greed, avarice, and rapacity in most of its forms, still continue to believe in the existence of this ideal land, and pay up every year for another tour. I hope the social historian is keeping track of a movement which has now become a kind of Jerusalem-less crusade, and, as the mediaeval pilgrim was recognized by his corded gown, his broad hat, and his staff, so the modern world, seeing a man dressed as a small boy, blistered by the sun, and festooned with cameras, recognizes a tourist. Italy has known the religious pilgrims of the early centuries, the scholars of the Renaissance, the aristocrats of the Grand Tour, the plutocrats of the last century; now she welcomes with composure, and that inability to be either shocked or surprised which is history's gift to her, the Not So Grand Tour, the latest, the most spectacular, and the most profitable phase in the long story of her traffic with the world.

It is my own theory that perhaps the present phase of bulk travel may be traced to mechanized warfare. The lorries which delivered armed men to all parts of Europe in the last war have become the comfortable coaches of peace; the officers, the N.C.O.s, and interpreters, are now the guides; and I fancy that this intricate operation is probably watched from the map-rooms of travel agencies by traffic managers who once commanded motorized battalions, and now plot with coloured pins the infiltration of their clients into the art galleries and museums of Europe.

One is constantly reminded of the metamorphosis. Troops had the habit of arriving abruptly in precisely the manner of a coachload of tourists in an Italian piazza. The guide emerges, as once the officer did, to survey the scene, and instead of soldiers festooned with equipment and strangely camouflaged, there descends a platoon of matrons, young girls in tights, men in shorts and Bermuda shirts, hung about with photographic equipment, and wearing a soldierly air of stoic obedience. Nor is it too fanciful to see in the advance of tourists upon an art gallery the civilian version of the liberation of some public building. Led by a gesticulating guide, who might be exhorting his followers to some heroic act, the tourists storm the steps and invade the lifts, while the main body, anxious to come to grips with Botticelli, surges up the main staircase led by trousered matrons and sandalled maids.

The autostrada is succeeded by a causeway that strikes off upon a three-mile course across the shallow salt lagoon in which, according to the poets, Venice floats, but in which the geologists and engineers say she is sinking at the rate of a yard every five hundred years. Somewhere, parallel with the causeway but invisible, runs the water-main that pumps fresh water into Venice from wells fifteen miles inland. Until eighty years ago the only fresh water was filtered rain-water stored in huge underground cisterns and carried round from door to door by sturdy mountain girls from Friuli, like the couple I had seen carrying water up the Euganean Hills. Electricity marches boldly across the lagoon upon pylons, each one standing upon its own little Venice of concrete.

The causeway ends in what is something of an achievement: a really ugly Italian piazza, a place called, in a grandiloquent moment, the Piazzale Roma. This horrid spot, blue with exhaust fumes and diesel smoke, crowded with parked coaches from every part of Europe, congested by confused travellers, is dominated by the six storeys of what must be the largest garage in Italy. Here the motorist must leave the car, which is of no further use to him.

I turned to watch crates of beer, bags of flour, and various other things unloaded from mainland vans and lorries and transferred to Venetian barges, each barge in charge of a vociferous, reliable-looking mongrel dog. In one of the parked coaches I noticed a number of tired American college girls in the last stages of exhaustion; in another were Germans from Hamburg; a third had come from Bradford, Yorkshire; there was a fourth from Oslo; a fifth from Copenhagen; a sixth from Lyons, and two from Vienna. And suddenly amid the confusion, the backfires and the clouds of diesel smoke, the piazzale was invaded by a group of caravanners from a near-by 'camping'. It is a pity that Charles Lever could not have seen the shorts and shirts, the toreador trousers, the blistered arms and shoulders, and the air of privileged eccentricity which proclaimed a temporary release from the tyranny of an industrial world.

They crowded into a *vaporetto*. The porter dumped my suit-cases on the deck. I jumped down and sat on them. We all faced the same way, like Moslems greeting the rising sun, as we set off down the Grand Canal.

CHAPTER EIGHT

Arriving in Venice – The Beadle of S. Mark's – The Theft of S. Mark's Body – The Greek Horses – A Table at Florian's – The Doges of Venice and the Dogaressas – A Gondola on the Grand Canal – Byron's Palace – The Old German House – Brother Fabri

§ 1

It was twenty-five years since I had been in Venice, and I contrasted my rather squalid arrival now with my former entry by train, the best of all ways to arrive. I recall following the porter along the platform to a terrace which was washed by the water of the Grand Canal. There it was, the Venice one had seen so often in books and art galleries: the old palaces, the striped mooring poles, the black gondolas, and a slight wind blowing up the canal, whipping the shallow waters into miniature waves to each one of which Canaletto sometimes gave a little arc of Chinese white. Venice and Rome are alike in offering not the sharp stab of discovery but the gentler nudge of recognition: it is almost as though one were living a second time and visiting scenes familiar in a former life.

Everything seemed much as it was twenty-five years ago as the *vaporetto* thrashed its way down the Grand Canal and passed beneath the Rialto Bridge, where they were still clearing up after the morning's fish and vegetable market. There had been a shower of summer rain in the night and the air had that silken shine which delighted the Venetian painters. The palaces, in faded pastel washes of green, brown, and Venetian red, formed an unchanging background, and across their wavering reflections the gondolas passed and re-passed, sometimes drawing up at mooring-poles brilliantly striped in armorial colours, or at some aged palace that had descended in the social scale, whose front door opened on *pali* like asparagus sprouting from a bed of ink.

The *vaporetto* sped on its way down this wonderful main street whose buildings still recall the names in the Golden Book, edging every now and then to the side to pull up for a few moments at a glassed-in waiting-room on a floating landing-stage, where some passengers disembarked while others came aboard. As the Venetians crowded in, I listened, enchanted by the sound of their voices. It is the prettiest, most bird-like chatter. The Italian 'g' becomes 'z' in Venice and the sound of 'c' becomes 'x'. This rippling, liquid dialect goes well with the surrounding water. At last we approached the best-known sight of all, where the two granite columns stand and where the Doge's Palace, like a piece of oriental lace, shines in the water. When we pulled into the S. Zaccaria landing-stage, a porter took my suit-cases and told me that my hotel was quite close. He led the way to a narrow crack of a street called the Calle delle Rasse.

The gondoliers painted by Carpaccio, and their fathers before them, roofed the cabins of their gondolas with a tough black fabric called *rasse*. The material was imported from one of the old regions of Serbia, Raska or Rassia, and was used so much in Venice that nothing else was sold in the Calle delle Rasse. The Danieli is on one corner, and the narrow calle terminates in a charming little campo and a busy fruit market. Here you can sit at a café table and watch people buying peaches and plums or slices of crimson water-melon, or maybe segments of coconut, which are exposed for sale on a curious ironwork stand that squirts a jet of water over them. Somehow in Venice the sight of coconut does not suggest a shooting-gallery, but sends the mind wandering off to the Spice Islands. There is an excellent baker's shop at one corner and, opposite, a cookshop where you can eat exotic dishes at a counter, or take away, on a beautifully packed cardboard tray, anything from half a roast chicken to scampi and tunny-fish.

While discovering the meaning of *rasse*, I solved a mystery which may perhaps have puzzled others: why window-blinds of a type never seen in Venice should be called 'Venetian'. The explanation is that during the eighteenth century, when this kind of blind was first made, the slats were bound with a strong canvas similar to *rasse* known as *Venetian*. Today you could not buy an inch of either in the Calle delle Rasse, which is now devoted to small fish restaurants, whose windows are filled with oysters, mussels, eels, tunny, ink-fish, cuttle-fish, octopus, shrimps, prawns, langouste, spider crabs, the ingredients of one of the best Venetian dishes, *fritto misto di mare,* and scampi.

This is the street in which I lived. My bedroom overlooked, not the Calle delle Rasse, but a parallel alley that also led to the campo. In order maybe to counteract the rude noises that rose from this alley, bringing with them echoes of a rough, cantankerous world, some woman had papered the walls with a pattern of delicate pale rosebuds tied with blue ribbon, which gave the room an improbable schoolgirl charm. The dressing-table wore a skirt of chintz. It was the sort of room in which you might find yourself when visiting friends in a country cottage. ('We've given you Jane's room now she's away at school!') It was odd to glance from the window of such a chaste little room straight into the eyes of Shylock, who lived on the other side of the alley, a fork-bearded, Rembrandtesque figure in a black skull-cap. We could have shaken hands from window to window across the narrow lane. The old man appeared to be independent of oxygen. The window was fast closed, and he would probably have gone without air all day but for his beloved canary. The bird lived in a beautifully-made cage of thin bamboo, which he placed out in the morning sun. It was the only sun the bird saw all day, and it did not shine for long in that narrow canyon. Sometimes a bright chain of song would bring Shylock from his shadows to whisper to the bird and smile, a sight Rembrandt would have enjoyed, then the sun went overhead and the little alley was dark until tomorrow.

Every morning I was awakened by quarrelsome voices and snatches of song. I would gaze down upon the straw-hats of a company of gondoliers who, at the same time every day, their oars upon their shoulders, swaggered down to the Riva degli Schiavoni, a narrow slit of which I could see at the end of the alley. Nothing I could do took the girlish simper from my room, which, in spite of books, maps, and tobacco smoke, remained unconquerably sweet. It was extraordinary to know that just round the corner were the Doge's Palace and S. Mark's.

§ 2

During the tourist season the most notable person in the Piazza is the beadle of S. Mark's. He wears a cocked hat, a suit of eighteenth century cut, and buckled shoes; and he stands at the west door grasping a brass-bound staff. His function is to prevent insufficiently clothed women from entering the basilica. Tightly buttoned and cravatted on the hottest day, with sword at hip, he himself is a rebuke to the carefree habits of the modern world; he is also perhaps the nearest thing this age can show to the Angel with the Flaming Sword. With a perceptible shudder, he will sometimes refuse admission to a man with hairy legs, but his real quarry is Eve. Watching him, I gained the impression that his duties have given him a rare insight into feminine character. He knows at a glance the kind of woman who will be deterred by a cautionary finger, who will blush and melt away, just as he recognizes in a flash the more militant type who, with an indignant shrug of bare shoulders, will try to force her way past him into the church.

It is amusing to notice how many women are unconscious of their offence. Standing in a state of near nudity which would not have been permitted on the stage thirty years ago, they innocently believe the beadle is anxious only for them to cover their heads. Having borrowed a handkerchief, they think they can take their bare arms and legs into S. Mark's, and at such moments the beadle is at his best. He has an eloquent range of expressions and gestures, indicative of disapprobation. His sigh can convey everything from sorrow to despair, and when neither glance nor sigh are adequate, the hopeless shrug of his shoulders is almost equivalent to a papal encyclical. Once only did I see this censor swept off his balance. Suddenly deserting his post, and taking a few steps forward, staff in hand, sword slanting from coat-tails, he bent down and, with a transformed expression which linked him at last with the human race, impressed a kiss upon the face of an infant in a perambulator.

Whenever I think of the superb Piazza, I see the important little figure in eighteenth century dress; I hear in imagination the sudden thunderclap of pigeons; I hear the hour being struck by the Moors (who are not Moors at all but Greenwood men in skin tunics); I see the sunlight, hot and white upon the enormous open space where a tide of grey feathers continually ripples round, and recedes from, advancing feet; and in the background glitters the Byzantine splendour of S. Mark's, wearing its domes like a synod of patriarchs. It appeared to Ruskin as if the great square had opened 'in a kind of awe' from the vision of S. Mark's, 'a treasure heap, it seems, partly of gold, and partly of opal and mother-of-pearl'. This is true enough now, as it was in his time.

I was not displeased to find that the much abused tourists lend an air of gaiety and vitality to Venice. The enormous crowds that drift about the Piazza and feed the pigeons, or sit at the tables of Florian's or Quadri's, eating ices or drinking coffee to the sound of the tireless string orchestras, almost provide the illusion that this city is still the Adriatic Queen and her inhabitants 'lords of the gold of all Christendom'. I looked in vain for a turban, which was a feature of the Venetian crowd as recently as the nineteenth century, but the only orientals I saw were a group of Japanese photographers and one willowy Indian girl in a sari and golden sandals, a vermilion spot in the centre of her smooth forehead. In 1782 Beckford was struck by the great number of eastern people and 'heard Turkish and Arabic muttering in every corner'; nearly a century later W. D. Howells, the American consul who wrote a charming book about his life in Venice, was interested in a group of Albanians 'with an Albanian boy, who being dressed exactly like his father, curiously impressed me, as if he were the young of some oriental animal – say a boy elephant, or infant camel'. Though the turban may have vanished, what could be more exotic than the costumes to be seen in S. Mark's Square today: the shorts, the beach pyjamas, the coloured stove-pipe trousers, the wide-brimmed Mexican straw hats, which no matter how unsuitable they may appear elsewhere, here in Venice have an almost traditional rightness. They are as much part of the Venetian scene today as the jaunty full-skirted figures of Canaletto or the masked dominoes of Longhi; possibly in a hundred years someone will think them just as charming and picturesque.

In 1851 Ruskin wrote: 'You may walk from sunrise to sunset, to and fro, before the gateway of S. Mark's, and you will not see an eye lifted to it, nor a countenance brightened by it. Priest and layman, soldier and civilian, rich and poor pass it by alike regardlessly.' No one could say that today. The crowds are fascinated by S. Mark's, and no doubt Ruskin has helped in this. They photograph it from every angle; they climb wherever possible inside and out, and you can see them, still aiming their cameras above the portico, as they stand beneath the gilt hoofs of the shining steeds of Lysippus.

When the first S. Mark's was burned down in A.D. 976, Greek architects began to erect the present basilica three years before Duke William invaded England. It took ten years to complete, and during that time Venetian captains, before they set out on their eastern voyages, were commanded to bring back some precious object or stone for its adornment. This bizarre church, glittering like an encrusted reliquary, is the most impressive reflection of the Eastern Roman Empire still alive and in daily use. When we see it for the first time our wonder reflects the surprise of all northern people who, arriving in Constantinople in ancient times as traders, travellers, pilgrims, or members of the Varangian Guard, saw the exotic and sophisticated society of Byzantium revolving in state round the figures of the Emperor and the Empress.

The architectural inspiration for S. Mark's was the imperial mausoleum in Constantinople, the Church of the Holy Apostles, where Constantine the Great had been buried in A.D. 337. Although S. Sophia was built shortly after, the earlier church continued to be the burial place of the imperial line. Theodosius the Great was buried there, also Justinian, Julian the Apostate, and many others. These emperors were still lying dressed in their imperial mantles, as they had rested for centuries, when the Latins of the Fourth Crusade sacked Constantinople and, breaking open the imperial tombs, stripped the embroidery and gold from the bodies of the emperors and used their coffins as horse troughs. When the Moslems conquered Constantinople in 1453, the

Church of the Holy Apostles was pulled down to make way for the Mosque of Mohammed II.

In the meantime three versions of the church had been transplanted: in Venice, in Ephesus, and in Périgueux in France. Those who have been to Ephesus will perhaps have wandered through the ruins of the Church of S. John on the hill, and many who have visited the town of truffles and *pâtés de foie gras* have wondered how such a strange domed church as the cathedral of S. Front came to be built in France. Of the three copies of Constantine's church, the only one that survives in its splendour is S. Mark's.

It is odd to think that S. Mark was not the original patron saint of Venice, for the Venetians annexed him so completely, and publicized his Lion in every corner of the world, that one is ready to believe that the Evangelist was himself a Venetian. But their first patron was an obscure martyr named S. Theodore, who had enjoyed a brief cult in remote ages, then for some reason lost his popularity; a fatal defect in a state like Venice, where success was everything.

S. Theodore's statue may be seen on one of the two columns in the Piazzetta in the act of spearing a crocodile, which symbolizes Evil. The movement to supersede him by a more powerful saint was a sign of the growing ambition of Venice. Naturally the superannuation of a patron saint is a tricky business, but one which an artful community was capable of carrying out with skill. From the moment S. Mark was elected, S. Theodore was forgotten in Venice, though it is good to know that he is still remembered in Rome in a strange little round church in the shadow of the Palatine Hill, where he is affectionately known as 'San Toto'.

Whether S. Mark's remains came to Venice in the ordinary way of business, or whether the Signory deliberately ordered their theft, is unknown. But the circumstances of their arrival is the key to Venetian psychology. Legend says that S. Mark had been martyred and buried at Alexandria, in Egypt, in a church near the Eastern Harbour. One day in A.D. 827 two Venetian sea-captains, who were trading with the Moslems, made a proposition to the guardian of S. Mark's tomb. 'Messer,' they said, according to Da Canale, 'if thou wilt come with us to Venice and bear away the body of Monsignor S. Marco, thou shalt be a rich man.' The guardian, attracted by this offer, pointed out that he was afraid to do as they suggested because the Moslems, who also revered S. Mark, would certainly kill him were the theft discovered. 'Wait until the blessed Evangelist command thee,' said the crafty sea captains.

That moment was not long in coming. The saint conveyed to the guardian that he would like to be disinterred, and the deed was completed at night. S. Mark's tomb was opened, the saint's remains were removed, another body was substituted and the tomb closed. The Venetians had already decided upon a plan of action. They placed the sacred remains in a basket beneath cabbages and pork, which they knew the Moslems would not investigate, and so made off for their ship: but the Evangelist himself nearly betrayed them. 'At the very moment when they opened the tomb, so sweet and so great an odour spread through the midst of the city that all the spiceries of Alexandria could not have caused the like. Whereupon the pagans said, "Mark is stirring", for they were wont to smell such fragrance every year.' They ran to the tomb, but were deceived by the substituted body, and those who went to the Venetian ship saw only a basket of pork slung up on the mainmast. So the Venetians got safely away with their precious cargo; and a new era began in the history of Venice.

Having stolen S. Mark, it now remained to prove that it was not a theft and that the new patron had had some former association with Venice. The first was easy. It was obvious that the saint wished to be rescued from a Moslem country, and had he not wished to be taken to Venice how simple for him to have raised a storm at sea and to have sunk or diverted the galley! But, as Venice did not exist during the lifetime of S. Mark, it was a little more difficult to link him with the city. Nevertheless, this was done. It was recalled that once when the Evangelist was on his way to preach in Aquileia, his ship had been driven by a tempest to a desolate island in the lagoon, the future Venice. As S. Mark stepped ashore, he was greeted by an angel who said 'Peace to thee, Mark, my Evangelist', and announced that one day his body would rest and be venerated in that spot.

339

The incident is typically Venetian, and one can already detect as early as the ninth century the qualities of craft and diplomatic guile which were to distinguish the affairs of the Republic in centuries to come. Also, to me there is something very Roman about the theft of S. Mark: it might be a companion story to the *Golden Ass*. The policy of the Republic in showing, not a benevolent bishop as their patron, but a fierce and threatening lion was, of course, also clever: the Lion of S. Mark, so arrogant and so alert, adequately expressed in symbolic form the policy of a great commercial empire. Why a lion should have been the symbol of S. Mark has been explained in a number of ways, but perhaps the best is that the Gospel of S. Mark stresses the regal status of our Lord, the Lion of the tribe of Judah. Wherever Venice set her foot the Lion of S. Mark was seen with a paw upon a book, which was open at a page on which the words '*Pax tibi Marce*' are inscribed, the greeting of the angel who met the Evangelist when he was shipwrecked on the island in the lagoon.

It is curious that the most sceptical people in history should have become the greatest collectors of relics. The acquisition of S. Mark began a truly amazing assortment of saintly bones. Wherever the Venetian fleets went, they were ready to traffic in relics and, if necessary, to steal them from their churches. The fearful sack of Christian Constantinople, instigated by Venice in 1204, choked the treasuries of Venetian churches with bones until a perfect *cordon sanitaire* of miraculous remains surrounded the plague-prone island. I have counted fifty-five complete bodies listed in 1519 by Giacomo Zoppi, in addition to an infinite number of heads, arms, and fingers; and I should not be surprised to know that I have underestimated them.

§ 3

At the beginning of the century, E. V. Lucas was struck by the 'friendliness' of S. Mark's. 'Why such an intensely foreign building of great size should exert this power of welcome I cannot say,' he wrote, 'but the fact remains that S. Mark's, for all its Eastern domes and gold and odd designs and billowy floor, does more to make a stranger and a Protestant at home than any cathedral I know.' To me it offers no welcome at all. It strikes me as a remote, withdrawn, and mysterious temple, austere, solemn, and infinitely impressive, a fit background for Byzantine emperors and Greek patriarchs.

It is a museum of mosaics and marbles. Someone once compared it to a den in which pirates keep their treasure. The mystery of Venice, something much more subtle than canals and gondolas, culminates in this church. You feel that Venice has nothing to do with Italy: its parent is Constantinople. On the Grand Canal, where the palaces are split up into flats and at low tide the water is seen sucking at foundations like the crust of an old Stilton cheese, one is well aware of the decay of Venice. Only in S. Mark's, where the same Mass is said every day which the Doge once followed from a private room in his palace, may one feel that something still lives on. Monsignor San Marco is still, in his own quiet way, stirring.

To the right of the rood screen, which is almost a Greek ikonostasis, is the ample marble pulpit in which the newly elected Doge was shown to the people. What a moment that must have been; and how one sympathizes with the man singled out for that honour, who then had nothing further to look forward to than a life sentence in scarlet and ermine. One of the many amazing things about Venice is the prison discipline which she managed to impose upon her leading citizen.

I went behind the rood screen to look at the high altar. It is said that the sarcophagus which lies there contains the remains of S. Mark. A verger showed me the famous Byzantine *Pala d'Oro,* a sheet of gold and enamel studded with precious stones. He told me it was made in Constantinople for the Doge Pietro Orseolo in A.D. 976, and that it contains one thousand, three hundred pearls, four hundred garnets, ninety amethysts, three hundred emeralds, and so on; and he also taught me how to tell the original stones from those inserted to replace those stolen by the French army in 1797: the originals are cut *en cabochon,* the new in facets. He smiled when I mentioned I had read somewhere that the undulations of the pavement are an intentional symbol of the sea. He said that no doubt the '*architetto di San Marco*', a doctor always in attendance, wished they were, instead, as they really are, a sign of the weakness of the foundations.

A small door near the main entrance leads by way of a stone stairway to the outer gallery. This is my golden moment in Venice: to stand beside the four horses from Constantinople and to look down upon the Piazza and up at the Campanile, to contrast the brilliance of the scene with the twilight of the church below. The four horses are among the most venerable, yet at the same time the most youthful-looking horses and certainly the proudest, on earth, as they step forward with arched necks into some fragrant Greek morning. Few, I fancy, who bend under their golden bellies to take photographs of the Clock Tower have any idea of their age. They were made about three hundred years before Christ, some say by the Greek sculptor Lysippus, and though they are always called the 'bronze' horses, ancient Greek writers say they were cast from an amalgam of copper, silver, and gold.

They are almost certainly the horses which Theodosius II took from Chios to decorate the imperial box, the Kathisma, in the Hippodrome of Constantinople. They stood upon the roof of what was a large building where the Emperor and the Empress and their court assembled to watch the chariot races. The Kathisma was a complete imperial residence in itself, connected by a staircase with the palace; it had dining-rooms, a throne-room, and robing-rooms where the Emperor and the Empress retired to change their costumes, as required by Byzantine ceremonial. All this was complete when the Christians of the Fourth Crusade sacked Christian Constantinople. The four horses escaped by some miracle. Their beauty and their splendour, as they stood proudly above the circus, penetrated even minds debased by greed and hatred, and instead of being hacked to pieces or melted into coin, they were carefully loaded in the galley of Morosini and consigned to Venice. It is said that on the way back the hind foot of one was broken, and Morosini, upon his arrival in Venice, received the permission of the Senate to keep it. He set it up outside his house in S. Agostini, where it remained for centuries, and was seen at the end of the fifteenth century by Marin Sanudo. Where, one wonders, is it today?

Evidently the Venetians did not know what to do with the Greek horses. At first they were placed among the menagerie of stone lions outside the Arsenal, then someone had the extraordinary idea of placing them in the gallery above the west doors of S. Mark's. It is a preposterous situation. Only their supreme beauty could carry it off, and the fact that time has hallowed this position. Here it was that Petrarch, seated beside the Doge, watched a tournament in the Piazza, then unpaved, and summed up the Venetians of his time as 'a nation of sailors, horsemen, and beauties'.

I do not think there is a single horse in Venice today nearer than the Lido, and Mrs Thrale, when she was there in 1784, mentions seeing people pay a penny a time to look at a stuffed one. But there were thousands of horses in Venice during the Middle Ages and the Doge, Michel Steno, is said to have had four hundred in his stables, which for some reason he dyed yellow, perhaps to match the golden steeds of S. Mark. Among famous speeches one would like to have heard was the outburst of Pietro Doria, when Genoa and Venice were at war, before a number of Venetian ambassadors. 'By God, Venetian Senators,' he cried, 'ye shall never have peace with the Lord of Padua or our Republic till we have bridled the bronze horses which stand in your square of S. Mark. When we have the reins in our hands we shall know how to keep them quiet.' But the horses were never bridled. They were, however, taken by Napoleon and sent to Paris for some years; and Samuel Rogers, who was in Paris after Waterloo, mentions that he saw English engineers taking them down from the Arc du Carrousel in preparation for their return to Venice. Except for a trip to Rome during the First World War, they have remained in Venice ever since. The last word about them was written by James Morris. 'I have often seen them paw the stonework, at starlit Venetian midnights,' he wrote, 'and once I heard a whinney from the second horse on the right, so old, brave and metallic that St Theodore's crocodile, raising its head from beneath the saintly buskins, answered with a kind of grunt.'

In a gallery that runs round the church I came upon a tapestry by some unknown artist of the fifteenth century which struck me

343

as lovely and unusual. The scene is Christ before Pilate. While Pilate washes his hands and is about to consign Jesus to His enemies, unnoticed by anyone in the group and easily overlooked by the hasty visitor, Pilate's little white dog is sitting up near the throne begging for the Saviour's life. The genius of the anonymous artist was such that he managed to introduce into a much painted scene what, to me, was an entirely new and unexpected poignancy: Christ, the despised and rejected of men, has at the end only one friend, a humble representative of the animal kingdom. I went back several times to look at this tapestry, and every time I thought it touching and beautiful.

§ 4

I enjoyed the Piazzetta and the Piazza before the day's sight-seers arrived. Walking down the Calle delle Rasse before eight o'clock, I would pause a moment to say good-morning to Signor X, who was usually marshalling the day's fish in the window of his restaurant. Crouched in the narrow road, his hair on end, his eyebrows bristling, he conveyed the impression that a monster prawn had escaped and was signalling to its companions. He would make abrupt signs, nodding his head and waving his arms, while a lad in the back of the window would interpret these gestures and ask urgently in dumb show what to do with a handful of eels. A charming colour scheme was always composed, the pink of shrimp and mullet contrasting with the silver of sardines, the greyness of octopus, and the dark red of spider crab with the brighter lobster. Signor X always returned my greeting with a bow and the news that crabs or oysters were particularly good that morning, though I never had the courage to eat Venetian oysters, especially in a r-less month.

Turning to the right at the Riva, I would linger a moment on the hump of the Ponte di Paglia and glance along the narrow canal to the Bridge of Sighs, which is not really a bridge in the Venetian sense but a fly-over from the old prison to the ducal palace. I suppose no one would look twice at it but for Byron, and most of the sighing was over by the time it was built; indeed

I cannot remember a single pitiful or heroic character associated with it. There is more genuine horror and tragedy in the Tower of London than in the dungeons of Venice and the Bridge of Sighs, yet nothing would have convinced our forefathers of this. A pleasant memory is of the creator of *Hiawatha*, who was sketching the Bridge of Sighs on a summer morning in 1828 when 'a wench of a chambermaid emptied a pitcher of water from a window of the palace directly upon my head. I came very near slipping into the canal'. Longfellow was not then an impressive bearded bard, but a young American of twenty-one on the first of several visits to Italy.

I would walk on to the Piazzetta which is, I think, above all places the one that exudes a feeling of cheerfulness and well-being on a sunny morning in summer. How far away and improbable appear those grim sights, of which the Piazzetta has seen so many. After their execution enemies of the State were often hung up between the two columns, the most public warning that could be given in Venice. The first thing William Lithgow saw when he landed on the Piazzetta in 1609 was 'a great throng of people, and in midst of them a great smoake'. He was told that a Franciscan friar was being burnt to death 'for begetting fifteen young Noble Nunnes with child, and all within one year; he being also their Father confessor'. Sometimes Venetians, on their way to work in the morning, would see a dead body, richly dressed, swinging by one leg between the columns, and would know from the humiliation of this attitude that someone had been executed for treason. Yet upon a sunny morning it seems impossible that such a charming scene should have witnessed anything except stupendous Veronese-like embarkations and arrivals.

Though the Piazzetta has been designed upon heroic lines, it is at the same time light and happy, and if buildings may be said to laugh and sparkle these do so in that wonderful marriage between stone and water. The Doge's Palace is one of the most exotic of buildings, an Arabic spice-box or a sandalwood case for a Greek Testament. As you approach Venice from the Lido on still evenings, there is a point at which you can see a pink flush in the water and as you draw nearer, you see the palace with its Gothic arcade and the arabesques of its loggia reflected in the canal. A strange thing about the Piazzetta is that, unlike most places which have been in constant use for centuries, it has not altered: it is today essentially the same landing-stage that one sees in early Venetian woodcuts.

In old pictures of Venice the golden Bucentaur was to be seen moored there upon the morning of Ascension Day, waiting for the Doge to embark for his marriage with the Adriatic. Now a number of gangways lead to a flotilla of gondolas. The gondoliers climb about their craft arranging the artificial roses in the little metal vases, punching up the cushions and making everything shipshape for the tourists. I would look through the fence of mooring-poles upon which are transfixed the domes of S. Maria della Salute across the water; near at hand, against the morning sky, I could see the statues on the roof of Sansovino's library; the two granite columns; the pink walls of the palace and the south angle of S. Mark's, where a spark of light burns all night by the will, it is said, of some long-dead mariner: and I felt how good it was to be alive and how fortunate I was to be in Venice.

There are memories of travel, unimportant when they happen, which nevertheless return at intervals to delight one, and among these, for me, is a table at Florian's in the early morning. The waiter, with the air of some grandee doing it for a wager, places a tray of coffee and rolls on the table, and the greedy pigeons immediately press forward and nod around my feet. The old women who sell maize arrange their trestle tables; the street photographer, who trustfully keeps an antique plate camera on its tripod in the square all night, comes along and unties it from its waterproof bag, a camera that has perpetuated the expressions of many generations. The first tourists arrive in twos and threes, then in boat-loads, then in conducted parties in charge of guides. All over the square tourists are kneeling amid a flutter of wings, aiming their cameras at wives and children, every arch of the colonnade shelters a photographer who directs his machine at S. Mark's, at the Clock Tower, at the Campanile. One wonders what happens to all these photographs.

As I sit idly watching the crowds, a guide gathers his chickens and announces in English, then in French, that they are looking at S. Mark's basilica, and shortly he will take them to the Doge's Palace. I intercept a cry of help from man to woman, from husband to wife. I hear an American ask: 'Say, honey, what are these Doges?'; and the wonderful reply – 'The kings of Venice!'

I smile to myself and remember the story, told by James Morris, of the Paddington householder, in London's 'Little Venice' on the Regent Canal, who fixed the notice to his gate, 'Beware of the Doge'. What an inspired pun it is, for it could well have been the motto of Venice down the ages. Fear that the Doge might make himself king runs through Venetian history, and explains why that functionary had to accept restrictions on his personal freedom which are unique in the history of ambition.

'Who were these Doges?'

What a question it is, the kind with which children so often confound one. I wondered how I should have answered it, had I been a guide. Perhaps I should have taken the easy way and said, 'They were the elected heads of the Venetian Republic and the word Doge means Dux, or Duke.' But if I really wished to give my flock a feeling for the ducal palace, and some interest in the extraordinary events that took place there, it would involve quite a long speech. When the Venetian Republic was brought to an end by Napoleon in 1797, there had been a hundred and twenty Doges in direct and unbroken succession from Paolo Lucio Anafesto, who was elected in 697. The Popes and the Doges were the two most ancient dignitaries in the world. The Roman Curia and the Venetian Signory were the only two organizations inherited intact from classical antiquity, thus the College of Cardinals and the Councillors of Venice, seated in state in their purple, had more than an outward resemblance. Possibly the many peculiarities of the Venetian constitution, its cynicism, the impression it gives of being an adult in a world of children, and its fear of the Doge, which seem to turn the pages of history back to Caesar and Cicero, may be explained by the fact that Venice was the only Roman community unconquered by the barbarian.

Of the hundred and twenty Doges, nine abdicated, four of whom became monks, two were killed in battle, three were murdered, three were executed, three were deposed, two were blinded and deposed, and two were exiled, one of whom was first blinded. One might conclude from this that being a Doge was a dangerous occupation, but all these tragedies took place before 1423, after which nearly every Doge, down to the last, Ludovico Manin, died in his bed.

One might ask what it was about the dignity and fame of being a Doge that made it worth while for men, century after century, to bow their necks to humiliating limitations to their liberty. 'Beware of the Doge' was such an anxiety complex with Venice that the leading citizen, with his own consent, became a gorgeously dressed prisoner in his own palace; a man who was given the state and dignity of a king but was not allowed to open his own correspondence. In 1275 the Doge was forbidden to hold land outside Venice; his sons were not allowed to marry foreign wives without the consent of the Council; his wife was forbidden to contract any debts or to receive presents disguised as samples from merchants and tradesmen. Such restrictions were always embodied in the oath, or *Promissione,* which the Doge took at the time of his coronation, and they became meaner and more stringent as time went on. In the fifteenth century the Doge was forbidden to speak in private with ambassadors and foreign envoys, and in public he had to confine his conversation to trivialities. The Doge, Antonio Grimani, who before his election loved to go duck shooting on the lagoon, found when he became Doge that his expeditions had to be confined to four occasions in the year approved by the Council; Andrea Gritti was forbidden to leave the city, and letters, even from his own children, had to be opened in the presence of Councillors. Upon one occasion when this patriot, seated in the Council Chamber, said that he would lead the Venetian fleet against the Turk, he was told sharply to study the terms of his *Promissione,* and to keep within bounds. On another occasion an entirely opposite opinion was expressed. The Doge Cristofero Moro, having objected to the ill-fated crusade proposed by Pius II, was told that if he did not go willingly, he would be taken by force. Michel Steno, when seated in state, was once told to hold his tongue.

Naturally, the Doge was surrounded by spies. Everything he did and said was noted by the secret service. About fifty years ago, during some alterations to the ducal apartments, a staircase was discovered which led to a listening post directly behind the Dogal bed. Immediately a Doge died, and during the interregnum, three magistrates were chosen by the Council, 'the Inquisitors upon the deceased Doge', whose task it was to hold a solemn trial of the dead man and to review every act of his life. The findings were passed on to five other magistrates, called 'Correctors', who were charged with drawing up the *Promissione* of the new Doge, and, if necessary, tightening up the regulations in the light of his predecessor's reign.

An organization that was able to impose such penalties upon its ruler was, of course, unique. Venice was really an aristocracy that preferred to call itself a republic, and the Grand Council was a House of Lords to which every noble whose name was in *The Golden Book* automatically belonged on his twenty-first birthday. This large body elected a smaller Senate which, with the Doge and six Privy Councillors, was the head of the Government. The operative power, however, came in time to be the famous 'Council of the Ten', a body sworn to secrecy, that controlled the police, the judicial machinery, and the secret service funds, and whose reputation, probably because of the speed and secrecy with which it could act, was sinister and dramatic. The Ten received no pay. They were elected for only twelve months, then they retired into private life. They knew everything that happened in Venice and everywhere else. How good their intelligence was is suggested by the story that Queen Elizabeth's love letters were regularly read to the Senate almost before the ink was dry! The Ten were the officials who opened the *Bocche del Leone,* and the calculated fear they inspired, not only in Venice, but all over Europe was like that felt in Nazi Germany for the Gestapo.

One wonders whether the horrific stories told of them are all true or are merely part of their legend. It is recorded that when Montesquieu was in Venice he was told by a leg-pulling friend that the Ten were watching him, and he immediately packed up and returned to Paris! The Ten had studied the psychology of fear. Sometimes a man would be tapped on the shoulder and told that 'their Excellencies would like to see you', but upon arriving at the Doge's palace, where the Ten had their meetings, would be kept in a waiting-room for an hour, then, without an explanation, be dismissed. It was said that sometimes the Ten would question a suspected person in darkness, though the phrase 'being put to the question' was something entirely different. This meant that the person questioned, with his wrists tied together, was hauled off the ground on a pulley, and in that position was interrogated.

The Ten were notorious for their swift political assassinations, executed by soft-footed stranglers who could enter a man's bed-room at dead of night and finish him off without making a sound. On the night of April 20, in 1622, a strangler visited a cell in the ducal prisons, and on the following morning Venice observed the body of a distinguished nobleman, Antonio Foscarini, dangling by one leg from the gallows between the two columns of the Piazzetta. His 'execution', or murder, was notable for a number of reasons. In four months' time he was proved to have been innocent, and the Ten appeared before the Grand Council, admitting their error and expressing regret. Also, arising from the murder, the Doge and the Grand Council were, for the only time in their history, publicly put in their place, and by an English-woman who was living in Venice. She was Althea, Countess of Arundel, and wife of the first great English art collector. She had rented the Mocenigo Palace where, two centuries later, Byron was to live.

She and her husband had been friendly with Foscarini in Lon-don when he was Venetian ambassador to James I; and it was now rumoured that Foscarini had been in the habit of going secretly and at night to the Mocenigo Palace to meet the agents of foreign governments. It was whispered that the Countess of Arundel was implicated and had been ordered to leave Venice within three days. Naturally the English ambassador was worried and, knowing his Venice, feared for the safety of the Countess. He was the attractive Sir Henry Wotton, who later became Provost of Eton and used to go fishing with Izaak Walton on the Thames at 'Black Pots'. Finding that the Countess had gone to Padua to see her sons, who were at the University, Wotton sent an urgent messenger to tell her the stories that were in circulation and strongly advised her to keep away. The messenger intercepted the Countess on the road to Venice, but instead of accepting the ambassador's advice, she stormed into Venice and demanded to be publicly exonerated in the presence of the Doge and the Grand Council.

Though such a request was preposterous, her demand for an audience was granted. Seated upon the right of the Doge, with the Grand Council ranged before her in the Great Chamber, the Countess indignantly denied that Foscarini had ever visited the Mocenigo Palace, and demanded a public apology. The Doge, Antonio Priuli, disarmed her with the softest of answers. Her name, he said, had never been mentioned in evidence, and he promised that those who had spread the calumnies should be punished. The Grand Council passed a resolution declaring its confidence in her innocence and instructed the Venetian Ambassador in London to convey such sentiments to the Earl of Arundel and also, if Lady Arundel wished it, to the Monarch himself. They also voted a hundred ducats to provide a present of wax and sweetmeats, which were formally presented to the Countess on fifteen salvers. Still further to soothe the feelings of the wife of the Earl Marshal of England, a state galley was sent to take her to the annual Wedding of the Sea, and she was given a public banquet. She returned to England, taking with her a blackamoor and a gondola.

Four months after Foscarini's death, positive proof was obtained that he had been 'executed' on false evidence, and the Council of Ten made their unique admission and apology, recommending that the wronged man should be exhumed and given a splendid funeral. ('The last of miserable remedies,' was Wotton's comment.) A curious epilogue to the case was mentioned by Mrs Thrale in her book of Italian travel. She says that among the charges against Foscarini was that after dark he went in disguise to the house of the French ambassador. Forty years later, she continues, an old lady died in Paris, confessing with her last breath that, while living in Venice as a companion to the wife of the French ambassador, she was visited in secret by an amorous nobleman whose name she never knew. 'So was Foscarini lost,' comments Mrs Thrale, 'so died he a martyr to love, and tenderness for female reputation.'

That the rule of the Ten, founded on suspicion and a depressingly cynical view of human nature, should have worked for more than a thousand years, is one of the many amazing things about Venice. For centuries the rest of Europe looked at the Republic with awe and envy as an example of a miraculously stable state, one that went on its glorious golden course age after age, untouched by internal strife or dynastic or religious wars. Even after Vasco da Gama had found the Cape route to the spice country, and Columbus had discovered America, there was no sign of decline, and to the casual onlooker Venice appeared as dynamic as ever. Those who were privileged to see the Doge seated in state, with his Council before him in their red gowns, felt that they were witnessing a scene from the classical world, as indeed they were. They were also witnessing Aristocracy's longest triumph.

History has few sadder footnotes to greatness than the decline of Venice in the eighteenth century. As trade grew less, life became more costly and spectacular, and Venice became the gayest city in Europe. The last Doge, Ludovico Manin, surrendered Venice to a young man of twenty-eight, a Corsican with untidy hair and a general's sash across a yet slim waistline. The Doge left the Council Chamber under the gaze of his mighty predecessors, and entered his apartments to be disrobed by his valet. Removing the *corno* from his head, the symbol of Venetian greatness, he handed it to the man with the remark that he would not be needing it again. Napoleon saved his last insult until the end. He sold Venice to Austria.

§ 5

One morning I joined the crowd that gathers at the gateway to the Doge's Palace. In high relief above the gate one sees the Doge, Francesco Foscari, kneeling before the Lion of S. Mark. It is an angry headmaster of a lion, and it appears to be teaching a backward Doge some trick, or perhaps, with paw on open book, trying to give him a lesson. Passing through this gate, I saw one of the most stately courtyards in the world.

The guides ask their charges to look at the staircase where, between the two statues called the Giants, the Doges were crowned, the culminating moment in an election which seems to have been unnecessarily complicated. The election of a new Doge began in the oddest of ways. The youngest of the councillors was told to go out into S. Mark's Square and seize the first boy he met there. The lad was taken to the Great Council Chamber, where he saw the nobility of Venice seated row upon row in their red gowns. All the lad had to do was to pick papers out of a hat. After inconceivable complications and re-balloting, forty-one councillors were selected to form an electoral college, and everyone else withdrew. The councillors now placed the names of those whom they wished to put forward as candidates into an urn, and one name was withdrawn. If this man did not receive twenty-five votes or more, another name was taken from the urn and the process repeated until one of the candidates received this vote. A deputation then left at once to bring the Doge-elect to S. Mark's, where he was shown to the people in the marble pulpit on the right-hand side of the church. After Mass, he swore to obey the laws of the Republic and made his *Promissione*. He was then clothed in the ducal mantle and handed the Standard of the Republic, and, like the Pope in his *sedia gestatoria*, was carried in a chair round S. Mark's Square, scattering largesse to the crowds. Finally, as he stood at the head of the ducal staircase with the banner of S. Mark in his hand, the youngest councillor fitted the cambric cap, the *vittà*, on his head, the little cap with strings which the Doge never removed even in church, while the oldest councillor added the dogal cap, the *corno*. All the bells of Venice then sounded, cannon were fired from the warships in the Arsenal, and the city abandoned itself to feasting and rejoicing. From that moment the Doge became the slave of Venice.

The crowds pass the superb courtyard with scarcely a glance, and ascend the stairs into a succession of marble halls, with heavy encrusted ceilings. The palace, where no Doge has ruled for more than a century and a half, is now admittedly dull and oppressive. One glances gratefully through its windows at unusual glimpses of S. Mark's, where white saints mounted on pinnacles remind one of Milan. One has to be a tremendous enthusiast to be genuinely interested in the enormous river of Venetian history which flows round the walls and overflows on the ceilings: Venice triumphant; Venice resurgent; Venice conquering the Turk; Venice capturing Crete; Venice always successful. It was an unwritten law that one had to be successful. No matter what a man's past triumphs, should he fail, it was assumed that there was treachery somewhere and he was probably impeached. In contrast to the modern cult of personality, Venice cultivated impersonality. The individual was nothing: Venice was everything. She was probably the only state that erected memorials not to her heroes, but to her evildoers. Under the arcade of the Doge's Palace is a tablet which says that Girolamo Loredan and Giovanni Contarini were banished for ceding the fort at Tenedos to the Turks; another commemorates an embezzler named Pietro Bintio, and I suppose one could find others. The true Venetian monument was not a tribute but a warning.

The faces of the Doges gaze down from the walls of their palace. That is inevitable. E. V. Lucas was reminded of city councillors and thought them 'incorrigibly municipal', and how right he was, but not, I fancy, in the sense he intended. There is nothing of the well-fed burgomaster about them, nothing that links those grandees with Rembrandt's *Night Watch*: they are 'municipal' in the sense that the Roman world was municipal, and their faces recall that long parade of stern and oddly Victorian faces in the galleries of the Capitoline Museum in Rome. The inflexible Doges and senators are classical, like a continuation of Roman portrait painting.

Famous names echo through the halls and corridors as the guides expound the history of Venice. I heard the name Dandolo – Enrico Dandolo – that great and terrifying old filibuster who, though blind and over eighty, led the ruffians of the Fourth Crusade to the attack on Constantinople, and died there and was buried in S. Sophia two hundred and forty years before the Turkish conquest. The old hero's armour, his spurs and his sword, were given by Mahomet II to Gentile Bellini who, after a visit to Constantinople as court painter to the Sultan, returned to Venice with them, also with a Turkish title, a pension, and many fine clothes. His portrait of Mahomet II was discovered in Venice a hundred years ago in a deplorable condition by Sir Henry Layard, the excavator of Nineveh, and is now one of the treasures of the National Gallery in London. I heard a guide mention the name of the Doge Leonardo Loredano, another portrait familiar to those who go to the National Gallery, and whose thin, ascetic face might be that of a Roman consul of the Augustan Age. Another guide was telling his flock about Sebastian Vernier, commander of the Venetian galleys at the battle of Lepanto, but he did not tell them that one who had seen the admiral at war, proud, arrogant, and quarrelsome, and later saw him in Venice after he had become Doge, could scarcely believe his eyes as he watched the great man strolling about the Piazza and chatting to friends as if he were an ordinary citizen. There is a fine modern statue of this Doge in S. Zanipoli, an arrogant, bearded figure striding confidently forward wearing body armour over a chain shirt, a baton in one hand, in the other a double-handed sword; the very embodiment of the dynamic state.

The little gesticulating figures in their circles of obedient listeners pointed to walls and ceilings and spoke the name of Francesco Morosini; and I remembered how in the chilly autumn of Venetian history this man brought back the fires of spring, and how the Lion of S. Mark grew new claws in his time and sprang upon the Turk in Crete and Greece, lending to the last years of the seventeenth century the splendour of the fourteenth. But all in vain, if indeed bravery and love of one's country, and faith in one's self, are ever in vain. The great leader died in Greece, but his body lies in S. Stefano in Venice.

I passed through a series of apartments designed on the same scale of magnificence, all more or less alike, though some are merely ante-rooms to great assembly halls. The golden ceilings are heavily moulded and frame a great deal of wasted painting, for who can honestly enjoy standing with his head tilted back, trying to make out something forty or fifty feet above? There is also a vast acreage of sombre panelling, some of which, one suspects, probably slides at the touch of a button to reveal a listening post or a secret stair. A room which no one wished to see was the Room of the Black Door. Here is the most sinister of all the Lions' Mouths, a letter-box for secret communications actually in the apartments of the Ten; and here it was that those summoned before the Ten would wait until called into their presence. The black door of this room leads to the Council Hall of the Three State Inquisitors, and also to a staircase on the way to the Bridge of Sighs, altogether an uneasy room.

I came at length to the Great Council Chamber which was designed for the seating in state of fifteen hundred noblemen. The vast hall is now merely an acreage of spotless polished floor beneath an encrusted ceiling. At the far end is the dais where the Doge and his Privy Council sat beneath Tintoretto's *Paradiso,* where some five hundred figures are all airborne, with draperies flying, a scene of the utmost intricacy and vigour that recalls the final canto of Dante. It was perhaps the artist's last work, painted with great love and piety when he was seventy-two. He refused payment for it, but eventually consented to accept a present from a grateful and delighted Senate.

In this great hall one can perhaps imagine better than anywhere else what a stupendous spectacle the Doge and the Grand Council must have been, a sight which those who saw it thought the most impressive manifestation of civilized life in the world. One must try to imagine the high benches from which the Chancellor and his clerks conducted the proceedings, the desks of the orators, the enormous double benches that seated the fifteen hundred nobles. We must imagine the Doge in his golden state mantle, as in

Bordoni's *Miracle of the Ring*: the councillors in their scarlet robes; the three inquisitors in purple; the Great Sage in violet; the five Sages of Law and War in blue; here and there the red stoles of the Procurators and the golden stoles of the Cavaliers; and the immense floor occupied by the aristocracy of Venice, robed in red. What an ordeal it must have been to appear before this assembly, even as a friend. An ambassador, presenting his credentials, had to salute three times. If he came from an emperor or a king, everyone save the Doge rose to his feet and uncovered his head at the first salute; after his third salute, the ambassador was conducted to the dais and to a seat on the right of the Doge, from which he delivered his address. The Doge would reply in polished phrases which meant nothing. After the assembly had dispersed, in some small, panelled room beneath sportive cherubs, the Ten might have been observed analysing the ambassador's speech and his letters, and slowly, like lawyers drawing up a lease, composing the official reply, weighing each word and balancing each comma in the light of centuries of successful statecraftiness.

To many visitors the great thrill is to cross the Bridge of Sighs and inspect the dungeons, which are neither damp nor under water. No prison cell is attractive, but I reflected that I have stayed in many a hotel bedroom almost as comfortless but by no means as quiet.

And what of the Dogaressa? One hears a great deal about the Doge, but hardly a word about his wife. Those shadowy and generally matronly ladies, the Dogaressas, had no authority and no official position; all that was expected of them was that they should appear upon state occasions with their husbands, looking decorative and expensive, and wearing the miniature *corno* as prescribed for them.

Queens have often deputized for kings, and have even commanded the royal armies, but there is not a single instance in the long history of Venice of a Dogaressa acting for a Doge. Though her role was a minor one, it is said that the first question asked by the electoral committee, once the name of a dogal candidate had been drawn from the urn, was, 'What's his wife like?' Her most important qualification was an upright and commanding figure on which the official state robe – the *dogalina* – would look well. The only Dogaressa who made an impression on history was the Byzantine princess, Theodora Ducas, daughter of the Emperor Constantine X, who arrived in Venice with new and exotic scents and lotions, and a two-pronged instrument of gold with which, to the curiosity of beholders, she delicately speared her food, which had previously been cut for her. This, it has been said, was the first fork seen at a European dining-table.

A memory I treasure of the Doge's Palace is of the courtyard at one o'clock in the morning with moonlight spilling into it. The concert which the orchestra of the Fenice Theatre gave there did not begin until after eleven. As the violins sounded in that incredible scene, it seemed as if the joys and sorrows of the Palace had found their way from corridor and gilded hall and had come to dance for a moment in the green wash of Venetian moonlight. The orchestra played a Brahms concerto, an arrangement by Maurice Ravel of four of Mussorgsky's compositions, and '*tre antiche arie di guerra scozzesi*', arranged by Carlo Franci. I recognized 'Red is the path to glory' and 'Mother, mother hear the news'.

In the interval I went out and walked about the deserted Piazzetta as if I were a member of the Senate. Everything was quiet, and the moonlight cast dark shadows. The pigeons had gone to sleep and the Piazza was a green lake of moonlight, and above, upon the gallery of S. Mark's, the four gold horses of Chios stood as if waiting for their Delphic charioteer. Two wise-looking tabby cats regarded the scene with doge-like solemnity.

§ 6

To appreciate a gondola a man must be twenty and in love, to travel in one alone and in later life may be restful but cannot be romantic. The gondolier, too, loses interest and, instead of lifting his voice in snatches of song, grumbles about the cost of living and deplores the parsimony of the modern tourist. One night, having selected the least voluble-looking gondolier on the Riva degli Schiavoni, I asked to be taken up the Grand Canal. It was a warm, windless summer's night, and the Canal was floodlit. One might have fancied, but for the shuttered silence of the palaces and their empty balconies, that Venice was still engaged in the extravagances of the eighteenth century. The floodlighting, skilful and effective though it is, lacks, of course, the life and movement of the flambeaux and oil-lamps familiar to past ages. The *pali*, or mooring-stakes for the gondolas, which are such a picturesque sight by day, become at night the lamp standards from which a dramatic greenish glow is directed upon the ancient buildings. There is a heartless publicity about this illumination which is entirely modern: the unwavering electricity casts into relief a hundred defects and blemishes, though the effect in general is pleasing, rather like an attractive dream from which one has no desire to awaken. So one drifts along enjoying, when out of earshot of a motor-boat or a water-bus, the faint liquid plop of the pole as the black shell slides silently over the canal.

As we advanced, the lights of other gondolas approached and receded, and I admired the statuesque movements of the gondoliers, and noticed that those who sang were propelling a man and a woman and were happily fulfilling their romantic tradition.

The sight of them brought to the surface of my mind a memory long since buried and forgotten. I must have been perhaps twelve years of age when, during some school holiday, greatly daring and alone, I took a boat out on the Avon at Stratford upon a gnat-haunted summer's night as calm and warm as this. It was twilight before I had splashed my way to the centre of the river, and, once there, appalled by the lateness of the hour and anticipating unpleasantness when I returned home, made as hastily as I could for the boat-house. As I did so, I was alarmed to see a light bearing down upon me with what seemed terrifying speed. Passing within a few feet of me in the twilight, I saw a curved, black and noiseless craft in which a plump little elderly lady, dressed in white, reclined upon cushions, and, if memory serves, swathed in grey gossamer veiling. But the figure that impressed me most was that of a tall man, clad in white from head to foot save for a scarlet sash, who, standing splendidly upon the poop, moved the craft easily over the water. I was told afterwards that I had narrowly escaped being run down by Marie Corelli. Anyone under the age of fifty will probably have to be told that her fame at that remote period was greater than that of any popular novelist writing today.

As I remembered that moment, I wondered how many gondoliers had left the Grand Canal for England. Two were sent with a gondola as a present from the Serenissima to Charles II; the Countess of Arundel took back with her a gondola and a negro who, like the negro in Carpaccio's *Miracle of the True Cross,* was probably a gondolier; and Disraeli, when in Malta, met Byron's gondolier, Tita Falsieri, who was down on his luck, and took him back to England. Tita, who had been with Byron in Greece and had moistened his dying lips, became deeply attached to Disraeli and, says Sir Harold Nicolson, 'after residing many years at Hughenden, where his portrait is still preserved, and after marrying Mrs Disraeli's maid, was appointed Home Service messenger in the India Office'.

As we passed along, my gondolier sang out the names of the palaces as we came to them. Though Napoleon had burnt the Golden Book, which held the titles of the Venetian nobility, the Grand Canal preserves most of the important names. 'Palazzo Rezzonico!' came the cry; and I glanced up to see the rusticated walls of the vast palace in which Robert Browning died. From the way Browning has been associated with the Rezzonico, I am sure many must think that the poet lived and worked there for years. The truth is that he never wrote a line there, and lived there only for about five weeks while on a visit to his son. November was not the best time for a man of seventy-seven to visit a draughty palace on the Grand Canal, and Browning caught a chill which led to his death.

My gondolier thrust his pole into a swirling lake of amber and purple and, nodding towards the opposite bank, pointed out a slumbering palace which stood transfixed in the limelight, the Palazzo Mocenigo. The wild happenings there are part of the Venetian story, and it is impossible to travel up the Grand Canal without remembering the fantastic household of fourteen servants, a dog, a wolf, and a fox, where, amid feminine screaming and passionate scenes, Byron somehow managed to write the first part of *Don Juan*. This is the palace to which Byron dragged the reluctant Thomas Moore, insisting that he should stay there, though Moore, having a fair idea of the confusion he would encounter, would rather have gone to an inn. 'As I groped my way after him though the dark hall,' wrote Moore, 'he cried out, "Keep clear of the dog!" and before we had proceeded many paces farther, "Take care, or that monkey will fly at you!" ' More violent than mastiff or monkey was the peasant girl of twenty-two, the wife of a baker, whom Byron had met while he was out riding. Her name was Margarita Cogni, 'a fine animal,' said Byron, 'but untameable'. The poet, who was a magnet to unbalanced runaways, tried to get rid of her; he even called the police when she arrived at the palace, but she said she had left her husband and intended to remain as Byron's mistress.

She could neither read nor write, and she arrived wearing her peasant's dress, which she soon cast aside as she began to acquire fashionable clothes. Byron threw hat after hat in the fire, but the girl persevered and was seen eventually dressed in a gown with a train, which she called 'a tail'. She dominated the palace, terrified the servants, and would knock down any woman whom she suspected of being a rival. Byron allowed her to run the place, with the result that the fourteen servants began to work, and though everything seems to have been done in fear and trembling, the place was beautifully clean and the housekeeping bills were halved.

Margarita did not inspire any Byronic verse, though her concern for him prompted the finest letter he ever wrote. 'In the autumn,' he wrote to John Murray, 'one day, going to the Lido, with my Gondoliers, we were overtaken by a heavy squall, and the Gondola put in peril – hats blown away, boat filling, oar lost, tumbling sea, thunder, rain in torrents, night coming, and wind increasing. On our return, after a tight struggle, I found her on the open steps of the Mocenigo Palace, on the Grand Canal, with her great black eyes flashing through her tears, and the long dark hair, which was streaming drenched with rain over her brows and breast. She was perfectly exposed to the storm; and the wind blowing her hair and dress about her tall thin figure, and the lightning flashed round her, with the waves rolling at her feet, made her look like Medea alighted from her chariot, or the Sibyl of the tempest that was rolling around her, the only living thing within hail at that moment except ourselves. On seeing me safe, she did not wait to greet me, as might be expected, but calling out to me – *Ah! can' della Madonna, xe esto il tempo per andar' al' Lido?* ("Ah, Dog of the Virgin, is this a time to go to Lido?") ran into the house, and solaced herself with scolding the boatmen for not foreseeing the "temporale". I was told by the servants that she had only been prevented from coming in a boat to look after me, by the refusal of all the Gondoliers of the Canal to put out into the harbour in such a moment: and that then she sat upon the steps in all the thickest of the Squall, and would neither be removed nor comforted. Her joy at seeing me again was moderately mixed with ferocity, and gave me the idea of a tigress over her recovered Cubs.'

At the safe distance of a century and a half, one is fascinated by the tigress, one of the most preposterous women to seduce Byron. But the time came when even he was exhausted by her emotion and her scenes, and exasperated by her jealousy (she once tried to learn to read to see if his letters came from women), told her that they must part. She was furious but left without a fight. The next night, however, the sound of falling glass was followed by Margarita, who strode into the room where Byron was dining and wounded him in the thumb with a table-knife. Byron's long-suffering valet, Fletcher, disarmed her and the formidable Tita escorted her to the palace steps, from which she jumped into the Canal. She was rescued dripping and, after a doctor had been called, was sent home. 'Byron superintended her resuscitation with a calm efficiency bred of long experience,' wrote Peter Quennell, 'he was no great believer in feminine suicides.' Nevertheless it was the end of the affair. Byron saw her only twice again, once in the distance and again at the opera.

I asked the gondolier to take me over to the Mocenigo Palace, where we drifted in the floodlights while I examined possibly the very steps from which Margarita took her celebrated dive into the Canal. Some may have wondered what happened to that passionate virago. In the year 1860 W. D. Howells arrived in Venice as American consul and remained there for five years. In the course of a charming book, he said that an old woman who kept a butter and cheese shop in a street leading from the Campo Sant' Angelo to San Paternian was pointed out as one of Byron's mistresses. In one of the only unkind and priggish sentences in his book (but, after all, he was only twenty-three) he described her as 'a fat sinner long past beauty, bald and somewhat melancholy to behold'. Were she Margarita Cogni she would have been seventy-four, and Byron had been dead for thirty-six years.

As we continued our progress, I heard the gondoliers crying warningly as they turned into the dark side-canals, but I fancy the old cries of *Premi* and *Stali* ('right' and 'left'), mentioned by Ruskin and so many writers on Venice, are no longer to be heard. I agree with James Morris that the modern gondolier just yells 'Oi!' which, of course, can be made to look more romantic if spelt 'O-ië' or 'A-oë'. While we were on our way, I heard music and saw, emerging from a side-canal, a procession which at first I took to be an illuminated funeral. There came slowly and ponder-ously a large barge hung everywhere with electric lights, but instead of the catafalque which I had expected it carried a piano and a small orchestra, while behind it, like a school of lethargic but musically-inclined sharks, followed a dozen gondolas filled with Americans. This was evidently the *Serenatine in gondola* which I had seen advertised. Two or three members of the party lifted their cameras) and let off electronic flashes, and a soprano voice floated charmingly over the waters in a well-known aria.

The multiplication of palaces, all with the same name, is con-fusing, and as we came to two Giustiniani palaces, the gondolier told me that it was in the second one that Wagner had composed part of *Tristan*. I looked up and wondered which was the balcony mentioned in his *Autobiography*, where he stood and said, as he looked down on the Grand Canal, 'Now I am living in Venice', and 'here I would complete *Tristan*'. He was forty-four when he arrived in 1858, longing for peace and quiet, with his unfinished opera in his head. Tired of the hotel, he had rented a large stately room in the palace with a bedroom adjoining, but, finding the walls a distressing grey colour, he concealed them with hangings of cheap red cloth. He then sent for his grand piano and his own bed. How one's heart warms to Wagner! To be able to sleep in one's own bed, as so many travellers did in the past, must have compensated for many of the hardships and irritations of travel. Wagner's routine was simple. He worked until two o'clock, then he took a gondola to the Piazza for luncheon and afterwards walked in the public gardens ('the only pleasure ground in Venice where there are any trees'), where there is now a statue of him. He would return to his rooms before dark and work until eight. Sometimes he went to the theatre. At that time Venice was, of course, ruled by Austria, and military bands played in the Piazza in the evening. Wagner, while quietly eating his dinner, was, he said, 'often suddenly startled towards the end of my meal by the sound of my own overtures . . .' He noted with a professional ear that the acoustics of the Piazza are excellent, and he noticed, too, that the loathing of the Venetians for the Austrians was so great that, though people could not keep away from the music, 'no two hands ever forgot themselves so far as to applaud'. It was a proud moment for the regimental bandmasters when Wagner went to the barracks one evening and attended a band practice. He met all the officers and noted modestly that he 'was treated by them with great respect'.

How fascinating to know from Wagner himself that the long note of the horn at the beginning of the third act of *Tristan* is probably an echo of a cry heard on the Grand Canal in 1858. Unable to sleep one night, he stepped out on his balcony and heard in the stillness, and from the direction of the Rialto, 'a rough lament' which was answered 'in the same tone from a yet farther distance in another direction. This melancholy dialogue, which was repeated at longer intervals, affected me so much that I could fix the very simple musical component parts in my memory'. This was the famous song of the gondoliers, of alternate stanzas of Tasso's *Jerusalem*. On a subsequent occasion, as Wagner was travelling home late one night, his gondolier uttered a deep wail, 'not unlike the cry of an animal: the cry gradually gained in strength, and formed itself, after a long-drawn "Oh!" into the simple musical exclamation "Venezia!" This was followed by other sounds of which I have no distinct recollection, as I was so much moved at the time . . . they remained with me until the completion of the second act of *Tristan*, and possibly even suggested to me the long-drawn wail of the shepherd's horn at the beginning of the third act.'

Wagner may not have known that he was repeating the experience of his countryman, Goethe, who seventy-two years previously had been attracted and moved by the cries of the gondoliers. Even in 1786, the date of Goethe's visit, the 'song' had to be asked for, as it was even then a curiosity that belonged to the past. Having arranged with his singers, Goethe met them at night. 'I entered a gondola by moonlight,' he wrote, 'with one singer before and the other behind me. They sing their song, taking up the verses alternately . . . In order to let me hear it, they landed on the bank of the Giudecca, and took up different positions by the canal. I walked backwards and forwards between them, so as to leave the one whose turn it was to sing, and to join the one who had just left off. Then it was that the effect of the strain first opened upon me. As a voice from a distance it sounds in the highest degree strange – as a lament without sadness : it has an incredible effect, and is moving even to tears . . .'

I asked my gondolier if the 'song' is ever heard nowadays, but he gave me the usual inconclusive answer – Isabella d'Este's motto, *Forse che si, forse che no* – 'Perhaps yes, perhaps no'. However, he promised to ask his friends. Centuries of guile, stealth, and keeping its mouth shut seem to have left a cautious sediment in the Venetian mind.

As we passed under the Rialto Bridge, I saw on my left the fish and vegetable markets, cleaned and swept for the next morning, and, looking up on the right, I wondered which house it was from whose windows Aretino described an early morning scene which he called the pleasantest view in the world: the Rialto crowded with merchants; barges full of grapes; twenty boats loaded with melons, making an island on which men walked counting them, smelling them, and pinching them; beautiful young housewives shining in silk, with gold and silver round their necks, while from a near-by tavern Germans piled into a boat, which overturned and threw them into the Grand Canal.

The revellers seen by Ariosto hailed from the near-by *Fondaco de' Tedeschi*, now the General Post Office, which sheltered German traders and their goods throughout the Middle Ages. They crossed the Alps, sometimes in winter, bringing German goods for sale in Venice, timing their arrival to coincide as near as possible with that of the Spice Fleet from the East. Then, having bought spices, Indian muslins, and Venetian silks and velvets, they would set off for home. The most fascinating account of mercantile Venice, and the kind of life led by the ordinary trader, is that of the Dominican of Ulm, in Germany, a man named Felix Fabri, who was in Venice on his way to and from the Holy Land nine years before the discovery of America. He saw Venice in the splendour of her golden age; he saw the Doge seated in state with the Senate; he saw one of the magnificent religious processions round the Piazza; he travelled in gondolas, not the black craft decreed in later times, but the gaily painted gondola of Carpaccio steered by graceful figures in striped tights. Brother Fabri was present on Ascension Day and saw the golden Bucentaur, shrouded with silken hangings and propelled by three hundred free oarsmen, move out into the lagoon to take the Doge to his annual Wedding with the Sea, while trumpets sounded and all the bells of Venice rang. He solved a problem, unanswered by any eye-witness account known to me: what happened to the gold ring after the Doge had cast it into the sea? I could not believe, if the Venetian temperament in 1483 were as it is today, that gold would be allowed to lie long in the water; and I was right. 'After the ceremony,' says Fabri, 'many strip and dive to the bottom to seek the ring. He who finds it keeps it for his own, and, moreover, dwells for that whole year in the city free from all the burdens to which dwellers in that republic are subject.'

Fabri's first act on reaching Venice was to go to the German House for news of home; and the first persons he saw were merchants from his own town of Ulm, who insisted that he should stay with them. Ulm's trade with Venice was in Eucharistic bread and – playing-cards! H. F. M. Prescott, who has written of Fabri's narrative with charm and scholarship, says that the *fondaco* was a building in whose double courtyard the merchants stored their goods while they lived in the upper rooms, which is the pattern of ancient *khans* all over the Middle East. Like every detail of life under the Venetian Republic, the lives of the merchants were regulated by law. They had to eat together in the refectory; they had to conduct their business with the knowledge of government departments; they had to be indoors by a certain hour at night. When the time came for them to return to Germany, they were obliged to declare their purchases and pay duty on them; they were not allowed to pack their own goods but had to hand them over to official packers, the width of the bales being determined by a narrow ravine on the Brenner; then, when everything was settled, the bales could be handled only by certain bargees or porters appointed for the purpose.

There were fifty-six bedrooms in the German House, some of which seem to have been rented by the year, whether the firms' representatives were in Venice or not. A firm in Nuremberg is said to have rented an apartment for eighty years; another, evidently familiar with the Venetian winter, installed a stove. The merchants sat together in the refectory in town groups, and Fabri was welcomed at the Ulm table.

This highly organized establishment, which had hummed with endeavour since the early Middle Ages, went up in flames one night in 1505, and half Venice seems to have helped to quench the flames. Among those who passed up the buckets were two artists, both aged twenty-eight; one was Giorgione, the other, Titian. Giorgione was to die of plague in five years' time; Titian was to die of it in seventy-one years' time. Both artists frescoed the new building, though not a trace of their work remains today, or, at the most, only a ghostly blur.

In a few moments we were passing the Gothic gem of the Grand Canal, the Ca' d'Oro – the palace of gold – which gives a better idea than any building in Venice of the background of a magnifico of the fifteenth century. On the other side of the canal we passed the stately little Renaissance palace, the Vendramin Calergi, where

Wagner died at the age of seventy, just a quarter of a century after he had composed *Tristan*. There is a story in Venice that his gondolier had a presentiment that his master was about to die, and sat about in the dark in his gondola at the water-steps, and, as he waited, he heard from a room in the palace above the notes of a piano. He was the last man to hear the great composer play.

We went up to the station, then back past the shuttered palaces. Only the *vaporetti* thrashing their way from pier to pier gave the venerable scene a purpose and linked it with modern life: but gaiety, and even wickedness, had departed. The blue lights searched the sad, impassive faces of the buildings, and, I hate to say it, gave to this famous highway the air of a lying-in-state.

CHAPTER NINE

The Pigeons of S. Mark's – The Arsenal of Venice – The Mediaeval
Assembly Line – Life in a Venetian Galley – Women of Venice –
Choppines – Tom Coryat and the Courtesan – Bellini and Carpaccio
– Painters and their Dogs – Titian and Aretino – Teriaca – The Glass
Works of Murano

§ 1

Anyone who has lived in the Italian countryside must often have marvelled that a thrush, lark, or sparrow can achieve maturity, indeed to see an adult small bird is to envisage a life of hairbreadth escapes at the cannon's mouth. This gives the pigeons of Venice an almost religious significance akin to that of the cows of Hindustan or the doves of Paphos. Here is the most shootable and eatable assembly of birds in Italy, yet not one feather of the nodding, greedy heads is ever touched, or has been touched as long as man can remember. Even the innumerable cats of Venice never stalk them, and they evidently teach their kittens to look the other way: they know that even to creep up on a pigeon in S. Mark's Square is at the top of the cat crime sheet.

The pigeons that befoul the National Gallery in London, and the British Museum, are protected by urban sentimentality and years ago, when it was suggested that their numbers should be reduced, there was such a pained outcry that the idea had to be dropped. In Venice no one would even dare to formulate such a scheme. When rations were short during the last war, no one in Venice ate pigeon pie, and I have been told by historians that it was the same during the Austrian siege of 1848. If you wish to see dismay upon an Italian face, just mention casually to a Venetian friend, as you tread among the mulberry-footed thousands in the Piazza, that you prefer *Piccione con Piselli* to the more usual pigeon pie and you will receive in reply an injured and reproachful glance

369

which may remind you of the day when by accident you stepped upon the paw of a favourite spaniel.

Why is it, in a country where no thrush or blackcap is safe, and where larks are sold in bunches, these sleek and corpulent pigeons are allowed to die of old age or over-eating? There are two explanations. One is that when Attila and his Huns were sweeping down upon the Roman cities of the mainland, the pigeons and the doves were seen to be deserting their nests in the town walls, which was interpreted as a sign from God that safety should be sought in flight. The inhabitants, following their example, were led to the islands of the lagoons, where eventually they founded the Venetian state. The second story is that during Holy Week, in the Middle Ages, the priests loosed thousands of pigeons from the façade of the basilica for the crowds to catch, presumably for the pot. The birds were weighted with screws of paper tied to their feet, so that great numbers were captured, but those which happened to escape were loudly cheered and granted immunity from capture ever after. This story has the ring of truth. The ceremony was obviously a skilful and sensible attempt to reduce the flock, and, at the same time, to overcome the ancient, possibly pagan, reluctance to eat the pigeons. The scheme did not work, however, since it was soon impossible to distinguish a free pigeon and its descendants from those liable to capture. The ceremony was therefore discontinued, and ever since, for something like five centuries, the pigeons of S. Mark's have continued to multiply in their sanctuary, a modern variant of the sacred geese of antiquity. The only reduction in numbers occurs when a city asks for pigeons (and, oddly enough, they do) and a few are caught at night, when Venice is asleep, and sent away by rail in crates. This actually happened while I was in Venice, and I was told that the consignment went to Brussels.

The birds use S. Mark's as if it were a cliff-face. The holes and crannies of the walls of Aquileia have been replaced by Byzantine moulding. They nest in the delicious narthex, and stain the faces of saint and apostle. Tender young squabs gaze fatly from Byzantine infoliation, looking forward to the time when they also will strut and preen with their generation, receding from the feet of advancing tourists, pushing and shoving in their unappeasable hunger, rising like a thunderclap at any unusual sound and flocking to the little marble bird-bath of fresh water, provided by the adoring city, which bubbles up in the Piazzetta dei Leoni on the north side of the church. The stones of Venice are now so thickly encrusted with their contributions that one feels sympathy for the most depressed figure on the Venetian scene, an old man with an iron-shod stick who is employed to scrape the marble of the basilica before anyone is up and able to observe him at his horrid task. I have watched that unfortunate functionary on his rounds as he hopelessly scrapes away and gathers up the morning's accumulation of feathers and addled eggs; and I have thought one might be watching some old priest of ancient Egypt prowling round the bird-cages where the sacred hawks lived on the fat of the land.

It is not true, as so often stated, that the pigeons of Venice are fed by the Municipality, a privilege which was gladly surrendered in 1952 to a generous insurance company, the Assicurazioni Generali, whose offices are just off the Piazza, in the Sottoportico Maruzzi. Every day during the winter the birds receive a hundred kilos of maize and wheat in two feeds, but in the summer, when visitors feed the pigeons all day long, the feed is reduced by half. It is a generous dole, and gives some idea of the size of the flock: a hundred kilos is roughly two hundred pounds, the weight of quite a massive human being.

It is worth while going to the far end of the Piazza, opposite the Correr Museum, at ten to nine in the morning to see what happens. At about that time a man wearing a peaked cap and a grey dust-coat will emerge from the neighbouring portico carrying a covered bucket marked with the initials A G. – Assicurazioni Generali. There is an expectancy in the air but no general descent, for the birds are aware that the grain will not be scattered until the clock of the Campanile strikes nine. A few hundred pigeons stroll about round the bucket, while an arrogant cock-bird mounts the rim and challenges any other bird that would like to do the same. The man stands waiting. A clock strikes somewhere, but neither man nor pigeons move: they know it is not the clock of the

Campanile. Then – bang – it happens. At the sound of the clock the man lifts the bucket and pours out the maize in the shape of an enormous A, followed by an enormous G. Simultaneously, with a rattle like several hundred Venetian blinds being released at the same moment, the air becomes full of wings as the birds swoop down from the roofs and chimneys, from the saints and domes of S. Mark's, to hang a moment in a flurry of blue-grey feathers before they hurl themselves into the tight mass that is ravenously pecking the grain with swift nods and prancing of little raspberry-coloured feet. Anyone would think they had not had a square meal for a week.

In the first few seconds the man is visible down to the waist, then you can just discern his head among the wings, and finally he vanishes completely in a cyclone of pigeons. If the man has a young son or daughter, his children might well fear, watching him feed the birds for the first time, that their beloved progenitor would never emerge; that, when the flurry of wings parts, there will be nothing on the pavement but the empty bucket, a peaked cap and a dust-coat! But no; a few thousand fly off to the left, a few thousand to the right; and there he is, like some early martyr, unharmed amid the turmoil.

§ 2

When the mediaeval V.I.P. visited Venice, the showpiece was the Arsenal. The stranger was shown a keel in the morning and, in the evening, he was taken to see a completed galley floating on the water. A speed record was set up in 1551 when the arrival of young Henry III of France threw Venice into a frenzy of hospitality. Upon that occasion the monarch saw a keel and ribs before he sat down to dinner, and when he had finished (though it must have been considerably later, for there were three thousand guests and twelve hundred dishes!), he watched a galley being launched from the slipway. During the war with the Turks, the Arsenal turned out a new galley every day for a hundred successive days, and this was possible because the Venetians were the inventors of the assembly line. A Spaniard named Pero Tafur, who visited the Arsenal in 1438, described how a newly-built galley was towed past a number of sheds, and, as she proceeded, one shed handed out cordage, a second, arms, a third, cannon, a fourth, food; and by the time the ship had reached the end of the dock-yard the crew were lined up ready to go aboard and take her to sea.

The Arsenal today is rather a pathetic survival to anyone who goes there remembering its past. Clustered round its imposing gateway are several stone lions brought back from various places by Venetian captains. One bears upon its rump Nordic runes, which some believe may have been cut by soldiers of the Varangian Guard; another, an elongated dachshund of a lion, came from Greece; it is one of a family that sits on trust among the white rocks of the heavenly isle of Delos. The visitor enters what is now a naval museum, though he catches a glimpse now and then of the famous dockyard, covering eighty acres, where sixteen thousand well-trained men once worked in a tumult of hammering and sawing, and where bubbling cauldrons of tar suggested to Dante the lake of boiling pitch in which fraudulent men were immersed in Hell; but the place is now silent, save for the occasional stammer of a pneumatic riveter or the bleat of a tramp steamer coming in for a minor repair.

The museum is full of arms, of captured ensigns, and of those long Lepanto pennants which also fly in many Spanish cathedrals; there are a few fragments of the Bucentaur, saved before that emblem of Venetian splendour was degraded in public on the Giudecca at the command of Napoleon, and all its gold-leaf melted down. What interested me most were the beautiful scale models of the various types of Venetian galleys. I saw the kind of craft that fed Europe with pepper, cinnamon, and cloves until the Cape route to India short-circuited the spice trade. All galleys of the same class were standardized, so that Venetian dockyards in all parts of the world had the correct spare parts, and a new crew could immediately take over a new ship, finding everything about it familiar. Venetian ships were 'as like to another as swallows' nests', as a fifteenth century writer put it.

They were also the finest ships of the time. The timber from the mainland forests was towed to Venice in great rafts, where it was laid down to mature for ten years in salt tanks at the Lido. Every nail, every rope, every scrap of sail was made in the Arsenal, and of the finest materials. The shipyard was not only the mainspring of Venetian wealth and power, it was also the pride of the Republic. I saw a trireme of the type in which I imagine Felix Fabri and his fellow pilgrims took ship from Venice to Jaffa in 1483. The hundred and eighty rowers were arranged in banks of three; the galley was about a hundred and forty feet long and could carry five hundred tons of cargo.

I know no other writer who describes, as Fabri does, the ordinary little details of how one booked a passage in a galley, how one arranged one's berth, how one ate, the kind of people one was likely to meet, and the ups and downs of a voyage in the fifteenth century. Looking at these models, one is struck by the beauty and elegance of their lines, and by the hardships of those who rowed them and the cramped quarters of the passengers. The only luxury was in the three-storey stern 'castle' occupied by the pilot and the helmsman (assisted, says Fabri, by 'certain cunning men, astrologers and soothsayers, who watch the signs of the stars and the sky', and could even detect omens in the smell of the bilge water); below were the captain's quarters and beneath them 'the place wherein noble ladies were housed at night, and where the captain's treasure is stored': but the ordinary pilgrims slept side by side, and foot to foot, in the long, barn-like space beneath the rowers. They lay on their own mattresses and in their own blankets, which were rolled up by day and hung on hooks. Beneath them was nothing but the ballast covered with boards that could be lifted in places. This the pilgrims often did to cool their wine bottles and eggs in the sand. Fabri tells us that if a poor man died at sea he was thrown overboard, but if a senator of Venice happened to die, his body was 'gutted like a fish' (an operation which Fabri was to watch with the greatest interest), and his coffin hidden deep in the ballast.

There were no regular sailings, but when sufficient pilgrims had gathered in Venice the Signory appointed certain galleys to take them across the sea. The moment Fabri and his companions had arrived, they went to the Piazza and saw, in front of S. Mark's, two flag-poles flying the crusading flag, a red cross on a white ground, a sign that passages could be booked there. Beside each flag stood the agents of the two galleys, each one canvassing for his own ship and disparaging the captain, the crew, and the accommodation of the other. As both galleys were at anchor off the Piazzetta, the pilgrims did the most sensible thing and went to look over both of them. They were greeted courteously by the captains, given a glass of Cretan wine and sweetmeats from Alexandria, and shown over the ships. Fabri and his fellow pilgrims decided on the trireme, as the larger, cleaner, and newer galley, and, having settled the price of their passages, went ashore and, in conference together, drew up a contract of twenty clauses, which the captain signed in the Doge's Palace before the notaries of the Republic. Some of the clauses are naturally rather curious. One bound the captain to protect the pilgrims, if necessary, from the crew, another bound him to provide sufficient space for the hens and poultry of his passengers, a third bound him, should any die during the voyage, not to fling them overboard but to bury them, when possible, on land.

Several weeks passed before the galley was ready to sail, but at last the passengers were told to go aboard with their bedding and food and find their places in the dark undercroft of the ship. It was a fearsome adventure for those who had never been to sea before and now found themselves in the bewildering community of mariners, carpenters, archers, barber-surgeons, and astrologers. All the pilgrims had previously consulted a doctor, who gave them a purge and written instructions on how to be healthy at sea. When the moment for departure arrived, the captain ordered the ship to be dressed. Sailors swarmed up the mainmast and decorated the top-castle with tapestry; several large banners flew out in the wind, the red cross of the Holy Land, the red Lion of S. Mark, the green oak tree and golden acorns of Sixtus IV, the reigning Pope, and the captain's flag quartered with the arms of Venice. The crew hauled up the anchors, the sails spread and filled with wind, and 'with great rejoicing we sailed away from the land: for the trumpeters blew their trumpets just as though we were about to join battle, the galley-slaves shouted, and all the pilgrims sang together *"In Gottes Nahmen fahren wir".*'

Those who say that Venice did not employ galley-slaves until the sixteenth century cannot have read Fabri, whose narrative proves that the system was already well established. He had a strong feeling of compassion for the wretched men who worked, ate and slept at their benches, but he adds nothing new to our knowledge of the hardships they endured. He tells us, however, that every galley-slave had something to sell hidden under his bench, and that their wine was considered superior to that served in the ship. Thirsty passengers could always obtain a drink between meals by buying one from the galley-slaves, while the alcoholically-inclined could leave the table as soon as a meal was over and go immediately to the galley-slaves and 'sit down and spend the whole day over their wine. This is usually done by Saxons, Flemings and other men of low class'.

The galley-slaves were not always straining at the oar: indeed, when the ship was under sail they had nothing to do but to 'sit and play at cards and dice for gold and silver, with execrable oaths and blasphemies'. Their food must have been revolting, and was prepared for them as they sat at their oars. Fabri says he often saw them eating raw meat. Now and again they had a windfall when rich nobles, disliking the ordinary menu, 'gave the cooks great sums of money to do separate meals of their own food, while they hand over the captain's food to the poor galley-slaves'. But they had their moments of freedom. Fabri mentions seeing them stream ashore at some little town carrying bundles full of objects for sale in the local market place. As they were to a man inveterate thieves, says Fabri, one wonders what treasures found their way to unlikely places via the rowing bench. Probably the privilege of making a little money was a relic of the old days when the citizen rowers of Venice were allowed to take a certain amount of duty-free goods for sale abroad. Molmenti mentions the odd custom among Venetian rowers of inviting S. Phocas to dinner every night when at sea, a peculiar guest, for he is the patron saint of Greek gardens and gardeners, and may be seen, spade in hand, among the mosaics of S. Mark's. As the saint never appeared, the cost of his dinner was put aside by the rowers day by day and given to the poor when the ship returned to port.

Though conditions of life at sea have changed, the passengers remain fundamentally the same, and among Fabri's fellow voyagers we can recognize some to be found on any Cunarder today. He mentions the sudden ship friendships and the equally sudden enmities. 'I have marked it for a fact,' he says, 'that the movement of all human passions is more violent on the water than elsewhere.' On calm days the pilgrims enjoyed themselves in a number of familiar ways. 'Some play for money, some of them with a board and dice, others with the dice alone, some with cards, others with chess-boards. . . . Some sing songs or pass their time with lutes, flutes, bagpipes, clavichords, zithers and other musical instruments'; an ordeal the modern traveller is happily spared, though it seems possible to recognize the predecessor of the deck-tennis enthusiast in those who 'show their strength by lifting heavy weights or doing other feats'. Darkness brought with it what must have been the most unpleasant moment in a galley – going to bed. The confusion, the noise, the dust shaken up as the pilgrims spread out their mattresses and made their beds, was appalling. Quarrels were frequent when those who had been sitting late on deck came down and blundered in the dark over the legs of their companions. 'I have seen some hot-tempered pilgrims,' says Fabri, 'throw their chamber-pots at burning lights to put them out', as 'some begin to settle the affairs of the world with their neighbours, and go on talking sometimes up to midnight . . .' These, after all, were the minor trials of life in a galley. 'There is,' said Fabri, 'among all the occupations of seafarers one which, albeit loathsome, is yet very common, daily and necessary – I mean the hunting and catching of lice and vermin. Unless a man spends several hours in this work when he is in a pilgrimage, he will have but unquiet slumbers . . . In the course of time mice and rats breed in a ship in great numbers, and they run about all night long, nibble at men's private larders, and gnaw their way into them and befoul the food, spoil pillows and shoes, and fall on men's faces while they sleep. . . .'

One looks at these model ships in the Arsenal with greater understanding, thanks to Fabri, and though they appear so neat and clean, one knows that beneath the benches was that foul tunnel where the pilgrims lay side by side. Fabri confesses that he sometimes stole over the prostrate figures of his fellows in the night and went up to breathe the fresh air on deck with the feeling that he had escaped from a stinking prison.

§ 3

I spent a pleasant hour in the palatial Correr Museum, which faces S. Mark's across the Piazza, where a number of curious relics of old Venice are preserved. I saw the robes of Doge and Senator, shoes and hats, masks and dominoes, these last rather creased and weary, and lacking in the jaunty air of wickedness so familiar in the pictures of Longhi and Guardi. What a singular object the ducal *corno* was, the Phrygian cap of liberty with which the Doge was crowned. It varied, not in shape, but in material from century to century. Sometimes it was plain, but more often jewelled, and always worn over the little white cap of fine cambric called the *vittà*. The miniature *corno* worn by the Dogaressa was an absurd enough little hat, but no doubt it looked impressive as the finishing touch to a majestic matron in a regal gown.

One of the most ludicrous eccentricities of fashion is to be seen here, *zoccoli* or *choppines*, which were worn by Venetian ladies for hundreds of years until, it is said, the good sense of a Doge's daughter abolished them in the seventeenth century. They were an exaggerated kind of patten, sometimes eighteen inches high, on which the wives and daughters of the nobility tottered about, as if on stilts, lifted head and shoulders above everyone else and resting their hands for support upon the heads of elderly attendants. In this position they were seen in 1645 and described by John Evelyn. 'It is ridiculous to see how these ladies crawl in and out of their gondolas by reason of their *choppines*,' he wrote, 'and what dwarfs they appear, when taken down from their wooden scaffolds; of these I saw near thirty together, stalking half as high again as the rest of the world.' Some think that this ridiculous fashion originated in the harems or bath-houses of Constantinople, others say that it was invented in Venice, possibly, as some cynic told Evelyn, to keep women at home. *Choppines* were beautifully made and light in weight, but nothing could render them elegant: all of them, even when gilded, look like old-fashioned surgical boots.

The Correr Museum has the original of Carpaccio's famous picture, *The Courtesans,* which launched Ruskin into one of his wilder eulogies. I agree with E. V. Lucas that there is nothing to suggest that these two dismal-looking females, perhaps mother and daughter, are not persons of unimpeachable virtue; indeed, if Evelyn was correct when he said that *choppines* were forbidden to courtesans, then the presence of a pair of these in a corner should have cleared their characters long ago. To me, these two women are a marvellous study in boredom. There are various degrees of boredom, and this is obviously the nadir. What makes their state so tragic is that they are dressed up and have taken enormous trouble with their hair, which has been washed, dyed, and sprinkled with gold dust, yet they have nothing to do, nowhere to go, and sit, relaxed and unsmiling, on some balcony or roof-top among birds and dogs which amuse them no longer. This picture proclaims the fact that Venice was a gay and wicked city for everyone but the wives and daughters of the upper classes, as these appear to have been. By a touch of irony these two flaccid and unattractive women have gone down the ages as courtesans.

I looked everywhere in the museum for some relic of the twelve thousand courtesans, the great tourist attraction of Venice for centuries, but I could not find even one of the red and yellow dresses 'like tulips', which they were supposed to wear at one period, or a picture of the most celebrated brothel in Europe, on the Rialto. It would have been interesting to have seen some portraits of these famous courtesans. I would like to know what Veronica Franco looked like, who fell so deeply in love with Henry III of France that after his brief visit to Venice she retired from business and devoted herself to good works and poetry. Most travellers had something to say of the Venetian courtesans. Montaigne was surprised to see them 'spending money like princesses on dress and furniture'; other writers mention that every gondolier was in the pay of a courtesan, and unless a passenger was firm and explicit he would find himself deposited at her door. Countless young men crossed the Alps for this very purpose. Lassels says that some young noblemen on their way to Venice could not rest properly until they found themselves in the city of their dreams. 'So infinite are the allurements of these amorous Calypsoes,' wrote Tom Coryat in 1608, 'that the fame of them hath drawn many to Venice from some of the remotest parts of Christendome.'

Coryat describes in his *Crudities* how he visited a courtesan because he wished to reform her – an explanation perhaps not heard for the last time – and the account of his reception, and the engraving which he published in his book, showing his meeting with Margarita Emeliana, '*bella cortesana di Venezia*', are interesting. Describing his arrival at the lady's house, he said, 'You seeme to enter into the Paradise of Venus. As for herself, she comes to thee decked like the Queene and Goddesse of Love.' This was the moment shown in his illustration. We see him, grandly dressed and cloaked, hat in hand, making a bow to a pretty young woman who advances to embrace him. Her hair is a mass of crisp blonde curls, she wears a necklace of pearls the size of bantam eggs, and a fashionable fringed gown of rich figured brocade and a ruff. Her gown stops short above the waist, exposing her breasts in that fashion which originated with the courtesans of Venice and was adopted by many virtuous women all over Europe. The revelation evidently surprised and shocked Coryat, though the type of dress was well known in England in his day. 'Almost all the wives, widowes and mayds do walke abroad with their breasts all naked,' he writes, 'and many of them have their backs also naked even almost to the middle, which some do cover with a single linnen, as cobwebbe lawn, or such other thinne stuffe: a fashion methinks very uncivil and unseemly.' Nevertheless, two Queens of England are said to have worn such gowns, Elizabeth I and Anne of Denmark, and Elizabethan writers often mention virtuous women with their breasts 'embared' and 'layed forth'.

As I went from room to room, I thought that any other museum of this kind would show a great number of feminine objects, relics of famous women, portraits and so on; but not in Venice. Perhaps

the strangest thing about a state which could claim the longest continuous history in Europe is the absence of distinguished women.
Only the courtesan of the earlier centuries and the emancipated
wife of the eighteenth century, with her *cisisbeo*, represent women
in the history of the Venetian Republic. In fact, the most memorable Venetian women were created in England – Portia, Jessica,
Nerissa, and Desdemona, while Byron's Margarita Cogni, the
'Fornarina', leaps out of anonymity with welcome clarity as a
creature of flesh and blood.

Some writers have said that the Venetian attitude to women was
semi-oriental, and this may be so; but I think the Venetians were
also afraid of women, or rather of feminine indiscretion. Centuries of guile, stealth, and spying had made Venice the most
cautious community on earth, a state so secretive and suspicious
than one rash word might ruin a man. It was typical of the Venetian attitude to women that an ambassador might take his cook
abroad, but not his wife. Venice did not trust its women: it had
too many secrets.

§ 4

Wonderful glimpses of the masculine world of Venice as it was
centuries ago are the famous scenes painted by Gentile Bellini and
Carpaccio, which draw thousands of people to the Accademia on
the Grand Canal. They were painted about 1495–1500, for the
Guild of S. John, to illustrate incidents in the history of the Guild's
treasured relic of the True Cross.

One day, while this relic was being carried along the Rio di S.
Lorenzo during a religious ceremony, it fell into the canal. Immediately men stripped to their underclothes and dived in – a
negro slave was just about to do so from a near-by house – but the
warden of the Guild, leaping in fully clothed, recovered the relic.
That was the incident chosen by Gentile Bellini. He also painted a
superb picture of S. Mark's Square during the procession of the
True Cross. We see the relic carried beneath a rich canopy hung
with the armorial shields of the Venetian trade guilds. It is escorted
by chanting priests holding candles, and followed by a long

procession of notables led by the Doge himself, walking beneath the state umbrella. This picture is a famous pictorial document. If the camera had been invented in 1496 it could not have told us more, if indeed as much. The square was paved with brick; the thirteenth century mosaics glittered on the front of the basilica; and the clock tower had not yet been built.

Carpaccio painted an equally splendid pictorial document – the Grand Canal in 1496. It is dotted with gondolas, but not the kind we know today. They are little painted canoes. The rule that they must be black in colour had not yet been made, neither had the distinctive *ferro* arrived, that curious steel blade with six notches that faces outward from the prow: but, strangest of all, was the gondolier himself, a decorative young man with hair down to his shoulders, a jaunty cap with a feather falling over one ear, a vivid tunic with slashed sleeves pinched in at the waist, and tights, striped red and white, or in black and white checks. The palaces along the canal are the mediaeval predecessors of the present buildings. They are mostly of red brick and marble, with Gothic windows, and roofs sprouting those curious funnel-shaped chimneys, some of which still survive in Venice. There is a wonderful glimpse along the Rialto, past the famous *bordello*, to the Rialto Bridge, which was made of wood, probably, I should think, by ships' carpenters. It was a covered bridge, as the present one is, and looks rather like two large wooden sheds or horse-boxes tilted upwards from opposite sides of the canal and joined in the centre by a drawbridge that could be raised to admit a ship. The incident depicted in this wonderful scene is the healing of a demented man. We see him standing in the foreground, on a palace balcony, surrounded by praying clergy, while the Patriarch of Grado, quite a young clean-shaven patriarch wearing a red skull-cap, holds the reliquary towards him.

Carpaccio's cycle of nine pictures, the *Legend of S. Ursula*, is to be seen in an adjoining room. Though it tells the story of the eleven thousand virgins of Cologne, Carpaccio, like a true Venetian, continues to paint a man's world and keeps the virgins in the background. There is, however, one immortal feminine picture in this series, the well-known *Dream of S. Ursula*. In this charming bedroom scene the young saint is seen chastely tucked up in one half of a double-bed. Her slippers are beside the bed just as she stepped out of them, her little dog is waiting for her to wake up. The morning sunlight is entering the neat Venetian room, illuminating the pot plants on the window-sill and also an angel, who enters on a golden beam to help Ursula solve her complex problem: how to reconcile her vow of life-long chastity with marriage.

I thought my favourite Carpaccio, *S. Jerome in his Study,* might be in the Accademia, but I looked in vain. I found it eventually not far from my hotel in the Scuola di San Giorgio degli Schiavoni. Within the last five or six years this picture has been renamed the *Vision of S. Augustine,* following an interesting piece of detection by Helen J. Roberts, who pointed out that S. Jerome was never a bishop, therefore the mitre and crozier seen in the background of this picture could not belong to him. Who then is the owner of this enchanting study, sitting, pen in hand, gazing doubtfully out of the window, a moment familiar to most writers? The scene evidently depicts S. Augustine, who *was* a bishop, at the moment when, according to a well-known story, he was writing a letter to S. Jerome, unaware that at that very moment the saint had passed away in his cell at Bethlehem. Augustine writes in one of the most pleasant and elegant work-rooms in Renaissance art, with green walls and a carved and gilt ceiling and an attractive and untidy desk near a window. The most prominent object in the scene, after the saint himself, is a small, curly-haired white dog, which perhaps should have given critics the clue long ago that S. Jerome, whose pet was a lion, could not possibly be the owner of this mouthful. The little creature gazes up at his thoughtful master with the expression of one who is anxious to help, and if any dog were able to provide a writer with the word that eludes him, this, one feels, is the animal.

I am sure that Augustine's pet could not have been painted by anyone who was not himself devoted to dogs, and to small, gallant, quick-witted ones in particular; and as I found my way back through narrow lanes and over arched bridges, I reflected that a pleasant book could be written by someone who knows all about dogs, like Brian Vesey-Fitzgerald, on the dogs of the great painters. One could find dozens of them. Carpaccio painted many. Surely the same curly-haired little dog in S. Augustine's study, or a near relative, is to be seen seated in his master's gondola in Carpaccio's picture of the Grand Canal? S. Ursula's small dog is a different breed, smooth-haired and crop-eared.

Some notable dogs were painted by Velazquez. I remember the big, drowsy long-haired dog who nods among the dwarfs in *Las Meninas*, in the Prado, in Madrid, while the little princess, tricked out in her bows and flounces, is posing for the painter. Another big, somnolent dog by Velazquez lies, tired out, old and far too fat, at the feet of young Don Carlos as he stands in hunting dress, grasping a musket in a gloved hand. I also remember a sympathetic brown dog of obscure ancestry seated sadly beside the dying Procris in the National Gallery in London, and among the top dogs of art is the bright-eyed little animal in Van Eyck's *Marriage of Giovanni Arnolfini,* also in Trafalgar Square.

§ 5

An absence of public statuary is a Venetian charm which possibly has not been sufficiently admired. It is true that since 1870 a few statues have arrived – Victor Emmanuel, Goldoni, Garibaldi – but one scarcely notices them, and they have an air of intrusion. No other great city has taken a more sombre view of its immortals, and possibly the reason is that a capitalistic state run by the secret service had too much in the files to become romantic about anybody. In any event, the Venetian temperament was, and, I think remains, basically sceptical, and it was easier to erect a memorial to an evildoer as a deterrent than to exalt Venetian virtue, which was assumed to be its own reward. It is this rarity of prancing horsemen, and even of comparatively harmless persons such as explorers and artists, which helps to make the statue of Colleoni so striking when you see it for the first time. I came upon it one morning after having examined the tombs of more than forty Doges in the Church of SS. Giovanni e Paolo, which the Venetian tongue fires off as S. Zanipolo. And there he was, the great *condottiere*, riding his splendid stallion over the edge of a narrow and graceful plinth, looking as fierce as if he had conquered Asia instead of having conducted a lot of bargains and gentlemen's agreements, and amassing an enormous fortune in the process.

I remembered his lovely little lace-like chapel in Bergamo and his farm in the hills not far away, and it is to me strange that, knowing Venice as he did, he should have left his fortune to her on the condition that his statue should be erected in the Piazza of S. Mark. Surely he must have known that the Signory would double-cross him? Such a tribute was entirely against Venetian tradition, and I can only think that the old soldier was so eaten up with jealousy at the thought of Gattamelata proudly riding his war-horse outside the basilica of S. Anthony at Padua, that he was blinded to reality. Venice, of course, banked the money and put the statue in an obscure campo outside the church of S. Zanipolo.

It was once gilded, and I think a discreet gleam, like that on Marcus Aurelius in Rome, might not be a mistake. It is one of those great works of art which killed its creator. Verrocchio, the sculptor, caught a cold while in the foundry during the casting of the bronze, and this led to his death. Before he died he asked that his pupil, Lorenzo di Credi, should complete the statue, but Venice had other plans. The Signory recalled from exile Alessandro Leopardi, who had been convicted of forgery, and told him to finish the work, which he did so well that he earned a pardon. So Gattamelata at Padua and Colleoni in Venice are the two first bronze horsemen of the modern world, and naturally they invite comparison. They are both so powerful that it is almost impossible to say which is the finer.

The campo is celebrated in the history of gallantry as the scene of Casanova's rendezvous with a pretty young nun whom he had spied in one of the convents. As he paced up and down waiting, she appeared alone, dressed as a gallant in black satin breeches and a coat of pink velvet in the pocket of which she carried an English pistol.

I thought it should be easy, with the help of a map, to walk across Venice from the statue of Colleoni to the Friary Church on the opposite side of the Grand Canal, and I started off with success, crossing to the other bank by the Rialto Bridge; but I found myself hopelessly lost. I regained the Grand Canal and took a *vaporetto*, which landed me near a large Franciscan church. It stands next to an awe-inspiring building, the State Archives of Venice, where unknown tons of documents are kept in some three hundred rooms. Here are the secrets of the world which Venice liked to possess, written long ago by candle-light in all the capital cities, east and west: hard facts about money and trade; gossip about love and adultery; stories of birth and death; all the countless fragments about governments and individuals which ambassadors, spies, merchants, and soldiers were continually scribbling for the Serenissima to piece together in order to chart the world's political reefs and undercurrents. Here is the great machine, motionless now, which made the Council of the Ten feared, the very cradle of 'the birthplace of statistics', as Burckhardt called Venice. Tons of these documents have never been read since they were received and filed away; the earliest was written when the Vikings were raiding England, the latest in the final year of the Republic.

The Friary Church was high and cool and empty. I thought it was bleak and disappointing, though I found what I had come to see, the tomb of Titian. When I was leaving, I looked towards the high altar and saw one of the artist's most famous Madonnas, thinking how strange that the floodlighting should have been left switched on in an empty church. I walked up to it with the idea of turning off the light, if I could find the switch, but found that there was no lighting except that which Titian had mixed with his paint.

It is said that he was ninety-nine, and still at work, when the plague carried him off, and of all the thousands who died at that time, he was the only one to be given a public funeral. He was an enormously prolific artist and I suppose his surviving canvases number many hundreds. His friendship for Pietro Aretino, blackmailer and pornographer, the Frank Harris of sixteenth century

Italy, has puzzled many of the artist's admirers, though surely there is nothing to wonder about. Genius has always made odd friends, and Aretino must have been marvellous company, a fascinating combination of vitality, generosity, and Rabelaisian laughter, a man who loved life and enjoyed the gutter as much as the palace. He circulated in the highest society and kept every letter written to him neatly documented in ebony cabinets – kings, princes, cardinals, dukes, duchesses, all had their separate files.

He lived in a rambling palace on the Grand Canal opposite the fish market, a house filled with ambiguous females whom he had befriended, children, the lame and the halt, who flocked to him and were never turned away. He was visited by the most exalted people of the time as well as by all kinds of rogues. He detested the idea of marriage and once made the superb remark that 'my children are legitimate in my heart'. Another was that he lived 'by the sweat of his ink'. He was thirty-four and Titian was forty-nine when the friendship began, and the two men, becoming inseparable, saw one another every day. If Titian felt he needed a change, he would go and paint in a well-lit room in Aretino's house; if Aretino's disorganized household got on his nerves, he would escape to Titian. If either received a haunch of venison or a jar of caviare from a noble patron, he would at once invite the other to share it. When Titian's lovely wife, Cecilia, died in childbirth, as so many women did in that age, the artist moved to a house on the Biri Grande with a view northward across the lagoon to Murano. There, at night under a vine-trellis, with the lights of the gondolas bobbing on the water, Titian would invite Aretino and his friends to dinner. There was a third friend, as devoted to Titian and Aretino as they were to him, Sansovino, the architect of the Library in the Piazzetta. He was married to a beautiful wife, Paola, who kept a firm hand on him, so one fancies that he was sometimes absent from the more hilarious parties.

It was through the influence of the extraordinary Aretino that Titian received a command to paint the Emperor Charles V, which was the foundation of his fortunes. Aretino never ceased to praise his friend to all his noble correspondents, and his championship of Titian became rather absurd. When it seemed to him that Tintoretto was receiving praise and commissions which should have gone to Titian, Aretino began to slander and libel the younger painter. Fortunately for him, Tintoretto's poverty saved him from blackmail, though the threadbare clothes which the proud young painter's wife patched up for him made him an easy target for Aretino's scorn. It is said that one day Tintoretto, baited beyond endurance, decided to have it out with Aretino. Meeting him in the street, he said that he would like to paint a portrait of him, and Aretino, delighted to get something for nothing, arrived at Tintoretto's studio on the following day. He took a chair on the dais and adopted an attitude, but Tintoretto said 'Stand up', and approached, holding a long horse-pistol. 'First, I must measure you,' said the painter, running the horse-pistol over his sitter, 'and I find you two pistols and a half high. Now – go!' It is said that from that moment all slander ceased, and Aretino began to praise and flatter Tintoretto.

When Aretino died at the age of sixty-four in the year 1556, Titian must have felt that some mighty natural force had been extinguished. Aretino's end was as characteristic as everything else about him. It is said that while listening to an improper story about his sister he fell out of his chair in uncontrollable laughter and died of apoplexy.

§ 6

Nothing surprised me more in Venice than the fact that you can still buy the world's oldest medicine there – *Teriaca*. It is sold in a chemist's shop called the *Testa d'Oro*, not far from the Rialto Bridge, and the sign, a golden head, overhangs the pavement. The shop has been in business since 1500, but started to make *Teriaca* late in the history of that remedy, in 1603.

The word 'treacle' comes from *Teriaca* or *Teriacle*, and as 'Venetian Treacle' it appears in all the travel books and letters of the seventeenth century. In those days a traveller might fail to have his portrait painted in Venice, or he might not take home with him a collection of Murano glass, but no one would dream of leaving Venice without a supply of the famous specific.

The history of *Teriaca* begins with Mithridates, King of Pontus, who died sixty-three years before Christ, a man who feared poison so much that he took a small quantity every day, followed by its antidote, but in doing this he became such a toxicological laboratory that when he really wished to take a fatal dose, after his defeat by Pompey, nothing would work; and he had to use a sword. Among the booty which fell into Pompey's hands was the king's medical library, with the prescription for *Mithridaticum*, the famous general antidote against poison. It was the result of years of research into the effect of every known kind of poison upon the bodies of condemned criminals.

The formula passed into the hands of Nero's doctor, Andromachus, who added various little touches of his own and launched it upon its astounding career as *Theriaca Andromachi*, which became the most famous cure-all ever known. It was recommended to Alfred the Great by Helia, the Patriarch of Jerusalem; it was taken to the Holy Land by the Crusaders; and among the treasures of Henry V of England was a 'triacle box'. The Middle Ages dosed themselves with *teriaca* for everything from toothache to the plague, and the Renaissance inherited a blind faith in it. Among the strangest of all survivals surely is the fact that *Teriaca* can still be bought in Venice.

Entering the *Testa d'Oro* one morning, I said to the chemist, 'I wish to buy some *Teriaca*.' I thought he looked surprised, and for a moment fancied he might ask me to sign the poison book.

'Just one tin, signore?' he asked politely.

I asked for two tins and he went to a cupboard, as if he were about to sell me aspirin and not a remedy that originated two thousand years ago, and returning, handed me two small cylinders which looked like spools of film in metal containers, but very dirty and rusty ones. Wrapped round each tin was a sheet of instructions, printed on paper that had turned brown with age. At the top was a pleasant woodcut of the 'Golden Head' surrounded by brimming cornucopias; and I read '*Theriaca Andromachi Senioris, Divinum Inventum*'. I saw that the purchaser was warned to guard against imitations and falsifications, as if counterfeit brands might be thrust on him at every street corner.

I commented on the obvious age of the tins and their wrapping. 'The last time we made *Teriaca*,' said the chemist, 'was thirty years ago. We still have a fair supply of it.'

'And what is it good for?' I asked.

He replied with the voice of Antiquity, of the Middle Ages, of the Renaissance. 'For *everything*,' he said. Then, perhaps thinking I appeared a little doubtful, he said it was a general tonic and particularly efficacious in cases of *affezioni intestinali* and *dolori di ventre*.

When I returned to my hotel, I unwrapped one tin and saw that in the course of the past thirty years some *Teriaca* had oozed out in a sinister way and had gummed down the lid. I chiselled round this with a penknife and prised it open. Inside, I saw a thick, black, shining fluid which was sticky, but had no smell. I poured some of it out and applied a match, half expecting a puff of smoke in which an alchemist might appear, but nothing happened: the fluid refused to catch fire but bubbled and sizzled and eventually formed a hard black bead. Curiosity now getting the better of discretion, I poured out a third of a teaspoon, which I noted is the dose for a child of four, and swallowed it. There was a bitter aftertaste, like quinine.

The next time I passed the *Testa d'Oro* I looked in and told the chemist that since taking *Teriaca* I had never felt better. At first he nodded solemnly, then we both burst out laughing. But *Teriaca*, he told me, still has those who believe in it as firmly as anyone in the time of Alfred the Great. Old residents of Venice, and the fisherwomen from the islands, would not dream of being without it in the house. I asked if he could give me the prescription. Certainly, there was no secret about it; but how sadly it has been cut down since the seventeenth century when it contained more than sixty drugs. Now *Teriaca* is made of nutmeg-butter, Gentian root, Comedrios, Ivatetica, hyssop, Imperico, and clarified butter. I must admit it is quite esoteric enough for me!

In the old days, I was told, in order to prevent fraudulent brews, *Teriaca* had to be made in public at certain stated times of the year and the process was supervised by the doctors and the health authorities. For several days beforehand the drugs to be used were displayed in garlanded jars in the windows of the chemists' shops, then, when the day arrived, mortars and cauldrons were placed in the street outside, and porters wearing white jackets and red breeches, yellow shoes, and blue caps with feathers in them, pounded away for hours. I was told that a cracked paving stone in Venice is often a sign that it once paved the way to a pharmacy.

Among the ingredients of the original *Teriaca* were Illyrian iris, myrrh, nard, and incense, Cretan dittany, Celtic spikenard, Balsam fruit, Opoponax, Balm of Gilead, Jewish bitumen, and earth from Lemnos. This was the most historic of all ingredients: it was known as early as the time of Herodotus as an antidote against poison, and was mined from a red hill on the island. In classical times it was mixed with goats' blood and made into little cakes and stamped with the image of Diana. This *terra di Lemnia* survived the end of paganism and was eagerly prescribed by mediaeval doctors; but perhaps, needless to add, not all of it came from Lemnos.

'After the drugs, spices, and the oils had been pounded or boiled, sometimes for days,' said the chemist, 'all sixty ingredients were mixed together with warm honey, and the brew was stirred continuously for three hours.'

The makers of patent medicines, who spend fortunes today in advertising their cures, could not buy such publicity as that given by the Government of Venice to the periodic brews of the famous cure. Everyone knew when this was to happen and everyone went to see it. When Evelyn was in Venice in 1645, he not only bought himself a supply of *Teriaca* (he may even have bought it at the *Testa d'Oro*), but he also witnessed one of the brewings, which he described as 'worth seeing' and 'extremely pompous'.

I should add that every city in Italy once made its own brand of *Teriaca*, but naturally that of Venice, Queen of the Spice Trade, was considered the best. It was exported everywhere and England consumed tons of it, though one regrets to say that the Italian profiteer and adulterator was at work even in Tudor and Stuart times. Queen Elizabeth's apothecary complained 'that straungers

doe dayly send into England a false and naughty kinde of Mith-
ridatium and Threacle in great barrelles more than a thousand
weight in a year', and in 1612, the Master and Wardens of the
Grocers' Company in London noted that 'a filthy and unwhole-
some baggage composition was being brought into this realm as
Tryacle of Genoa, made only of the rotten garble and refuse out-
cast of all kinds of spices and drugs, hand overhead with a little
filthy molasses and tarre to worke it up withal'.

The potion continued to appear in the *London Pharmacopeia*,
(together with earth worm and moss grown on human skulls),
until 1746.

§ 7

I could see nothing in the glass shops of Venice which I would
like to possess, indeed most of the glass on view looked to me
hideous and I thought it sad to see an ancient craft in decline.
Among the memories of such displays are windows full of glass
harelequins, some standing on their heads, figures from American
strip-cartoons, comic dogs, and vulgar little goblets dusted with
gold. I had the feeling that Venice has been making glass for so
long that the process has become too easy, and technique has now
replaced style and design. One longed to see something simple
and beautiful. Curiously enough, that is what people said in the
sixteenth century, when, looking round for something to take
home, they were repelled by drinking-glasses in the shape of ships,
whales, lions, and birds. Perhaps the present exuberance is therefore
only one of those periodic lapses which must be expected in an
art as ancient as this.

The morning I went to Murano, where the glass-blowers have
been grouped since the thirteenth century, was one of those pearl-
grey moments when the lagoon lies under a spell and the islands
loom up in the stillness like a mirage. The boat moved over water
that looked as if an enormous sheet of grey glass had spread from
Murano, and even our wake was vitreous: it spread slowly outward until it rocked the silhouettes of boats where men cut out of
grey paper were prodding the shallow water for shell-fish. The

boat was full of tourists, and I was seated next to an Australian woman who, unlike most visitors to Venice, was critical.

'Do you like Venice?' she asked, and when I appeared to hesitate, undecided in what way to frame a reply to such a peculiar question, she went on to tell me what *she* thought of it.

'The place needs a good clean up,' she said. 'All that trash floating about in the Grand Canal! Then those narrow streets full of people. Have you seen some just a few feet wide?'

'Yes,' I said, 'I live in one of them.'

'Oh you do,' she said. 'Does it smell? People come out of them just like rats from a sewer.'

'In my own particular sewer,' I said, 'we scurry.'

She looked at me disapprovingly.

'Then San Marco,' she continued,' I suppose you've been there. If ever a place needed a good wash! How different the English cathedrals are, so beautifully clean. I'm sure there isn't a speck of dust in the whole of Durham Cathedral.'

I said how pained I was that Venice had disappointed her.

'But I love it!' she cried. 'I think it's wonderful – but dirty! And have you been to the Lido? Well, take my advice, and don't go!'

She looked sternly at me. I was thinking of Goethe walking about the shore picking up shells like a delighted child (it was his first sight of the sea), and of Byron riding over the sands with Shelley.

'What is wrong with the Lido? Is it very dirty?' I asked.

'What is wrong with it is this,' she replied. 'You can't get near to the sea. Every hotel guards its little miserable bit of beach as if it were a gold-mine. You should see the beaches in Australia – miles of them and never a fence in sight! The place is also full of neurotics.'

I began to admire this iconoclast who seemed in my eyes to occupy a place among the select few who have refused to be bullied by the fame of Venice. 'This puddling in a tub continually is no charm to me,' said James, fourth Earl of Perth, in 1660. Dr John Moore also disliked 'being paddled about from morning to night in narrow boats along dirty canals', and even Mrs Piozzi, though so devoted to her 'dear Venetians', had much the same housewifely attitude to dirt as my Australian acquaintance, and deplored the Piazza 'all covered over in a morning with chicken-coops, which stink one to death . . .'

Suddenly the bright chatter in the boat was silenced as we saw, looming out of the greyness, a glimpse, startling and unexpected, of a more heroic age; a vision that for a fractional moment of time resembled the hooded queens bearing the body of Arthur to Avalon.

> *Then saw they how there hove a dusky barge*
> *Dark as a funeral scarf from stem to stern.*

And as we moved nearer the craft was revealed as a catafalque in the form of a carved gondola, black and silver, draped with purple, and with the Lion of S. Mark mourning in the prow, but, instead of the 'stately forms, black-stoled, black-hooded like a dream', which the apparition had seemed to promise for a second, we saw four old men, wearing black berets, bent above the oars. The Venetian hearse faded in the mist, and soon we saw the funeral isle of S. Michele, its cypress trees reflected in the still water, infinitely mournful and impressive. As we reached Murano the sun came out and the lagoon scintillated in the almost excessive brilliance of a Venetian morning.

A young salesman was waiting on a wooden jetty to take us to an adjacent glass-works where, in a dim cavern, we saw men with long blow-pipes extracting soft blobs of hot glass from furnaces. With little puffs, the obedient material expanded into the shapes required; it was snipped off with scissors, and, after a few more puffs and snips, another harlequin was born. Upstairs in a showroom we saw what the modern glass industry considers to be saleable, a fearful reflection on modern taste. I wondered how much glass is sold on these daily excursions, and if the boldly labelled crates consigned to London, Paris, New York, and so on, really contain glass. If so, who buys it? One fortunately never sees it anywhere.

I wandered off into Murano, over which brooded something of the untidy melancholy of Salford on a hot Sunday. In spite of such an uncompromising air, I liked the island and would love to have stayed there. It is really five diminutive islands linked together by wide curving canals, and upon the central isle I found a Byzantine basilica dedicated to S. Donatus. If, as I suppose, he was the Roman Donatus (the patron saint of Arezzo) martyred under Julian, perhaps he is honoured in Murano for having, among his miracles, put together a glass chalice broken by the barbarians in such a way that not a drop of the Sacrament was spilt. I promised myself that if ever I became tired of the brilliance of Venice, of the crowds, of the itching palms, I would retreat to Murano, which gives the impression of not caring a bit whether you go or stay.

Venice naturally takes all the limelight from Murano, though the island has a fascinating history. It is believed that when the mainland people fled to the lagoons from the Huns, the glass-workers among them opened workshops in their new home, and if this is so, Venetian glass has a pedigree that takes it back to the beautiful glass-ware of ancient Rome. Because of the danger of fire, all the furnaces were moved to Murano in the thirteenth century, and, as the export of glass was second in importance only to the seaborne commerce of Venice, the islanders were granted every kind of privilege. They were governed by their own magistrate, who was treated like a Doge, and the Venetian police had no power of arrest on Murano.

There was a carefully propagated story in the Middle Ages – an admirable example of sales talk – that Venetian glass would shatter at the first touch of poison: it was also said that glass-blowers who were bribed away from Murano by foreign governments or individuals would be hunted down and slain wherever they were. In spite of this, the history of European glass is that of Murano workers teaching their craft in other countries. Henry VIII of England, who collected Venetian glass, personally welcomed eight men from Murano and gave them a workroom near the Tower of London. They must have been doing well, or too well for the liking of Venice, since they were eventually recalled by the Council of Ten.

It used to be said of Venetian glass (and much the same thing is now said of Scotch whisky), that 'although one should transplant a glass-furnace from Murano to Venice herself, or to any of the little assembly of islands about her, or to any other part of the earth besides, and use the same materials, the same workmen, the same fuel, the self-same ingredients every way, yet they cannot make crystal glass in that perfection, for beauty and lustre, as in Murano'. The words are those of James Howell, the entertaining Welshman, who went to Murano in 1621 to lure some glass-workers to England, and offered the explanation that the glass-making virtues of the island were due to 'the circumambient air that hangs over the place' – no doubt another piece of propaganda.

If anyone should be surprised, as I was, by the unattractive objects produced today in Murano, he should, as a corrective, visit the Museo dell' Arte Vetraria on the island. There can be seen the Venetian glass of one's dreams: chalices, reliquaries, graceful cups, plates, and bowls as thin as air, some slightly blue or brown in colour, some crystal clear, and modern reproductions prove that, if the demand existed, the *maestri* of Murano could turn out glass today every bit as fine as that made by their ancestors.

I caught the boat with only a few moments to spare. My Australian acquaintance had kindly kept a place beside her and patted a cushion, on which I lowered myself obediently.

'So that we can have another nice talk,' she said.

As we moved away from the jetty, the young salesman, not looking too pleased with us, fired a parting sally at one of the tourists. 'We say here in Murano,' he laughed, 'that the first woman was made here, beautiful and – brittle!' There was an uneasy titter as the boat chugged off.

'Well, I wonder what that meant!' said my companion. She lit a cigarette and blew the smoke straight up into the air.

'Now,' she said, 'you must tell me what you thought of Murano.'

I listened with interest to her impressions all the way back to Venice.

§ 8

One morning I took a motor-boat to Torcello, which lies some way to the north of Murano, and is often described as an uninhabited island. This is not quite true: about a hundred fishermen live there. It was once one of the most distinguished of the twelve original settlements in the Venetian lagoon, and the ships' captains who stole the relics of S. Mark from Alexandria were men of Torcello and Burano.

The boat left me at a flight of four or five brick steps which led to what once may have been a landing-stage. There was not a soul in sight. The only building was a roofless shell, perhaps of a church, with a board fixed to the wall bearing the word 'Torcello'. Let into the wall was a statuette of the Blessed Virgin under a roofed shrine.

There is a touch of pathos in the very name of Torcello, which was the name of one of the towers in the city wall of Altinum. How sadly those Romans who remembered better days must have looked at this salty little island, and how they must have compared its rough makeshifts with the civilized urban life they had known. It was this urban homesickness, this Roman longing for an organized life under the law, that eventually drew the people of the lagoons together into the Republic of Venice.

A deserted and turgid canal led to the interior of the island, and, as I set off to walk along its banks, I saw a campanile ahead of me rising above the flat fields. The country all round had the ragged look of earth that had once held buildings and has not been given back to agriculture. The ploughshare would soon blunt itself in those sour fields upon the foundations of churches and palaces.

The canal led, as I had expected, to what was once the centre of a town, and here was a remarkable sight. A campanile almost as lordly as that of S. Mark's rose above a dead piazza where a cathedral, a second church, and various buildings, stood in utter silence. The grass was growing in what had once been the busiest centre of the town: shrubs and trees had taken possession of deserted courtyards, yet in the cheerful morning sunlight, so unwilling is one to admit death, the scene had a look of suspended animation, as if at any moment the doors of the cathedral might swing wide and out would pour the population. But, alas, I glanced around at the signs of decay, and knew that such a scene has not been witnessed in Torcello for centuries.

Then I saw that I was not alone. In the shade of some trees a short distance away two old fisherwomen in black dresses were standing at trestle tables, as if at a church bazaar, arranging ashtrays, lace, dinner-mats, and glass from Murano. I walked over and asked where their customers came from: they replied that several tourist boats would be arriving in the course of the day. While we were talking, I saw the only piece of Venetian glass I would like to have possessed: it was a simple oblong of polished brownish glass, a paper-weight, I think, which looked as though half a pint of peat water from a Highland burn had been frozen into a block. The price was trivial but the weight was formidable, and while former generations thought nothing of buying a marble well-head or a granite sarcophagus, we of today are appalled by an extra pound. I have never ceased to regret that I walked away and did not buy it. If there is anything in predestination, I was intended to do so, but something went badly wrong: and the more I think about that bit of glass the more delightful it appears to have been.

Entering the cathedral, I found myself in an austere Byzantine church which was founded in the year A.D. 639. The dome of the central apse glittered with mosaics of haloed saints: another mosaic contained hundreds of figures in the confusion of the Last Judgment. Behind the altar was the marble throne of the bishop, with a semi-circular curve on each side for the clergy, a seating arrangement which the early Church borrowed from the Roman law court. I explored the fields behind the cathedral and traced the vanished streets and buildings, whose stones had been carted away when the island was abandoned.

The cause of this desertion was malaria. Perhaps some visitors to Venice do not know that lagoons are of two kinds, alive and dead, and when the tides cease to cleanse a lagoon every day the anopheles takes over and malaria appears. Venice has fought a battle with river silt for centuries. Torcello was not so successful: gradually the tides no longer freshened the lagoon, the canals became stagnant and the population was obliged to emigrate to other islands. Thousands of tons of stones and precious wood were removed from the abandoned buildings of Torcello, all of it now incorporated in the architecture of the other islands.

When I returned to the cathedral a tourist boat had landed a number of gaily dressed visitors, who were rambling about taking photographs and watching the lizards. I was glad to see that the two old women were doing well with their lace and their post-cards. On the way back, I passed the only inn on the island, from the outside a humble-looking place. Entering, I found a sophisti-cated hotel with the latest kind of cocktail bar, and a restaurant that overflowed to a terrace upheld by marble columns, genuine Byzantine columns too, where, beneath a prolific vine, tables were set for lunch.

The name Locanda Cipriani upon the humble exterior should have warned me that the gay world had set foot upon the deserted island; and I was indeed grateful for that curious and totally un-expected offshoot of the Hotel Cipriani when, seated beneath the vine, and facing the magic of the garden, I ate the best risotto and scampi that one could find anywhere. Afterwards, the daughter of the proprietor took me over the hotel whose chromium-plated bathrooms gush water from the only taps in Torcello. Through the windows of bedrooms and sitting-rooms I caught occasional glimpses of the lonely campanile and the old roof-tiles of the silent churches. If any author of independent means is in need of that peace which is popularly supposed to aid creation, here under the vine in this garden he would quite likely find it.

§ 9

I was sorry to say goodbye to Venice and faced without pleasure the world of wheels. In spite of all the hard things that have been said of water-buses and speedboats, I thought the mechanization of the canals a good deal easier to live with than the deadly tumult of the modern road. I had found Venice a comparatively quiet and restful place and, above all, a wonderful place to walk in. I loved to explore the network of lanes, the succession of little arched bridges, the little *campi* with their ancient cisterns: and I thought the person who does not walk about Venice misses half its charm and beauty.

Thinking that I would leave the autostrada to the touring coaches, I decided to go to Padua along the old road that follows the curves of the Brenta. Technically a river but a canal in actual fact, the Brenta is the last section of the great system of north Italian waterways still used by travellers, and, rounding a bend, I saw coming towards me the modern version of that Brenta boat which delighted Goethe so much, now a long, low motor-boat with a covered top. The tourists sat in the shade gazing from bank to bank at the villas which were such a spectacular feature of the Venetian spending spree of the seventeenth and eighteenth centuries.

They stand amid their gardens, some large, some small, a few in good repair, many neglected, and all of them an eloquent expression of the Venetian longing to get away from the lagoon and have a garden, stables, and a coach-house. The villa which Byron rented is still standing at Mira – the Villa Foscarini dei Carmini – and it was while he was out riding one day on the banks of the Brenta that he first encountered the formidable Margarita Cogni. The largest of the villas, built on a graceful bend of the river a few miles from Padua, is the Villa Pisani at Stra, which would be a landmark in any city in Europe. The guide leads his charges through apartments designed entirely for shows and pageants, and points out the room where Napoleon slept, and the vast ceiling upon which Tiepolo glorified the deeds of the Pisani family, his last work before he went to Spain; and some think his best.

I went from Padua to Bologna, where I spent a night, and in the morning encountered the Autostrada del Sole. This wonderful road will soon be open from Milan to Naples. It is the finest road to be constructed in Italy – indeed in Europe – since the great consular highways, the Via Flaminia, the Via Emilia, and other backbones of civilization. It runs to Naples by way of

Bologna, Florence, and Rome, a distance of about three hundred miles.

The speedway occasionally is lifted above the surrounding country upon concrete columns which give it the appearance of a classical colonnade on a vast scale: it crosses rivers upon graceful girder bridges, and vanishes into mountains by way of a hundred tunnels to emerge again into the sunlight, straight here, curving there, and all the time resembling some mighty engineering achievement of antiquity. It is, of course, useless to the traveller who wishes to explore towns and villages, but by attracting a great proportion of through traffic it is going to make the old roads much pleasanter than they are.

The section from Bologna to Florence is a triumph. After following the valleys of the Reno and the Selta for miles, it strikes off on a new and original path across the Apennines, in and out of the mountains by way of innumerable tunnels, and giving one a glimpse of the inaccessible country between Castiglione and Futa, where there are practically no roads.

Having made this painless journey, the motorist may care to reflect how Pius II was once jolted over the Apennines, sometimes in a coach, then, when the road was too bad, in a chair. How grateful he would have been for the Autostrada del Sole: above all, how proud the Caesars would have been of it.

The speedway joins the road to Florence and one is soon finding one's way through the western outskirts.

CHAPTER TEN

Florence – The Ponte Vecchio – The Pazzi Conspiracy – The Secret of the Medici – The Benefactress of Florence – The end of the Medici – A modern troubadour – The Gozzoli fresco – Innocents at play – Alone in a Palace – The Boboli Gardens – The Brownings and the Anglo-Florentines

§ 1

I paid little attention to the letter confirming the reservation of my room in Florence, which mentioned that I would have a good view of the Ponte Vecchio. The hotel idea of 'a good view' is not always that of the guest. I thought that with luck, and by leaning out of the window, I might possibly be able to see a small portion of the bridge in the distance. I was therefore surprised to find myself poised above the Ponte Vecchio with such a good view of it that I could count every roof-tile. The hotel, they told me, had been built on the site of an ancient tower which the Germans blew up in 1944 to block the approach to the bridge. It was the only bridge in Florence to survive the last war because, says Harold Acton, 'Hitler is said to have admired it.' Perhaps Hitler might have changed his mind had he known, as Carlo Francovitch says in *La Resistenza a Firenze*, that a telephone line ran across it, linking the Committee of Liberation with the British army.

It was delightful, morning after morning, to draw the blinds and look down on the Ponte Vecchio. From where I sat at my bedroom window the bridge resembled a number of red-tiled potting-sheds set side by side. The oddest little pipes, with galvanized caps to them, sprouted from the tiles, too small to be chimneys but perhaps the vent-pipes of furnaces in which the jewellers, whose shops line both sides of the bridge, melt their gold.

How pleasant it was to sit there in the morning, eating my meagre Italian breakfast and gazing down upon a sight as Florentine as the Red Lily or the Medici *palle*. The old bridge bears its double line of shops across the Arno with such an air of grace, like some aged beauty who has posed for all the artists of her day. Shrunk by a rainless summer, the river moved almost imperceptibly beneath the domesticated arches, and in the gentle morning sunlight the well-known scene glowed with a hundred pastel shades in browns, yellows, and reds. There was usually an enthusiastic oarsman urging his shell across the water, as he sped through the arches to some imaginary winning-post; and there were always two fishermen casting from a barge moored near the bank, casting and never in my experience catching anything, but beginning each day like symbols of Hope.

It was a lovely glimpse of Florence in the freshness of the morning. At that early hour there was not a hint of the international hordes so soon to descend upon the city from 'campings' and coaches: in the peace of that moment two or three waiters, and a maidservant talking loudly, would pass across the bridge to the hotels on the other bank of the river: one by one the jewellers would unpadlock their shutters – some of these nail-studded like dungeon doors – and the old bridge was ready for another day. At such times, I thought, I might have been back in the nineteenth century with the Brownings, across the water at the Casa Guidi, and the Grand Duke of Tuscany asleep in the Pitti Palace beneath a flight of golden cupids.

When Cosimo I, Duke of Tuscany, decided to live on the other side of the river – the first Medici ever to do so – the Ponte Vecchio was occupied by the butchers, scarcely the most attractive approach to a palace, and that was the reason why the Duke replaced them by the jewellers, who have been there since 1565. Another of his works was the overhead corridor which connects the Uffizi with the Pitti Palace and crosses the river on the upstream side of the bridge. This furtive and eccentric construction, which Vasari proudly said he designed and built in five months, gave the Duke a secret covered way between his palace and the seat of government. One is reminded of the corridor which links the

Vatican with the Castel S. Angelo, and perhaps Cosimo remembered how his kinsman, Clement VII, had escaped to safety by way of that passage only thirty years earlier, during the Sack of Rome. From my vantage point I could see how cleverly Vasari had carried this corridor across the Arno, using the upstream buildings of the Ponte Vecchio and building the corridor as an extra storey. If the parent of this passage were the Corridoio di Castello in Rome, another of its interesting children would be the Grande Galerie of the Louvre, which Catherine de' Medici planned in imitation of it.

On my first morning in Florence I resolved not to enter a museum or a gallery, but just to walk about and recognize places. Florence is a city most people have known at second-hand all their lives. Stendhal was delighted to find himself perfectly at home there from the moment of his arrival; and I think this is not an uncommon experience.

In my first five minutes I was patting the head of the bronze boar in the Straw Market. The graceful lines of this loggia have now been hidden beneath festoons of straw hats and baskets, but a determined investigator may discover in the interior, submerged beneath handbags, the stone on which bankrupts were pilloried in days when the bankers occupied the market. The bronze boar, *il Porcellino*, is one of the favourite statues of Florence. His snout is bright with the endearments of many generations. Hans Andersen wrote a story about a poor boy who climbed on his back one night and was whirled away on many a strange adventure. It is not as good a story as that which was once told, and may still be told, in the nurseries of Florence, that the boar was once able to transform himself after dark into a man 'as beautiful as a Saint Sebastian freshly painted', and in that form fell in love with a girl. He confessed his secret to her, but warned her that if she told it to anyone he would be unable to see her again, and would be for ever frozen into bronze. She promised to keep the secret, but felt that she had to tell her mother. Under the most binding of oaths, the mother told her best friend, with the result that before an hour was out the whole of Florence knew it. Since then, it is said, the bronze boar has been a statue, and the girl? She became a frog, for, as everyone knows, frogs are human beings who were unable to control their tongues.

I walked on and, taking a street to the right, entered the Piazza del Duomo. The cathedral, sheathed in geometrical marbles in tints of white, green, and red, the first great effort of united Italy (for the marble covering is not old), gives to the piazza an air of tremendous splendour, and even of gaiety. It forms a background more suited to the eccentric garb of today's tourists than the more sombre garments of our forebears. Indeed, as I admired the intricate screen of marble, there happened to pass across the square a young woman tossing tangled hair out of her eyes, her legs in red tights; and it required no effort of the imagination to see her as a mediaeval page in the act of hurrying back to a love-lorn master with some message of hope. Even the odd-looking young man whom she greeted, bearded and spectacled, and wearing in the intolerable heat what appeared to be a leather jacket, seemed in the heady Florentine sunlight to be in character with the scene.

What can I say of Giotto's lily tower? It is larger and even more graceful than I had imagined, and I felt that I was standing in the presence of genius.

Across the road was the famous Baptistry, and I heard a guide telling his listeners that all Florentines are baptized there, though I find this difficult to believe. I found myself eventually pressed into the front rank of the crowd that surrounded Ghiberti's bronze doors, and heard an English voice at my elbow explaining to a friend how figures in such high relief are cast.

'You're from Sheffield?' I said.

'Noa – Huddersfield,' replied the voice.

To this visitor, the beauty of the gates and their place in art meant nothing, they were merely a technical problem; and I thought it probable that Ghiberti would have preferred this admirer, possibly a fellow craftsman, to many who have stood there and have committed their impressions to writing.

The cathedral, exquisitely called S. Mary of the Flower, is a dark uncluttered Gothic temple which offers sanctuary from the noise, the heat and the crowds outside. The first thing I saw, high on the wall, was Uccello's painting, to imitate marble, of an Englishman much loved in Florence five hundred years ago, the *condottiere*, Sir John Hawkwood, the commander of the famous 'White Company'. He was born at Sible Hedingham, in Essex, where there was once a Hawkwood Chapel in the parish church, and some say he was knighted on the field at Crécy. His name was spelt 'Aucud' in contemporary documents, which suggests that mediaeval Englishmen dropped their H's, and modern Italians call him Giovanni Acuto. The 'White Company' was one of the most famous of the mediaeval war bands. The men were well trained and well armed. They carried ladders in sections which, when fitted together, could reach the tallest town walls in Italy. Hawkwood was an expert on night manœuvres, which were considered poor form.

The fresco shows him prancing forward on a war-horse, dressed in armour covered with a surcoat, and wearing one of those round hats like a cake, fashionable at the time. There is a local story in Essex that after Hawkwood's death his family returned to England and, with the help of Richard II, persuaded the Signoria to return his body for burial in his native village.

The choir repeats the octagonal shape of the tower and is separated from the nave and transepts by marble screens which occupy the same place as the wooden screens over which Lorenzo the Magnificent vaulted in 1478, and so saved himself from the daggers of the Pazzi conspirators who tried to murder him during High Mass.

Behind the high altar I came to a haunting piece of statuary on which it is said Michelangelo was working at the time of his death at the age of nearly ninety. It is a Descent from the Cross. The old sculptor has carved his own features as those of Joseph of Arimathaea. It is the face we know so well from portraits and sculpture, though infinitely aged and saddened, with the nose broken in youth by Torrigiano, the sculptor of the tomb of Henry VII in Westminster Abbey. It is not known for certain whether it was this Descent from the Cross, or the even more pathetic group in the Castle at Milan, on which the genius was at work at the time of his death; the claim is made for both of them.

A short walk through narrow, crowded streets took me to a café whose coloured tables were grouped on the pavement within a territory defined by lemon trees in tubs. I sat among a flock of American girls who were writing postcards and exchanging information. 'Say, Carol,' said one of them, 'do you remember what the guide said about the Patsy Conspiracy? It was kinda cute. Did he say those guys were hung up from the windows right ahead or round the corner . . .'; and, following the direction of a pointed pencil, I saw on the opposite side of the piazza, lit by the morning sun, the Palazzo Vecchio, with Michelangelo's tall David, white as snow against the brown stones and, at right angles, the elegant Loggia dei Lanzi where Cellini's Perseus stood holding aloft the dripping head of Medusa.

Here was the classic view, the companion picture to the Ponte Vecchio, two pictures which are recognized everywhere, or almost everywhere, as Florence. The scene was as I expected it to be, but somehow more brilliant, and, like everywhere else in Europe now, seething with strangers. I have already said that those who have emancipated themselves from normal fashions look picturesque in the Piazza del Duomo, and in the Piazza della Signoria they are even more harmoniously in tune with a background that suggests rough and unshaven days. I was interested to watch girls and young men of many different nationalities wheel out their bicycles from the spot where Duke Cosimo I once stationed his lancers.

It is curious that when Dante, in the loneliness of his exile, thought of his beloved Florence, he was thinking of a Florence that lacked nearly all of its now familiar landmarks. It is even doubtful whether Dante saw the completed Palazzo Vecchio; indeed the only famous building in Florence which the greatest of Florentines would recognize, if he returned today, would be the Baptistry. When he left Florence in 1302 the Duomo was not built, the Campanile was undreamt-of, the Ponte Vecchio with its houses did not exist, the great churches were just being erected – S. Croce, S. Maria Novella – while the Bargello and Or San

Michele were not to be planned for another thirty to fifty years.

While I was crossing the piazza, I came upon a group of people who were gazing down at a stone set in the pavement which said that Savonarola had been burnt at the stake there in 1498. On more or less the same spot, during the days of his triumph, the great reformer had lit his Bonfire of Vanities, composed of false hair, jewels, cosmetics, books, and pictures. Such a memorial, and such a memory, suit a square dominated by the uncompromising outline of the Palazzo Vecchio. It was here, I think, that I encountered the guide who had impressed the American girls with his account of the 'Patsy' Conspiracy. He was bidding his hearers to look at the side windows of the Palazzo from whose mullions, he told them, the conspirators had been hanged. I think probably the 'cute' bit was his description of Archbishop Salviati's red stockings kicking in the air.

Murders in church are singularly horrifying and have been called a typically Renaissance crime. They were the easiest way to wipe out a well guarded family at an unguarded moment, and the signal to strike was usually some particularly sacred moment in the Mass, such as the Elevation, when, as an expert at the time commented, the victims' heads would be inclined ready for the blow: but there were no really good schools for murderers, as in our own enlightened age, and things were sometimes bungled by amateurs, as in the Pazzi attempt to murder Lorenzo and his brother Giuliano.

What lifts this conspiracy out of the sordid back streets of crime is that the Pope himself, Sixtus IV, was involved, and the would-be murderers were in and out of the Vatican all day, though, as one of them confessed afterwards, the Holy Father, anxious as any of them to see a revolution in Florence and the end of the Medici, drew the line at murder.

He was a good Pope who did a great deal for Rome. He built the Sistine Chapel and the Ponte Sisto, he founded the Capitoline Museum, and he restored the Trevi Fountain (the predecessor of the present one), but he was an early exponent of the strange papal vice of nepotism. The length to which aged bachelors would go in order to establish their often ambiguous nephews in palaces is a curious psychological study. Sixtus IV had four nephews upon whom he doted, and one can see this happy family together in Melozzo da Forli's wonderful picture: the Pope, plump and worldly in a red velvet chair, and the nephews, good-looking, richly dressed, and deferential.

The Pope was always hard up and was financed by the Medici; however, when he asked for a loan of forty thousand ducats to establish his nephew, Girolamo Riario, in territory on the boundary of Florence, Lorenzo de' Medici took fright. The forty thousand ducats were much less important than the danger to Florence of a new power in the Romagna. When Lorenzo refused to lend the money, the Pope closed his account and transferred it to the rival Pazzi bank. The head of this bank in Rome was a fiery little dandy called Francesco Pazzi, who was not only delighted to provide the Pope with all the money he wanted, but was anxious to whip up hatred against the Medici, until eventually a plot took shape. Only two years before Milan had been weakened, when Galezazzo Maria Sforza had been murdered in church by young fanatics; and now a similar murder was planned to weaken Florence.

An eager recruit was a churchman of ill-repute, Francesco Salviati, Archbishop of Pisa, who had his own grudges against the Medici. The only likeable member of the gang was a soldier, Giambattista Montesecco, whose task it was to go to Florence and reconnoitre the ground. He possessed some remnants of good feeling and when he encountered Lorenzo de' Medici's genial charm, he began to feel sorry that he had agreed to kill him. This feeling, which was to grow as the plot advanced, was one of the reasons why it failed.

Towards the end of April in the year 1478 all the conspirators were in Florence. At the last minute it was decided to kill the brothers not at a banquet, as originally planned, but during High Mass. When Montesecco heard of this he backed out. He did not object to killing a man in the street or at a banquet, but he refused to kill him in church, 'where God would see him'. Thus the only professional slayer withdrew, and his place was taken by two priests who had no such tender scruples.

On Sunday, April 26, the Duomo was crowded. The Medici

brothers were not seated but were strolling about, as Continental Catholics still do, chatting in low voices, ready to drop to one knee at certain moments. Contemporary writers do not agree on the precise point of the Mass selected by the murderers for their attack: some say it was the ringing of the sanctus bell: some the *Agnus Dei*, some the words, *Ite missa est*. Suddenly one of the murderers stabbed Giuliano and caused him to stumble against Francesco Pazzi, who began to attack him like a maniac, thrusting and stabbing so violently that he even managed to wound himself in the thigh. As Giuliano lay dead, one of the two priests, Antonio Maffei, a dagger in one hand, placed the other amateurishly upon the shoulder of Lorenzo de' Medici in order to take better aim, with the result that Lorenzo shook him off and, drawing his sword and wrapping his cloak round his arm as a shield, vaulted over the low wooden rail into the choir. Friends now surrounded him and together they ran through the crowd of frightened priests and choristers to the north sacristy, closing the heavy bronze doors (which are still there) in the face of the assassins. Though the gay Giuliano lay dead pierced by sixteen dagger wounds, Lorenzo was alive; and the Pazzi Conspiracy had failed.

How often some simple unexpected fact has wrecked the best-laid plot. None of the conspirators knew that the Gonfalonier, an alert and suspicious magistrate called Cesare Petrucci, had recently fitted a self-locking device to the doors of the Palazzo Vecchio; so when, taking advantage of the confusion in the cathedral, those conspirators charged with the task of capturing the building entered it, they locked themselves in! They were easily overpowered, and were soon suspended from the windows of the Palace.

Botticelli was asked to paint upon the walls of the Palazzo Vecchio a picture showing them swinging there, but all trace of this work has long since vanished.

One is so accustomed to the idea that a statue in a public place should be a memorial to someone, a king, a general, a statesman, or a poet, that an outdoor gallery of sculpture selected for public enjoyment as works of art, which is what the Loggia dei Lanzi is, strikes one as a great novelty. When Cellini took a wax model of his Perseus to Duke Cosimo I, the Duke said, 'If you could only execute this little model, Benvenuto, with the same perfection on a large scale, it would be the finest piece in the piazza.' That is how Florence thought of the Piazza della Signoria: a place where a critical public could admire 'fine pieces'.

Of course they are not all fine pieces. I thought Ammanati's fountain disappointing and found it difficult to understand why Cosimo preferred it to Giambologna's greatly superior fountain, designed in competition for this spot and rejected, which is now the pride of Bologna. I thought Neptune too large and coarse, and so muscle-bound that he could not descend at night, as legend says, and go round the piazza talking to the other statues! On the other hand, Michelangelo's David looks as though he could not only walk round the square but leap right over the fountain, if he wished to do so. A committee of artists decided where this snow-white Greek God should be erected, and they chose a good place. He stands out luminously from the wall, and looks best at that time of day when the building is in shadow and the sun is on the piazza. The present David is a copy and appears perfect until you have seen the original in the Accademia.

In June, 1504, forty men drew the original to the piazza in a huge crate from which only the head protruded. The journey took four days and nights, and such was the envy which Michelangelo, who was then only twenty-nine, inspired in mean spirits, that stones were thrown at the David on the first night, and a troop of guards was ordered to watch the statue until it was safely delivered to the site. Everyone who visited Florence between the years 1504 and 1882 saw the original David in position, but in that year it was feared exposure to the weather was damaging the marble and it was removed.

Another beautifully-placed statue is the Perseus. He looks splendid from every angle, and the arch of the Loggia provides him with an attractive frame. After one has read Cellini's auto-biography, one looks at that statue with intimate affection. Never perhaps have the joys and sorrows of designing and casting a famous statue been more dramatically recorded. Cellini describes the making of this work from the first moments of conception (the idea was Cosimo's), and he recounts his troubles with his patron ('more a merchant than a duke'), and with the paymaster ('a flimsy little fellow with his tiny spider's hands and a small gnat's voice'); and so on to the crazy scene in the foundry when the statue was being cast, and everything seemed to be going wrong until Cellini, in one of his frenzies, flung all his pewter plates, dishes, pots, and pans into the bubbling metal and, as the mould began to fill, 'fell down on my knees and with all my heart gave thanks to God'.

Walking over to the gates of the Palazzo Vecchio, I stepped for a moment into the small entrance courtyard and knew that I had found one of the perfect places in Florence. Never has a forbidding exterior offered a more charming and unexpected contrast. Outside was the crenellated thirteenth century, here was the grace and elegance of the late Renaissance. At first I did not take in the richly decorated columns which support the arcade, or the walls covered with grotesques: I saw only the central fountain, where a lovely little winged infant stands upon one foot, grasping a dolphin as infantile as himself. His smile is not that of a boy who has caught a fish, but that of a child who is playing with a friend. Verrocchio made this bronze for one of Lorenzo's country houses, and it was brought here years after when the old palace was modernized and redecorated for Joan of Austria, the bride of Ferdinand, son of Cosimo I. Has a bride ever been offered a more charming welcome?

In the days that followed I was to explore the Palazzo Vecchio from floor to roof, and to be impressed and delighted by its painted halls and their massive ceilings, and by the windows. which offered unexpected glimpses of Florence and its red roofs, One thinks of Vasari as the author of *The Lives of the Painters*, but here he is seen as the painter of immense, confused battle-scenes. Probably he would have been astonished and saddened could he have known that his studio gossip would be more treasured by posterity than his plunging horses.

I walked on and came to a spacious oblong piazza, the Piazza di Santa Croce, where tournaments were once held, and where, in the rose-tinted days of 1475, the great *giostra* was staged in honour of the pale and lovely Simonetta, the wife of Marco Vespucci, a cousin of the man who gave his name to America, and some say the model for Botticelli's Venus. Dante, in white marble, now presides over the scene, a little grimly, I thought, as if aware that the monument is an overdue atonement for his exile. The far end of the piazza is occupied by the Franciscan church of S. Croce, which has been called the Westminster Abbey of Italy. The greatest men buried there are Michelangelo, Machiavelli, and Galileo, then come Leonardo Bruni, the poet Alfieri, who ran off with Bonny Prince Charlie's wife and made her extremely happy, and the musician, Rossini.

The church is glorious: a huge Franciscan temple with a vast nave and a distant gleam of stained glass. But how disappointing it is, in this capital city of Sculpture, to see so many frightful tombs. One can well imagine that any sculptor, faced with the task of designing a tomb for Michelangelo, would find the work difficult, though it is unbelievable that anyone could have considered the three inconsolable maidens, representing Sculpture, Architecture, and Painting, a fit memorial to this genius. It would be a kindness to his memory could they be replaced by the tragic Pietà in the Duomo, which perhaps the artist intended for this very purpose.

Dante's empty sepulchre also struck me as unfortunate. The poet is seated in pensive mood with his immortal work upon his knee, while a female (Florence) points to him sadly, and another female (Poetry) weeps. It is a great relief to cross the nave and admire the simplicity and dignity of Settignano's memorial to Carlo Marsuppini, the work of an age that knew how to say good-bye.

In the cloisters I saw a memorial tablet to Florence Nightingale, who was born in Florence and named after the city. Her fame gave a great impetus to the revival of the name, with its inevitable shortening to Flossie, Flo, and Florrie, though it is a much older name and was popular with men as well as women in the Middle

Ages: it had nothing at all to do with the city, but with the Roman names Florentius and Florentia. I think this dignified and pleasant name is possibly out of fashion in this age of Joans, Carols, and Marilyns.

At the end of a path bordered by shrubs and grass, I saw one of the most exquisite little buildings in the world, the Pazzi Chapel. It is a tribute to the good taste of that ancient and aristocratic family which ruined itself in its attempt to destroy the Medici. Compared with the Pazzi, the Medici were of recent and obscure origin. It was a crusading Pazzi who brought back from the Holy Sepulchre the flints from which, to this day, at Easter, a torch in the shape of a dove is ignited, which travels on a wire from the altar of the cathedral, exploding a car full of fireworks in the piazza outside.

The Pazzi Chapel was the work of Filippo Brunelleschi, whose insignificant appearance Vasari compared to that of Giotto. This mighty little man built the dome of the cathedral of Florence a century before S. Peter's dome was built, and it was the architectural wonder of the fifteenth century. But there are no problems of engineering in the Pazzi Chapel: it is an exercise in the mysteries of proportion, and an expression of that search for perfection inspired in ardent and romantic minds during the Renaissance by the ruins of Rome. When he was a young man, Brunelleschi went off to Rome with his friend Donatello, and there they filled notebooks with measurements and sketches, and returned to Florence longing to adapt such wonders to the needs of their own age.

The building is small and simple: it has the effect on one of a chord of music heard in a garden of box hedges and cypress trees. Donatello added a frieze of angels' heads, and one can fancy the two friends opening their Roman notebooks and selecting their favourite columns and pilasters and their most attractive acanthus leaves. Beauty did not, however, protect the remains of old Jacopo Pazzi, who was buried here after his execution for his part in the Pazzi Conspiracy. Lack of rain being attributed to his interment in sacred soil, he was dug up and dragged round Florence by small boys. Some writers describe the ordinary folk of Florence as if they were angels who spent their time in creating or admiring masterpieces, but it is obvious from the history of their riots that they were just as horrible as any other mob in history: and they were as imaginative in their cruelty as mediaeval Chinamen.

Someone had told me that there was a good restaurant on the Piazzale Michelangelo, high up at the back of Florence: and there I went, to find myself alone with an enchanted view of the valley of the Arno. I saw the river below and the bridges; I saw Giotto's Campanile, and the white-ribbed, red dome of Brunelleschi, and, some way to the left, the embattled bell-tower of the Palazzo Vecchio. Hundreds of red-tiled roofs, domes, and towers filled the valley, while, upon the opposite slopes, white roads threaded their way up to Fiesole, and, higher still, to hilltop towns and belts of woodland. This is one of the most civilized views on earth, and now more precious than ever in our new dark age.

I climbed flights of steps at the back of the Piazzale, and stood alone in the church of S. Miniato before the superb classical tabernacle which Piero de' Medici erected over a miraculous crucifix. There is an altar in the crypt where the remains of S. Miniato lie, a Roman soldier who was martyred in A.D. 250.

I walked down to the restaurant, an elegant building with an air of distinction and an inscription in honour of Poggio, and I was given a table under a stone-pine. Glancing across a bed of scarlet cannas, I saw a bronze copy of Michelangelo's David looking down towards Florence, the very embodiment of Italian vitality. Preparations were being made near me for a large party. The waiters stood expectantly, flipping dust from chairs and tables as they anxiously watched the road from Florence.

We heard the sound of approaching Fiats as they climbed the hill, and soon a wedding-party converged on the tables under the trees. It was a simple wedding, the men in black Sunday suits, the women neat and hatted, the girls charming and poised. I have now reached the age when all brides and bridegrooms seem to me absurdly young and helpless, and this couple was no exception. The occasion was more formal than it would have been in

England and expressed a nice mixture of affection and family piety: indeed perhaps the most honoured guests were two or three aged men and women, who must have been the grandparents. When the priest arrived on a scooter, respect for the Church was added to the stately manners of this exemplary gathering.

No people, except maybe the Spaniards, succeed in looking so like their ancestors as the Italians, and one cannot be in Italy even for a day without noticing, behind the counters in shops, in banks and in the streets, faces which recall those painted by the great masters. The scene under the trees was an ancient one. Even the attitude of the wedding-guests at table, their gravity on an occasion which is so often an excuse for jokes and merriment, reminded me of something I had seen or read. Though the wedding party was neither rich nor noble, it was linked by custom and conduct to that famous wedding procession on the *cassone*, in which, to the sound of trumpets, members of the Ricasoli and Adimari families walk gravely two by two beneath a canopy to the Duomo.

I walked back to Florence down a hot and tawny hill, and on the way came to one of the city's most popular 'campings'. There may have been fifty, indeed there may have been a hundred, trailer caravans of all makes, size, and colours parked beside the motor-cars which had brought them there. Though there was a restaurant, many of the campers had eaten in green canvas tents pitched near their caravans, and were now extended upon the grass in the northern belief that the sun is a benevolent orb. Never since the days of the great barbarian invasions have so many members of the Teutonic races, with their wagons, their wives, and families, descended upon Italy. 'And when they come to a place rich in grass, they place their carts in a circle and feed like wild beasts,' wrote Ammianus Marcellinus of the original 'campings' of A.D. 390. 'As soon as the fodder is used up, they place their cities, as we might call them, on the wagons and so convey them: in the wagons the males have intercourse with the women, and in the wagons their babes are born and reared: wagons form their permanent dwellings, and wherever they come, they look upon as their natural home.'

Much the same sentiments were expressed to me by a hotel proprietor at Ravenna, who deplored the German caravan invasion of the Rimini coastline. 'They come in their caravans, they bring their own food and off they go without leaving a penny!' he said.

Down in Florence the striped and panelled Baptistry, the Duomo and its companion tower stood soaked in sunlight during the temporary hush of the siesta. I explored a network of narrow streets where men wearing the paper caps of sculptors were at work, some in the street itself, gilding wood, stamping leather, and doing a hundred jobs that are best done by hand. Suddenly the siesta came to an end, shops lifted their noisy shutters, churches opened their doors; and soon Florence was awake again.

I was looking for a firm of camera repairers which had been recommended to me. I had noticed that my small, costly camera had shed a chromium screw which, though it did not appear to impair the efficiency of the instrument, was irritating, and I was anxious to have it replaced. At length I located the firm in the basement of a scabrous building in a slum, and I paused, unwilling to trust my precious machine to such a place. However, I descended some steps into the basement and found myself in a dark room separated from another by a glass door. In this inner room two young Italians were leaning gracefully against a lathe. The shelves were covered with every conceivable make of camera, old and new. I rapped on the counter, but the young men were studying what I took to be the racing page of a newspaper; however, when they turned at the sound of my knocking, I saw they were studying with clinical care a different kind of form, and, putting down the picture of a film star, one of the young men opened the door and advanced to me with a smile urbane and crafty. It was the smile which a Florentine ambassador might have employed on a Doge, but when he saw my camera his professional manner changed.

'How beautiful!' he cried. 'This is the new XY 3, the first I have seen. How beautiful! Please excuse me!'

He took the camera into the workroom, where both young men admired it and handled it as Cosimo's jewellers might have fondled the ducal crown: but he returned crestfallen. Alas, the missing screw was of a particular kind made only by the manufacturer of the camera. It would be difficult, if not impossible, to match it. However, if I would leave the camera with him he would see what could be done. I returned the next day to find the screw had been replaced. 'We made one,' said the young man. When I asked for the bill, he became again the polished ambassador.

'Please,' he said, 'it is I who am in your debt for the pleasure of seeing and handling the beautiful XY 3.'

When I told this to a man who was complaining about the rapacity of the Italians, he could scarcely believe it: but had the camera not appealed to the Florentine eye, I am sure the bill would have been formidable.

§ 2

The Medici, whose name meets one at every corner of Florence, were late-comers to Florentine banking. Long before they had been heard of, while they were probably still tending their vines and their oxen in the valley of the Mugello, the Bardi, the Peruzzi, the Scali, the Frescobaldi, the Salambini, and many others, were well known to the chronically hard-up kings of mediaeval Europe. It is interesting to think of those sophisticated Florentine financiers with their letters of credit and their double-entry (which, incidentally, they had inherited, by way of the Papal Chancery, from Ancient Rome), operating in a mediaeval world where kings carried round the currency of their realms on mule-back from castle to castle, and hid the crown jewels under the bed.

Artistic Florence is well known, but financial Florence is still much of a mystery. Nearly all the bank ledgers are believed to have perished, though anyone who has seen the scale on which archives are preserved in Italy may wonder what remains to be discovered. I should like to read a book on the Florentine bankers which would humanize those shadowy characters as they sat at their green baize tables, juggling with their golden florins or whispering in their back rooms with branch managers from London or Lyons.

In the bank almost opposite the Ponte Vecchio, where I too often cashed travellers' cheques, I admired, while waiting for the evanescent notes, a pleasant modern mural depicting a respectful Bardi, upon bended knee, lending money to Edward III of England. Nearly all the Plantagenets borrowed in Florence. The Frescobaldi helped to finance Edward I's crusade: Edward II drew on the Salambini and the Scali banks: Edward III, the greatest debtor of all, absorbed as many florins as he could get, and helped to pay for Crécy and Agincourt with his Florentine money. When in 1339 he stopped repayment, he caused a series of crashes which reduced some of the greatest Florentine bankers to poverty. I was surprised that a bank should have chosen to perpetuate the memory of such an unsatisfactory client: but bankers are resilient characters. They were soon helping Edward IV to fight the Wars of the Roses! What interesting conversations must have taken place in the head offices in Florence; what secrets of royal extravagance; what warnings and suspicions, as Bardi and Peruzzi went into conference with their agents.

The bankers have all been forgotten, save the Medici, and they are remembered not for their florins but for their patronage of art. Though forgotten, the bankers have left something behind, in addition to their massive palaces: they have given the vocabulary of banking its most essential words: cash (*cassa*), bank (*banco*), debt (*debito*), credit (*creditore*), ditto (*detto*); and the 'florin', a word still flowering in England, was originally the famous gold coin minted at Florence in 1252, stamped with the Florentine lily.

It was impressive to walk, especially after dark, past the massive palaces of the bankers. In the night they seem to draw defensively closer, as if at the whisper of a royal bankruptcy. Like all buildings which have anything to do with money, they have a wary look, and an architect must glance at them with respect as the first of their kind. The Medici Palace is the parent of the Italian palazzo: it was the first Renaissance palace ever built, a style that spread to every city and town in Italy, then across the Alps to the cities of Europe. The massive rustication of the lower

storey, like some Etruscan town wall, has been repeated everywhere, in mansions, Government offices, and clubs, all over
the world, but now, with the triumph of termite architecture,
the Renaissance palazzo may perhaps be said to have run its
course. The Medici Palace, though larger than when the Medici
knew it, is still the most attractive, while the Strozzi Palace is the
most massive, a cautious elephant of a building, and one to break a
burglar's heart.

Among the most admired pictures in the Uffizi is Botticelli's
Adoration of the Magi, in which the Virgin is seen, robed in red and
blue, seated in a rough shelter contrived in a Roman ruin. A group
of brilliant, stylish people stand round her, most of whom appear
to be more conscious that they are having their portraits painted
than that they are present at the Nativity. One of the three kings,
a lean old man, kneels before the Child, offering his gifts; and we
see him in profile. There is something familiar about him. Where
has one seen him before? Surely he was the peasant who was working in a garden at Fiesole yesterday, or was he the man with the
ox-cart on the road to Empoli? One has seen him everywhere in
Tuscany, observing the world with wary eyes: the brown skin is
drawn tightly over his skull, his mouth is a thin line, the prominent nose is probing into some bargain at a cattle sale. This is a
portrait of the greatest of the Medici, Cosimo the Elder, the Father
of his Country.

The descendants of this peasant family, who migrated to the
city at about the time of Dante, controlled Florence almost
continuously for three centuries. They pervade every corner of the
city. We visit their palaces, we enter buildings erected by them,
we admire the pictures and the sculpture which they commissioned, we see the cell in S. Marco where Cosimo retired to
meditate, we stand beside the family tombs in S. Lorenzo, and we
see the red *palle*, or roundels, of the Medici arms everywhere, with
the feeling that a family has never been more closely associated
with a city.

In theory Florence was a democratic republic governed by the members of her trade guilds. As in Venice, elaborate safety devices were fitted to the constitution to prevent a take-over by a military dictator. Two citizen councils elected the chief magistrates, who held office for only two months, and were then succeeded by others. During their two months, the Gonfalonier of Justice and the six (later eight) Priors had to live together in the Palazzo Vecchio, which, as well as the seat of government, was a first-class club. The best food in Florence was reserved for the table of the *signori*, and everything was done to make their two months' stay pleasant and luxurious. When Iris Origo's Merchant of Prato went shopping in Florence, he was delighted to be able to buy veal that had been reserved for the Priors' High Table, and was the best to be had, and another shopper explained his failure to buy the kind of fish he wanted because it had been reserved for the Palazzo Vecchio, where the 'old *signori*' (the out-going Priors) were giving a dinner to their successors in office.

The Palazzo Vecchio was the scene of continual governmental changes, and Florence was always in the throes of ballots, and elections for the coveted distinctions. Immediately he was elected, a Prior could wear the *Lucco*, a gown of pink, violet or crimson, and he took up residence in the Palazzo Vecchio, where a staff of servants in green livery ministered to his wants. The *signori* lived amid the tapestried halls: they ate their excellent meals together at tables loaded with silver-plate: there were singers, musicians, and comedians to cheer them if they were bored: altogether it was democracy at its plutocratic best. Below this decorative head, however, was a sturdy body of committees which would fascinate any student of red tape.

The power of the Medici was founded on money and tact. Cosimo the Elder, who died in 1464, perfected the art of controlling the curious Florentine political machine from a distance: in public, he was the genial, munificent millionaire, but in reality the manipulator of the ballot-box and the puller of strings. The Medici secret was very simple: it consisted in having their own men in all the key positions. If men of other parties held office, they had to be men of no ability or character. It says much for the political strategy of Cosimo and his successors that they were able to persuade one of the most quick-witted and brilliant communities in the history of Western civilization that Florence was a republic! Cosimo was, of course, an astute money-maker and a lavish spender. Something of his sardonic wisdom lies in his advice to a friend who had been made magistrate in a distant city: 'Dress in red and keep your mouth shut!' Pius II, who was an adept at the acid character sketch, described him as 'more cultured than merchants usually are. He had some knowledge of Greek: his mind was keen and always alert; his spirit neither cowardly nor brave. . . . Nothing went on in Italy that he did not know, indeed it was his advice that guided the policy of many cities and princes.' The Pope said that the Bishop of Orta once remarked in his presence what a pity it was that Florence had no husband, to which Pius replied, 'Yes, but she has a paramour', meaning Cosimo. Pius also said that on one occasion Cosimo attempted to kiss the papal slipper but was unable to bend because of gout, an ailment which he handed on to his descendants. It is possible that this crippling infirmity was a severe form of arthritis. Cosimo spent his last year in a wheel-chair, and his son, Piero, could scarcely move hand or foot; Piero's son, Lorenzo the Magnificent, was in his turn stricken by the malady at the age of thirty and ended his brilliant life at forty-three.

Lorenzo once frankly defined the reason for the Medici control of Florence. 'In Florence,' he said, 'one can ill live in the possession of wealth without control of the government'; so one might call the Republic a financial dictatorship disguised as a democracy. Lorenzo was a third-generation millionaire and was more interested in statecraft and the arts than in making money. He was an ugly, sallow man who had no sense of smell and a harsh voice, but the moment he spoke his ugliness was forgotten. His death mask shows a rough face, stern and powerful, indeed if one did not know it was the face of Lorenzo, one might think it to be that of some tough soldier of fortune.

Unlike his father and grandfather, who were trained as merchants and bankers, Lorenzo was brought up as a prince and, when the time came for him to marry, a great alliance was sought, and his remarkable mother set off for Rome to inspect Clarice, daughter of the ancient Roman family of the Orsini. She wrote home to her husband, Piero, 'the Gouty': 'The girl has two good points: she is tall and fair: her face is not pretty, but it is not common, and her figure is good. . . . Her breasts, I could not see, as they are completely covered here, but they seemed to me well proportioned.' Clarice and Lorenzo were married with an incredible display of wealth, and in course of time had a family of three boys and four girls.

No great man should be considered without reference to his mother. That remarkable woman, Lucrezia Tornabuoni, of an older banking family than the Medici, survived her husband for eighteen years and watched over Lorenzo's life until she died in 1482. Lorenzo sent twenty-seven letters announcing her death to various rulers. 'I am plunged in grief,' he wrote, 'I have lost not merely a mother but my only refuge in many troubles and the comfort of my labours.' He never did anything without consulting her. He could see only large issues; she saw all the details, and it was said that her decisions were often wiser than his. When her death was announced, his envoy in Rome wrote warning him that he must expect conspiracies now that his mother could no longer 'save you from them as she used to do'.

Books have been written about Lorenzo's statecraft, his love of learning and art, and his contribution to Tuscan poetry, but less has been said about his triumph in a sphere of life where rich men are not always successful: he was a devoted and adored parent. He loved to romp and joke with his children and he allowed them to call him Lorenzo, which Machiavelli thought undignified. When they were away in the country at one of his villas and he was in Florence, his eight-year-old Piero wrote to him, while Clarice sent him partridges and said the children were always asking 'When will Lorenzo come?' Old laughter and happiness lie embalmed in their brown faded letters. One child asks for a pony: then comes a letter of thanks, saying how beautiful the pony is, 'so handsome and so perfect'. At the age of eight Piero was able to write to his father in Latin. 'We are all very well and studying,' he began. 'Giovanni is able to spell. You can see for yourself how my writing is getting on. As for Greek, I work at it with Martino's help, but do not get very far. Giuliano can only laugh [he was an infant in arms], Lucrezia sews, sings and reads [she was nine], Maddalena knocks her head against the wall but does not hurt herself. Luigia can talk quite a lot. Contessina makes a great noise all over the house. Nothing is wanting to us but to have you here.'

In spite of such a happy domestic scene, it was an uneasy time. Lorenzo was facing the greatest crisis of his life. He was at war with the Pope and with Naples, and all the enemies of the Medici were hoping for his collapse. In the Medici nursery were three small boys who had not yet attracted the attention of the Furies, and were destined to bear the Medici name into a changed world. Piero, the writer of the letter, was to become a spectacular failure and to go down in history as 'the Unfortunate'; Giovanni ('who can spell') was to become Pope Leo X; Giuliano (who could do nothing but laugh) was to make no mark on history and to die in his thirties.

Two years after Lorenzo's death, Piero, then twenty-three, was faced by the French invasion of Italy. He could not handle the enemy and was hissed in the streets of Florence while the crowds 'wagged the tips of their hoods at him' – a supreme insult – and, in fury, drove him and his family into exile. They remained away for eighteen years. One wonders whether a more crowded eighteen years have ever been recorded. They included the reigns of the Borgia Pope, Alexander VI, and that of the warlike Julius II. During the first, the wicked Caesar Borgia, king of all Italian gangsters, failed to hew a princedom for himself in Italy; during the second, Pope Julius in person stormed the walls of pro-French cities and, in calmer moments, tried to bully Michelangelo.

Without the Medici, Florence reverted to her political dream, the Republic. At first the city was controlled by the arch-hater of the Medici, the Dominican reformer and visionary, Savonarola, who filled the churches and called upon the wicked to repent. Pyres were made of finery. Horrible gangs of children paraded the streets with crucifixes, entering private houses and confiscating musical instruments, cosmetics, books and pictures, to cast on the Bonfire of the Vanities. Many artists saw the error of their ways. Botticelli confined himself to religious themes ever after, and among other converts were Lorenzo di Credi, Perugino, and Pollaiuolo, while it has been said that Michelangelo never forgot the sound of Savonarola's voice. The end came when the Dominican attacked the morals of the Pope, and his reward for much good advice to the Borgias was martyrdom in front of the Palazzo Vecchio.

The next great character of the Republic was Machiavelli, a Florentine genius and perhaps the most misunderstood character in Italian history. The adjective Machiavellian in English, in French *Machiavélique*, and in Italian *Machiavellico*, are used every day to describe some action which is judged crooked or guileful to the point of dishonesty, and the Italians even describe political craftiness as *Machiavellismo*. But these words were coined long ago; no one now, in an age of brain-washing and wireless propaganda, could possibly think of Machiavelli as anything but a promising beginner in the art of achieving results by any means.

As an individual, he was honest and likeable and, as he once said of himself, his poverty was proof of his loyalty. He saw more clearly than anyone that Italy's tragedy was the system of mercenary armies which worked well enough while the country was a collection of city states and war was not a very serious affair, but was useless against France and Spain. As the foremost writer on military matters, he was once invited by the great general, Giovanni delle Bande Nere, to drill troops on parade. What happened was amusingly described by the novelist Bandello in a letter to Giovanni.

'You must remember that day,' he wrote, 'when that most ingenious Messer Niccolò Machiavelli came to us beneath the walls of Milan, and proposed to perform a manœuvre with the foot soldiers, according to the rules laid down in his *Art of War*. I need not remind you of the difference there is between one who knows, and one who has put in practice what he knows . . . Experience is the master teacher . . . Messer Niccolò kept us in that place for two hours under the burning sun, trying to arrange the men in the prescribed order, but never could succeed in doing it. All the time, he talked so well and so clearly, and by his discourse showed that the thing was so extraordinarily easy, that I, in my ignorance, lightly believed that I could myself have arranged this infantry in battle order . . . Seeing that there was no chance of Messer Niccolò finishing the business for a long time, you, Signor Giovanni, said to me: "Bandello, I must get our men out of this difficulty, in order that we may go and have our dinner!" Then, when you had told Machiavelli to retire, and to let you take command, in the twinkling of an eye by the help of drums all the troops were at once marshalled in various manners and positions, to the extreme admiration of the spectators . . . At dinner Messer Niccolò laughed pleasantly at the misadventure of the morning and, turning to you, remarked: "Signore Giovanni, I feel quite sure that if you had not come to my help we should still be there in the open field with the burning sun shining down on us!"'

Any young soldier who remembers saying 'left' when he meant 'right', especially under the bleak eyes of authority, will always have a fellow feeling for poor Machiavelli. With the fall of the Republic, and the reinstatement of the Medici with the help of a Spanish army, Machiavelli was cold-shouldered and retired to his small estate to write his books. Among the curious habits of authors must be placed his custom, after a day with rustics in the open air, of putting on court dress when he retired to his library to write.

Eighteen years had passed since the Medici had been driven into exile, and now in 1512 they returned to dominate the life of Florence again. Did any of them remember, one wonders, as he re-entered the scenes of his childhood, that half a century or so before, and in a different Italy, when the power of the Medici was at its height, the great Cosimo had foreseen the exile. I have noticed that some men of truly exceptional ability, either in the realms of thought or action, are gifted with a cold-blooded sense of future events which appears like second sight; and this Cosimo the Elder possessed. The old banker, in the act of returning the proceeds of his usury to God in the form of churches or altars, once remarked, 'I know the humours of this city. Fifty years will not pass before we are driven out; but the buildings will remain.' The old man had no illusions about Florence, about the Medici, even about money, but he knew that Donatello, Brunelleschi, and Michelozzo held the gift of immortality.

If anyone were to write a play about the Medici, I fancy that he would find his plot in the twenty-five years of the restoration, which saw the end of the senior branch of the family. Bastards and murder had played little part in the succession of the earlier merchant bankers, but now the rise of the Medici to princely prominence was paid for in tragedy and melodrama. The head of the family was Lorenzo's son Giovanni, the little boy 'who is able to spell' in the nursery letter of long ago. At the age of thirty-seven he became Pope Leo X, and his ambition was the glorification of his family. He married his nephew Lorenzo, the son of his brother Piero the Unfortunate, to a French princess, and established him in control of Florence. Husband and wife died within a month of one another, leaving an infant daughter, who, except for the Pope himself, was the only legitimate descendant of the Elder Cosimo.

In this crisis the Pope decided to rule Florence from Rome and sent there as his representative his friend and adviser, Cardinal Giulio de' Medici. He was the illegitimate son of the gay Giuliano, Lorenzo's beloved brother, who had died of dagger wounds on the pavement of the cathedral during the Pazzi Conspiracy. His existence was unknown until after the assassination, when Lorenzo gladly recognized him as his dead brother's child and brought him up with his own children. Now, more than forty years later, the illegitimate Medici, whose existence was rooted in the brilliant far-off Florence of Botticelli, found himself ruler of the city and alone in the silent palace with the last legitimate member of the family. In the history of the Medici there can have been no stranger or more touching moment than that when Cardinal Giulio, parting the curtains of the cradle, looked down upon the infant girl, presumably the last Medici of the senior line. Who could have guessed that she would become Catherine de' Medici, the Queen of France and the mother of three French kings?

In two years' time Leo X died, and in two more Cardinal Giulio de' Medici mounted the papal throne as Clement VII. From Rome he announced his plans for the future government of Florence.

Himself a bastard, the Pope revealed the existence of two young Medici, both illegitimate, whom he sent as rulers of Florence under the guidance of a cardinal. The parentage of the two boys has never been settled. One of them, Alessandro, was the oddest of all the Medici. His dark skin and woolly hair proclaimed African blood, and some believed that he was the Pope's son by a slave girl.

This fantastic member of the family was expelled during the renewal of the Franco–Spanish war for Italy, but with the victory of Spain was reinstated and married to the illegitimate daughter of the Emperor Charles V and given the title of Duke of Tuscany. Alessandro was then twenty, and the Florentines detested him. Glimpses of his five-year rule occur in Cellini's autobiography: it was Cellini who designed his coinage and made no attempt to disguise his patron's negroid features.

The early Medici were not given to murder, as were some of the families of the time. Now, however, the senior line was to be extinguished by a murder as sensational as any. The duke's inseparable companion in his revels and escapades was a member of the junior branch of the family, which sprang from the brother of Cosimo the Elder. There was no love lost between the two branches, and the junior Medici always remained tactfully in the background. The young man was named Lorenzo, or, because of his slight build, Lorenzino, and all the time he was pandering to his relative he was planning to do away with him. One night he arranged for the Duke to meet him in a house next to the Medici Palace where, instead of a complaisant lady, Alessandro was confronted by a bravo, and his dead body was not discovered until the morning. Cellini tells how at the time of Alessandro's murder he was out duck shooting near Rome with a friend. As they rode home in the twilight they were astonished to see a fiery light in the direction of Florence, and said, 'Assuredly we shall hear tomorrow that something of vast importance has happened.'

The junior branch of the Medici had made no mark in history until Lorenzino murdered his kinsman and so brought the dynasty of Cosimo the Elder to an end. One of the mysteries of history is why, in an age that condoned tyrannicide, he should have fled to Venice, where he was eventually assassinated, instead of claiming the dukedom as next of kin. His behaviour was so odd that it has been assumed he was mad. His flight opened the way for his cousin Cosimo, son of Giovanni delle Bande Nere (the general who extricated Machiavelli from his difficulty on the parade ground), a young man not quite eighteen, strong, powerful and, as he appeared before the authorities to claim the dukedom, quiet, docile, and submissive. He gave the impression that he would give no trouble, and, as new political pressures indicated another duke, he was granted the succession.

Before he was twenty, the young Duke proved to Florence that she had found a master. The republican pretences of the earlier Medici were now cast aside and the Florentines became the humble subjects of a sovereign who believed that the first duty of government is to be strong and, secondly, if possible, just and merciful. No voice was raised in protest when he transformed the home of Florentine republicanism, the Palazzo Vecchio, into his private palace. There he brought his haughty Spanish wife, Eleanor of Toledo, and there she bore her four sons, two of whom succeeded to the Duchy.

Cellini gives some admirable descriptions of Cosimo and Eleanor as he saw them at the Palazzo Vecchio when he called to discuss his work, especially the Perseus. Eleanor was hot-tempered and Cosimo was an exasperating autocrat with no real love of art yet, as a Medici, with obligations towards it. Cosimo I reigned for thirty-seven years and became the first Grand Duke of Tuscany, and his dynasty, at first from the Palazzo Vecchio, then from the Pitti Palace, ruled Florence and Tuscany for two hundred years.

The early Medici were more attractive than their grand ducal successors chiefly because of their friendships with the great men of the Renaissance. From the time of Cosimo the Elder to that of his grandson, Lorenzo the Magnificent, artists and sculptors ate with the family in the Medici palace in the Via Larga, and feckless geniuses such as Fra Filippo Lippi evidently had a studio there.

The story is that on one occasion Cosimo the Elder locked the idle friar in a room as the only way to get him to finish a canvas, but the artist is said to have knotted his bedclothes together and to have escaped by the window. The architect Michelozzo was so devoted to Cosimo that he went into exile with him, and, in the eyes of Donatello, Cosimo could do no wrong. This was indeed an attraction of opposites: Cosimo, the millionaire banker, and Donatello, a genius who had no money sense at all and kept his florins slung up to the ceiling in a basket where anyone who needed money could help himself. Disturbed by Donatello's shabbiness, Cosimo once gave him a costly red gown which the sculptor wore once and then returned as being too grand. On his death-bed, Cosimo charged his son and successor, Piero the Gouty, with the care of Donatello, then nearly eighty, and when the old sculptor died he was buried, as he had wished, near his patron.

Poor Piero the Gouty, in his invalid chair, had many friends among the artists. 'Most illustrious and generous friend,' is the way Domenico Veneziano began a letter to him, while Benozzo Gozzoli, who painted the famous fresco in the Palazzo Medici, wrote to Piero affectionately as *amico mio singolarissimo*. Lorenzo's affection for Verrocchio and Botticelli – 'our Botticelli', as he called him – is well known. The most celebrated of all the stories is that of Lorenzo watching a young lad carving the face of an old satyr and remarking that such a venerable creature would surely have lost a tooth. When he saw the lad at work again, he noticed that one of the satyr's teeth had been knocked out and the gums had been aged, which so impressed him that he took the young artist to live in the Palazzo Medici with his family. The young man was Michelangelo.

Such stories ended when the senior branch of the family was succeeded by the Grand Dukes of Tuscany. The friendly bridge between wealth and genius was broken down. The artist now approached his patron on bended knee. It is inconceivable, for example, that Cellini should have called Cosimo I his *amico singolarissimo*! The relationship was that of servant and master, and if the master were ignorant and a bad payer the servant could do nothing but cringe and hope for a smile. Nevertheless the Grand Dukes, who have had many detractors, were intelligent and perceptive patrons, and most of them were kindly and benevolent; even in decline they retained the intellectual interests which had always distinguished the Medici.

The only truly great ruler among the later Medici was Duke Cosimo I, who created the Grand Duchy with the aid of a few hand-picked, humbly-born secretaries (none of them Florentines) and left it after thirty years the strongest state in Italy. As everyone knows who has been through the Palazzo Vecchio with a guide, he was succeeded by his son Francesco, an amateur chemist who conducted his experiments in a jewel-casket of a room with a secret door which led to a smaller room where, presumably, the Grand Duke kept his precious stones, powders, and liquids: but it is difficult to believe that this was ever a serious laboratory, though it is said that Francesco sometimes greeted his secretary of state with bellows in hand. He it was who began to arrange the rooms in the government offices – the Uffizi – as an art gallery, a task which his successors continued.

When his Grand Duchess died, Francesco married Bianca Cappello, the Venetian beauty who had run off with a bank clerk. She had been his mistress for years and, aided by Bacchus, it is said, they remained devoted until eventually they died within a few hours of each other, and everyone, of course, suspected poison. Montaigne saw the lovers in their middle age when he was taken one day in 1580 to see them dine in public . . . 'The Duchess is handsome,' he wrote, 'according to Italian ideas, a pleasant and dignified face, big bust, and breasts as they like them.' He thought she was 'quite capable of having bewitched this prince and of retaining him at her feet for a long time'. They had no family, but by his first wife Francesco was the father of Marie de' Medici, who, in the following reign, married Henry IV and became the second Medici to be Queen of France. She was the mother of Louis XIII, of Elizabeth, who married Philip IV of Spain, and of Henrietta Maria, who married Charles I of England, thus in the tenth generation from old Cosimo the Elder the three principal thrones in Europe were occupied by a Medici.

Having no male heir, Francesco was succeeded by his brother Ferdinand, who without much difficulty divested himself of a cardinal's robes to become Grand Duke. He proved himself to be a good and popular ruler. He was also a discriminating art collector and acquired the Venus de' Medici. But his life's work was to carry forward the scheme his father, Cosimo, had originated: to create the port of Leghorn. It was Ferdinand who gave the building of this port an unusual interest by making it a refuge for the persecuted of all nations. Those who built its fortunes were Jews from all countries, English Catholics flying from Protestant England, Protestants from France, Flemings from the Spanish Netherlands; and all found a welcome at Leghorn. This was the moment when Robert Dudley, son of Elizabeth's Earl of Leicester, eloped with his pretty cousin, Elizabeth Southwell, and arrived in Florence in time to help the Grand Duke with his scheme. I have mentioned that the later history of the Dudley family is to be sought in Bologna, but Tuscany was the scene of Robert's success, first as a shipbuilder, a marine architect, and engineer, and then as a courtier. His later years were spent in the Pitti Palace as Grand Chamberlain.

Ferdinand's son and successor, Cosimo II, is remembered for protecting Galileo from the Jesuits, and appointing him 'Chief Mathematician to the Grand Duke' at a good salary and with freedom to carry out his scientific experiments. In gratitude, Galileo wrote the name of his patron in the sky, and the four moons of Jupiter, which Galileo was the first to see, are known to science as *Stellae Medicae*. Science and the making of scientific instruments (the barometer was invented in Florence at this period) occupied the Medici of the time as art had done during the Renaissance.

The next two reigns covered more than a century: Cosimo's son, Ferdinand II, reigned for fifty years and his son, Cosimo III, for fifty-three, but by that time the doom of the Medici was imminent ... The last Cosimo was a weak bigot who was cursed by a miserable marriage to a French princess whose loathing for him approached mania. To get away from her, Cosimo travelled through Europe and made a tour of England during the reign of

Charles II. The bulky and boring book compiled from these travels is notable for an unusual preface in which Cosimo frankly described his wife's short-comings, and the narrative proves how little a prince, trundling round with coaches full of courtiers, can see of a country; though he did give a good description of Charles II touching for the King's Evil at Newmarket.

By the time Cosimo III died in 1723 an uncanny silence had fallen upon the Pitti Palace. Though three successive generations had between them produced twenty-four children, there was now no male to carry on the line. Cosimo's elder son, Ferdinand, had died, and his younger son, then a drunkard of fifty-two, succeeded to the throne. The fourteen-year reign of Gian Gastone was a shocking end to a great story. This unhappy man had contracted a hateful marriage and, like his father, had separated from his wife. He lived with failure and disillusion, the bottle as his friend and comforter, hidden by his courtiers, who dreaded his rare public appearances, until, taking to his bed, he lingered on and died at the age of sixty-six, proof that the process of drinking oneself to death often takes a long time. So ended in the male line one of the world's most distinguished families.

§ 3

The *Venus* of Botticelli, rising from a sea of tourists, is a familiar memory of Florence. In the Uffizi, which is now an art gallery with top lighting and pastel walls, the crowds are funnelled by structural inevitability to the most admired pictures; and Botticelli is today what Ghirlandaio was to the Victorians.

Though the sound of guides instructing in all the languages of Europe may fill the gallery, if you manage to reach the front row of spectators you will enter a region of church-like whispers – that 'estranging reverence' defined by Berenson – as the crowds find themselves in the embarrassing presence of greatness. Reverence of any kind is such a rare quality these days that one must respect and welcome it when one can; and I was surprised by the awed attitude of people to a picture which most of them had seen in reproductions all their lives. I think perhaps the first feeling is one of astonished discovery that the ethereal goddess formerly seen on a postcard is really four feet high. Also, no reproduction, no matter how admirable, can convey the exquisite lyrical quality of this composition or the strange, early morning tone of the colours.

The crowds which surge all morning round the picture, and its companion, *Spring* (that dreamland where it is possible to reconcile apples with primroses), are unburdened by theories, and are not interested in Neo-Platonism, or whether the pictures were inspired by Poliziano's famous poem on Venus riding on the seashell. They are, however, powerfully influenced by popular taste, and the little group in which I found myself, which was harangued by an unusually good guide, was most interested to learn that Venus has been recognized by scholars as the reigning beauty of Florence in 1470, Simonetta Vespucci, who died of consumption at the age of twenty-three. Probably the happiest person is the tourist who has never read a line of art criticism and enjoys Botticelli as he would a bed of spring flowers.

How interesting are the fluctuations of taste. A hundred years ago the tourists would have given scarcely a second glance to Botticelli, but would have gathered round Ghirlandaio – now, alas, considered to be merely a decorator. 'Sandro Botticelli was not a great painter in the same sense as Andrea Mantegna,' wrote John Addington Symonds less than a century ago. And, to Symonds, there was an even greater than Mantegna, one who possessed 'the keenest intuitions, the deepest thought, the strongest passion, the subtlest fancy, the loftiest imagination' – Ghirlandaio! So one may well wonder where the crowds will be gathering in the Uffizi in a hundred years' time.

As we were swept onward past Mantegna, past the famous battle scene of Uccello (which once hung in Lorenzo's bedroom), past sweet Madonnas by Filippo Lippi, to remain stationary for a short while before Michelangelo's *Holy Family*, we were eventually propelled by those behind us into the Tribune. Here an even more remarkable revolution in taste was obvious. The centre of this gallery is occupied by the Venus de' Medici, once the most admired female figure in the world. She stands as she did when she

434

was adored by our ancestors, but clothed now in familiarity; and no one gave her a second glance. Hundreds of small green replicas of this Venus once penetrated every corner of the world, though it is a long time since I have seen one on the top of a bookshelf. As the crowds passed her indifferently, I remembered the days when William Beckford could write that he went to the gallery 'to worship the Venus de' Medici' and, having seen her, felt that he could have stayed there for ever. Addison reverently felt her wrist; Lady Anne Millar, with a tape-measure, found that she was four feet nine and three-quarter inches high; but the greatest of all her admirers was Samuel Rogers, who could be seen every morning in 1821 seated opposite 'as if he hoped, like another Pygmalion, to animate the statue; or perhaps that the statue might animate him', as Mrs Jameson put it rather unkindly; for Rogers was notably desiccated in appearance. So well known was his infatuation that one day, taking his seat as usual, he noticed that the statue was holding a note addressed to him (the work of a young English visitor) in which the Venus begged Rogers not to ogle her every day, for, though partial friends might deem him still alive, she knew that he had come to her from the other side of the Styx.

As the visitors flow through the superb gallery, some may wonder why, of all the ducal capitals of Italy, Florence is the only one to have preserved its family treasures. This was indeed the question that puzzled me from the moment I arrived in the city. How had this happened?

In Milan the castle in which the Visconti and the Sforza lived has been rebuilt; in Pavia they tell you how the French sacked the great library; in Mantua the empty palace of the Gonzaga echoes to the daily tramp of the town guide and his flock, even the *studiolo* of Isabella d'Este is a ruin, and if you mention pictures they tell you of the Gonzaga sale to Charles I of England; in Ferrara only the typists of the Prefecture give life to the ancient castle; in Modena they tell you how the Este pictures made the artistic reputation of Dresden. All these great collections have been dispersed, and if you wished to trace them your journey would take you from Paris to the city that was once called St Petersburg. Yet Florence has been able to resist the auctioneer. An art collection, which even a dealer would be unable to value, has survived the death of the family that created it, and is seen today on the walls and in the rooms of the same palaces for which it was originally designed.

This miracle was the work of a woman whose name is rarely heard even in Florence. She was the Electress Anna Maria Luisa, only daughter of Cosimo III and sister of the last Grand Duke. She was born in 1671, and the only picture I have seen of her, in the Pitti Palace, shows a tall, neat-waisted young woman in a hunting costume heavily braided with gold. She wears a tricorne hat decorated with ostrich feathers from which her dark curls descend to her shoulders. Her right hand holds a flint-lock musket, her left rests on the head of a hunting dog. This charming girl was married to the Elector Palatine at the age of twenty-four, and spent the next twenty-six years in Germany. Upon the death of her husband she returned to Florence, a woman of fifty, to end her life there and to witness the downfall and degradation of her family.

Six years after her return, her father's long and dreary reign ended and the old Grand Duke, aged eighty-one, was succeeded by his only surviving son, Gian Gastone, aged fifty-two. In spite of his weakness, the people liked him, far gone as he was in dissipation and melancholia. His bust in the Uffizi shows a preposterous face with a self-indulgent, pouting little mouth, gazing out from an enormous periwig in a pathetic attempt to look like Louis XIV. Resigned now to be the last Medici Grand Duke of Tuscany, the unhappy man isolated himself in the Pitti Palace. There is probably a psychological reason why an elderly aristocratic alcoholic should dote on the lowest companions he could scrape out of the gutter, and, if so, this would apply to Gian Gastone.

When Anna Maria arrived in Florence she discovered that the widow of her late brother, Ferdinand, Princess Violante, had been installed as hostess in the palace, and since she did not like Violante, and as Gian Gastone did not like anyone, the royal establishment was split into three exasperated groups. Fortunately, palaces are designed to cushion a great amount of ill-will, and there was room enough in the Pitti to contain an overload of incompatability.

Gian Gastone would sometimes show himself to his subjects, hopelessly drunk, but they seem to have had some sympathy for his problems, and they were also grateful to him for certain reforms and for having swept the palace and the government clear of the priests and the spies who had ruled Florence in the time of his father. As his reign of fourteen years proceeded, his natural misery of spirit overwhelmed him, and he began to retire more and more from public events and to drink in secret. It is strange to imagine the two haughty dames and the middle-aged toper living their separate lives under the frisking cupids of the Pitti, surrounded by the works of the world's greatest artists.

Anna Maria had been in the habit of giving her brother good advice – no doubt one of the reasons why he disliked her – but now, as she saw him in his degeneration, she knew that he could not be helped. That a family of great collectors should be about to terminate in one who was himself a collection of psychopathic disorders held that touch of irony which fate sometimes reserves for such occasions. Like many alcoholics, the Grand Duke was able to astonish his courtiers by sudden unexpected shafts of wisdom and common sense, generally delivered in sardonic asides, almost as if another personality, a finer, better Gian Gastone, had risen to the surface only to be pulled down again by his demon. Still, such disconcerting flashes gave the impression that he knew perfectly well what was going on.

The Electress upheld the dignity of the Medici in public. Sometimes she would drive through Florence in the evening to attend a church or to take the air, and was to be seen travelling at a snail's pace in a huge gilt coach drawn by eight horses and attended by a mounted guard. One day she received Horace Walpole, who described how she stood beneath a black canopy and, after speaking a few words, dismissed him.

In *The Last Medici*, Harold Acton gives a horrifying account of Gian Gastone's degeneration. For the last thirteen years of his life the Grand Duke never dressed properly, and for the last eight rarely left his bed, where a Spanish ambassador described him as 'lying motionless as a lunatic'. Once, when it was rumoured that he was dead, a public appearance was judged to be advisable, and to fortify himself for the ordeal the unhappy man drank heavily beforehand. 'It were well to skate over the rest,' writes Harold Acton, 'how the inebriated Grand Duke, as he was driven in gala through the streets of Florence, turned now and then to vomit out of the chariot window, while his peering people bowed or curtseyed or doffed their hats. This bloated, broken-looking bibber: was this the last male descendant of a family which had embodied the perfection of human culture?

'At the Prato Gate he was helped on to the terrace whence yearly the Grand Dukes had witnessed the races of barbs. His humiliated courtiers stood as far as possible out of the royal reach, but Gian Gastone was evidently enjoying himself in spite of his puking, for he kept raising his querulous voice and calling to them incoherently, hiccoughing deplorable remarks at the pages and ladies-in-waiting. Then he fell into a dozing torpor; his servants deposited him furtively in a litter, and carried him back to the Pitti. At the Pitti he remained.'

Such was the last Grand Duke's final appearance in public. Hidden away in his apartments in the Pitti, he surrendered himself to the entertainments devised by his favourite, a servant named Giuliano Dami, who for years had acted as his pander. Dami had recruited an army of males and females from the very dregs of the population and introduced them into the palace to minister to his master's peculiarities. 'Their salaries varied with the antics they performed,' says Harold Acton, 'often he [the Grand Duke] required them to insult him and knock him about like a clown; from the fact that they were paid on Tuesdays and Saturdays in ruspi (a ruspo being a Florentine sequin formerly worth ten francs) they became notorious as *Ruspanti*. . . .'

One day, while his sister and sister-in-law were at Mass, Gian Gastone, hearing the sound of drums and trumpets in the forecourt of the Pitti, saw some Poles with dancing bears. This delighted him so much that he asked the men to his apartments, where he started drinking with them, then, becoming drunk, began to throw wine in their faces; they, drunk as well, retaliated, and the noise brought anxious chamberlains to the scene, who saw the Grand Duke, like an angry bear, struggling with one of the Poles.

There were worse stories, but it is kinder not to tell them. His condition belonged to medicine rather than to morals, and one feels pity rather than contempt for this tragic member of a great family. Some days before his death at the age of sixty-six, a strangely different Gian Gastone came for a moment to the surface. No *Ruspanti* came near him. He repented with tears and, having received the last sacraments, died. No sooner was his last breath drawn than the great powers of Europe, who had been brooding like vultures over the Tuscan Succession, disregarded the obvious claims of the Electress Anna Maria to reign in her own right as Grand Duchess, and gave Tuscany to the Duke of Lorraine on the understanding that he should, in return, give Lorraine to France.

Anna Maria, the last of the Medici, continued to live in her apartments in the Pitti, observing, without a change of expression, the horde of vulgar and ignorant Lorrainers who now ruled Tuscany. She was immensely rich. No one could touch her personal fortune or the Medici art collection, which belonged unquestionably to her. In the last years of her life she performed an act as fine as any in the long history of her family: she left the greatest art collection in the world to the State of Tuscany on the condition that it should never be removed from Florence and should be kept for the benefit of the public of all nations. In doing so, she created the Florence of today. Whatever the failures of her unfortunate brother, Anna Maria atoned for them and made it possible for the Medici to make their bow to history with dignity and magnificence.

I think perhaps the strangest thing about Florence is that, in a city of sculpture, one looks in vain for a statue of the greatest benefactress the city ever knew.

§ 4

Charles Godfrey Leland's reputation as a humorist – he was the author of *Hans Breitmann* – has obscured the fact that he was a pioneer folk-lorist. It is probable that his skit on the German-American is still bringing down the house at rural concerts though his real work is unknown to most people, and even those aware of it, so perilous is humour, may be a little suspicious of him. He was an American with the gift of tongues who spent his last years in Florence, where he died in 1903. In company with an Italian friend, he went about collecting stories and legends 'truly gathered from old wives', as he put it, which he published in 1895 as *Legends of Florence*.

I picked up his book by chance and was soon lost in a marvellous world of *foletti*, *fate*, *diavoli*, *strege*, and *maliardi*, all of them spirits who were evidently the old pagan gods, nymphs, satyrs, and the rest who, surprisingly, I think, haunted the peasant's fireside as recently as seventy years ago. I wondered how many of these stories are still told on winter evenings in Tuscany.

I remembered these legends when I was visiting the Uffizi because it seemed so interesting to think that painters of the Renaissance probably needed no instructions from their learned Neo-Platonist patrons when asked to paint the old gods. Here, for example, is the kind of scheme, or *storia*, for a picture which might have been suggested to Botticelli.

There was once a poor man who lived in squalid misery with a wife and two children, one of whom was blind, the other crippled. The poor fellow often wept with despair and would say:

> '*The wheel of Fortune turns, they say,*
> *But for me it turns the other way;*
> *I work with good-will, but do what I may,*
> *I have only bad luck from day to day.*

'Now it happened that very late one night, or very early one morning, as one might say, between dark and dawn, he went to the forest to cut wood. When having called to Fortune as was his wont – Ai! what was his surprise to see – *tutta ad un tratto* – all at once, before his eyes, a gleam of light, and raising his head, he beheld a lady of enchanting beauty passing along rapidly, and yet not walking – on a rolling ball – *e ciondolava le gambe* – moving her limbs – I cannot say feet, for she had none. In place of them were two wheels, and these wheels, as they turned, threw off flowers from which there came a delicious perfume.

'The poor man uttered a sigh of relief seeing this, and said: "Beautiful lady, believe me when I say that I have invoked thee every day. Thou art the Lady of the Wheel of Fortune, and had I known how beautiful thou art, I would have worshipped thee for thy beauty alone."'

The goddess, remarking that she was not always in the habit of casting her favours on those who deserve them, asked the poor man whether he would prefer to pick one of Fortune's flowers for himself, or to pick two and bring fortune to two other human beings as miserable as himself. Unselfishly, he elected to bring good luck to others, but, as he advanced to pick the two flowers, the goddess, with her usual caprice, suddenly told him to pick a third for himself!

This pretty little story is surprising for its perfect picture of the Roman Fortuna on her golden wheel, scattering sweet flowers to right and left, as described by a Tuscan peasant only seventy years ago.

It is surprising to find Michelangelo in the role of a pagan god, a kind of Pan. The story told to Leland was that his spirit haunts woods and groves, often at night. He amuses himself by teasing lovers 'and when he finds a pair who have hidden themselves under leaves and boughs to make love, he waits until they think they are well concealed, and then begins to sing. The two feel a spell upon them when they hear his voice, and can neither advance nor retreat'. But Michelangelo's favourite quarry was the lady artist. When seated at her easel in some pleasant wood, she would notice that her sketch had become covered with meaningless scrawls, which she was unable to rub out or rectify. If she lost her temper, she would hear a laugh, loud and startling; on the other hand, if she took fright and hurried home she would discover that her sketch, so far from being ruined, had become a superb drawing in the style of Michelangelo.

'It is marvellous how the teasing faun or Silvanus of the Romans has survived in Tuscany,' commented Leland. 'I have found him in many forms under many names, and this is the last. But why it should be Michelangelo, I cannot imagine, unless it be that his face and stump nose, so familiar to the people, are indeed like those of the faun. The *dii sylvestres*, with all their endless mischief, riotry and revelry, were good fellows, and the concluding, and rather startling touch that the great artist in the end always bestows a valuable picture on his victim is really godlike – in a small way.'

Though scholars have traced the inspiration of Botticelli's two most famous pictures to the poem by Poliziano, I thought them just the sort of scenes which a Tuscan peasant might expect to see if he awakened in a haunted wood.

§ 5

When the Germans blew up the water and gas mains of Florence during the last war, they also destroyed the bridges, except 'the most artistic one' (the words are Hitler's); and while the Pitti Palace, overflowing with refugees, looked like a slum with washing hanging out of every window, the galleries of the Uffizi were ankle-deep in water. That was the moment when the city was caught between two opposing armies.

Few, if any, remember this today as they pass with delighted murmurs from room to room in the Uffizi; yet all the masterpieces there (and in every other gallery in Europe) have returned to the walls after incarceration in caves, tunnels, mines, cellars, and secluded castles. If men ever deserved the praise and gratitude of their fellows, they are the little-known group of scholars and administrators, the curators of museums and art galleries in all countries, whose task it was to safeguard the art treasures from air raids and other perils of modern war. Happily, the directors of the Florentine galleries hurried their treasures into safety as war came to Tuscany.

Readers of Sir Osbert Sitwell's autobiography will remember that what he pleasantly calls 'the rarest of all house-parties' gathered during his absence in 1940 at his castle near Florence, Montegufoni. The 'guests' included Botticelli's *Primavera*, Uccello's *Battle of San Romano*, Cimabue's *Virgin Enthroned*, and hundreds of other pictures from the Uffizi which had been sent there for safety by the Italian Government during the war. Though the castle was later on occupied by the Germans, all the pictures came through safely except Ghirlandaio's circular *Adoration of the Magi*. This picture, which has a diameter of more than six feet, was damaged 'because the Germans used it, face upwards, as a table-top (though the table beneath had a top of its own), and it was stained in consequence with wine, food, and coffee, and with the marks which the soldiers made on it with their knives'.

The 'house-party' at Montegufoni was not exceptional. There were in Tuscany alone about thirty-seven similar collections hidden in hilltop castles in the nine provinces of the Region. The story of their recovery and restoration has been well told by Mr. Frederick Hartt in *Florentine Art Under Fire*, a book that should be issued as a paperback in all European languages and made compulsory reading for art students who visit Florence. One is reminded with pride that when the Allies invaded Italy the British and American Governments put a plan into operation to preserve the art treasures. Commissions had been appointed in both countries to decide how best the cultural treasures could be saved in war areas, with the result that when the Allied armies moved in, art historians, archivists, architects, and scholars trained in museums and art galleries, English and American, were appointed to the staffs of the military commanders. It was their task to locate hidden collections, to assess damage, and to render first aid. The devoted co-operation they received from their 'enemy' opposite numbers, the Italian art historians and curators, is one of the fine stories of the war. There is, of course, no gratitude in international affairs, but one likes to think that perhaps someday in the future the historian of Europe may give praise to Britain and America for having remembered the things of the spirit during the heat and fury of conflict.

I never looked at the pictures in the Uffizi, displayed so serenely upon the well-lit walls, glistening in their frames as if they had never known such squalor as a mildewed cellar, without remembering those devoted Allied officers, bumping over dusty roads in jeeps, in search of lost masterpieces while the landscape still shook with shellfire. Mr Hartt, an American art expert, was assigned as Monuments and Fine Arts officer to the provinces of Florence, Siena, and Arezzo, and many were the glimpses afforded him of immortality in the strangest surroundings. On one occasion, with German shells passing overhead, he succeeded in making his way to an old mansion standing in vineyards where, in a hall which the Germans had used as a garage, he discovered enormous crates full of statuary. 'Unable to suppress an exclamation of shock and wonder,' he writes, 'I climbed over the crates, identifying with great emotion one after the other until I found myself gazing through the bars of a crate into the agonized face of Michelangelo's *Dawn*, every tragic lineament disclosed by the light from the door.'

In the town of Montagnana he came to a villa which had received a direct shell hit, where he found Rosso Fiorentino's *Descent from the Cross*, dusty and scratched, and 'in the middle of all the rubble, dirt, and disorder of the villa was the haunting beauty of Pontormo's uninjured *Deposition* from Santa Felicia in Florence, whose grief-stricken figures seemed to soar above the desolation in an unearthly realm of silver light and rose and green shadows.' In this villa he reflected that 'the visitors who came in such hundreds to see the Studiolo of Francesco I de' Medici in the Palazzo Vecchio would have been most surprised if they could have beheld the paintings which form the walls of that little jewel box, scattered about the chapel. . . .'

He also found casualties, such as Pontormo's *Visitation*, which had fallen under a bombed wall and had also been stamped on by men in hobnailed boots so that plaster and brick-dust were ground into the painting. With the expert's unconscious humour, the author reflects: 'It is a tribute to the durability of Cinquecento panel painting that there was anything left.' I like his story of the English brigadier who was so interested in the art treasures which had to be removed from the danger of his headquarters that he demanded a brief lecture on each piece as it left the castle. 'This I had to deliver,' says Mr Hartt, 'to the thunderous accompaniment of the General's artillery and the whistle and crash of German shells so near that more than once the workmen ran for cover.' I also like the story of the commanding officer of a South African Field Dressing Station, a Major Morton, who was worried to hear that, through some misunderstanding, he had established his hospital in a villa full of art treasures which was itself also an artistic monument. 'Major Morton's concern for the safety of the villa and its contents was touching in the extreme,' writes Mr Hartt. 'The strictest orders were given to all his men, and these orders were meticulously complied with ... Before he left, Major Morton wrote to thank me for the use of the villa. During the period in which his unit was there, he said 199 severe battle casualties were treated – before the frescoes of Pontormo, Andrea del Sarto, and Alessandro Allori.'

A grim story is that of the hundreds of stolen pictures, but the Allied organization was able to foil the Germans, who had planned the greatest art robbery since the time of Napoleon, indeed the author calls it 'the greatest single art-looting operation in recorded history.' Among the loot captured on its way to Germany were *Adam* and *Eve* by Cranach, which Goering desired. As the author saw the first consignment on its way back to Florence, escorted by military police, 'it gave me not only unspeakable personal satisfaction,' he writes, 'but a deep pride in the Allied cause ...'

I have an idea that the full story of 'Operation Art' has not yet been told. Mr Hartt, of course, deals only with his own three provinces, but what was happening, one wonders, in other places. How, for example, did Venice fare? Surely this story should be set down in the fullest detail while those are still alive who took part in what is the most civilized operation ever planned in wartime.

§ 6

The heat of the day lingered in the streets, but in the evening it was cool beside the Arno. It was the moment I often chose to find some small restaurant. As the best wine in Italy is rarely found in a bottle, so the best cooking is often to be enjoyed in a cellar or a room that contains no more than ten tables. It is all a matter of luck, but you must find such places before the owner has become prosperous enough to hire a chef. When that happens, it is time to move on to another cellar where the husband sits at the cash desk while his wife does the cooking.

I had discovered a restaurant in one of the back streets of Florence which I would enter straight from the pavement, and, pushing aside a bead curtain, would find myself in a room papered from floor to ceiling with cigarette cartons. I had just finished dinner one night when I became aware that a street musician – a distressing feature of Italian restaurant life to me – had entered, and was preparing to tune up. He stood with one foot on a chair, gently thrumming the strings of a mandolin, but I paid no particular attention until he began to sing in a pleasant English voice:

Have you seen but a bright lily grow,
Before rude hands have touched it?
Have you mark'd but the fall of the snow
Before the soil hath smutch'd it?
Have you felt the wool of the bever?
Or swan's down ever?
Or have smelt o' the bud of the briar?
Or the nard in the fire?
Or have tasted the bag of the bee?
O so white! O so soft! O so sweet is she!

The effect of this upon the room was interesting. I myself was astonished. The few Italians present, none of whom I imagine understood the song, applauded loudly, appreciating, with their natural good taste, that they had been listening to something out of the ordinary. The young man bowed his acknowledgements and, after a few preliminary strums, sang Purcell's *Man was for the*

Woman Made. He was a young fellow in his twenties with blue eyes and a mop of yellow hair and a thin golden beard, which gave him the indolent, rather crafty look of an Elizabethan Englishman. When he came to my table to collect alms, I asked if he would prefer to sit down and have something to eat.

'Thank you,' he said, 'but first I must park my lute.'

He stowed the mandolin away on a ledge. 'No musical instrument, except possibly the oboe,' he explained, 'was designed to take out to dinner.'

Most young people appear perilously carefree to their elders, and this young man seemed to me abnormally buoyant. He was like a legend or a fairy-tale in reverse: a bird that had become a man. He did not trouble to look at the menu.

'Can I have a steak?' he asked.

He attacked the enormous Florentine steak with delight and cast glances at me from time to time from those watchful blue eyes, wondering why I had not begun to ask questions. I let him wonder all through the crême caramel and the cheese, then I said, 'I was surprised to hear Ben Jonson and Purcell in a place like this.'

'I am very fond of them,' he replied. 'Do you know Campion's *Oft have I sighed*? Or *Sweet Kate* by Robert Jones, or Thomas Ford's *Faire, Sweet Cruell*? There are also some very good modern folk songs. An American student taught me a Spanish miners' song which he learnt from a man who was in the Spanish Civil War. I sang it yesterday on the Ponte Vecchio and got into trouble with the police.'

There was an echo of the North Country in his voice, the unmistakable tang of Yorkshire. He told me that he was at Hull University and, having decided to write a thesis on the Renaissance, thought he must see Florence.

'But I had no money,' he explained, 'so I decided to sing my way to Italy and get lifts along the road – I've always loved the Elizabethan madrigals. I got here within a fortnight, which isn't bad, in fact it's very good indeed. It's about the time taken by a Florentine courier of the time of Lorenzo *il Magnifico*, to reach Paris! But then, you see, when I moved, I moved fast, in big American touring cars!'

I expressed surprise, and confessed that the ugly gesture of the hiker thumbing a lift dried up the wells of human kindness in me.

'I agree with you,' he said, 'it is quite hideous. If I ever have a motor-car I shall never give anyone a lift. But you must realize that all hitch-hiking is psychological warfare. The thumb gesture arouses in the minds of many motorists an acute guilt complex, a why-should-I-be-sitting-here-while-that-poor-chap-is-standing-in-the-road kind of feeling. It is not therefore to be despised by anyone like myself, who has to travel without money. But it is entirely loathsome, common, and beastly. I am myself in favour of a graceful wave of the hand, and a slight bow in the direction I wish to go. But it is not nearly so effective as the jerked thumb.'

'I should have thought your graceful bow, in conjunction with the "lute", would be practically irresistible!' I said.

'Well, I've nothing to complain of. But, of course, I've studied the psychology of hitch-hiking and have developed a technique. It is a good idea to look tired, but you must never look dirty. You must never try to attract attention by a gay smile. The driver, who may not be feeling very cheerful himself, thinks "let the blighter walk", and drives on! It is essential to have a pack, a heavy-looking one, and often a little Union Jack is a help. A good-looking girl in shorts with a pack and a Union Jack need never walk a yard! But it's rather different for a man. What you've got to remember is that you have only a few seconds to create an agreeable reaction in the mind of someone travelling towards you at seventy miles an hour!'

I asked about food and sleeping quarters. Farmers would sometimes give him a bed and nearly always let him doss down in a barn. During a warm summer, however, it was delightful to sleep out in some places, like the caves in various parts of southern France and the beach at Nice. He found that madrigals were the perfect introduction wherever he sang them. He said that people who, at first, were indifferent or even hostile, thawed as soon as he began to sing; and this I could easily imagine since his general effect was that of a carefree, rather threadbare, but still in some way elegant, young troubadour. He must surely have awakened many an ancestral memory when he thrummed his 'lute' in those regions of the south where Bertran de Born and Peire Vidal used to sing.

'And has Florence justified your pilgrimage?'

'In every way,' he replied. 'The trouble is the necessity to make a little money now and then. It takes time which could be more usefully employed. My mainstay in Florence has been a Dominican who is anxious to learn English, but the wretched fellow is off to the States next month, and I shall have to look for someone else.'

He looked at the end of his cigarette and laughed.

'Something will turn up! It always does!'

We said good-bye under a lamp in the street outside. He leaned against it negligently, holding his mandolin as if he were about to break into song, and I was reminded of Nicholas Hilliard's beribboned gallant leaning against a tree. I asked what he intended to do when he had seen Florence. He replied in a memorable phrase.

'I shall sing my way back to Hull.'

I saw him twice again, once in the street, singing to a puzzled crowd of German tourists, and again in the library of the British Institute, where he was helping to classify and rearrange the English books. When I inquired for him there some time later with the idea of asking him to dinner, I was told that he had gone to Rome. The words suggest a train or a motor coach, but I had a vision of him standing by the roadside, perhaps making a graceful bow in the direction of the Eternal City.

§ 7

Those sooty London relatives of the Florentine palaces, the clubs of Pall Mall, resemble their ancestors in scale, and also in their air of sombre defensiveness. Anyone who has read a book about Florence knows what an exceptional building the Palazzo Medici is, yet who can doubt that if it were to be discovered some morning squeezed in between the Travellers' and the Reform quite a number of people would not notice anything out of the ordinary.

Indeed it might be imagined that members of the Travellers', who never speak to each other, having entered by mistake, would be found seated there in unquestioning silence.

Cosimo the Elder built this massive pile about 1440 as a new family mansion, and all the earlier Medici lived there for the next hundred years, until, in the time of Piero the Unfortunate, they were driven out and all their portable treasures sacked by the mob. What the first home was like, no one knows. It was probably one of those cheerful structures seen in Giotto's frescoes, with plenty of coloured marble decoration and balconies upheld on slender columns: but Cosimo wanted something more modern. He asked Brunelleschi to design a new palace for him, but this the wary old banker rejected as too splendid and therefore likely to create envy. It is said that Brunelleschi was so wounded, or angry, that he smashed his scale model into innumerable fragments – *in mille pezzi* – and Michelozzo, Cosimo's favourite, supplied the winning design. Thus the Medici Palace at the corner of the Via Cavour, one of the busiest streets in Florence, is not only the first Renaissance mansion, it is also a measure of the degree of grandeur permitted by fifteenth century Florentines before they began to say that a banker was getting too big for his boots.

I went there one morning with a flock of visitors and was impressed to think that when this sophisticated building was designed, one which, as I have said, would cause no surprise in London or any other modern city, there were thousands of old soldiers alive who had fought at Agincourt. The palace is now the Prefecture, but visitors can get a glimpse of the courtyard and are taken upstairs to see the tiny family chapel so gaily frescoed by Benozzo Gozzoli.

The courtyard is lovely, and anyone passing beneath the archway in the time of Lorenzo would have seen two Davids presiding over the atrium, one by Donatello, the other by Verrocchio. The garden, now a formal one of geometrical beds divided by tessellated paths, was full of fantastic topiary in the old days. The hedges were cut into the shapes of hounds, stags and elephants, and in the middle was Donatello's Judith, now on the steps of the Palazzo Vecchio.

The visitor will be disappointed if he goes to the palace in the hope of capturing some intimate memory of the Medici; even the marble steps with their beautiful shallow treads which lead into the palace have never felt the footstep of even a later Medici, as the whole palace was reconstructed when the Marchese Riccardi bought the building in the seventeenth century. All Italian palaces are designed to contain a teeming family, and they are not large when one thinks of them housing six or seven sons with their wives, families, and servants. In his old age Cosimo, wracked with 'gout', grieved over the smallness of his family. A son and a grandson had died; he had only his ailing heir, Piero the Gouty, and two grandsons. He was heard to sigh one day, as he was carried in his chair through the palace, 'Too large a house for so small a family!'

The little chapel is much as the Medici knew it. I sat in one of the chestnut stalls and admired Gozzoli's famous cavalcade, the Three Kings on their way to Bethlehem, which covers the walls and is pictured in nearly every book on Italian painting. Someone as barbarous as those who made a door in Leonardo's *Last Supper*, has inserted a window and a door, both of which cut into the fresco.

I suppose no finer glimpse exists of the kind of princely procession which wound its way over the Italian countryside during the Renaissance. The Three Kings are on their way to a Tuscan Bethlehem. They have come down from the mountains with their nobles and retainers along a road that winds out of the gates of shining hilltop towns and passes through woods of cone-shaped trees. It crosses arched bridges and passes through domed meadows, sloping vineyards, and groups of cypress trees. It is the enchanted landscape of a fairy-tale, and it is difficult to believe that anyone was ever unhappy there.

The travellers ride in silent reverence without sound of fife or trumpet. Some sit on saddles of red velvet and hold embossed and embroidered bridles. Their horses are caparisoned in scarlet and gold. As they pass down from the mountains, a rider detaches himself and gallops after a buck; another unleashes a hunting leopard; a falcon that has just killed a hare stands unconcerned almost under the horses' hoofs, and a duck swims in a little stream, unfrightened by grooms and horsemen.

One of the Three Kings is a white-bearded old man who rides a dappled mule and is clothed in dark red; another is a King of middle-age with a chestnut beard, who wears his crown over a cap of ostrich feathers and rides a white stallion; and the third is a fair-haired young man gorgeously clothed in cloth-of-gold, who rides proudly forward, his feet in golden stirrups. There is not one smile in the whole procession. Only the Tuscan landscape smiles as the travellers go gravely on their way to Bethlehem.

I listened while the guide told the legend that has recently been discredited: that the cavalcade commemorates the Council of Florence and that the young king is Lorenzo the Magnificent. It was always an unconvincing story. Why the Medici should have wished to perpetuate a theological wrangle that achieved nothing has never been explained. Cosimo had financed it out of friendship for the insolvent Pope (prudently accepting the town of Borgo Sansepolcro as security!) and one would have thought that bankers, who were accustomed to writing off bad debts, would have been only too glad to forget the inglorious Council instead of living with it in their private chapel. And the guide went on to tell us what a splendid spectacle it was, this meeting of the Greek and Latin Churches, a brilliance which Gozzoli, he said, who had probably seen the processions, reproduced in his fresco. But the truth is that it was not splendid or brilliant, and the people of Ferrara, where the Council began, were bitterly disappointed by the dull appearance of the seven hundred sombre Greek bishops and priests in black or violet, and the monks in threadbare robes of grey, considering their own Latin bishops and abbots more spectacular. And when the Council moved to Florence the pageantry was ruined by rain, and the Emperor John VIII rode through the dripping streets under an umbrella.

Nevertheless, the guide insisted on the splendour and told us that the old king was the Patriarch Joseph, the middle-aged one was the Emperor, and the young one was Lorenzo the Magnificent as a boy. Having lived for something like twenty years with the picture of the young king (in the form of a large unavoidable lamp-shade) I have had plenty of time to wonder how anyone who has ever seen the death-mask of Lorenzo could imagine that, even in the most angelic moments of childhood, the sallow, harsh-faced Medici with his broad nostrils could have resembled the fair-haired boy in the fresco. Consequently, I was delighted to see that in 1960 E. H. Gombrich traced the story that links the Gozzoli fresco with the Council of Florence to a French guide book, *Guide Souvenir de Florence* by J. Marcotti, published in 1888. 'Always eager to give life and substance to the shadowy events of the past,' writes Mr Gombrich, 'tourists and even historians have seized on this interpretation without reflecting on its improbability.'

The writer then notes that Gozzoli has taken over whole groups, including the Three Kings, from Gentile de Fabriano's famous picture on the same subject, now in the Uffizi. There you will find in a picture which is dated 1423 – twenty-six years before Lorenzo was born – the good-looking young king of the Gozzoli fresco. Gozzoli was evidently greatly attached to this figure. He painted him again in the now destroyed frescoes at Pisa. A good reproduction is to be found in *The Mural Painters of Tuscany* by Eve Borsook, where the young man is seen with the same kneeling figure, who is removing his spurs, as in Fabriano's picture. And I do not think Gozzoli was the only artist to copy this graceful lad. I think I am right in recognizing him again, and also the middle-aged king, in the charming fresco which Fra Angelico painted on the walls of the cell in S. Marco to which Cosimo the Elder retreated from time to time.

Has it ever occurred to anybody that the visit of the Magi was perhaps Cosimo's favourite religious theme, and understandably so in one who himself had poured out so much gold, frankincense, and myrrh? Not only was this the incident pictured on the monastery cell where he went to meditate, but it is also the scene by Botticelli, with Cosimo himself as one of the kneeling kings, painted a few years after Cosimo's death for an altar in S. Maria Novella.

I listened while the guide concluded his story, wishing that I were one of those brave characters whose love of truth transcends the embarrassment of contradicting someone in public.

§ 8

The church of the Santissima Annunziata stands at one end of the exquisite Piazza dell' Annunziata: and if you linger there long enough you will see a taxi arrive from which will step a bride and her bridegroom. Entering the church, the bride will leave her bouquet at an ornate altar on the left of the main door. If you look to the right of the church you will see the earliest foundling hospital in Europe, the *Ospedale degli Innocenti*, in whose gardens romp and totter hundreds of innocents, blissfully unaware of the significance of bridal bouquets. The juxtaposition, though not deliberate, is effective.

The square is the most beautiful in Florence. In the centre rides the Grand Duke Ferdinand I, who became a cardinal but prudently never took holy orders, so it was a simple matter for him to resign the purple and accept the crown of Tuscany when his brother failed to produce an heir. He was the Medici who, as I have mentioned, built the Villa Medici in Rome and brought to Florence a number of famous statues, including the Venus de' Medici.

The Grand Duke rides a horse with a peculiar pedigree. It was cast by Giovanni da Bologna from Turkish guns when that sculptor was in his eighties. When Marie de' Medici heard of it, she was planning a mounted statue of her deceased husband, Henry IV of France, and fearing that the artist might not be spared to make many more such steeds, coolly suggested to her uncle, Ferdinand, that, as France did not possess a sculptor capable of making such a horse, would he kindly send it to her and have another made for his own statue! That did not appeal to Ferdinand. However, he obligingly had a second horse cast from the same mould, and this was sent to France. It fell into the sea near Havre but was retrieved and was eventually erected on the Pont Neuf with Henry IV in the saddle and a parchment inside giving details of its odd history. Unhappily this fascinating animal was removed during the French

Revolution, and, reverting to the original medium of the parent horse in Florence, was melted down into cannon. The existing, and more recent, statue of Henry IV on the Pont Neuf also has a strange history. It was cast from the statue of Napoleon which once stood on the column in the Place de la Concorde.

When I entered the church of the Annunziata, which is full of beautiful things, I happened to have chosen a moment when three brides followed each other and prettily knelt down in their white dresses and placed their bouquets at the shrine of the miraculous Virgin. And what an unexpected shrine it is: an ornate classical tabernacle designed by Michelozzo for Cosimo the Elder, and now hung about with as many votive lamps as a Greek altar. It would be pleasant to see such an exercise in classical ornament more clearly. It is the only monument in Florence which carries, as far as I know, a revealing glimpse behind the scenes of Medici munificence. It bears the surprising inscription: *costò fior. 4 mila el marmo solo* – 'the marble alone cost four thousand florins'. It is as abrupt and angry as the sudden bang of a closed ledger. I thought that even Cosimo may have been a difficult character when it came to paying up!

That full-blooded genius, Benvenuto Cellini, is buried in the cloisters of this church. One stands at his tomb as at that of an old friend, remembering not only the Perseus and the gold saltcellar, but a hundred not always creditable stories from one of the world's greatest autobiographies. The crucifix which he designed for his tomb is, alas, not there. It was a nude Christ in white marble upon a black marble cross. I remember seeing it in Spain in a small room at the Escorial. A cloth was twined round the waist, and I was told that it replaces a handkerchief with which Philip II, in a moment of reverent prudery, had covered the figure nearly four hundred years ago.

I crossed the square to the Foundling Hospital. The front of this building brings a delighted gleam of recognition to the most sated eyes. In the spandrels of the arches are fourteen infants in swaddling bands, each one in a slightly different pose, and each standing within its heavenly circle of Della Robbia blue. A flight of steps leads to the arcade where, in a discreet corner, I found a small window, now covered with an iron grating, beneath a quotation from the Psalms: 'When my father and my mother forsake me, then the Lord will take me up.' The window once held the *ruota*, or wheel, on which unwanted infants were placed, accompanied by a hasty tug at the bell rope, generally at night. An inscription states that the wheel was used as recently as 1875.

The hall of the hospital leads into a garden where I was courteously invited to watch the *innocenti* at play. There were perhaps a hundred between the ages of four and six, running and tumbling on the grass while two young nursemaids sat under the trees in charge of them. I was fascinated by a sight such as this in the very headquarters, as indeed Florence is, of infantile pulchritude. How many times, I wondered, had Ghirlandaio and Botticelli and, of course, Verrocchio and Donatello, stood there sketch-book in hand, and Luca della Robbia certainly, when he was designing that group of laughing, romping children on the singing-loft, now in the museum of the cathedal. I was watching an almost identical scene. While I smiled to think that I had perhaps discovered the place where all the best Renaissance child models came from, an infant tottered and fell and was unable to rise. One of the young nurses ran to him and, carrying him back, sat soothing him in the shade of trees, a perfect Filippo Lippi Madonna.

I walked on down the garden path and found I was not the only visitor. A well-dressed young woman sat on a garden seat with one of the infants, and, as I passed, she gave me a swift smile, almost of recognition, which puzzled me until it occurred to me that it was a glance of complicity, and that she thought I had come, as she had, to adopt a child.

An official of the hospital agreed that for five centuries the playground was the most accessible and satisfactory place for an artist to study a number of small children in action, but the records of the institution do not mention the names of any artists who may have found their infant Christs there. The hospital was built at the expense of the Guild of Silk and opened its doors in 1444. In those days the boy foundlings, when old enough, were apprenticed to the shipmasters of Leghorn: nowadays children who are not adopted by foster parents, as many are, are sent to religious institutions when they are six years of age.

The beautiful old building, which was designed by Brunelleschi, is as up to date inside as any modern children's hospital with its bright and sunny wards, where I saw a younger intake than that in the garden, lying asleep in the abandoned attitudes of infancy, or clamouring for attention by shaking the sides of cribs and play-pens. The mothers of the children are allowed to visit them, some even nurse their own children there.

It was a novel and interesting experience to be alone in a Florentine art gallery where the treasures of the hospital are displayed in five rooms. The great attraction is Ghirlandaio's *Adoration of the Magi*, which is dated 1488, a year later than his painting of the same subject in the Uffizi. I think I prefer the painting in the *Innocenti*, and I liked particularly the two adorable little foundlings in their nightgowns reverently kneeling in the foreground.

I came to a show-case in which a number of letters from distinguished visitors have been preserved. I noticed the signatures of Heine, Garibaldi, Messonier, Longfellow, Alma Tadema, and a letter of thanks from 'Samuele Smiles, scrittore e moralista scozzese,' congratulating Signor De Sanctis on his singing.

§ 9

I think the least attractive statue in Florence is the bovine version of Giovanni delle Bande Nere in the Piazza S. Lorenzo. The fiery parent of Cosimo I is seen, dressed in Roman armour, seated upon a magnificent plinth that was surely designed for something resembling the Nelson Column. Instead, it ends abruptly with this warrior, who has the air of having climbed up there and is wondering how to descend. The sculptor was that boastful and envious character, Baccio Bandinelli, whom, after reading Vasari's account, one dislikes almost as much as Cellini did. He evidently had a pull with the Grand Duke, possibly because Bandinelli senior, a goldsmith, had saved the Medici gold plate during the family exile.

It is typical of Florence that within a few yards of this distressing figure is one of the world's sublime works, Michelangelo's Medici Chapel in the church of S. Lorenzo. This is the church where the Medici were christened, married, and buried, and where its leading members from the fifteenth to the eighteenth centuries still lie in death. With the exception of the two Medici Popes, Leo X and Clement VII, there is hardly a distinguished Medici absent from the sepulchral conclave.

The family is interred in three separate buildings, the Old Sacristy, the New Sacristy, and the Chapel of the Princes, and it is unfortunate that one is sometimes shown these in the wrong order. First one should visit the Old Sacristy, which is a small, beautiful companion to the Pazzi Chapel, indeed Brunelleschi designed it just a year or two before. Here the early Medici are buried, and I thought Verrocchio's sarcophagus the most beautiful early Renaissance tomb in Florence. One should then go to the New Sacristy, which Michelangelo built at the request of Leo X, whose fanatical passion for his family I have mentioned.

The moment I stepped into this chapel, I had the feeling that I was in some classical tomb. In design, it is a Roman hall with windows and pilasters, and though, like a pagan tomb, it counterfeits life, its business is death, as Michelangelo chillingly conveyed by making the pilasters and other architectural features in stone darker than the walls, as if they are in mourning drapes. It is disturbing and melancholy. 'If life pleases us we ought not to be grieved by death, which comes from the same Giver', was one of Michelangelo's sayings, but I could find nothing of that cheerful resignation in this muffled drum of architecture. The chapel itself, with its mourning pilasters and its sad, uneasy figures poised upon the sarcophagi, the brooding statues in the niches above, give the feeling that one is in a tomb oneself; and I looked round amazed to see my fellow tourists flipping the pages of their guide books completely unawed, as if they themselves were immortal.

One would not think that even that supreme jester, Time, would care to perpetrate a joke in such surroundings, nevertheless surely the grimmest joke in Florence is that the most splendid of the Medici tombs commemorate two of the least splendid of the Medici. The sarcophagi are memorials to the two young men drawn out of obscurity by Leo X to give a new lease of life to a dead branch of the family. One was Giuliano, the grandson of Lorenzo the Magnificent, a good and kindly man who reigned only for a year, and the other was his nephew, Lorenzo, of whom there is nothing to say except that he was the father of Catherine de' Medici. The contrast between the greatness of the memorial and the achievements of those commemorated must strike anyone who knows the family history.

For whom then, one asks oneself, could such a tomb have been erected? The answer, surely, is Dante. In the year before the work began on this Tomb Chapel, Michelangelo was one of those who wrote to Leo X asking him to obtain the bones of Dante from Ravenna; and Florence had reason to believe that the poet's remains would lie there in the 'worthy sepulchre' which Michelangelo had agreed to build. But Ravenna, warned in time, produced a carefully emptied sarcophagus, and so the scheme came to nothing. The design for Dante's tomb remained, however, in the mind of Michelangelo, though how much of it is reflected in the memorial which he erected to the two Medici, I suppose we shall never know. At any rate, to one visitor at least the New Sacristy seemed to have nothing to do with the Medici but quite a lot with 'the architectural grandeur', as Dorothy Sayers expressed it, of the *Divine Comedy*.

The Chapel of the Princes is the last to be visited, where, amid a strange museum of coloured marble let into the walls and selected for its cost, stand statues of the Grand Dukes of Tuscany. The family had indeed travelled far since the days of old Cosimo, father of his country, who strolled about in his red gown talking to everyone and offering good advice. These haughty princes in ermine mantles, crowned, and grasping sceptres, belong to a different world, and how Cosimo, the old cynic, would have smiled could he have seen them in their ducal splendour!

Few visitors see the grim reality of these chapels. In the crypt below is a dusty vista of coffins, each one carefully placed beneath the appropriate monument above. There can be few other family tombs as complete as these, except maybe the tombs of the Kings of England and the Spanish royal tombs in the Escorial. The Grand Dukes of Tuscany had a reluctance to be crowned with the regalia of their predecessors, or perhaps it would be more accurate to say that each Grand Duke was buried with his own crown and sceptre and new ones were made for his successor. The presence of so many bejewelled bodies in the vaults of Florence was an invitation to the tomb robber rarely exceeded in promise since the days of the Pharaohs. Accordingly, in 1857 the Government decided to find out how much theft had gone on, and how many of the Grand Dukes still retained their crowns and sceptres. The Pope, Pius IX, visited the mausoleum and inaugurated the Government Commission with special prayers. Forty-nine coffins were opened and examined under the eyes of armed sentries, who were present to see that the workmen employed by the commissioners did not pocket any of the remaining jewels.

The report of these proceedings must be the most macabre Government publication ever issued, rivalling in necrophilic appeal the revelations of the royal vaults, which form a gruesome appendix to Dean Stanley's book on Westminster Abbey. When the coffin of Giovanni delle Bande Neri was opened, his bones were found inside a suit of his famous black armour, the visor down. Doctors who saw how his right leg had been amputated were not surprised that he had expired. It is recorded that the surgeons asked for ten men to hold him down while they sawed off his leg, but he scornfully said that twenty could not hold him if he did not wish it, and bore the operation alone, only crying out twice. When he knew he could not recover he cried, 'I will not die amongst all these poultices', so he was moved to a camp-bed, where he died.

Only two coffins had been unrifled, which was really surprising since those connoisseurs in exhumation, the French armies of 1801, had occupied Tuscany. The intact burials were those of Cosimo III and the last Grand Duke, Gian Gastone, both of whom were discovered crowned, holding their sceptres, and wrapped in their cloaks as Grand Masters of the Order of S. Stephen. The remains of Eleanor of Toledo, the wife of Cosimo I, were immediately recognized when her beautiful dress of figured brocade was seen again after two hundred and ninety-five years, the same dress so well known from Bronzino's portrait in the Pitti.

§ 10

As in Venice, the visitors to Florence follow a well-worn but limited path, and it is not difficult to be alone. I found that, in contrast to the surging corridors of the Uffizi, other galleries and museums (they number about forty) were almost empty; and some of my happiest memories are of mornings in the Pitti Palace and of afternoons in the Boboli Gardens. There is no better description of the Pitti Palace than that of Sir Osbert Sitwell, who calls it 'the sort of residence a sea god would have erected for himself, so that you could almost perceive the weed still clinging to the huge rusticated buildings of the retaining walls, from which it seems the ocean has only just receded'. How apt that is: a bronze ring pendant from the rustication suggests not a horse but a boat, and the building has the appearance of some vast quayside palace in a fresco, even the stones seem eroded by the tides.

Time has treated the leviathan in a most gentlemanly way. It looks today precisely as you see it in prints made in the last years of the Tuscan dukedom when grenadiers in bearskins, the officers in white breeches and looped-back tunics, marched across the sloping parade ground, watched by Victorians in stove-pipe hats, the ladies in crinolines, the young girls holding parasols and wearing little boots and striped stockings.

The difference between the Uffizi and the Pitti is that the first is a review of Italian art from its beginnings, arranged according to period, school, and artist, while the Pitti wears the less clinical air of a private collection. This is aided by the splendid surroundings of the ducal palace; indeed, as I lingered, often alone, beneath the chandeliers, admiring chairs, tables, tapestries, as well as pictures, and inspecting the involved happenings on painted ceilings, I might have been a guest of the Grand Duke wandering about by myself on one of those days when the court had gone hunting.

Some might possibly deplore the sight of so many great paintings arranged haphazardly with the idea only of decoration and of establishing an impression of splendour. This I happened to like. I thought it delightful to see these pictures covering the walls from top to bottom, many of them possibly in the same places they occupied in the days of the last of the Grand Dukes. I thought it impressive to see a profusion of Titians and Raphaels in magnificent frames clustered anyhow on the walls, just as they were seen long ago when they cost £100 each. In all this I was conscious of the gratitude one owes to Princess Anna Maria. Apart from the privilege of examining the works of genius, she has made it possible for later ages to gain some idea of the wealth and splendour of ducal life in the seventeenth and eighteenth centuries.

The atmosphere of the Pitti was pleasant and friendly. The attendants had time to stop and chat. One of them told me that the Medici kept a corps of chairmen to convey visitors up and down the marble stairs, and this might explain the apparent disregard for leg muscles shown by the architects of palaces. When wandering round the splendid rooms, it was amusing to hear the furtive hiss with which the Italian custodian indicates that he wishes to attract one's attention, then to find myself ushered mysteriously through a little door in the gilt panelling to stand surprised in a marble bedroom and bathroom of the eighteenth century. I also saw something of the short cuts, the unexpected corridors, the concealed doors – such a convenience to the lover and the assassin – which exist here, as in all palaces.

I counted seven Titians and nine Raphaels – though there may be more – and the impression I always took away was of dukes, cardinals, princes, and princesses gazing gravely from their golden frames. I came upon two Englishmen in the collection, one an arrogant and supercilious young man with a weak chin, painted by Holbein. He was Sir Richard Southwell, who inherited great wealth in the time of Henry VIII and edged his way tactfully through the reigns of Edward VI and Mary: but not a nice fellow, not the type one would trust! The other, an unknown Englishman by Titian, was a pleasanter person, and surely one of the finest portraits ever painted. Against a dark background, this tall, auburn-haired young man, perhaps twenty-five or thirty years of age, wearing a black gown touched at the neck and wrists with white linen, and holding a new pair of brown leather gloves, regards the world with blue, experienced eyes. There is a tradition that he was the Duke of Norfolk.

And there was a third Englishman. How did Oliver Cromwell find his way to the Pitti Palace? This seems quite improbable. I was told that, in the course of his championship of the Waldensian Protestants, Cromwell had written to the Pope to say that unless persecution ceased an English fleet would appear in the Tiber, and the threat so alarmed Alexander VII that persecution did cease. Impressed by Cromwell's action, the Grand Duke, Ferdinand II, wrote to the Protector and asked if he would consent to be painted by Lely. Cromwell replied that he would gladly do so, and would like to present the portrait himself to the Grand Duke's gallery.

Nobody could tell me whether this was the portrait which inspired Cromwell's famous warning: 'Mr Lely, I desire you would use all your skill to paint my picture truly like me, and not flatter me at all; but remark all these roughnesses, pimples, warts and everything, otherwise I will never pay a farthing.' If it is the picture, Lely failed dismally in the eyes of one English critic. When Francis Mortoft visited the Pitti in 1658, the year of Cromwell's death, he wrote, 'there is also a picture of the dead Lord Protector of England, though nothing like him'.

The woman's face that remained most vividly in my memory was that of Eleanor of Toledo, by Bronzino, with her little son, Giovanni, at her side. She wears the dress in which she was buried, a gown of oyster satin covered everywhere with an intricate raised design in black and brown velvet. Her oval Spanish face, with its arched eyebrows and long pinched nostrils, wears a haughty expression, which could as easily develop into laughter as rage. This unresolved look can still be seen almost anywhere in Spain when the girls come out in the evening to show themselves off in the *paseo*. This was the Duchess with whom Cellini was so often in trouble. There was a vein of bumbling coarseness in him, and I think he handled her badly, either fawning on her in the hope that she would put in a good word for him with the Grand Duke, or else enraging her with some tactless compliment. She was the daughter of the Viceroy of Naples, and her marriage with Cosimo I was a happy and fortunate one, though it ended in tragedy. In 1562 she and two of her young sons died within a month of each other from fever caught in the Maremma Marshes.

The day I went to the *Museo degli Argenti* of the Pitti, I found myself alone there. This is a surprising place, full of those precious pocketable objects which have a habit of vanishing, no matter how well protected, when princes die. There was an exquisite little head of Tiberius carved in turquoise in the first century A.D. and made into a miniature bust with the addition of a gold pedestal by one of the great jewellers of the sixteenth century. There were beautiful vases of rock crystal with silver lips attributed to Cellini, and cups of jasper, amethyst, sardonyx, and other poetic minerals, made for Lorenzo the Magnificent; there were cups of lapis lazuli and the famous cameo on which, it is said, Vincenzo de' Rossi spent five years carefully carving Cosimo I, Eleanor of Toledo, and their family. Cosimo, in bearded profile, looks rather like Edward VII when Prince of Wales, and the family are crushed together as if they were standing in a small lift, so that one feels sorry for de' Rossi, slaving away year after year at such unresponsive material. Jewellery, and the art of the goldsmith in general, seems to be either exquisite or undisciplined, and interesting only as costly novelties fit to amuse an ailing princess: but in Florence all ancient jewellery is interesting, especially if you are living above the Ponte Vecchio. I recalled how many great painters and architects gained their first experience when, as apprentices, they swept up the gold dust.

After a morning in the palace I would eat a sandwich in an unexpected place in the Boboli Gardens. This is a tower whose spiral stairway leads to a room at the top where a young man in a white jacket, who presides over snacks and cold drinks, makes a superior toasted ham sandwich. I believe the tower dates from the time of Gian Gastone, who during his unsullied youth studied science or astronomy there; and I shall long remember the pleasant moments on the outside balcony, the tinkle of ice in a glass of *aranciata*, and the brilliant little segment of Florence (including the window of my bedroom) visible between the trees.

The Gardens, which lie on the hillside at the back of the palace, were a charming retreat, and were deserted during those two hours of the siesta when Florence locks its churches and pulls down the shutters. I loved the dark avenues of ilex and cypress from which, as from a tent of leaves, one sheltered from the incandescent whiteness of the afternoon. All the well-known features of the Italian Garden were there: the statues under the ilexes; the sound of water dripping in a marble basin; the box hedges planted strategically with a Latin eye to the trapping of little birds, and the lizards, like green whiplashes in the dust, or lying upon hot stones motionless save for the pulsing of their throats.

The hippodrome at the back of the palace, with tiers of stone seats for thousands of spectators, was the scene of tournaments and wedding pageants. Every one of the disastrous marriages of the later Medici was celebrated there with a magnificent show for which famous artists were glad to design scenery and costumes. How elaborate these were may be seen in the *Museo Topografico* and the print-room of the Uffizi.

Flights of steps lead from the arena to a fountain where Neptune stands upon a rock in the centre of a lake, grasping a trident from whose prongs fall slow drops of water. Higher still, and you come to the statue of Abundance, which has a melancholy history. It began as a statue of Joan of Austria, the wife of Francesco I, who lost interest in it when he fell in love with Bianca Cappella. Poor Joan, neglected in stone as in life, stood amongst the undergrowth for years, until it occurred to Ferdinand II to transform her into a tribute to his administration. So Joan of Austria emerged as Abundance.

As you climb the terraces, you are rewarded with glimpses of Florence until, at the top, you see the city lying below, a haphazard collection of red roofs, still surprisingly mediaeval in appearance, from which rise the immortal domes and towers.

One day when I left the garden, I went to look at the ducal stables and coach-houses, which form a wing at right angles to the palace. A pleasant old man opened the door and led the way straight into the seventeenth century. The coaches and carriages of the Medici stretched to the end of a long hall, all beautifully cared for and polished, as if a messenger from the Grand Duke might arrive and order them into action. The old man went round opening the doors and letting down the steps, and gently swinging the coaches on their leather braces. The doors of the most costly motor-car may be banged, but those of the gold and silver state coach of the Grand Dukes of Tuscany can only be closed; and they close with a precise, crisp click which in itself is the echo of a more elegant world. My favourite coach was that in which Catherine de' Medici, seated like a precious object in a gilt cabinet, was drawn through the streets by horses jingling with red and gold harness.

In past centuries visitors would go to the stables to see the zoo. In early times lions were kept at the back of the Palazzo Vecchio as symbols of the Republic, and the Florentine lion, *Il Marzocco*, is still seated upon a pedestal in the piazza, holding a ducal shield with a Florentine lily upon it. The animals were later moved to the Pitti, and it was here, in 1644, that John Evelyn bought a leg of mutton for the lions. A few years later Richard Lassels said that the Grand Duke and his court sometimes stood above the pit and watched the animals fighting. When the fight was over, the lions were driven back to their dens by 'a fearful machine of wood made like a great Green Dragon which a man within it rowles upon wheels, and holding out two lighted torches at the eyes of it, frights the fiercest beast thereby into his den'.

It is pleasant to contrast such moments with the story of the giraffe that arrived in Florence in 1488, a gift from the Sultan of Egypt. This creature became the pet of Florence, and people were never tired of admiring his grace and mildness, and the gentle way he would accept apples from children. When winter came there was much anxiety and large fires were kept burning to warm him, but, to the grief of Florence, he died in the following year.

§ 11

A large and rambling old palazzo with stone balconies, many windows, and a railed-in courtyard stands at the corner of the Via Gino Capponi, not far from SS. Annunziata. From certain positions on the pavement you can see an iron vane on the roof in the form of a flag, and with a pair of field-glasses you might be able to make out that the flag is pierced in the form of the letters 'C.R.' and the date '1777'. The letters stand for 'Carolus Rex' and the date is the year in which Bonnie Prince Charlie bought the house, which incidentally has the distinction of being the only property ever owned by the Stuarts during more than a century of exile.

As the owners of the house were not in Florence, I had to be content with a glimpse of the outside, and a conversation with a delightful old retainer who might have stepped out of some seventeenth century print. He was one of the most courteous watch-dogs I have ever met, and while we were talking I glanced into the entrance hall and saw, emblazoned in fresco upon the walls, the complex Royal Arms of Stuart England. Someone told me later that another relic of Charles Edward exists in a small room frescoed, incredible as it sounds, in Royal Stuart tartan.

The palazzo is the most interesting relic of the Stuarts in Italy. Charles halted his unhappy wandering life for a few years when, at the age of fifty-seven, he settled there with his lively young wife, Louise of Stolberg. He was already a mass of nerves and grievances and far gone in dissipation, and he bored Louise with rambling accounts of his adventures in the Highlands, and some-times, when in his cups, was not responsible for his words or his actions. Outside the house, Charles and his wife were known as the Count and Countess of Albany; the moment they entered, and ascended the stairs beneath the Royal Arms, they became Charles III and his consort; and every detail of royal etiquette was observed. This was the period when Charles was spied on daily by Sir Horace Mann for the British Foreign Office.

Shortly after their arrival in Florence Louise met the handsome and charming young poet, Count Vittorio Alfieri, and they fell deeply in love. It was from this palazzo that she ran away from her husband's jealousy and the violence of his drinking bouts, eventually joining Alfieri, with whom she lived happily until his death some twenty years later.

Abandoned and still further humiliated, Charles Edward nevertheless managed to pull himself together and make one of the few successful decisions of his life. He asked his daughter, Charlotte, then in her thirties, to come and live with him in Florence. She was a devoted and charming woman, the child of his affair with Clementina Walkinshaw, whom he met during the '45, and she was able to recall her unhappy parent to a sense of his dignity, and to bring some happiness and tranquillity into the last three years of his life. Scotland remembers her as 'the bonnie lass of Albany'.

There is another building with Stuart memories in Florence, which, by some strange chance, remains in British occupation. This is the British Consulate in what used to be the *Casa Alfieri*, on the Lungarno Corsini. It was in this palazzo, after the death in Rome of Charles Edward, that Louise, Countess of Albany, settled with her lover. If anyone today wishes to have a visa on his passport or to have it renewed, the stamp will descend upon it in the little study where Alfieri once wrote his tragedies. Upstairs, the painted ceilings are those beneath which the Countess of Albany, called by some the Queen of England and, by others, the Queen of Florence, held her famous *salon* in her old age, attended by the whole of Florentine society and by every celebrated visitor to the city. After her poet's death she lost interest in her appearance, and some complained that she was dumpy and dowdy and her receptions boring, though they all accepted invitations to them. Her tomb in S. Croce bears above it the last lion and unicorn to support the armorial dignity of a Stuart sovereign.

§ 12

The unification of Italy was celebrated in Florence, as in Rome, by an architectural fandango, in the course of which many a fine old landmark was swept away. In Florence – for a short time the capital of the new realm – the town wall, with its gates and towers, was sacrificed to make way for the Viale de Circonvallazione, a boulevard which changes its name every few miles. The Brownings and their contemporaries were the last generation to see the old town wall of Florence, which had a special significance for Englishmen since they came to rest at last within its aged arms, in a little graveyard planted with a double line of cypress trees.

As you travel today towards the Porta S. Gallo, along that stretch of the boulevard known as the Viale Antonio Gramsci, you come to a remarkable object in the centre of the road. It is a rise of ground upon which grow a number of venerable trees; and as you approach nearer, and see the road dividing respectfully on each side, you realize that this must be the old *Cimetero degli Inglesi*, in the Piazza Donatello. The graveyard is no longer used, and as you stand looking at the shrubberies behind the spiked railings, from which a tombstone can be seen protruding here and there, it seems a little sad that the champions of the Risorgimento should have been consigned to a traffic island.

It was a warm and sunny afternoon when I went there to wander over the rough grass among the briar roses and the oleanders. Yellow butterflies were flickering above the wild flowers, and the only other person in sight was a figure appropriately enough sharpening a scythe. The first name that caught my eye was 'Arthur Hugh Clough, sometime Fellow of Oriel College, Oxford. Died at Florence on November 13, 1861, aged 42'. I seemed to hear Winston Churchill's voice during a bad moment of the last war:

> *For while the tired waves, vainly breaking,*
> *Seem here no painful inch to gain,*
> *Far back, through creeks and inlets making,*
> *Comes silent, flooding in, the main.*

And not by eastern windows only,
When daylight comes, comes in the light,
In front, the sun climbs slow, how slowly,
But westward, look, the land is bright.

What could have been more appropriate to the hoped-for entry of the United States into the war, yet surely Clough is the least likely of English poets to have supplied the right word in a moment of national crisis. Florence, where he died from a fever caught during a journey in search of health, was a significant name in his life. He married Florence Nightingale's cousin, and Florence herself found the poet a willing horse and drove him hard as she involved him in her various schemes and reforms.

Near by, I came to the grave of another English poet, Walter Savage Landor, who died in 1864, aged eighty-nine. The man with the scythe approached to cut the adjacent grass, and agreed that the lettering on the tombstones is a disgrace to the Florentine stonemasons. Hardly an inscription carved only a century ago is clearly legible now. I suppose Landor is remembered chiefly for the lines found in so many anthologies:

I strove with none, for none was worth my strife.
Nature I loved and, next to Nature, Art:
I warm'd both hands before the fire of life;
It sinks, and I am ready to depart.

Landor often said good-bye to himself. The above valediction was written when he was well over seventy, but he continued to live on to be nearly ninety. He was the most irascible of men and his life was a series of rows, disputes, financial confusion, and libels in Latin, a tongue whose vituperative power he found superior to that of English.

I found the grave of Elizabeth Barrett Browning, 'died 1861 aged 55'. 'The funeral was not impressive, as it ought to have been,' wrote the American sculptor W. W. Story, the devoted friend of the Brownings. 'The services were blundered through by a fat English parson in a brutally careless way, and she was consigned by him to the earth as if her clay were no better than any other clay.' Near at hand I saw the grave of Isa Blagden, the kind, self-sacrificing little woman who adored the Brownings, and a few paces away the grave of 'Fanny , the wife of W. Holman Hunt, 'who died in Florence, Dec. 20. 1866, in the first year of her marriage'. I came to the grave of Frances Trollope ('Francesca' on the headstone), who died in 1863, aged eighty-three.

I asked the man with the scythe if many people visit the English cemetery now. He said no, just an occasional visitor like myself. Sometimes people in a hurry asked where the grave of the English *poetessa* was to be found, and they would go to the grave of Elizabeth Browning, and perhaps leave a flower.

I happened to mention the English cemetery to an Italian friend who is familiar with the Florentine archives, and we talked of the fascinating group of people who left England a century ago to settle in Florence. He told me that Landor's conflicts with authority, and his rows with Italian artisans, are still carefully filed away in the records. Landor, he reminded me, made continual warfare on those who went up to his villa to do odd jobs. One carpenter was so severely assaulted or abused that the very account of his experiences when he reached home gave his wife a miscarriage.

I suppose we should now call Landor a schizophrenic: one side of him was the gentle poet who loved flowers so much that he refused to have them picked; the other Landor would instantly knock down anyone who dared to wear a rose! He adored children and animals, and the countless pilgrims who found their way to the Villa Gherardesca to burn their incense (and in the nineteenth century he was more famous in Florence than Lorenzo the Magnificent), would see a charming host brimming over with laughter and gaiety and full of charm and courtesy. Perhaps the best Landor story is that of an argument with his cook. Suddenly losing his temper, the poet picked up the Italian (Landor was a big, powerful man) and flung him through the window, then, as the body hit the earth, cried in anguish, 'My God, I've forgotten the violets!'

Sir Henry Layard, the excavator of Nineveh, who spent his

boyhood in Florence, remembered the strange Landor menage and the impressive figure of the poet, who was to be seen, and heard, as he roamed the Tuscan hills declaiming his hexameters; and he also recalled the Landor children, barefoot and wild, dressed as peasants and subject to no discipline until their parent lost his temper. It was one of Landor's theories that children should be taught Greek before they could speak English. His warfare with his wife was more or less continuous, and during one of their disagreements, Landor, at the age of sixty, suddenly packed up and went home to England, where he remained for the next twenty-three years. There he plunged into troubles, financial, emotional, and legal. He indulged his old vice of libels in Latin which were immediately answered by writs (a tribute to the learning of the eighteen-thirties!), and at the age of eighty-three was bundled back to Florence. In the meantime he had conveyed his income and property to his wife and family, and they turned the poor old man out penniless into the street.

There on a hot day, straying aimlessly about, the old poet met Robert Browning, who took him home and befriended him. 'Shortly after this Browning brought him to me at Siena,' wrote Story, 'and a more pitiable sight I never saw. It was the case of old Lear over again; and when he descended from his carriage with his sparse white hair streaming out, and tottered into my house dazed in intellect with all he had suffered, I felt as if he were really Lear come back again.'

Genius has been variously described as a capacity for taking pains, infinite patience, and so forth, but a constant ingredient is abnormal vitality; and this Landor possessed. Under the care of Browning and Story, the old man revived, and it is recorded that he sometimes rose before anyone else was astir and sat under a cypress tree in the first light of morning, writing Latin alcaics. When he moved into lodgings he had recovered so much of his old spirit that now and then a dish he disliked would go flying through the window. One day shortly before he died, an excited young man with a mop of red hair climbed the stairs to his lodging. He was Swinburne. The old poet and the young – the Georgian and the Victorian – sat talking together and Swinburne described Landor as 'alert, brilliant, and altogether delicious'. He added, 'I should like to throw up all other things on earth and devote myself to playing the valet to him for the rest of his days.' Instead, he wrote the verses which are still legible on Landor's grave:

> And thou, his Florence, to thy trust,
> Receive and keep,
> Keep safe his dedicated dust,
> His sacred sleep.

§ 13

Why did so many talented people desert England for Florence in the nineteenth century? The financial and other entanglements that sent Landor there were fairly common; health (Elizabeth Browning); the desire to live abroad (Mrs Trollope); the belief, in the words of Shelley, that Italy was the ever sunny 'paradise of exiles' all played a part, though probably the most important single reason was the cheapness of living there. A writer estimated in 1814 that a man with £150 a year could live in Italy like a gentleman and frequent society, though he added apologetically that he could not expect to keep a carriage! Frances Cobbe, who shared a villa near Fiesole with Isa Blagden, the friend of the Brownings, wrote that 'poverty in Florence permitted us to rent fourteen well-furnished rooms in a charming villa, and to keep a maid and a manservant. The latter bought our meals every morning in Florence, cooked, and served them. He swept our floors and he opened our doors and announced our company and served our ices and tea'. Frances says that the bills never exceeded £20 a month.

A new phase in Anglo-Italian relations began when members of the middle-class came to live beneath what they confidently expected would be an eternally sunny sky. Those who arrived during a bad winter had to face a period of adjustment. The aristocrats of the former century, accustomed to their own vast, draughty houses, had taken the Italian winter in their stride, though Horace Walpole did remark that, as most of the walls were painted in fresco, 'one has the additional horror of freezing with imaginary marble'. When English people arrived who were accustomed to small rooms and fireplaces, we hear that the Italian palazzo lacked 'snugness'. Mrs Leigh Hunt, faced by a villa 'with marble steps to the staircase and a marble terrace over the portico', thought it 'anything but snug', and Henry Matthews, wintering at Pisa in a house 'with marble floors and staring casements', dreamt longingly of 'the warm carpet, the snug elbowed chair, and the blazing coal fire of an English winter evening'. Italy has suffered almost as much as she has gained from her lovers, but now and then the legend of the eternally lovely land grew dim and was replaced by a longing for 'snugness'. Even Lady Blessington, when staying in a villa on the Brenta which should have suited her, commented petulantly on the statues that 'desecrated' the façade, and 'thought of our beautiful villas in dear England, hid amid umbrageous trees, feathering down to velvet lawns'. Most startling of all was Browning's sudden piercing cry, 'Oh to be in England now that April's there.'

The new Anglo-Florentines differed from the travelling nobility of the eighteenth century in their comparative poverty, their morality, and the fact that they had no desire to learn Italian. As their social status did not automatically admit them into Italian society, the only Italians many of them ever knew were their servants, tradesmen, and peasants. Also the reverence for Italy as the mother of the Arts was now replaced by a feeling of affection tinged with patronage, and many no doubt contrasted the haphazard charm of Italy with their own now rich and powerful homeland. Landor expressed this new attitude in his usual extreme way when, speaking of Italians, he announced proudly, 'I admit none of them within my doors', and once he was as good as his word when an Italian called, and, entering the room wearing his hat, was promptly assaulted and flung out. He happened to be his landlord. The novelist Charles Lever held the same ideas. 'The Italians are falsehood incarnated,' he declared, 'their whole lives, a long practical lie'.

One may imagine with what amusement a nation which has always enjoyed the foibles of humanity regarded those strange self-contained persons, and how much was excused natives of a remote island almost always invisible in a covering of mist and fog. No wonder they were all a little mad!

The Brownings lived for fourteen years in a flat in the Casa Guidi. It is almost opposite the Pitti Palace, and I often walked there across the Ponte Vecchio. Sometimes I would see English students taking snapshots of the building, perhaps wondering which of the windows had once framed the pale little face of Elizabeth with its dark nodding ringlets. The Casa Guidi would not be out of place in the Gray's Inn Road, and it is still split into flats whose tenants gaze down, just as the Brownings did, from Casa Guidi windows upon the church of S. Felice.

I had always assumed that the abode of two poets and the scene of an idyllic love affair might have been a little more attractive in appearance. Certainly Elizabeth Browning's verse does not prepare one for the commonplace building in which most of it was written. The visitor who is not in too much of a hurry will discover three memorials to the Brownings, one in the Piazza S. Felice, which mentions most delightfully the 'golden ring' which Elizabeth's verse forged between England and Italy; another, in the courtyard of the house itself, with a bronze bust of Robert; and a third, in the Via Mazzetta, erected by the municipality, which quotes, in Italian and English, the lines from *Casa Guidi Windows*.

> *I heard last night a little child go singing*
> *'Neath Casa Guidi windows by the church!*
> *O bella libertà, O bella!*

To us, the Brownings are models of sober rectitude, a change from their immediate predecessors on the Italian scene, Byron and Shelley: but to the Florentines who saw them every day, the Brownings must have appeared just as crazy. One wonders if anyone ever tried to describe the Wimpole Street household to an Italian of the period in an attempt to explain why a man of thirty-five, after marrying a frail little invalid of forty-one, should have parted at the church door, then, later, have eloped with her like a young lover, with a faithful maidservant and a dog. The robust poet, so tenderly careful of his little wife, must have struck the Italians as an odd variation on a theme they had known in more carnal guise in the past. They were unquestionably a strange-looking couple: the sturdy Robert, the evanescent Elizabeth, 'a pale, small person hardly embodied at all', as Hawthorne said, while Frederick Locker, less kindly, described 'curls like pendant ears of a water-spaniel, and poor little hands, so thin that when she welcomed you she gave you something like the foot of a young bird'.

The true eccentricity of the Browning household was probably not revealed until their son, Pen Browning, reached the age of ten, and was still dressed like a girl. The poets, accompanied by this ambiguous figure, caused many a passer-by to stare back at his embroidered trousers and the fair ringlets nodding to his shoulders. Poor Browning, who knew well what a fool and a prig his wife was making of their boy, could do nothing about it. When she was a little girl in Paris, Henriette Corkran met Pen Browning and his doting mother, and described the meeting in later life.

'Penini,' she wrote, 'had long golden ringlets; he wore white drawers edged with embroidery; these peculiarities impressed me for I thought he looked like a girl . . . After a few moments of general conversation, which I thought extremely dull and commonplace for such great poets, Mrs Barrett Browning beckoned to me. I approached her feeling shy. What was that little, but *great* woman going to speak about with a small child like me? I was soon put at my ease. In a feeble voice she said: "You and Penini must be friends, dear. He is my Florentine boy", stroking his head lovingly. "Has he not got beautiful hair? so golden – that is because he was born in Italy where the sun is always golden." Then she kissed me and placed my hand in Pen's . . . During most of her visit Mrs Barrett Browning kept her right arm round her little son's neck, running her long thin fingers through his golden curls . . .'

At the age of thirteen, when his mother died, poor Pen was still dressed like a not so little Lord Fauntleroy, and one of the first things Robert did was to alter his son's appearance. 'The golden curls, the fantastic dress is gone,' wrote Browning, 'he has short hair, worn boy-wise, long trousers, is a common boy all at once.' One looks up at Casa Guidi windows knowing that one member of the trio had been bottling up his feelings for years.

The only real cloud on what Edmund Gosse described as 'sixteen years of unclouded marital happiness' was Elizabeth's interest in spiritualism. She revolted against the 'grave's disgrace', and her longing for a sign brought her in touch with that extraordinary character, Daniel Home, the medium. Here we see table-turning, rapping, levitation, and spirit hands, lifted from the suburban parlour into the palaces of nineteenth century Europe. Even the battle of Sedan comes into the story! Never have the denizens of the other world been introduced to so many distinguished inhabitants of this one. The music of string orchestras at royal receptions fades out to the sound of guitars plucked by ghostly hands; gilt tables gyrate with their messages, and unseasonable blossoms flutter down upon the tiaras of startled grand duchesses. Yet one is left wondering whether Home was a gigantic fraud (as Dickens and Browning believed), or whether, as many scientists thought, his phenomena were genuine interruptions of natural laws.

The Brownings met him in London when he had arrived from America at the age of twenty-six. He was not an American, but a Scot who had spent his childhood and youth with an aunt in the United States. Browning detested him on sight. He was tall and slim, not particularly good-looking, with blue eyes, which many found attractive. In the course of a seance at Ealing, a wreath of clematis was placed by a ghostly hand upon the head of Elizabeth – '*how*, I was unable to see', commented the doubting Robert.

Home wintered in Florence one year, much to Browning's disgust. One dark night, when the medium was returning to the villa where he was staying, someone attempted to kill him and he was slightly wounded. It has, however, never been suggested that

Browning was responsible for any revenge more piercing than *Mr Sludge, the Medium*. Notwithstanding Browning's dislike, Home was irresistible to many important people. While in St Petersburg, he married a god-daughter of the Czar. Four years later he returned to Russia to hold seances in the Winter Palace and, his wife having died in the meantime, to marry another member of the Russian aristocracy. Among his greatest admirers was William, King of Prussia, who became the first German Emperor. Home was present with him at Sedan and accompanied the German army to Versailles. The Browning correspondence does not enlarge on the supernatural: it was evidently too painful a topic.

§ 14

It is usually said that Walter Savage Landor was the most eccentric member of the English colony in Florence, though I would award the distinction to Seymour Stocker Kirkup. They were the two oldest residents, and in the 'sixties were rated only slightly below the Venus de' Medici among the sights of Florence. Kirkup was an accomplished artist. The son of a London jeweller, he had inherited an adequate fortune and had been led to Italy by a weak chest while he was still in his twenties. It may be encouraging to others with a similar weakness to know that he continued to live there to be a hale and hearty ninety-two. He painted busily all his life, but became interesting as a 'character' only in his eccentric old age when letters of the time refer to him as 'dear old Kirkup'.

He lived in an ancient building which cannot have been far from my hotel, since it was among those blown up by the Germans to block the approach to the Ponte Vecchio. Here he was to be found surrounded by a confusion of old furniture, pictures, and books. He was a venerable, white-haired figure dressed in old clothes. 'His long white locks hung over his shoulders,' said Henry Layard, who knew him well. 'His sharply chiselled features, hooked nose and bright, restless eyes gave him the aspect of one who practised the black arts'; and he was, in fact, a spiritualist in daily touch with his idol, Dante. He even possessed a portrait which the poet had autographed in the spirit world. When he was nearly seventy Kirkup married his medium, a pretty peasant girl named Regina, aged nineteen, who settled in with her mother and family, and soon there was material proof of their collaboration, a child called Imogen. 'The weird old man with the tiny child beside him seemed to have stepped out of an illustration to the *Old Curiosity Shop*,' wrote Giuliano Artom Treves in the *Golden Ring*, an excellent summary of the Anglo-Florentines.

Layard, who was in the habit of calling on Kirkup in his tower, says that one day, after a long absence, he knocked at the door but without meeting any response. Kirkup had become stone deaf, and the only way he could tell whether he had a visitor was by noticing if his dogs were barking. However, at the time of Layard's visit the dogs had long been dead, and so, after hammering for some time, Layard was just on the point of leaving when the door was opened by the old man himself. 'He led the way silently, and with a mournful expression such as I had never seen before, into the inner room,' wrote Layard. 'There, laid out on the floor, and surrounded by lighted tapers and flowers, lay the body of Regina, dressed in her holiday garments, a cross upon her breast, her beautiful features still unchanged ... Some years afterwards when nearly ninety years of age, he married her sister in order that she might inherit the little property that she and her family, after years of plunder, had left him.'

As the child Imogen grew up, the spirits urged her to persuade her venerable parent to sever his long association with Florence and move to Leghorn, where, as it happened, she had a lover. As Kirkup never questioned 'the voices', the move was made and Imogen married her lover. Kirkup died aged ninety-two and lies buried in the Protestant Cemetery. To the quizzical eyes of the Florentines, as they observed the odd antics of the exiles from the misty island, how exquisitely appropriate it must have seemed that the old necromancer should have been also the British Consul!

Another who almost lived up to the high standards set by Landor and Kirkup was the novelist, Charles Lever. He was a large, outwardly merry, bouncing character who is always described as Irish though he was born in Dublin of English parents. This now little known writer (*Harry Lorrequer, Charles O'Malley, The O'Donoghue*) wrote his novels by instalments, in the Dickensian fashion, and they were illustrated by 'Phiz' or Cruickshank. They are apparently still mildly collected, since recently I received a second-hand book catalogue in which forty-four were offered for three guineas. When Lever decided to live abroad with his wife and three children, he settled first in the Austrian Tyrol, then decided on Italy. One day in 1847 Florence fancied that a travelling circus had arrived as the Lever family rode in on piebald ponies, wearing Tyrolean clothes and little hats adorned with peacock feathers. Lever was soon a popular figure at all parties, balls, theatrical performances, and card-tables. He rode with his family in the Cascine, never rising in the saddle but seated firmly like a trooper riding to attention. He said it was good for the liver. He could scarcely speak a word of Italian, but was so expressive that he once defended himself in an Italian law court and won his case. Like most humorists, he could not bear funny people.

He had inexorable high spirits and garrulity in public, but in private he relapsed into a nervous, irritable melancholy as he churned out his weekly instalment. He worked hard and was the Edgar Wallace of his day. It was said of him, as of Wallace, that he could keep two novels going at the same time. Those who saw him bouncing round the ballroom, his wife in his arms (the polka had just arrived), would have found it difficult to believe that only some hours previously he had been writing gloomy grumbling letters to his publisher about money. The truth was that Lever had to have his carriage and pair and spent every penny as it came in, though he was quite well off. The steady £1,200 to £2,000 a year, which his novels brought in, may be multiplied by six, perhaps even more, to find the modern value. His novels are full of high spirits, humour, and observation, but neither his readers, nor those who met him over a dinner-table, could have imagined in what blood, sweat, and tears they were produced. In his later years he became British consul in Trieste, a place he detested, and he died there, writing to within a year or so of his death, at the age of sixty-six.

Another forgotten best-seller who basked in the sunshine of that distant Florence, but as a visitor, was G. P. R. James, the author of more than a hundred historical romances, probably not one of which is remembered today. Perhaps he, rather than Lever, should be called the Edgar Wallace of the time. He had read a lot of history and, after a kind word from Walter Scott in his youth, was off on a profitable canter down the centuries, his armour rattling. He produced a new novel every nine months for eighteen successive years. (*Agincourt, Arabella Stuart, The Smuggler, Ticonderoga*, are some of his titles.) Most of his novels were written to a recipe and often began: 'One evening, as the sun was setting, a solitary horseman might have been seen . . .'; and all were immensely popular. One admirer – Landor, as it happens – described his work as 'always pure and hopeful, and distinguished by a chivalrous respect for ladies, and a true sense of honour'.

Photographs show him to have been a large, heavy man with clear-cut features, wearing those no doubt beautifully hand-made garments which, owing to some peculiarity of early photography, are revealed as full of creases, so that even the most eminent of the Victorians appear to have slept in their clothes. His grandfather was the inventor of 'James's Powder', the great cure-all of the eighteenth century. Dying at Venice at an advanced age, the novelist was laid to rest in the solemn little isle of S. Michele, on the way to Murano.

§ 15

Two things strike one about the English colony in Florence: the number of distinguished women who belonged to it – Elizabeth Barrett Browning, Anna Jameson, Frances Trollope, and Mary Somerville – and the great age attained by most of its members. Landor lived to be eighty-nine, Mary Somerville to be ninety-two, Kirkup to be ninety-two, Frances Trollope eighty-three, Thomas Augustus Trollope eighty-two; and the oldest of them all was the rich Temple Leader, who reconstructed the immense fortress of

Vincigliata, still one of the sights of Florence, and lived to be ninety-three. I cannot recall any other group of associates which could boast so many near centenarians, perhaps a tribute to the climate of Tuscany or, more likely, due to the fact that those sturdy Victorians were not injected by their doctors, on the slightest pretext, with some new drug.

Mary Somerville, who has been called the most remarkable woman of her generation, was in her seventies when she arrived in Florence in 1851 with her adoring old husband and two mature spinster daughters who, the neighbours said, were unreasonably devoted to the piano. They lived in a house with a little rose garden at the back, in the Via del Mandorla, where Mary Somerville awed everyone by her intellectual distinction, at the same time astonishing them by the simplicity of her manner and appearance. Everyone knew her story: how as a girl, the daughter of Admiral Sir William Fairfax of Jedburgh, she had taught herself Latin and mathematics, and, encouraged by her husband, Dr William Somerville, she had continued her studies and had become internationally famous at fifty. What the Florentines and the pilgrims to her shrine found so difficult to reconcile was the dear little old lady, who would be discovered pruning the roses or quietly sewing, with the author of such works as the *Violet Rays of the Solar Spectrum*, and honorary membership of most of the learned societies of Europe. That anyone so erudite should appear so ordinary caused astonishment all her life. Charles Greville was the first to voice this when he met her in London in 1834, when she was fifty-four. 'The subject of astronomy is so sublime,' he wrote, 'that one shrinks into a sense of nothingness in contemplating it, and can't help regarding those who have mastered the mighty process and advanced the limits of the science as beings of another order. I could not then take my eyes off this woman, with a feeling of surprise and something like incredulity, all involuntary and very foolish; but to see a mincing smirking person, fan in hand, gliding about the room, talking nothings and nonsense, and to know that La Place was her plaything and Newton her acquaintance, was too striking a contrast not to torment the brain.' Much the same impression was expressed in the following year by Lady Morgan, who met Mary Somerville, also at a London party. 'Mrs Somerville struck me as being a simple little woman, middle aged,' she wrote. 'Had she not been presented to me by name and reputation, I should say one of the respectable twaddling chaperones one meets with at every ball, dressed in a snug mulberry velvet gown and a little cap with a red flower. I asked her how she could descend from the stars to mix amongst us? She said she was obliged to go out with her daughter (who was dancing with my niece in the same quadrille.)'

A delightful glimpse of the scientist in Florence was given by another clever woman, the American astronomer, Maria Mitchell, then at the start of her career. Calling at the Via del Mandorla as a reverent pilgrim, she was shown into a large room where a fire was blazing, 'very suggestive of American comfort'.

'After some little delay I heard a footstep come shuffling along the outer room, and an exceedingly tall and very old man entered the room, in the singular headdress of a red bandanna turban, approached me, and introduced himself as Dr Somerville, the husband. He was very proud of his wife, and very desirous of talking about her . . . Mrs Somerville came tripping into the room speaking at once with the vivacity of a young person. She was seventy-seven years old, but appeared twenty years younger. While Mrs Somerville talked, the old gentleman busied himself in toasting a slice of bread on a fork. . . . An English lady was present, learned in art, who, with a volubility worthy of an American, rushed into every little opening of Mrs Somerville's more measured sentences with her remarks upon recent discoveries in *her* specialities. Whenever this occurred, the old man grew fidgety, moved the slice of bread backwards and forwards as if the fire were at fault, and when at length the English lady had fairly conquered the ground and was started on a long sentence, he could bear the eclipse of his idol no longer, but, coming to the sofa where we sat, he said testily, "Mrs Somerville would rather talk on science than on art".'

This was a rebuke to the redoubtable Mrs Anna Jameson, for she it was who wished to speak, probably about legends of the saints. When the adoring old husband died, followed five years later by the death of her only son, Mary Somerville sought relief from her sorrow in writing *Molecular and Microscopic Science* at the age of eighty-five. Such was the astonishing old lady whose name is perpetuated in Somerville College, Oxford.

In the Victorian age an unsatisfactory husband was one of the keenest spurs to successful female authorship, and should perhaps not be despised even today. Two fine examples are to be noted among the Anglo-Florentines, Mrs Anna Jameson and Mrs Trollope. Mrs Jameson's books may still be found by anyone strolling along the Charing Cross Road – *Legends of the Saints; Legends of the Madonna; Legends of the Monastic Orders*. They are, in their way, unique: and though there have been better art critics, no one has more industriously collected the stories behind the pictures and told them more charmingly. The author first appeared as a gay, talkative, red-headed governess named Anna Murphy, who had the good fortune to travel abroad with her employers and meet many distinguished people. Her marriage to a young barrister, Robert Jameson, was not a success, and he eventually went to Canada, where he had a distinguished career, becoming Chancellor of Toronto and afterwards Speaker and Attorney-General. In an attempt to make her marriage work, Anna joined him in Canada, but in two years' time returned to Europe to become an indefatigable professional writer.

She was at the height of her popularity when she lived in Florence in the eighteen-fifties, no longer, of course, a dashing red-head, but, as Maria Mitchell's interview with Mary Somerville proves, as talkative as ever. Nathaniel Hawthorne, who was shown round Rome by her, described 'a rather short, round and massive personage of benign and agreeable aspect, with a sort of black skull-cap on her head, beneath which appeared her hair, which seemed once to have been fair, and was now almost white. I should take her to be about seventy years old'. (She was actually sixty-four.)

No one knew the Brownings better than Mrs Jameson. She was one of the few who had been admitted to the darkened room in Wimpole Street where Elizabeth Barrett lay stretched upon her invalid couch, with her dog, Flush, at her feet. Later, when in Paris, she was astonished to come across her friend with Robert Browning, and to learn that they had eloped, if the word, which suggests young lovers, can be applied to such mature runaways. Herself such a capable traveller and organizer, Mrs Jameson was appalled by Browning's helplessness in everyday affairs – 'the worst manager I ever met with' – and the poets were only too thankful to put themselves in her experienced hands. She took them first to Pisa, and afterwards helped to settle them in Florence. She herself lived just round the corner from the Casa Guidi, in the Via Maggio.

Anna Jameson managed to live by her pen and support two helpless sisters. She found compensation for her unhappy marriage in her independence and her popularity, and in lavishing friendship on her women friends of whom Lady Byron was the first, with Elizabeth Browning and Ottilie von Goethe good seconds. This forceful, industrious, and gallant member of the Florentine circle caught a fatal chill one winter's night as she was returning from the reading-room of the British Museum, where she was writing the *History of our Lord*, and died at the age of sixty-six.

The misadventures of Mrs Trollope's marriage were of a different kind from those which led Mrs Jameson to literary fame. As Frances Milton, she married a quick-tempered young lawyer, Thomas Trollope, who scared off all his clients and then took up farming. He has been described as a man pursued by failure 'with almost demoniac malice', but when one knows that he put his money in a scheme to sell fancy goods in Cincinnati, one begins to wonder whether he may not have invited the demoniac pursuit. With child-like innocence, Mrs Trollope went off to the United States and erected a bizarre building in Cincinnati to house European goods. This building continued to be known as 'Trollope's Folly' long after it had become a billiard saloon, then later, some say, a house of ill fame.

However, the more uncouth aspects of the American scene inspired Frances Trollope to write a book, which is still most readable, and was among the first English travel books which infuriated American critics. She concentrated on revivalist meetings, and other emotional excesses, and denounced slavery; and the book, which is a first-rate piece of descriptive writing and acute, though one-sided, observation, brought her celebrity and money. After her return to England, Trollope fled to the Continent to escape his creditors, while his wife continued to write travel books and to support him until he died.

A family of writers who publish books under the same name can be confusing, and, as Mrs Trollope had imparted her fluent talent to her two sons, Thomas Adolphus and Anthony, the bookshops were soon flooded with Trollopiana. It has been estimated that, between them, mother and sons produced three hundred and six books, Anthony out-writing his mother by twenty novels. He is the only member of the family whose books have survived, and the Barchester cult keeps six of his novels in print. In addition to writing, he was an active and much travelled post office official, and I have read somewhere that he originated the pillar-box.

When Mrs Trollope arrived in Florence, she was sixty-three and an esteemed best-seller, and her elder son, Thomas Adolphus, then aged thirty-three, decided to make his life in Italy with her. She continued to produce a novel a year, while he devoted himself to Italian subjects. Anthony, however, remained at home, to rise in the postal hierarchy and to write the Barchester novels.

At first the English colony accepted the arrival of Mrs Trollope with some reserve. She had the frightening reputation of 'putting people into her books', and some, notably the Brownings, thought her works vulgar, and herself not quite the sort of person they would care to know. However, the numerous Trollope 'fans' sought her out, and many would rather have missed Botticelli than the authoress they admired.

Four years after their arrival, the Trollope household was transformed by the appearance of an exotic stranger. She was a dark, large-eyed young woman of twenty-three named Theodosia Garrow. She was fashionably frail in health, fluent in Italian, a poet, and a regular contributor to the *Athenaeum*. Thomas Adolphus, who was thirty-seven, fell in love at sight. Theodosia's origins were unusual. Her grandfather, when in India, had married a high-caste Indian girl ('a Brahmin sultana', as T. A. Trollope described her), and their son – Theodosia's father – married at the age of twenty-five a Jewess of forty-eight with a grown-up family. At the time of Theodosia's birth, it is said that her mother was fifty-nine.

Shortly after the marriage of Thomas Adolphus and Theodosia, it was decided to acquire a pleasant villa, which became famous in the social and intellectual life of Florence as the Villino Trollope; and one can find it today in the Piazza dell' Independenza, not far from the central station. Here Mrs Trollope lived with her son and daughter-in-law, and now that another pen had been added to the family the Trollopian ink flowed, if possible, faster than ever. Visitors took away with them the memory of marble halls, suits of armour, Florentine chests and majolica, and a terrace where a special brand of iced lemonade was served as the now aged authoress entertained the guests with undiminished vitality, while her son and Theodosia discussed with them the future of Italy.

Years of productive work followed: novels from Mrs Trollope (sometimes two in one year), poems and articles on Italian freedom by Theodosia, and admirable historical works by T. A. Trollope which do not deserve the oblivion which has overtaken them. Like a true Anglo-Florentine, Mrs Trollope lived to be eighty-three, and in two years' time Theodosia followed her to the grave. Unable to live in a house which held so many memories, Trollope sold it and eventually moved to Rome. In gratitude for Theodosia's championship, the municipality honoured her with a tablet on the house in the Piazza dell' Independenza, on which you may read, charmingly expressed in Italian, that she wrote in English with an Italian heart.

§ 16

I walked back from Fiesole on an unforgettable summer's evening. I looked down over the olive trees to the Valley of the Arno, where the domes and towers of Florence could be seen illuminated by the last half-hour of sunlight. The sky was already pink at the edges, offering that delicious Italian assurance that the sun would shine tomorrow. The cicadas were trilling in the fields and gardens, and the stone walls held the heat of the day. As I picked out Brunelleschi's dome and Giotto's tower, I heard a stealthy clatter near at hand, and, glancing over a stone wall, saw on a lower level two white oxen, with horns like harp frames, come slowly under the olives behind a plough. The farmer, like an Irishman, was stealing a scratch crop. I called down and asked what he intended to grow. He looked up, and I found myself gazing at the lean, taut face of Cosimo de' Medici.

'Melons,' he replied.

I had been to visit two English friends, rich and elderly, who were trying to find peace in a troubled world. They had tried South Africa, where they had doubled their capital in a gold-mine merger, but it was too far from Europe. Perhaps Italy was the answer. I was anxious to see them, for, of course, there is no answer to their problem! Peace, if it exists, exists only in one's self.

They had rented a villa below Fiesole, quite in the old style. There was nothing the English colony of a century ago would not have recognized: the brown-washed building with its central tower, standing in its *podere* of farmland: the box-edged garden, with its fountain and the double line of lemon trees in terracotta tubs; the tiled shelter in which the lemons are placed under sacking in winter. It was all there, even to the Italian family: the butler-handyman in white linen coat and black trousers, ready to receive guests; the cook, his ample, sallow wife; a dark-eyed daughter busy about some household task. It looked the same on the surface, but, of course, it was all different. The wages alone would have ruined the Brownings in a month. Rent was high, living was expensive, but, above all, it was lonely. There is now no English colony in the old sense. Today the villas of Tuscany are prestige homes for wealthy manufacturers from Turin and Milan.

'I think,' said my friend, 'when our lease is up next spring, we shall probably try Monte Carlo.'

I said good-bye, feeling that the Anglo-Florentine sunset has definitely set over Fiesole. But one well-known English pen continues to write on those hills. In the beautiful *La Pietra*, which dates from 1460, Harold Acton has written his distinguished books on the Medici and the Bourbons of Naples. The Italian garden which his father created so skilfully, a wonderful composition of box hedges, terraces, fountains, statues, and even a greenwood theatre, deserves to be remembered as an English contribution to the Florentine scene.

I walked on to the main road through steep and narrow lanes confined by stone walls. The sloping hillside was dotted with villa after villa, each one escorted by guardian cypress trees: a landscape unchanged in appearance since the nineteenth century. What an age it was. There will surely never be another haven like Florence, where artists and writers with small means could live in leisure and sunlight. It is perhaps easy, in the insecurity of our own age, to exaggerate the felicities of nineteenth century Florence, nevertheless it was a period when a great number of contented English expatriates managed to produce an enormous amount of work, and, looking back, it appears to have been an enchanted backwater.

A feature of the time was the association in Italy of English and American writers and artists. The first American invasion of Europe was that of a great number of cultured and talented individuals, particularly sculptors, who had come to study and to produce works to satisfy the demand for public statuary in the developing United States. It was the period when the Capitol in Washington was still incomplete and the State House in Boston was being enlarged, when public buildings of various kinds all over the country demanded heroes in stone and bronze. Among the most distinguished American sculptors were Horace Greenough, Hiram Powers, Thomas Crawford, father of the novelist Marion Crawford, and Browning's great friend, William Wetmore Story. They were attended by what Henry James called 'that strange sisterhood of American lady sculptors', who, incidentally, were the first American women to be studied by the Italians. 'One of the sisterhood, if I am not mistaken,' wrote James, 'was a negress, whose colour, picturesquely contrasting with that of her plastic material, was the pleading agent of her fame; another was the "gifted child" (speaking by the civil register as well as by nature) who shook saucy curls in the lobbies of the Capitol and extorted from susceptible senators commissions for national monuments.' This era, on the eve of Italy's national unity, when the Grand Duke of Tuscany still slept in the Pitti and the Pope in the Quirinal, is as picturesque as any that had gone before. In a Florence still encircled by her wall, and in a Rome, small, countrified, and full of the rush and whisper of fountains, the American sculptors exported their statesmen; and the consignments read like the passenger list of a cruising liner – Josiah Quincy; Chief Justice Marshall; Professor Henry; Francis Scott King . . . and so on. For over a century now those distinguished Americans, reborn in Italian marble, have gazed down upon far-off city square and campus.

In their letters, rather than in anything they wrote for publication, Story and Browning preserved the magic of past days in Florence, of long talks in each other's houses and homeward walks at night, still talking, under a full moon. It is a wonderful world of tranquillity into which we look in these letters. Both the Brownings and the Storys loved picnics. In the heat of summer they would take their food with them and spend a day in the mountains or beside a stream, or in some ancient garden like that at Pratolino, near Florence, where the giant statue of the kneeling *Penino*, representing the Apennines, suggested to Elizabeth a pet name for her tiny son. One of their most ambitious destinations was the mountain top near Bagni de Lucca with the beautiful name of *Prato Fiorito*, the field in flower. This involved a long ride on horseback or donkey. 'Here we lay for half an hour and talked and gazed at the tumbling waves of mountains below,' wrote Story, and, of another occasion, he wrote: 'After dinner we sat on the rock by the stream and sang, and I made me a long pipe-stem of a cane-pole and smoked and smoked.' (It was a pity that Browning did not smoke, thought Story. 'It is his greatest fault,' he once said.) And again: 'The whole day in the same woods with the Brownings. We went at ten o'clock, carrying our provisions. Browning and I walked to the spot, and there, spreading shawls under the great chestnuts, we read and talked the live-long day . . .'

Henry James said, of mid-nineteenth-century Florence, 'I find I can live in it again with any old ghost whatever who will so much as hold out a finger.' And I feel as he did. Probably few visitors now, when everything has to be seen in a few hours, are even aware of the ghostly fingers of their not so remote compatriots; but they are there, beckoning in the Casa Guidi, the Villa Landor, the Piazza dell' Independenza, and upon the hills of Fiesole; and I think we owe them a smile of recognition as we pass.

CHAPTER ELEVEN

The Towers of S. Gimignano – Siena and the Palio – The Sienese Contrade and their Origins – Blessing the horse – The Race – A Pope's Adventures in Scotland – Arezzo – The House of Vasari – The Madonna of Carda – La Verna and S. Francis – The Hermits of Camaldoli – The Improvvisatori *of Tuscany*

§ 1

Upon a hill above the valley of the Elsa, halfway between Florence and Siena, stand fourteen towers, the towers of S. Gimignano. They are like nothing else one has ever seen. To call them mediaeval skyscrapers is silly: they are the unique expression of a knightly society at war with itself and with the merchant guilds, and powerful enough to impose such ridiculous, pugnacious gestures upon the community. Every mediaeval town in Italy once sprouted them until the warlike nobles, who built them in rivalry with each other, were tamed by the urban, mercantile spirit and persuaded literally to come down to earth. The fourteen towers of S. Gimignano are the last group, or clump, in Italy, and they give one an idea of the extraordinary appearance of the larger cities of the Middle Ages, for example Bologna, which had two hundred of them.

Nowadays the towers of S. Gimignano are a tourist attraction, and if any traces of later periods ever existed in the town, these have been carefully eliminated, and one is persuaded that nothing has happened there since the twelfth century. During the last war the Germans shelled the town for two days with 280-millimeter shells: and not one of the fourteen towers fell down! It was reported in the United States that the old town with its art treasures had been obliterated, but, though much damage was done, when the Allies eventually reached S. Gimignano, expecting a pile of rubble, they saw the fourteen towers – all erect and smartly at attention. I do not pretend to know how this happened, especially as the object of the bombardment was the destruction of a supposed French artillery observation post in one of the towers.

I explored the battlements during one of those magic days in Tuscany when there appears to be no limit to one's vision. I looked north beyond the horizon to Florence, and east to Arezzo, while, only ten miles away, Siena sat enthroned upon her hills in knightly vigil, and so close she seemed in that spun air that I might have shot an arrow into her, or perhaps have tossed a gauntlet into the Campo, or maybe have shouted some taunt that would have been clearly heard and resented. Such thoughts are natural in the shadow of these towers.

I looked down, too, upon the Chianti country, those ridged lands above the hot valleys where the wine tastes better than anywhere else. They drink it when it is six months old and draw it from casks, like cider in Devon, and, as you drink it, you know that someday you will contrast it with the travel-weary fluid of the same name in London.

Though the bombardment spared the towers, it damaged many of the old buildings and the frescoes for which S. Gimignano is famous. A shell penetrated the *Crucifixion* by Barna da Siena, carrying away a yard of it; *S. Sebastian* by Benozzo Gozzoli was damaged by shrapnel; a shell went through the *Paradise* of Taddeo di Bartolo; and there were other casualties, but you would never know unless you were told. Happily Ghirlandaio's lovely *Burial of S. Fina* was untouched.

She was one of those strange child saints, a poor little invalid who lay paralysed for ten years upon a wooden bed, unable to defend herself against rats. She has not been able to escape from them, even in art galleries, where she is always pictured with a rat in attendance. They will tell you in S. Gimignano that on the night she died the church bells rang by themselves, and when she was lifted from her wooden couch, it was found that she had been lying upon a soft bed of white violets. They say also that the violets of S. Fina still flower among the stones of the fourteen towers.

There are, needless to say, many in S. Gimignano who have no difficulty in understanding why the town of S. Fina had such a fortunate escape during the bombardment.

§ 2

Arriving in Siena a day or so before the Palio, I could find nowhere to stay. It seemed that every tourist in Italy had descended upon the ancient city, and I was on the point of returning to Florence, which is only about forty miles away, when I was introduced to Giulio.

He was, I was told, a Giraffe, which is to say he lived in that contrada, or ward, of Siena known as the Giraffe, and he was in fact a flag-bearer and a teacher of *sbandierata*. This is the art, seen nowhere else, I think, but in Siena, of casting a flag into the air and catching it by the staff as it descends. It is practised by two men, who toss their flags to each other and catch them in mid-air, often twirling them between their legs with a follow-through movement before they fling them into the air again. The art is practised in all the seventeen districts, or contrade, into which Siena is divided, and is exercised twice a year during the Palio, in July and August.

I saw in Giulio a lean young Italian with a bright and acquisitive eye. He thought it would be a pity for me to return to Florence, since the days which led to the Palio were so full of interest and excitement. After a confusing afternoon, in the course of which I met a great number of his friends and relatives, an empty furnished flat was found, which I agreed to take.

I admit that I was badly shaken by it. It was in a scabrous building in one of the most forbidding streets in Giraffe territory. Once the abode of some knight or merchant, it was now split up into flats. An ominous stone stairway ascending in almost total darkness, reminiscent of those in the slums of Edinburgh, mounted to sinister landings. It was rather an alarming place for a stranger to find himself in a foreign city. As I fumbled with the key and opened the door, I began to wonder whether I had not been rather foolish to allow my anxiety to see the Palio to lead me into such a situation. The flat was in darkness, and when I opened the wooden shutters to let in what little light there was in the narrow old street, I turned to survey an incongruous scene. I was in a prim little home contrived in this savage old building. It simpered back at me in a hire-purchase suite, a piano draped with lace, and an uncomfortable velvet sofa. It reminded me of the neat suburban interiors which wives of warders compose in the blood-stained turrets of the Tower of London. It was amazing that some young wife should have been able to defy and dominate the old building and to have transformed it to her way of thinking. The bedroom contained a brass *letto matrimoniale* and a wardrobe full of women's clothes. All I could tell of the creator of this unlikely abode was that she was small and fond of blue. I had often longed to see the Palio, and had listened for years to the descriptions of those who had seen the race, but never could I have imagined such an introduction to it, or indeed that such genteel little homes were Siena's solution to the problem of living with the Middle Ages.

Later that evening I ran across Giulio, who introduced me to the Captain of the Giraffe Contrada, who welcomed me as an honorary Giraffe and courteously invited me to dinner on the eve of the Palio.

§ 3

When we talk about the Derby we mean the race, and not the Stakes, and in the same way the Palio, which is really the prize, has come to be applied to the race. The Palio in its original form was a *pallium* or cloak of rich velvet or brocade; in Siena today it is a silk banner with an image of the Virgin upon it. The lords of the Renaissance were always talking about 'bringing home the Palio', and among the racing men one recalls are Francesco Gonzaga, the husband of Isabella d'Este, Lorenzo the Magnificent, and Caesar Borgia. These men either went themselves or sent their horses and jockeys to the many open events which were organized by towns all over Italy during religious festivals. I have never seen a racing calendar of Renaissance Italy, but it must have been a crowded one.

The Palio in Siena is, of course, not a race at all in the true meaning of the word. It is a burlesque with a touch of cruelty about it which relates it to the comic races of the Italian Middle Ages and to the fist-fights of the period. Such races were held on feast days and were probably the most popular part of the entertainment. Unlike the bloodstock races, which were held outside the town, the comic races were run through the streets. There were ass and buffalo races, races for Jews in Rome, in Milan for prostitutes, and in Florence for the old horses on which the dyers' boys loaded cloth to be washed in the Arno. There were even races for riderless horses. The animals had spikes attached to them, which drove them frantically through the streets between screens of canvas.

The French and Spanish invasions of the fifteenth century disrupted the racing of bloodstock, but new amusements arrived with the invaders. Under the Spaniards a form of bull-fight – *caccia di tori* – became popular in Siena and was held in the main piazza. Each contrada provided its bull, which was led round with much ceremony, and the contrade went to considerable trouble and expense to design a *macchine*, or, as we should say today, a decorated float, into which the bull-fighters could retreat at moments of danger. This was the age of pageantry and triumphs, and the machines were ingenious and beautiful. When bull-fights were abolished in Tuscany in 1590, their place was taken during the annual festivals by a revival of the old burlesque races. To add a touch of splendour to them, the competing contrade organized a procession of cars, which were grander versions of the old *macchini*. It is from these cars that the seventeen contrade of Siena derive their puzzling names: the Tortoise, the Snail, the Wood, the Eagle, the Wave, the Panther, the Ram, the Tower, the Unicorn, the Owl, the Shell, the Dragon, the Goose, the Giraffe, the Caterpillar, the She-Wolf, and the Porcupine.

In true Renaissance fashion, most of the cars were classical tableaux or allegorical compositions. The car of the Dragon told the story of Cadmus. He was seen standing, spear in hand, upon a rocky landscape of canvas, having killed the dragon. As the float reached the grandstand, he extracted the dragon's teeth, which he cast about him, and wherever he threw them the canvas was agitated as an armed man sprang up. The car of the Goose represented the city of Rome being warned of the Gothic attack by the Capitoline geese. Roman soldiers were seen standing round battlements on which stood a goose, while Father Tiber reclined in a corner. The Giraffe car was a gilded enclosure in which the model of a gigantic and unusual giraffe was attended by Moors: the animal's hide was white and its spots were red. The car of the Owl was an allegorical tableau which represented Wisdom and Intelligence. Its chief character was Minerva, who sat enthroned among classical deities while a boy walked in front holding a silver vase on which a live owl was perched.

A delightful car, which I should like to have seen, was that of the Caterpillar Contrada. It was escorted by gardeners wearing green jackets, yellow breeches, and bandoliers of flowers. Green and yellow ribbons fluttered from their hats and they carried a flag of yellow, green, and blue (the same colours are carried today), in the centre of which a green caterpillar stood upon a sprig of olive. This beautifully escorted car was a garden in the form of steps which led to an arched arbour and a fountain. As the car encircled the piazza, musicians seated upon the steps were heard playing their instruments.

So one could take every contrada in Siena and trace its name to the car it devised centuries ago; and it is interesting to think that the colours worn by the contrade, and the emblems they bear, are the last living vestige of the courtly pageantry of the Renaissance; a pageantry, incidentally, which became the parent of masque and ballet.

Some scholars think that these contrade go back to the armed bands of the Middle Ages; others believe that they are no older than the Renaissance and, like the *festaioli* of Florence, were groups of men who planned and organized the annual pageants. Whatever their origin, it is clear that they now preside over a number of ancient customs. The race for the Palio goes back to the burlesque races of the Middle Ages; the way the jockeys attack each other with whips provided for the purpose is a relic of the fighting contests of ancient times, while the *comparse*, the great pageant of mediaeval costume, is in direct descent from the Renaissance. Most

important of all, the pageant and the race are held in honour of the
Virgin.

§ 4

There were moments when I thought Siena the most beautiful
town I had seen in Italy, Florence not excepted, but one should not
compare them; one cannot compare the fourteenth century
with the fifteenth. When I went into the country and looked back
at Siena, mounted above the ridged vineyards, I saw a vision of the
Middle Ages that filled me with delight. If one could return either
to the fourteenth or the fifteenth century, what a difficult decision
it would be: at least I thought so as I walked the narrow hilly
streets lined with old palaces; and again, as I stood in the striped
cathedral, and as I admired the tender, tenuous Virgins of Lorenzetti and Simone Martini as they leaned against their gold backgrounds, dreaming of Byzantium. What a problem it would be
indeed: the century of S. Catherine or that of Lorenzo the
Magnificent?

Curiously enough, just as the swarming crowds in Venice had
lent vitality and colour to the Piazzetta, so the crowds in Siena,
infected with the Palio fever, brought from the past a memory of
the city's violent rivalries. These crowds, however, were content
to pack the streets, to watch men putting down cart-loads of sand
on the outer perimeter of the Campo, where the race would be
run. They wandered about happily and bought the mediaeval
sweetmeat, *Pan Forte*, or the almond cakes called *Ricciarelli*, which
reminded me of the little marzipan cakes of S. Teresa, which are
made at Avila, in Spain.

Apart from the cathedral, which was packed from morning
until night, the crowds kept to the main roads, and I found the
picture galleries to be comparatively empty. I had no idea how
much I was to enjoy them. Here I seemed to find myself in a
curious cul-de-sac of art; a marvellous collection of enlarged
miniatures, a development, if you like, of book illustration or
illumination, which appeared to be moving towards the Renaissance, yet never arriving there. What a perfect town Siena must

have been for a conservative! To a Sienese of the Renaissance, how revolutionary, almost blasphemous, Florence must have seemed with its peasant Virgins! Here in Siena, as befits the Virgin's own town, the Queen of Heaven is always a lady. It is this wistful and almond-eyed aristocrat, sometimes dreamy and melancholy, her Child in her arms and a halo of burnished gold behind her head, who presides over an enchanted land.

I passed from room to room marvelling at this beautiful mediaeval world, full of miracles and grace, where celestial beings hung suspended in the air with nothing to proclaim their origin save that their feet were in the clouds; a world where any goose-girl could meet a saint, or the Queen of Heaven herself, standing among the olive trees; where kings and queens wore their crowns, even in bed; a world where angels and devils mingled with the people in the narrow streets of castellated cities. At a time when Uccello and his contemporaries were wrestling with the problems of perspective, these painters of Siena, only forty miles away, were still painting uphill tables and floors, painting with their backs to Florence and their faces to Ravenna.

I enjoyed the sight of sunlight filling that superb piazza of herring-bone brick, the Campo. It is often compared to a shell, though I think it looks more like an open fan. Its nine ribs radiate outward from the handle – the Palazzo Pubblico – and form a colossal semi-circle, each segment a marvel of brickwork. The Campo hummed with effort. Carpenters were putting the final hammer blows to the grandstands which obscured the lower storeys of the old palaces, now shops, while men were spreading six inches of sand along the crazy racecourse; and carts were arriving piled with mattresses, which were stacked up to block the entrance into the Via San Martino. This is the Beecher's Brook of the Palio. As the bareback riders come round the bend of the piazza and gallop downhill towards this street, a horse unfamiliar with the course will generally bolt into the Via San Martino. Even now, I was told, though the entrance is blocked with hoardings and padded with mattresses, there are often bad falls at this place.

Here, I thought, was a memory of Italy which I should never

forget: the sunlight on the red bricks of the tall Mangia tower; the town hall with the white and black shield of Siena, the *Balzana*, above each pointed Gothic window; the tourists and country folk wandering over the immense slope of the piazza; a man selling balloons and sweets; the noise of hammering; the carts grinding over the sand with timber and mattresses; and a little girl holding a red and yellow balloon on a string as she watched the pigeons drinking at the *Fonte Gaia*.

In 1297, the year after Edward I of England had removed the Stone of Scone from Scotland, the Sienese stood in this piazza watching workmen beginning to build the Palazzo Pubblico. Now, more than six and a half centuries later, the municipality still occupies the ground floor and the visitor, ascending the stone stairway, is allowed to wander through the painted chambers above. This is a fantastic building. No Vasari, as at Florence, has ever brought it up to date and swept the knights and ladies from the walls, or removed wrought-iron screens and inconvenient walls. Here are the surroundings in which a mediaeval commune conducted its affairs. From the Room of the Priors you can glance down and see the Campo fanning outward to its fringe of buildings and, turning, admire walls that were decorated in 1407. The chapel, dim and mysterious, and covered everywhere with frescoes of saints and heroes, leads through painted arches into the *Sala del Mappamundo*, though the map of the world has long since vanished. However, a splendid picture remains, which Simone Martini was commissioned to paint by the city fathers in 1315, when he had returned in triumph from Avignon, where he had met Petrarch and Laura and had painted frescoes that pleased the Pope. This picture, which fills the wall, shows Our Lady seated in queenly state beneath a canopy held by saints. Though there is not a king or a knight in the picture, the group of saintly personages belongs to a world of chivalry.

When Philip de Commines was in Siena with Charles VIII in 1495, he thought the city 'governed the worst of any in Italy', and always 'divided by factions'. Perhaps he had been looking at the two famous frescoes, painted a hundred and fifty years before his time, by Ambroglio Lorenzetti in order to illustrate the difference between good and bad government. Though 'Bad Government' is now much the worse for wear, it is easy to see what a Council of merchants wished to impress upon their contemporaries in these two paintings. In 'Good Government', Justice is enthroned, surrounded by the figures of Magnanimity, Temperance, Prudence, Strength, and Peace, while overhead fly Faith, Hope, and Charity. We see a wonderful view of Siena, the piazza, the streets, palaces, and gates, where men are at work, a professor is teaching, girls are dancing together, pack-horses are coming in loaded with merchandise; and in the countryside beyond the walls the ploughman is busy on the terraced hills, and men are tending vines, while happy hunting parties roam the hillside and river bank. Then we see 'Bad Government'. A satanic horned figure is enthroned, with one foot upon a black ram, which represents Tyranny. The figures that sit on each side are Cruelty, Betrayal, Fraud, Fury, Discord, and Treachery. In the air above are Avarice, Pride, and Vanity; on the ground below Justice lies bound. The joyless landscape is stripped, empty and bare: the fields are untended, and the vines unpruned; men have been murdered and women raped.

Several centuries ago, to people who were unable to read, these two allegories must have been equivalent, in modern terms, to a year's subscription to a daily newspaper. They still hold good. They are still true and, as far as the message goes, they might have been painted yesterday.

I took away with me the memory of a resolute little man on horseback. He was the *condottiere*, Guidoriccio da Fogliano, who was elected for six months as Captain of War in 1326, and did so well that Siena kept renewing his agreement for seven years. He is seen fully armed, wearing a long surcoat emblazoned with his arms, black diamonds and green foliage, while his horse is similarly barded. Both horse and rider are animated by an air of resolute endeavour, and although one can see only the horse's eye, it is an eloquent one: this excellent charger obviously knows that his master is riding to demand the surrender of the walled town that can be seen in the distance. The painting is small, yet it is full of power. The little armed figure grasping his baton, and so firmly in the saddle, remains in the memory as one of the four horsemen of Italy, all *condottieri*, who are still riding confidently down the ages – Hawkwood in Florence, Gattamelata in Padua, Colleoni in Venice, and de Fogliano in Siena.

§ 5

During Palio time in Siena the sound of a drum sends people running towards it. As the drum taps echo in the old streets, the palaces look as if they know all about it and approve. Glancing round on such occasions, you may see at the end of a street a brief vision of a man in red and yellow tights passing with a brilliant flag. It is something to do with the Palio, some preliminary ceremony. One afternoon, as I was climbing the Via dei Fusari to the cathedral, I heard a ruffle of approaching drums, and when I came into the piazza I found it crowded with people, all gazing in the same direction, while the Archbishop of Siena, vested in cope and mitre, and accompanied by the clergy and the choir, stood on top of the steps at the west doors.

In a few moments I saw a wonderful sight. Uphill into the sunlight of the piazza there emerged from the darkness of a street four of the great white oxen of Tuscany, yoked two by two to a heavy tumbril. The wagon jolted and ground its slow way over the pavement, while beside it marched a guard of young men in the dress of 1450, one leg white, the other black, pleated tunics caught in at the waist, and upon their heads cocky little hats of felt. From the wagon flew banners and the black and white flag of Siena. More young men leaned from the wagon in the same costume, and proudly recognized friends in the crowd.

This was my first sight of the *Carroccio* of Siena, indeed of any *carroccio*. So this was what the battle-cars of the Middle Ages looked like: a glorified farm wagon, a consecrated hay cart. The spokes of its wheels were beautifully shaped and the sides of the wagon were painted. From the mainmast floated the long white and black pennant of Siena, and half-way up the mast a brass bell was suspended which every now and then was tolled by a picturesque attendant who pulled a cord attached to it. As the car drew level with the cathedral steps, four varlets in brown sack-cloth went to the heads of the oxen while the brilliantly clad attendants in the car lifted down a painted silken banner. This was the Palio, which was to be lodged in the cathedral until the day of the race. Then an object, which had at first puzzled me, was lifted down and carried up the steps by a group of men. It was a wax candle five feet high, the gift of the contrade to the church. By this time all the bells of history seemed to be ringing. Everyone who has been inside a Catholic church will have admired the beautiful custom, which Christianity borrowed from paganism, of burning candles at shrines, but never did I think it would be my good fortune to see an official gift of light to a cathedral, as this was.

Siena Cathedral has the look of a bishop who, by some strange accident of highway robbery or shipwreck, has been obliged to assume an oriental costume. Nothing could be more Christian than the outlines of this noble church, and nothing more Moslem than the horizontal stripes of white and black marble with which it is built. As one looks at it, memories of other Gothic cathedrals are mingled with thoughts of Cairo, Damascus, and Còrdoba, and one wonders how those restless alien stripes came to the hills of Tuscany.

As the Palio and the candle were carried in procession up the nave, I realized that never before had I seen one of the great cathedrals fully alive. Only the pageantry of the Church remains today, one misses the pageantry of the people: the blaze of heraldry, the splendour of ancient costume. Here in Siena one can see twice a year one of those gorgeous spectacles which have elsewhere vanished from the earth.

During the week of the Palio the inlaid pavement of the cathedral is visible, a pavement so precious that it is boarded up and invisible for most of the year. A door on the left aisle leads into the famous library which Pope Pius III built in memory of his uncle, Pius II, the famous Sienese poet, diplomat, and eventually, pope. Today one goes there not to look at the books but at the frescoes which Pinturicchio painted between 1505 and 1507. They look so fresh and brilliant that they might have been painted yesterday. I was delighted by this vivid picture biography. These frescoes should, I suppose, rank as 'decoration', though Berenson has a kind word for them: they have 'undeniable charm' and reflect processions and ceremonies in an 'enchanted out-of-doors'. And what more suitable background could there be to the life of a much travelled pontiff than this 'enchanted out-of-doors' where the sea and galleys, and little rocky harbours, are never far away? We first see Pius setting out to seek his fortune as a handsome young fellow with fair hair falling to his shoulders, then as a trusted diplomat and orator, later as a bishop in the act of blessing an emperor and his modest bride, and, finally, as pope.

My favourite scene shows Aeneas Sylvius Piccolomini, as he then was, being received in audience by James I of Scotland. This was a secret mission on which the future pope was sent in 1435, and he gives a vivid account of this adventure in the *Commentaries*, which he wrote later in life. His ship, he says, was blown to Norway in a gale, then blown to sea again, and when all hope had been abandoned was cast up somewhere on the east coast of Scotland. This must have been between North Berwick and Dunbar since Aeneas, in fulfilment of a vow, weak, numb, and barefoot, walked ten miles to the shrine of Our Lady at White-kirk. This was a famous shrine whose spring of miraculous water had been famous since 1294, when the Countess of March, fleeing wounded after the Battle of Dunbar, drank the water and was cured. Unfortunately, the pope-to-be does not say how he reached the Scottish King, how he obtained fresh clothes, or whether the King was at Edinburgh or Perth.

Pinturicchio, to whom Scotland was merely a name, has painted a purely Italian scene. James I (who died in his early forties) is pictured as a venerable white-haired figure in a brown garment, his knees covered with a blue wrap. He is seated on a dais approached by a strip of Turkey carpet. A crowd of graceful Italianate Scots stand about, dressed in Renaissance fashions, and through a colonnade of marble columns (the like of which was never seen in the Scotland of James I!) we see a river winding through a gentle landscape that might be that of Lake Maggiore. Aeneas, in a scarlet robe, stands in an oratorical attitude addressing the aged monarch. It must be the strangest picture of fifteenth century Scotland ever conceived. For the real Scotland of 1425, as seen by Aeneas, we have to go to his account of the mission. 'It is a cold country,' he wrote, 'where few things will grow and for the most part has no trees. Below the ground is found a sulphurous rock, which they dig for fuel. The cities have no walls. The houses are usually constructed without mortar; their roofs are covered with turf; and in the country, doorways are closed with oxhides. The common people, who are poor and rude, stuff themselves with meat and fish, but eat bread as a luxury. The men are short and brave; the women fair, charming, and easily won. Women there think less of a kiss than in Italy of a touch of the hand.'

He decided to return through England disguised as a merchant. Crossing the Tweed in a small boat, he came to Berwick. He called at a farmhouse door whose owner upheld the northern reputation for hospitality and, sending for the local priest, provided dinner. 'Many relishes and chickens and geese were served, but there was no bread or wine.' Men and women gathered round the farmhouse and asked the priest whether the future pope was a Christian!

'When the meal had lasted till the second hour of the night, the priest and the host together with all the men and children took leave of Aeneas (he always refers to himself in the third person), and hastened away, saying that they were taking refuge in a tower a long way off for fear of the Scots, who were accustomed, when the river was at ebb-tide, to cross by night and make raids upon them. They could not by any means be induced to take him with them, although he earnestly besought them, nor yet any of the women, although there were a number of beautiful girls and matrons. For they think the enemy will do them no wrong – not counting outrage a wrong. So Aeneas remains behind with two servants and his one guide among a hundred women, who made a circle round the fire and sat up all night cleaning hemp and carrying on a lively conversation with the interpreter.

But after a good part of the night had passed, two young women showed Aeneas, who was by this time very sleepy, to a chamber strewn with straw, planning to sleep with him, as was the custom of the country, if they were asked. But Aeneas, thinking less about women than about robbers, who he feared might appear any minute, repulsed the protesting girls, afraid that, if he committed a sin, he would have to pay the penalty as soon as the rovers arrived. So he remained alone among the heifers and the nanny goats, which prevented him from sleeping a wink by stealthily pulling the straw out of his pallet. Some time after midnight there was a great noise of dogs barking and geese hissing, at which all the women scattered, the guide took to his heels, and there was the wildest confusion as if the enemy were at hand. Aeneas however was afraid that if he rushed outside, in his ignorance of the road he might fall a prey to the first person he met. Accordingly he thought best to await events in his own room (it was the stable), and very soon the women returned with the interpreter, saying that nothing was wrong and that the new-comers were friends, not enemies. Aeneas thought this was the reward of his continence.'

Surely the strangest of papal reminiscences?

It should be said that the writer was a gay young layman at this time who had no thought of taking Holy Orders; in after years, as pope, he asked people to forget Aeneas and his writings and remember him only as Pius. The pictures which show him thirty-three years later as pope, reveal a pale old invalid of only fifty-three. He had a poor digestion. The frost-bite which had lamed him in Scotland lasted all his life and developed into what was called gout. One picture shows him as pope, pronouncing the canonization of his townswoman, S. Catherine of Siena. He sits enthroned, wearing the tiara, a blue wrap over his knees, while cardinals in scarlet gaze down upon the body of the saint. Stretched on a bed, S. Catherine (who had been dead for eighty-one years) lies as if asleep, clothed in a Dominican habit and holding a lily.

I wish Pinturicchio had painted Pius enjoying a picnic in the Sienese *contada* and transacting business with his cardinals in the shade of a chestnut tree. He loved to do that, and was able to capture such occasions so that the magic of lost spring-times continues to live in his words. He wrote, when seeking a cure for his gout:

'The Pope then carried out his intention of going to the baths. It was the sweet season of early spring. All the hills about Siena were smiling in their vesture of foliage and flowers, and luxuriant crops were growing up in the fields. The Sienese country immediately around the city is indescribably lovely with its gently sloping hills planted with cultivated trees and vines or ploughed for grain, overlooking delightful valleys green with pasture land or sown fields, and watered by never-failing streams. There are also thick forests planted by nature or man where birds sing most sweetly and on every hill the citizens of Siena have built splendid country seats. Here are noble monasteries where holy men live; there private palaces built like fortresses. Through this region the Pope travelled in a happy mood nor did he find the baths less pleasant. They lie ten miles from the city in a valley two or three stades wide and quite eight miles long. It is watered by the Mersa River, a tributary of the Ombrone. This never dries up and is full of eels which, though small, are very white and sweet. . . . Around the baths are simple houses used as inns. Here the Pope passed a month and though he bathed twice a day, he never omitted the signatura or other state business. About the twenty-second hour he was accustomed to go into the meadows and, sitting on the riverbank where it was greenest and grassiest, he heard embassies and petitioners. Every day the wives of the peasants brought flowers and strewed the path by which the Pope went to the baths; and the only reward they expected was permission to kiss his feet.'

With that picture for company I was happy to roam the battlements of Siena and to look down upon that enchanted countryside where to this day a man may walk straight into the background of an Annunciation and eat his sandwiches beside one of those rivers between domed hills which, as everyone who has been to an art gallery knows, ran through Bethlehem.

§ 6

The Palio temperature chart continued to rise several degrees every day, indeed almost every hour. The fateful moment came when, to prove there was no dirty work, the contrade drew their horses by lot from a glass jar. The animals had been released from cart shafts and various humdrum duties for the great occasion, and though they looked unlikely race-horses, some, no doubt, were better than others to the practised eye. Whenever a contrada drew what it considered a *cavallo buono*, there were shouts of joy and men danced together and embraced their animal; though if it were deemed to be a *cavallaccio*, groans of despair were heard and people abused the unfortunate horse. Then came the *prove* when, during a burst of late afternoon sun, the horses galloped bare-backed round the Campo in a series of trial races with their jockeys clinging to them.

I met Giulio during a *prova*, wild with joy because the Giraffes had drawn a good horse. Now, he whispered, they must take care to see that their jockey was not bribed to lose the race! It was common knowledge, he told me, that, as the Goose Contrada had drawn the favourite, two rival contrade had come together and were planning to ruin its chances. How, I asked? 'Oh, there are ways!' replied Giulio. 'For example, a winning jockey can be attacked with the *nerbi* of rival jockeys' (a *nerbo* is the ox-hide whip which every jockey carries to beat, not his horse, but his competitors) and 'it is possible to make an arrangement so that the winning jockey goes slow when he should go fast'. And here Giulio made that curious little gesture, common to *homo Mediterraneus*, of raising his right hand and gently rubbing the thumb against the forefinger, indicating money.

I had long since suspected that the Palio is an Italian state of mind, and here was proof of it: I heard all the qualities which Machiavelli had recommended to the attention of princes proudly expounded and advocated. I did not dare to remind Giulio that all this plotting and scheming was in honour of the Blessed Virgin.

When the evening of the Giraffe dinner came, the night before the Palio, I wandered lost in the heart of mediaeval Siena, pausing now and then in the light of a lamp to decipher a misleading map drawn by Giulio. Dare I ask the way? Suppose I had strayed into an enemy contrada! This would not have been difficult. The Giraffes are bounded on the north by the Caterpillars and on the south by the Owls and the Unicorns. Fortunately I heard the sound of revelry and, venturing to peep through the crack of a door, caught a glimpse of Giulio in the act of pouring out wine.

The dinner was being held under a trellis in a stable-yard. The floor was strewn with wood shavings. Two long tables and a head table occupied the whole length of the yard. There were oil-lamps on the white tablecloths, and each place was set as if in a restaurant. Some of the *alfieri*, the flag-bearers, had been refreshing themselves and stood in a circle singing. Giulio handed me a tumbler of Chianti, and as I was talking to the Captain of the Contrada, I heard a muffled bang behind me and, turning, saw that I was standing in front of a stable door. The Captain, thinking I would like to see the animal on which the hope of the district depended, asked one of the guards to open the upper half of the door. Inside, a rough little horse was comfortably bedded down with plenty of straw. An electric light was burning before a shrine of the Virgin. The horse looked out into the lamplit yard, and at the sight of him the *alfieri* recharged their glasses and solemnly toasted him.

Eventually we were seated, and the priest said grace. At the top table the President of the Contrada (a Piccolomini, I was told), sat with the Captain and some distinguished guests, and also a small Sicilian who wore the red and white racing colours of the Giraffes. He was the *fantino*, the jockey, and they said he was a good one. but expensive. He made enough money at a Palio to live comfortably for the rest of the year.

Plates of salami and ham appeared under the trellis, followed by great bowls of spaghetti, to be succeeded in turn by cold roast chicken and salad, and custard cake and peaches. The Chianti, decanted from a cask, circulated generously, and the *alfieri* sang

happily throughout dinner and had to be hushed when at length
the President rose to make a speech.

As I said good night, Giulio reminded me to be at the church
on the following afternoon to see the horse blessed, and I returned
through some of the most sinister-looking streets in Europe. I
must have taken a wrong turning and have strayed over the
Giraffe boundary, for I came upon another feast, just on the
point of breaking up. All the women were in the street, and every
window-ledge within sight of the yard where the dinner had been
held, was occupied by sightseers. Whether they were Owls or
Caterpillars, or even Unicorns, I shall never know. Such is the
sense of faction implanted by the Palio, even in alien breasts, that I
turned and stole back to the main street as quickly as I could.

The next day I found my way in the afternoon to a church
called S. Maria della Suffragio. The priest, whom I had met at the
dinner, took me to the church rooms and showed me the wardrobe of the Giraffes. Glass-fronted cupboards completely lined one
room, and inside hung the red and white garments of the contrada, made of expensive cloths and silks, suspended in moth-proof
cellophane bags. There were also leather boots, gloves, tights,
embroidered belts, swords, shields, and suits of armour. Everything had been pressed, brushed, and, if necessary, dry-cleaned.

The church was small and there was no aisle. The rugs and
carpets had been removed. The priest told me it was quite true
that if during the Benediction a horse behaved unconventionally,
it was regarded as the most fortunate of omens. Some horses, he
said, did not mind being sprinkled with holy water, but others
objected. While we were talking, the church filled, and we heard,
coming down the hill, the sound that never stops during the Palio,
the tapping of drums. We heard hoofs on the pavement as the
horse was led into the church by the jockey and a member of the
contrada in his costume of red and white. The sacristan had lighted
the altar candles and the priest came out, wearing a surplice and
stole. He looked at the horse, and began the prayers. The animal
behaved well, listening quietly to every word. Then, making the

sign of the Cross, the priest cautiously approached the horse and said in Latin: 'Let this animal receive Thy Blessing, O Lord, whereby it may be preserved in body and freed from every harm by the intercession of the Blessed Anthony, through Christ, our Lord. Amen.'

He took an aspergillum and flicked some drops of holy water over horse and jockey. The animal stood quietly through this short ceremony. All over Siena similar blessings were taking place in the other nine competing contrade. Everything now depended on the will of heaven – and the machinations of Siena.

§ 7

The Palio – at last! It came during the last few hours of sunshine, when the heat of the day was over. I stood at a window opposite the starting point and saw the central space of the Campo filled with humanity which really did appear to be 'seething'. It had every reason to do so. It was packed so tightly that people who fainted were propped up against their companions and had to be lifted above them to the track. The grandstands round the Campo were full, and from nearly every window-sill hung a red and gold cloth.

The sun shone upon the pink brick of the Mangia Tower and upon the Palazzo Pubblico. Above every window of the old building, and there are twenty facing the Campo, was the white and black shield of the Republic of Siena, exactly as they may be seen in Sano di Pietro's picture of S. Bernardino preaching. A feeling of anticipation vibrated in the air and was intensified by the tolling of the Mangia bell, which was being rung by a man whose tiny swaying figure might be seen outlined against the sky. He had climbed over four hundred steps to the top and had then, so I was told by a friend of his, plugged his ears. It is said in Siena that if the wind is in the right direction, the Mangia bell can be heard in Rome. It is also often claimed that it has never been rung by an automaton, which is probably incorrect since the word Mangia comes from *mangiaguadagno*, a casual labourer, a name inspired by an automatic figure's intermittent efforts. A distant rattle of drums added greatly to the excitement. It penetrated to the Campo through a dozen stone crevices and alleys; and I felt that at any moment now the banners would be unfurled and we should march against Florence!

There was a flourish of trumpets as there poured into the outer circle of the Campo the most colourful and romantic procession to be seen in the world today. All the seventeen contrade of Siena take part in the pageant, but only ten, selected by lot, compete in the subsequent race. First came the twelve trumpeters of the Commune in black and white tights and red tunics; from each trumpet fell a flag which quartered with the white and black of Siena what I took to be the Florentine Marzucco on a red field. Behind rode a horseman carrying the flag of the Commune, but there was nothing Florentine about this: it was plain white and black. There was a tremendous flutter of heraldry as the thirty-six standard bearers of the estates and castles of the Republic came into the sunlight, followed by the flags of the trade guilds – mercers, apothecaries, painters, blacksmiths, stonemasons – but where were the immortal bricklayers? – then rode the *Capitano del Popolo* astride the right kind of solid charger: he wore plate armour and his page walked ahead bearing his sword and shield.

What impressed me, as the procession unfolded, was its seriousness. In England one goes to a pageant prepared to smile at the absurdity of modern people pretending to be their ancestors: but in Siena a great part of the male population walks with ease into the fifteenth century. Of the hundreds of men and boys taking part, not one looked out of place or embarrassed. The art galleries had been carefully consulted, and I noticed figures that recalled Mantegna, Carpaccio, and Pisanello. Though, as I say, there was not a false note, I must confess I did see one of the heralds glance furtively at his wristwatch.

Each of the seventeen contrade was led by a drummer and followed by two flag-bearers; then came the Captain of the contrada on horseback, and in armour, with men-at-arms and pages, a standard bearer, and more flagmen. Last of all rode the jockey upon a parade horse, while the horse he would ride later in the race was led behind him, a rich cloth flung over its back.

A neighbour told me that should a contrada's horse be killed during the *prove*, as indeed happened fairly recently, when a horse broke a leg and had to be shot, the contrada cannot draw another one, but parades in mourning with a draped drum, crêpe hanging from cap and helmet and a hoof of the dead horse borne sorrowfully on a silver dish.

Each contrada was easily identified by its flag, whose colours were repeated in the gorgeous costumes of the contingent. The Eagles carried a flag on which the black, double-headed eagle of the Emperor Charles V was emblazoned, with black and blue bands on a yellow field. The tunics of the contrada were yellow with a black and blue edging, their hose were yellow, and the calf of the left leg was encircled by two blue bands. The Snails carried a yellow and red flag with pale blue piping, and wore red tunics with wide slashed sleeves turned back to show a fawn lining: one leg was yellow, the other striped yellow and red. The Porcupines had a white flag with black, red, and blue stripes, and wore tunics to match: one leg was red, the other black and white, and upon their curly wigs they wore those little pork-pie hats seen so often in portraits of the fifteenth century. I watched with pride as the Giraffes marched past with their red and white check flag, looking extremely fine in their red and white tunics embroidered with silver, and with red caps edged with white fur. Giulio, a flaxen wig to his ears, strode nobly forward with his flag as if he had stepped out of a Pinturicchio fresco in the cathedral.

I was impressed by a display of his art. As the contrada drew level with my balcony, the drummer turned inward and gave a roll on his drum, a signal for the contrada to halt and for a display of *sbandierata*. Giulio and his companion, facing each other, cast their flags up thirty feet into the air, catching them as they descended shafts first. As if this were too easy, they would turn their backs on the falling flags and catch them as they came down; they would twirl them beneath their legs and toss them into the air, throwing them from a distance of twenty feet to each other. The whole Campo was soon encircled by tossing flags as the various contrade halted and gave their display.

A charming sight was a double file of young pages linked together, shoulder to shoulder, by a rope of evergreens. They divided the ten competing contrade from those which were not competing. I was puzzled by six knights in armour who rode with their visors down. I was told that these represented six dead, or non-existent contrade: the Bear, the Viper, the Lion, the Cock, the Sword, and the Oak. 'If a contrada fails to win the Palio in fifty years,' someone explained, 'it must die.'

It took two hours for the procession to pass. Then came what was to me the great moment when, to the sound of its bell, the *carroccio* lumbered into sight drawn by its four white oxen. The Palio was mounted in front of the car, a long streamer of silk on which a picture of Our Lady could be seen within a painted oval. A guard stood in the wagon and, as the trumpeters sounded a fanfare, and the bell tolled, the strangest sound in the pandemonium of cheering and drum tapping, the white oxen lumbered along gently swaying, as they do on all the roads of Tuscany.

And now, as the last contrada departed, the ten rough horses, each with its bareback jockey, cantered to the starting rope. The jockeys wore crash helmets and the colours of their contrada. Each carried a whip, the notorious *nerbo*, and already, as they crouched over the withers, they looked savagely at each other. The crowd, which had roared and cheered and shouted itself hoarse for two hours, now became demented. There was an explosion and a cloud of black smoke from some archaic starting system, and as the rope dropped the horses got off to a fearful start (one was facing the wrong way), the jockeys taking cuts at one another with their *nerbi*. As they turned the corner and went downhill towards the Via S. Martino, a roar went up as, sure enough, two horses crashed into the mattresses and their riders lay on the sand: but the other eight came on. Pandemonium broke loose. The favourite was in front. I looked anxiously for the Giraffe. He was lying well back on the rails, the little Sicilian inflicting *nerbate* on any jockey within range. One horse was galloping along riderless. Suddenly there was a stampede immediately below me. One of the horses had run into the crowd. knocking down several policemen and many spectators. The jockey was flung clear, while the crowd, storming over the barriers began to kick and hit him. The unfortunate man held his hands over his face to protect his head, while his assailants continued to rain blows upon him with sticks, fists, and feet.

'They say he did it on purpose!' shouted my neighbour. 'They want to kill him!'

I heard afterwards that a rival had cut his bridle. An old trick! The victorious contrada went mad. They kissed the jockey and the horse. They carried the jockey shoulder high and would have done the same with the horse had it been possible. All over the Campo quarrels and disputes were in progress which would last until the next Palio. Out of this chaos of ill-will and vituperation the victors – they were the Goose Contrada – marched in a sedate way towards the *carroccio*, where the magistrates bestowed the Palio upon them. To see the victors, with their fair hair ear-length or dropping to their shoulders, such innocent smiles upon their faces, one thought of many a saintly picture by Duccio or Lorenzetti.

When I could do so, I edged my way to the Palazzo Pubblico, where I found the Giraffes in heated argument. Giulio was white with fury. Those dirty Geese! Did I see what they did to the Giraffe horse on the second time round? I left him to his fury and looked round with curiosity. Among the armour, the swords, the helmets and banners lying about in the crypt of the town hall, I saw an ox ready to be roasted, its heart on a spit.

All night long the drums were beating through the streets and the flags were waving. I was told there was much less fighting than usual.

§ 8

I gave up my flat after the Palio and went to an hotel in the Goose Contrada, a short climb from the old fountain, Fonte Branda, and within a few yards of the church of S. Dominic and the house of S. Catherine. The hall porter was a triumphant Goose who radiated satisfaction, but the waiter confessed to me in a whisper that he himself was an Eagle and his wife a Caterpillar; and both were disconsolate.

The house in which S. Catherine was born was only a hundred

yards or so away, in a network of steep streets that rises in a series of red roofs towards a view of the distant cathedral, quite the best view of it, I thought, in Siena. The hilly streets were those which S. Catherine knew in the fourteenth century: the steps leading to her home might be those on every one of which, as a child of five, she used to kneel and salute the Blessed Virgin; indeed the exact spot is shown where she was standing in the valley of Fonte Branda when, at six years of age, she looked up and saw Christ enthroned above the church of S. Domenico, smiling at her from the sky.

Many of S. Catherine's visions and ecstasies took place in that tall, red-brick church on the slope of the hill near her home. I wandered about it one morning, putting off as long as possible the sight of the saint's head and finger which the church possesses, as it announces in three languages. I wonder what S. Catherine would have said of this, she who hated, despised, and eventually conquered her body and lived only in the spirit. Sometimes after receiving communion she would remain in a trance for hours, and she was able to live on the Sacrament until her stomach rebelled against anything else. Like many saints, she was ashamed of an appearance of eccentricity and sometimes, to avoid talk, would sip water in public and would chew a few mouthfuls of food, but always with great physical suffering. She told her confessor and biographer, Fra Raimondo, that she had found it more difficult to conquer sleep than hunger: but she did conquer it and was able to sleep for only half an hour in two days and nights, spending the rest of the time in prayer.

The full story of her austerities is amazing, and so, too, is the punishment she gave herself if she felt fear or disgust. She died worn out at the age of thirty-nine – 'that poor little body' as one of her followers commented – having corresponded with popes, emperors, and kings, and having been the moral force behind one of the great events of history, the return of the Papacy from Avignon to Rome.

I was shown her head behind a gilt grille. I believe it to be genuine since there is evidence that before her funeral in S. Maria Sopra Minerva in Rome, where her body, or what is left of it, lies under the high altar, Fra Raimondo sent this relic, and the finger, to Siena. The head has been built up with plaster over the skull, but it is not quite so macabre as the skeleton in the same church of Andrew Gallerani, who wears artificial flowers in his ears.

More appealing, indeed, I thought haunting, is the only contemporary portrait of S. Catherine, by her follower, the artist and politician, Andrea di Vanni. The ancient panel, painted six hundred years ago, shows a pale, wraith-like figure in a Dominican habit with a Madonna lily in the crook of her left arm and her right hand blessing a kneeling woman. The cracked paint has caught something of the saint's strange, withdrawn face, sad, unearthly, and deeply touching. I remembered how great scholars and theologians sometimes went to defame her, or find fault with her, but, having seen her and talked with her, went away convinced of her holiness.

The red-brick house in which S. Catherine was born is only a few steps away. It has now been transformed into a series of chapels, and when largely rebuilt during the Renaissance, it was given a charming little loggia on the first floor. Her father, a prosperous dyer, needed a house as large as this since Catherine was his twenty-fifth child. Piety has, of course, disguised the structure, though I was shown a convincing little cell where the saint had slept and prayed as a girl, once her doubting parents were convinced that she was following no earthly voices. I was shown the vinaigrette which she used when she went to nurse plague victims, the handle of her walking-stick, a portion of her hairshirt, and the cloth in which her head was wrapped when it came from Rome. As always with the earth-bound, I had a sense of standing before the incomprehensible, yet this brings with it, in the words of Evelyn Underhill, 'a strange exhilaration as if we were brought near to some mighty source of Being', and were at last 'on the verge of the secret which all seek'.

Some of the frescoes and pictures which cover the walls recall her political achievements for, like many of the saints, she was a mixture of spirit and common sense. More extraordinary, I think, than that a dyer's daughter brought up in one of the back streets of Siena should have advised cities and dictated a course of action to the Papacy, far more extraordinary is that one who had renounced the world, and had done her best to become purely spirit, should have had such a firm grasp of mundane affairs.

'I beseech your Holiness, in the name of Christ crucified, to make haste,' she wrote to Gregory XI when he was wavering between the French interest and removing from Avignon to Rome. 'Adopt a holy deception,' she continued, 'let it seem that you are going to delay for a time, and then do it swiftly and suddenly . . .' And this is S. Catherine speaking, not Machiavelli! In other moods she addressed the pontiff colloquially as 'daddy', calling him, 'Oh my sweet, most holy babbo', or even 'sweet babbo mine'.

S. Catherine knew no Latin and, like Dante, wrote her letters in the Tuscan of her day. About four hundred have survived. Sometimes she would write them herself, but as her correspondence grew she would dictate them to her followers. One of these has described how the saint sometimes dictated three letters simultaneously to three young men, one a letter to the Pope, another to Bernabò Visconti, and a third to an unnamed person. As she dictated, S. Catherine would often cover her face with her hands, sometimes she would look up as if for inspiration, and at others she would become rapt in ecstasy and the sentences would pour out. At such difficult moments the young men would cease writing and, looking at each other in bewilderment, would appeal to S. Catherine, asking for which of them a particular sentence was intended. 'Dearest sons,' she would say, 'do not trouble, for you have done this by the work of the Holy Spirit; when the letters are finished, we shall see how these words fit in with our intention, and then arrange what had best be done.' When the words had been sorted out, they were all found to belong to three separate letters. Another observer noted that S. Catherine dictated rapidly without a pause as though she were reading from a book. Nearly all her letters began *Al nome di Jesù Christo crucifixo et di Maria dolce,* and ended with the words, *Jesù dolce, Jesù amore.* 'Love carries the soul as the feet carry the body,' was one of her sayings.

I looked with awe round the building where so many great events began, if indeed they did begin there and not in 'some mighty source of Being'. I thought that the saints belong to a family of their own with marked characteristics, and remembered that Saint-Martin noted this and said that 'all mystics speak the same language, for they come from the same country'. I shall never forget the red-brick house in the hilly street where one of those unearthly travellers began her earthly pilgrimage.

§ 9

On my way to Arezzo I admired the Tuscan landscape which lay ahead, each hilltop holding a castle or a town. It was early in the morning, and as I went on I met country people on their way to market in Siena with eggs, vegetables, and crates of hens. I passed a young farmer standing upright in a cart, as poised as the charioteer of Delphi, while a lad walked at the head of two white oxen, whistling, singing, and from time to time speaking to them. With each step the great beasts swayed and nodded solemnly as if they understood the ox language he addressed to them, probably Etruscan, I thought.

The marriage of the Tuscan landscape to the New Testament has been the happiest of unions. The brown, silvery-grey countryside with its chestnut woods, its dark groves of cypress, its red-tiled farms, its outcrop of volcanic boulders, roofed by the blue Italian sky and palpitating to the sound of the cicada, is the most civilized rural scene on earth. It is embroidered everywhere by human living, and there is scarcely a hill, a stream, a grove of trees, without its story of God, of love or death.

I passed many a farm perched on the hillside. They were all the same: a Roman-like enclosure with an arched entrance, stalls for the oxen, pig-sties, stables for the mules, and above them, reached by an outside stair, the gaunt living-rooms of the family. Each farm had its own conical hay-rick built round a pole, always with a flower-pot on the top, and in each farmyard was a pile of rich manure ready to go back into the land. Though much has been written about the Tuscan landscape, I think few, perhaps, have placed among its beauties those black mounds which maintain the natural rhythm of agricultural life. No bags of chemicals have gone into the land, which is nourished, as Nature intended, by the sheep, pigs, mules, and those massive presiding deities of Tuscany, the white oxen, the Maremmana and the Chianina. In this mechanical age, a natural, hand-tended landscape, fertilized by its own livestock, is an unusual sight, and that Tuscany looks like a garden is due not entirely to conservatism, but to the steepness of the land, some of which cannot be broken with ploughs, but must be dug with a spade.

To the townsman almost any rural scene appears a happy one. He generally sees it in the summer, during a temporary lull in the farmer's constant conflict with the elements. In the summer in Tuscany you might think the countryside looked after itself, that the vines and the olives never needed pruning; that the steep fields were a joy to plough; that water never froze in winter and that the happy farmer had nothing to do but wait in glorious sunlight for the harvest, undeterred in his cheerful musings by thoughts of the *fattore*, or of the middleman who adulterates olive oil and wine almost before it has travelled a mile from the farm.

On the hilly road near Grillo I saw a farmer standing on the roadside in his best suit, and thinking perhaps that he wanted a lift to Arezzo, I stopped. No, he said, he did not want a lift: he was waiting for his daughter, who was coming in the autobus from Monte S. Savino. He told me an old story: young people were leaving the land for the cities, and the cost of everything was so high that it was impossible to make both ends meet. One of his sons was in Rhodesia, another was studying to be a television engineer in Milan, and his daughter was a nurse in Arezzo. He didn't blame them. He smiled and I went on, carrying with me the memory of a lean, brown face with a long intelligent nose.

I continued over a steep mountain road with hills on either side, planted with vines and olives, and at the top, where scrub oaks grew among rocks and boulders, I entered the Province of Arezzo. Away to the left I saw, far off in the haze, a glimpse of the Arno Valley, then the road looped down into gentle country where the oxen wore red tassels on their flat foreheads and before me stood Arezzo, the birthplace of many famous men.

§ 10

Wherever the Romans went, they took with them plates, dishes, and bowls of red pottery which had a brilliant hard gloss like that of sealing-wax. It is dug up on Roman sites everywhere. It is brittle stuff, and careless Roman servant girls must always have been breaking it. It is to be found in every museum in Europe. Fragments, and even complete vessels, have been found all over London, even under S. Paul's Cathedral in the nineteen-twenties, when the dome was strengthened; and there are rooms full of it in the Guildhall and London Museums. Old-fashioned archaeologists called it 'Samian ware', though a better name is 'Aretine ware', since its manufacture began at Arezzo and then spread all over Gaul.

Some of the bowls are exquisitely encircled with raised decorations which show hunting or mythological scenes, and the best pieces were signed by the potters in a small cartouche in the base of the bowl or dish. Hundreds, perhaps thousands, of potters' names are known, and also the dates when their workshops were producing, so that this pottery is almost as good as coinage in dating a find.

I first became interested in it towards the end of the First World War, when I was convalescent in the military hospital at Colchester. Reading that one of the main Roman roads lay under the grounds, I received permission to do some digging, and, much to my astonishment, I soon struck a Roman cemetery and unearthed a glass urn full of bones which, upon examination by the local museum, proved to be those of a sporting Roman lady and a gamecock. This triumph led me to further efforts, in the course of which I found many fragments of Aretine ware, and among them the stamp of a potter called Flavius Germanus, whose work had never before been noted in England. I have always intended to go back to Colchester and look for these objects in the museum there. I built up a fine collection of potters' stamps during the nineteen-twenties, when the odds and ends of the great nineteenth century collections were to be found in the junk shops of London, or were auctioned for a few shillings at Sotheby's, though I am sure you could tramp London today without finding a single example.

Having been interested in Aı tine ware, and having spent so many Saturday afternoons in my youth searching for it, I was delighted to be in Arezzo, where this beautiful pottery originated, but astonishment was added to delight when, opening a parcel that was waiting for me in the hotel, I found three of the most splendid Aretine bowls I have ever seen, each one signed by the best Augustan potter, M. Perennius. I could hardly believe my eyes. All three pots were decorated with friezes in high relief: a bear hunt; a bear attacking a hunter; and goddesses, each figure separated from the next by those classical decorations which, when discovered centuries later in ruins and grottoes by Raphael and his contemporaries, were called 'grotesques'. The pots were, of course, modern reproductions made from actual moulds in the Arezzo museum, and were the gift of a distinguished citizen whom I had not yet met. It seemed to me so strange that Arezzo should welcome me in a way that revived a hundred youthful enthusiasms, almost as though the ancient spirit of the place wished to reward me for the affection I had once shown for the work of its artists.

I placed the pots on a table where they would be the first things I should see when I awakened in the morning, and I smiled to think that this was what I used to do with a new book or a toy when I was a child.

§ 11

Signor Alberto, who had given the Roman pots to me, turned out to be a more authentic Etruscan than the marble merchant whom I had met at Parma. He had the full dark eyes, the pointed beard, the long, inquisitive nose, and the Mona Lisa smile of a terracotta tomb figure. He was the only Italian I have known who, after two or three meetings, invited me to his home and introduced me to his wife and his two children. He had been a regular officer in the Italian army, but during the final stages of the war had joined the Partisans and had raided the retreating Germans from the fastnesses of his own mountains. It was an odd experience, he said, to come down into Arezzo in disguise to meet his friends and relatives. When I told him what pleasure the Aretine pots had given me, and of my interest in Aretine ware, he laughed delightedly and, hitting himself on the chest, cried, 'We Etruscans have the second-sight – *prescienza!*'

We visited the museum together and, thanks to his influence, cases were unlocked and we were able to handle some of the finest Aretine pottery to be seen anywhere, complete bowls and plates of a quality rarely exported to such barbaric provinces as Britain. Signor Alberto was surprised to hear how much Gaul-made Aretine pottery has been found in England, particularly beneath the City of London, though now, with the erection of tall buildings whose foundations penetrate below the Roman level, no more can remain to be discovered.

Arezzo is a small city and a charming one, simple, uncongested, comparatively quiet, and friendly, an enchanting backwater in the mainstream of tourism. My friend was proud of his famous fellow Aretines : Maecenas, the rich friend of Horace and Virgil, Petrarch, whose birthplace, now an Academy, was bombed during the last war, Guido of Arezzo, who devised musical notation, Leonardo Bruni, the historian of Florence, Pietro Aretino, the notorious journalist, feared and hated by so many, yet the bosom friend of Titian, and the artist-biographer, to whom all writers on art owe so much, Vasari, the author of *Lives of the Painters*. None of these, however, seems to have remained in his native town : Maecenas went to Rome, Petrarch to Avignon and Padua, Guido to Ferrara, Aretino to Venice ; and the only one who established a home in Arezzo was Vasari, though it cannot have seen much of him.

His house exists much as it was in his time, and we walked up to the Via Venti Settembre to look at it. It is a fair-sized stone building of two storeys, and one enters it straight from the street to find oneself in the surroundings of a prosperous artist of the sixteenth century. How interesting it was, after having seen in Florence numbers of ducal walls decorated by Vasari and the suites of rooms designed by him in the Palazzo Vecchio, to stand in the simple surroundings which he designed for his own retirement. I was reminded of Giulio Romano's house in Mantua. It must have been pleasant for these artists and architects, after labouring for years on enormous rooms and lying on their backs painting ceilings, to come down to normal proportions and to rooms designed not to impress the beholder, but for ordinary living.

The chief room in Vasari's house has recessed windows and window-seats; there is a huge fireplace, and the walls and ceiling are richly decorated with the maze of classical allegory from which Vasari could apparently not extricate himself even in private life. However, even with a life-sized Venus over the mantelpiece, matched at the opposite side of the room by a many-breasted Diana of Ephesus, the room is a comfortable one in which a man could read and write and look out of the window to watch his friends passing in the street.

Unlike many artists, Vasari seems never to have been seriously short of money. He was a likeable, talented man with a tremendous capacity for work, and he must have been easier to get on with than geniuses who were temperamental and dilatory. Aged popes and cardinals, for whom time was a matter of some urgency, could feel confident, if they employed him, that the work would be done on time, and that was probably the foundation of his success. He was the son of a potter (which may explain the name Vasari), and he did not marry until he was well established and forty years of age. Having acquired his house when he was twenty-nine, the girls of Arezzo must long since have given him up as a confirmed bachelor. His eventual marriage, however, seems to have been a happy one, though childless.

How surprised he would have been could he have known that future ages would value his writings more than his painting. His great classic was born one night at dinner when Cardinal Farnese suggested it would be a good idea to write the lives of Italian painters, sculptors, and architects. The year was 1544, when Vasari was thirty-three, and seven years later the first edition of his book was in print. All through his forties and fifties, while he was painting and building in Florence and Rome, he was gathering material for a second edition. This insatiable worker died in Florence at the age of sixty-three and was buried in Arezzo. We stood in his house and thought of Monna Vasari's years of solitude there while her husband was busy with the affairs of pope and duke, both of them perhaps dreaming of the time, which never came, when he would be able to retire to his comfortable stone house in Arezzo.

'It is a great mistake,' said Signor Alberto, 'to let ambition lead a man away from his own town . . . I would rather be a little fish in Arezzo than a whale in Milan or Rome!'

Alberto was not really interested in Roman pottery: his passion was Piero della Francesca. We stood in the dark choir of the church of S. Francesco, half-way up the hill in the centre of the town, while he called for electric lights, and the sexton floodlit the frescoes for us. On each side and above us there opened out in scene after scene, like windows on a brilliant, dignified world, the extraordinary mediaeval legend of the True Cross.

It is puzzling to see a work of genius which former generations failed to recognize, for Piero della Francesca was not placed among the immortals until about forty years ago. Now critics speak of this choir in Arezzo in the same breath with the Raphael Stanze and the Sistine Chapel. I like to think that, had I never read a word about him and had come across the frescoes by chance, I should have recognized their greatness.

Born in a little town called Sansepolcro, just too far off for him to have been annexed as one of Arezzo's famous sons, Piero seems to have been a deliberate mathematician who took his time in creating upon the walls of sacred buildings a world brilliant and beautiful to look at, but as dispassionate as Euclid. I asked Alberto if any stories or legends about him remained in the province, but he said no, Piero's personal life was a mystery. It is not even known why he was called *della* Francesca instead of *dei* Franceschi, because he was not illegitimate; his father was Piero de Franceschi and his mother was Romanà di Perino da Monterchi.

Alberto admired him for resisting the lure of Florence and for returning to his native town in middle age, where he became a town councillor. Blindness afflicted him in old age, but little else is known of him. Even Vasari, who wrote of him about fifty years after his death, was unable to discover any biographical details, and only one anecdote: that having painted frescoes of grooms and horses in some stables, a horse took a dislike to one of Piero's horses and, believing it to be alive, repeatedly kicked it.

'Nowadays,' said Alberto, with one of his faun-like smiles, 'one would not be surprised to be told that Piero's horse kicked back!'

The records say that he died in Sansepolcro on October 12, 1492. That was the day when, far away on the other side of the world, Christopher Columbus landed in America.

Some critics discover a heavenly beauty in Piero's women, but I can only see a haughty disdain. I asked Roberto if in his opinion these aloof females were models or imaginary women.

'I will show you,' he replied. 'They are purely Aretine. Like myself, they are Etruscan, and you will see the same type in Sansepolcro today, indeed right through the Tiber Valley.'

We motored a mile or so out of Arezzo to a jewellery factory. After an introduction to the owner, I was taken to a large workshop where about a hundred and fifty girls were busy.

'There,' whispered Alberto, indicating a girl, 'pure Piero della Francesca! And look at that one with the brown hair . . . the Queen of Sheba!'

When I was prowling about Arezzo one afternoon, I came upon an interesting scene. Six small boys in jerseys and shorts were playing a noisy game on the long, balustraded terrace in front of the Law Courts. The Piazza Grande, in which this building stands, is a steeply canted open space surrounded by ancient buildings, archways, and the entrances to alleys. One of the boys held at arm's length a square of cardboard while the others took it in turn to run towards it, holding a broomstick pressed beneath an arm. From the curvetting and prancing before the boy with the broomstick set off on his run, I understood that he was a mounted lancer, then it dawned upon me that they were playing at Arezzo's great annual event, the *Giostra del Saracino*, or the Joust of the Saracen. This is a tournament which goes back in origin to the thirteenth century, in which mounted competitors in armour ride at a quintain in the form of a wooden figure. The 'Saracen', unless hit squarely, swivels round and delivers a powerful blow on the back of the horseman.

I thought that this was a game which small boys must have played in every town during the Middle Ages before a tournament was held.

§ 12

The Tiber and the Arno rise in the mountains north of Arezzo and flow south on parallel courses for some way, then the Arno, instead of flowing through Arezzo, turns a 'scornful snout', as Dante put it, and, swinging west in a great loop, makes for Florence, Pisa, and the Tyrrhenian Sea. The Tiber flows on steadfastly southwards to Rome.

The valleys through which these rivers flow are among the greatest beauties of Italy, indeed it is almost impossible to decide which of the two is the more attractive. I suppose many people would prefer the wilder upper reaches of the Arno, known as the Casentino, where among the mountains and the falling streams are towns and villages whose history goes back to Rome. Their modern names all carry an echo in Latin: Subbiano – *Sub Janum*; Campogialli – *Campus Gallorum*; Pieve al Bagnoro – *Plebs Balnei Aurei*; Cincelli – *Centum Cellae*; Traiana – *Trajanus*; Campoluci – *Campus Lucii*; Capolona – *Caput Leonis*; and so on. Upon the highest points of the Central Apennines in the Casentino are two monasteries, Camaldoli, and La Verna, where S. Francis received the Stigmata.

To me the Tiber Valley appealed quite as much as the Casentino. It delighted me to see the youthful Tiber babbling over its stones on its long journey to Rome. I thought the peasants in these two rich valleys different from those round Florence and Siena, and wondered whether the old way of life was stronger here. In the Valley of the Tiber I really did see the haughty type of young woman painted by Piero della Francesca.

In a maze of side-roads that twist in all directions three or four miles west of the young Tiber, a hill covered with the white, red roofed buildings of a small town rises from the plain. Its name is Monterchi, which is the modern corruption of *Mons Herculis*; and it was the birthplace of Piero's mother. The view from its ramparts is magnificent. I looked north across the Tiber Valley to the Alpe della Luna and south into Umbria. It was wonderful to stand there on a summer's morning and to follow the white threads of the lanes between the vineyards and the orchards, and to hear, borne up upon the hot and lazy air, such country sounds as the barking of farm dogs, the song of some invisible worker in the fields, and the creak of an ox-wagon as it wound its way round the hill up to the quiet, pretty little town.

On the flat land at the foot of Monterchi a double line of cypress trees leads up to the cemetery on the hillside opposite the town, and in its tiny mortuary chapel Piero della Francesca painted one of his most famous frescoes – *Madonna del Parto* – the Pregnant Madonna. The chapel contains only an altar below the fresco. When I entered there was no one there but a peasant girl who had just lit a lamp on the altar and, turning, revealed herself to be in the same condition as the Madonna. Above the altar Piero has painted a dome-shaped pavilion, much the same kind of circular tent in which Constantine is sleeping in the Arezzo frescoes, but richer and more ornate. Two winged angels gracefully lift the entrance to this tent to reveal inside a young woman in a light blue gown of fifteenth-century cut, evidently a maternity gown of the period, unbuttoned down the front, accentuating her condition.

She is one of the most beautiful of Piero della Francesca's women. Like all of this artist's pictures, this lingers in the memory, and afterwards I was haunted by it and wanted to see it again, as I was to do on three occasions. Every time I returned to see the fresco, it refreshed my mind like a great poem one has committed to memory.

The second time I was there two pregnant women came up the cypress avenue and placed on the altar two little tins which they filled with olive oil, then, having placed a wick in the oil and set it alight, they prayed and went out. The village girls for miles around make this offering to the *Madonna del Parto*, asking her for an easy delivery.

How strange to see this procession of life to a cemetery. Quite often birth and death must meet at the door of this chapel; and that is probably what Piero della Francesca intended.

A few miles from Monterchi I crossed the infant Tiber and, travelling through a rich land of vines, olives, and fat, white cattle, came to Sansepolcro, the artist's birthplace. I found a small town gathered, with its ridged red roofs, within crumbling ramparts. It was market day and a number of booths had been set up where vegetables, secondhand clothes, and agricultural tools were being sold. When I asked a passer-by to direct me to the *Resurrezione*, he pointed to an old building approached by a double flight of steps, which turned out to be the Law Court. Through an open door I saw a lawsuit in progress: a policeman was standing by, an advocate was arguing a case, while the magistrate was solemnly writing notes, wearing what looked like an undergraduate's gown. I thought I had come to the wrong building until the caretaker, uttering that hissing sound made by Italians on such occasions and scratching the air with the fingers of one hand, signed for me to follow him. In the next room, a large gaunt hall, I saw, facing me upon the end wall, the *Resurrection* by Piero della Francesca.

It is early morning. The rising sun has touched with pink a few thin clouds that lie in a blue sky. Four Roman soldiers have fallen asleep beside a marble sarcophagus. They have watched all night, but now, with the dawn, have dozed off in awkward attitudes: three of them have not even removed their helmets. Above them rises a tremendous revelation of strength. Christ has emerged from the grave and stands above the four figures, gazing straight ahead, with his bare left foot upon the marble. A pink cloak, touched with the morning light, falls in thick folds over His left shoulder, leaving His right arm and the right side of His body bare. He holds a banner bearing a red cross and on His body, below the breast, is a red lance wound. His figure appears real, yet it belongs to the other world: if one were ever to have a vision, I thought, it would have this startling impact upon one.

The expression of suppressed strength in the Saviour's attitude and face is like no other painting of Christ I have ever seen. He is nearer in appearance to the Pantokrator with wide searching eyes who gazes straight at you from the semi-dome of Byzantine churches, than to the gentle, compassionate Christ of Christian Art. The contrast between the relaxed figures of the sleeping men and the taut, upright figure, so wide-awake, is like the culminating moment in a drama. How can those men continue to sleep with that stupendous apparition above them? And as I looked at the bearded face of this powerful, unsentimental Christ, the words ran through my mind: 'He descended into hell; The third day he rose again from the dead.'

§ 13

Two or three years ago I happened to go into a secondhand bookshop in Cape Town to buy a fairly scarce book on Florence. The bookseller, whose name is Anthony Clarke, spoke of Italy as he had seen it as a gunner officer in the last war.

'I always like to think,' he said, surprisingly, 'that I am responsible for the safety of Piero della Francesca's *Resurrection* in Sansepolcro.' I asked him to tell me the story, which he later put into writing. 'It was sometime in 1944,' wrote Mr Clarke. 'I was then a troop commander in the Chestnut Troop "A" Battery, 1st Regiment, R.H.A. Our regiment was the artillery support for the independent 9th Armoured Brigade, and "Chestnuts" were supporting the 3rd Hussars. For a while, I recall, we were based around Città di Castello and then moved north. It was during this move that I was ordered to establish an observation post overlooking Sansepolcro.

'At first light I moved forward in my tank on the eastward slopes of the hills on the east, and then, with a signaller and a portable wireless, walked over the crest onto the forward slopes. We cleared out the inside of a large bush, made ourselves as comfortable as possible – for we were going to be there all day – and settled down to watch and wait. We were not in direct communication with our guns (this might have some bearing on what took place later) as our wireless had not the range. We were in communication with our tank, and the tank's wireless was in touch with the Battery.

'I ordered one round of fire from one gun on a particular range and bearing somewhere in the middle of the valley, so should I need gunfire in a hurry I would have a fair idea what order to give without having to fuss around with a map and protractor. Our guns were about two to three miles south.

'Then we waited. The sun came up in a cloudless sky and Sansepolcro lay clearly before us. I was told over the wireless that the enemy were suspected of being in the town and that I was to shell it prior to our troops moving in. So I ranged on the town and put down two or three rounds of troop fire (4 guns). My battery commander, Marcus Linton, M.C., R.H.A., informed me over the wireless that ammunition was plentiful and that I could go ahead and use as much as I liked. An attack was going to be launched the next morning and it was up to us to clear the town first. So I shelled Sansepolcro. In the meantime I was scanning the town almost yard by yard and was unable to see any sign of the enemy anywhere, though, of course, that did not mean they were not there! At the back of my mind a small question kept nagging. Why did I know the name of Sansepolcro? Somewhere I had heard the name and it must have been in connection with something important for me to remember it. But when or where I could not remember.

'Then my signaller and I had a visitor. He was a ragged youngster with a dog. We said, "*Tedeschi* – Sansepolcro?" and pointed to the town. He shook his head and grinned and pointed to the hills. The Germans had vacated the town, a further support of my own opinion. Then I remembered why I knew the name of Sansepolcro – ("the Greatest Painting in the World!"). I must have been about eighteen when I read that essay of Aldous Huxley's. I recalled clearly his description of the tiring journey from Arezzo and how it was worth it for at the end of it lay Francesca's *Resurrection*, "the greatest painting in the world!"

'I estimated the number of shells I had fired and was sure that if I had not destroyed the greatest painting I had done considerable damage. So I fired no more . . . We sat, the signaller and I, under our covering bush watching for, but never seeing, any enemy. When it was dark we withdrew and returned to the gun position.

'The next day we entered Sansepolcro unmolested. I asked immedately for the picture. The building was untouched. I hurried inside and there it was, secure and magnificent. The townsfolk had started to sandbag it, but the sandbags were only about waist-high. I looked up at the roof: one shell, I knew, would have been sufficient to undo the admiration of centuries. And that is that. Sometimes I wonder how I would be feeling now if I had happened to destroy the *Resurrection*. At one time I thought of writing to Aldous Huxley. The incident might, I suppose, be a fine illustration of the power of literature, and that the pen is mightier than the sword!'

I went to see the picture again with Alberto, who took a camera and a flash-gun with him. It was an unusual experience, remembering the reverent atmosphere of the Uffizi, to observe the homely casualness with which the masterpiece is treated in its native town. When Alberto said he wished to take a photograph, a stout table was immediately produced for him to stand on, and helpers emerged on every hand; I think I recognized even the magistrate.

In the afternoon we went to visit one of Alberto's many friends, who has a house on the ramparts of Sansepolcro. He happened to be out, but his wife insisted that we should drink a glass of vermouth as we walked about the garden, gazing on one side over the ridged roofs and chimney-pots of Sansepolcro to the silver thread of the Tiber in the valley beyond, and, on the other, into the Buitoni factory. Miles of macaroni and spaghetti now carry the name of Sansepolcro to all parts of the world. We were shown over the model factory and admired shining machines which pressed out the pasta and passed it on to others, which packed it. All this began in the last century with Grandmother Buitoni, whose primitive, cast-iron spaghetti machines are to be admired in the factory's museum.

§ 14

Some of the small towns in the Casentino and the Tiber Valleys are visible from miles away, seated proudly upon their hills; others, like Anghiari, you see when high above them on a winding road which gives an eagle's view into their streets – you can even see if it is market day – then, as you wind your way down, the view changes and you can no longer see within the walls but, with every bend of the road and each new vista, the walls grow higher until, as you descend into the valley, you look up and see the town high above you on its rock.

The smallest of these places would not be embarrassed to entertain pope or king. Though the inhabitants may be small farmers, and the most important people are the priest, the chemist, and the *Maresciallo dei Carabinieri*, they know how affairs are conducted in the great world. It is surprising what splendour can be unearthed for a special occasion, maybe even a theatre, as in Anghiari. This is an unexpected little Scala to find in a small mountain fastness, and the inscription *Teatro di Anghiari del l'Accademia de' Ricomposti* links the little place, if not perhaps with Plato, at least with the age of academies. Now, of course, times have changed. I noticed a florid poster showing a woman cowering before a revolver, an advertisement for a film called *La morsa si chiude*.

I remember Anghiari for having sheltered me during a heavy downpour when the piazza became a lake into which every hilly street poured its torrent. Water shot in the most graceful curves from every roof and blocked-up gutter. I took refuge in an antique shop into which I had to creep sideways, so full was it of old chestnut and mahogany chests-of-drawers, washstands, copper pans, basins and jugs, old pictures in battered frames, chairs, tables, and the rest. I discovered the owner seated with a couple of friends among piles of chairs and tables, eating a water melon. Moving aside a few armchairs and a card-table or two, they smiled pleasantly and welcomed me with a scarlet segment. There was an old inlaid chestnut writing-table that I could have had for almost nothing, but it was heavy and in these days there are no warships waiting to take a traveller's purchases to his native land.

My favourite town is Poppi, which I think of as the capital of the Casentino. One meets mediaevalism all over the north of Italy, but this town seemed to me to be a living fragment of a remote past. It is a town of enchanters, knights, and maidens with long hair at castle windows. Even the small bus that links Poppi with Arezzo might, by a small stretch of the imagination, be an enchanted dragon, or a dragon condemned by a sorcerer to imitate a diesel engine with its groans and its shrieks and its sudden jets of smoke. It is a town of stone arcades which lead up to a castle, clearly a relative of the Palazzo Vecchio in Florence. After dark, when the lamps are lit, Poppi becomes quite sinister, and a couple of amiable citizens, as they play a game of dominoes in a wine shop, might be the first and second murderers. The centre of the town is not large enough to be called a piazza, but is at the top of a hilly street where several roads meet. In the centre an octagonal baroque oratory is dedicated to Our Lady of the Plague, and the story is that during a visitation of the plague centuries ago, the priest walked round the town with the image of the Virgin, whereupon the plague instantly ceased. The words *Ave Maria* are written over the altar. Ten o'clock is past bedtime in Poppi, and at that late hour a little group of people sometimes waits in the darkness for the last bus to arrive from Arezzo. It can be heard some way off in the valley, as it gnashes its teeth and snorts along from Bibbiena, then it growls menacingly and seems to pause and gather strength for its uphill pull to the town, where it arrives fuming. It almost exactly fits some of the narrow streets, and as it comes to a stop with a belch of rage and draconian puffs of diesel oil, those inside, led by the village priest, stand up and, as if performing the same physical exercise, or some religious act, stretch their arms in unison and lift down suitcases, wicker-baskets, and brown paper parcels. The priest is the first to descend, his steel spectacles gleaming, his shovel hat like a ruffled cat, a large parcel beneath his arm. There is much kissing of children and cries of welcome; relatives and friends, thank God, are safe within the walls of Poppi again!

The caretaker of the castle of Poppi is Leonido Gatteschi, who is eighty years old. He wears a black beret and carries a cane with a gold knob. He will tell you, as he stands on the ramparts above the plain, looking out to the mountains where you can see La Verna and Camaldoli, that he has looked after the castle for sixty-five years and his chief worry is that no one will take over from him. He is inclined to blame the younger generation – striplings of forty and fifty – for having no sense of responsibility. If the Counts of Guidi ever had a devoted seneschal, his spirit must have been reborn in Leonido Gatteschi.

It is an impressive castle and in such good condition that you could move in tomorrow with your men-at-arms and serving wenches, and make it quite comfortable with a few tapestries. I don't think I have ever seen a more decorative and dramatic courtyard, with its picturesque staircase emblazoned with coats-of-arms and a balustrade of nearly a hundred miniature stone columns. Signor Gatteschi led me over the castle, talking all the time and waving the gold-topped cane, which in his hands became a wand of office. I saw a chapel where ghostly frescoes of the Giotto School were struggling through the whitewash; I saw gaunt halls in which the knights of the Middle Ages managed to make themselves massively comfortable; and, most interesting of all, I saw the bedroom of the Guidi Counts, a large room notable for some excellent mediaeval plumbing. The water, which was laid on, was filtered through charcoal, and I noticed above a stone wash-basin the name Panosco Ridolfi and the date was 1469. The town library is kept in this room. How incredible it is, and how typical of Italy, that a library of twenty thousand volumes, including nearly eight hundred incunabula and six hundred illuminated manuscripts, also town records that go back to 1330, should be seen incidentally as one rambles over a mediaeval castle.

When we were on the ramparts, we looked to the north and saw in the valley beneath us the site of the battle of Campaldino, in which Dante fought, when the Ghibbelines of Arezzo were beaten by the Florentine Guelphs on a summer's day in 1289. So began Arezzo's long history as a colony or subject city of Florence.

We turned away from that depressing sight and looked to the south. Seeing the old man on the ramparts waving his gold-topped cane above the distant valleys, one might have imagined that he was seeking some flash of the sun on helmet or lance-point, a sign that his lord would not be late for dinner.

§ 15

'I wish to introduce you to a beautiful lady,' said Alberto one morning. 'Please don't ask me any questions, but just come with me.' We motored north from Arezzo into the Casentino, where the Arno advances and retreats from the road, sometimes, as at Subbiano, flowing beside it for miles, dark and reed-fringed. At a little place called Rassina, we turned into a side road and were soon approaching a mountain called the Pratomagno. Such roads are one of the surprises of the Casentino. They often expire, as if from sheer fatigue, upon the flanks of the mountains, where mule-tracks continue up to hill villages which appear to be as remote, though only a few miles from Florence or Arezzo, as if they were still in the Middle Ages.

We met nothing on our road but mules loaded with wood, moving in single file. Suddenly, rounding a bend, we saw that the road went no farther. When Alberto cut off the engine, we heard the rush of water tumbling from a wooded ravine and, looking up, we saw a white village high above us.

'That is Carda,' said Alberto. 'We shall have to leave the car and climb up by the path.' We could see this track winding round between immense boulders. 'But first let us see whether my friend is about.'

There were some brick buildings surrounded by a high fence at the foot of the mountain. We entered the enclosure and saw a man in waders feeding ravenous trout. The long, concrete channels of a trout hatchery boiled with fish as the man cast chopped liver into the water. In some channels the fish were little fingerlings which looked, as they fought for their food, as if someone had thrown a bowl of silver into the water; others were about a pound in weight, while some were enormous.

'Those are the ones the trout fishermen buy if they cannot catch anything in the mountains!' remarked Alberto. 'Oh yes, of course,' he added, noting my look of surprise, 'no fisherman would face his wife with an empty basket!'

The man locked up the trout hatchery, and together we climbed up the mule track to Carda. We arrived at a picturesque group of stone houses built on various levels, with a tiny church and its bell-tower on the highest point, facing a small, open space, the so-called piazza, from whose boundary wall I looked into a valley far below. Everything was granite-grey, and there was not a tree or shrub in sight. Hens and geese ran in and out of the houses, and on every side were ravines and precipices and a view of the Pratomagno rolling away into the distance. It was astonishing to think that Florence was less than thirty miles to the north-west as the crow flies, and Arezzo about twenty miles to the south, yet we might have been in Tibet.

The inhabitants gathered round, the men talkative and interested, the women standing inquisitively in the doorways, the hostile geese lengthening their necks at us and hissing.

'You are now going to see the beautiful lady,' whispered Alberto.

We entered the little church where, above the altar, I was shown the Madonna of Carda.

'She is said to be the work of Andrea della Robbia,' said Alberto, 'but you will find no picture of her in any book on art or on the della Robbias, and she is one of the most beautiful Madonnas ever made by Andrea. The people of Carda believe that the lost secret of the della Robbia glaze is concealed in her head, but, of course, that is a story you hear of other della Robbia master-pieces.'

The villagers glanced at us, delighted with our interest in their treasure. They all talked at once, anxious to tell us the epic of Carda: how the Madonna came to the mountain village. The story is that in 1554, when Florence was at war with Siena, two men of Carda were fighting with the Florentine army. One day they came to a ruined church in that part of the Chiana Valley which then belonged to Siena, and, entering this church, they saw the Madonna above the ruined altar and fell on their knees. They promised that should she bring them safely through the war, they would carry her away from her ruined church and instal her in their own church in Carda. First carefully hiding the statue where they could find it again, they rejoined their troop; and when the war was over, they recovered the Madonna and, in spite of its weight, took it in turns to carry it on their backs to Carda. It is life-size and of white glaze, and one of the most beautiful works of this master that I have seen. She has been attractively mounted in a niche against a blue background.

The manager of the trout farm invited us to his house, which was built on the hillside in such a way that the door was at roof level and we went downstairs to the kitchen. Here his wife brewed coffee while he produced a bottle of vermouth and some local cheese, which was the best I have ever tasted. This sheep's milk cheese varies from town to town throughout Italy; in some towns it is as hard as parmesan, in others it has the texture of gruyère, and it can also be soft, though I think perhaps the right name for this kind of cheese is *cacio pecorino*. When I said that I had seen no sheep on the mountain, our host told me that the village owned a large communal flock which was pastured on the other side of the hill. There was a shepherds' rota in the village so that everyone took his turn in looking after the flock. 'It is worth while to come back to Carda in the evening,' he said, 'to see the sheep flowing like a river in the lanes and each one finding its own way home.'

Alberto chaffed him about Carda's annual carnival, which must also be a sight worth witnessing. A competition is held for original ways to eat spaghetti; the winner last year had eaten it out of a shoe! Anyone found at work on carnival morning is tied up and carried to the space in front of the church, where he is obliged to empty glass after glass of wine until he can hardly stand, and at that moment is elected King of the Carnival.

'Did I keep my promise?' asked Alberto on the way back.

'You did,' I replied. 'She is one of the beauties of Tuscany.'

§ 16

A few miles to the north-west of Sansepolcro, upon the mountains that slope down to the valley of the Tiber, a narrow winding road of the kind described as *non carrozzabile* leads to the hamlet of Caprese. Later ages have added to Caprese the name of Michelangelo. It was here, upon the sixth of March in the year 1475, that an unexplainable miracle occurred when a nice, commonplace couple brought a genius down to earth. And the little heart that began to beat that day on the hilltop at Caprese was to go on beating for eighty-nine years, at the end of which time a sad, tired, disillusioned old man with burning eyes, a broken nose, and a long white beard, one who felt that he had failed and had been frustrated by the vanity of popes, caught a cold and died in Rome.

On the way up to the village I saw nobody except a gang of road workers who were removing a rock fall, then I came to a few houses and, after several more hairpin bends, arrived at the top of the hill and to a group of old stone buildings which stood deserted, with a locked-up air about them. It was a strange place in which to find a monument. I walked to it and saw in bronze relief the infant Michelangelo starting up from his cradle in surprise at the sight of a vision of his *Night* from the Medici Tombs and, in the background, the *Moses*. This extraordinary conception is perhaps a little too dramatic. What is so appealing about the infancy of genius is that there is nothing to distinguish it from ordinary infancy. It is only in later childhood that the first of those signs appear which indicates that a human being may have been set apart to achieve more, and to sorrow more, than ordinary men. Remembering Michelangelo's troubles with Julius II, I thought it a little unfair to give him such an early vision of the *Moses*!

Upon the side of a double-storey building erected on the edge of the mountain, and approached by way of an outside stair, I read an inscription which said that Michelangelo had been born there. The building was locked and the houses opposite appeared to be empty. I was about to leave when a small car arrived containing a young man and an old one whose face might have been carved out of walnut shell. The young man was the village schoolmaster, with a roll call of sixteen, he told me; the old man produced some keys and we unlocked the birthplace and opened the windows.

The house has been transformed since Ludovico Buonarroti and his wife Francesca dei Neri went to live there. It is now a gaunt hall with some photographs of Michelangelo's work on the walls and a few books and magazines in an adjoining room called the library. Next to the birthplace is a chapel in which Michelangelo was christened, a humble, barnlike place which has recently been restored. These two buildings, and the foundations of an ancient castle which had just been discovered a few paces away, were all there was to be seen.

It is not possible to imagine the young Michelangelo crawling about this hilltop, or learning to walk there, since, while still an infant in arms, he was taken to the family property at Settignano, a few miles from Florence, and put out to nurse with a stone-cutter's wife. 'If there is anything good in me,' he once said to Vasari, 'it comes from the pure air of your Arezzo hills where I was born, and perhaps also from the milk of my nurse with which I sucked in the chisels and hammers with which I used to carve my figures.' Certainly there was nothing in his family history to explain his genius. His father was an impoverished man of good family who thought it beneath his dignity to be a merchant or a mechanic and preferred to haunt the Medici and beg for odd jobs. That the temporary post of magistrate at Chiusi and Caprese had fallen vacant for six months, and had been accepted by Ludovico Buonarroti, is the reason why Michelangelo happened to be born there. Though the elder Buonarroti declined to soil his own hands, he had no compunction at all in receiving the proceeds of Michelangelo's handiwork when his son became famous; indeed as long as his father and brothers lived, Michelangelo sent them money to maintain their farm, but was never able to satisfy their needs.

We closed the windows and locked up the house, and as I went off down the hill, the idea that appealed to me was not that of an infant haunted by future greatness, but of two infants: Michelangelo on the hill, and the Tiber in the valley below, both at the beginning of their journey to Rome.

I had arranged to meet Alberto on another hilltop, at Sigliano, for a picnic with the *Associazione Amici della Musica di Arezzo*. There was a scene of bustle and excitement on this hilltop. Motor coaches had arrived with the musicians and their friends, and they were now strolling about admiring the view of the vineyards as they sloped down to the infant Tiber and inspecting the only building on the hill, a venerable little church which contained an early fresco of S. Christopher and the Infant Jesus.

Most of the excitement was caused by about thirty young women, all of them, I was told, aspiring professional pianists, who had come from various countries to a musical finishing-school, and as they tripped over the hilltop in their high heels, they vied with each other in winning a smile from their host, a celebrated musician. It was delightful to watch so much international charm in action, but, alas, the maestro, who was accustomed to it, wore the air of a languid god.

The old priest stood beaming in his worn cassock, delighted by the invasion and by the smell of grilled steak which rose from a corner of the west wall of his church, where waiters in dinner-jackets – incredible touch! – were busy with a charcoal grill. The old man took me into his house to wash in a tin basin. The building was as bleak and lonely as a hermit's cell. I could see few books, but the vegetable garden was admirable. We stood above the sun-drenched world, looking down the hillside where the olive trees stood, each with its little circle of shade, towards the valley where the Tiber was sliding over its pebbles.

Tables, their white cloths held down by stones, had been set out in the shade of the olive trees, and the waiters carried round casks of red and white Chianti and filled the carafes. Some of the more robust spirits, including Alberto, proposed many toasts before the meal began, so that when eventually we sat down to gigantic Florentine steaks, the party had reached that state of exhilaration which usually occurs much later. On my left was an American woman who seemed to have no connection at all with the Society, but she was a distinct acquisition to it.

'Have you noticed,' she asked, 'the number of country people around here who have steel dentures?'

'No, I haven't.'

'Well, just watch out,' she said, 'and don't say you haven't been warned! I guess there was some shortage of porcelain, or whatever it is, during the war, so they fitted them out with steel instead. It's terrific! When they smile at you, you want to run for your life!'

The meal ended with pears and *pecorino*, then came the speeches, so full of flourishes, tributes, and compliments which had to be delivered to the last syllable. We were grateful to the priest's dog for chasing a cat up a tree and driving the hens under the main table round the feet of the maestro himself; but the speeches continued.

What a picture it was. Beyond the shade in which we sat, the white world blazed with heat, and we could hear the drowsy sounds of afternoon coming up from the valley. The pretty girls leaning on their elbows at their table in the dappled shadow, making eyes above their wine glasses, lighting their cigarettes, and adopting in the spattered light a dozen relaxed attitudes that would have delighted Renoir, turned the mind away from the speeches to other times. Nothing is new in Tuscany, we were merely the latest of those who had laughed and joked upon that hilltop under the same blue sky.

§ 17

In the autumn of the year 1224, when S. Francis was forty-three years of age, he went to Mount La Verna with three of his friars to fast and pray. During this time he received the Stigmata upon his hands, his feet, and his side, and was the first saint to bear upon his body the wounds of crucifixion. With his genius for compressing a story into three lines, Dante wrote:

> There he received from Christ, upon the bare
> Ridge between Tiber and Arno, that last seal
> Which two years long his body lived to wear.

Because of his wounded feet, which made walking too painful, S. Francis was carried back to Assisi, where two years later he hailed death with the words, 'Welcome, Sister Death, for thou art to me the gate of life.'

As recently as fifty years ago travellers thought the ascent of La Verna something of an ordeal. A mule-track wound in, out, and around the mountains, and the journey took the best part of a day. Now there is a motoring road, full of hairpin bends and blind corners, which leads the traveller to the holy mount in an hour or two. When I was near the top, I looked up and saw the monastery perched above upon enormous pillars of rock. I drew into the side of the road to let a man who was leading two white oxen go past, and as he did so, I asked if those marvellous creatures belonged to the Franciscans. He said they did: Moro was the name of one, Spadino that of the other. I went on thinking how much 'the little poor man of Assisi' would have approved of Brother Moro and Brother Spadino, who were so faithfully and patiently tilling the earth of the holy mountain. Parked near the main gate was a costly Packard, and I wondered what devotee of Lady Poverty had come so far to pay his respects.

The mountain wears its monastery like a cap or a helmet. The buildings appear to be a prolongation of the most geologically contorted portion of the rock, and from some of the windows the monks look down into ravines almost as sheer as those of Meteora. There is one large church and several chapels and conventual buildings constructed round a piazza. Like Franciscans everywhere, the monks are jolly and smiling, carrying out their founder's command that they should be the troubadours of God. 'Let the friars beware of being sad and gloomy, like hypocrites,' said S. Francis, 'but let them show themselves joyful in the Lord, gay and pleasant.'

In company with a courteous friar, I explored the mountain and looked down on one of the great views: upon one side I saw the valley of the Arno and on the other, the valley of the Tiber. All the mountain torrents on the west flow into the Arno and go on their way to glide in time beneath the Ponte Vecchio; while to the east they fall into the Tiber and advance through Umbria towards the bridges of Rome.

As I looked down over the mighty stretch of Tuscany, which

rolls away beyond Arezzo to a spoonful of blue which was Lake Trasimeno, I thought how notable it was that of all the castles of Tuscany, whose ruins I could see on every hilltop, the only one to remain alive is the Castle of Brotherhood which S. Francis built on La Verna. What is Brotherhood, or rather what do we mean when we talk about it nowadays? I have never forgotten something which G. K. Chesterton said in his book on S. Francis. The Franciscan ideal of Brotherhood, he said, should not be confused with the modern idea of back-slapping Democracy. 'It is assumed,' he wrote, 'that equality means all men being equally uncivil. . . .'

'Do you think,' I asked the friar, 'that there is more hatred in the world now than in the days of S. Francis?'

'It is difficult to say,' he replied gently. 'Perhaps we hear more about it.'

We went to the various chapels and admired the collection of altar-pieces by Andrea della Robbia. He was the nephew of Luca della Robbia and inherited the family genius, which he was even able to transmit to his sons. Many of the altar-pieces have not been moved since they were erected centuries ago, and there is not a scratch on them: they are as fresh as on the day they were glazed, and they are, of course, impervious to the damp of winter.

A covered passage connects the church with the little Chapel of the Stigmata, which is visited twice in twenty-four hours by the community, once just after midnight. The friar told me the well-known story of the winter's night before the passage was enclosed, when a snowstorm forced the brethren to give up their usual midnight prayers in the chapel. But in the morning they were ashamed, and their frailty rebuked, when they saw in the snow the footprints of those animals and birds which had gone in their place.

I happened to notice a rebuke of another kind on the walls of the passage, addressed to that national pest, the Italian graffitist, who is capable of writing his name on the Cross itself. It read:

Se credi, prega!
Se non credi, ammira!
Se sei sciocco, scrivi il
Tuo nome sul muro.

'If you believe, pray; if not, admire; if you are stupid, write your name on the wall.'

I noticed among the frescoes in the corridor a picture of S. Francis preaching to the birds, and one of the Saint with the ferocious bandit known as the Wolf, whom S. Francis converted and re-named the Lamb.

When the Saint came to the mountain with three companions in September, 1224, the place where the chapel now stands was a rocky cleft that could be reached only by throwing a tree trunk across to form a bridge. S. Francis chose the spot because it was out of earshot of his companions, a place where he could be alone with God. 'Now return to your dwelling and leave me alone,' he said to them, 'for with God's help I intend to keep this fast without being disturbed or distracted in mind; so let none of you come to me. But only you, Brother Leo, come to me once a day with a little bread and water, and again during the night at the hour of Matins. Then come in silence, and when you reach the end of the bridge, you are to say "*Domine, labia mea aperies*" ("Lord, open Thou my lips"), and if I answer, cross over and come to the cell, and we will say Matins together, but if I do not answer you, then go away at once.' And S. Francis said this because he was at times so rapt in God that he was not conscious of anything through his bodily senses. And with these instructions, S. Francis gave them his blessing, and they returned to their own dwelling.

So they departed, leaving their beloved master alone with only a nesting falcon for company. The bird always awakened the Saint in time for Matins by flapping her wings and would not go away until he rose to pray. 'And whenever S. Francis was more weary than usual, or weak or ill, this falcon, like a wise and compassionate person, used to utter her cry a little later. S. Francis took great delight in this holy time-keeper, for the falcon's solicitude banished all sloth and summoned him to prayer, and furthermore the bird used often to spend the day with him.'

In spite of the Saint's instructions, Brother Leo, the favourite disciple, knowing how ill and exhausted his master was, joined the falcon in keeping watch over him. On more than one occasion the friar was amazed to see the Saint in ecstasy levitated several feet from the earth. Before dawn on the Feast of the Holy Cross, as S. Francis was praying in his retreat, 'his fervour grew so strong within him that he became wholly transformed into Jesus through love and compassion'. He saw a Seraph descending with six shining, fiery wings and upon it was the form of a man crucified. He was filled with great fear, and at the same time with great joy, sorrow, and wonder. During the vision Christ appeared to him and said, 'Do you know what I have done to you? I have given you the Stigmata, which are the marks of My Passion, so that you may be my standard-bearer.'

When his companions next saw the Saint they noticed that he tried to conceal his hands and feet and he could not put his feet to the ground. At last they saw with awe the marks of the Stigmata. 'So his hands and feet appeared to have been pierced through the centre by nails, the heads of which were in the palms of his hands and the soles of his feet, standing out from the flesh; and their points issued from the backs of the hands and feet, so that they seemed to have been thrust through the bend outside the flesh as through a ring; and the heads of the nails were round and black. Similarly in his right side appeared an unhealed lance wound, red and bleeding, from which blood often flowed from the holy heart of S. Francis, staining his habit and under-garment.'

In the *Fioretti* there is an account full of lifelike touches which describes how S. Francis, in company with Brother Leo, returned to Assisi, riding an ass, and how the people of the various towns came out to welcome him, and how he tried to hide his bandaged hands, but was obliged to let them kiss the tips of his fingers. He seems to have remained in a state of trance and did not know where he was. A long time after they had passed through Sansepolcro, he asked, 'When shall we be nearing Borgo?'

All the places mentioned in the *Fioretti* are to be seen on the mountain: the place where he was greeted by the birds; the place where he was assailed by Satan; where the Wolf, who became Lamb, lived; but most appealing of all, I thought, was the rock where he retired to meditate, and his stony bed. The friar led the way down a stairway cut in the rock which took us to a mighty overhanging ledge that appeared to be about to slide forward and crush whatever was beneath; in a neighbouring chasm a rough wooden cross marks the hard stones where it is said S. Francis used to sleep.

While we stood talking, we were joined by a man, a woman, and a little girl who wore an iron boot. They knelt and prayed, then we all went up together. Waiting at the top was a chauffeur in a white dust-coat, and my mind sped back to the car I had seen at the entrance. I was to learn that the man was a doorkeeper in some large office building, who, when his child contracted polio, vowed with his wife that should the child recover, they would make a pilgrimage to Assisi and La Verna; and this they were now doing with tears of gratitude and happiness in their eyes and – in the Packard provided by an American employer. So the little flowers continue to blossom on the rocky soil of La Verna.

The saints as animal lovers is a subject which, I think, has probably attracted the painter more than the writer. In England it is true to say that nothing has endeared S. Francis more than his love of animals; but in this he was not exceptional. The lives of the hermits and anchorites of Egypt, and also the Celtic saints, are full of animal stories. Though S. Jerome was only an honorary hermit, he was entirely in the fashion of the desert when he adopted a lion as a pet after he had taken a thorn from its paw, and there is a Franciscan touch in the story that the lion became the guardian of the donkey that carried the monastery firewood. The story goes on that when the donkey was stolen, S. Jerome believed (as S. Francis never would have done), that Brother Lion had eaten Brother Donkey, and as a punishment he made the lion carry the wood! This charming creature (one remembers his beguiling expression in Carpaccio's picture in Venice) performed his task patiently and willingly, but one day, noticing his old friend the donkey plodding along with a caravan of merchants, he bounded out, anxious to clear his character, and stampeded the camels into the monastery yard together with the donkey. One hopes that S. Jerome apologized.

The fauna of the Thebaid was, of course, much fiercer than that known to S. Francis, the lion predominating. S. Anthony, the first of the hermits, lived in a rock cave, not unlike the top of La Verna, which overlooked the Gulf of Suez, and his most pleasant visitors were animals, the rest being mostly devils. When he was burying the Hermit Paul, two lions appeared which licked his hands and feet and then helped as best they could with their paws to dig the grave.

It is said that the great Macarius of Alexandria was followed about by a loving buffalo that provided him with milk; the same saint cured a young hyena of blindness; another hermit, Theon, attracted so many animals that you could find your way to his cell by following the tracks of wild asses, gazelles, and buffaloes. One aged monk taught a lion to eat dates; another shared his food with a she-wolf; and a third was attended by an ibex which taught him what plants to avoid.

Again, the *Fioretti* reminds one of the *Vitae Patrum* whenever the devil appears, as he does quite often. He is, however, rather a crude, knockabout devil lacking in the fearful subtleties and refinements of his Egyptian days. Only once in the *Fioretti* did he show that he was still capable of his old tricks, and that was when he appeared to Brother Ruffino in his worst form, disguised as Christ. When S. Francis realized what was happening, his advice was worthy of any Egyptian anchorite. He told the afflicted friar that when the false Christ next appeared, he was to say, 'Open your mouth, and I will drop my dung in it', whereupon the devil would depart. He did. But there is nothing in the *Fioretti* like the tug-of-war between God and Satan that went on continuously in the Egyptian desert, and neither did the first Franciscans tease and irritate the devil, and spar with him, as the hermits did, in order to pit their spiritual strength against him and to make war upon him from their fortresses of prayer. This warfare gives to the ancient eremitical life the air almost of a sporting event, or perhaps of the arena, and it was all part of the saintly athleticism, a form of flexing the spiritual muscles. However, the Franciscans were never assailed by Satan in his innumerable and bewildering disguises, including that of his almost irresistible daughter, but appeared merely as a rough bully bent on knocking friars about and hurling them over precipices, and behaving with crude physical violence, as he did one night when S. Francis encountered him in an abandoned church.

I would like to have stayed some time on La Verna, and in my brief stay there I sensed the extraordinary Franciscan peace which I have known before in the Franciscan shrines in the Holy Land. I said good-bye with regret and went on down the winding road.

§ 18

A falcon from La Verna which happened to fly on a course to the north-west could alight, in ten miles or so, upon another and even more ancient monastery called Camaldoli. An earth-bound traveller, as he follows the winding road from Poppi into the mountains, does not find the journey so simple, as he ascends first through forests of beech trees, and then through dense plantations of firs and pine. Although only a few miles away and part of the same mountain, La Verna was a place not so much of trees as of rocks. There were beech woods, but I remember chiefly funnels and chasms and projecting ledges from which I looked down into ravines. At Camaldoli the bones of the mountain were covered and the hot summer air was impregnated with the smell of pine; the characteristic sound was that awful series of splintering crashes which a great tree makes as it dies under the axe of a forester.

The founder of Camaldoli was a man who was born in Ravenna two hundred and seventy years before Dante was buried there. He was nearer the Exarchate than the Middle Ages, and in our own country at that time the Saxon kings were repelling the Vikings. S. Romuald, as he became, was a Benedictine abbot whose monks were always rebelling against the strictness of his rule. In despair at what he considered the easy-going laxity of monastic life, he decided to found an Order of his own, and so retired with five companions to the mountain of Camaldoli. Here they lived as hermits in silence and solitude. They arrived wearing the black Benedictine habit, but, owing to a dream, S. Romuald changed it to white. And today, some nine hundred and fifty years later, you will find white-robed hermits still living in silence and solitude on Camaldoli. The world has changed, yet there they are, the hermits of Camaldoli, obeying the rules laid down for them by their founder at the end of the Dark Ages.

When I arrived, I saw a clearing in the forest in which what looked like a village stood grouped closely about a church with twin towers. The roofs were at all kinds of queer angles and everything wore the patina of antiquity. What gave the monastery the appearance of something one has seen in a dream or a picture was the stout stone wall that encircled it, as if to hold at bay a forest of gigantic firs that had advanced to within a few hundred yards. On a smiling morning, as I saw it, there was nothing menacing about the forest, indeed it seemed to offer a hundred delightful walks through scented shade, but somehow the wall turned my thoughts to misty days in winter when, no doubt, such a barrier would be a comfort.

The first thing that interested me was the heraldic device of the Camaldolese Order, which shows a dove on each side of a chalice. It indicates that the Order is composed of two classes, monks and hermits, and that both, the active life and the contemplative, are united in Christ.

Like most visitors to Camaldoli, I wanted to visit a hermit and to find out how these men lived. The first monk I saw was obviously not one, but a jolly, 'clubbable' kind of monk, as the Doctor might have said. He told me that the *Eremo* was a thousand feet higher up the mountain. Yes, he said it would be perfectly simple to visit the hermits, in fact he was going up there himself later on and would be glad to show me the way.

I entered the monastery and found myself in an ancient pharmacy where nothing had apparently been altered since the Middle Ages. A dusty alligator hung from the rafters and beneath it a bustling young lay brother in horn-rimmed glasses stood behind a rampart of objects on a well-stocked counter. Near the door, where in other chemists' shops there is usually a weighing machine, I noticed an upright coffin in which a skeleton was propped. I went to examine it and read an inscription : 'In this glass you see yourself, foolish mortal. Any other glass is not telling the truth.' On a shelf near by I saw a good selection of pickled vipers and I noticed some badger skins, which I seemed vaguely to remember are infallible in cases of sorcery.

There must be a mediaeval hypochondriac hidden away in me, for this was the place I had always hoped to find : the apothecary's shop in which one could ask for half an ounce of crabs' eyes or a packet of powdered coral, or perhaps even a jar of hart's horn jelly, the wonder drugs of yesterday. And it did indeed look at first sight as though, isolated upon this Apennine, men were still searching for the Elixir of Life. Who could say what the countless little drawers held in the beautiful, age-blackened walnut panelling ; what, in spite of his horn rims and his modern air, might not the lay brother have under the counter? Fascinated, I stepped into smaller room full of mortars and pestles and retorts (and another alligator), a room which gave the impression that an alchemist had just slipped out to look up something in Galen. A stuffed armadillo gave a homely touch to one corner and upon the wall, framed perhaps for ready reference, I read a formula which contained the words *grasso umano* – human fat.

When, however, I approached the counter, I was preceded by a man who was buying a packet of razor blades and by a woman who bought a bottle of eau-de-Cologne and a jar of face cream. This, of course, as any follower of Don Quixote will know, might have been enchanter's work. Unhappily it was not, since two pharmaceutical worlds met at the counter and, in spite of all evidence to the contrary, the world of razor blades and face creams was the real one. It remains a fact, however, that had I asked the lay brother for half an ounce of black hellebore, which as everyone knows will cure gout and kill wolves, he would have been puzzled, yet he would have produced the more mysterious butabarbital or penicillin without turning a hair!

I asked where his customers came from. He said they were living at the hospice up the road and were on holiday. Every year people came to spend a week or two in the pine-scented air of the mountains, to walk, to ride, and to fish; and the pharmacy was the village shop.

Monks everywhere love to dabble in distilling, in the hope maybe of discovering something as good and profitable as Benedictine or Chartreuse. In Camaldoli they make three liqueurs: one is *Laurus*; another is *Elixir dell' Eremita*; and the third is *Lachryma d'Abeto* – the tears of the fir tree.

Hearing a laugh at my elbow, I turned to find the merry monk whom I had met on my arrival. He said he would like to show the church to me, after which perhaps I would like something to eat. As we set off together, I was surprised to hear that this delightful man had been a hermit for two years. I was amazed to think that he had been able to remain silent for two minutes! It occurred to me that his merriment and volubility were not, as I had thought, that gaiety of soul which is said to be so necessary to a monk, but Nature's revenge on a naturally sociable individual after two years of silence.

'How did you endure it?' I asked.

'It was hard,' he said, 'but I felt it necessary to submit myself to the discipline.'

We made our way through the Baroque church, in which there is a beautiful della Robbia, and eventually set off for the Hermitage along a steep road through the forest. My companion was a picturesque figure in his white robes, to which he had added a straw hat of immense proportions, and as we went along, he told me how a hermit lives. There are about sixteen of them at the moment, each one living in silence in his cell. Except for the recluses, who are rarely, if ever, visible, the ordinary hermits leave their cells seven times in twenty-four hours to sing the Divine Office in their little church. Their first attendance is at one-thirty in the morning for Matins and Lauds; the first Mass is at seven o'clock; there is another Mass at nine; eleven-forty-five is the hour of Nones; four-thirty of Vespers; and so on. Not a word is spoken as they make their way to and from their cells to the church in all weathers, sometimes through thick snow and in torrential mountain rain and mist; and in silence they return. Twelve times a year they speak on certain feast days, when they take a common meal together, but this is eaten in silence : it is only afterwards that they are allowed to talk.

'Do they talk much?' I asked.

'No,' he replied, suddenly sombre. 'One gets out of the habit.'

Each hermit eats in his cell; the spare, meatless diet of bread and vegetable soup is placed on a revolving wheel by a lay brother. On Fridays only bread and water are taken, and each hermit keeps two Lents every year.

'Look!' said my companion suddenly, pointing upward to the path ahead, where some distance away stood a white figure, absolutely motionless. 'A hermit!' he added.

As we advanced, the figure remained as if frozen and, as we drew level, I saw that he was reading a book. He did not look up at us and though it seemed uncivil in such a remote spot to pass another human being without a 'Good Afternoon', there was a reserve about the man which conveyed to us that to speak would have been a breach of manners : but I must say he disappointed me. Fresh as I was from the Uffizi and pictures of John the Baptist and unkempt anchorites, emaciated and in shaggy skins, standing at the entrances to caverns, this well-dressed person with a white beard and a spotless robe, who had obviously washed, did not seem a real hermit.

We came to a walled enclosure in the forest. The stout gate was locked and barred. When the monk pulled a bell-rope, the gate was unlocked by a lay brother. Inside, I saw about twenty or thirty solid little one-storied buildings, each roofed with red tiles and each one exactly like the next. They were grouped with the mathematical precision of a military camp at equal distances from one another, and they lined each side of a paved road that led to the church. I noticed how cleverly they had been set out, the front of one towards the back of the next, so that the inhabitants should have nothing distracting to look at. While the monk went off to transact his business, I glanced through the gates which led into the enclosures and saw that each building had its own patch of garden, most of them planted with beans, peas, and potatoes, and a few enlivened by geraniums and dahlias. Even flowers, however, could not dispel the bleak air of penitence.

When the monk returned, we walked up the main avenue while he pointed out objects of interest, notably the cell (for that is the name given to these buildings) in which a Belgian hermit has been immured for seven years. In order to indulge in such austerities a hermit has first to receive the permission of the Father Superior. I expressed some surprise.

'Oh, but it is nothing,' cried the monk. 'In 1951 a hermit died in that cell over there who for twenty-three years had lived on bread, water, and vegetables, and had no fire in the winter.'

I said that he was perhaps anxious to hasten his departure.

'On the contrary,' replied the monk. 'He was eighty-five!'

We went to the little church, where a lay brother was at work. 'You must see the Blessed Mariotto Allegri,' cried monk and lay brother together. 'He is as fresh as the day he died.'

'When did he die?' I asked.

'In 1478,' they replied, 'that's nearly five hundred years ago!' In the vestry was a box with a glass lid.

'Isn't he wonderful?' they said. I looked down and saw an old man like brown paper. He was dressed in a white habit and had been Abbot of the Order when Lorenzo the Magnificent was alive. Perhaps, I suggested, they had even met. 'But of course they met,' they said. This was the great Platonist, Mariotto Allegri, who, as described by Christoforo Landino in his *Disputationes Camaldulenses*, had invited Lorenzo and his brother Giuliano to bring their learned friends of the Platonic Academy to the Abbey as his guests in 1468. I returned to look at him. How amazing to think that those brown-paper lips had spoken to the Medici.

On our way from the church to the gate, my companion paused at a cell and knocked. The door was opened by a hermit who was introduced to me as Don Domenico. For some reason not clear to me, he had been absolved from the vow of silence and seemed pleased to see us. I was delighted when he invited us to enter. Again, to me, as I think to most people, a hermit's cell suggests the forbidding cavern we have seen in the works of the great masters; but even the eremitical life has changed with the times. I entered a neat little cottage as compact and tidy as the master's cabin in a ship, or it might have been the quarters which a kindly governor had allowed a carpenter inmate to construct in some ideal prison. It was austere and bare, but everything was well made and evidently the result of centuries of planned solitude. A small study, in which there were neat bookshelves and a writing-desk of plain pine, led into a bed-sitting-room with a chair, a table, an unshaded electric light, and a bed built into a wooden alcove. I sat on it and found it as hard as iron. As Don Domenico was a priest, a tiny oratory led from the bedroom where he said Mass every morning.

One would have to live in a monastery to know whether malice, which mediaeval kings said was the curse of monasticism, still exists, but, as a casual visitor, I cannot remember ever having met a miserable or an unpleasant monk. I recall two main types, the lean ascetic who radiates serenity, and hearty men of God who, one has even suspected, sometimes overdo the cheerfulness, as if anxious to live up to some popular conception of Friar Tuck. Without wishing to deny that both serenity and cheerfulness are founded on spiritual discipline and values, I have often wondered in what measure lack of money troubles, or marital disturbances and parental disappointments – to say nothing of the woes of the outside world – assist the spiritual calm. Don Domenico, with his kindly, gentle smile, belonged to the saintly category, and indeed, I thought that in his white habit, seen against a rocky background, he would have appealed to Giotto and Mantegna.

It is not always easy to make casual conversation with the unworldly, but I happened to notice on his shelves several books on the planets and found that he was an amateur astronomer. He produced a telescope which he had made, as Galileo might have done, from old lenses and a piece of sheet tin, and he told me that in the small hours he often took this instrument into his garden and counted the moons of Jupiter.

We left as the hermits were going to Vespers. The doors of the severe little houses opened silently and from each stepped a cowled figure in white. They walked slowly, with heads bent and their folded hands concealed in their ample sleeves. Each one was enclosed in a ghostly detachment as if unaware of his fellows. Some were old, white-bearded men, some were hale and middle-aged, and as they slipped into the church I watched them with admiration. They had voluntarily embraced that condition which few of us are brave enough to endure, complete solitude. When I thought of the horrors that can assail one at night, and how one longs for the first streak of dawn and the sounds of common life, it seemed to me that these men, who had vowed themselves to years of solitude and wakefulness, had never been better described than in that ancient term, 'athletes of God'.

We went down the hill through the pine woods, and once more laughter and gaiety possessed my companion, and I think I know why. One remark of his, I thought, illuminated the frugality of monkish life. When describing to me the period of the year in which something had happened, he said: 'It was at Easter. No, it was not Easter! It must have been at Christmas, because I remember we had walnuts after dinner!'

§ 19

'When I was in the mountains with the Partisans,' said Alberto one day, 'I often went off at night in the winter-time to farmhouses to hear the *contadini* extemporizing. We call these rhymes *canti estemporanei*, and in some of the valleys they speak a classical sixteenth century dialect and use words long since obsolete. It was fascinating to hear farmers and peasants in crowded farmhouse kitchens, men who cannot read, describing with eloquence the events of the day, the sowing of crops, the ploughing of land, the clouds, the birds, the passing of aeroplanes, all in beautifully turned *ottava rima*.

'I wish you could hear the *stornelli* and *rispetti* as I heard them during the war, when one man would impersonate Hitler, another Churchill, and a third Roosevelt. I know that many people, even writers about Italy, think that this old gift has vanished, but it is not so. Electricity, the radio, and television have not succeeded yet in separating the *contadini* of Tuscany from the age of Homer.'

The *improvvisatori*, he said, can be found all over Tuscany today, and when I asked whether it would be possible for me to hear one, he said nothing could be easier. He promised to make arrangements.

The improvisation of verses on any given theme, which I believe survived until recently, and may even still survive in Wales, goes back, as Alberto suggested, to remote ages. I can remember at least one Roman reference to it. The *improvvisatori* descended from Rome by way of the Middle Ages to the Renaissance. One day at a state banquet Cardinal Giovanni de' Medici asked a celebrated *improvvisatore*, Silvio Antoniano, if he could compose a poem in praise of the clock, which could be heard striking from the palace belfry. The young man immediately improvised, and continued to do so to such good effect that when Giovanni de' Medici became Pius IV, he made Antoniano a cardinal.

English visitors to Italy in the eighteenth century were fascinated by these poets. A celebrated *improvvisatore* named Talassi was in England in 1770 and was invited to Streatham by Mrs Thrale, where Dr Johnson, himself no mean performer on the spur of the moment, was delighted with him. When Dr Burney was making his musical tour of Europe, he met the *improvvisatrice*, La Corilla, in Florence; for women as well as men were gifted. La Corilla once demonstrated her powers upon the Capitol before a distinguished audience, which included the Duke of Gloucester, when she is said to have rhymed with equal success on Physics, Metaphysics, Legislation, Eloquence, and Mythology. Another famous *improvvisatrice* was Isabella Pellegrini, whose gifts surprised Madame de Stael. Probably the most celebrated of all was the eighteenth century *improvvisatore* Berdinadino Perfetti, who became transfigured when reciting and appeared to compose in a trance. After one of his public displays on the Capitol, he was crowned with laurel by Benedict XIII and made a citizen of Rome.

In a day or so Alberto asked me to meet him in the evening at a trattoria on the road from Arezzo to Montevarchi. He introduced me to two ordinary-looking Italians, who might have been farmers in their town suits or small shopkeepers. Actually, I was told, they both sold plastic buckets and razor blades and suchlike at open-air markets. One was named Elio Piccardi and the other was Matteo Mattesini. The plan was for us to have dinner together and afterwards they had agreed to display their powers by extemporizing on any theme I cared to suggest. Alberto took me aside and said that he had brought his tape-recorder so that I should have an accurate version of the rhymes if I wanted it. 'These *canti* should not really be written down,' he said, 'for a part of their impressiveness is due to the atmosphere, the interplay of expression between the two men, the sudden fits and starts of inspiration. Anyhow, you'll soon see what I mean. . . .'

A little room with a window on the road had been reserved for us and dinner was ready. We ate mounds of steaming spaghetti. One of the men told me that he had begun life herding sheep, and to wile away the time had composed poems which he addressed to his flock; the other told me that when they both met at the same market, they often indulged in *canti estemporanei* from stall to stall to the admiration of the whole piazza. This love of the spoken word is surely something we have lost with Caxton.

I noticed that our guests drank little and thinned down their Chianti with water. When dinner was over, they sat facing each other across the table and asked me to give them a theme. They said they would like a *problema*. After some consultation with Alberto, I said, 'A river is in flood and a man is crossing it with his mother and his wife. Suddenly there are cries for help and the man sees that both women are being swept away by the flood. He can save only one. Which shall he save, his mother or his wife?' The *improvvisatori* listened carefully, nodded and, without a moment's hesitation, Elio Piccardi lifted a hand in an oratorical manner and began to intone in a voice pitched in a high bardic key:

> 'Rimettiamo la lingua in movimento
> ora ci hanno dato un delicato dramma,
> sarebbe un contrasto, sai, di sentimento:
> cantare su una moglie e su una mamma.
> Ambedue trovandosi nel cimento,
> a ripensarci sai, 'l cuore s'infiamma,
> ma per mantener nel mondo l'energia
> io difendero la moglie mia.'

This says, in effect, let us give voice now that we have a delicate drama. To sing of wife or mother in peril would be a conflict of sentiments, but, in thinking of it, the heart takes fire, and, to ensure the future of the world, he would save his wife.

While listening to him, and admiring the way he picked his rhymes out of the air, I thought it is much easier to do this in Italian than in English. For every English rhyme there must be at least four Italian ones. At the sound of the high-pitched, chanting voice, first one head peeped round the door, then another, and eventually, unable to resist the entertainment, eight or ten country-men who had been drinking in the trattoria entered quietly and lined up near the window. They followed each word with gusto. Their eyes never left the face of the poet. Such audiences are not often seen in a world of literate men. Each word was important to them.

Having completed his eighth line, Piccardi paused for his friend, and Mario Mattesini plunged in, full of mother love. He said that the devotion of a mother for her child was no idle fantasy. From the moment she brought her infant into the world, she nursed him, gave him her energy, and never ceased to love him. His two concluding lines won the approval of the audience who murmured agreement. These said that a man did not always hear the truth from his wife, but his mother never failed him.

Piccardi then came in again strongly for the wife, ending with the lines:

> per la mi' moglie, con quel ricciol biondo,
> fo annegar tutte le mamme che c'è al mondo.

For his wife, with her blonde curls, he would let all the mothers in the world drown! This seemed to shock the audience, who shook their heads. Mattesini then sang that his friend's soul must be barren and shallow if he could say such things of a love to which all the world pays homage. 'The mother's grey hair was also blonde once,' he reminded us.

Piccardi then said that when he went to war 'in the infantry', he heard men dying, some from America, some from England. They did not call upon their mothers: they invoked their poor wives and their children. Mattesini contradicted this. In his experience, when a bomb dropped, a man did not think of his wife and family at all, but cried, '*O mamma mia!*' He went even farther and said that men were bad who did not call upon their mothers in moments of peril.

There were fourteen verses, and it was obvious to me that Mattesini had the easier task. One of his most telling couplets was:

> *Se ti muore, una mamman 'un la ritrovi,*
> *ma de le mogli cento ne rinnovi.*

'. . . if a mother dies, she cannot be replaced, but you can find a hundred wives!' This was a line that a land of matriarchy had evidently been waiting for: smiles and nods of approval, grunts of approbation and some back-slapping for Mattesini, concluded the first *canto*.

The next one was rather a poor subject and I cannot think how it was chosen and approved – *Il Traffico Stradale* – the traffic on the roads. This was followed by an argument for and against fat women, in fifteen verses, and the evening concluded with a gracefully worded *Saluto* to myself. As they knew nothing about me and had met me only that evening, the poem was a peg for some charming, old-fashioned ideas of England as ruler of the seas and the guardian of Liberty, seasoned with some high-flown tributes to 'Ciurcillo', as they Italianized the name Churchill.

I was greatly impressed by the poets and the audience, and I wished that I had been able to paint the scene. It was straight out of the Homeric age: the wandering minstrel entertaining workers from vineyards and sheepfolds. When I came to read the tape transcriptions, however, I was surprised to find that it had really been an exercise in verbal dexterity and quickness of wit: there was no poetry. It had been ordinary conversation expressed in *ottava rima*. Alberto was right; *canti estemporanei* should be enjoyed at the time, but not printed afterwards: but where else in the world would you find a couple of street vendors who were proud to call themselves poets and who on request could express themselves fluently in rhyme? They were men who had inherited a literary tradition that went back beyond Dante, perhaps to Provence, possibly to Homer.

CHAPTER TWELVE

*Into Umbria – Hawkwood's castle – S. Margaret of Cortona –
Perugia, the city of Popes and Conclaves – Rise of the Flagellants – Visit
to Gubbio – Assisi – S. Francis – How the Saint's body was lost and
found – A bird sanctuary – The Waters of Clitumnus*

§ 1

I left Arezzo regretfully and took the road that leads south out
of Tuscany into Umbria. It traverses a lovely valley which was
once a fearsome malarial marsh, but now, drained and cultivated, is one of the best-groomed farmlands in Tuscany. It was
one of those hot days in summer when the landscape stretches
ahead, white and quivering, and the eye is grateful for the pools of
shade under the olive trees. The pulse of the heat was the rhythmic
song of the cicada; and I thought how blessed is rain, how cool
and how life-giving.

Beyond the hill-town of Castiglion Fiorentino I came upon the
only movement in that sun-stricken world, where a young farmer, burned brown as a walnut, was guiding his plough under the
olive trees. The oxen, their white bodies yellowed with sweat,
moved with slow elephantine grace, shaking their vast horns every
now and then to move the red tassels on their flat foreheads to
dispel the flies. I asked the name of the place whose battlemented
walls we could see on a hill some miles away. He replied that it was
the castle of Sir Giovanni Acuto, its name Montecchio, and he
implied that Sir John Hawkwood had lived and died there. This I
knew was not so. It was just one of several castles which he sold
to Florence in an attempt to become solvent. He must have been
a mighty spender. Even though the expense of keeping a thousand
men fighting fit must have been enormous, he made a fortune out
of the various state quarrels, yet was always hard up. Some measure of his fame as a general, and the advisability of having him

on your side, was the large retaining fee paid to him in his last years by Florence, which included a special allowance for his wife. Bankers are not usually so generous without good reason.

A rough track leads up to the battlements and to a heavy old gate studded with nails the size of half-a-crown: but there was nothing to see save a farmhouse built in the ruins and a sentry walk whose loop-holes look north to Arezzo and south to Cortona. The farmer's wife knew that she was living in the castle of Giovanni Acuto, but who he was she neither knew nor cared.

I went on and took a series of hairpin bends and loops that swung up to the dizzy fortress town of Cortona. It was so high that it was perceptively cooler there, and from the ramparts I looked down upon Lake Trasimene and the road to Perugia. What an eyrie it is! As I looked at it, I wondered if anyone now reads George Dennis, the English consul of the last century whose book, *Cities and Cemeteries of Etruria,* is still the most readable work on the subject. How Cortona amazed and delighted him. It was one of those Etruscan cities which caused him to gather his readers solemnly, as it were, in a hushed group as he addressed them in archaic thou's and thee's, current language being inadequate to express the awe with which the antiquity of Cortona filled him. 'Ere the days of Hector and Achilles, ere Troy itself arose – Cortona was,' he said dramatically.

It was too hot to do more than walk round the town and enjoy the darkness of churches and the coolness of museums. I took away some odd memories: the iron hooks outside what is now the post office placed there, I was told, in the Middle Ages for hanging up criminals; the pea-green Etruscan candelabra in the museum ('wonder of ancient wonders' to Dennis), and a chastity belt in a near-by case. I remembered too a curious conversation overheard in the little restaurant in the main piazza where I had lunch. Two men were seated at the next table having a political argument with a third, a fierce little hunchback. If they were baiting him in the hope he would blow up, they were successful, for, pushing back his chair he strode towards the door, then hesitated and, returning, said in a low menacing whisper, 'I am a son of the stones of Arezzo,' then, pausing to let that sink in, added, 'and if you really want to know I'm a – *Ghibelline!*' The little man then left the room with great dignity. His companions burst into a roar of laughter. The waiter told me that the hunchback was a man of good family from Arezzo; he detested Florence and the Florentines and could not bear to be reminded of the battle of Campaldino, fought in 1289, when Arezzo was forced to submit to Florence! He once caused something of a sensation in the Uffizi by declaring in a loud voice, 'These men,' referring to Michelangelo, Vasari, and others, 'are not Florentines. They are Aretines!'

Cortona is steeped in Franciscan memories. A woman who has been called the Mary Magdalen of Franciscanism, and a man who has been called its Judas (and also its S. Paul), once lived there. She was S. Margaret of Cortona; he was the famous Brother Elias who, after the death of S. Francis, swept away the ideal of poverty and brought the Franciscan Order in line with a materialistic world.

To the people of Cortona, S. Margaret is still a living presence. She is their beloved *poverella*, and in all the trials and perplexities of life they go to pray at her tomb in the highest part of the town. She was born in 1247, and grew into a strikingly beautiful girl. Falling in love with a well-born young man from Montepulciano, she went to live with him and bore him a son. They were ideally happy and, though her lover spoke of marriage, they were never united by the Church. This did not seem to matter to them since every day was happier than the one before. This ideal life ended in nine years' time when her lover's murdered body was discovered in a wood.

Margaret's grief created in her one of those spiritual crises not unusual in the lives of the saints. Convinced that her beauty had been the cause of her lover's downfall, and that his death was a punishment for sin, she vowed herself to a life of penitence. Once she was tempted by the devil, who came to her as she was mourning under a fig tree and whispered that her dazzling beauty would bring her the love of many great ones of the earth; then she heard the voice of Christ bidding her take her broken heart to the Franciscans at Cortona. First giving away all she possessed, she walked barefoot with her child to the hill-town where, in the extravagance of her grief, she desired to go back naked to Montepulciano with a rope round her neck and make public penance. The good Friars soothed her, and she settled down to a life of prayer and service to the poor and the sick. One day, as she was praying before a crucifix, she saw the head of Christ inclined towards her, a sign that her sins were forgiven.

She was received into the Third Order of S. Francis and embraced the love of God with the same passionate intensity she had devoted to an earthly lover. She was a mystic, a worker of miracles, and, like so many saints, a practical woman who founded a great mediaeval hospital and, anticipating S. Catherine of Siena by a century, took a hand in politics and tried to reconcile the warring factions of Tuscany. 'It is strange,' wrote Edward Hutton, 'that Cortona should have held almost at that same time two such different Franciscans as Frate Elias and S. Margaret – the one a great statesman who abhorred poverty, the other a poor woman who loved it. . . . And it is she who is the victor, not he, for all his power and wealth and greatness of mind. He is forgotten by all men save a few historians, while her name is still familiarly dear on the lips of peasants and children, who invoke her, their all-powerful friend, as we may hear any day in the fields or the byways about her home:

> O Lily of our friends,
> O Violet of humility,
> O little Sister of the Seraphs,
> Ora pro nobis.

The road to Perugia runs for miles along the shores of the hot, stagnant Lake Trasimeno. Napoleon once thought of draining it, but nothing has yet been done. Some day I would like to go back and explore it and find the place where the Roman army was defeated by Hannibal. It is sometimes dangerous for an army to be commanded by an agnostic. The Consul Flaminius scorned all the omens. He fell from his horse on the morning of the battle, the legionary standards remained fixed in the earth and had to be dug out, and, much worse, the sacred chickens (coops of these accompanied every Roman army), refused to eat. No wonder that before the day was over Flaminius and most of his army were dead.

One can fancy red faces above the togas in the clubs of Rome. 'What else could you expect from such a fellow?'

§ 2

The city of Perugia, seated upon its mountain like the Ark on Ararat, looks as it did in the Middle Ages. You see the grey stone buildings forming an uneven outline far off, against the blue sky of Umbria, and if you have been to the Lebanon, you will probably compare it to the castles which the Crusaders built there with a lordly disdain for the problems of labour.

Perugia is a city apart. It never really joined in the hurly-burly of Italian politics as did Milan, Florence, Siena, or even Lucca and Pisa: it remained on its mountain, introspectively apart, locked away with its own mixture of violence and piety, especially violence. 'The most warlike of the people of Italy,' was Sismondi's description. To train themselves for fighting, the Perugini played a ferocious game in which the male inhabitants divided themselves into teams and, having padded themselves with clothing stuffed with deer hair, and assuming beaked helmets like the heads of eagles or hawks, stoned each other savagely until the streets were strewn with casualties. It was quite usual for ten or twelve men to die or to be wounded in these encounters, but their relatives are said to have accepted their deaths calmly and bore no resentment.

When I saw the city standing a thousand feet above the Tiber, and nearly two thousand above the Tyrrhenian Sea, and looked at the road winding up to it, I realized why so few distinguished travellers used to go there. The most notable was Goethe, who liked the city. Among the Englishmen, Smollett was an improbable visitor as he angrily drove up the hill and, being accident prone, had a nasty coach mishap on the way. When Samuel Rogers went to Perugia, he found teams of oxen stationed at the foot of the road to give extra power to horse- or mule-drawn carts and carriages. Compared with the few who attempted the ascent, hundreds must have passed Perugia by. An anonymous English pilgrim who did so in the Middle Ages referred to it as 'the terrible city of Perugia'. Evidently he had heard of its blood baths, and maybe of the Flagellants, who orginated there, and went masked through the countryside lashing themselves until the blood flowed as they begged God to forgive their sins.

The road today is as perilous as in Smollett's time. It is haunted by small, angry-looking Fiats which go charging up, changing gear every fifty yards, accelerating and cutting their corners in an attempt to retain momentum. I never actually saw an engine die on this road, but it must sometimes happen, just as the horses and mules must have panted to a standstill in the old days.

As I mounted, the view of the heavenly Umbrian plain became even more wonderful. I saw the Tiber, no longer an infant as in Tuscany, describing wide loops of silver as it moved confidently onward to Rome. A few miles away, against the background of Mount Subasio, was Assisi. What a strange juxtaposition: Perugia the violent, and Assisi, the birthplace of the apostle of peace and kindness; and it is pleasant to say that it is of S. Francis and not of the violent Baglioni, the lords of Perugia, that one thinks as one climbs this road. And one also remembers that S. Francis was buried in secret to prevent the Perugians from stealing his body and transporting it to their fastness.

Passing beneath a massive gate, I found myself in a labyrinth of ancient streets. It was late afternoon and most of the shops were closed. There were few people about. Though I had a map, it was of little use. I was lost. Eventually, by the merest chance, I found my way to the main street, where I was stopped by a hand in a white cotton glove. *Scusate!* The Corso was closed to traffic: it was the hour of the *passeggiata*! And in a glance I took in a remarkable scene. The descendants of the violent warriors, and of those who had survived the stone game, were strolling up and down, smiling and bowing to each other in a faint aroma of cigar smoke. There were hundreds of neat little girls in twos and threes, hundreds of young men, their parents and grandparents, all strolling about on the top of the mountain. Coming to the end of the Corso, where a terrace wall has a drop of a thousand feet to the rocks below, they would turn and saunter back to the Fountain.

Eventually I found myself in one of those large hotels, now almost period pieces, which were built for the travelling aristocracy of the railway age. It must have been the last word in hotels in 1900 and it is still a good one, though the enormous lounges and writing-rooms (what a lot of writing was done in those days), appear to be mourning a lost world. Like everything else, my bedroom was on a large scale, and its great attraction was a view eastward over the plain to Assisi: and directly beneath my window I could watch the *passeggiata*.

First impressions of a new place are often memorable, and I shall certainly not forget my impetuous plunge into the warrens of Perugia on my first night. All I can say is that if you wish to find out what a mediaeval town must have looked like, you should wander haphazardly about Perugia after dark. I found myself enclosed by massive stone buildings in narrow lanes and alleys, all of them sloping either up hill or down; Cyclopean archways led, by way of long ramps, to new levels; and once I came to a terrace overlooking a ravine whose opposite slopes were covered with palaces, houses, and churches, their roofs rising one above the other as they followed the contour of the hill. Again I was reminded of the East. There are streets in the Old City of Jerusalem like the streets of Perugia, and the *souk* at Aleppo has the same sinister archways, the same thick walls of finely-hewn brown stone. What a city for assassinations! Yet it was the poison phial and not the dagger that was notorious in Perugia. The poison was Aquetta, a colourless fluid much prized and feared in the fifteenth century; it was said to have been prepared by rubbing pork with white arsenic and collecting the juice.

As I walked on, there were often the strangest of illusions: a man walking a few paces ahead would suddenly vanish, and when I reached the point of his disappearance I would see that he had quietly slipped down a flight of steps to a lower street: in the same way men emerged head first, as if climbing out of a cellar or a manhole, to vanish again into the mediaeval labyrinth. I was on the look-out for a *porta del mortuccio*, or door of the dead, which every house of standing once possessed; and I found two, both in old, shuttered palaces. They were narrow and pointed and were bricked up, next to the main doorway, and in centuries past were used only for the passage of a coffin, owing to the Etruscan superstition that where Death had once entered, he would enter again.

I think the impressive climax of my walk was to come unexpectedly upon an extraordinary monument. It was a massive old wall and gateway now enclosed by the city, but once obviously the boundary of the Etruscan town. The lower stones were those huge black Etruscan blocks which were revived as 'rustication' in the palaces of Florence. The upper courses were Roman, and above the gate I read by the light of a street lamp the words 'Augusta Perusia'. What a discovery to come across at night upon a mountain. This was one of the gates built some forty years before Christ, when Augustus rebuilt the city after it had been destroyed during his war against Antony and Cleopatra.

I came suddenly out of the dark streets into the short Corso Vannucci, where the *passeggiata* takes place. How admirable it is of Perugia to have resisted the temptation, to which more than half of Italy has succumbed, to call a street the Corso Garibaldi or the Corso Vittorio Emanuele, but to remember the real name of that painter of tender Madonnas, Pietro Vannucci, who is better known as Perugino. And here in a few yards were the distinctive features of Perugia: that wonderful group of buildings which, under the influence of history and the Italian genius, is capable of such infinite variety. Here were the Cathedral, the Fountain, the Palazzo dei Priori, and the Collegio del Cambio, all the well-known ingredients of the lovely architectural compositions which greet one in every city in this inspired land.

Perugia's variation on this noble theme is one to be remembered with the *piazze* of Florence, Siena, Bologna, and Ferrara. Whenever in the future I hear the name Perugia, I shall think of this scene. First, the Cathedral, attractive and yet ugly, with its wall that has never been covered with marble, approached by a fine flight of steps upon which Pope Julius III, in green bronze, is seated in an attitude of benediction. Near the porch a stone pulpit juts out from the building, from which S. Bernardino used to tell the Perugini of their shortcomings; and above the main gate, behind plate glass, is a large crucifix placed there six hundred years ago by a contrite gunner, who by mistake sent a shot into the Cathedral at that point. Perugia's usual gestures of violence and penitence!

A few paces from the Cathedral is the famous Fountain, now almost black with age, its sculptured figures frayed by Time, a structure like the two lower tiers of some gigantic mediaeval wedding cake. Only a few paces away stands that striking fortress-like building – Perugia's Palazzo Vecchio – with square Guelphic battlements and rows of beautiful perpendicular windows, and a flight of stairs which leads to a noble doorway. Above this, standing out upon stone brackets, are the Griffin of Perugia and the Guelphic Lion, and suspended between them are some relics which are claimed to be the bars of gates carried off from Assisi or Siena by the Perugians in 1358. This is not so, however: the iron bar and chains vanished, I was told, one night in 1799, and what are seen now are only the rods and chains from which the trophies were suspended.

I returned to my hotel with a mind filled by mediaeval pictures. More dramatic upon its mountain even than Siena upon her hills, and evoking memories of the more sinister aspects of the mediaeval world, Perugia, I thought, is one of the most convincing survivals from the past that I had seen. Before I went indoors, I walked over to the terrace wall outside the hotel and looked down into a great bowl of warm darkness. I could make out by starlight the white roads crossing the plain. Muffled night sounds came up: the bark of a farmyard dog; the distant clatter of a train; then intense silence. Pin-point sparks far below marked the position of houses and farms; and not far away a whole constellation on a hillside, matching those in the wide night sky above, told me that Assisi was not yet in bed.

§ 3

In the course of his spiteful life of Perugino, Vasari said that the Umbrian painter came from a home so poor that he was haunted throughout his life by the fear of poverty and would do anything for money. He dismissed as commercial pot-boilers most of the paintings of Assumptions, Nativities, Crucifixions, and gentle Madonnas which proceeded so smoothly from this master's brush.

There is, of course, nothing unusual in this, since artists have to live and take care of their wives and families; but when Vasari went on to say that Perugino was an agnostic and 'would not believe in the immortality of the soul', he dealt him a fatal blow. People prefer their saints to be painted by Christians.

Perugino's portrait in the Cambio at Perugia shows a tough-looking, ugly little man with a thin mouth and eyes which are calculating and at the same time apprehensive: the eyes of a man who expects the worst to happen and tries to prepare for it. Though it may not be a kind face, it is a pathetic one, and Perugino must have been fundamentally unhappy and melancholy. Vasari says that when the painter arrived in Florence as a lad to learn his art, he was so poor that he slept for months in a chest. Then he quickly developed the technique which made him famous, and we are told that dealers were soon buying up his work and selling it profitably, even outside Italy. Centuries later his most unlikely admirer was Napoleon who, strange to relate, shared with nuns an admiration for the modest eyes and the gentle dreaminess of Perugino's Madonnas.

The artist married a young girl and took pleasure in her dress and appearance, 'and he liked her to wear pretty headdresses both out of doors and in the house,' says Vasari, 'and is said to have often dressed her himself.' I recalled having read years ago a charming little story by Maurice Hewlett in *Earthworks out of Tuscany*, in which a visitor disturbs Perugino in the act of dressing his wife's hair in the courtyard of his house. Some time afterwards I read it again and found it just as elegant and amusing, and written in a courtly prose that has now passed out of fashion.

I was shown a house in Perugia where the old master and his young wife are said to have lived, but the tenancy is conjectural, and probably a more authentic association is the fine corner building, with an arched doorway and pointed windows of red marble, in which it is believed he had his studio. Even more interesting is the disused church of S. Severo, which was closed when I tried the door, until I discovered the usual old woman with the keys. Here I saw a fresco which shows two rows of saints, the upper row painted by Raphael at the age of twenty-two, when he was a pupil of Perugino. Years after Raphael's death, when Perugino was over seventy, the old man added the lower row. I wonder whether there is another picture which displays the strong sunrise of a great pupil and the uncertain sunset of his master.

Of Perugino, Berenson wrote: 'He had a feeling for beauty in women, charm in young men and dignity in the old, seldom surpassed before or since.' He went on to describe some of Perugino's women as 'tall, slender, golden-haired, dainty – Shakespeare's heroines in disguise. Then there is a well-ordered seemliness, a sanctuary aloofness in all his people which makes them things apart, untouched and pure'.

It is pleasant to read such a counterblast to Vasari's mean account of the Umbrian master. And if you wish to see the 'Shakespeare's heroines in disguise', there is no better Arden than the National Gallery of Umbria, in Perugia's Palazzo dei Priori. What inhabitant of Perugia in the stormy fifteenth century could have believed that Perugino's brush would prove to be more powerful than Baglioni's sword, and that Pinturicchio would one day move into the Palace of the Priors?

The art gallery is well lit and admirably arranged, with a charming and friendly background for the works of that tender school which, together with the gospel according to S. Francis, is the most enduring product of Umbria. I duly admired in many a Perugino the lovely Shakespearean heroines – some a little too devout, surely, for Rosalind and scarcely robust enough for Portia – and admired, too, the exquisite glimpses of Umbria, with its rocks and trees, which this artist always placed in the background, each one a golden little landscape in its own right. How extraordinary to think that so much tranquillity was produced at a time when Florence and Perugia were passing through a period of violence. Perugino had the secret of shutting out the noise of battle and murder when he was creating his ideal world, where no sounds but celestial music and benedictions ever broke the reverent hush.

During his lifetime the city was terrorized by the Oddi and the Baglioni. Murders followed each other; papal legates turned back from Perugia, afraid of being torn limb from limb; the countryside was burnt and devastated; indeed Perugia was in real life the picture of that Bad Government which Signorelli painted on the wall in Siena. And Florence was hardly better. During Perugino's life, Charles VIII invaded Italy; the Medici were driven out of Florence, and Savonarola was burnt at the stake there. A little later Louis XII conquered Milan and drove out Ludovico Sforza, and at much the same time Leo X solved the tyranny of the Baglioni by decoying the head of the family to Rome and executing him. How fortunate was Perugino to have had access to his magic world of peace and gentleness, where the Madonna sits half-smiling as she listens to the songs of angels.

I shall always think of this Gallery as the haunt of exquisite musical angels. A whole flock, by Benedetto Bonfigli, is surely the most elegant escort ever seen in Heaven, wearing upon their blonde heads pink hats and haloes which might have come from Paris. In another picture, the Virgin is entertained by endearing little angels who, as they sing, hold music written in the oddest notation, perhaps a system used in Heaven, or on earth before the time of Guido of Arezzo. Then I came to the 'Madonna dell' Orchestra' by Boccati, whose real name was Giovanni di Piermatteo. He pictures the Virgin as a prim little maid listening with clasped hands to an angel band of children as young as herself. They stand upon the balustrade on each side of her throne. One plays a mandolin, another a harp, a third clashes cymbals, a fourth blows an odd-looking pipe, and a fifth has a curiously shaped violin tucked under her chin. They are singing as they play, some with wide open mouths, while on either side of the throne sit two fat cherub performers, one playing what looks like a toy organ and the other, his fat arms tucked into his body, taps a xylophone. And while I admired this heavenly concert, I became aware of something sinister and essentially Perugian. I saw four Flagellant donors being led to the Madonna by S. Francis and S. Dominic. All four held lashes, two were hooded with that peculiar pointed cowl with slits for eyes which, originating in Perugia, was adopted by the Inquisition, and is still to be seen in Italy and Spain among the Confraternities of Mercy. There were other pictures which showed the same strange, distressing penitents. Some held lashes and had a space cut out of their gowns at the back to reveal their bleeding flesh.

It is said that this morbid epidemic, certainly one of the strangest ever known in Europe, began in Perugia in 1265. A young monk much given to flagellation had a vision in which saints joined him in his penance and, as they whipped themselves before the high altar, they told him that it was God's will that mankind should expiate its sins in this way. He confessed his vision to the bishop, who preached about it. The idea appeared to offer a remedy for the agony of the times. Men's minds were deranged by the disorder of the age: the murders, the wars, the plagues, and the strife between Pope and Emperor, all of which seemed to prove that the devil was in control. The bishop's words satisfied a desire to propitiate God. It became widely held that to punish the body with lashes drove out sin and pleased God; indeed a regular tariff of redemption had been drawn up, so many lashes, so much remission of sin.

Soon the groans of the Flagellants sounded on the mountain-top and descended to the Umbrian plain, as bands of penitents, stripped to the waist, visited neighbouring towns and exhorted others to follow their example. The emotional epidemic spread like a fire all over Italy. Whole towns closed down for thirty-four days – the age of our Lord – while their Flagellants took to the road on a penitential pilgrimage. The idea spread in France, Germany, Hungary, and Poland, and soon half Europe was whipping itself. The Flagellants were at first led by priests and crosses, then, as the movement degenerated and was joined by rogues and harlots, the Church realized that it was basically heretical in that it replaced the sacraments and penances of the Church by private penance. The cities closed their gates, Milan erected eighty gallows as a warning to the blood-stained processions, but it was not until the Pope had condemned the movement that it was put down with the aid of prisons and the stake. It broke out again, however, after the Black Death.

There was nothing new or original about it: all religions in all times have known flagellation, and it is still practised every year in Iraq, as anyone knows who has seen the Shia pilgrims whip themselves through Baghdad. That gruesome spectacle is seen at night when thousands of fanatics, eight or ten abreast, advance in torchlight to a series of grunts and groans as the lashes rise rhythmically above their bleeding backs. It is the same sight which Europe witnessed in the thirteenth century.

One is apt to judge a movement in its decline and degeneration, but I found myself thinking, as I saw the masked penitents among the Virgins and the angels, that, horrible as they became, the Flagellants were at first an expression of man's pathetic longing to see the reign of Christ's peace and mercy upon earth.

I left the Gallery and walked over to the Fountain outside, with the intention of going into the Cathedral to see the Virgin's wedding ring: but, standing entranced by the sunlight on the old stone, the colour of new-baked crusty bread, I stood listening to the Fountain, which happened to be working that morning. Thinking still of the Flagellants and the later violence in the time of Perugino, it seemed to me that the Middle Ages, untamed in Italy by kingship or chivalry, lingered in Perugia longer than anywhere else north of Rome.

Yet how easily swayed and impressionable those violent people were; how anxious to be good; how conscious – maybe the beginning of virtue – of their sins. I stood under the outside stone pulpit in which S. Bernardino preached. It is honey-gold and waist-high, and was entered by way of stairs inside the building and a little door in the wall. When S. Bernardino stepped into it, he looked down upon a scene made familiar by several pictures of the time: he saw people on their knees, men on one side, women on the other, divided by a wooden partition. And it was upon such an occasion that he faced the fierce yet contrite Perugini and, incredible as it sounds, persuaded them, not without great difficulty (*con pena grandissima*, he said), to give up their terrible *Battaglia de' Sassi*, the Battle of Stones. How well he knew human nature! Not content with having convinced them in the pulpit of the wickedness of their traditional sport, he insisted on the drawing up of a statute, and from that moment the game ceased.

I entered the Cathedral and was taken to the shrine of the Virgin's wedding ring; the ring itself is visible only three or four times a year. The stone, I was told, is a pale agate that changes colour according to the nature, or character, of the person who holds it. The care taken to guard it is a measure of Perugia's reverence. I was told that it lies in a leather case, locked by a golden key which is kept by the bishop. Fifteen iron and steel boxes, one within the other like a Chinese puzzle, each with its key, and all fifteen keys in the keeping of a different functionary, terminate in a heavy iron chest, studded with nails and banded with steel.

The history of the ring is peculiar. It was sold by a merchant in Jerusalem to a Marchioness of Tuscany in some remote age, and had been stolen from a church at Chiusi.

§ 4

In one of the transepts I was shown an urn which contains the remains of two popes who died in Perugia, Urban IV and Martin IV. It is believed that the first pope was poisoned and the second met what seems to have been an exclusively mediaeval doom, a surfeit of eels. The great Innocent III, the contemporary of S. Francis, also died at Perugia, but his remains were removed to Rome in the last century. The hazards of a papal visit to Perugia seem to have been considerable, since a fourth pope, Benedict XI, died there of poisoned figs, and reposes beneath a Gothic tomb in the church of S. Dominic.

Such a high papal death rate in a provincial city deserves an explanation. Perugia had been part of the Patrimony of S. Peter since the Dark Ages, but the Holy See never attempted to exert any control over it for centuries, doubtless feeling that such a nest of wild cats was better left alone. The first pope to cultivate Perugia was Innocent III, familiar in English history as the pontiff who excommunicated King John and placed England under an interdict. He approached his violent city cautiously, almost play-fully, presenting himself in the guise of *padrone,* as he put it; and he managed to carry it off.

Perugia found a pope irresistible as long as he appeared in person. Cardinals were regarded as victims to be intimidated and bullied, and, if necessary, killed: but the moment God's Vicar appeared before them, faction fights ceased and an unnatural calm descended upon the mountain. It is strange to think that when the anarchy of Rome became unendurable, many a mediaeval pope went to Perugia for peace and quiet! The scene of their rustication was the old Canonica near the cathedral. The cloisters are still visited by people who stroll through them with no idea what an interesting old place it is, and how many important events occurred there. Here were held four papal conclaves, which elected Honori-us III in 1124, Honorius IV in 1285, Celestine V in 1294, and Clement V in 1305.

In the times of Innocent III, and of his successor, Honorius III, the first Franciscans were living in their thatched huts at Assisi, and both popes knew S. Francis. It was Innocent III who authorized the new Order and experienced the celebrated dream in which he saw the Saint propping up the tottering columns of the Church. Though there is no record that the pontiffs, while at Perugia, ever visited S. Francis, it would have been contrary to human nature had they not done so; and how delightful it would be had we an account of such visits. One imagines the papal procession winding down the long road to the Umbrian plain and the meeting of the harassed high priest, weighed down by the complexity of the world's problems, with one who found life so simple.

Among the cardinals, however, was one who did visit S. Francis in his hut, a man who, we are told, loved to cast aside his princely garments and put on the rough robe of a Franciscan. This was Ugolini Conti, Cardinal-archbishop of Ostia, who, a year after the death of S. Francis, was elected pope as Gregory IX. He was a frequent visitor to Perugia and while there at the beginning of his reign, in the year 1228, he canonized S. Francis. It was also at Perugia that he had the vision, described in the *Fioretti,* which convinced him of the miracle of the Stigmata. 'Pope Gregory IX

577

had certain doubts about the wound in Saint Francis's side, as he later admitted. One night Saint Francis appeared to him, and raising his right arm a little, he showed him the wound in his side. And it seemed to the Pope that it was filled to the brim with blood mingled with water flowing from the wound; and from that moment all doubt vanished.'

The most extraordinary of all Conclaves was held in the Canonica in 1292. The cardinals had been travelling all over Italy for more than two years, unable to elect a pontiff, and they came at length to Perugia. A devout cardinal happened to mention a hermit named Pietro di Morrone who lived in the mountains and was famed for his sanctity. Forgetting that a good Christian may make an indifferent pope, the Conclave, in a moment of exasperation and despair, elected the hermit. When informed of this in his mountain fastness, the poor old man, who was eighty years old, tried to run away, but was captured, made a bishop, and dressed in pontifical vestments. For five months Celestine V lived a bewildered life in an artificial cell contrived for him in a palace, and was then mercifully allowed to abdicate.

A few years later, in 1304, Perugia was the scene of a famous papal story. When Benedict XI, the son of a shepherd in Treviso, in Venezia, was staying there, his old mother arrived, longing to see her son. The women of Perugia dressed the old peasant in the latest fashion, and so she was announced at the court. Benedict rather unkindly pretended not to recognize her, saying that his mother was a poor old woman and not a fashionable lady. She was whisked away to return in her own clothes, when he received her with the utmost tenderness. Poor Benedict was, however, fated never to leave Perugia. His brief reign of a year was terminated one day when a man said to have been disguised as a nun appeared with a silver dish full of superb figs, a gift from the Abbess of S. Petronilla. The Pope was as fond of figs as his predecessor Martin IV of eels, and the next morning he fell sick and died. Scholars have detected a number of possible assassins, but Philip IV of France would appear the most likely one.

At the Conclave that followed the death of Benedict, the French

Archbishop of Bordeaux was elected as Clement V. It is said that a secret arrangement existed between him and Philip; at any rate, immediately the election was over Clement invited the cardinals, most of whom were French, to follow him, not to Rome, but to France. And so in Perugia began the seventy-seven-year-long exile of the Papacy at Avignon.

The absence of the popes did not make the Perugian heart any fonder; in fact when the Papacy returned to Rome, Perugia became one of the most bellicose portions of the papal dominions. There is a record of at least one Renaissance pontiff cowering in a barricaded monastery as he listened to the fighting in the streets, then, during a lull, slipping away to Assisi. It was Paul III who decided to call Perugia to order; and I was interested to discover that I was sleeping every night above a notable relic of papal rule. The terrace on which my hotel was built was formed by the demolition of the great papal fortress, La Rocca Paolina, which the Pope built to subdue the city. There is not a sign of that mighty construction above ground, but a friend showed me a collection of engravings which prove it to have been one of the strongest fortresses in Italy, and a massive tribute to the pugnacity of the city it was built to overawe.

First the Pope sent a large army which destroyed the palaces of the Baglioni, together with four churches and four hundred houses, and upon this demolished quarter of the city rose the great fortress. Its guns commanded not only the plain and the road to Rome, but also the Corso and the chief buildings of Perugia. Probably no building in Italy roused greater hatred. For more than three centuries it symbolized the subjection of the proud city, and the moment the Perugini could do so – during Italy's fight for independence in the last century – they blew it up and hacked it to pieces. Anthony Trollope was in Perugia just before the fortress was demolished, and again a year or two later while it was still being destroyed. On his first visit he described how he toured the underground tunnels and dungeons, and on his second visit how he watched the enthusiastic townsfolk pulling the place to pieces. He was particularly struck by an old gentleman with a long white beard who sat happily every day watching the proceedings and, asking who he was, was told that he had been a papal prisoner for many years.

The most unusual experience that befell me in Perugia was to be taken by a town engineer on a tour of a series of streets which had once formed part of the fortress, and are now underground. The entrance is an Etruscan gateway that had been incorporated in the walls of the fortress, the Porta Marzia. This gate is kept locked. Whoever had built it in Etruscan times had the idea of reproducing above the arch a terrace divided into five compartments in which five life-sized human figures, now much battered and eroded, are leaning. For some reason the modern inhabitants tell you that they represent an Etruscan, or Roman, family which had died from eating poisoned mushrooms. Perhaps this obsession with poison is natural in a city that once specialized in the notorious *Aquetta*.

We passed under the arch and entered a mediaeval Pompeii. Before us stretched narrow lanes and archways, a ruined church, and houses of three storeys, with gaunt windows, last inhabited four centuries ago. No footfall broke the silence. It was as I imagine a mediaeval city must have appeared during a visitation of the plague.

'We sometimes have dances down here,' said my guide, unconscious, as the young so often are, that he was being macabre: a dance of death would have been appropriate, I thought, as we plunged deeper into streets which wore the ghostly air of subterranean places that had once been open to the sunlight. Had we put to flight a coven of witches in the act of brewing *Aquetta*, I should have thought it quite appropriate.

§ 5

The old church of S. Pietro was built a thousand years ago on the edge of the mountain. I have never seen a more decorated church; every inch is covered with fresco and, as if this were not sufficient, it is full of framed pictures. The people of Perugia have a specially warm place in their hearts for S. Pietro, since the monks who were in residence a hundred years ago, during the final phases of Perugia's resistance to the Holy See, took the side of the citizens. When Perugia had the unusual distinction of being sacked by the Pope's Swiss Guard, certain patriots took refuge in the church. The guide told me how the good monks secretly cut down their bell ropes and lowered the wanted men to the rocks below.

While we were talking, a group that always delights me entered the building: an old priest with a party of rustic parishioners. They had come from some place forty miles away. The villagers were wearing their best clothes, and several of the old women wore dresses of a cut which had been in fashion long ago. It was a group of a kind that no one will see in ten years' time, a little fragment of another world. The priest was persuaded to sit in the organist's seat, and one of the old women timidly suggested that he should play the instrument. He shook his head severely, then, to lighten the rebuke, playfully touched one of the keys. A silvery note of unusual beauty trembled in the air. The priest was as surprised as his flock, and, as they stood rapt and expectant, he touched one or two more notes which went gambolling round the building like cherubs at play. Greatly daring, the old man now struck a chord which filled the church with celestial harmony, then, very gingerly he ventured into a simple voluntary. His flock stood watching, forming a group that would have delighted any painter; indeed it almost seemed as if one of the frescoes had left the walls and had come down into the nave. The attention of the old people, and their pride and wonder, could not have been exceeded had they discovered the form of S. Cecilia in the organ loft, guiding the plump fingers of their old shepherd.

The spell was broken by the guide who, determined that no one should miss any of the pictures, opened a door in the choir to admit more light. Through this I looked across a burning afternoon to Assisi and beyond to Spello. The hills stood drenched in sunlight, crested with their towns and castles. Here again was the background of Umbria which painters like Perugino placed behind their Virgins. The guide droned on, demanding that we should admire this or that painting, unaware that he had offered us a picture finer than any in the church.

.   .   .   .   .

One morning I was taken to have coffee in a brightly frescoed bar in the basement of a palace which houses the *Universita Italiana per Stranieri,* which is now nearly forty years of age. It has in that time attracted something like thirty thousand students from ninety-three nations, Germany, the United States, France, Japan, and England providing the greatest number, more or less in that order.

The bar was crowded with pleasant young people from many countries who offered, I thought, a happier picture of united nations than the one more familiar to us. The students learn Italian and devote themselves to Italian history, philosophy, literature, and archaeology, and are awarded diplomas and certificates. They can live extremely cheaply in a hostel, or as expensively as they like in lodgings or hotels. The atmosphere was that of a pleasant holiday school, and I thought the young people were having a wonderful introduction to Italy.

I met a young man from London and another from Stratford on Avon. The University has attracted about three thousand English students to Perugia since it was founded. Though no one I met appeared to be more than twenty-five, I was told there is no age limit. I was shown a flight of marble stairs on which the oldest student, from Germany, had just stumbled.

'How old is he?' I asked.

'Eighty,' I was told.

This pleased me: it linked Perugia with the Rome of the eighteenth century where, as Peter Beckford said in 1788, he knew 'an old Irish boy turned of eighty' who had gone there to 'finish his education'.

§ 6

Readers of the *Fioretti* will remember that the wicked wolf which was converted by S. Francis was a native of Gubbio. The town is twenty miles north of Perugia as the crow flies, but the windings of the road must make it more like forty miles. They tell you in Umbria that Gubbio was one of the first five towns founded after the Flood.

Hearing that I was going there, a young man, whom I had met casually, asked for a lift part of the way as he was going to one of the hill villages. I found him an amusing companion as he told me stories of the isolated mountain people with whom he had become friendly when he was working with the Partisans during the war. He had a sharp eye for the oddities of human character and, pointing to a remote mountain on which we could just discern a cluster of buildings, said that it was the home of a curious religious sect called the Biribini. It appeared that a peasant from the mountain, when on military service near the Austrian frontier, happened to meet an American Quaker. Becoming converted, he returned home announcing that he was a 'Quakere' and anxious to make converts. The doctrines of Quakerism had, however, suffered a strange change in him, and he led his fellow villagers into a thinly disguised paganism, which included mixed bathing in mountain streams at midnight. It is curious, remarked my companion, that Pan and the old gods are still lurking about the mountains, ready to catch anyone who strays from the fold. The village priest is reputed to have said of the sect, 'Well, live, and let live! Some of them are better than my flock, who go around stealing hens and uttering atrocious curses!'

Every hill held its castle or its church; the slopes were grey with olives and outside each farm stood a cone of hay where the golden hair of the perpendicular fields was coiled round a long pole. There was not a building, a stream, a tree, an odd-looking hillock, or a strangely-shaped field that was not the scene of some story. The moment the illiterate peasant leaves his cottage, he steps into a library of fiction for which a weekly newspaper seems a poor substitute. I asked my companion about a ruin on one of the hills. It was a Byzantine watch tower, he replied, and part of a chain of signal stations between Ravenna and Rome. He said it used to take a day for a message to reach Rome in that way, semaphore by day and firelight at night.

I left him on the roadside, and went on through the enchanted land. When I came to Gubbio, I saw the old town climbing the lower slopes of a hill, backed by an immense mountain on which there was a church. Just before the road mounts to the town, I came to the ruins of a small Roman theatre, its semi-circle of seats complete, and cushioned in soft turf. I sat on one and looked up at the iron-grey old town whose buildings rise on ledges or terraces. I could see narrow lanes winding between stone walls to a large turreted castle erected on arches, but it proved to be, not a castle, but the Palace of the Consuls, which was the grand name given to the seat of government in the Middle Ages. Like so many Umbrian towns, Gubbio was always a town of soldiers. I was soon to hear that a thousand men of Gubbio went on the First Crusade, and a rake and three lilies on the arms of the town were, I was told, the insignia of Godfrey de Bouillon. These memories are still fresh in Gubbio, and the names of Bohemund and Tancred are often mentioned in the *stornelli* of the mountain poets. They also say that when Don John of Austria took command of the papal fleet before Lepanto and found that so many of his officers and men came from Gubbio, he exclaimed, 'What then is this Gubbio? Is she greater than Naples or Milan, or what is she?' Bearing such things in mind, it seems appropriate that the first object that catches the eye as one enters is a memorial to the Forty Martyrs of the Resistance, forty men of Gubbio who were executed during the last war.

Ox-carts mingle with motor-cars in the busy square at the foot of the hill, but as I climbed into the old town I found myself in silence. Massive houses of five or six storeys are now tenements, and I was amused to watch women leaning from the top windows with ropes in their hands, pulling up their groceries in buckets. There are wonderful old churches in Gubbio for those with strong leg muscles, but the finest sight is the terrace built upon arches, a magnificent piece of mediaeval engineering, upon which stands the noble and elegant Palazzo dei Consoli. From its windows and balconies one can imagine the consuls and the bishop of the day saying farewell to the brave lads off to the Crusades; and that the mind of Gubbio still loves to linger on far-off things I saw for myself when some men entered the piazza and began to erect what I took to be a loom or some primitive musical instrument. It was a cross-bow to be used in a contest with the cross-bowmen of Sansepolcro! Inside the palazzo is a vast mediaeval hall large enough, it seemed, to contain London's Guildhall several times; upstairs the consuls transacted their business and could walk out on a delicious loggia with a view downward to the Roman theatre and the plain. Under the roof-tiles, as in Venice, were the prisons – the opposite of dungeons.

I was shown Gubbio's great possession, the famous Eugubine Tables, which are seven bronze plates inscribed about two hundred years before Christ and intended to be bolted to a temple wall. They gave the priests in the minutest detail the correct liturgical movements in various forms of augury, including that of bird flight. If the priest moved in the slightest degree, or stood in the wrong attitude, the whole prognostication was cancelled and had to be done all over again. As an enthusiastic bird-feeder myself, I was anxious to find out if the Tablets had hints about omens, but the guide was unable to satisfy my curiosity.

An even greater treasure is the body of S. Ubaldo, the bishop and patron saint, who died in 1160. He lies in the church on the top of the mountain. An hour's walk past crumbling walls, lines of cypress trees and hill farms, with the view becoming grander at every bend, brought me to quite a large church and a monastery. There was not a soul about, but the church was open. Facing me, as I entered, was a glass coffin: inside, wearing a gold mitre, was the body of the saint, with an electric light shining on his brown face.

A monk, hearing someone moving about, entered and gave me a brief history of S. Ubaldo. He also told me that the saint had a French manservant who came from a town called Thann in the Vosges Mountains, who, after his master's death, cut off three of his fingers. He returned with the precious relics to his native town, where a beautiful church was built to enshrine them. And, continued the monk, representatives of the town of Thann travel to Gubbio every year to attend the *Festa dei Ceri*, held on the anniversary of the saint's death.

We entered an adjoining room, or hall, where three unusual objects were lying side by side on the floor, the famous *ceri* of Gubbio. A *cero* is a candle, but these *ceri* do not look in the least like candles. They are not easy to describe. They are about thirty feet long, heavy, and made of wood covered with painted canvas; in shape they reminded me of gigantic Christmas crackers. Once a year they are taken down from the mountain, bolted to wooden stands with shafts on them, and shouldered about the town and up the mountain by relays of sweating men. Each *cero* has its patron saint whose statue is fixed on top during the *festa*: S. Ubaldo, S. George, and S. Anthony.

'You must see the *festa*,' said the monk, 'there is nothing else like it in Italy.'*

'What is its origin?' I asked.

He hunched his shoulders and spread his hands; and I knew that he was going to say, '*Chi lo sa?*'

A pleasant memory of Gubbio is the little chapel which commemorates the meeting of S. Francis with the wolf of Gubbio. It is in a country lane near a railway crossing, on the flat land just outside the town. The chapel was locked, but seeing a woman sewing in a garden with a black and white cat on her lap, I asked her if she knew where the key was; and she had it in the pocket of her apron. Going inside, I saw near the altar a picture of Brother Wolf giving his paw to S. Francis. The woman told me that there was another church, in Gubbio itself, which is built on the site of the grotto where Brother Wolf lived after his conversion; but I must have misunderstood her direction, for I never found it.

§ 7

Assisi is only about fifteen miles from Perugia, down the long mountain road and across the lovely valley of the Tiber. I had been watching the sun rise over it for some time, and now I decided to go and find out for myself if, as I had been told by some who have lived there, it has its own special air of peace and graciousness. I went all the more willingly as that morning the daily newspaper reflected more than the world's normal amount of hatred.

The most interesting spot on the way, in unlikely juxtaposition with a railway crossing, is a famous Etruscan sepulchre, the Tomb of the Volumnii. Surely one of the many extraordinary things

* See Appendix, p. 611.

about that inscrutable race is the way they crept to rest under cornfields and in all kinds of ordinary places, as if they were hibernating dormice. Nowadays the entrance to an Etruscan tomb is often a hut like a gardener's tool-shed in the centre of a field of maize; and this tomb, a few yards from a railway crossing, had the usual unexpected quality. It was discovered over a century ago, when an ox that was being driven across the field vanished and was found uninjured, having crashed into the vestibule. This was the tomb that inspired George Denny to study the Etruscans. That great enthusiast could not always conceal beneath Victorian prose the whoop of joy with which he greeted each new discovery. He thought this tomb 'like enchantment'; it was 'the realization of the picture of subterranean palace and spell-bound men, which youthful fancy had drawn from the Arabian Nights'.

I descended several massive steps into a chamber cut in the volcanic rock. Although it was a hot day, the place was chilly and smelt of dust and death and, for me, lacked the 'enchantment' it had for Denny. It was a family vault in which the Volumnii reposed in urns and sarcophagi, a gathering presided over by the head of the family, whose name was Aruns. Like most wealthy Etruscans, Aruns wished to enter the next world in evening clothes and in a party mood, at least that is the impression conveyed by Etruscan tomb sculpture, which shows the deceased in festal attire, reclining on a banqueting couch. Aruns is shown actually eating something from the melon-shaped bowl which he holds so gracefully, and with the air of an accomplished diner-out, in his left hand.

On each side of him are two winged angels, which anyone at a first glance might take for an early work by Michelangelo. How, I asked myself, did two Christian angels get into an Etruscan tomb? Then I saw that there were snakes in their hair, and it dawned on me that these were not angels but two of the Furies, the awful goddesses usually seen with fang-like teeth and wings, which symbolized the swiftness of their vengeance. But here they appeared noble, benevolent, and protective; and I remembered that it was such bad luck to mention their real names that men called them the Kindly Ones and even deflected them, as I saw now, in sculpture. No wonder Aruns looks so composed and confident with two such escorts: two placated Furies who seem to promise that they will look after him wherever he has gone.

I crossed the Tiber, which flows here over a chalky white bed and is now a vigorous stream, and soon I saw Mount Subasio ahead, the pretty town of Assisi encircling a lower spur. On its outskirts, built on arches like a church erected on an aqueduct, is the basilica and monastery of S. Francis.

Crowds of tourists were flocking to the basilica, and I thought I would postpone my visit until I had seen something of Assisi. I told myself that, in any event, I would rather see some of the places where S. Francis had lived before I saw his tomb. So I passed on to Assisi, smiling to think that I was repeating the reprehensible conduct, but not from the same motives, of the only recorded traveller who had done the same thing. This was Goethe, who confessed without shame that he passed the Church of S. Francis 'with aversion' and hurried on into Assisi to admire the Temple of Minerva in the piazza. Those who have criticized him perhaps forget that he was a man of the eighteenth century and the temple was the first intact memorial of the classical world he had so far seen.

I thought Assisi an endearing and lovely little town, rising in a series of shelves or terraces on the mountainside, like Gubbio. Some of the buildings, which rose straight from the street, with arched doorways, looked old enough to have been there in the days of S. Francis, though that is hardly possible. Many a street was too narrow for traffic, and some were not even lanes, but winding flights of steps. Flowers enlivened the town on every side. They grew in window-boxes and in pots, they cascaded from balconies and hung in festoons from ancient walls and archways, giving an air of Franciscan gaiety to Assisi, and reminding visitors that they had come to the town of the poet and mystic whose life has been told in the *Fioretti*.

When I came to the busy little piazza, I understood Goethe's enthusiasm for the Temple of Minerva and its six exquisite fluted columns, a temple clearly of the Augustan period. It stands in line with the other buildings in the street, in neighbourly contact with the *Torre Comunale,* as if it might be the office of some splendid bank. This was a sight that was familiar to S. Francis all his life, as a gay young man of Assisi, as a reviled beggar and, at last, as a revered saint. The worn old steps now lead to a church, and three small boys sat on them, feeding a flock of rapacious pigeons which perched on their shoulders and fluttered round their heads.

Next to the temple is a small museum which admitted me to an entirely unexpected scene, indeed I believe it was one of the most surprising experiences I had known in Italy. Some steps led down beneath the piazza of Assisi to the pavement of its predecessor, the forum of Asisium. The relationship between forum and piazza is something one takes for granted in many an Italian town, but to be able to walk about a forum under a piazza is quite extraordinary. In this dark and chilly underworld, lit by electric light, I walked on Roman pavements and noted an open gutter that carried off the rains nineteen centuries ago. The huge blocks of travertine beneath my feet were scored and chipped by the traffic and the chariots of a dead world, and I found an impressive flight of steps which are the lower steps of the Temple of Minerva, now concealed from those who walk in the sunlight above. In Roman times this temple stood half as high again above the forum as it now does above the piazza. In front of it, probably somewhere near the centre of the modern roadway above, I came to the base of a statue of Castor and Pollux which once stood in the centre of the forum. The twins have vanished, but an inscription remains which says that a banquet was held in Asisium to celebrate the dedication of this monument. Exploring this phantom world, I found that farther on, probably beneath the shops on the far side of the piazza, where you can buy films and postcards, was the tribune of the Roman town, flanked by two small temples, one to Jupiter, the other to Esculapius. I came up into the daylight dazzled by my discovery in more ways than one. If only Goethe could have seen this. . . .

The hotel was a Tower of Babel. I shared a table with two middle-aged English women who had come over from Perugia in the 'bus. They talked a lot about 'dear Saint Francis' and his love of animals. It is not unusual in England to hear people speak of S. Francis as if he were an honorary Englishman and a noted president of the R.S.P.C.A.; and, indeed, it is pleasant to think that the Saint himself would have had nothing but approval for those homes where Sister Cat and Brother Dog are always to be found in the best chairs. Yet what an odd English delusion it is that all other nations are unkind to animals! After lunch, my companions hurried off to visit the wood where S. Francis sang his duet with the nightingale.

§ 8

When you stand on the hill at Assisi and look down on the Vale of Spoleto, you see the river Chiascio flowing in a series of silver loops to join the Tiber. The level farmland is broken about a mile off by the dome of a huge church. This is S. Mary of the Angels, where the real life of S. Francis began and where he died. It is now a gigantic and flamboyant building with a more than life-sized gold Madonna above the portico, but it was once a little woodland oratory where in remote ages some pilgrims or hermits from the Holy Land deposited a fragment of the tomb of the Virgin. One day angelic voices were heard singing in the woods, and the oratory became known as S. Mary of the Angels.

The church is gaunt and enormous and at first I did not see its peculiar feature: beneath the dome stands the tiny oratory of S. Mary, which once stood in the wood. The huge church was built to enclose and preserve the precious little building where S. Francis set out on his search for Reality, where his disciples joined him, and where, at the age of forty-five, he gave back his spirit to the God whose splendour he had seen everywhere around him. Piety has, of course, disguised the outside of the shrine, but inside the walls are still of rough stone and the building, which could hold perhaps twenty or thirty people, looks much as it must have done in the time of S. Francis.

The saint's father was a rich cloth merchant who used to visit the French fairs, and his interest in France explains why he named the son, whom he hoped would carry on the business, Francesco.

It is also claimed that his baptismal name was John, and that he was called Francesco because he loved to sing French songs and to speak French. It seems to me astonishing that we know so much about a man who was born in 1181 or 1182 and who died in 1226. He was born when Richard I, the Lionheart, was reigning in England; he was thirty-five when Magna Carta was sealed, and he died in the reign of Henry III. Among his contemporaries were Saladin and Genghiz Khan. Yet we know more about S. Francis than about many a modern man because those who had worked with him were encouraged to write their recollections after his death; and these accounts have survived.

When he was twenty, Francis fought against Perugia and spent a year as a prisoner of war. Upon his release he is said to have become the leader of the gay young men of Assisi, though one fancies that gaiety in that little town must always have been rather limited. Before he was twenty-five he began to experience the self-hatred and dissatisfaction with life which are the mystic's first step along the road to Illumination. A psychic transformation occurred. In the agony known to mystics as 'the Dark Night' he turned his back on life, left his family, even stripped himself of the clothes his father had given him, and went off to lead the life of a hermit and a beggar. His old friends laughed at him and called him mad. To the man of the world, a saint always appears mad, just as to those of the spirit, worldly values seem insane. What is believed to be Reality to the one is not so to the other. In his conquest of self, Francis, like other saints, forced himself to do many things he once hated. This reversal of character is chiefly responsible for the charge of madness so often brought against the elect. It is natural that this should be so. If a man suddenly begins to court those whom he detests, to eat everything he dislikes and generally to behave in a way opposite to that of his nature, he would be at once suspected of insanity. This was always happening to the saints as they put off the 'old man' and put on 'the new'. Some of the things saints have done to conquer themselves, and notably sensitive women like S. Catherine of Siena and S. Catherine of Genoa, make one feel sick; compared with them, the means taken by S. Francis to correct his loathing for leprosy – the kissing of lepers, eating with them, and the care of them – are almost pleasant.

Of all who have answered the call of Christ ('sell that thou hast and give to the poor, and thou shalt have treasure in heaven: and come and follow me.'), S. Francis was the most literal, the most ardent, and the most successful. Poverty is the mystic's key to spiritual wealth, indeed S. Francis was so aware of this that he once threw away his belt-buckle, considering it too grand a thing to own, and used a piece of rope. Could he have found something commoner and cheaper than rope he would have used that. His magnetism was great even when he was flexing his spiritual muscles and he soon drew disciples to himself. The first was a rich and noble friend, Bernard of Quintavalle, who sold all he had and gave it away and went to join Francis in the leper colony; the second was another well-known man, Peter Cataneo, a canon of the cathedral.

In spite of his physical frailty and a diet of scraps, S. Francis had enormous vitality. He tramped everywhere on foot, sometimes singing with joy and playing an imaginary fiddle, and preaching in three or four different towns or villages in one day. What exhausting miles he must have covered; and to this day the Umbrian version of 'Shanks's mare' is *Il cavallo di San Francesco*.

When he had twelve disciples, S. Francis went to Rome and received from Innocent III authority for his Rule. Francis himself was never a priest and consequently never said a Mass or heard a confession, and all his first twelve followers, save one, were laymen. The dress they chose was the costume of the humblest labourer of the time, a coarse gown of the cheapest grey material. In later centuries the Franciscans adopted the brown colour that is familiar today, though Franciscan cardinals and bishops still wear the original grey, as does the Father Custos in Jerusalem, the only grey Franciscan among the brown-habited guardians of the Holy Places. The grey habit is also remembered in the name of Grey Friars in London, where the Franciscans arrived two years before the death of their founder.

As one stands in the little stone building under the dome of S. Mary of the Angels it is not difficult to imagine the life that went on in the woodland clearing seven and a half centuries ago. The Benedictines who owned the chapel and the ground, which they called the Porziuncola – the 'little portion' – gave it to Francis and his followers to be their mother-house. On each side of the chapel, in two lines facing each other, the brothers built themselves rough wattle huts thatched with straw. Their routine was simply to go out into the highways and by-ways and preach the Gospel.

They had been settled in the Porziuncola a short time when Clare, the beautiful eighteen-year-old daughter of a nobleman, a girl who had been converted by S. Francis and longed only for the life of the spirit, fled from her father's castle and arrived late at night at the clearing in the woods. S. Francis himself cut off her hair while she stepped from her fine dress and accepted the rough Franciscan habit and took the vow of Poverty. I often thought of her when I went to the Porziuncola, and of the strange scene on the Monday following Palm Sunday in 1212, when the friars came out with torches to light her through the wood. Midnight was long past when S. Francis and the girl crossed the plain to the Benedictine nuns at Bastia Umbra, where she lived until the first convent of Poor Clares was founded, of which she was the superior. It was in the garden of her convent that S. Francis wrote his *Canticle of the Sun*, with which Italian poetry begins. What song did he sing, I wonder, as he walked back to the wood that early morning; and – was Clare's long hair still lying in front of the stone altar with her dress and her jewels?

It is an historical fact that within seven years the twelve disciples had grown to five thousand Franciscan brothers, who arrived at the Porziuncola from all parts of Italy to attend the first Chapter of the Order. The pavement of the great church today probably only partially covers the site of the encampment grouped round the chapel, where the visiting friars built themselves shelters of straw and leaves. Of course S. Francis had made no preparations of any kind, but the delighted townsfolk of Assisi flocked down to the plain with food and fed the visitors until they departed as if they were a flock of precious migrant birds. It is said that among the interested spectators were two guests, S. Dominic and Cardinal Ugolini Conti, a great friend and supporter of S. Francis, who became Pope Gregory IX. This was the occasion when the future pope is said to have removed his scarlet and to have replaced it with the rough grey habit.

Soon after, in all the towns and villages of Europe people became aware of poor men in grey who were speaking urgently and movingly of God, and the friars even invaded the Moslem East. At that moment, the year 1219, S. Francis himself stepped into secular history in the most extraordinary way: he arrived in Egypt to convert the Sultan, al-Malik al-Kamil, when the Crusaders were besieging Damietta. Of all the situations in which we are able to visualize S. Francis – tramping the roads of Umbria, preaching to the birds, tending hares and fish, praying on La Verna – surely this is the most fantastic, as the siege engines battered the Moslem walls and the Greek fire came hissing down to the screams and curses of the armies. 'He had come to the East,' writes Steven Runciman, 'believing, as many other good and unwise persons before and after him have believed, that a peace-mission can bring about peace.' Nevertheless, incredible to relate, he received permission to see the Sultan and was sent to the enemy lines under a flag of truce. After a moment of suspicion, it was 'soon decided that anyone so simple, so gentle, and so dirty must be mad', and he was treated 'with the respect due to a man who had been touched by God'.

There was a story that the Sultan had placed a carpet decorated with crosses in front of his divan. 'If he treads on the cross I will accuse him of insulting his God,' he said; 'if he refuses to walk on it, I will accuse him of insulting me.' As S. Francis walked straight on the carpet, the Sultan taunted him, and S. Francis replied: 'You should know that our Lord died between two thieves. We Christians have the true cross; the crosses of the thieves we have left to you; and these I am not ashamed to tread upon.'

The Sultan was charmed with the Saint's simplicity and sincerity, and, after listening to him with the respect and courtesy which all cultured Moslems give to a holy man, sent him safely back to the crusading army; and so ended one of the most remarkable encounters in history. The incident is elaborated in the *Little Flowers of S. Francis*, but there is one story often omitted in some versions from prudish reasons, which seems to me typically and beautifully Franciscan. It is that in the course of his wanderings in Egypt the Saint came to an inn in which there was a woman 'who was outwardly very beautiful but inwardly corrupt, and this wretched creature tempted him to sin'. L. Sherley-Price gave the story in his translation in the Penguin Classics.

'Saint Francis said, "I am willing; let us go to bed." And she led him to her room. Then Saint Francis said, "Come with me", and he led her to a hot fire that was burning in the room, and in fervour of spirit he stripped himself naked and lay down before the fire on the hot hearth. And he invited her to come and strip and lie down with him on this soft and beautiful bed. And when Saint Francis had remained there a long time with a cheerful face, and was neither burned nor scorched, the woman was frightened and pricked in conscience by such a miracle; and not only did she repent of her sinfulness and wicked intention, but was fully converted to the Faith of Christ. And she attained such holiness that many souls found salvation through her example in that country.'

The story seems to me entirely in character, first with the Crusades, when every inn was filled with prostitutes, and again with S. Francis, who acted with his usual disconcerting simplicity, and at the same time saw good shining beneath evil.

The wonderful animal stories which express the Saint's vision of God in every created thing have perhaps obscured, in popular accounts of him, the spiritual battle towards the Ultimate which led to the ecstasy on La Verna and the Stigmata. After the blinding vision, his sight failed and in two years he died. In his last years he knew that his twelve disciples had grown into an international movement, but worldly success was the last thing he ever wanted: his whole life had been a flight from the world to eternal values. In this crisis he abdicated and handed over to others. 'Lord,' he said in his resignation, 'I give Thee back this family which Thou didst entrust to me. Thou knowest, most sweet Jesus, that I have no more the power and the qualities to continue to take care of it. I entrust it therefore to the ministers.'

His blindness increased and he had to be led about. Some days before his death the brothers carried him down from Assisi to S. Mary of the Angels and placed him in the infirmary, a few paces from the chapel. The place is now the ornate *Cappella del Transito* at the entrance to the chancel. In the whole course of his life he had never asked for any material thing, but now, as Sister Death was waiting, he made a touching request. He wrote to a friend in Rome, Madonna Giacomo dei Settesoli, telling her that he was dying, and asking her to come to him, bringing his shroud, wax for candles and some of the little almond cakes – *mostaccioli* – which she had once given him when he was ill in Rome. She hurried to Assisi and saw him before he died. His last hours were spent on the bare earth, praising God, his face radiant with happiness. His life had been so short that many of his original disciples, including his first convert, Bernard of Quintavalle, were with him at the end. He asked them to sing his *Canticle of the Sun* and he joined in when he was able. So died S. Francis at the age of forty-five, the only human being who had relived the life of Christ.

Visitors are shown the garden which grew thornless roses after S. Francis had flung himself among the thorns to subdue Brother Ass, as he called his body, but most people are more interested in a statue of the Saint in the cloisters in whose hands a pair of living white doves have been persuaded to nest.

§ 9

The eastern gate of Assisi, the Porta Nuova, leads down through olive groves to the old church of S. Damiano. At the outset of his spiritual quest, S. Francis went there to pray one day and heard Christ speak to him from a crucifix, saying, 'Go, Francis, and repair my falling house.' In later years when S. Clare fled to him, and he was faced with the problem of female converts, S. Francis obtained the old church, then disused, as the first house of Poor Clares, and so it remained for forty years until the death of S. Clare. After this the nuns moved into the town to the present church of S. Clare.

A friar showed me over S. Damiano, which retains unaltered the original church in which the first Poor Clares worshipped more than seven centuries ago; and I have never seen, even in remote Coptic villages in Egypt, a more primitive Christian place of worship. The nuns were evidently too poor to employ a carpenter and their tiny choir with its rough oak boarding and clumsy old benches, and what looked to me like an old dove-cote turned into a lectern, is visible evidence of the first Franciscan rule of absolute Poverty. I realized that a nun renounced much more than a friar. He at least had the open air and the freedom of the world, while the Poor Clares were immured in what, to a worldly eye, appear depressing and squalid surroundings.

The friar told me that the crucifix which spoke to S. Francis is now to be seen in the church of S. Clare in the town, and I walked back through the olives and the mulberry trees and, passing through the gate, soon came to a mediaeval building of striped stone. A small convent of Poor Clares is living there in strict seclusion. Leading from the nave is a chapel divided into two parts by one of the high metal grilles usual in convents. As I approached it, a curtain was drawn back and, facing me on the other side of the screen, stood a hooded figure, erect and immobile. She had the effect of some apparition, and a rather alarming one. When she spoke, it was to ask in a toneless voice my nationality and what language I would prefer to speak. Continuing in good English, the figure told the story of the crucifix which I could see beyond the grille: a large primitive wooden cross with the figure of Christ painted upon it in the Byzantine manner. Having finished, not giving me time to say 'thank you', the hooded nun silently stretched out a hand and swiftly drew the curtain back into place. I have heard of nuns who teach ballet or make gramophone records, but I could imagine nothing like that happening here: but then I may be wrong. How can one tell when listening to someone without a face? For all I know, the nun, in her own lonely sphere, may be the soul of Franciscan joyousness.

I descended into the crypt, and saw, lying in a coffin, the body of S. Clare, who had died over seven hundred years before. The books say her body is incorruptible. If this is incorruption, surely it should be hidden. Her face was black. She clasped a book in her mummified hands and held an imitation lily. I was horrified. Sister Death was not this macabre horror; and I hurried up the steps and out into the open air, appalled, not for the first time, by this gruesome preoccupation with holy bones.

Anyone who wishes to find the true Franciscan atmosphere should go to the lonely hermitage of the Carceri, which is an hour's arduous walk up the hill, but on a hot day, allowing for breathless pauses beside stone walls and in olive groves, it is much longer. The old monastery lies plastered like a swallow's nest upon the side of a gorge and is almost invisible among the trees. S. Bernadino gave it its present form but left intact the primitive cells and the chapel where S. Francis and his followers loved to retire and meditate.

A few Franciscans look after the hermitage and are glad to show you the bed of S. Francis, an uncomfortable shelf of rock, and the venerable oak, propped up like some incredible cripple, beneath whose branches it is said the Saint once stood. This would make it more than seven hundred years old, which seems a long life for an oak in a hot country. Still, it is a wonderful old tree, even if it is only the son or grandson of the original Brother Oak. The silence of the gorge was broken by the rarest sound in Italy, the song of birds. I was told that the hermitage is a bird sanctuary and that snares, traps and guns are not allowed anywhere near it. I remarked to the friar that the birds seemed aware of this as they hopped confidently about and flew fearlessly from tree to tree, knowing perhaps that no one was going to serve their poor little carcasses on a mound of polenta. He nodded his head and said I ought to hear the nightingales. They sing there now as they sang in the thirteenth century, and no doubt they are linked by a chain of nightingales' eggs with the birds S. Francis heard. Indeed, it was in this dense ravine that the Saint held his celebrated contest with the nightingale, each trying to outsing the other to the glory of God the whole night through, until S. Francis, weary and voiceless, admitted himself vanquished.

It is sometimes said that this is the place where S. Francis preached to the birds. However, the *Little Flowers* states explicitly that this occurred at Bevagna, which lies to the south, near Foligno. One day, intoxicated with God, the Saint ran into the fields crying, 'I would preach to my little brothers the birds,' and, as they gathered round, stretching their necks and regarding him with their beady eyes, he began, 'My little brethren birds, ye ought greatly to praise and love the Lord who created you, for He provides all that is necessary, giving you feathers for raiment and wings to fly with.' The birds listened reverently all through the sermon until he made the sign of the Cross, and gave them leave to fly away.

Birds attracted S. Francis as they have appealed to other mystics, and for obvious reasons: they inhabit the air and appear absolved from bondage to the earth. They have an outward resemblance to the angels, and the Holy Spirit has always been visualized as a dove. But S. Francis also loved birds for themselves and showed towards them as to all dumb creatures, an affectionate, half-humorous understanding and a respect for their dignity which is entirely modern, or at least different from the attitude of his superstitious contemporaries, who so often detected the devil in the shape of animals. This S. Francis never did, though he was living in a world where men saw a flight of crows as questing devils, and recognized the Evil One in a pig, a cat, a toad, a bat, or any creature which seemed to them to be behaving in a suspicious way.

Though the devil appeared to the first Franciscans disguised as Christ, he never appeared in the guise of a sparrow as he did to their great contemporary, S. Dominic. And one feels that no matter how suspicious the sparrow, or how fiendish its chirpings, S. Francis would have given it the benefit of the doubt. He must have been the least mediaeval-minded of men. It was not in his nature to believe that God would allow the animal creation to be used for purposes of evil; indeed we read that after suffering the assaults of devils on La Verna the birds came to console him.

Some such thoughts passed through my mind as I wandered along the forest paths in the gorge, listening to the chirpings and the pipings as the birds sang their fearless songs in praise of their little brother Francis. Here, if anywhere, I thought, a man who is far enough along the road might expect to meet the Saint standing in the sun shadows under the oak trees. He does not seem too far away.

Jokingly I selected a stone cell in the monastery and asked the friars to keep it for me. It looked straight into the bed of a dry torrent. One of the friars, an old man with a silver beard as fine and thin as silk, regarded me with uncomplicated blue eyes. 'You will come back?' he said solemnly. 'Yes, we will keep it for you. It could be arranged.' Suddenly my little joke had become serious and I wished I had not made it. Sadly, I shook hands and went away, knowing that I should never go there again.

§ 10

The time came when I thought I should do as most people do the moment they arrive in Assisi, visit the tomb of the Saint. Its story is a strange one. . . .

When S. Francis was carried down from Assisi to die, as he wished, in the Porziuncola, his followers asked for an armed guard to prevent the dying Saint from being captured by the Perugini. They were hovering like vultures in the hope that they might secure his body and bury it in their city. This was characteristic of the time. It was believed that piety justified the theft of a sacred relic, and that even a stolen saint reflected celestial benefits upon the town in which he was buried and revered.

The man who was determined that Perugia should not steal the body was the most interesting, though not the most saintly, of the original disciples, Brother Elias. He was about the same age as S. Francis and was the son of a mattress-maker of Bologna. He first appears in history as Elias Buonbarone, a schoolmaster of Assisi, and was sent by Francis to the Holy Land on a mission, and after the Saint's death took control of the Order. He has been reviled by some as a worldly and ambitious man; others have seen him as the S. Paul of Franciscanism, a man who realized that a world order cannot proceed in a condition of apostolic simplicity.

With Elias the sweet idyll of Franciscanism came to an end and entered what the world believes to be reality or one might say that an Order which S. Francis had wished to found on heaven was brought down to earth by his worldly-wise successor. At any rate, it is to Elias Buonbarone that the world owes the preservation of the body of S. Francis which, beyond all doubt, rests today in the sanctuary where Elias secretly buried it in the year 1230.

No sooner was the Saint dead than this remarkable man, with the approval and support of the Pope, drew up plans for the mighty church which stands today. The speed with which it was built under his direction and inspiration was one of the outstanding achievements of the Middle Ages. Two years after his death, S. Francis was canonized by his old friend and admirer, Pope Gregory IX, and at the same time, in the year 1228, the Pope laid the foundation stone of the great church. In another two years, on May 25, in 1230, two white oxen harnessed to a funeral car drew the body of S. Francis from the church of S. George in Assisi to the enormous crypt, or lower church, which was then ready to receive it. A great crowd had gathered, but immediately the body was inside, the doors were locked and barred by order of Elias. There were howls of rage from those who had come to see the burial, but Elias had made his plans and was determined to have no witnesses. S. Francis was buried deep in the rock in a tomb designed like that of a Pharaoh to defy the robber. In another nine years it seems the entire church was complete, even to the belfry, an astonishing achievement when one considers how many mediaeval cathedrals lingered on incomplete from generation to generation.

How well Elias had done his work was seen in succeeding centuries when repeated attempts were made, but in vain, to find the bones of the Saint. At length in modern times the Franciscans approached Pope Pius VII for permission to make a scientific search, and this was granted in 1818. The excavators worked for two months behind closed doors, pushing out tunnels beneath the altar in the crypt, before they came upon the tomb. It was in the depth of the rock just as Elias had sealed it in 1230. He had hidden it as if in the heart of a pyramid, making a tomb-chamber of heavy slabs of travertine which he had taken from the Roman wall near the Temple of Minerva. There, lost in the bowels of the earth, they found a limestone sarcophagus enclosed with an iron grating.

When the lid was lifted the bones of S. Francis were seen lying in dust, perhaps the disintegrated shroud which the Lady Giacomo da Settesoli had brought for him. Several silver coins had been slipped into the coffin, among them some of Lucca dated 1181 and 1208, also a red cornelian ring of the second century showing Pallas holding a Victory in her right hand. It was then announced to the world in a Papal brief that the body found under the basilica was that of S. Francis.

I followed a crowd into the church; many were there because it was a 'sight' that had to be seen, some were devout people who wished to kneel at the tomb of S. Francis, and others were aware that the church is one of the richest art galleries in Italy. Every inch of its walls is covered by the best artists of the thirteenth and four-teenth centuries, and you cannot open any illustrated book on Art without coming across reproductions of these frescoes.

Some of the more observant visitors were no doubt surprised to find the custodians of the church to be not the familiar brown-robed Franciscans, barefooted in sandals, but friars in black habits wearing well-polished black shoes. They are nevertheless Francis-cans, the Friars Minor Conventual, who at the command of the Popes, for this is a patriarchal basilica, have performed duties there and have conducted the services for centuries.

It is not often that one sees a great mediaeval sanctuary as it appeared to people centuries ago, every stone coloured and every wall surface decorated with paintings and frescoes. The effect is unusual to an English eye accustomed to the bleached dignity of an undecorated cathedral. Even the roof and the vaulting are coloured blue and scattered with golden stars, while on every hand are pictures designed to tell a story to those who could not read. This is one of the world's largest and most beautiful picture books;

and it is not always easy for the literate to imagine what it meant to the lively minds of the Middle Ages, and how it coloured thoughts and dreams.

The dark crypt is more impressive than the beautiful church above, and if it is true, as some say, that Elias himself designed these buildings, or was at least the man who inspired them, there is surely a symbolism in the purgatorial gloom of the crypt and the brilliance of the church above, or possibly that most earthly of Francis's followers remembered the caves and caverns in which the Saint prayed in his early days as he was struggling towards Illumination. That at least was the effect upon me; and the church is so designed that the proper way to see it is to begin in the darkness below and move upwards into the light.

Steps lead from the gloomy Lower Church to the even deeper darkness of the Saint's tomb, which stands in the centre of an impressive and austere crypt of rough undecorated stone. The limestone sarcophagus, in which the bones of S. Francis were found, may be seen exposed to view in a massive pier of rock above four altars, back to back, where visiting priests sometimes say Mass from early morning until noon. Several lamps burn in the crypt, and a special votive lamp hangs immediately in front of the sarcophagus. Every year the oil for the lamps is given by a different Region of Italy, and upon the morning of October 4, the day on which S. Francis died, the mayor of the Region's chief city fills the votive lamp, while branches of olive and laurel are placed on the altars.

Some may think it strange that his bones, which meant so little to S. Francis, should repose in one of the most impressive shrines in Italy: but that is not all. As one walks round the central tomb, one comes to four other tombs which one learns with amazement and a warm feeling of affection are those of four of the original disciples – Brother Leo, whom S. Francis called 'the little lamb of God', Brother Angelo, 'the gentle knight', and Brother Masseo who once, when they came to cross-roads, was made to spin round by S. Francis until he became dizzy, who then stopped him and selected the road the friar was facing. All three accompanied the Saint to La Verna and were with him when he received the

Stigmata. The fourth tomb is that of Brother Rufino, who was so holy that S. Francis sometimes called him 'Saint Rufino'.

It is almost certain that S. Francis would disapprove of his tomb, unless maybe the four beloved companions, who share it with him, could point out, and no man was ever more ready to listen, that earth-bound humanity needs such anchors for the mind; that to many the awakening of the spirit might well come in such a sepulchre in the same way that a crucifix once spoke to him in S. Damiano. It is sad to reflect that the feeling of peace and beauty which surrounds the tomb of S. Francis should, but does not, surround the tomb of Christ.

The best-known artistic treasures of the basilica are the twenty-eight frescoes in the Upper Church in which Giotto told the story of S. Francis. Some who have studied the subject believe that the artist began to paint them in the year 1296, when he was about twenty-nine years of age. Should this be so, the Saint had been dead for only seventy years.

One of the extraordinary aspects of the Franciscan epic is the speed with which S. Francis was canonized, the rapidity with which his sanctuary was erected, and the efficiency with which those in authority asked companions of the Saint to commit their recollections to writing. I am sure historians must wish that other events of the century had been documented with equal zeal. The first to order a life of S. Francis within a short time of his death, and while thousands were living who had known him, was Gregory IX, who asked Brother Thomas of Celano, who had joined the Order in 1215, to undertake the task. In 1244 the General of the Order sent round to all who had known S. Francis, asking them to write their recollections and send them to him at Assisi; and among those who did so were many of the original disciples. In 1260 S. Bonaventura, then General of the Order, who had all this material to work on, wrote what was then the official life; and this was Giotto's guide book. His frescoes are indeed illustrations to Bonaventura's *Legenda*.

It added greatly to my enjoyment to know how near the artist was to the events he pictured. It was as if a modern artist had painted happenings as near to us as the last years of the reign of Queen Victoria. There were men still alive – Giotto must have met them – who remembered Brother Elias, dead for only forty years, and though the original disciples had departed, a younger generation was living who had known them and had heard from their lips the story of the Franciscan idyll.

This near contemporary glimpse of the world of S. Francis is a precious thing, and what a brilliant, unusual world it was, the Italy of 1300. The frescoes show marble palaces with delightful balconies supported by columns, with charming *loggie* like little temples, and if many a window is still mediaeval and church-like, there are columned porticoes whose architraves are decorated with marble medallions as if already prepared to blossom into the Renaissance. Outside and inside, the buildings were decorated in the Cosmatic style with the elaborate geometrical mosaics made popular by masons who, searching the classical ruins for rare marbles, cut them into many-coloured cubes.

As pictured by Giotto, S. Francis is not the little man of mean appearance mentioned by one or two of his contemporaries: he is an attractive and well-built figure, as one would imagine he must have been. His first appearance was as a soldier fighting for his town, and before his conversion he wished to lead the life of a knight. It may be, of course, that Giotto was told to paint a hero, but I like to think that he may have been following a contemporary memory. Certainly the figure of S. Francis being honoured by the village idiot in front of the Temple of Minerva is that of a courtly young nobleman; while, again, he is a good-looking young friar, and certainly a muscular one, as he casually shoulders the tottering Lateran, while the Pope dreams in bed near by in full regalia, mitred and gloved. Giotto never deviated from the official life, and though the *Little Flowers of S. Francis* had not yet been compiled, there is nothing that would puzzle a modern reader of that book. I think Giotto may have had some difficulty with the Seraph in his picture of S. Francis receiving the Stigmata, and he imagined a really extraordinary object, and this he seems to have felt himself since in later years he created an improved Seraph when he painted the same scene in S. Croce, in Florence.

Of all the hundreds of pictures, the one that printed itself on my memory is Giotto's allegory in the Lower Church of the mystical marriage of S. Francis to Lady Poverty. Painted on an impossible concave vault above the altar, the artist seems to have been inspired by this theme, which is perhaps strange as Giotto detested poverty and saw nothing ennobling in it. Nevertheless he painted a scene one can never forget. Upon a rock stands a tall, slim woman dressed in a patched and tattered gown. Her feet are in thorns and she wears a wreath of brambles from which spring lilies and roses. Christ holds her right hand and joins it to that of S. Francis. On one side Hope holds a ring and, on the other, Charity offers a heart to the bridal pair. A chorus of angels surrounds the three central figures, and many of the wedding guests, clutching their money bags, seem to wonder indignantly why they have been invited and make ready to depart. In the foreground a boy throws a stone at the bride and a dog barks at her. It is surely the strangest wedding scene ever painted.

Beneath the columns of a cloister I found the excellent Franciscan shop. I bought a gramophone record of the *Canticle of the Sun*, also a charming little tile which depicted Brother Wolf offering his paw to S. Francis. The shop was doing such excellent business that two friars were hard at work behind the counter. If anyone were conscious of irony in the fact that such traffic should be associated with the saint who refused to handle money, even in a good cause, he did not show it. And the noise of the old dispute made by those who believed that Brother Elias had transformed Lady Poverty into Lady Rich, which rumbled round the Lateran, Avignon, and the Vatican for centuries, has happily died away. All over the world the Franciscans are loved and respected for their simplicity, their poverty, and their care of the poor.

The thoughtful visitor, who has traced the steps of S. Francis upon the white roads of Umbria and has knelt at his shrine, may ask what happened to Brother Elias. His leadership split the Order into those, known sometimes as the Zealots, who wished to observe the rule of apostolic poverty, and others who believed that

Elias was shaping an unrealizable ideal to the needs of a material world. The propaganda of the two parties may be detected even in the early 'lives' of the Saint. During his leadership, and with the support of Gregory IX, Elias concealed the body of his leader and built the magnificent church to enshrine it; he was then deposed by his enemies and retired to the mountain town of Cortona.

He was, of course, a worldly churchman. His enemies were never tired of criticizing his vanity and even the fact that he kept a good cook! His association with the atheist Emperor, Frederick II, who valued him as a brilliant statesman, brought Elias into conflict with the Holy See, and he was excommunicated. He again retired to Cortona, where he built a Franciscan church and convent for his followers. In his seventies, feeling death to be imminent, he sent a friar to Rome to beg for absolution, which the Pope, then Innocent IV, granted. Hurrying back, the friar was in time to console the dying man and to see the fulfilment of his last wish, which was to be clothed again in the grey habit of the Order. It is said that after his death his body was dug up by a Zealot and flung on a dunghill.

Few probably think of him as they stand in the crypt beneath his basilica, yet he it was who saved the body of S. Francis from desecration, and he was the architect of more than the mighty building which enshrines it.

§ 11

On one of those hushed mornings in early autumn when the grapes, the olives, and the chestnuts are nearly ready for the harvest, I left Assisi with the idea of reaching Rome that night, for Rome is only a hundred miles away. I had packed some sandwiches, to which a kind friend had added a basket of ripe figs picked that morning; and so I set off down the hill and across the valley. I had made to myself the most difficult of all promises in Italy, that I would not pause or dawdle on the way, that I would not be lured by hilltop towns, or be beguiled for any reason at all, with one exception: the Waters of Clitumnus.

I was soon travelling south along the Via Flaminia, which was the Great North Road of the Romans, and I saw the old towns standing high in sunlight upon the hills, echoing their Latin names, – Spello, *Hispellum*; Foligno, *Fulginium*; Trevi, *Trebia* – and I had the feeling, not easy to explain, that I had been here before; that some tree or rock or some river or bend in the road might unlock the gates of memory and resolve the mystery. Of all the Regions of Italy, Umbria is the most subtle, the most tranquil, and the most mysterious. One has the feeling that the roots go down even deeper than usual, beyond the Etruscans to unknown people speaking a lost tongue, and that the mountain-tops have seen star-gazers of whose existence history has no record. It was no accident that S. Francis was an Umbrian. A chain of religious faith and speculation links the *Canticle of the Sun* with the Eugubian Tablets of Gubbio; and as the pagan world revered the Umbrian Schools of Divination, so the modern world finds at Assisi the shrine of the greatest of all the Umbrian seers. It is curious that the augurs saw the will of the gods in the flight of birds in that same countryside where many centuries later S. Francis loved birds as a manifestation of the divine spirit.

When I came to the Waters of Clitumnus I saw a beautiful, rich and well-watered valley, lying between two ranges of thirsty hills. The little river went sliding on its brief course to join the Tiber, and I soon arrived at its source. A path led from the road to a farmhouse where I asked permission to go down to the Waters, for they are private property. The farmer's wife nodded pleasantly towards the gate that leads to the Waters – *fonti* she called them – and I came to a scene of entrancing beauty.

The 'Fountains', or Waters of Clitumnus, look at first sight as if some landscape gardener of great talent had designed perfect surroundings for the clearest water on earth, water so limpid and translucent that it appears as if it had been filtered in some under-ground laboratory. Then you notice that it is not ordinary water: it is strangely alive, not with the ascending bubbles of mineral gas but with a slow, curious, and gentle quivering for which there seems no explanation until you look into the depths. There, upon beds of silver sand and clean gravel, you see the 'eyes' of hundreds of springs welling up out of the earth. The water is rarely more than two or three feet deep and it is fascinating to look down, as through a sheet of glass, and see the 'eyes' bubbling, each one agitating a little wisp of the finest sand. Tall poplars grow round the pools and are reflected in the glassy water; willows bend above them, and anyone at all sensitive to atmosphere would recognize, and rightly, another Umbrian shrine.

Virgil, Juvenal, and Propertius (who was born near Assisi), are among those who mentioned the Waters of Clitumnus and their strange quality of whitening the cattle that bathed in them, and their more than curious habit of reflecting not a person's physical appearance, but his nature. This must have changed since Pan died for, looking down rather fearfully, I saw myself! The Emperor Caligula paid a visit to the Clitumnus, so did Honorius, who turned aside to see the Waters when on his way to Rome. No doubt they saw the special breed of white oxen dedicated to the gods which grazed upon the banks of the Clitumnus in Roman times. They were never broken to the plough or mated, but were fattened on the rich pastures until the time came when they were led garlanded to the altar.

I looked into one of the springs and saw that the sands were covered with silver coins. So the old pagan custom of casting an offering to the river god still continues, as it does at the Fontana di Trevi in Rome. I do not know why this particular spring should have been selected for the offerings, and I wondered if it were the same in which nineteen centuries ago Pliny noticed a shower of coins. When he was there many shrines had been erected to the various deities who presided over the pools, and he read inscriptions on walls and columns written by visitors who wished to testify to the virtues of the presiding gods. 'There are many of them,' he wrote, 'you will greatly admire, as there are some that will make you laugh.' The chief deity of the pools was the god Clitumnus whose statue, says Pliny, stood in a shrine near by, clothed in a toga.

While walking along the bank of the river I came upon this shrine, or one remarkably like it, standing higher up near the road. It is a small temple with just room for a priest and a few visitors who had come to consult Clitumnus, who was an oracular god. I saw that the place where the oracle once stood in his toga is now occupied by a disused Christian altar.

I returned to gaze again into the crystal pools, fascinated as men have been for thousands of years by their furtive and mysterious movement. I have never seen any place in which the pagan world seemed nearer. I thought of Pan and the Naiads, and I wondered about the local people. An old man came from the farmhouse and dipped a kettle in one of the pools. Yes, he said, it was good water; and that was that. I wondered what he really thought about it, and whether he liked wandering out to fill the kettle after dark. I wondered too, if at times when the moon is full, he has ever heard the white oxen going down to drink.

I continued my journey through the enchanted land, a land so warm with life and so rich in experience, and late that night I slept in Rome.

APPENDICES

The Elevation of the *Ceri* at Gubbio

When May 15 came round again I went to Gubbio, full of curiosity, to attend the Feast of S. Ubaldo and to see the elevation and procession of the *Ceri*. The streets were so crowded that I left my car in a garage and walked to the upper town. While on the way I encountered hundreds of excited and exhilarated young men, arm in arm and singing, an unusual spectacle in a country where intoxication is thought to be disgraceful. They were dressed in white trousers and wore red neckcloths, with shirts of either red, yellow, or black. They were the *Ceraioli*, who later in the day would carry the heavy *Ceri* through the streets and finally run with them to the top of the mountain.

I was grateful to the mayor, who had sent me a ticket for the old palace, in the piazza, which is now the town hall. From its windows I looked down upon a crowd in which there did not appear to be room for one more human being. Opposite rose the lordly Palazzo dei Consoli, with a tall mast in front from which the town flag was flying. When the bell sounded all eyes looked up to the bell-tower where the figure of a man was seen in the arches, outlined against the sky, as he rang the bell not with a rope, but with his feet. Bracing himself and grasping supports, he trod upon a wooden platform which was attached to the beam of the bell. He swung the platform up until the bell was just on the point of turning over, then he released it and brought down the bell with a tremendous bang.

At the same time I noticed that the three *Ceri*, which on my first visit I had seen in the sanctuary on the summit of Monte Ingino, were lying side by side in the piazza, while teams of *Ceraioli* were preparing to bolt them to the heavy platforms, or stretchers, on which they would be erected and carried round the town. They are extraordinary objects, in shape two octagonal prisms joined together by a narrow waist, and again I thought they resembled nothing so much as gigantic Christmas crackers.

The final touch was the attachment to the top of each *Cero* of a saintly statue: S. Ubaldo in golden vestments, S. George on horseback, a blue cloak fluttering from his shoulders, and S. Anthony, in a cope of red and black. These garments were not painted on the statues, but were made of brocade and cloth. While this was happening I was able to identify the three teams of *Ceraioli*: those in yellow shirts were the bearers of S. Ubaldo, those in blue of S. George, and those in black of S. Anthony.

At last the *Ceri*, now upright, towered up as high as the first-floor balconies, and with a wild shout the excited teams flung themselves upon the poles of the stretchers, and before one realized what was happening the *Ceri* were moving at a rapid Bersagliere jog-trot. The strained faces of the *Ceraioli* were some indication of the weight that was being carried and, as they ran, men ran alongside ready, if a bearer dropped out, to take his place. The three fantastic objects – totem poles, idols? – after a quick turn round the piazza – *un breve carosèllo* – vanished in the direction of the lower town. It was just after mid-day. They would not appear in the piazza again until six o'clock, when the final race up the mountain would begin. In the interval the *Ceri* would be carried to all parts of the town. Flowers would be thrown down to them from balconies; at certain places they would be halted while the *Ceraioli* would be entertained to more refreshment.

In spite of the three saints, it seemed to me that I was witnessing a pagan ceremony which had descended from remote ages, and the *Ceraioli*, flushed and beside themselves with excitement, recalled the fanatical priests of some pagan deity like Cybele. There are only two other ceremonies in Italy which may be compared with Gubbio's annual feast, in both of which enormously heavy objects are carried round the town. During the Feast of S. Rosa at Viterbo, on September 3, a ninety-foot-long illuminated float is carried round at night, while the street lights are dimmed. But a closer resemblance to the *Ceri* is the Feast of the *Gigli* (lilies), which is held at Nola, near Naples, on the last Sunday in June. Eight huge obelisks, eighty feet high, accompanied by a decorated ship, are carried through the streets. The ship and obelisks are said to be a memory of the welcome given to S. Paulinus of Nola in A.D. 431 upon his return from Africa. The eight obelisks are believed to represent the gift of lilies to the saint by the eight trade guilds. Perhaps if a lily can grow in the course of time into an eighty-foot-high obelisk, the three *Ceri* of Gubbio may, as their name implies, have once been candles.

A protracted civic luncheon occupied the afternoon. The great hall of the Palazzo dei Consoli resembled a larger London Guildhall on a festive occasion. A band played in the minstrels' gallery and a posy of spring flowers lay beside each plate. The bishop was seated with the mayor at the top table, with a few distinguished guests, a cabinet minister, and military officers. Six courses slowly followed one another, and the wine waiters had evidently been told to see that no glass was ever empty. Speeches of great length were delivered to the last word, and in the relief which followed them the guests pelted each other with flowers. When a carnation had missed the bishop's purple skull-cap by inches, he decided to retire, but, in any event, he was on duty. The time had come for him, accompanied by the clergy, to take the statue of S. Ubaldo, and a relic of the saint, to the lower town to meet the *Ceri* and to bless them.

I retired to my window again to wait for six o'clock. Every now and then an excited official would arrive from the lower town with news of the happenings there, and this would be communicated to the enormous crowd. At the last moment some attempt was made to clear a passage, only just in time, for, to the sound of harsh cries and the shuffling of feet, the *Ceri* arrived in clouds of dust. The *Ceraioli*, having carried their burdens up the steep streets, appeared exhausted, and the *Ceri* dipped and slanted like a three-masted ship that was about to run on the rocks. The sweating men were glad to lower the stretchers and accept draughts of wine.

As the mayor, standing at the window of the palace, dropped a handkerchief, the *Ceraioli*, rushing to their *Ceri*, put their shoulders to the shafts and were off at the double. Three times the *Ceri* encircled the square amid frenzied shouting and orders which no one could hear. I have a memory of a man with a drawn sword insecurely seated upon a shaggy horse, who seemed to have a perhaps nominal command of the situation, and another, also on horseback, who, when able to do so, blew a trumpet. More than once a *Cero* leaned dangerously, but the slant was quickly righted, and as the saints passed on a level with my window I noticed how beautifully carved they were, particularly S. George and his horse, the work of a fine artist.

When the *Ceri* had left the piazza, the sound of shouting higher up told us that the final exertion was approaching, the ascent of Monte Ingino. Making my way as well as I could through the crowd, I found a place where I could see the mountain. All the way to the top were hundreds of running figures, and the three *Ceri*, like carnival giants, slanting a little to left or right, were carried at a running pace to the summit.

Having reached the sanctuary, the *Ceri* would be detached from their platforms and laid side by side upon the floor until May of the following year. The three saints would be carried down the mountain and escorted to their respective churches. So once again Gubbio had paid tribute to a beloved patron saint who had died eight hundred years ago.

Famous Families of Italy

THE VISCONTI OF MILAN

The family rose to power in 1262 as Archbishops of Milan. When *Archbishop Giovanni* died in 1354 the state was divided between his three nephews: *Matteo* (d. 1355) *Bernabò* (d. 1385) who married *Regina della Scala*, and *Galeazzo* (d. 1378). The latter's son, Gian Galeazzo, became the 1st Duke of Milan. He was the most powerful of the Visconti and was preparing to make himself King of Italy when he died of the plague (1402).

The dynasty ended with his two inept sons: *Giovanni Maria*, 2nd Duke, who was murdered in 1412, and *Filippo Maria*, 3rd Duke, who died in 1447 leaving an illegitimate daughter, *Bianca Maria*, who married her father's general, Francesco Sforza (1401–1466).

THE SFORZA OF MILAN

Francesco Sforza seized Milan and made himself 4th Duke. The 5th Duke was his son, *Galeazzo Maria Sforza*, who was assassinated in 1476. His heir, *Gian Galeazzo Sforza*, was a boy of seven. He became 6th Duke, though the duchy was controlled by his uncle, *Ludovico il Moro* (1451-1508), under whom Milan achieved its greatest brilliance. He married *Beatrice d'Este* (1475-1497) and employed *Leonardo da Vinci*. After Gian Galeazzo Sforza's untimely death, aged 25, Ludovico succeeded as 7th Duke of Milan. He fell from power during the French invasion of Italy and ended his life in a French prison.

The French claim to Milan was based on the marriage of *Valentina Visconti*, daughter of Gian Galeazzo Visconti, 1st Duke, with Louis, Duke of Orleans. Their grandson, *Louis XII*, regarded himself as the rightful Duke of Milan and considered the Sforzas to be usurpers. The French claims to Milan and Naples brought France and Spain into conflict on Italian soil.

THE GONZAGA OF MANTUA

This distinguished military family became Lords of Mantua in 1328 with the title of Captains-general. The first Marquess of Mantua was *Gianfrancesco* (1395–1444), who was succeeded as 2nd Marquess by his son *Ludovico* (1414–1478), who was followed by his son *Federigo* (1442–1484) as 3rd Marquess. Both *Ludovico* and *Federigo* married German wives.

The 4th Marquess, *Francesco* (1466–1519), married *Isabella d'Este* (d. 1539). Their son, *Federigo* (1500–1540), became the 1st Duke of Mantua.

His two sons succeeded as 2nd and 3rd dukes respectively, *Francesco* (1533–1550) and *Guglielmo* (1538–1587). The 4th Duke was Guglielmo's son *Vincenzo* (1562–1612).

The 5th, 6th and 7th Dukes were sons of Vincenzo: *Francesco* (1586–1612), *Ferdinand* (1587–1626) and *Vincenzo II*, (1594–1627). With the last named the direct line came to an end. He was the Duke who sold the famous Mantuan art collection to Charles I of England.

The dukedom was carried on in the person and descendants of *Charles of Nevers* (1580–1637) and the 10th, and last Duke was *Ferdinand Charles*, who died in 1708.

THE ESTENSI OF FERRARA

The oldest and most aristocratic ruling family in the N. of Italy, tracing descent from the time of Charlemagne. *Azzo VI* (1170–1212) was elected ruler of Ferrara by the citizens. Through *Welf IV*, who obtained the Duchy of Bavaria in 1070, the Estensi became connected with the princely houses of Brunswick and Hanover from whom the English reigning House of Windsor is descended.

Nicholas III (1384–1441) was succeeded by three sons: *Lionello* (1407–1450), one of the great Renaissance patrons of art, *Borso* (1413–1471) and *Ercole I* (1431–1505), the father of *Isabella* and *Beatrice d'Este*. His son, and successor, *Alfonso I* (1486–1534) married, as his second wife, *Lucrezia Borgia*.

Their son, *Ercole II* (1508–1558) was succeeded by his son, *Alfonso II* (1533–1592), with whom the main Este line terminated. At his death the Holy See assumed control of Ferrara, and the family, continuing in the descendants of a cousin, ruled as Dukes of Modena. *Alfonso IV* (1634–1662) was the father of *Mary of Modena*, consort of James II of England.

With *Ercole III* (1727–1803) the line of the Estensi of Modena ended. His heiress, *Marie Beatrice* (d. 1829) married the Archduke Ferdinand, son of the Emperor Francis I, and until 1860, when Modena was incorporated in Italy, the title was held by Austrian archdukes.

THE SCALIGERI OF VERONA

The founder of the family was *Mastino della Scala* (d. 1277) the son of a weaver or, as some said, a maker of ladders (*scala* is Italian for ladder). The citizens asked him to be lord of Verona in 1262. His benevolent rule was terminated by his assassination in 1277. He was succeeded by his brother *Alberto I* (d. 1301) who, according to a contemporary, was 'sublime in soul and perfect in his ways'. He was succeeded by three sons.

1. *Bartolomeo della Scala*, who reigned for less than 3 years. He was the first Scaliger to welcome Dante to Verona.

2. *Alboino* (d. 1311)

3. *Cangrande I.* (d. 1329) the greatest of the Scaligeri to whom Dante dedicated the *Divine Comedy*. He was succeeded by two nephews:

1. *Mastino II* (d. 1351) father of *Regina della Scala*, wife of Bernabò Visconti, who gave her name to the land on which the Scala Opera House was eventually erected in Milan.

2. *Alberto II.* (d. 1352)

He was succeeded by two sons of *Mastino II – Cangrande II* (d. 1359) and *Cansignorio* (d. 1375), under whose sons and grandsons the dynasty melted away.

Verona was seized by Gian Galeazzo Visconti, after whose death, in 1402, it was peacefully incorporated in the Venetian Republic.

THE MEDICI OF FLORENCE

This family of international bankers controlled Florence from 1434 until 1737, first as citizens, later as Grand Dukes. The first great Medici was *Cosimo the Elder* (1389–1464). He and his son *Piero the Gouty* (1416–1469) and Piero's son, *Lorenzo the Magnificent* (1449–1492), were crippled by an hereditary infirmity which they called 'gout'. Among Lorenzo's sons were *Piero the Unfortunate* (1471–1503) and *Giovanni* (1475–1521) who became *Pope Leo X*.

The Medici were exiled from Florence during the French invasion of 1494 but returned in 1512. The senior line died out in 1537 with an illegitimate Medici who was murdered. The junior branch then came to power as the Grand Dukes of Tuscany. They were.

Cosimo I (1519–1574) who was succeeded by his sons:

Francis I (1541–1587)

Ferdinand I (1549–1609), then son succeeded father as follows:

Cosimo II (1590–1621), *Ferdinand II* (1610–1670), *Cosimo III* (1642–1723) and *Gian Gastone* (1671–1737), the last Medici Grand Duke of Tuscany.

THE BORGIAS

The Spanish family of the Borgias, or Borjas, came from Jàtiva south of Valencia. Eight Borjas each bearing the famous shield of a red bull on a gold ground were present when Valencia was captured from the Moslems. *Alfonso Borja*, Bishop of Valencia, was present with Alfonso I at the conquest of Naples in 1444; in the following year he was elected pope, as Calixtus III.

Interest is concentrated on *Rodrigo Borgia* (1431–1503), Pope Alexander VI, his son *Caesar Borgia* (1476–1507) and his daughter *Lucrezia* (1480–1519). She married, as her third husband, Alfonso d'Este, brother of Isabella and Beatrice d'Este. Upon his accession, she became Duchess of Ferrara.

The character of the Borgia Pope was in contrast to the sanctity of a later member of the family, *S. Francis Borgia* (1510–1572) Duke of Gandia, who become the third General of the Jesuits and was canonised in 1671.

BIBLIOGRAPHY

I have confined this list to works in English which have been of use to me in writing this book and, in doing so, I gratefully acknowledge my debt to their writers.

Acton, Harold, *The Last Medici* (Methuen, 1958)

Ady, C. M., *Lorenzo dei Medici and Renaissance Italy* (English Universities Press, 1955)

Bates, E. S., *Touring in 1600* (Houghton Mifflin, Boston and New York, 1911)

Bellonci, Maria, *A Prince of Mantua* (Weidenfeld and Nicolson, 1956)

Berenson, Bernard, *The Italian Painters of the Renaissance* (Phaidon Press, 1959)

Borsook, Eve, *The Mural Painters of Tuscany* (Phaidon Press, 1960)

Brand, C. P., *Italy and the English Romantics* (Cambridge University Press, 1957)

Brinton, Selwyn, *The Gonzaga – Lords of Mantua* (Methuen, 1927)

Burchard, Johann, *At the Court of the Borgia* (Folio Society, 1963)

Burckhardt, Jacob, *The Civilisation of the Renaissance in Italy* (Phaidon Press. n.d.)

Cartwright, Julia (Mrs Ady), *Isabella d'Este, Marchioness of Mantua 1474–1539* (John Murray, 1903)

Cartwright, Julia (Mrs Ady), *Beatrice d'Este, Duchess of Milan 1475–1497* (J. M. Dent, 1920)

Cellini, Benvenuto, *The Life of* (Phaidon Press, 1949)

Chabod, Federico, *Machiavelli and the Renaissance* (Bowes and Bowes, 1958)

Clark, Kenneth, *Leonardo da Vinci* (Cambridge University Press, 1939)

Collison-Morley, L., *Italy after the Renaissance* (George Routledge, 1930)

Collison-Morley, L., *The Story of the Borgias* (George Routledge, 1932)

Collison-Morley, L., *The Story of the Sforzas* (George Routledge, 1933)

Coryat, Thomas, *Crudities* (Glasgow, 1905)

Crawford, Francis Marion, *Gleanings from Venetian History* (Macmillan, 1905)

Dante Alighieri, *The Divine Comedy* (new translation by Dorothy L. Sayers and Barbara Reynolds in the Penguin Classics, 1949–62)

David, Elizabeth, *Italian Food* (Macdonald, 1954)

Dennis, George, *The Cities and Cemeteries of Etruria* (John Murray, 1883)

Dombrowski, Ramon, *Mussolini: Twilight and Fall* (Heinemann, 1956)

Fabri, Felix, translated by Aubrey Stewart (Palestine Pilgrims' Text Society, Vols 7 to 10, 1892)

Forrest, Alan, *Italian Interlude* (Howard Timmins, Cape Town)

BIBLIOGRAPHY

Gardner, Edmund G., *The Story of Florence* (J. M. Dent, 1901)

Gardner, Edmund G., *The Story of Siena* (J. M. Dent, 1905)

Gardner, Edmund G., *Saint Catherine of Siena* (J. M. Dent, 1907)

Goethe, Johann Wolfgang v., *Travels in Italy* (Bohn, 1883)

Gombrich, E. H., *The Story of Art* (Phaidon Press, 1950)

Gould, Cecil, *An Introduction to Italian Renaissance Painting* (Phaidon Press, 1957)

Hale, J. R., *England and the Italian Renaissance* (Faber, 1954)

Hale, J. R., *The Italian Journal of Samuel Rogers* (Faber, 1956)

Harcourt-Smith, Simon, *The Marriage at Ferrara* (John Murray, 1952)

Hartt, Frederick, *Florentine Art under Fire* (Princeton University Press, New Jersey, 1949)

Hibbert, Christopher, *Benito Mussolini* (Longmans, Green and Co., 1962)

Hood, Stuart, *Pebbles from my Skull* (Hutchinson 1963)

Hutton, Edward, *The Cities of Lombardy* (Methuen, 1912); *Siena and Southern Tuscany* (Methuen, 1923); *Florence and Northern Tuscany* (Methuen, 1924); *The Cities of Umbria* (Methuen, 1905); *Ravenna* (J. M. Dent, 1913)

Italian Renaissance Studies, edited by E. F. Jacob (Faber, 1960)

Kirby, Paul Franklin, *The Grand Tour in Italy (1700–1800)* (S. F. Vanni (Ragusa), 1952)

Lucas, E. V., *A Wanderer in Florence* (Methuen, 1928)

Masson, Georgina, *Italian Gardens* (Thames and Hudson, 1961)

Masson, Georgina, *Italian Villas and Palaces* (Thames and Hudson, 1959)

Memoirs of a Renaissance Pope, the Commentaries of Pius II. Trs by F. A. Gragg and L. C. Gabel (Putnam's, New York)

Miller, Betty, *Robert Browning, a Portrait* (John Murray, 1952)

Morris, James, *Venice* (Faber, 1960)

Mortoft, Francis, *His Book, being his Travels through France and Italy* (The Hakluyt Society, 1925)

Nicolson, Harold, *Byron, the Last Journey* (Constable, 1948)

Noyes, Ella, *The Story of Ferrara* (Dent, 1904)

Noyes, Ella, *The Story of Milan* (Dent, 1908)

Okey, Thomas, *The Story of Venice* (Dent, 1907)

Oliphant, Margaret, *Francis of Assisi* (Macmillan, 1902)

Origo, Iris, *The Last Attachment* (Cape and Murray, 1949), *The World of San Bernardino* (Cape, 1963)

Parks, G. B., *The English Traveller in Italy, Vol I. The Middle Ages (to 1525)* (Edizioni di Storia e Letteratura, Rome, 1954)

Peniakoff, Vladimir, *Private Army* (Cape, 1950)

Pope-Hennesey, John, *Italian High Renaissance and Baroque Sculpture* (Phaidon Press, 1955–63)

Prescott, H. F. M., *Jerusalem Journey* (Eyre and Spottiswoode, 1954)

Quennell, Peter, *Byron in Italy* (Penguin Books, 1955)

Roberts, H. I., *St. Augustine in "St. Jerome's Study": Carpaccio's Painting and its Legendary Source* (The Art Bulletin. XLI. 1959)

Ruskin, John, *The Stones of Venice* (Dent, Everyman, 1935)

Schevill, Ferdinand, *The Medici* (Gollancz, 1950)

Sells, A. L., *The Italian Influence in English Poetry* (Allen and Unwin, 1955)

Shirley-Price, L., new trs. of *The Little Flowers of St Francis* (Penguin Classics, 1959)

Sismondi, J. C. L., *History of the Italian Republics in the Middle Ages* (Routledge, n.d.)

Staley, Edgcumbe, *The Guilds of Florence* (Methuen, 1906)

Stendhal (M. H. Beyle), *Rome, Naples and Florence* (John Calder, 1950)

Stendhal (M. H. Beyle), *The Charterhouse of Parma* (Penguin, 1958)

Stoye, John Walter, *English Travellers Abroad 1604-1667* (Cape, 1952)

Symonds, J. A., *Renaissance in Italy* (Smith, Elder, 1897)

Symonds, Margaret and Lina Duff Gordon, *The Story of Perugia* (Dent, 1904)

The New Cambridge Modern History, I. The Renaissance (Cambridge University Press, 1957)

Trevelyan, J. P., *A Short History of the Italian People* (Allen and Unwin, 1956)

Treves, G. A., *The Golden Ring, the Anglo-Florentines 1847-1862* (Longmans Green, 1956)

Underhill, Evelyn, *Mysticism* (Methuen, University Paperbacks, 1960)

Vasari, Giorgio, *The Lives of the Painters, Sculptors and Architects* (Dent, Everyman, 1949)

Vernon, H. M., *Italy from 1494 to 1790* (Cambridge University Press, 1909)

Villari, Pasquale, *The Life and Times of Girolamo Savonarola* (Fisher Unwin, n.d.)

Wall, Bernard, *Italian Life and Landscape, Vol. 2, Northern Italy and Tuscany* (Paul Elek, 1951)

Weiss, R., *Humanism in England during the Fifteenth Century* (Blackwell, Oxford, 1957)

Whitfield, J. H., *A Short History of Italian Literature* (Penguin, 1960)

Wiel, Alethea, *The Navy of Venice* (John Murray, 1910)

Wiel, Alethea, *The Story of Verona* (Dent, 1902)

Young, G. F., *The Medici* (London, 1909)

INDEX

SELECTED TRAVEL TITLES AVAILABLE FROM METHUEN

	ISBN	TITLE	AUTHOR	PRICE
☐	0413 74750 6	Orchid Fever	Eric Hansen	£6.99
☐	0413 75930 X	Stranger in the Forest	Eric Hansen	£6.99
☐	0413 75940 7	Motoring with Mohammed	Eric Hansen	£6.99
☐	0413 69120 9	The Literary Guide to Dublin	Vivien Igoe	£12.99
☐	0413 75130 9	The Literary Companion to Edinburgh	Andrew Lownie	£9.99
☐	0413 54490 7	In Search of England	H. V. Morton	£8.99
☐	0413 54850 3	In Search of Ireland	H. V. Morton	£8.99
☐	0413 18470 6	In Search of London	H. V. Morton	£9.99
☐	0413 54480 X	In Search of Scotland	H. V. Morton	£8.99
☐	0413 40740 3	In Search of Wales	H. V. Morton	£8.99
☐	0413 75430 8	A Traveller in Italy	H. V. Morton	£10.99
☐	0413 75440 5	A Traveller in Rome	H. V. Morton	£9.99
☐	0413 75420 0	In the Steps of the Master	H. V. Morton	£9.99

• All Methuen books are available through mail order or from your local bookshop.

Please send cheque/eurocheque/postal order (sterling only) Access, Visa, Mastercard, Diners Card, Switch or Amex.

Expiry Date:_____ Signature: _____

UK customers please allow £1 for the first book and 50p thereafter up to a maximum of £3 for postage and packing.

Overseas customers please allow £1.50 for the first book and 75p thereafter up to a maximum of £5 for post and packing.

ALL ORDERS TO:

Methuen Books, Books by Post, TBS Limited, The Book Service, Colchester Road, Frating Green, Colchester, Essex CO7 7DW.

NAME: _____

ADDRESS:_____

_____

_____

Please allow 28 days for delivery. Please tick box if you do not wish to receive any additional information ☐

Prices and availability subject to change without notice.